The Savage Wars of Peace

To the memory of

Dilmaya Gurung
of Thak

1953–95

The Savage Wars of Peace

England, Japan and the
Malthusian Trap

Alan Macfarlane

Published 2003 by
PALGRAVE MACMILLAN
Houndmills, Basingstoke, Hampshire RG21 6XS and
175 Fifth Avenue, New York, N.Y. 10010
Companies and representatives throughout the world

PALGRAVE MACMILLAN is the global academic imprint of the Palgrave
Macmillan division of St. Martin's Press, LLC and of Palgrave Macmillan Ltd.
Macmillan® is a registered trademark in the United States, United Kingdom
and other countries. Palgrave is a registered trademark in the European
Union and other countries.

ISBN 978-1-4039-0432-4

First published in hardback 1997 by
Blackwell Publishers Ltd.

This book is printed on paper suitable for recycling and made from fully
managed and sustained forest sources.

A catalogue record for this book is available from the British Library.

Library of Congress Cataloging-in-Publication Data
Macfarlane, Alan.
    The savage wars of peace: England, Japan, and the Malthusian trap / Alan
    Macfarlane.
       p. cm
    Originally published: Oxford, UK; Cambridge, MA: Blackwell Publishers,
1997.

       1. England – Population – History.   2. Japan – Population – History.
       3. Demographic transition – England.   4. Demographic transition –
    Japan.   I. Title.
HB3585 .M33 2003
304.6'0941 – dc21

                                                                    2002030259

10   9   8   7   6   5   4   3   2   1
12   11   10   09   08   07   06   05   04   03

Transferred to Digital Printing 2009

Take up the White Man's burden –
The savage wars of peace –
Fill full the mouth of Famine
And bid the sickness cease;

Rudyard Kipling, *The White Man's Burden.*

Contents

Acknowledgements

My interest in Japan was first kindled by Kenichi and Toshiko Nakamura of Hokkaido University, who were kind hosts during two visits to Japan. Their friendship and patient answering of hundreds of questions have made it possible to begin to attempt to understand Japan.

On the Japanese material, Emiko Namihira, Emiko Ochiai and Hiro Watanabe read and commented on earlier drafts or background materials and Akira Hayami discussed some of the central ideas with me. Osamu Saito read through the whole book and provided invaluable guidance on Japanese demography and economic history. Funding for visits to Japan was kindly provided by the British Council, Hokkaido University and the Japanese Ministry of Education.

For help with the medical and scientific background I would like to thank H.B.F.Dixon, Derek Bendall and Nicholas Mascie-Taylor. Patricia Bidinger kindly read the chapters on specific diseases. My students and colleagues in the Department of Social Anthropology and King's College provided their usual stimulus and support.

John Davey of Blackwell Publishers was his usual encouraging self and gently steered the book back from various extremes of length. The text has in fact gone through twelve drafts, at its maximum reaching twice its present length. Most of these were typed by Penny Lang and her careful deciphering of my scribbled suggestions made it possible to produce the book at all. She also helped check the notes.

Iris Macfarlane and Mark Turin read the whole book and suggested various improvements. Cherry Bryant read the text through twice and improved the presentation and argument immeasurably.

Gerry Martin helped in numerous ways; he provided several key books, brought numerous ideas to my attention, read through the text twice and made helpful comments. More generally his support and that offered by the Renaissance Trust were invaluable and I am deeply grateful to him for his friendship and kindness. I also thank Hilda Martin for providing the context for many stimulating discussions.

As always, my deepest debt is to Sarah Harrison. Much of the argument was developed in discussions with her and the final product is in many ways a joint venture.

Frequent fieldwork visits to Nepal were made possible through funding from the Economic and Social Research Council and the University of Cambridge. I would like to thank my 'other family' in Thak for the opportunity to become involved in another world and for their innumerable kindnesses.

Much of this book revolves around the role of women, in particular the stress put on their bodies by childbearing, breast-feeding and constant toil in the house and fields. My growing realization of the importance of the contribution of women largely grew out of my conversations, filming and observation of my 'sister' Dilmaya Gurung, whose tragic death at the age of 42 in April 1995 exemplified many of these themes. This book is dedicated to a remarkable person whose self-sacrifice and abilities shaped much of my thought.

References, Conventions and Measures

Normally, much of the materials in a monograph would be one's own. This book, however, is a work of synthesis. Much of what I know is derived from the scholarly work of others. I could have tried to absorb their work and then synthesize it into my own words with brief acknowledgements but I have decided not to do so.

One reason is that my competence in many areas is such that readers could well ask on what authority statements are made. Why should my views on Japanese history, for instance, be taken seriously when it is only too obvious that I am by training an historian of England? It seems better to let the reader see as much of the original expression of facts and opinions as possible. Consequently this book is a patchwork of quotations and examples with a concomitant effect on the style. On the other hand I hope that the authenticity of many first-hand accounts will enrich the argument.

Spelling has not been modernized except in a few old English quotations (from before the fifteenth century) where the meaning would be obscure for a modern reader. American spelling (e.g. labor for labour) has been left as in the original. Italics in quotations are in the original, unless otherwise indicated. Variant spellings in quotations have not been corrected.

Round brackets in quotations are those of the original author; my interpolations are in square brackets.

The footnote references give an abbreviated title and page number. The usual form is author, short title, volume number if there is one (in upper case Roman numerals), page number(s). The full title of the work referred to is given in the bibliography at the end of the book, where there is also a list of common abbreviations used in the footnotes.

Where several quotations within a single paragraph are taken from the same author, the references are given after the last of the quotations. Each page reference is given, even if it is a repeated page number.

Measures

A number of the early quotations refer to English systems of measurement, some of which are now no longer in use:

Value: four farthings to a penny, twelve pennies (d) to a shilling (s), twenty shillings to a pound (£). One pound in the seventeenth century was worth about 40 times its present value (in 1996).

Weight: sixteen ounces to a pound, fourteen pounds to a stone, eight stone to hundred-weight (cwt) and twenty hundred-weight to a ton. (Approx. one pound (1b) equals 0.454 kg.)

Liquid volume: two pints to a quart, four quarts to a gallon. (Approx. one and three quarter pints to one litre.)

Distance: twelve inches to a foot, three feet to a yard, 1760 yards to a mile. (Approx. 39.4 inches to 1 metre.)

Area: an acre. (Approx. 2.47 acres to a hectare.)

Frequently Cited Early Authors

The observations of the following writers between the fifteenth and early twentieth centuries are frequently quoted. The works from which quotations are taken are listed in the bibliography.

Japan

Alcock: Sir Rutherford Alcock, British diplomat. Visited Japan on two occasions between 1859 and 1864. Travelled in various regions.

Bacon: Alice Bacon, American visitor to Japan in the late nineteenth century.

Bird: Isabella Bird, British traveller. Toured through central and northern Japan for seven months in 1878.

Chamberlain: Basil Hall Chamberlain, British teacher. Lived in Japan for most of the period 1873 to 1911 and travelled widely.

Geoffrey: Theodate Geoffrey, American visitor to Japan in the 1920s.

Griffis: William E.Griffis, American teacher. Visited Japan in 1870–4, travelling to various places.

Hearn: Lafcadio Hearn, Irish-Greek parentage, author and educator. In Japan for much of the period 1890–1904.

Inouye: Jukichi Inouye, Japanese author, who spent a number of years in Europe as well as Japan.

Kaempfer: Engelbert Kaempfer, German, employed by the Dutch trading company as a doctor, also a keen botanist. Visited Japan between September 1690 and November 1692. Mainly resident in Nagasaki, but made two trips to Edo (Tokyo).

King: F.H.King, former chief of the Division of Soil Management of the U.S. Department of Agriculture, who travelled through Japan, Korea and China in the early 1900s.

Morse: Edward L.Morse, American zoologist and art expert. Visited Japan on three occasions between 1887 and 1883 and travelled widely.

Nagatsuka: Takashi Nagatsuka, Japanese author of *The Soil*, written in 1910 and based on a hamlet 44 miles to the northwest of Tokyo.

Oliphant: Laurence Oliphant, Private Secretary to Lord Elgin and author of the narrative of his mission in 1857–9.

Pompe: Pompe van Meerdevort, Dutch, employed by the Dutch trading company as a doctor. In Japan 1857–63, mainly in Nagasaki.

Saga: Dr Junichi Saga, Japanese, collected and published the oral history of an area to the north-east of Tokyo, roughly covering the period 1890–1930.

Scidmore: Isabella Scidmore, American visitor to Japan in the late 1880's.

Thunberg: Carl Pieter Thunberg, Swedish, employed by the Dutch trading company as a doctor, also a keen botanist, Visited Japan from August 1775 to November 1776. Mainly resident in Nagasaki, with one trip to Edo.

Von Siebold: Dr Philipp Franz von Siebold, German, employed by the Dutch trading company as a doctor. Visited Japan from 1823 to 1830 and 1859 to 1862. Mainly in Nagasaki, but visited Edo.

Willis: William Willis, British doctor. Lived in Japan and travelled in various areas, 1862–77.

England

Black: William Black, late-eighteenth-century doctor and statistician.

Blane: Sir Gilbert Blane, early-nineteenth-century doctor.

Boorde: Andrew Boorde, sixteenth-century doctor.

Buchan: William Buchan, mid-eighteenth-century doctor.

Chadwick: Edwin Chadwick, mid-nineteenth-century public health reformer.

Creighton: Charles Creighton, late-nineteenth-century medical historian.

Culpepper: Nicholas Culpepper, mid-seventeenth-century herbalist and medical writer.

De Saussure: Cesar de Saussure, Swiss traveller who visited England for a number of months during the period 1725–30.

De Rochefoucauld: Francois de la Rochefoucauld, French philosopher who visited England in 1784.

Fortescue: Sir John Fortescue, chief justice of the king's bench, who wrote his account of English law and society in the 1460s while in France.

Franklin: Benjamin Franklin, eighteenth-century American scientist and author.

Gouge: William Gouge, early-seventeenth-century Puritan divine.

Heberden: William Heberden, late-eighteenth-century doctor.

Kames: Lord Kames (Henry Home), mid-eighteenth-century Scottish judge and philosopher.

Malthus: Thomas Malthus, late-eighteenth-century economist and demographer.

Moryson: Fynes Moryson, early-seventeenth-century traveller.

Place: Francis Place, late-eighteenth- and early-nineteenth-century social reformer and analyst.

Stubbes: Philip Stubbes, later-sixteenth-century Puritan writer.

The Main Japanese Periods

710——794——1192————1336————1467————1603————1868——1912
　　Nara　Heian　Kamakura　Muromachi　Sengoku　Tokugawa　Meiji

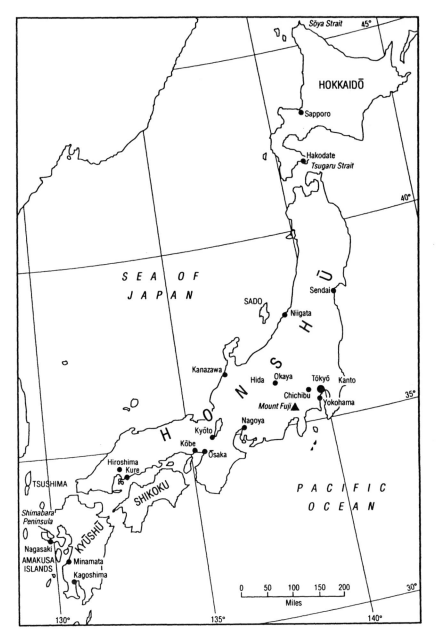

Map 1: *The Main Islands of Japan*

Map 2: *Modern Japanese Prefectures*

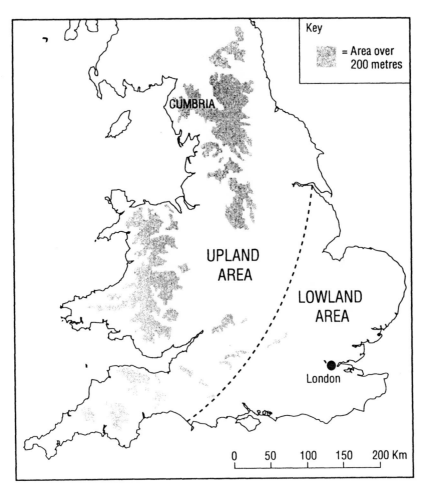

Map 3: *Upland and Lowland England*

Epilogue to the Paperback Edition

The Savage Wars of Peace (*SWP*) is based on the assumption that there was something unusual about English and Japanese civilizations in contrast to many of the neighbouring continental Empires and that this divergence went back to the middle ages. Although not directly addressing this argument, events at the end of the twentieth century were seriously challenging any overtly Euro-centric vision of the world.

What many saw as the most significant event of the 1990s was the rapid growth of China and Chinese related economies. Talk spread of a new type of 'Confucian' world civilization, others remembered that the ascendancy of Europe had, in world terms, only been very brief, basically from the 1830s to 1980s. A number of books came out lambasting the Euro-centric models of the world, arguing that not only China but also Japan were just as rich, powerful and 'advanced' as Europe until at least 1800. From different angles, the work of Blaut, Goody and Gunder Frank are examples of this new wave.[1] They argue that since we now know that rapid economic growth was occurring outside the Euro–American zone, any idea that there is something special about Europe in terms of mentality, social structure, political freedom, must be mistaken.

While the attack is usually on Max Weber, by implication the whole Enlightenment problematic is seen as misguided, if not mischievous. There was no European miracle, there is no necessary link between freedom and economic growth. Look at China, Taiwan, Thailand, Hong Kong, South Korea, Japan, Singapore, Malaysia and you will see that what happened in the west was fairly insignificant. It was an accident that it happened there first. East Asia was always the world leader, and it just had been temporarily delayed, probably by European imperialism, its wealth sucked away. If Europe had never existed, East Asia would quite soon have developed its own form of industrial civilization.

The one example of this new argument I have found related to Japan is by Susan Hanley. Her *Everyday Things in Premodern Japan* (1997), mainly consists of revised versions of earlier articles on material life. As such it is a valuable collection of many of the articles which I used extensively as the background to *SWP*. Hanley shows convincingly in her book, as she did in her articles, the following. The material standard of most Japanese improved between 1600 and 1868; compared to most of Asia, the Japanese were well fed, clothed and housed through this period; compared to Europeans they were extraordinarily clean and enjoyed a high level of sanitation; there was no dramatic change in material culture at the Meiji restoration; the unusually high standard of material culture by Asian standards was a necessary, if not sufficient, background to rapid industrialization.

However, she tries to push the argument further. She argues that Japanese civilization was at the same level of material culture as Britain in 1800, and that fundamentally the differences between the two occurred after that date. This is less convincing. In her zeal to prove that the Japanese were not as miserable as many have portrayed, Hanley tends to omit the central fact of Japanese life when compared to Europe. This is that Europeans, especially the English, made very great use of nonhuman energy (wind, water and particularly animals) and that this lightened the labour load considerably. The Japanese had to achieve their extraordinarily high material standard of living (for an agrarian society) largely through enormous self-discipline, sophisticated social cohesion and incredibly hard work. They had taken the rice path to agricultural involution and without discussing this we cannot really understand why Japan was both materially so well off, and yet so far from the European experience. That she also omits any serious discussion of the other two components of the Malthusian trap, namely war and disease, also takes it in a different direction to *SWP*.

While Hanley's book is based on older research, to my mind the best of the new genre is the aptly titled *The Great Divergence* (2000) by Kenneth Pomerantz. The book consists of a detailed comparison of the economic situation in China (and to a lesser extent other parts of Asia) with Europe, particularly during the eighteenth and nineteenth centuries. There are detailed assessments of the standard of living, technologies, agricultural methods and yields, taxation regimes and other central indicators of economic performance. A very large amount of statistical information is gathered together to support a number of the basic conclusions. These may be summarized as follows.

Apart from the matter of shipping and international trade, there was no appreciable superiority of the west over China by 1800. The Chinese were as well fed, clothed, housed, lived as long, produced as much through their agriculture, as western Europe. It was only after 1800 that a divergence in standards of living and technical efficiency occurred. There was no significant structural difference in the economies of China and Western Europe before 1800. They were both 'agrarian' and subject to the same structural constraints. There was no 'divergence' until the nineteenth century.

Since there was no difference in either quantity or kind in the economies at the two ends of Eur–Asia by 1800, we are left with the puzzle of why differences developed so quickly between 1800 and 1850. The reasons were relatively small and entirely fortuitous, and both were centred in the first period on England. England had good coal supplies and it had a huge set of 'invisible acres' in the Americas that supplied it with the wealth for its 'take off'. China's coalfields were in the wrong place (the northwest) and it had no vast empty acres to pillage.

In many ways this is a refreshing thesis. Yet the danger of this new argument is that it obscures as much as it clarifies. My criticisms are basically methodological. Although western writers have in their ignorance lumped 'China' into one entity, or lumped 'Japan' and 'China' together – when they are very different – it does not help to mirror this shortcoming. Pomerantz treats 'Europe' over its thousand-year history as if there were really no major differences within it. Thus when he needs evidence to show that yields, or ratios, were no higher in 'Europe' than in 'China' he is happy to draw evidence fairly indiscriminately from Portugal, Italy, France, England, Scandinavia. Of course, once one does this, one can prove almost anything. In particular, he lumps England and the Continent, until 1800 at least. Once one assumes there is no difference it is not relevant to look at the different political or social histories of different parts of Europe. The difference between English and French feudalism, for instance, is deemed quite irrelevant.

In fact this lack of differentiation between parts of eighteenth-century Europe leads to a confirmation of the Enlightenment argument. Pomerantz provides detailed evidence and logical arguments which confirms the view that most of continental Europe had indeed hit the outer limits of the agrarian mode of production. There was no obvious escape from this, either in Europe, China, India or Japan. Unfortunately, however, by lumping England in with this picture until 1800, Pomerantz makes it almost impossible to understand how the situation was reversed.

The second point is that Pomerantz concentrates on quantities, that is outcomes, rather than processes. It may well be that the yield per hectare from wet rice is much higher than from dry grains and this is interesting. But equally interesting is the way in which wet rice cultivation has all sorts of social and economic consequences, for example by reducing the number of animals, increasing the demand for labour (and hence increasing population), reducing the size of holdings (and hence altering stratification), reducing the need for grinding machinery. Thus, from a statistical point of view in terms of output per unit of land or even unit of energy input, there may be little difference between an acre of wet rice in the Himalayan village where I work and the huge arable fields where I live in England. But a little reflection and some detailed first-hand observation of the two processes brings home a vast divergence. This over-emphasis on quantification – one can only count what one can count – rather than quality runs right through the book.

The difficulty is compounded by an overemphasis on cross-sections rather than dynamics. Pomerantz's basic point, that China was in many ways as affluent as much of Europe in the later eighteenth century was made by Montesquieu, Adam Smith and Tocqueville. But what the earlier writers who were living through the events also noticed was a difference in dynamics. They observed that the technology and sophistication of China when described by Marco Polo was enormous – but seemed to have changed little four hundred years later. There were a series of micro improvements and China had impressively maintained its standard of living with a larger population. Yet it was not becoming materially wealthier. Smith observed the same phenomenon for much of continental Europe by the eighteenth century. Even the Dutch had halted. Nevertheless, over the four hundred years up to 1700 there had been enormous change and growth, and England and America were still growing. So the west had until recently been dynamic. If one compared the technology of western agriculture in 1000 AD and 1750 there was an immense change, particularly in the use of non-human energy (wind, water, animals and increasingly coal in England). There was a dynamic momentum, though Smith saw it halting. In China, fundamental technological and economic change had largely halted after the fifteenth century.

Although one must resist the attraction of the Rostovian metaphor of 'take off', it is important to look at momentum. The English industrial revolution did not happen from a standing start. We can see the build up of capital and technology over half a millenium. After the event we can see the results. This is one of the many reasons which leads one to be certain that neither China nor Japan were 'moving towards' industrialization before the impact of the west.

Perhaps the deepest methodological weakness of Pomerantz's book, however is the narrow disciplinary foundation of the work. The problem of economic growth is far too important to leave to economic historians. The underpinning of growth in medieval Europe was not technical or economic, but rather political; the unification into nation states. Likewise, it seems likely that, if we are to understand the first industrial revolution, we will not get far if we stop at economic facts.

If we ask ourselves what information Pomerantz provides about the difference of social structures, the difference in political and administrative systems, the difference in religions and ideologies, as between China and parts of the west, the answer has to be 'practically nothing'. The rich, multi-stranded, Enlightenment vision has been abandoned. The problem is defined in purely economic terms and consequently it is not surprising that we find the answer in purely economic terms – coal and American resources. Yet the mind is not content with this, even at a superficial level. There was lots of coal in Japan, there was lots of coal in Germany and parts of France, so why was it not used? Many European powers had 'ghost acres' in various parts of the world, yet this often made them poor (Spain, Portugal) rather than rich. To proceed further we need to move beyond economic facts, though it is very useful to have them outlined so well.

Finally, there is the matter of science or, as some would prefer to call it, reliable knowledge. It is revealing that a book which, in many ways, could be seen as undertaking the same task as Joseph Needham, in other words to increase our respect for the ingenuity and sophistication of China, hardly alludes to Needham's work. Indeed it hardly mentions the scientific revolution at all. Now it has become fashionable to argue that scientific knowledge had no obvious effect on economic efficiency until the later nineteenth century. If we define science and efficiency very narrowly and confine ourselves to practical technologies that were developed in a laboratory and directly applied, this may be true. Yet, as Crosby has convincingly argued we need to define reliable knowledge much more widely.[2] As Needham himself so forcefully demonstrated, while China was far ahead in terms of technology and reliable knowledge by 1300 AD, there was not much major development in the following five hundred years.

Whatever we mean by the 'scientific revolution', it did not occur in China, but it did occur in Western Europe. That is to say a new attitude to truth, experiment, precision, measurement emerged and through long chains of causation influenced all sorts of things. Without the embedded and increasing reliable knowledge much of the technology of the west, from weaponry, through navigation, to glass and iron and pottery and steam engines, would not have occurred. To write a whole book on *The Great Divergence* between the two ends of Eur–Asia and to completely omit all of this is, to say the least, bizarre. It is as bizarre as not considering seriously the difference between Christianity and the Confucian–Taoist–Buddhist–Shinto mixes of East Asia. Or as bizarre as failing to discuss the differences between social structures (class and caste and ranks), between kinship systems (agnatic, cognatic) or between political systems (monarchical and republican, imperial and centralized).

It may be difficult for many western historians to criticize the new 'Orient-centred' vision for fear of being accused of being ethno-centric. Having spent much of my life as an anthropologist working on Himalayan societies and in studying Japan I have the highest respect and admiration for Asian civilizations. Thus I am perhaps in a better position than many to warn of the dangers of a new form of historical political correctness. While doing us a service by reminding us of what Smith and his successors always stressed – that is to say the majesty and sophistication of East Asian civilizations – it would be sad if in doing this we also lost sight of the central question. That question is why the

modern transformation to an industrial and scientific-based civilization occurred in western Europe and not eastern Asia. In answering that question we
have to use a much wider canvas than the purely economic and material.

The question of how and why the modern world, a compound of capitalism,
individualism, industrialism, democracy and many other features, emerged and
why it did so in western Europe is one I have pursued all of my adult life. A brief
account of the stages in this journey of exploration is given in the original
introduction to *SWP*.[3] This book is part of my answer.

SWP seeks to explain in some detail how the two islands of England and
Japan broke out of the normal tendency whereby rising population absorbs
increased resources and then overshoots to create a crisis through the intersec-
tion of war, famine and disease. This is what I called the Malthusian trap. It is
a trap which does not absolutely destroy a civilization, but inhibits and under-
mines it. The solution to the question of why England and Japan early escaped
from the Malthusian constraints turned out to lie in a combination of chance
factors, in particular islandhood. Since finishing the book in 1996 it has become
increasingly clear that the Malthusian trap is only one part of the story. Its
power cannot be understood without looking at precisely those dimensions
which Pomeranz and others tend to overlook, namely politics, law, social
structure and knowledge systems. So in a series of subsequent books I have tried
to look at the escapes from parallel traps, which combined in the past to make
the Malthusian one so deadly.

In *The Riddle of the Modern World: Of Liberty, Wealth and Equality* (2000), I
looked at the work of three great thinkers who asked the same central question
as that which lay behind *SWP*. This question is how was it possible to escape
from a world of war, famine, disease and poverty into one of relative liberty,
wealth and equality. Montesquieu, Adam Smith and Tocqueville all gave answers which help us to understand how England and then America escaped
from a series of traps as vicious as that outlined by Malthus. This is the normal
tendency for increased resources to feed not only into growing population and
hence war, famine and disease, but also into increased social inequality, political
centralization and authoritarianism. These three authors outlined the way in
which it was possible for something to occur which avoided the almost universal
tendency which they had observed in every preceding civilization in history.
They produced answers to these difficult questions by employing a wide and
broad comparative method which placed Europe, Asia and America alongside
each other so that they were able to note what was common and what different.
So they provided a coherent story of the political and social underpinnings of
that material and demographic transformation described in *SWP*. Thus *Riddle*
can be read as another part of the attempt to explore how our world came into
being.

Even at the end of Riddle, however, there were several unfinished arguments. One concerned the peculiar case of England and the nature of the bonds that hold people together in a capitalist civilization. Montesquieu, Smith and Tocqueville had pointed to the peculiar legal and social system in England, in particular its development of extensive associations or 'civil society' as it would now be called. Yet none of these authors had a sufficient knowledge of English history to be able to explore exactly how or why England had developed in this peculiar way. In *The Making of the Modern World; Visions from West and East* (2002), I explored this theme through an examination of the greatest of English historians, F.W. Maitland (1850–1906). I considered his work as a contribution to political philosophy and social history rather than as legal history. Maitland explained with great clarity when and why English society, polity, family system and law diverged from continental systems. In his later work he outlined the origins of civil society and modern liberty through the elaboration of the device and concept of the Trust.

While Maitland outlined a satisfying answer to how our modern world emerged, I felt it would also be valuable to look at the answers provided by these European thinkers from outside. How plausible were their ideas when regarded from a non-European civilization? Since Japan is the alternative civilization described in *SWP*, it seemed appropriate to take a Japanese thinker, and in the second half of *Making* I analyse the life and work of the greatest of modern Japanese social thinkers, Yukichi Fukuzawa (1835–1901). Fukuzawa recognized the central essence of what thinkers from Montesquieu to Maitland had stressed, that is the combination of tensions and balances which created the dynamism and openness of Britain and America. He explained how this system worked and helped his countrymen to import many of its institutional under-pinnings in education, commerce, clubs and elsewhere. So he helped to provide the right context for the importation of western science and technology. Within a generation, Japan had moved from being a relatively weak agrarian civilization on the edge of China to becoming the first industrial nation in Asia, powerful enough to defeat both China and Russia at war. If ever there was a demonstration of the accuracy of a set of social theories, this was it.

So between 1996 and 2000 I tried to understand how some nations have escaped from two further traps which feed into the Malthusian one, the political (authoritarian centralization) and the social (hierarchical inequality). One further major trap remained unexplored however. This was alluded to right at the end of *The Riddle of the Modern World* in the following way. 'There is still a large gap in the explanation of how the transition to the modern world has occurred. Overcoming the Malthusian trap is part of the story, and I have tried to provide a theory to explain how that happened. Partially overcoming political, religious and social predation is another part of the total picture and this book [*Riddle*] has provided a theory as to how that may have occurred. Yet there is a third trap which needs consideration. In order to complete the picture we need a thorough examination of the conditions which lead certain societies to go through an industrial revolution, and others an industrious one, some to go through a wisdom revolution and others through a knowledge (science) one. Or, put in another way, why did technological and scientific growth occur so spectacularly and rapidly in western Europe between about the twelfth and nineteenth centuries and why, during the same period, did it slow down, cease and even partially regress in other civilizations which had previously been far more "advanced" than Europe?"[4]

Over the last few years, working with Gerry Martin, I have been trying to explore this last part of the puzzle. It is what one might call the Mandarin trap, in other words the tendency for knowledge systems to become more rigid and conservative with time. It is rather similar to the other three addressed above. Resources and wealth accumulate as a result of chance or invention. This not only feeds into population growth and political and social inequalities, but it also puts more power into the hands of the intellectuals. It tends to increase the control of the lay and clerical forces who guard the thought systems of a civilization. There is a very strong tendency towards conservatism, a looking to the past and the known truths, amongst the literate. The past is littered with examples of different examples of this tendency; the Christian Inquisition, the Brahmin control of thought in India, the Confucian education system, the dominance of mullahs at certain periods in Islamic civilizations. Religious purity, social status and political expediency all tend towards suppression of intellectual innovation.

Yet we know that, counter to this normal tendency, at some period between about 1200 and 1700 a radical break in systems of thought did occur. A number of revolutionary shifts in method and substance came about to which we attach rough labels such as 'The Renaissance' and 'The Scientific Revolution'. An open system of understanding and representing the world was instituted, or re-instituted. This, in turn, was to provide the foundation for the new biology, chemistry, physics and medicine without which the escape from the Malthusian, political and social traps described in the earlier volumes could not have triumphed or been sustained.

To understand how and why this had happened is indeed a daunting task, to which many have devoted their lives without conspicuous success. How could one approach such a vast subject, the revolution in western paradigms of knowledge that led to the divergence of Europe from all other civilizations? Furthermore, if one did find parts of an answer, how could one present one's findings in a brief and comprehensible form? Gerry Martin and I decided to focus our analysis on part of the problem, an exemplar or typical case and one which seemed to lie at the heart of any solution to the question of what happened to shake Europe out of its tendency towards the dogmatic slumber of which Kant spoke.

In a short book on the social history and effects of glass, we describe the great divergence between an increasingly glass-saturated western Europe and an increasingly glassless world outside Europe.[5] We suggest that glass alone is obviously not a necessary and sufficient cause for the transformation of the quality of reliable knowledge. Yet it did have an amazing effect. It created a revolution in human systems of knowledge when conjoined with some of the other demographic, political and social elements outlined in previous volumes and also the inheritance of tools of thought and accumulated information which flowed through Islam from Asia and the Ancient World. It allowed a major shift in vision and confidence.

Glass made a new science and technology possible by providing the new instruments: microscopes, telescopes, barometers, thermometers, vacuum flasks, retorts and many others. At a deeper level it literally opened people's eyes and their minds to new possibilities and turned western civilization from the aural to the visual mode of interpreting experience. In the appendix to the book we examine twenty famous experiments which have changed our world, chosen at random. Fifteen of them could not have been performed without glass tools. Putting it another way, the collapse of glass manufacture in Islamic civilizations and the fading away in India, Japan and China made it impossible that they could have had the type of knowledge revolution that occurred in western Europe.

The following sciences would not have existed without glass instruments: histology, pathology, protozoology, bacteriology, molecular biology. Astronomy, the more general biological sciences, physics, mineralogy, engineering, palaeontology, vulcanology and geology would also have been very different. Without clear glass we would have had no gas laws, no steam engine, no internal combustion engine, no electricity, no cameras and no television. Without clear glass we would not have had the visualization of bacteria, little understanding of infectious diseases which is at the centre of the medical revolution since Pasteur and Koch.

Without the chemistry which depended crucially on glass instruments we would have had no understanding of nitrogen and so no artificial nitrogenous fertilisers. Much of the agricultural advance of the nineteenth century would not have occurred without glass. There would have been no knowledge of the moons of Jupiter and no obvious way to prove that Copernicus and Galileo were right. We would have no understanding of cell division (or of cells), no detailed understanding of genetics and certainly no discovery of DNA. Without spectacles a majority of the population in the west over the age of 50 would not be able to read this chapter.

So glass is both a giant and unforeseen accident and at the same time it follows a predictable pattern of movement round a triangle: deeper knowledge, innovation, multiplication of innovated artefacts which lead back to further knowledge. The movement round this triangle was confined to one region yet it was powerful enough to make the world we live in. It could only do so, however, as part of that package of demographic, political and social patterns outlined in the other books described above. If the modern world is like a garden barred by a combination lock, then unlocking the gate requires the accidental coming together of a series of different numbers which could neither be designed nor left entirely to chance.

Yet even at this point, the quest was not over. Returning to the most puzzling question behind *SWP*, the strange improvement in health in England and Japan in the early modern period, I have had further thoughts.

Part of my explanation in *SWP* for this previously unexplained change was that the introduction of tea was a primary factor behind the hitherto unexplained fall in mortality in eighteenth-century Britain. Hence tea drinking allowed the industrial and urban revolution to occur for the first time.[6] The television series which featured the argument spurred a publisher to ask my mother (a tea manager's widow) and I to write a general book on the history and effects of tea.[7] Research for that book has deepened my conviction that the link between the transition from agrarian civilization to our modern industrial world does, indeed, to a considerable and surprisingly large extent hinge on the huge accident of tea drinking. The theme is explored in the new book which also contains a wider survey of the effects of tea on health. To my considerable surprise, recent work on the medical effects of tea suggests that a number of other diseases may also be influenced by tea drinking. These include several touched on in *SWP*, including malaria, influenza, bubonic plague and various skin and eye diseases. It has also been suggested with some evidence that tea drinking may lower the incidence and effects of many degenerative conditions which I did not deal with such as gout, stones, arthritis, tooth decay, heart attacks, strokes and various cancers.

It is worth singling out one of these for further comment. One of the most striking yet puzzling findings in *SWP* was that malaria seems to have more or less disappeared in Japan between the fourteenth and seventeenth centuries. Likewise, in Britain where malaria had been a serious endemic ailment in the seventeenth century, it seems to have receded rapidly after about the first third of the eighteenth century in England and southern Scotland.[8] For example, writing at the start of the nineteenth century, Thomas Place noted that 'The ague [malaria], too, had its victims in large numbers. Towards the close of the seventeenth century, nearly one in forty, of those who were buried in London, are stated to have died of this disorder, which is now but seldom heard of, and kills nobody. Even those counties, where it was most prevalent and most fatal, are comparatively free from it, it being confined to much smaller spaces . . .'[9] I put forward various theories which experts have suggested in the past to account for this disappearance: better irrigation and land drainage which reduced the number of stagnant pools where mosquitoes breed; changes in livestock rearing which altered the relations between mosquitoes, livestock and humans; mosquito netting in Japan. None of these is satisfactory as a total explanation, even when they are united.

In light of the fact that some early writers from the seventeenth century argued that malaria could be cured or decreased in its effect by tea drinking, as well as the exact correlation between the growth of tea drinking and the decline of malaria in both these islands, it would seem worth re-examining this topic. It is known that certain plants contain substances that are effective against malaria, for instance the Neem tree in India and artemesia in China, as well, of course, as cinchona bark or quinine. Perhaps there is something similar in the tea camellia. It would certainly be worth further research. For instance, an epidemiological study might confirm whether after the introduction of tea drinking into Assam after the 1880s, or into India from the 1920s, the levels of malaria declined even without spraying or netting. Or whether countries which are tea drinking, such as China or Japan have lower incidence than those without tea. Even within a population, for instance Sri Lanka, there are considerable differences in the incidence of malaria; does this coincide at all with the incidence of tea drinking? It would be very good to see whether experiments showed any effects of tea on malarial parasites.

Although I hardly dealt with China in *SWP*, in so far as I did so, I assumed that it more or less conformed to the Malthusian 'crisis' model of high mortality (epidemic and periodic) and high fertility through young age at marriage for both males and females. Recent research has suggested that my assumptions were wrong. In particular the work of James Lee and his associates suggest the following characteristics of Chinese demography over the period from say 1700 to 1900.[10] Mortality was usually fairly low, roughly in line with that in England or Japan; famine and subsistence crises were not widespread; marital fertility was lower than that in Europe and roughly in line with Japan; while women married very young (in their early teens), men married late (in their late twenties or later) and many never married at all; female infanticide rates were very high, averaging between ten and twenty per cent of all live births. In this reappraisal, Chinese demography turns out to be different from both Europe and Japan, but certainly not a simple high mortality and high fertility regime.

In the context of health, what is particularly interesting is the low mortality rate. Like Japan, much of the best land in China was densely populated and there were very large cities. As in Japan or later eighteenth-century England there is the intriguing question of how mortality, particularly that caused by water-borne diseases, was kept in check in a situation where we would expect there to be increasing problems of dysentery, typhoid and other ailments. In *Green Gold* we have widened our argument, suggesting that the spread of tea drinking in China from the eighth century onward may be an important factor in the rise of the T'ang and Sung Empires by allowing dense population without serious water-borne disease. This, we argue, may be due not only to the universal use of boiling water in China, but also because of the anti-bacterial substances in the tea. If, as we suggest in the same book, tea may also inhibit a range of other diseases, including influenza, malaria and possibly even bubonic plague, as well as common diseases such as strokes, heart attacks and cancers, the reason for the surprisingly good health of the Chinese population may be connected to tea drinking in a much more dramatic way than merely the boiling of water.

Certainly this was the opinion of the Chinese themselves. As we quote at some length in *Green Gold*, both the Chinese themselves from the eighth century onwards, and the missionaries and diplomats who visited China from the sixteenth century, believed that the longevity and healthfulness of the Chinese was largely to be accounted for by tea drinking. Just to quote one among many examples, in a herbal reference by Li Shih-chen, published in 1578 but thought to contain material from a much earlier period, Li stated that tea would 'promote digestion, dissolve fats, neutralize poisons in the digestive system, cure dysentery, fight lung disease, lower fevers, and treat epilepsy. Tea was also thought to be an effective astringent for cleaning sores and recommended for washing the eyes and mouth.'[11]

A further way in which further work on tea drinking fits into the theses advanced in *SWP* is also worth mentioning. There is a good deal in the book on work, on the immense toil of pre-industrial life. In order to sustain the dense populations of Japan and China, very intensive wet rice cultivation was necessary, often on a very meagre diet without much protein or even many vegetables. In *Green Gold* it is suggested that tea drinking, by providing extra energy through the effects of caffeine on human muscle co-ordination and endurance, may have played an important part in making such agriculture possible. Furthermore, it is known that green tea contains high levels of vitamin C, and it may also contain enzymes which help the body to extract the maximum of this vitamin from fruit and vegetables (and help, among other things, to reduce scurvy). All of this is an important part of the health environment explored in *SWP*, just as the stimulating effects of the caffeine in tea, combined with the energy in sugar, we argue, are crucial to understanding what happened when enormous demands were put on generally ill-nourished workers during the British industrial revolution.

Since completing the book in the summer of 1996 I have learnt one more thing about tea which alters one argument in *SWP*. As noted, I argued that the polyphenols in tea destroyed harmful bacteria in water, for example those associated with dysentery and typhoid. This added to the effects of boiling the water to make tea and reduced water-borne disease. Yet I remained puzzled when I wrote the book as to how tea drinking by the mother could have protected breast-feeding infants, for one of the most striking facts about the sudden decline in water-borne dysentery in the middle of the eighteenth century in England was that it occurred not only among those who drank tea for the first time (mothers and fathers), but equally among infants in their first months. Trying to understand this, I suggested in the book that the link was a negative one. The mother was less likely to have dysentery so her nipples and hands and clothes would have fewer harmful bacteria. So the infant would be less likely to get the disease.

Later, a doctor explained to me that what a mother eats or drinks will almost immediately be passed on to the infant. As a result the anti-bacterial polyphenols in the tea will pass easily into the mouth and stomach of the baby. Hence the tea drinking of the mother could well have given the breast-fed infant direct extra protection. This would explain why it was both maternal and infant mortality from water-borne disease that simultaneously declined in tandem. It is yet another argument against feeding infants with dried milk products in those many societies which suffer so terribly from water-borne infections.

So a further part of the answer to the question of how the modern world came about is now in place. During the last five hundred years one civilization, and then others which have copied it, have, at least temporarily, deviated from the normal tendencies and traps which halt the increase in the wealth of nations.[12] The Malthusian link between production and reproduction has been weakened. The almost inevitable connection between increasing wealth and increasing political and social predation has been partially suspended. The powerful tendency towards intellectual rigidification has been temporarily lifted by developments in the methods of generating and transmitting accurate knowledge about the world.

This is not, of course, to say that these tendencies will not reassert themselves in the future. What has happened was the result of chance rather than design and there are plenty of examples of reversals. Not least among them are that in the middle of the twentieth century most of the nations on earth, including most of those in Europe, as well as China, Japan and Russia, were governed by people who were explicitly trying to destroy the liberty, equality and openness which earlier thinkers had believed to be so valuable. History has certainly not ended. Indeed, many of the tendencies, for instance the continued massive onrush of population, the spread of new and old diseases, the spending of huge quantities of money on weapons and aggressive 'defence' systems are all too obvious.

It is my hope, however, that this interconnected set of volumes, of which

SWP is one essential pillar, will give a broad outline to some of the dangers which history reveals to us and the underlying patterns and tendencies which have again and again caused infinite misery and the collapse of civilizations. James Riley in his review of *SWP* suggests that other nations were not in a position to emulate the English or Japanese model which allowed an escape from agrarian poverty.[13] This is obviously true of the eighteenth and even much of the nineteenth century. But we now live in a different world where ideas, technologies, cultures and social systems can move very quickly. It does not seem beyond the bounds of human creativity and rationality to be able to learn a little from our past and to build on this knowledge a safer, wealthier and more just future, based on an understanding of what those structural tendencies are which we must avoid, and how they have successfully been evaded from time to time.

SWP was in many ways the most difficult and laborious of the fifteen books which I have published. This was partly because of the difficulty of the subject. To comprehend the medical history of two civilizations over a period of one thousand years is a large task. Furthermore, to solve the problem of why, for the first time in history mortality started to fall in a sustained way in societies which were rapidly urbanizing and where the level of nutrition may have been decreasing, was very difficult. The fact that most of the data as well as the basics of medicine and biology were new to me at the start of the task made it even more difficult. It required the absorption of new data and techniques of analysis. I also had to rethink the theoretical framework and concepts of cause and effect which I had absorbed over the years as a historian and anthropologist. I had to elaborate new multidimensional, non-teleological, models to explain change. These are first elaborated in the last chapter of *SWP* and further refined in the subsequent volumes.

The difficulties of researching and writing *SWP* had two consequences which can be explored in relation to this paperback edition. One effect of the difficulty of the task was to make me very conscious from an early point that I was on an unusually long and complex mental adventure. So I decided to keep a diary of the writing of the book. I kept the papers, plans and daily diary entries and from time to time while writing the book took stock of these. This helped the writing and research itself, but I began to realize towards the end of the three years it took that I had accidentally also created what I facetiously refer to as 'An Autobiography of a Book'. In other words, alongside *SWP* I was writing an account of how a book is written and how intellectual problems are solved. This was written during the creative process itself and not afterwards.

There are a number of accounts of creative work written by poets, novelists, painters, mathematicians and others. There are also a larger number of accounts written with hindsight after a creative act, for example Crick and Watson's separate accounts of the discovery of DNA or Goody, Geertz and Levi-Strauss's accounts of their intellectual work in anthropology based on reconstructions after the event.[14] What I have not found is a full-length book written by a social scientist or historian describing what happens as the problems are actually being posed and resolved, rather than after the discoveries have been made.[15] Without such an account almost all those who are being trained to undertake research in the arts, humanities and social sciences absorb a distorted and confused image of how they should proceed, as I did myself. By reading only the final outcome of work in the shape of a finished and polished monograph or article, people assume that this must bear some resemblance to how a book was originally written or a discovery made. This is far from the case.

Until now it has been very difficult to publish a parallel account of a large piece of creative work. The commentary will only take on a meaning when placed alongside the finished product and will only appeal to a specialist audience. This may help to explain why such an account has never been published. Now, with the advent of a reasonably priced paperback, in conjunction with the entirely new dimension of the internet, it becomes possible for the first time to attempt something more ambitious to be done. So, on my website I have put some of the background thinking and experience that went into the writing of *SWP* in the hope that it will interest some readers to see what a chancy, uncertain yet exciting business it is to write a long book.[16]

There is another consequence of the laborious nature of *SWP*, combined with the fact that for a long time I was very unsure as to where to proceed. As all those who try to do so will know, almost always when one write or creates in other ways, one produces too much. There is usually about a quarter or a third of the writing which has to be left out of the final 'published' version. In the case of writing, this is a necessary process, even if it feels wasteful. This extra writing creates mental scaffolding round the object in creation and allows one to build it, but it will finally be dismantled and vanish when the final object appears. Most of it is of interest to a few of the readers who want to go down the by ways of the subject, or into some matter in greater depth. Some of this may go into an appendix. On the whole, however, constraints of cost and attention from the 'average' reader leads to the abandonment of nearly all of this invisible writing.

As with all my books, this process occurred when writing *SWP*. Yet it was on a much larger scale than I recall in any other instance. This was partly because it was in the end a very long book, so cutting one quarter of the original length would constitute many thousands of words. Yet the amount that disappeared was much greater than this. The original text was made even larger because I was not sure where clues and arguments were fruitful and I needed to explore them in depth, partly because I needed to explain to myself many areas bordering on the central theme which, in the end, were not absolutely essential. So I wrote many drafts, which became longer and longer. In the end, something like 100,000 words have been omitted from this published version.

These omitted sections may be of use to some specialists who want to pursue topics touched on in *SWP* in greater depth. There are 36 'appendices'. The first six, to give an idea of their nature, are as follows: abortion methods in England, Japanese adoption, irrigated rice cultivation tasks in Japan, air-borne disease, domesticated animals in Japan, the bath in Japan. All are now available on the website.

Retrieving these omitted passages is worth doing for another reason, for they add another significant dimension to the account of how a book is written. They illustrate, as has seldom been done before, how much material and of what kind tends to be squeezed out of a book when it is published. They are, to paraphrase the title of a book by Max Muller, 'chips from an English workshop'. That these chips can now be added back to enrich the book is, of course, another fruit of the internet revolution. To have distributed them as a CD with the original book or paperback copy, as I had previously considered, would be expensive and complicated and it was for this reason, among others, that I decided not to do so. In any case, most readers would not want all or even any of the extra material. Yet for those who do want to go down some of the paths I took while writing the book, and then abandoned in the published version, it is now possible to see this material.

So the republication of the book in paperback form gives me the opportunity to create an unusual set of materials. The central text is the 'stand-alone' book which you have in your hands. This is a retrospective and edited account of an adventure or exploration, the published account of the voyage of discovery written after it was finished. Alongside this there is a website which contains various contextualizing materials. It contains a fuller account of why and how the book was written in the very moment when the search for solutions was in progress. If one carries on the metaphor, they are the diary or log of the voyage as it happened, interspersed with various tentative plans and sketch maps of possible ways to go. There are also descriptions of a number of the paths down which I strayed and on which I found curious facts, but which were finally left out of the final published account. Finally, to give some sense of the author and his search, there are 12 short film extracts. In these I pursue the puzzles narrated in the book on location in Japan, Nepal, Australia, Venice and England. More widely, the whole adventure is, as described, but one voyage which fits in with the others to understand the interlinked nature of the unlikely escape into the modern world.

Notes

1 J.M. Blaut, *The Colonizer's Model of the World* (1993); Jack Goody, *The East in the West* (1996); André Gunder Frank, *ReOrient* (1998).

2 Alfred W. Crosby, *The Measure of Reality* (1997), now dates the 'great divergence' in thought systems even earlier, roughly in the period 1250–1450.

3 A longer and more detailed account of the attempt to solve some of these problems is given on www.alanmacfarlane.com.

4 Macfarlane, *Riddle*, pp.293–4.

5 The book was published in 2002 as Alan Macfarlane and Gerry Martin, *The Glass Bathyscaphe: How Glass Changed the World* by Profile Books in Britain, and as *Glass: A World History* by Chicago University Press in the US.

6 *SWP*, 132–53.

7 To be published in 2003 as *Green Gold: The Empire of Tea*, by Alan and Iris Macfarlane.

8 *SWP*, 196.

9 Francis Place, *Illustrations and Proofs of the Principle of Population* (1822:1930), 251.

10 James Z. Lee and Cameron D. Campbell, *Fate and fortune in rural China: Social organization and population behavior in Liaoning 1774–1873* (1997) and James Lee and Wang Feng, 'Malthusian Models and Chinese Realities: The Chinese Demographic System 1700–2000', *Population and Development Review* (25:1), 1999. See also William Lavely and R. Bin Wong, 'Revising the Malthusian Narrative: The Comparative Study of Population Dynamics in Late Imperial China', *Journal of Asian Studies* 57, no.3 (August 1998).

11 Jill Anderson's *Introduction to Japanese Tea Ritual* (1991), quoted in Bennet Weinberg and Bonnie Bealer, *The World of Caffeine* (2001), p.36.

12 It is a failure to analyse these normal tendencies, and hence to see the peculiarity of the deviations from them, which is among the reasons for the failure of interesting books such as David Landes, *The Wealth and Poverty of Nations* (1998) or Jared Diamond, *Guns, Germs and Steel* (1997) to provide a convincing account of the development of civilizations.

13 For the review, see www.alanmacfarlane.com.

14 Francis Crick, *What Mad Pursuit* (1989); James D. Watson, *The Double Helix* (1968); Jack Goody, *The Expansive Moment* (1995), ch. 8; Claude Levi-Strauss, *A World on the Wane* (1961); Clifford Geertz, *After the Fact* (1996).

15 What there is, has been mined in a number of interesting general works on creativity, including more general works on creativity such as Arthur Koestler, *The Act of Creation* (1964) and Margaret Boden, *The Creative Mind* (1990).

16 For this account, see www.alanmacfarlane.com.

Bibliography

All books are published in London, unless otherwise indicated.

Blaut, J.M., *The Colonizer's Model of the World*, New York, 1993.

Boden, Margaret, *The Creative Mind*, 1990.

Crick, Francis, *What Mad Pursuit*, 1989.

Crosby, Alfred W., *The Measure of Reality; Quantification and Western Society 1250–1600*, Cambridge, 1998.

Diamond, Jared, *Guns, Germs and Steel; the fates of human societies*, 1997.

Frank, André Gunder, *ReOrient; Global Economy in the Asian Age*, Berkeley, 1998.

Geertz, Clifford, *After the Fact; Two countries, four decades, one anthropologist*, Harvard, 1996.

Goody, Jack, *The Expansive Moment; the rise of social anthropology in Britain and Africa, 1918–1970*, Cambridge, 1995.

Goody, Jack, *The East in the West*, Cambridge, 1996.

Hanley, Susan, B., *Everyday Things in Premodern Japan*, Berkeley, 1997.

Koestler, Arthur, *The Act of Creation*, 1964.

Landes, David, *The Wealth and Poverty of Nations; why some are so rich and some so poor*, 1998.

Lavely, William and Wong, R. Bin, 'Revising the Malthusian Narrative: The Comparative Study of Population Dynamics in Late Imperial China', *Journal of Asian Studies*, 57, no.3, August 1998.

Lee, James Z., and Campbell, Cameron D., *Fate and fortune in rural China: Social organization and population behavior in Liaoning 1774–1873*, Cambridge, 1997.

Lee, James Z., and Feng, Wang, 'Malthusian Models and Chinese Realities: The Chinese Demographic System 1700–2000', *Population and Development Review* vol. 25, no.1, 1999.

Lévi-Strauss, Claude, *A World on the Wane*, 1961.

Macfarlane, Alan, *The Riddle of the Modern World: Of Liberty, Wealth and Equality*, 2000.

Macfarlane, Alan, *The Making of the Modern World: Visions from West and East*, 2002.

Macfarlane, Alan, and Martin, Gerry, *The Glass Bathyscaphe: How Glass Changed the World*, 2002; American edition titled *Glass: A World History*, Chicago, 2002.

Macfarlane, Alan and Iris, *Green Gold: The Empire of Tea*, forthcoming, 2003.

Place, Francis, *Illustrations and Proofs of the Principle of Population*, 1822: reprint 1967.

Pomerantz, Kenneth, *The Great Divergence: China, Europe, and the making of the modern world economy*, 2000.

Watson, James D., *The Double Helix* 1968.

Weinberg, Bennet, and Bealer, Bonnie, *The World of Caffeine*, 2001.

Introduction

This book attempts to solve part of a problem that has haunted me for over thirty years. My first memory of being really stirred by the question of the origins of industrial civilization, and in particular the relations between population and economic development, was as an undergraduate reading history at Oxford when writing an essay on the causes of the industrial revolution in England. Surveying the state of the argument as to whether it was rising birth rates or falling death rates which had led to the surge of population in England from the middle of the eighteenth century, it appeared that scholars were almost equally divided on the degree to which population growth was a cause or a consequence of the industrial revolution in England, and what caused that growth. I still remember my excitement at discovering a problem which was so clearly a puzzle to some of the best historians of the period.

It seemed obvious that mortality was dropping, yet all the theories to explain why this happened were clearly inadequate. 'Higher living standards' seemed to be important, but what these were was left vague; of particular medical changes, the disappearance of plague was mentioned though it was not clear why this had happened; changes in the habits of lice, better nutrition, absence of war, improvements in hygiene, medical improvements, even a change in the virulence of disease were canvassed. Scholars appeared to be circling round a large problem yet unable to resolve it – better at knocking down theories than building them up. It was possible for me as an undergraduate to show that the decline of plague had happened too early (it disappeared two generations before the rapid growth of population); that there was no evidence of viral changes; that the medical improvements were insignificant, with the possible exception of smallpox inoculation, that the nutritional improvements were very questionable, as were improvements in hygiene.

Then there was a similar puzzle in relation to fertility. An almost equal number of authors believed that this was the crucial variable. But what caused the rise in fertility? The only reasons given were that it was due to the same rising living standards which affected fertility, perhaps by allowing people to marry younger. Yet again the arguments and evidence seemed weak and inconclusive.

Part of the difficulty appeared to be caused by the fact that data on mortality, nuptiality and fertility was so poor, as it was based on aggregative analysis (totals of baptisms, marriage and burials from parish registers). I did not then know that French demographers were developing a new technique, 'family reconstitution', which would transform our understanding of the past by giving much more precise statistics on marital fertility, infant mortality and age at marriage. The method was first applied to English data by E.A.Wrigley in his work on Colyton in Devon. Along with the exploration of early listings of inhabitants by Peter Laslett, this made the period of the mid-to-late sixties an enormously exciting one in English historical demography. The academic work was given practical relevance by a growing awareness of ecological and demographic problems at a world level.

Some of the results of these new findings were summarized in my first publication, an article in *New Society* (10 Oct. 1968) in which I wrote that 'We are discovering that there was birth control in Stuart England; that Europe had a "unique marriage pattern", combining high age at marriage with a large proportion of never married persons; that the small "nuclear" family predominated in most of the pre-industrial west; that one of the major factors permitting the accumulation of capital and hence industrial expansion in the late eighteenth century was late marriage and the consequent slow population growth – roughly one quarter of 1 per cent per annum in the 200 years before industrialization.'

Despite the new data and frameworks, the questions I had encountered in the early 1960s were still wide open. It seemed difficult to proceed any further in solving the large question about the relations between industrialization and population by remaining within the European context. This was one of the lessons to be drawn from the great step forward taken when, in 1965, John Hajnal published his essay on the European marriage pattern.[1] By setting the west European marriage data alongside that for eastern Europe and Asia, he was able to see both the major peculiarities of the west (late age at marriage and selective marriage) and the fact that there was a pattern or system. On a more limited scale a number of other demographers made such contrasts within Europe, for instance Wrigley between France, England and Scandinavia. Thus it became clear that only through a wider method of contrast would many

[1] Hajnal, *Marriage Patterns*.

of the central features of the English demographic past become visible at all.

In order to broaden my framework into a comparative one I went to Nepal in December 1968 for fifteen months, to work as an anthropologist among a people called the Gurungs.

It is difficult to analyse the effects of this experience, and of nine further trips between 1986 and 1995, in altering the way I approached the English past. Much of the influence was at a deep level of perceptual shift which alters both the questions one asks and the implicit comparisons one has in mind when evaluating evidence.

Witnessing the perennial problem of disease, the sanitary arrangements, the illness of young children, the difficulties with water, the flies and worms, the gruelling work and the struggle against nature in a mountain community made clear to me, in a way that books or even films alone could never do, some of the realities which the English and Japanese faced historically.[2] Of course it was different. Each culture is different. But to feel in the blood and heart and to see with one's eyes how people cope with a much lower amount of energy, medical care and general infrastructure makes one aware of many things. Without this experience I know that I could not have written this book. Trapped in late-twentieth-century western affluence it would be impossible to feel or know much of what has been important to the majority of humans through history. Watching and studying a village over the years also makes one more deeply aware, as does all anthropological work, of the interconnectedness of things, the holistic view of a society.

It is important to stress this experience, for in the body of this text Nepal is scarcely mentioned despite the fact that much of what I have seen when examining England and Japan has become visible by setting them against a backdrop of Nepal. De Tocqueville once explained, 'In my work on America. . . . Though I seldom mentioned France, I did not write a page without thinking of her, and placing her as it were before me.'[3] Nepal helped me to understand the Japanese case, which I shall shortly describe, and Japan helped me to get England into perspective. A straight, two-way, comparison of either England-Nepal or Japan-England would not have been enough.

At the theoretical level, the Nepalese experience enabled me to look at England, and indeed the whole of western Europe, from the outside and to see more clearly its demographic and economic peculiarities. In the last chapter of my book *Resources and Population* I tried to characterize these peculiarities by developing a model which incorporated both the work of European historical demographers and my Nepalese data. The model, further modified in chapter 1

---

[2] My general account of the society is in Macfarlane, *Resources*; a preliminary account of the medical situation is in Macfarlane, *Disease*.
[3] De Tocqueville, *Memoir*, I, 359.

of this book, differentiated between what I called 'crisis' regimes, such as that in Nepal in the past, where the rapid rise in population over the last hundred years was due to the elimination of war, famine and epidemic disease, and 'homeostatic' regimes, such as England in the past, where fluctuation in population were mainly due to changes in fertility rates.

When I returned with a whole set of new data, the English historical world began to look different. The work of Wrigley, Laslett and others inspired me to undertake my own family reconstitution studies to help resolve the puzzles. But since it was clear that demography was embedded in the wider economic and social context, Sarah Harrison and I developed a technique of 'total reconstitution' which used all the surviving documents of a community.[4] This enabled us to reconstruct the parish of Earls Colne and to a lesser extent Kirkby Lonsdale in Cumbria. A number of the factual questions were resolved by this method and one could make some progress.

The combination of a large data collecting and analysis exercise and the pressures of starting to teach anthropology meant that I only came up for air in 1977 and it was then that I explicitly realized that my perception of English history had completely changed. Using the comparative anthropological framework, I suspected that much of the theory which had been developed to understand English history since the 1950s needed revision.

In 1977, I was tugged away from the themes of marriage, family and fertility about which I had long been brooding and felt compelled to write *The Origins of English Individualism* which represents a re-assessment of aspects of English history in the light of my Nepalese experience and of my growing immersion in comparative anthropology. Hardly had the main writing of this book been finished when I returned to the subject of English fertility, in particular reflecting on what effects my shift of interpretation of the English past had on my understanding of that part of the demographic puzzle concerned with fertility.

Looking back, my book on English individualism helped to break a deadlock in my own thought. Wrigley and Hajnal had shown that the marriage and fertility side of the English situation were very important. But the puzzle of why there was this unusual marriage pattern remained. It seemed that peasantry, or a domestic mode of production, was deeply association with high fertility and a low age at marriage. Yet England deviated from this. The assumption that the English had been 'peasants' in the normal anthropological sense appeared to be wrong. The general theory connecting high fertility and peasantry remained, it was just that England might well be an exception.

In essence, I began to understand why fertility was often low and attuned to

---

[4] Macfarlane et al., *Reconstructing Historical Communities*, and for the documents themselves, published and indexed in full, the Earls Colne microfiche.

the needs of a market economy in England. In true 'peasant' societies, based on the domestic mode of production, to expand family size was rational. In England, with its early concepts of private property and individual rights, there were considerable 'costs' in having children. These ideas were expanded and published in my book on *Marriage and Love in England 1300–1840* (1986) in which I attempted to explain the reasons for the unusual demographic history of England and in particular that part concerned with restrained fertility.

It had become obvious since Hajnal's work that the key lay in the European marriage system and in particular a late and selective marriage pattern which could be varied in some sort of complex relation to the economy. I explored the various pressures which lay behind a system which Thomas Malthus recognized in his discussions of the 'preventive check' in the second edition of his *Principles of Population*. In the final chapter I attempted to show how marriage was linked to economic growth, and arose out of the early capitalist and individualistic nature of English society which I had described in *Individualism*. With this book I felt I had come to grips with the conundrum which Wrigley had identified – how did the marriage system work and what were its correlates.

The other half of the problem, that concerning mortality, had not been addressed. I had noted that historically English mortality patterns seemed to be unusual.[5] Yet I had made no progress in analysing this other side of the demographic puzzle. This was partly because the difficulty of solving the problems in the field of mortality were even greater than those in relation to fertility. With fertility, the mechanism of how certain levels were maintained in Western Europe had become clear after Hajnal's paper. In the case of mortality none of the arguments put forward to explain the sudden decline in English mortality from the middle of the eighteenth century carried conviction. We knew that it happened, but we did not know either how or why it happened. With fertility, one is mainly out in the open, dealing with visible human motivations and institutions. With mortality, the solutions are less visible, involving complex chains of bacteria and viruses affected by many human and non-human forces.

Apart from posing fresh questions by suggesting a great contrast between the English and Asian case, the Nepalese experience did not really help in its solution. Nepal's rapid population growth from the middle of the nineteenth century confirmed that medical improvements were not needed for population growth to occur. It showed that the elimination of war and famine was enough to let natural fertility cause a doubling of the population in each generation. But none of this really helped with the English puzzle. I had come to an insurmountable obstacle and it was only a chance invitation to visit Japan in 1990 that opened up another way of approaching the problem.

---

[5] Macfarlane, *Culture*, 155–6.

I had long been struck by the similarity of England and Japan. Both were islands, both passed through an authentic 'feudal' period, both were noted for a puritanical form of world religion, and both became pioneers of industrialization in their respective regions. As I studied and re-visited Japan in the 1990s, the similarity in the shape of the population graph in England and Japan and the fact that both seemed, early on, to have separated production and reproduction suggested that it might be worth investigating the matter further.

What was particularly intriguing was that there now seemed to be two exceptions to the 'normal' population patterns, as represented by Nepal. By investigating these two cases side by side, might it be possible to resolve some of those problems which still baffled historians and demographers?

The possibility of real advance was made more likely by the rapid developments in social and demographic knowledge in both England and Japan. The general shape of what had happened in England was becoming much clearer, especially through the publication in 1981 of E.A.Wrigley and Roger Schofield's *Population History of England*. Furthermore, the work of a number of Japanese and foreign scholars, who had applied the methods of European demographers to the voluminous Japanese records, particularly that of Hayami, Saito, Yamamura, Hanley, Thomas Smith and, more recently in relation to epidemics, Jannetta, now made a real comparison possible for the first time.

In this book I start by looking at the major problem to be solved: how were some nations able to break out of the Malthusian trap of war, famine and disease? War and famine are the obvious starting place since their containment was the foundation upon which any sustained development would be built. If a country is subject to war or constantly ravaged by famine, or, more often, by both, there is little chance of proceeding to a level where the next threat, epidemic disease, can be overcome.

It is not too difficult to see how, through the chance of islandhood, England and Japan escaped from the interlinked curses of war and famine. But though this gave them an advantage it is still very difficult to understand how they increasingly avoided epidemic disease. While it was known that a number of diseases did decline in England from the later seventeenth century, and in Japan some centuries earlier, none of the possible causes for the decline seemed convincing.

There seemed few grounds for believing that the mortality decline could be the result of medical improvements, of environmental changes, of changes in the virulence of disease organisms, or even improvements in nutrition. It was much easier to prove that each cause was insufficient; even combined they could not be shown to lead to the decline that was to be explained.

In attempting to find an explanation I have adopted several strategies. Having dealt with war and famine as two parts of the mortality pattern, I decided to distinguish the various classes of disease. The obvious division was between the ways in which diseases were transmitted. Here I followed Macfarlane Burnett's distinction between three of the major branches of infectious diseases: those passing through water and food, those borne by insect or other vectors, and those travelling through the air.[6]

By examining each class of disease in parallel in England and Japan I found that a new set of questions emerged. For instance, the absence or presence of certain diseases in Japan threw light on the situation in England and vice versa. It became clear that the differences were the result of material and cultural features of the environment. The shock of difference led the search towards a number of aspects of the environment which would have remained largely invisible if one had remained within one culture area.

I felt that the way to proceed was to see which environmental factors were associated with each of the major branches of disease. This approach worked reasonably well with those bacterial diseases which are directly affected by human practices such as the keeping of animals, the nature of clothing, eating, washing and so on. Yet even when an explanation was given of how a certain set of environmental factors caused the rise or decline of a disease, there was often an area of cultural practice which in turn needed explanation. In the final section on disease I deal with those diseases which are most difficult to explain, namely the air-borne epidemics where the direct environmental approach seemed less likely to be fruitful.

The lowering of mortality was only one part of the escape. Having achieved less than maximum mortality a country was faced with the second of the Malthusian traps – runaway population growth. Malthus had foreseen that humans sometimes achieve, through a windfall resource or a new technology, a temporary lowering of their death rate for a generation or two. But this would shortly be offset by a rapid rise in population as the perennial high fertility rate operated. This would in turn bring them face-to-face with war, famine and new kinds of disease. How could this second trap be avoided?

Having established that English and Japanese fertility seems to have been kept well below the theoretical maximum over long periods at a time when wealth was increasing, I examine the three ways in which this could be achieved. I begin with exposure to sexual intercourse, that is the pattern of marriage and sexual relations which brings women and men together. I then look at the impediments to conception, in other words the biological factors (such as sickness, work strain, lactation) and contraceptive technologies which prevent conception in the first place. I then look at the third area, that is the treatment of unwanted conceptions, in particular abortion and infanticide. Yet even when I had established the different mechanisms used in the two countries

[6] Burnett, *Infectious*, ch.8.

which led to their lowered fertility, there was still the question of motivation, which I discuss in relation to heirship.

The difference between research and writing creates a contradiction which it may be helpful for readers to be aware of. As I proceeded I became more and more aware of the symbiotic relations between all aspects of what I was studying. This was true of the relations between different types of disease, for instance the vector-borne and water-borne diseases. It was true of the relation between mortality and fertility, for example the ways in which infants were fed was important in both respects. The interrelations between war, famine and disease were equally strong. The connections and mutual inter-effects of housing, clothing and hygiene were very powerful. My central theme became the complex set of links between hitherto apparently rather remotely connected phenomena.

Yet the book has to 'murder to dissect', to split apart in order to be read sequentially. Only in the conclusion is it possible to bring all the threads together by considering the chains of cause and consequence which led to the unusual outcome whose effects we see around us now. I make some conjectures about the extent to which the developments suggest conscious design or random chance, in other words how far they indicate the Darwinian process of 'blind variation and selective retention'. Thus, starting with Malthus we end with Darwin.

Part I

The Trap

1

The Malthusian Trap

'For nation shall rise against nation, and kingdom against kingdom: and there shall be famines, and pestilences, and earthquakes, in diverse places. All these are the beginning of sorrow.'[1] In the words of the gospel such was the state of humankind.

It was a world from which it seemed impossible to escape. In 1788 Edward Gibbon completed his great work on *The Decline and Fall of the Roman Empire*. The following year he surveyed the world around him. There seemed little improvement over the last two thousand years. 'The far greater part of the globe is overspread with barbarism or slavery: in the civilized world, the most numerous class is condemned to ignorance and poverty. . . . The general probability is about three to one that a new-born infant will not live to complete his fiftieth year.'[2]

Gibbon's world was one with a population of less than one thousand million inhabitants. As we stand at the end of the twentieth century, only a little over two hundred years later, there are more than seven times as many humans on earth. Yet we see a world in which many millions have escaped from a daily fear of war, famine and disease. For the privileged living in parts of Europe, America and Asia, there is wealth and stability undreamt of by peoples in most past civilizations.

It is easy to assume that this change was inevitable; because this happened, it had to happen. Yet when we regard the many millions who are still trapped in poverty, disease and the fear of war, and when we remember that the escape into

[1] Matthew, 24:7–8.
[2] Gibbon, *Autobiography*, 217.

relative security has only occurred within a brief space of time, we are reminded that it was not inevitable.

In order to gain a full sense of how unlikely were the events which have unfolded over the last two hundred years it is helpful to go back to the writings of a man who stood at the transition point between the old world and the new. In 1798, nine years after Gibbon's *Memoir*, Thomas Malthus published his *Essay on the Principles of Population*. In this short essay he laid out the reasons why agrarian civilizations seemed to be trapped for ever in misery. Alongside Adam Smith's *Wealth of Nations*, it is the clearest analysis of the structural tendencies of *ancien regime* societies and their intrinsic limits to growth.

In the second edition of his *Principles* Malthus himself came to revise his views and to write of strong *tendencies* rather than iron *laws*. Furthermore, we now know that some of his predictions were wrong and others seem to have been suspended, at least temporarily. Indeed, that is one of the major themes of this book. Yet without subscribing either to his views of 'progress' or to his representation of the iron laws, it is nevertheless essential to outline in stark detail his early vision. Only then can we fully understand the unlikeliness of the transition which has taken place.

Malthus drew attention to three facts. The first is that human beings are very strongly motivated by a desire for sexual intercourse. 'The passion between the sexes has appeared in every age to be so nearly the same, that it may always be considered, in algebraic language, as a given quantity.'[3] All else being equal, men and women will mate as soon as possible after puberty. If such mating is only permitted within marriage, 'Such is the disposition to marry, particularly in very young people, that, if the difficulties of providing for a family were entirely removed, very few would remain single at twenty-two.'[4]

The second fact is the high fertility of humans. If this high fertility is combined with a reasonable rate of mortality, such early and frequent mating will lead to rapid population growth. He cited examples of populations which had doubled in twenty years or less. In fact, he deliberately erred on the conservative side. As Alfred Sauvy points out, 'a population not practising contraception and benefiting from present-day medical science could in an extreme case double in thirteen years.'[5] This is because of the natural fecundity of human beings: 'If a couple comes together at puberty, stays together until the woman's menopause, and has no recourse to contraception, its average number of children will be about ten. In a population living in the best possible conditions this would probably increase to twelve.'[6] Numbers can thus easily

---

[3] Malthus, *Population*, I, 312.
[4] Malthus, *Population*, II, 52.
[5] Sauvy, *Population*, 410.
[6] Sauvy, *Population*, 349.

double in each generation and this means that a vast population will build up very quickly.

The third fact is that economic resources, and in particular food production, cannot keep pace with this population growth within a basically agrarian economy largely dependent on human labour. This is due to the law of diminishing marginal returns. While there may be periods when rates of growth in agriculture rise to three or four percent *per annum*, which is equivalent to a doubling of food in a generation, such periods cannot be sustained for more than a few decades.

The result of these facts was a powerful tendency for population to outstrip resources. 'Population, when unchecked, increases in a geometrical ratio. Subsistence increases only in an arithmetical ratio. A slight acquaintance with numbers will shew the immensity of the first power in comparison of the second.' 'Assuming then my postulata as granted, I say, that the power of population is indefinitely greater than the power in the earth to produce subsistence for man.' Malthus did not find this particularly cheering. 'It is, undoubtedly, a most disheartening reflection that the great obstacle in the way to any extraordinary improvement in society is of a nature that we can never hope to overcome. The perpetual tendency in the race of man to increase beyond the means of subsistence is one of the general laws of animated nature which we can have no reason to expect will change.'[7]

Malthus identified two types of check to population growth which might operate. There were the 'preventive' checks: 'moral restraint', referring to delayed or non-marriage, and 'vice', by which he meant all kinds of artificial birth control. Secondly there were the checks which raised the death rate, what Malthus termed the 'positive' checks. These were again divided into what he termed 'vice', that is man-made destruction, and 'natural' disasters. He distinguished them thus: 'Of these positive checks, those which appear to arise from the laws of nature may be called exclusively misery; and those which we bring upon ourselves, such as wars, excesses of all kinds, and many others, which it would be in our power to avoid, are of a mixed nature. They are brought upon us by vice, and their consequences are misery.' He included in the positive checks a very wide range of causes of death. 'The positive checks to population include all the causes, which tend in any way prematurely to shorten the duration of human life, such as unwholesome occupations; severe labour and exposure to the seasons; bad and insufficient food and clothing arising from poverty; bad nursing of children; excesses of all kinds; great towns and manufactories; the whole train of common diseases and epidemics; wars, infanticide, plague, and famine.'[8] These 'positive' checks tended to act in concert. 'The vices

[7] Malthus, *Principle*, 71, 79, 198–9.
[8] Malthus, *Summary*, 250.

of mankind are active and able ministers of depopulation. They are the precursors in the great army of destruction; and often finish the dreadful work themselves. But should they fail in this war of extermination, sickly seasons, epidemics, pestilence, and plague, advance in terrific array, and sweep off their thousands and ten thousands. Should success be still incomplete, gigantic inevitable famine stalks in the rear, and with one mighty blow levels the population with the food of the world.'[9]

Malthus believed that unless people espoused the path of 'moral restraint', delaying their marriages or not marrying, all other measures would be in vain. For instance, all attempts to eradicate poverty would be hopeless. 'It is not in the nature of things that any permanent and general improvement in the condition of the poor can be effected without an increase in the preventive check; and unless this take place . . . everything that is done for the poor must be temporary and partial: a diminution of mortality at present will be balanced by an increased mortality in future.'[10] Likewise, attempts to eradicate particular forms of misery, whether war, famine or disease, would merely deflect mortality into another 'channel'.

The idea of the 'channel' is an important one in Malthus' thought. He seems to have taken the concept from Heberden. 'Dr William Heberden published, not long since, some valuable observations on this subject deduced from the London bills of mortality. In his preface, speaking of these bills, he says, "the gradual changes they exhibit in particular diseases correspond to the alterations which in time are known to take place in the channels through which the great stream of mortality is constantly flowing."' To tamper with particular channels is therefore a waste of time. 'Now if we stop up any of these channels it is perfectly clear that the stream of mortality must run with greater force through some of the other channels; that is, if we eradicate some diseases, others will become proportionally more fatal. In this case the only distinguishable cause is the damming up a necessary outlet of mortality.' This means that 'we should reprobate specific remedies for ravaging diseases; and those benevolent, but much mistaken men, who have thought they were doing a service to mankind by projecting schemes for the total extinction of particular disorders.'[11]

This leads Malthus from what Boulding calls the 'Dismal Theorem' to the 'Utterly Dismal Theorem'. 'Since equilibrium between resources and population can be maintained only by misery and/or vice, and since population tends to rise to the limit of available subsistence, any improvements leading to an increase in the production of food must increase the equilibrium population,

---

[9] Malthus, *Principle*, 118–19.
[10] Malthus, *Population*, II, 252.
[11] Malthus, *Population*, II, 180,181,179.

and hence, presumably, increase the sum of human misery and vice.'[12] Malthus half seriously contemplates the corollary of this. If people are not prepared to use the preventive checks, they should try to diminish misery by encouraging the 'positive' checks to operate as soon as possible. 'To act consistently, therefore we should facilitate, instead of foolishly and vainly endeavouring to impede, the operations of nature in producing this mortality; and if we dread the too frequent visitation of the horrid form of famine, we should sedulously encourage the other forms of destruction which we compel nature to use.' 'Instead of recommending cleanliness to the poor we should encourage contrary habits. In our towns we should make the streets narrower, crowd more people into the houses, and court the return of the plague.'[13]

This is indeed Utterly Dismal, yet it flows directly from his argument that, without the preventive check, 'distress and poverty multiply in proportion to the funds created to relieve them.'[14] This may be a bitter pill to swallow, as he admits. Yet there is no point in trying to avoid the facts: 'discouraging as the contemplation of this difficulty must be to those whose exertions are laudably directed to the improvement of the human species, it is evident that no possible good can arise from any endeavours to slur it over or keep it in the background.'[15]

Malthus was not alone in outlining the world of misery within which agrarian societies appeared to be trapped. His ideas were fully consistent with those of many of the other great classical economists and social scientists. Those who first began to analyse with precision what was happening were the brilliant set of political economists who worked in Scotland mainly during the period between 1740 and 1790 – Ferguson, Millar, Kames, Robertson, Hume and Smith. It was obvious to such thinkers that humankind was caught in a trap, whereby population would always outstrip resources. David Hume pointed out that 'Almost every man, who thinks he can maintain a family, will have one; and the human species, at this rate of propagation, would more than double every generation. How fast do mankind multiply in every colony or new settlement.'[16] The harder people worked, and the more technologically ingenious they were, the more their numbers would grow. Ferguson wrote, 'If a people, while they retain their frugality, increase their industry, and improve their arts, their numbers must grow in proportion.'[17]

The most forceful expression of the argument was by Adam Smith. His *Wealth of Nations* was the blueprint for a new age and suggested the 'Natural

[12] Kenneth Boulding, quoted in Malthus, *Principle*, 47.
[13] Malthus, *Population*, II, 179.
[14] Malthus, *Population*, II, 274.
[15] Malthus, *Principle*, 199.
[16] Hume, *Essays*, 224.
[17] Ferguson, *Essay*, 142.

Progress of Opulence'. Yet his message is inconsistent, for in relation to the laws
of population he seems to have realized that it was impossible for sustained
economic growth to occur. There was a built-in contradiction which would
forever trap agrarian societies and prevent their escape from eternal misery. It
was clear that 'Every species of animal naturally multiples in proportion to the
means of their subsistence, and no species can ever multiply beyond it.' Mankind was just another species in this respect, for 'men, like all other animals,
naturally multiply in proportion to the means of their subsistence.' He pointed
out that an improvement in wealth would lead to a decline in mortality among
the common people, hence more children would survive and the population
would increase. Likewise, increased wealth through increased wages would lead
to increased fertility. 'The liberal reward of labour, therefore, as it is the effect
of increasing wealth, so it is the cause of increasing population', or, as he put it
in a marginal note, 'high wages increase population.'[18]

E.A.Wrigley has summarized the position of the classical economists. As far
as Smith was concerned 'his view of the prospects for growth in general induced
him to discount the possibility of a prolonged or substantial improvement in real
wages, and to fear that the last state of the labourer would prove to be worse than
the first.' His successors 'developed arguments that served to reinforce the
pessimism that Smith displayed about the secular prospects for real wages.'
Thus 'looking to the future, they saw no likelihood of significant further advance and some danger of regression.' The capitalism they described 'was not
expected by them to produce the changes now termed the industrial revolution.'
For while they predicted increases in output 'they expected them to be broadly
matched by increases in population, leaving the ratio between the two little
changed.'[19] In other words, there was no escape from the circle of misery. The
only question was whether a country would be 'trapped' at a low or high
equilibrium, in other words with sparse or dense populations. As Wrigley notes,
'pre-industrial societies were by definition in a position of negative feedback.
Each period of economic growth was eventually cut short before reaching the
point at which it was self-sustained and progressive.'[20]

Malthus' first edition of the *Essay* provided little in the way of proof for the
theory, though this was to be supplied in the much expanded second edition.
Yet the Malthusian analysis has largely been borne out as a description of most
civilizations before the nineteenth century. Almost all agrarian societies have
conformed to his predictions. If there were gains in resources, these were soon
swallowed up by rapidly rising population through a high fertility rate and
lowered death rates. This would lead to denser populations which in turn led to

[18]   Smith, *Wealth*, I, 89,163,90.
[19]   Wrigley, *Two Kinds*, 99,101,103,103.
[20]   Wrigley, *Population and History*, 111.

the negative feed-back of a rise in mortality. This cycle prevented long-term and sustained economic growth. As David Landes summarized the evidence 'An amelioration of the conditions of existence, hence of survival, and an increase in economic opportunity had *always* been followed by a rise in population that eventually consumed the gains achieved.'[21]

Wrigley has described the Malthusian world as one 'where fertility and mortality are high, population is large relative to available resources and growth is curbed principally by the positive check.'[22] In fact, within the long period when it was mortality which tended to be most important in checking the growth of population there were two distinct patterns. Conventional population theory assumed that in the thousands of years up to the 'demographic transition', since mortality and fertility were clearly balanced, this was achieved by 'perennial malnutrition and everyday disease.' Thus it was suggested that year in and year out mortality ran at about the same level as fertility both at a high level.[23] Wrigley describes this situation as one where 'mortality was always high because the disease environment was so unfavourable . . . in this sense high mortality could be said to have 'caused' high fertility.'[24]

There are, however, very few cases of this pattern in recorded history. Much more common is the situation of dramatic crises of mortality, as described by the anthropologist Peter Kunstadter. 'A more nearly accurate model of demographic conditions . . . within which most non-modern men have lived may have been high fertility (beyond the level needed for replacement in normal years) with low-to-medium death rate, with occasional or periodic variations in death rates due to natural disasters (floods, earthquakes, climatic fluctuations . . ., insect plagues, crop failures, . . . etc.) and probably more recently, epidemic diseases.'[25] In this situation 'the disease environment was less deadly but social conventions made early and universal marriage mandatory. As a result, fertility was high and because rapid growth had to be short-lived, mortality was high too.'[26] What Wrigley implies is that the mortality now took a different form. Instead of perennial high mortality, in most years mortality was considerably below fertility, but every few years or generations the growing population would be hit by a 'crisis', one or more of the Malthusian positive checks, namely war, famine and disease.

---

[21] Quoted in Chambers, *Population*, 10 (Chambers' italics).

[22] Wrigley and Schofield, *Population*, xxiv. The 'positive check' is, of course, mortality. This has been termed a 'high-pressure regime' by Wrigley.

[23] Macfarlane, *Resources and Population*, 305; this 'classic' model has more recently been termed the 'west African' model by Wrigley because it has been observed in that part of Africa.

[24] Wrigley and Schofield, *Population*, xxiv–v.

[25] In Harrison and Boyce, *Structure*, 315. Wrigley has termed this the 'Chinese' model.

[26] Wrigley and Schofield, *Population*, xxiv.

Agrarian civilizations have almost all been characterized by a situation where the normally high fertility is periodically balanced by the mortality crisis. The model and the evidence for it was described by Carlo Cipolla. He wrote that 'the material available suggests that any agricultural society – whether sixteenth-century Italy, seventeenth-century France, or nineteenth-century India – tends to adhere to a definite set of patterns in the structure and movements of birth- and death-rates. Crude birth-rates are very high throughout, ranging between 35 and 50 per thousand. . . . Death rates are also very high, but *normally* lower than the birth-rates – ranging generally between 30 and 40 per thousand.' As a result of these usual figures, the 'population of an agricultural society is characterized by a normal rate of growth of 0.5 to 1.0 per cent per year.' Such a growth rate would mean, over long periods, a staggering growth of population. If it had occurred, for instance, since 10,000 BC, population 'would form today a sphere of living flesh many thousand light years in diameter, and expanding with a radial velocity that . . . would be many times faster than light.'[27]

This continued growth has clearly not happened, not because of perennially high mortality, but rather as a result of periodic 'crises'. It has been avoided 'because throughout the demographic history of agricultural societies, death-rates show a remarkable tendency to recurrent, sudden dramatic peaks that reach levels as high as 150 or 300 or even 500 per thousand.' These peaks were the result of wars, epidemics and famines, which Cipolla notes, 'wiped out a good part of the existing population.' It was the 'intensity and frequency of the peaks' that 'controlled the size of agricultural societies.'[28]

In 1960, Cipolla noted that the detailed demographic records for agrarian societies were still 'poor'. In the following years information improved greatly and a good deal of it was summarized by T.H.Hollingsworth in 1969 in his work on *Historical Demography*. The evidence he assembled on India, China, Egypt and other great agrarian civilizations fully supported the picture which Cipolla had outlined.

The history of China is a classic example of these difficulties. China in 1700 was well abreast of Europe in terms of technology, as Joseph Needham and his collaborators have shown.[29] Its population at this date was about 160 million. The peace and stability of the Chi'ing dynasty, combined with an apparent absence of widespread epidemic and endemic disease, allowed the Malthusian tendency towards rapid growth to occur. The population doubled to about 310–30 million in the hundred years to 1800 and increased to 420–40 million by

[27] Cipolla, *World Population*, 76.
[28] Cipolla, *World Population*, 77; see also Cipolla in Glass and Eversley (eds), *Population*, 573.
[29] Needham et al., *Science and Civilization*.

about 1850.[30] The result, according to many, was the growing misery of the bulk of the population. People had to work harder and harder, for 'Despite enormous growth in population and food supply, the Late Imperial era saw a decline of productivity per labourer in agriculture.'[31]

Malthus noted that 'The Jesuit Premare, writing to a friend of the same society says, "I will tell you a fact, which may appear to be a paradox, but is nevertheless strictly true. It is, that the richest and most flourishing empire of the world is notwithstanding, in one sense, the poorest and the most miserable of all. The country, however extensive and fertile it may be, is not sufficient to support its inhabitants. Four times as much territory would be necessary to place them at their ease." '[32] In the words of James Nakamura and Matao Miyamoto, the tendency was 'to push the level of per capita income down toward the subsistence level – that is, there was no escape from the Malthusian trap.'[33] The 'crisis' came in the form of famines and the devastation of the Taiping rebellion of the mid nineteenth century in the aftermath of which many millions died.[34]

Turning to the west, it would appear that most of Europe hit a Malthusian ceiling in the late sixteenth century. Research on European populations supported the universal and devastating nature of the crises that affected the population. Fernand Braudel noted the effects of the 'biological *ancien regime* . . . the balance between births and deaths, very high infant mortality, famine, chronic undernourishment and virulent epidemics.' He noted that towards the end of the sixteenth century 'Man's very progress became a burden and again brought about his poverty', for in 'probably the whole Western world, population again became too dense. The monotonous story begins afresh and the process goes into reverse.'[35] Jan De Vries asks 'Could Europe have reached an economic ceiling in the early seventeenth century in which a precarious balance between population and food supply was constantly threatened by inadequate harvests?' He answered in the affirmative, pointing to the fact that 'In Ireland, Germany, Poland, Denmark and the Mediterranean countries varying combinations of plagues and chronic warfare and insecurity caused a substantial decline in population.'[36] In a recent survey of the evidence, Massimo Livi-Bacci has given a similar description. 'The situation for the various European countries is not much different from that of Siena. The sixteenth,

---

[30] Nakamura and Miyamato, *Population*, 247; Fairbank, *Paradox*, 168.
[31] Fairbank, *Paradox*, 170.
[32] Malthus, *Population*, I, 130.
[33] Nakamura and Miyamato, *Population*, 264.
[34] Spence, *China*, 170–84.
[35] Braudel, *Capitalism*, 53,3.
[36] De Vries, *Economy*, 6–7,184.

seventeenth, and early eighteenth centuries are characterized by subsistence crises, with the attendant adverse demographic consequences, at a rate of two, three, or more per century.[37]

Italy was a particularly dramatic example. 'Italy in the decade 1620–30 embarked on a long period of economic decline which lasted beyond the middle of the eighteenth century and during which levels of living progressively deteriorated.'[38] Principally as a result of disease, 'During the first half of the seventeenth century, Italy as a whole declined from 13 to 11 million inhabitants, while northern Italy, the industrial heartland of Europe, lost a quarter of its population.'[39] France was in the same predicament. 'The population of the French kingdom within its frontiers of 1700, whether we look at it as a whole, or in its age groups . . . oscillates vigorously from minimum to maximum around a sort of equilibrium position representing possibly 19 million Frenchmen. In 1700 it probably stood nearer the minimum than the maximum point.' In the early eighteenth century, France may have been trapped in the usual positive feed-backs of war, famine and epidemic: 'decisive changes did not occur in France before the second half, and maybe not before the end, of the eighteenth century.'[40] Even prosperous Holland seems to have some kind of Malthusian ceiling in the middle of the seventeenth century.[41] In Mediterranean Europe, for instance in parts of Spain, parish register evidence suggests that 'crisis mortality continued to be important well into the nineteenth century.'[42]

It is not difficult to see how powerful the 'positive' checks were. The first and most destructive was war, not only because of deaths in battle, but much more significantly through the disruptions it caused leading to famine and epidemics. The shadow of famine hung over the world until very late. The demographic position at the end of the seventeenth century is made clear by K.F.Helleiner. 'Certainly, as far as the demographic situation of this period is concerned, there was little if anything to herald the impending changes. Man was still very much at the mercy of the elements. As late as the 1690s a succession of poor and indifferent harvests created severe subsistence crisis in almost all countries of Europe. So far from growing, the population declined here and there, as dearth and starvation stalked through the lands from Castille to Finland, and from the Scottish Highlands to the foothills of the Alps.'[43] Such famine would bring disease in its wake.

---

[37] Livi-Bacci, *Population*, 81.

[38] Cipolla in Glass and Eversley (eds), *Population*, 574.

[39] De Vries, *Economy*, 4–5.

[40] Goubert in Glass and Eversley (eds), *Population*, 473.

[41] Van Bath in Daedalus, *Fertility*, 610ff.

[42] Richard Smith in Bynum and Porter (eds), *Companion Encyclopaedia*, 1675.

[43] Glass and Eversley (eds), *Population*, 79.

Thomas McKeown pointed out that many diseases are density dependent: 'in the early phase of human existence, from the beginning of the pleistocene up to about 10,000 years ago, infectious disease due to micro-organisms specifically adapted to the human species was almost nonexistent.'[44] As Alfred Crosby put it, 'Hunters and gatherers had their personal vermin – lice, fleas, and internal parasites – but few of the nomad humans remained long enough in one spot in sufficient numbers to accumulate filth enough to enable mice, rats, roaches, houseflies and worms to multiply in armies. The farmers, however, did just that.'[45] Or as Kenneth Kiple writes, 'so long as humans lived in small isolated bands their disease difficulties would have been largely limited to chronic infections with low infectivity.'[46]

With the establishment of permanent cultivation in about ten thousand BC, and particularly with the growth of urban civilizations from about four thousand BC, new diseases emerged. 'Almost all studies that attempt to reconstruct the history of infectious diseases indicate that the burden of infection has tended to increase rather than decrease as human beings adopted civilized lifestyles.'[47] This was partly the result of increasing dirt and increasing poverty. 'The aggregation of large, malnourished populations created the conditions required for the propagation and transmission of micro-organisms and so led to the predominance of infectious diseases as causes of sickness and death. This established a high level of mortality which limited the rate of population growth.'[48] But above all, increased density of population allowed a whole new disease ecology to emerge. 'With the domestication of plants and animals beginning in the Near East some 8,000 to 10,000 years ago, humans summoned forth a host of new diseases and in so doing set in motion changes in their disease ecologies that are ongoing today.' These new diseases were supplemented by others as the rise of the first literate and urban civilizations created enough density for viral and other diseases to establish themselves. We are told that 'smallpox and measles, together with influenza, chicken-pox, whooping cough, mumps, diphtheria, and a host of other diseases, arose with growing human populations. These were the illnesses that pass quickly and directly from human host to human host and need no intermediary carrier; in other words, they became the diseases of civilization.'[49] Thus a basic contradiction between economy and health begins to build up.

---

[44] McKeown, *Modern Rise*, 79. Certain diseases, such as malaria, were of course to be found very early in human evolution.

[45] Crosby, *Ecological*, 29; see also 31.

[46] Kiple in Bynum and Porter (eds), *Companion Encyclopaedia*, 358–9.

[47] Cohen, *Health*, 32. See chapter 4 of Cohen, and especially 48, 53–4 for an excellent account of the way in which increasing human density leads to the growth of disease.

[48] McKeown, *Modern Rise*, 162.

[49] Kiple in Bynum and Porter (eds), *Companion Encyclopaedia*, 360, 362.

As a country's wealth and commerce grows, it is often most economically rational to concentrate this in densely populated areas, towns and cities. In economic terms this is efficient, overcoming the 'friction of space' and bringing various advantages in terms of division of labour, economies of scale and so on.[50] De Vries summarizes the growth of large cities in western Europe from the sixteenth century: 'Paris, London and the *Randstad* in the 1570s collectively embraced some 370,000 inhabitants. In the next century each grew to surpass the 400,000 mark. By 1700 one and a half million people lived in them.' By 1650 Paris and London were both approaching the half million mark, 'unprecedented in western Europe.'[51]

At the same time, 'Urban populations died at higher rates because the city was crowded and filthy, its streams and rivers polluted with industrial and human waste, its air thick with particles from wood and coal fires, and its streets strewn with waste.'[52] With reference to London, Malthus quoted Graunt's mid-seventeenth-century estimate that it required an annual influx of six thousand people a year just to make up for its population deficit.[53] Wrigley and Schofield estimate that London always killed more people than it produced but that its relative size meant that it was mainly during the period between 1625 and 1775 that it had its decisive effect on national population. In the last three quarters of the seventeenth century it acted as a depressant on population growth and in the 'eighteenth century London continued to act as a severe drain on the surpluses being produced elsewhere; even as late as the second quarter of the century it offset about a half of the national baptism surplus.' It looks as if England had hit a buffer. 'The conditions for a relatively high-level equilibrium trap were beginning to become apparent in late-seventeenth-century England.'[54]

Other civilizations where urban populations were growing faced a similar Malthusian feedback. By the seventeenth century Japan was extremely densely populated. When Engelbert Kaempfer visited it he found that 'The Country is populous beyond expression, and one would scarce think it possible, that being no greater than it is, it should nevertheless maintain, and support such a vast number of inhabitants.' He found many large towns and cities 'the chief whereof may vy with the most considerable in the world for largeness, magnificence, and the number of inhabitants.' The capital, 'Jedo', later Tokyo, 'is so large, that I may venture to say, it is the biggest town known.'[55] He was right, for with a population of about a million it was the largest city on earth. It is not surprising

[50] See Davis and Golden in Heer (ed.), *Readings*, 55.
[51] De Vries, *Economy*, 155,151; the *Randstad* is the central Netherlands area around Amsterdam.
[52] Riley, *Sickness*, 122.
[53] Malthus, *Population*, I, 243.
[54] Wrigley and Schofield, *Population*, 169,472.
[55] Kaempfer, *History*, 3,306,307.

that Japanese demographic historians have detected a similar negative influence in Japan. Akira Hayami argues that 'Owing to the high death rate in cities, which teemed with workers who had migrated from the depressed countryside, the Kanto and Kinki regions (which included Edo, Kyoto and Osaka) were subject to the negative-feedback function and their populations stagnated.'[56] The thesis seems to have been accepted by Susan Hanley and Kozo Yamamura: 'while the evidence is only starting to come in', what we do have 'confirms Hayami's hypothesis – and E.A.Wrigley's with regard to premodern Europe – that the cities drained the surrounding countryside of population, thus creating negative growth rates in the areas immediately surrounding cities.'[57]

We are left with a puzzle. It is difficult to see how the 'great transformation' from the world of high mortality and fertility occurred and how the 'Wealth of Nations' was achieved. In order to escape from the trap, societies had to increase their productive power, that is their agricultural and manufacturing wealth. As they did so, they had to avoid too-rapid population growth and the rise of the positive checks of war, famine and disease that seemed inevitably to emerge as populations became more dense. This growing burden of disease and malnutrition as humans moved from hunter-gathering through the phase of early civilizations to the early modern period has been outlined by Mark Cohen.[58] The growing levels of epidemic disease associated with the higher density of agrarian civilizations are surveyed by Kenneth Kiple.[59] As Braudel noted, 'until the eighteenth century, the population was enclosed within an almost intangible circle'. Only then 'were the frontiers of the impossible crossed and the hitherto unsurpassable population ceiling exceeded.'[60]

The difficulty of achieving this change is made clear by Ronald Lee. On the one hand, 'Entrance to a higher ellipse can be gained only from the population densities and levels of technological attainment characteristic of the highest development of the previous technology.' On the other hand, 'Populations such as the Chinese, entrapped in a medium-technology agricultural regime, through prematurely dense population, would not be well situated to make the transition to an industrial economy.' Some variant of the Chinese fate was a common one, and 'many populations would get stuck at relatively low-level equilibria, and thus make no further progress. The more obvious and cheaper technological developments would occur, but those requiring larger collective investments and higher living standards might not.'[61]

[56] In Jansen and Rozman (eds), *Japan*, 293.
[57] Hanley and Yamamura, *Economic*, 304.
[58] Cohen, *Health, passim* esp. 53–4,130–2,140–2.
[59] In Bynum and Porter (eds), *Companion Encyclopaedia*, 358–62; see also Polgar, *Evolution* and Crosby, *Ecological*, 29,31.
[60] Braudel, *Afterthoughts*, 9.
[61] Coleman and Schofield (eds), *Population*, 122.

Only in very exceptional circumstances could the various negative feed-back mechanisms be avoided. 'Only populations blessed with the most advantageous institutions governing reproduction, surplus extraction, and use of surplus, would be able to pass through the neck of the hyperbola and continue to progress into the next higher technological regime.' For instance, 'Premature population growth, or premature restraint, might render the passage from one stable equilibrium to a higher one much less likely.'[62] It is all a matter of balance, and the factors that allow that balance are many and delicate. What is significant is the narrowness of the room for manoeuvre.[63]

In order to establish what factors were important and the ways in which the balance was achieved, we need to examine cases where the escape from the Malthusian trap apparently occurred. One case might give some possible clues. But if two cases, widely separated in culture and geography, and largely independent historically, could be found, we should be able to penetrate more deeply into the necessary and sufficient causes of the unlikely emergence of a different demographic pattern.

---

[62] In Coleman and Schofield (eds), *Population*, 122,122,123,128.
[63] Well illustrated in the diagram in Coleman and Schofield (eds), *Population*, 123.

2

Two Islands

The first and best documented escape from the Malthusian trap occurred in the island kingdom of Britain and particularly in England. The demographic peculiarity of England began to become apparent to historians in the mid 1960s when the systematic reconstruction of the population history of England was undertaken by members of the 'Cambridge Group for the History of Population and Social Structure'. 'Indeed the more deeply the English experience is probed, the more unusual it appears to be.'[1] Wrigley, Schofield, Laslett and others showed that somehow England had moved from a situation where there were periodic crises caused by war, famine and disease to a much lower and steadier level of balanced mortality and fertility well before the eighteenth-century industrialization process began.

The central feature was that for much of the period population was held in check as much by lowered fertility as by mortality. England was the one well-documented and long-established exception to the Malthusian pattern of high mortality balancing high fertility. This equilibrium between population and resources was achieved 'not by sudden, sharp mortality spasms, but by wide, quiet fluctuations in fertility, which in their downward phase reduced fertility levels to the point where population growth ceased even though mortality was still low by the standard of other pre-industrial societies.' This is a total contrast to the 'mortality-dominated' equilibrium 'sometimes regarded as generally present in all pre-industrial societies' England was exceptional in that it 'experienced a fertility-dominated' system.[2]

[1] Wrigley and Schofield, *Population*, xxix.
[2] Wrigley and Schofield, *Population*, 247,248,451.

Malthus was one of the first to note that there was something unexpected and unusual about mortality in England. Firstly, he suggested that contrary to the view that agrarian societies were very unhealthy and disease-ridden, this was not the case in England. Particular parishes were surprisingly healthy. 'In the parish of Ackworth, in Yorkshire, it appears, from a very exact account kept by Dr Lee of the ages at which all died there for 20 years, that half of the inhabitants live to the age of 46.' He believed that the number of deaths per thousand of the population per year in country villages was of the order of 20 to 25 per thousand.[3] On the basis of this and other figures he concluded that 'it appears from the clearest evidence that the generality of our country parishes are very healthy.'[4]

What was even more surprising was that while cities were growing, the mortality rate seemed to be dropping. 'The returns of the Population Act in 1811 undoubtedly presented extraordinary results. They showed a greatly accelerated rate of progress, and a greatly improved healthiness of the people, notwithstanding the increase of the towns and the increased proportion of the population engaged in manufacturing employment.' Malthus noted that in the *Observations* on this act 'it is remarked that the average duration of life in England appears to have increased in the proportion of 117 to 100 since the year 1780.' He believed that 'So great a change, in so short a time, if true, would be a most striking phenomenon.' He was somewhat sceptical, believing that part of the explanation lay in migration and military service, which would lead some deaths to occur abroad. On the other hand, he accepted that 'as the increase of population since 1780 is incontrovertible, and the present mortality extraordinarily small . . . much the greater part of the effect is to be attributed to increased healthiness.'[5]

In terms of what happened, Malthus believed that there had been a major shift some time in the eighteenth century. 'We do not know indeed of any extraordinary mortality which has occurred in England since 1700.'[6] Deaths from certain diseases had declined, but others had increased. He noted 'the extinction of the plague' as one significant change. The other was 'the striking reduction of the deaths in the dysentery.' On the other hand, 'consumption, palsy, apoplexy, gout, lunacy, and small-pox became more mortal.'[7] Nevertheless, the total balance had shifted towards lower mortality.

---

[3] Malthus, *Population*, I, 243,241. This calculation, namely the number of deaths per thousand per year in the general population, not taking into account sex or age, is known as the 'crude death rate' and will be the one I mean when I refer to 'death rate'.
[4] Malthus, *Population*, I, 240.
[5] Malthus, *Population*, I, 251,245.
[6] Malthus, *Population*, I, 250.
[7] Malthus, *Population*, II, 182.

Three contemporaries of Malthus also noticed the unexpected change that seemed to have taken place. One was Sir Gilbert Blane who published a table comparing the situation in London between 1693 and 1789 showing for example that the expectation of further life at age five had risen from forty-one to fifty-one. 'Whoever will cast his eye on this, will perceive with mingled surprise and satisfaction the highly improved value of life in the age in which we live.' In general he thought the expectation of life had increased by about a third. He noted further that the improvements had particularly affected one group. 'Accounts have been kept in the bills of mortality since the year 1728, of the numbers who have died at different ages, and it appears that the number of deaths, under two years, from that time till 1750, was annually from 9 to 10,000. In the latter half of last century they fluctuated from 6 to 7,000; and since the commencement of this century they are averaged under 5,500.' Not only were infants less prone to die, but there had also been a 'notable diminution of the number of deaths in childbed.' It appears that 1790 was the first year in London in which the number of births exceeded the number of deaths.[8]

Francis Place gave similar figures to those of Blane, showing that London 'was more healthy in the eighteenth than the seventeenth century' and that 'the salubrity of London has, upon the whole, gone on increasing for more than a century past.' He thought that the change was especially marked in the period 1740–1800. 'The principal amelioration in the health of the metropolis, however, seems to have been more particularly brought about within the last sixty years. Until nearly the middle of the last century, mortality kept pace, in some measure, with the increasing population.' He believed the changes had spread 'all over the country.'[9]

Thomas Bateman reflected:

> In comparing the catalogue of diseases, and the extent of the ravages occasioned by them, as exhibited in the Bills of Mortality, and the writings of physicians of our own times, with those contained in the Bills of the 17th century and in the works of Sydenham, Morton and Willis . . . we are naturally struck with the great diminution of the fatality, and with the total disappearance of some of the most formidable of human maladies, and the comparative rarity of others, in our present annual Bills . . . the healthy condition of the metropolis seems to have been more particularly produced within the last 50 years, during which period it has most rapidly increased in extent and population.[10]

---

[8] Blane, *Dissertations*, 180,122,123,172.

[9] Place, *Illustrations*, 248–9,253.

[10] Quoted in Buer, *Health*, 89. For the views of mid-nineteenth-century statisticians such as Farr and Finlaison who agreed with these authors, see Chadwick, *Report*, 14,12.

The decline in mortality in the eighteenth century only emphasized a situation which was already unusual. Research on the mortality patterns of early modern England by Wrigley and Schofield has shown that contrary to previous expectations, for most of the period between the sixteenth and nineteenth century England enjoyed low mortality rates for a pre-industrial population. Crude death rates fluctuated between 22.5 per thousand and about 30 per thousand so Wrigley and Schofield are able to assume a constant rate of about 25 per thousand. This is about 15 to 20 points lower than what we would expect to find from the experience of most agrarian societies in the past.

This relatively low death rate led to a reasonable expectation of life. For instance, in the period 1566 to 1621 it averaged over 38 years at birth, reaching a peak of 41.7 years in 1581. Even in the period 1820 and 1870, the expectation of life at birth was only about two years higher than that in the later sixteenth and early seventeenth century. Much of the mortality, of course, occurred in the first year and in childhood. If they survived the early years, 'during most of English history between Elizabethan and Victorian times a young man or woman of 20 could look forward on average to a further 35–40 years of life.'

The peculiarity of this escape from high mortality is emphasized when we compare England to her nearest neighbour on the Continent. In France for much of the period up to the end of the eighteenth century, death rates were about 40 per thousand per year. The expectation of life at birth was on average about 28 in France, up to eight years lower than England. As the work of Jean-Pierre Goubert on the Beauvais and others have shown, France was a country 'in which the positive check cycle was a major feature of the mechanisms keeping numbers and resources in balance.' France was characterized by an 'equilibrium between population and resources that trapped most men in poverty and misery.'

The absence of any 'extraordinary mortality' since 1700, which Malthus had noted, was a much earlier feature. 'There were a few brief periods . . . when the relative tranquillity of English mortality was severely disturbed . . . but such occasions were probably less common and less severe in England than elsewhere in western Europe.' England was not 'afflicted by many of the crises experienced abroad.' Wrigley and Schofield note 'England's prominent exemption from the common experience of north-west Europe.'[11] Furthermore, there is plenty of evidence that conditions in southern and eastern Europe were even less favourable than those in north-western Europe.[12] Even within a relatively favoured zone, England was exceptional. Bisset Hawkins in 1829 stated that 'the mortality of Great Britain, its cities and its hospitals, is greatly inferior to that of any other country in Europe . . . this superior value of life in Great Britain is not confined

[11] Wrigley and Schofield, *Population*, 182,234,236,453,479,452,479,451,453,342,341.
[12] For the demographic disasters in the south see e.g. Kamen, *Iron*, 44–6; Kunitz, *Speculations*, 355–63.

to any particular districts, or classes of individuals. . . . It is indisputable, that the average proportion of deaths in England and her cities is less than that of any other country in Europe.'[13]

It is not easy to accept this discovery for it runs against both intuition and sentiment. As Roger Schofield and David Reher observe:

> We must wait until 1870 before again finding as high a value for life expectancy as the 41 years observed during the 1580s. These surprising results have naturally aroused some scepticism. Is it really possible that during these somewhat remote periods, before the health transition was under way, life expectancy had reached the levels of the late nineteenth century? If this were really the case, would it not be necessary to revise completely our views of the factors which have generally been associated with the first phase of mortality decline?[14]

Mary Dobson remarks that 'it may occasion some surprise that individual parishes could boast expectation of life at birth as high in the 16th, 17th and 18th centuries as those attained nationally only about 1920.'[15] As Petersen puts it, 'The supposition that the stinking cities of early industrialism could be the sites of a longer average life was a notion repugnant not only to the "nature poets" and Engels, not only to Chadwick and Ruskin and the Webbs, but also to a very large sector of nineteenth-century British opinion of all political orientations.' Nevertheless, 'according to the universal judgement of modern scholarship life expectation rose appreciably during the development of the industrial system.'[16] Nor did it rise from a very low base – it was not the case that middling misery replaced awful misery. What appears to have happened is that relatively low mortality rates achieved by at least the later sixteenth century rose somewhat in the seventeenth century. Instead of continuing to rise, they dropped again from at least the middle of the eighteenth century. There are thus two things to explain. The basically low mortality rates before the eighteenth century and the fact that these became even lower as population rose rapidly and people crowded into the cities and factories.

There are still other questions to answer. One concerns the point at which the unusually low mortality rates began. The Wrigley and Schofield evidence only takes us back to 1541. It seems likely that the relatively low mortality found then had been established as a pattern a good deal earlier. For example, David Loschky and Ben Childers have argued that 'All available material indicates that a substantial fall in mortality occurred in the fifteenth or early sixteenth

[13] Quoted in Buer, *Health*, 237.
[14] In Schofield et al. (eds), *Decline*, 23–4.
[15] Wrigley, *Death*, 137–8.
[16] Petersen, *Malthus*, 158.

century.'[17] Elspeth Moodie has suggested an even earlier change, 'Wrigley and Schofield's discovery that national mortality crises were neither as frequent nor as severe in the early modern period as we previously believed could well also be true of the late fourteenth and fifteenth centuries.'[18]

Equally contentious is the dating of the *further* reduction in mortality in the eighteenth century. The general consensus now, based on Wrigley and Schofield's work, is that the major drop in mortality started in the 1740s or 1750s and continued until the 1830s, when it halted, only to progress again in the later nineteenth century.[19] It may be, however, as Alfred Perrenoud has argued, that 'it was towards the end of the seventeenth century, and more particularly around the 1690s that a new mortality pattern emerged.'[20]

Several further aspects of the decline in mortality are worth noting. One is that a considerable part of the improvement took place in cities and particularly among infants and young children. The point was made by Malthus in his pinpointing of the decline in infant dysentery. M.W.Beaver gives evidence for the 'remarkable decrease' in child and infant mortality in the period 1730 to 1829.[21] John Landers analyses the decline of infant mortality in London between 1680 and 1820 showing that infant mortality fell by rather more than half in the century after 1740.[22] England had the lowest infant mortality rate in Europe by the nineteenth century, despite the fact that it was suffering the first urban and industrial revolutions. After about 1830 there were no further changes in infant mortality rates until they began to drop in about 1903–8.[23] Thus we need to look 'to innovations that account for lower mortality in the common diseases that had caused heavy losses among infants and children (the enteric diseases, especially dysentery, and malaria).'[24]

Secondly, it has been argued that it was not so much the incidence of disease that changed, but the case fatality: 'Riley's work indicates that this improvement in longevity was attributable not so much to a reduction in the amount of illness suffered by the population, but rather to a reduction in the number of cases with a fatal outcome.' This has implications for how we explain the decline. Decline in case fatality is 'a phenomenon eminently compatible with an explanation couched in terms of better standards of living.'[25]

---

[17] Loschky and Childers, *Early*, 85.

[18] In *Review Symposium*, 165.

[19] See Guha, *Decline*, 90–1.

[20] In Schofield et al. (eds), *Decline*, 33. Razzell believes that the change occurred mainly in the first half of the eighteenth century (Razzell, *Essays*, 199,206).

[21] Beaver, *Milk*, 245–7.

[22] Landers, *Death*, 192; for details see esp. 95,139,228 and the graphs on 99,103,147,170.

[23] Smith, *People's Health*, 66,113.

[24] Riley, *Insects*, 844.

[25] Guha, *Decline*, 113,106.

At first sight Japan does not seem to constitute an exception to the Malthusian tendency. Until the 1960s, conventional Japanese historiography, based on a Marxist and crude Malthusian model, made the mortality regime the centre of the analysis. Malthus himself had thought that Japan's demographic pattern was identical to that of China, with its population controlled by war, famine and disease.[26] The standard demographic history of Japan by Irene Taeuber endorsed this view and it has been supported more recently by Carl Mosk.[27]

Yet it is worth looking a little more closely at the general pattern of population in Japan. If we start with estimates of the earliest known totals, it is suggested that 'the population of Japan, about 3 to 5.5 million people in AD 645, was much larger than European populations at that time.'[28] It appears to have gone through a period of Malthusian 'crises', particularly famine and epidemics, between the eighth and eleventh centuries. W.Wayne Farris believes that this was a time of very high fertility and mortality, with rates of about 50 per thousand. But he admits that there are considerable inconsistencies in the data and is doubtful about his calculations.[29] 'Sawada Goichi estimated the population of Japan at 6 million in the eighth century, and it is unlikely that population grew significantly through the year 1050.'[30] Given the rocky and somewhat barren island with its inhospitable climate, the early-eighth-century population of about six million people was already extremely dense by any standards.[31] It then fluctuated considerably. One guess is that in 1185–333 it was 9,750,000, while in 1572–91 it was 18,000,000.[32] This latter figure is very unreliable and almost certainly far too high; it is generally thought to have increased to between 10 and 18 million by the start of the seventeenth century.[33]

The agricultural improvements of the sixteenth and seventeenth centuries, combined with administrative advances and peace, meant that in the seventeenth century the population of Japan soared. 'Hayami estimates a population of no more than 10 million at the beginning of the seventeenth century, which grew rapidly to 30 million by 1720 (the uncertainty of the sources induces him to adopt a safety margin of plus or minus 5 million), maintaining an average annual growth rate of between 0.8 and 1 per cent for over a century.'[34] More recently, it has been suggested that 'Although accurate statistics were not kept

[26] Malthus, *Population*, I, ch.xii.
[27] Taeuber, *Population of Japan*; Mosk, *Patriarchy*.
[28] Jannetta, *Epidemics*, 41, note 16, drawing on Farris, *Population*.
[29] Farris, *Population*, 43,45–6.
[30] Farris in Kiple (ed.), *Disease*, 380.
[31] Jannetta, *Epidemics*, 69.
[32] Taeuber, *Population of Japan*, 20.
[33] Hanley in *Cambridge History*, 4, 664.
[34] Quoted in Livi-Bacci, *Population*, 66. For original estimates, see Hayami, *Population Growth*.

at that time, some demographers and historians place the growth rate in the range of 0.78 to 1.34 per cent annually between 1550 and 1700 . . . the country's total population grew from roughly 12 million persons to approximately 26 million to 30 million at the time of the shogun's census in 1721.'[35] Whichever figures we take, there cannot be any doubt that Japan's population was growing rapidly during the seventeenth century. It looked as if it was heading straight into the Malthusian trap even if remarkable developments in urban infrastructure and agriculture had allowed this growth to occur.

Thus the situation in Japan in 1720 was very similar to that in England in 1620. There had probably been a doubling of population in a little over a century and suddenly there was a check. In England there were dearths and a rising mortality rate in the 1620s as part of a Europe-wide recession. In Japan, a serious famine occurred in certain areas in 1732. Then the population in Japan did exactly what it did in England, it ceased growing for over a century.

The broad statistics are fairly clear. 'In 1721, the population was 26.1 million; in 1846, 26.9 million.' Moreover, there had been no dramatic fluctuations in between. 'The highest figure recorded in these surveys is 27.2 million; the lowest, 24.9 million.'[36] In fact, the change in the pattern seems to have occurred before the end of the seventeenth century. Hayami claims that the population of Japan was almost level from 1671 to 1851.[37] Furthermore, Arne Kalland and Jon Pedersen have noted that 'at least as early as 1690 the population was not allowed to grow freely, as the unbalanced sex ratio indicates. Consequently, population control was introduced early.'[38] Nakamura and Miyamato concluded that 'Population growth starts to slow down in some domains (*han*) from around the middle of the seventeenth century, and this change extends widely throughout Japan for the next century.'[39]

The stability at a national level masked considerable local variations. In particular, the population of eastern Japan dropped, while that of western Japan rose. 'Generally speaking, in the Kanto and Tohoku areas, population decline was the rule; in Kyushu, Shikoku, and Chugoku, increases predominated; and in central Japan, there was a slight population decrease in the Kinki region and an increase in Hokuriku.' Hayami suggests that this was due to economic forces. In the eastern Kanto area, the commercial economy had already reached its limit and hence population remained stationary. In the 'developing' area of the Inland Sea 'village industries and peasant by-employments were developing during this period.' and this allowed a modest increase.[40]

[35] Nakai Nobuhiko in *Cambridge History*, 4, 539.
[36] Hayami in Jansen and Rozman (eds), *Japan*, 287.
[37] In Laslett and Wall (eds), *Household*, 477.
[38] Kalland and Pedersen, *Famine*, 71.
[39] Nakamura and Miyamoto, *Population*, 233.
[40] In Jansen and Rozman, *Japan*, 291,301.

Looking at mortality rates, it was long believed that people in Japan before the later-nineteenth-century Japanese industrial revolution lived in that state of high mortality to be found in the majority of agrarian societies. Then from the 1960s evidence began to emerge from detailed studies that perhaps the mortality rates were much lower than expected. At first the evidence was rejected as mistaken, since there was so strong an expectation of high mortality in such a society. In the first major western account of Japanese demography, Taeuber wrote, 'Unfortunately for the validity of this inference from the records, both death and birth rates are so low as to be improbable. A 'normal' crude death rate of 30 per 1,000 total population in Tokugawa Japan would mean that levels of mortality were as low as those achieved by such prefectures as Fukui and Ishikawa in the years from 1925 to 1930.'[41] Even in the 1980s, 'Estimated life expectancies for the same samples are higher than many Japanese scholars find believable.'[42]

Using the excellent census and vital registration records for Japan, a number of scholars have applied the techniques of 'family reconstitution', that is linking births, marriages and deaths. Results showed a surprising situation during the eighteenth and first half of the nineteenth century, even more extreme than that of England. In terms of death rates, the work of Hayami showed that in the village of Yokouchi death rates fluctuated between 16.4 and 25.5 per thousand per year over the period 1671 and 1871 while the average over the whole period was 20 per thousand.[43] In a study by Thomas Smith of the village of Nakahara the death rates fluctuated between 18 and 32 with a mean average of 26.5 per thousand.[44] A third study of four villages showed 'death rates in the villages ranged in our samples from about 25 per thousand to 18 or 19, and these averages included famine years.' Hanley and Yamamura comment that such rates 'seem extraordinarily low for a premodern society.'[45]

Given very low mortality, it is not surprising to find that the expectation of life was unexpectedly high. In two Japanese villages in the eighteenth and early nineteenth century it fluctuated between thirty and seventy-five at birth.[46] Smith found the expectation of life at age one in Nakahara between 1717 and 1830 to be forty-six for males and fifty-one for females. Other villages varied between thirty-four and sixty.[47]

The impression from this work is that mortality rates in the second half of the Tokugawa period were even lower than those in England at the same

[41] Taeuber, *Population of Japan*, 29.
[42] Hanley in *Cambridge History*, 4, 699.
[43] Cited in Hanley and Yamamura, *Economic*, 297.
[44] Smith, *Nakahara*, 39.
[45] Hanley and Yamamura, *Economic*, 325, 212.
[46] Hanley, *Fertility*, 139.
[47] Smith, *Nakahara*, table 4.4, 56.

period. In the city of Takayama, with about forty-five thousand inhabitants in the eighteenth century, death rates were between 27 and 31 per thousand.[48]

It is likely that these findings will need to be qualified in various ways. First, there was clearly much regional variation. For instance, mortality rates were obviously a good deal higher in the remote and economically backward northern area of Hida where Ann Bowman Jannetta has carried out detailed studies based on temple registers. Yet even here the 'most extraordinary finding is the near-constancy of life expectancy at birth at a level of between 30 and 40 years from the late eighteenth century to the mid-twentieth century.[49]

Secondly, there were enormous variations over time. One of the most interesting findings is that, as in England, there seems to have been a drop in mortality well before the famous late-nineteenth-century transition. But whereas this happened in at least two waves in England in the fifteenth to sixteenth centuries, and then in the eighteenth, it happened much earlier in Japan.

The period between the eighth and mid eleventh centuries witnessed constant epidemics. Farris lists '34 epidemics for the eighth century, 35 for the ninth century, 26 for the tenth century (despite a marked decline in the number of records), and 24 for the eleventh century, 16 of which occur between the year 1000 and 1052.' Epidemics then seem to have declined in severity. 'The era from 1050 to 1260 marks a time of declining importance of disease in Japan. There were fifty epidemics over 210 years, an average of one outbreak every 4.2 years, compared to one epidemic every 2.9 years in the 700s and one every 3.8 years in the poorly documented 900s.' Thus 'by 1365 neither infection nor famine nor war was restricting the growth of Japan's population.'[50] The situation by the seventeenth century, when there was another spurt of population, seems to be one where, as early European accounts suggest, the densest settled population in the world was enjoying a relatively disease-free environment. The unusually low later Tokugawa figures give us a glimpse of the end of this process.

Nevertheless we should remain cautious about the figures. Many of the calculations are based on records which tend to ignore deaths in very early infancy. Furthermore, it is often difficult to distinguish *de jure* from *de facto* populations in reconstitution studies. For both these reasons, Hayami among others would push up the mortality rates somewhat, finding, like others, the life expectancies suggested by Hanley and Yamamura and Smith to be 'impossibly high'.[51] Hayami guesses that in fact something like 20 per cent of infants may have died in the first six months, and hence guesses at infant mortality rates of

---

[48] Yoichire Sasaki in Hanley and Wolf (eds), *Family*, 137.
[49] Jannetta and Preston, *Two Centuries*, 426.
[50] Farris in Kiple (ed.), *Disease*, 377, 381, 384.
[51] Hayami, *Myth*, 7.

up to 200 per thousand, which would place it on the level of England at the same time.[52] Osamu Saito has calculated figures of 279 per thousand for three villages in central Japan for the period 1751–1869.[53]

Yet even if we push up the death rates from the low to the high twenties, we are still dealing with an unusual situation which needs explanation. It places Japan in the same league as England or Holland, namely as a nation with normal mortality below that of most agrarian societies. The Japanese case is all the more surprising given what we know of the densely packed countryside and large towns and cities. For Japan to have achieved mortality rates by 1600 which would not be improved on until the mid twentieth century is a considerable achievement. Both England and Japan had somehow overcome the 'hump' of high mortality.

It becomes apparent that Japan as a whole, like England, was exceptional in its demographic pattern, having a long period of stationary population for about six generations. As Spencer long ago noted, Tokugawa population stabilized 'when population was growing rapidly in most other parts of the world' and 'this is a rather remarkable demographic event in world history.'[54] Hollingsworth makes the same point. 'Japan, as always, is an exception. . . . The picture here is of a stable population, one of the very few pre-industrial stable populations that is well documented.'[55]

The second important impact of recent work in Japanese demography has been to suggest that the adjustments in population growth rates in Japan, as in England, were as much the result of fluctuations in the fertility rate as in the mortality rate. This emerged as a result of similar intensive work on registers of births, marriages and deaths and other demographic materials in Japan. The resulting change is noted by Thomas Smith. 'The rapid growth of Japanese population in the seventeenth century, followed by virtual stagnation from about 1700 to 1867, is a phenomenon that has long been of great diagnostic interest to historians; and until recently they were nearly unanimous in explaining it in Malthusian terms.'[56] Now, however, it has been suggested that, as Kalland and Pedersen have argued, the stable population was 'not a result of high death rates, but rather of low birth rates.'[57]

What this suggests is that in Japan, as in England, a 'homeostatic' pattern was developing, in which the 'preventive checks' of lower fertility were at work. Fertility was reduced, as in the eighteenth century. However, if economic

[52] Hayami, *Class Differences*, 11–12.
[53] Saito, *Famines*, 12.
[54] Spencer, *Asia – East by South*, 383.
[55] Hollingsworth, *Historical Demography*, 76.
[56] Smith, *Nakahara*, 8.
[57] Kalland and Pedersen, *Famine*, 34.

conditions altered rapidly, fertility could rise. As in England, as proto-industrialization developed, the fertility controls weakened and the population began to grow. The population 'began increasing from the start of the nineteenth century' and 'after the 1820s, this trend of stable growth held true for virtually all localities.'[58] The growth was, however, modest until the middle of the century. Then 'In the *bakumatsu* period and following the Meiji Restoration, the population growth accelerated.'[59] As in England, this was not merely the result of a drop in mortality but 'stemmed mainly from an increased birth rate.'[60]

There was no real 'demographic transition' in early modern Japan from a situation where population was mainly held in check by high mortality to one where it was mainly checked by low fertility. Susan Hanley writes 'In many ways demographic patterns in the eighteenth and nineteenth centuries were similar to modern Japanese patterns: a relatively high degree of urbanization, small families, deliberate population control through social practices and birth control, relatively low birth rates . . . low rates of adult mortality.'[61] Hanley and Yamamura write that, 'we believe that the concept of a 'demographic transition' in the sense of a transition from high fertility and mortality to low, should be rejected as inapplicable to Japan.'[62]

What happened was that in the burst into industrialization in both England and Japan fertility was allowed to rise. Then, when industrialization was achieved, the balance changed and fertility was again restricted. In England the restriction occurred about one hundred years into the industrial revolution, in the 1870s. In Japan it was effected about 80 years after the start of rapid industrial growth in the 1950s. The power of the preventive check in Japan was well illustrated then. 'When the 1950s ended, Japan's people had accomplished an all-time first among twentieth-century nations: in ten years they had cut their crude birth rate in half, from 34 births per thousand in 1947 to 17 in 1957, a level that they have maintained ever since.'[63]

---

[58] Hayami in Jansen and Rozman (eds), *Japan*, 315.
[59] Gibert Rozman in *Gambridge History*, 5,560.
[60] Hayami in Jansen and Rozman (eds), *Japan*, 315.
[61] Hanley, *Fertility*, 127.
[62] Hanley, *Economic*, 314.
[63] Coleman, *Family Planning*, 34.

Part II

Wars of Peace

3

Natural Environment, Culture and Human Labour

In order to understand the ways in which the Malthusian checks of war, famine and disease were controlled in England and Japan, we need to know something about their geology, geography and technology. Engelbert Kaempfer wrote that Japan 'may in different respects be compar'd to the Kingdoms of great Britain and Ireland, being much after the same manner, tho' in a more eminent degree, divided and broke through by corners and forelands, arms of the Sea, great bays and inlets running deep into the Country, and forming several Islands, Peninsula's, Gulphs and Harbours. Besides, as the King of Great Britain is Sovereign of three Kingdoms, England, Scotland and Ireland, so likewise the Japonese Emperor hath the supreme Jurisdiction of three separate large islands.'[1]

Japan consists of the four main islands of Honshu, Shikoku, Kyushu and Hokkaido. The total area of Japan is 142,766 square miles, about one-quarter larger than the whole of the British Isles. It currently has more than 120 million inhabitants, over twice the population of Britain. It is volcanic with 60 active volcanoes and 450 defunct ones. Volcanic lava covers more than a quarter of the country and the frequent earthquakes to which it is prone are connected with the outward thrust of Asia towards the Pacific. Physically, almost the whole of Japan is rugged hill and mountain country, plains occupying less than one-sixth of its surface. The flat lowlands are fragmented into tiny valleys surrounded by mountains and coastal patches. Much of the lowland area is covered with coarse gravel fans laid down by the mountain streams.

In winter Japan is strongly influenced by a very cold air-stream which comes from the continental anticyclone. Parts of Hokkaido, for instance, experience

---

[1] Kaempfer, *History*, I, 100.

four months with sub-zero temperatures. In the summer, however, warm, moist air from the Pacific is sucked in so that at low altitudes it is very hot. The climate is extreme for an island, both within the year, and in variety from the semi-frozen north to the tropical south. The huge variations in climate can be better understood when we consider the length of Japan. F.H.King explained to his American readers that 'The Island Empire of Japan stretches along the Asiatic coast through more than twenty-nine degrees of latitude from the southern extremity of Formosa northward to the middle of Saghalin, some 2,300 statute miles; or from the latitude of middle Cuba to that of north Newfoundland and Winnipeg.'[2] It has heavy rainfall in the summer, receiving most of its average of forty inches a year at that time. It is also very humid in early summer, with typhoons in late summer and autumn. The mountains have severely limited the land available for cultivation with five-sixths still covered by wild vegetation, mainly forest. Agriculturally it is an irrigated rice growing country with some pasture land, particularly in Hokkaido.

Britain lies off the coast of France, Belgium and Holland at roughly the same latitude as northern Japan. The land is a mixture of old and new rock with no active volcanoes. There are only occasional minor earth tremors and no severe earthquakes. Physically much of Britain is relatively flat and cultivable, with rich soils and good drainage. Because it lies in the gulf stream, it enjoys a comparatively mild climate with few extremes of heat or cold. It receives a reasonably constant supply of rainfall throughout the year, with up to sixty inches of rain on the high, westerly, hills. The land is broadly divided into two main zones, both of which have been cultivated for many centuries, with pastoral farming in the 'upland' area of the west and north, and arable farming in the 'lowland' area of the east and south. The main crops are wheat, rye and barley in the south, and oats in the north.

The physical differences are large, but even more pronounced are the cultural and historical contrasts. The people of Japan are of Mongoloid origin; those of Britain of Indo-European background. The Japanese speak a unique language whose origins puzzle experts but which has some affinities to other Asiatic languages. The English speak a Germanic language of the Indo-European group. The written language of Japan is a mixture of several scripts, heavily influenced by the pictographic script of China. English is written in alphabetic form, based heavily on Greek and Roman roots. The Japanese political system is an amalgam of Chinese models, with later internal variations and western importations. It has historically been very different from the unusual form of constitutional monarchy that grew up in England. The philosophic and religious traditions in Japan are based on an ancient amalgam of Shinto, Buddhism,

---

[2] King, *Farmers*, 424–5.

Confucianism and Daoism. That of England is a particular brand of western Christianity. The culture of Japan, based on China, is in almost every respect different from that of England based on classical and Germanic roots. The history of the two countries over the last thousand years can also be contrasted. Japan was only periodically influenced by outside pressures, from China and Korea, then the West, while England has received a constant stream of influences from a basically Roman and Christian continent. England spread outwards to set up the largest Empire the world has ever known, Japan turned inwards except for a few short interludes and was without an Empire. From the eighteenth century England developed the first industrial society in the world while Japan industrialized with outside inspiration over a hundred years later.

Turning to specific connections with mortality, it is well known that disease patterns are strongly affected by climate and ecology. The island climates of England and Japan may well have been one of the necessary ingredients for their mortality patterns. Both England and Japan, because of their position, were unusually rainy and windswept. 'Rain has a very cleansing effect on air, it carries down the dust and draws down the higher and purer strata of air. A rainy and wind-swept area is usually healthy, although it may not have a pleasant climate.'[3] Furthermore, in the case of malaria, and possibly some other diseases the fact that there are sharp winters with temperatures below freezing may be beneficial.

Historically, the patterns of disease have been affected by foreign trade, exploration and conquest. The pressure on Japan from the west in the later nineteenth century introduced a number of diseases into that country. It is difficult to allow for these 'macro' changes for they are often so large that they escape our notice. Yet the pattern of the migration of diseases is becoming more apparent to historians.[4] The general tendency from the sixteenth century was for disease levels to rise as mobility increased both between different parts of the globe and within specific countries. Dobson suggests that one reason for the rise of mortality in seventeenth-century England was 'the increased global and regional population movements of the time.'[5]

The geographical positions of England and Japan may have been important in this respect. As Macfarlane Burnett pointed out some time ago, 'it is self-evident that if the microorganism responsible is not present in a community then no cases of that disease will occur. It is one of the great advantages of Australia that as an island nation remote from the continental sources of most infectious disease it is relatively easy to prevent entry of disease.'[6] There can be no doubt that the exclusion of disease was very important in Japan. The absence

[3] Lane-Claypon, *Hygiene*, 64.
[4] cf. Crosby, *Ecological*.
[5] Dobson, *Hiccup*, 419; cf. also 420–1.
[6] Burnett, *Infectious*, 118.

of a number of epidemic diseases before the later nineteenth century may well
have been the result of a combination of a wide sea and a deliberate policy to
keep out foreigners and to confine the few who were allowed in to small,
quarantined, port enclaves. Though much less significant, the North Sea may
have helped to keep out some epidemics from England. There were times when
it appears that effective action was taken, for instance in relation to plague.[7]

Both mortality and fertility are affected by the amount and nature of human
labour. If people are exhausted by too much physical work, they are more
susceptible to certain diseases. Work in certain jobs, such as those in mines or
with textile fibres, will increase mortality rates. Similarly if women have to work
very hard during pregnancy and soon after birth, this will affect both maternal
health and infant survival, as well as fertility rates.

As early as the fifteenth century, Sir John Fortescue commented that England 'surmounteth all other lands in fruitfulness' and 'bringeth forth fruit of it
self scant provoked by man's industry and labour.'[8] In the sixteenth century, van
Meteren from Antwerp, who lived in England for many years, noted the high
standard of living. English wealth came from sheep, rather than from hard
labour: 'the people are not so laborious and industrious as the Netherlands or
French, as they lead for the most part an indolent life . . . like the Spaniards; the
most toilsome, difficult, and skillful works are chiefly performed by foreigners,
as among the idle Spaniards. . . . They keep many lazy servants, and also many
wild animals for their pleasure, rather than trouble themselves to cultivate the
land.'[9] Lupold von Wedel, visiting in 1584–5, thought that 'the peasants and
citizens (of England) are on the average rich people,' adding that 'I have seen
peasants presenting themselves statelier in manner, and keeping a more sumptuous table than some noblemen do in Germany. That is a poor peasant who has
no silver-gilt salt-cellars, silver cups, and spoons.'[10] Similarly, David Hume
commented that 'Lord Bacon, accounting for the great advantages obtained by
the English in their wars with France, ascribes them chiefly to the superior ease
and plenty of the common people amongst the former.'[11]

Between the fifteenth and mid eighteenth century, England was able to
produce considerable surpluses with an amount of human labour which amazed
outsiders. It was a relatively affluent country, second only to Holland, but with
a much larger and more diverse population. This was the economic base from
which it launched into rapid urbanization and industrialization, a process that

---

[7] Flinn, *European*, 60.
[8] Fortescue, *Commendation*, 66.
[9] Rye, *Foreigners*, 70.
[10] Quoted in Appleby, *Diet*, 102.
[11] Hume, *Essays*, 157.

paradoxically increased the need for human labour to service the new 'labour saving' machines. There is considerable debate as to what happened after 1750. A vast amount of literary and historical material suggests that people were forced out of a relatively relaxed work pattern into working much longer hours in terrible conditions. Stendhal 'felt at once the absurdity of the eighteen-hour day of the workman.' He added that 'My companions thought me quite mad when I added: the excessive and crushing toil of the English workman avenges us for Waterloo and four coalitions.'[12] Yet, at the same time, we should remember that many argued that until the end of the eighteenth century conditions for the English labourer were better than those in many countries. For example both Malthus and Arthur Young agreed that conditions were far worse in France.[13]

In England, much of the strain on the human body was reduced by the use of animals: horses and oxen for carriage and power, sheep, pigs and cows to produce clothing and protein. The contrast with Japan could not be more dramatic and the nature of work patterns in Japan can only be understood if we note two glaring absences.

It was Isabella Bird, coming from animal-rich Britain in the later nineteenth century, who most graphically described the absence of domesticated animals in Japan. She was struck by the silence and emptiness of the countryside. 'As animals are not used for milk, draught, or food, and there are no pasture lands, both the country and the farm-yards have a singular silence and an inanimate look.' She missed the sounds: 'a mean looking dog and a few fowls being the only representatives of domestic animal life. I long for the lowing of cattle and the bleating of sheep.' Furthermore, 'there is little traffic, and very few horses are kept, one, two, or three constituting the live stock of a large village.' 'Cows and coolies carry much of the merchandise, and women as well as men carry heavy loads.'[14]

The situation two centuries earlier may have been somewhat different for there are suggestions of a more extensive use of animals. In 1613, Captain Saris had noted that pigs, goats and even cows could be purchased cheaply, though there may have been special provision for the Dutch traders.[15] Kaempfer's account shows that 'There are Horses in the Country: They are indeed little in the main, but some of them not inferior in shape, swiftness and dexterity to the Persian Breed. They serve for state, for riding, for carriage and ploughing.' Yet even in the most pastoral area of the mountains 'we saw no cattle grazing any where all day long, excepting a few cows and horses for carriage and ploughing.'

---

[12] Wilson (ed.), *Strange Island*, 165.
[13] Malthus, *Population*, I, 230–1.
[14] Bird, *Tracks*, 49,49,128,131.
[15] Purchas, *Pilgrims*, 147. This may have been specifically for the foreign residents in Yokohama.

Elsewhere, 'They have a sort of large Buffles, of a monstrous size, with hunches on the back, like Camels, which serve for carriage and transport for goods only, in large Cities.'[16]

There are a number of possible explanations for the marked absence of large numbers of domestic animals. The ecological arguments would stem from the nature of the volcanic soil. Japan lacked the possibility of pastoralism except in certain areas in the west and north. This argument is then supported by a second, that given the small area of cultivable land people could not afford to keep animals which would compete with grain production. The 'opportunity cost' of giving up precious land to livestock was too high. It was necessary to use every piece of fertile ground to produce the basic grains in very densely settled areas.

It has been observed that raising animals is an expensive option – for instance, to feed grains to chickens may produce meat and eggs but many people in the world cannot afford to use the grain in this way. The fairly desperate struggle to grow enough rice and other foodstuffs may have made animals a luxury the Japanese could not afford. Indeed, as population built up in the seventeenth century, the cereal rather than animal husbandry option may have become increasingly attractive. Carl Pieter Thunberg at the end of the eighteenth century was aware of the absence of pasturage and animals: 'Meadows are not to be met with in the whole country; on the contrary, every spot of ground is made use of either for corn-fields, or else for plantations of esculent rooted vegetables.' He implied that it was the low number of grazing animals that led to the absence of pasture. 'They have few Quadrupeds; for which reason there is no occasion to lay out the land in extensive meadows.'[17] As the agronomist F.H.King pointed out when he visited Japan in the early twentieth century, 'By devoting the soil to growing vegetation which man can directly digest they have saved 60 pounds per 100 of absolute waste by the animal.' He calculated that '1,000 bushels of grain has at least five times as much food value and will support five times as many people as will the meat or milk that can be made from it.'[18] On this reckoning, the agricultural area of Japan, if it had been based on pastoral agriculture, could only have supported six million, rather than the thirty million actual inhabitants it supported in 1800.

A similar theory was put forward by the anthropologist Richard Beardsley and his co-workers in the 1950s: 'Land shortage accounts particularly for the rarity of grazing animals. On arable land, crops grown for direct human consumption are much more efficient than natural vegetation or fodder crops for

[16] Kaempfer, *History*, I, 194; II, 376; I, 195.
[17] Thunberg, *Travels*, IV, 81,94; a very similar passage is in Alcock, *Tycoon*, I, 69.
[18] King, *Farmers*, 135.

grazing animals.' There is not enough waste or spare grazing for larger animals.[19] This view is supported by the agricultural economist Ester Boserup: 'Draft animals fed on produced fodder are not an efficient source of energy supply. The mechanical energy supplied by them is probably only some 3–5 per cent of the energy contained in the fodder they consume.'[20] This suggests that the relatively sparse population of England allowed people to 'waste' land and grain on animals. There was, furthermore, no religious proscription on the use of animals products, unlike Japan.[21]

In England, a further set of technologies which provided an alternative to human labour were centred on the use of the wheel. Wind and water mills were two of the obvious devices to use the powers of the elements. In Japan, the wheel, though well known, was only used at the margin, and indeed its use may have declined over the centuries. Just to take one simple use of the wheel, we may note the curious absence of the wheelbarrow in Japan. This device was traditionally of enormous importance in China. 'For adaptability to the worst road conditions no vehicle equals the wheelbarrow, progressing by one wheel and two feet. No vehicle is used more in China, if the carrying pole is excepted, and no wheelbarrow in the world permits so high an efficiency of human power as the Chinese ... where nearly the whole load is balanced on the axle of a high, massive wheel with broad tire.'[22] Yet in Japan the wheelbarrow was not adopted, unlike most things Chinese. For the medieval period, we are told 'The wheelbarrow seems to have been unknown (whereas it was used in China) and earth was carried either in baskets, or thrown on to a screen made of straw or rushes drawn by hand and slid along the ground.'[23] Towards the end of the nineteenth century, 'Japanese rural economy knows nothing of wagons or wheelbarrows.'[24] There was also a relative absence of larger carts drawn by animals to carry human or other loads.[25]

Until the nineteenth century, Japan had a productive technology which was in many ways no more efficient in terms of its use of non-human labour than the remotest parts of some of the poorest countries today. My description of the technology of the Gurungs of Nepal, written twenty-five years ago, would apply reasonably well to Japanese agriculture. 'The Gurungs have a pre-wheel culture in which the human back lifts and moves everything, and the human arm and leg

[19] Beardsley, *Village*, 177.
[20] Boserup, *Technology*, 49.
[21] See the chapter on food for a discussion of this proscription.
[22] King, *Farmers*, 237–9.
[23] Frederic, *Daily Life*, 129.
[24] Chamberlain, *Things*, 20.
[25] See for example, Kaempfer, *History*, III, 202; Thunberg, *Travels*, III, 108,134; Oliphant, *Elgin's Mission*, 139; Alcock, *Tycoon*, II, 477; Morse, *Day*, I, 347,425.

does most of the grinding and pounding.'[26] How then did the Japanese feed their large population? The answer is through incessant physical work and a high degree of co-operation.

The immense pressure put on the human body, possibly unparalleled even in China or India, is widely acknowledged by historians of Japan.[27] Thomas Smith quotes a passage from a mid-nineteenth-century advice book for farmers which shows the obsession with work and time: 'If the farm family would escape poverty, it must treat time as precious (*koin oshimubeshi*). By rising early and shortening the daily rest period, two additional hours a day can be worked. That is seven hundred and twenty hours a year; the equivalent of sixty days, or two months, when no food is consumed, no wage paid, no oil required for lighting. . . . Thus can the farm family escape the pain of poverty.'[28] Beardsley and his colleagues wrote that 'By far the largest amount of work is accomplished through human energy in Niiike.' In 1949, an average acre of rice required 870 man hours of labour. This was thirty times more than what it would have required in the United States.[29] Likewise, visiting agronomists saw the gruelling work undertaken. King's figures of work showed 'something of the tense strain and of the terrible burden which is being carried by these people, over and above that required for the maintenance of the household.' He found that 'The oriental farmer is a time economizer beyond any other. He utilizes the first and last minute and all that are between.' He could do nothing but admire, 'This marvelous heritage of economy, industry and thrift, bred of the stress of centuries.'[30] The burden of work was also alluded to by native Japanese.[31]

Kaempfer realized that it was partly the poor terrain which forced the people to work so hard and thought this a benefit. 'But even in this particular nature hath been exceeding kind to this Country: this seeming defect in the soil, this want of culture, is what keeps up in the inhabitants that so much commendable spirit of labour and industry.'[32] Thunberg wrote that in general 'The diligence with which the husbandman cultivates the soil, and the pains they bestow on it, are so great as to seem incredible.' Every tiny scrap of land was used with the utmost care. 'The pains which a farmer takes to cultivate the sides of even the steepest hills, is almost incredible. If the place be even no more than two feet square, he nevertheless raises a wall of stones at the bottom of the declivity, fills the part above this with earth and manure, and sows this little plot of ground

---

[26] Macfarlane, *Resources*, 33.
[27] See Saito, e.g. *Gender*.
[28] Smith, *Native Sources*, 210,199.
[29] Beardsley, *Village*, 177–8.
[30] King, *Farmers*, 430,261,165.
[31] See for example Saikaku, *Storehouse*, 140; Inouye, *Home*, 151.
[32] Kaempfer, *History*, III, 313.

with rice or esculent rooted vegetables.'[33] Alcock described how 'Men, women, and children may be seen in the fields early and late, and the labour is chiefly manual.'[34] Edward Morse noted that 'The extensive rice-fields everywhere indicate the enormous amount of labor involved, not only in making them, but in the yearly amount of labor expended in planting-time.' Almost everyone worked almost all the time. 'A few infirm old men and women and little children were seen, but everybody else was at work in the rice-fields or on the farms or busy with duties in the house.'[35]

The 'duties in the house' were not just household work, but bi-occupations which, as Thomas Smith has shown, were often as important and labour-consuming as agriculture.[36] Morse described some of these, noting:

the universal industry of the people. Everybody works; all seem poor, but there are no paupers. The many industries, which with us are carried on in large factories, here are done in the home. What we do by the wholesale in the factories they do in the dwellings, and as you ride through the village you see the spinning, weaving, the making of vegetable wax, and many other industries. In these operations the entire family is utilized from a child above babyhood to blind old men and women.[37]

The pressure, particularly on women, was remembered by many. Country girls 'had learned to eat their meals as fast as possible so they could get straight back to work; otherwise they were told off by their parents. They even used to pour water over their rice and barley to make it easier to swallow quickly.' 'We never had time in the morning to put on any makeup. The attitude then was that a girl who spent time in front of the mirror was no use to anyone.' 'The ideal girl got up in the morning, folded her mattress, dressed quickly, and went outside. Then, without even sitting down, she'd quickly run a comb through her hair ... all you had time to think about during the day was work, so you weren't expected to worry about how you looked.'[38] 'One peasant recalled, "We were taught that peasants must work from morning to night in order to stay alive. Whether bad weather caused crop failures or not, we lived believing that it was our predetermined lot to work." '[39] A young wife described the attitude of the family she had married into. 'They would complain, "Our young wife

[33] Thunberg, *Travels*, III, 257; IV, 83.
[34] Alcock, *Tycoon*, I, 319.
[35] Morse, *Day*, I, 9–10; II, 51.
[36] Smith, *Native Sources*, ch.3.
[37] Morse, *Day*, II, 51–2.
[38] Saga, *Silk and Straw*, 141, 142–3.
[39] Hane, *Rebels*, 105.

takes a lot of time in the toilet" ...'[40] Her mother-in-law reputedly said, 'I sure hate to see a young wife wasting her time feeding the baby. She should be working the loom and making some money.' Saito has figures on the hours worked by the Japanese, particularly women, in the later nineteenth century. They appear to work something like twice as long as equivalent groups in western Europe.[41]

The effects of all this immense physical effort on women's bodies was noted by Isabella Bird. 'At Kayashima I asked the house-master's wife, who looked about fifty, how old she was ... and she replied twenty-two – one of many similar surprises.' 'The married women look as if they had never known youth, and their skin is apt to be like tanned leather.'[42] At the end of the century, Alice Bacon noticed the same rapid aging of women. 'A Japanese woman loses her beauty early. At thirty-five her fresh color is usually entirely gone, her eyes have begun to sink a little in their sockets, her youthful roundness and symmetry of figure have given place to an absolute leanness, her abundant black hair has grown thin, and much care and anxiety have given her face a pathetic expression of quiet endurance.'[43] The work was not only long, but extremely heavy; beating, carrying incredible weights and pumping water.

We see that despite their apparent similarities in geographical situation and size, the way in which the British and Japanese used their environment was quite different. For the British, the emphasis on pastoralism and the harnessing of the 'natural' power of animals, wind and water meant that before the industrial revolution, many lived a relatively easy life. In Japan, with a much denser population subsisting on inferior land under rice cultivation, the apparent decrease in domesticated animals and limited use of wind and water, meant that the physical work load became progressively greater, with women suffering in particular. This is what Hayami has called an 'industrious revolution'.[44] From this evidence it would appear that England was in a much more favourable position than Japan, and yet Japanese mortality levels were apparently comparable if not lower than those in England. It would seem that the environment, on its own, can provide few answers.

---

[40] Quoted in Hane, *Rebels*, 90.
[41] According to a talk on 'Gender, work and time in the farm household economy', given at the Cambridge Group for the History of Population and Social Structure on 3 March 1994.
[42] Bird, *Tracks*, 100,87.
[43] Bacon, *Japanese Girls*, 101.
[44] Hayami, *Transformation*, 6; Hayami, *Population Growth*, 37.

4

The Destruction of War

It was not by accident that Malthus put 'War' as the first of the great 'positive' checks in pre-industrial societies. For it is not merely the killing of thousands in battles, but also the much greater effects of dislocation, often leading to a huge number of deaths by famine and disease, which explain why war and conquest have tended to be the major form of 'crisis' in most agrarian civilizations. The destruction of a single campaign could undo most of those enormously laborious efforts to harness nature which we have witnessed in the previous chapter.

Perennial warfare is the basis of many tribal societies and makes for a world where it is difficult for 'civilization' to emerge. 'The social complexity and cultural richness of civilization depends on institutional guarantees of peace. Lacking these institutional means and guarantees, tribesmen live in a condition of war and war limits the scale, complexity and all-round richness of their culture.'[1] When civilizations based on writing, cities and settled agriculture arose, war was partially controlled, but when it did occur, its effects were far more devastating. For instance there was the massive destruction caused by wars in Egypt, India and China. The population history of Egypt shows that of the seven events which are believed to have led to massive declines in the Egyptian population between 664 BC and 1966, five were thought to be the result of the Persian, Macedonian, Roman, Arab and Turkish conquests. The other two were plagues.[2]

In India and the Middle East, 'the Mongol invasions of the thirteenth century were followed in the late fourteenth century by the conquests of Timur, who ranged from Anatolia in the West to India in the East and marked his

---

[1] Sahlins, *Tribesmen*, 5.
[2] Hollingsworth, *Historical Demography*, 311 (diagram).

victories with minarets and pyramids of skulls.' Landes gives a vivid picture of
the area: 'nomads from the steppe, Russians spreading southward and eastward,
the Afghan tribes and Mogul emperors to the east, the nations of Christian
Europe in the Danube valley and the Mediterranean. The land was forever
criss-crossed with armies; siege followed siege, massacre followed massacre.
Even the ghastliest carnages of the Thirty Years' War . . . pale alongside the
bloodbaths of Delhi.'[3]

In China, there were eras of peace, but when these ended the numbers killed
and the destruction was on an even greater scale. The invasions and devastations
of the Mongols are thought to have reduced the Chinese population to half of
its former level within fifty years, over 60 million people dying or failing to
be replaced.[4] Another catastrophe occurred with the Manchu invasion in the
1660s which E.L.Jones believed 'cost that vast land seventeen per cent of
its population. That was a loss of twenty-five million people.'[5] Again in the
nineteenth century, the Taiping Rebellion 'was the bloodiest war of the
nineteenth century. It lasted from 1850 to 1864, causing 20 million deaths.'[6]

Against this background western Europe, from the sixteenth century
until the world wars of the twentieth century, appears relatively secure. By
the sixteenth century, 'the only enemy that Europeans had to fear was other
Europeans; . . . the virulence of fighting diminished, particularly in that
north-western corner of Europe . . .'[7] Jones agrees that 'Europe probably lost
fewer men per 1,000 to warfare than did Asia, but it is likely that the ratio of
capital equipment she lost was much less still.' He gives details of the relative
destruction, noting in particular that the water-irrigated rice cultivation of
much of Asia was much more likely to be deeply damaged by warfare. The
consequence was often that famine ensued after war and then there were
epidemics. He concludes that 'Europe's overall losses seem markedly less serious than those of Asia.'[8] Indeed, 'Only those parts of Eurasia that were spared
the conquests of Mongols – Japan and western Europe – were able to generate
sustained technological progress.'[9]

Yet we should not forget that all this is relative. There was a state of periodic
warfare that beset much of western Europe from the fall of Rome through to the
nineteenth century. The Hundred Years War, the religious conflicts of the

---

[3] Landes, *Prometheus*, 34.
[4] Clark, *Population Growth*, 72.
[5] Jones, *Miracle*, 36.
[6] Wright, 'War' in *Encyclopaedia Social Sciences* (2nd edn), 458; Ho (cited in Dumond, *Population
Growth*, 304) puts it at nearly 30 million.
[7] Landes, *Prometheus*, 34.
[8] Jones, *Miracle*, 37,38.
[9] Mokyr, *Lever*, 186.

sixteenth century and, worst of all, the Thirty Years War of the seventeenth century were only the most serious and long-term of the wars which occurred.

In the case of the Thirty Years War, for example, on one estimate the consequences of the war is reckoned to have lowered the population of Germany from 21 to 13.5 million.[10] Kamen comes to the general conclusion 'that over the German lands as a whole the urban centres lost one-third of their population and the rural areas lost about forty per cent.'[11] The effects of these wars are obvious. Wars 'destroyed some of the most active centres of technological change in Europe, especially in the southern Netherlands (1568–90) and most of Germany (1616–48).'[12] Likewise, wars had earlier destroyed the rich potential of the Italian cities in the fifteenth century, and would be one of the major factors in the relative decline of Holland in the eighteenth. 'From a purely economic point of view, war was a much greater evil than the plague. . . . War . . . hit capital above all, and those who survived found themselves in conditions of the most abject misery.'[13] Geoffrey Parker writes of another of the regional conflicts, 'it seems clear that the prolonged conflict generated by the Revolt of the Netherlands served to retard the growth of the northern republic (and particularly of its landward provinces), to inflict permanent damage on the economy of large areas of the Spanish empire, and to ruin for two centuries the prosperity of "Belgium".'[14]

There are some grounds for believing that the level of devastation and destruction declined in much of Europe from about 1660 onwards. 'The destruction occasioned by war has unquestionably abated, both on account of its occurring, on the whole, less frequently, and its ravages not being so fatal, either to man or the means of his support, as they were formerly.'[15] Pitirim Sorokin was to develop Malthus's theme. He showed that warfare increased in Europe between the twelfth and seventeenth centuries, 'then by the seventeenth century Europe had attained a new integrated system of ultimate values. . . . Consequently there occurred the decline of the curve of war-magnitude during the eighteenth and nineteenth centuries.'[16]

J.U.Nef was one of those who suggested that war in Europe went through three phases; medieval warfare, which was moderately destructive, then a period of increased destruction with the introduction of guns and the religious disputes in the sixteenth century, and then a decline in the severity of warfare from the

---

[10] Russell, *Violence*, 182.

[11] Kamen, *Iron*, 43.

[12] Mokyr, *Lever*, 76.

[13] Cipolla, *Before*, 133–4.

[14] In Winter (ed.), *War*, 66.

[15] Malthus, *Summary*, 254; cf. also Malthus, *Population*, I, 315.

[16] Sorokin, *Society*, 512.

middle of the seventeenth century. The rising tempo of war in the sixteenth century was obvious: 'With religious zeal so little relieved by the supreme Christian virtue of charity, and armed on all sides with weapons unknown to the violent of earlier ages, an almost universal slaughter became possible.' Yet even in this period, there were restraints: 'terrible as warfare on the Continent became, especially from 1562 to 1648, the devastation and the destruction of life might have been much greater than they were. It was restraints upon war which prevented a general collapse of European civilization following the Reformation, a collapse which . . . would have prevented the genesis of industrial civilization in the north of Europe.'[17]

Perhaps the most significant underlying conclusion we can draw from Nef's account is that Europe began to enter a virtuous, instead of vicious, circle. Up to the seventeenth century, as wealth and population grew, so did the negative feedback of predatory warfare. From that date, the balance shifted; enough surplus was fed back into the forces controlling violence and there was enough desire to make money by means other than open violence. The violence of market capitalism, the Mandevillian world of concealed warfare through the war of all against all in trade and production, began to take over from the ethos of earlier centuries where it was destruction and predation which were the paths to wealth.[18]

William McNeill notes how the ravaging mercenary armies of the fourteenth century gave way to better paid and organized armies from the seventeenth century. It became possible to 'support professional standing armies on tax income without straining the economic resources of the population too severely.' 'Such armies could and did establish a superior level of public peace within all the principal European states' so that civil wars decreased. This, he argues, started a positive feedback loop. Peace 'allowed agriculture, commerce, and industry to flourish' and hence raised the taxable wealth, which kept the armed forces in being. 'A self-sustaining feedback loop thus arose that raised Europe's power and wealth above levels other civilizations had attained.'[19]

It is quite easy to overlook an absence and the case of warfare in England is a good example. For instance, the monumental *Population History of England* scarcely mentions the relative absence of the most potent of the Malthusian positive checks. There is only one brief reference to 'warfare' in the index where Hakluyt is approvingly quoted as drawing attention in the 1580's to 'our long peace and seldom sickness.'[20]

---

[17] Nef, *War*, 115,117.
[18] cf. Hirschman, *Passions and Interests*.
[19] McNeill, *Pursuit*, 139,117.
[20] Wrigley and Schofield, *Population*, 234.

In considering war in England there is first of all the question of foreign invasions. Unlike many continental countries that continually faced the threat of, if not actual, invasion, with the exception of the Scots in the eighteenth century, England was not invaded by a large 'foreign' army after 1066. The Armada of Philip II nearly reached the coast but was destroyed by storms. This absence from actual, and for long periods from threatened, invasion is of considerable significance. One of the restraints on economic growth is a political variant of the law of diminishing returns. As a country becomes richer, it becomes the envy of its neighbours. It is likely to be attacked and its delicately built infrastructure and capital destroyed, as happened time and again in historic Europe and over many parts of Asia. If a nation wishes to protect itself against this hazard, it has to devote a larger and larger proportion of its wealth to defence, as happened in Holland from the later seventeenth century. England was able to avoid both of these fates. It was not ransacked by conquerors for many hundreds of years, so that its wealth could accumulate and the intricate organization of communications and institutions was not disrupted. Nor did it have to spend an inordinate amount of wealth on defending itself. Of course its powerful navy was essential to its defence, but it had the distinct advantage of a sea border which meant that it could not easily be overrun. On land, a combination of feudal levies and well-placed fortifications could hold at bay threats coming from Wales or Scotland.

The danger of foreign predators, combined with the desire to raid the wealth of richer countries outside one's borders, led to the need to keep standing armies in all continental countries in Eurasia. This had a serious effect leading to the destruction of the accumulated wealth of the ordinary population, because of the cost of keeping a large army permanently supplied. John Aylmer in the sixteenth century described the contrast between what he saw in England and continental countries. 'O England, England, thou knowest not thine own wealth: because thou seest not other countries penury. . . . The husbandman in France, all that he hath gotten in his whole life, loseth it upon one day. For when so ever they have war (as they are never without it) the kings soldiers enter into the poor mans house, eateth and drinketh up all that ever he hath.'[21] Fortescue, who had spent much time in France, also spoke of the oppression of the rural population by troops a century earlier, 'so that there is not the least village there free from this miserable calamity, but that it is once or twice every year beggared by this kind of pilling [pillage].'[22]

The absence of invasion was complemented by relative internal peace. Much of the destruction caused in continental Europe, whether in Italy in the fifteenth century, France in the sixteenth, or Germany in the seventeenth, was the result

---

[21] Reynolds and Orwell, *British Pamphleteers*, 29–33.
[22] Fortescue, *Commendation*, 180 (spelling modernized).

of civil war, often caused by religious differences. The English were practically
free of this, as Charles Creighton, who was particularly sensitive to the medical
effects of warfare, noticed. 'Although the history of the last year or two of John
and of the earlier years of Henry III is full of turbulence and rapine, yet we hear
of no general distress among the cultivators of the soil.' Creighton cites evidence
to show that 'the whole of that period, and of the years following until 1234, is
absolutely free from any record of wide-spread distress among the lower class.'
He is reminded of the observation of Philip de Comines on the Wars of
the Roses in the fifteenth century: 'England has this peculiar grace that neither
the country, nor the people, nor the houses are wasted or demolished; but the
calamities and misfortunes of the war fall only upon the soldiers and especially
the nobility.' Creighton does note some exceptions, as in the incursions of the
Welsh and Scots on the borders and the battles between Simon de Montfort and
the King in 1264 but he concludes that 'on the whole we may take it that the
paralysing effect of civil war seldom reached to the English lower classes in the
medieval period.' He finds that concerning 'pestilence due to war and invasion',
the 'domestic history from first to last is singularly free from such calamities.'[23]

Even the English Civil War of the 1640s was, by continental standards, a
relatively minor affair. We are told, for instance, that 'Most of the clashes
between the Parliamentary and Royalist armies were skirmishes resulting in few
deaths. In terms of fatalities, the most serious battle was Marston Moor in July
1644, when the combined deaths on both sides totalled 4,000. . . . More typical,
though, was the battle of Roundway Down in July 1643, when the Royalists
destroyed a Parliamentary army . . . only 600 were killed, and the rest were
captured.'[24] The absence of mass destruction was noted by most foreigners.[25]
The disturbances of the English Civil War were however serious enough to
show the dangers of ensuing disease, principally of typhus which struck in 1643
and 1644.[26]

This is not, of course, to say that the English were not involved in warfare
elsewhere. Sorokin showed that between 1100 and 1900 the English were
engaged in one war or another for over half the time. There was no diminution
of war, nor in the numbers involved.[27] In the later period, for example it is
calculated that in the years between 1689 and 1815, England was at war for 73
of the 126 years. Many of these, for instance the Napoleonic Wars, were of major
dimensions.[28] The point is that these wars were fought on other people's

---

[23] Creighton, *Epidemics*, I, 37–8,38,13; see also 547.
[24] Clarkson, *Disease*, 119.
[25] For example see De Tocqueville, *Memoir*, II, 378.
[26] Creighton, *Epidemics*, I, 547,556.
[27] Sorokin, *Sociological Theories*, 324–5.
[28] See C.N.Harley in Mokyr (ed.), *Industrial*, 219.

territories. What is certain is that the chief Malthusian positive check had been brought under control in England from 1485 at the latest, and probably from the eleventh century, after the Norman invasion. On a population graph of England, the deaths in the Wars of the Roses and the Civil War would hardly be discernible. The correlated famines and epidemics which war brought on the continental land masses of Europe and Asia were also absent. The most dangerous threat to human kind, the chief form of insecurity and brake upon planning, was thus largely eliminated in England many hundreds of years ago. It is difficult not to see this as a key element in its unusual development.

That Japan was likewise effectively protected from the threat of foreign invasion by sea was obvious to Kaempfer. 'The Sea, which encompasses the Islands of Japan, is very rough and stormy, which with the many rocks, cliffs and shoals, above and under water, make its navigation very dangerous.' 'There is but one good port known, fit to harbour ships of any considerable bulk: this is that of Nagasaki, the entry whereof is very narrow.' Hence, 'Japan is so well guarded by nature itself, that it hath still less to fear from a foreign enemy. An invasion was attempted but seldom, and never with success. This valiant and invincible nation never obey'd any other commands, but of their own Princes.'[29] Thunberg noted 'that no foreign war should have been waged for centuries past, and interior commotions should have been prevented . . . this must appear as improbable, and, to many as impossible, as it is strictly true, and desiring of the utmost attention.'[30]

There were only three recorded attempted invasions of Japan in the fifteen hundred years before 1945. The first was at the end of the eighth century. It was repulsed after initial successes.[31] The second and third were those by Kublai Khan in 1274 and 1281. Both were unsuccessful, due to a combination of stormy weather, rocky coasts and the mobilization and determination of Japanese warriors.[32] No-one attempted another invasion until 1945. Even the threat of invasion was largely absent throughout Japanese history and the country was never pillaged by outsiders. Japan's shield was even stronger than that of England and, given the tempestuous sea, it was not even necessary to build up a defensive navy. Not until the American war ships arrived off the Japanese coast in the 1850s was the inadequacy of the sea defences felt.

The wide sea also made it unattractive for Japan to invade other countries. The only large external attack launched by Japan before the 1880s was in 1592 when Hideyoshi invaded Korea. Ultimately the campaign was not a success and

---

[29] Kaempfer, *History*, I, 160; III, 306,309.
[30] Thunberg, *Travels*, III, vii.
[31] Kaempher, *History*, I, 298; Thunberg, *Travels*, III, 261.
[32] See Kawazoe Shoji in *Cambridge History*, 3, 411–23 for details.

it was not repeated. Thunberg was almost right when he wrote that 'The Japanese have never given way to the weakness of conquering other Kingdoms, or suffering any part of their own to be taken from them.'[33] Japan was therefore free from the need to raise heavy taxation for armies and of the destruction caused by international warfare. Furthermore, 'people who have already secured the fundamental elements of civilization find the partial seclusion of an island environment favourable to their further progress, because it permits their powers to unfold unhindered, protects them from the friction of border quarrels, from the disturbance and desolation of invading armies, to which continental peoples are constantly exposed.'[34]

Being an island does not necessarily ensure internal peace and Japan often gives the impression of being a society which had many of the trappings of war. Kaempfer regarded the Japanese as a 'warlike people' and it was in his work that Malthus found what he thought was the solution to the puzzle of how a country which Thunberg described as filled with people who lived in 'such happiness and plenty' could nevertheless control their population. Kaempfer's extracts from Japanese chronicles showed 'bloody wars', and as compared to China 'the greater frequency of wars and intestine commotions.'[35] Yet, if we examine the history of Japan over the thousand years up to 1900 Malthus's solution does not fit.

After the pacification of Japan by Nobunaga and Hideyoshi in the last quarter of the sixteenth century, up to 1850, Japan had the most complete and lasting period of absence from any kind of war, external or internal, that any major agrarian society has ever known. Yukichi Fukuzawa in the later nineteenth century wrote that 'the 250 years of Tokugawa rule during which there was no warfare is unmatched in world history' allowing the Japanese to 'live in this incomparably peaceful society.'[36] This peace was not inevitable. There had been many disputes and battles previously. It was a triumph of organization and ability, based on the ruthless and astute politics of Nobunaga, Hideyoshi and Ieyasu. The delicate machinery which kept the powerful daimyo in check for several centuries was undoubtedly helped by the absence of land neighbours with whom they could ally, but it was nevertheless in large part due to governmental organization. It is tempting to see this as totally contrasted to a period of 'feudal anarchy' and bloodshed before Nobunaga. But just as it is a mistake to assume that England was awash with war and blood before 1485, so it would seem that devastating civil wars were largely absent in Japan even before the Tokugawa era.

---

[33] Kaempfer, *Travels*, III, 258–9.
[34] Semple, *Geographic*, 434.
[35] Malthus , *Population*, I, 138.
[36] Fukuzawa, *Civilization*, 167.

The first lengthy history of Japan in the English language was written by George Sansom who believed that internal war had only a limited destructive impact within Japan. The most extreme period of civil war occurred in the years preceding 1428. 'The armed conflict . . . had lasted for fifty years . . .', so that 'It might be supposed that the national economy would suffer from the plague of armies and the depredations of greedy barons.' Sansom however argues that 'medieval warfare was not in fact especially deadly or destructive.' The 'damage done by warfare to the true economic foundation of the country, its rice fields and its forests, was almost negligible. The industrious cultivators were usually unhurt, though from time to time they were inconvenienced by being conscript- ed for war service.' After all, whoever won the battle would continue to want the revenues from the countryside. This was an internal conflict, not the marauding of foreign armies intent on plunder. 'Even the country's total loss in manpower was not serious, for death in battle was not so common as the military romances would have us believe, and few civilians were killed.'[37] An interesting insight into the kind of small-scale and limited warfare practised in Japan at this time is given by Louis Frederic. When the Mongol troops invaded Japan, 'the Japanese were utterly astonished to find that the Mongols did not fight in accordance with the laws of chivalry practised by the samurai: the first horsemen who advanced towards the disembarked Mongol troops, loudly shouting their names and challenging their adversaries to come and pit their strength honourably against them in single combat, were met by showers of arrows and promptly surrounded by a multitude of soldiers who massacred them.'

Sansom's account is not contradicted by the recent survey of Japanese history contained in the 'Medieval' volume of the *Cambridge History of Japan*. The index refers to the Gempei War of 1180–5 and the Onin War of 1467–77. There are three references, to the 'Kanno disturbance (1350–2)', the 'Nambokucho disturbance (1336–92)' and the 'Nigatsu disturbance (1272)'. Otherwise there is no reference to war. Although there were undoubtedly many provincial wars and conflicts, there is very little in the volume to suggest a society which was seriously devastated by civil wars; rather we have a picture of an affluent and largely peaceful country, where small sections of warrior knights fought small- scale battles from time to time. As in England, it would seem that a largely homogeneous population, undifferentiated by language or religion, did not descend to such barbarities as the large scale destruction of crops and animals. The prize was power, not plunder, and a would-be ruler would not benefit from destroying his future subjects. Such island civil wars seem to have been elevated strategic games, kept within an arena, and avoiding the real damages which international wars create.

---

[37] Sansom, *History*, II, 181.

The situation for medieval Japan has been described, perhaps a little whimsically, by Frederic. He believed that 'The Japanese, a fearless and courageous fighter, despising death, was for all that not really a man of war. He was first of all a . . . "countryman" who loved his small plot of native land, his province, and who rejoiced to see order and peace prevailing there. He was deeply distressed by a state of war, even shocked by its unseemliness.' The paradox was that the Japanese 'did not think of war as other than an opportunity for winning personal glory. Poetic knights despising death, they were not really warriors at heart.'[38]

Some support for Frederic's views can be found in two otherwise unexplained facts. The first was the history of the samurai after 1600. That a warrior class could continue in existence almost unchanged for 250 years without fighting a single battle or even skirmish is difficult to understand, unless we realize that it was the ethic, Bushido, that was important, and not the fighting. Their war-like ethic, combined with absence of actual fighting, is reflected in the paradoxes of the zen art of war.[39] Secondly, in the medieval period 'one fact is a continual source of wonder' namely that the Japanese were 'equipped with sadly inadequate weapons (except in single combat when their swords performed wonders) . . .' Even when they encountered superior weapon systems, they did not emulate them – an unusual lack of interest for a nation which often accepted and adapted superior technologies from outside with great alacrity. When the Mongols attacked, the Japanese encountered 'powerful bows, cross-bows, swivel-guns, bombs', yet 'they did not think of equipping themselves with better arms!'[40] Limited, single-combat, close warfare by a few warriors was what they liked. When, in the middle of the sixteenth century, a new range of gunpowder-based weapons were brought to their attention by the Portuguese, they were rapidly copied and even improved on. Nobunaga and Hideyoshi used them to overcome feudal resistance. But then they were banned and largely abandoned.[41] Cannon and hand-guns were not wide-spread. Thus when Kaempfer visited Japan at the end of the seventeenth century he could write, 'Guns they have none.'[42]

The absence of serious warfare in England and Japan is one of the central foundations for their unusual development. It arose largely accidentally out of their island position. The avoiding of the destruction of war was not only important in itself but also in relation to its effects on the other Malthusian checks, namely famine and disease. War usually kills many more through the

---

[38] Frederic, *Daily Life*, 177,175,179.
[39] See Cleary, *Art of War*.
[40] Frederic, *Daily Life*, 179.
[41] See Perrin, *The Gun*.
[42] Kaempfer, *History*, II, 306.

disruptions to agriculture and society leading to famine and epidemics, than are directly killed in battle. The effective absence of the first Horseman of the Apocalypse needs to be assessed in conjunction with that of the second, famine.

5

The Nature, Causes and Elimination of Famine

Famine is the second of the great scourges which act as an automatic check to the progress of mankind. In agrarian civilizations, Malthus believed, any improvement in agricultural production would soon be swallowed up by increased population. Then, sooner or later, large scale famines would emerge.

'Famine is a state of extreme hunger suffered by the population of a region as a result of the failure of the accustomed food supply. It is to be distinguished from the more or less constant undernourishment of chronically poverty stricken districts.'[1] In many 'pre-industrial' societies, the majority of the population has lived so close to subsistence level, and the communications and storage devices have been so poorly developed, that bad weather, crop disease or the dislocation of agriculture through war often leads to famine. Weakened, people begin to die of starvation or disease. It might almost be said that famine and the old agrarian order were necessarily connected.

Malthus saw famine as a frequent occurrence in human history. He was struck by Dr Short's observations on the Bills of Mortality and in particular a table 'Of the 254 great famines and dearths.' Of these, 15 had occurred before the Christian era, so, subtracting these, 'it will appear that the average interval between the visits of this dreadful scourge has been only about seven and a half years.'[2] More recently Fernand Braudel has written that 'Famines recurred so insistently for centuries on end that it became incorporated into man's biological regime and built into his daily life. Dearth and penury were continuous, and familiar even in Europe.'[3]

---

[1] Southard in *Encyclopaedia Social Sciences*, 1st edn, under 'Famine'.
[2] Malthus, *Population*, I, 308.
[3] Braudel, *Capitalism*, 38.

Malthus saw China as one of the most terribly afflicted of all countries. It was a country where in 'times of famine' which 'are here but too frequent', 'millions of people' perished of hunger. The famines which followed unfavourable seasons 'are perhaps the most powerful of all the positive checks to the Chinese population.'[4] In China it is estimated that 'there was a drought or flood-induced famine in at least one province almost every year from 108 BC to AD 1911 (Mallory 1926).'[5] In the seventeenth century 'famines became common, especially in north China, worsened by unusually cold and dry weather;'[6] 'nine million fatalities were caused by the famine in north China from 1876 to 1879.'[7] Famine continued in parts of China until very recently. In 1920 and 1921 in certain provinces 'at least 500,000 people died, and out of an estimated 48.8 million in these five provinces, over 19.8 million were declared destitute.'[8] Between two and three million died in Honan province in 1943.[9] The bungled reforms of Chairman Mao meant another massive famine. The 'Great Leap Forward' led to 'famine on a gigantic scale, a famine that claimed 20 million lives or more between 1959 and 1962. Many others died shortly thereafter ... especially children, weakened by years of progressive malnutrition.'[10]

South Asia is another area where devastating famines have occurred until very recently. Malthus saw it as another of the great famine areas of the world: 'India ... has in all ages been subject to the most dreadful famines.'[11] The historical situation was surveyed in 1911. 'Famines seem to recur in India at periodical intervals. ... Every five or ten years the annual scarcity widens its area and becomes a recognized famine; every fifty or a hundred years whole provinces are involved, loss of life becomes widespread, and a great famine is recorded. In the 140 years since Warren Hastings initiated British rule in India, there have been nineteen famines and five severe scarcities.'[12]

Braudel refers to the 'terrible and almost general famine in India in 1630–1.' He quotes a Dutch merchant: 'People wandered hither and thither, helpless, having abandoned their towns or villages. Their condition could be recognised

---

[4] Malthus, *Population*, I, 131,135.
[5] Jones, *Miracle*, 19. There is a description of the 1,282 Chinese famines in the 2,019 years preceding 1911 in Ehrlich, *Population*, 13–15. Watkins and Menken, on the other hand, minimizes the severity of Chinese famines (Watkins and Menken, *Famines*, 653).
[6] Spence, *China*, 21.
[7] Southard, 'Famine' in *Encyclopaedia Soc. Sciences*.
[8] Spence, *China*, 309.
[9] Arnold, *Famine*, 20.
[10] Spence, *China*, 583.
[11] Malthus, *Population*, I, 119.
[12] *Encyclopaedia Britannica*, 'Famine', 167; for a history of early Indian famines, see Aykroyd, *Conquest*, 50ff.

immediately: sunken eyes, wan faces, lips flecked with foam, lower jaw projecting, bones protruding through skin, stomach hanging like an empty sack, some
of them howling with hunger, begging alms.'[13]

In 1769–70, it is estimated that about ten million people perished of
starvation. In Bengal about one third of the inhabitants are thought to have
died.[14] Famines continued throughout the nineteenth century. Paul Seavoy lists
some twelve major peacetime famines between 1812 and 1901, at least half of
which caused an estimated mortality of over one million persons.[15] The closing
decade of the nineteenth century 'was distinguished by the occurrence of
terrible famines', rough calculations suggest that '19 million persons' dying
'may be taken as a rough estimate of loss due to famines.'[16] Others suggest that
'ten famines in India between 1860 and 1900 are estimated to have resulted in
fifteen million deaths.'[17] A Census Report of 1901 stated that 'In ancient times
the occurrence of a severe famine was marked by the disappearance of a third or
a fourth of the population of the area afflicted.'[18]

The Bengal famine of 1943–4 has been extensively studied. It is reckoned
that it took between 1.5 and 3 million lives which was 'due in part to the
complications of war and the (British) administration's incompetence, but little
to do with crop failure.' A combination of 'food hoarding and speculation led to
very large increases in food prices', and people did not have the 'entitlements',
that is the earning power, to buy food.[19] Even in 1966–7 'only a major inflow
of food . . . saved India from famines in which hundreds of thousands,
if not millions, might have died.'[20] The 'Bangladesh-Bengal-Assam food
shortage of 1974–5 developed into a famine that claimed an estimated 1.8
million lives.'[21]

In Russia, famine continued as a threat and an actuality until the middle of
the twentieth century. 'Russia was scourged by major famines eleven times
between 1845 and 1922.'[22] The terrible famine of 1891–2, for instance, was
described by Tolstoy; that of 1921–2 killed at least three million people.[23]

---

[13] Braudel, *Capitalism*, 41.
[14] Berg, cited in Jones, *Miracle*, 29.
[15] Seavoy, *Famine*, 242.
[16] Cassen, *India*, 80.
[17] Southard, 'Famine' in *Encyclopaedia Social Sciences*, 1st edn.
[18] Cassen, *India*, 80, quoting the 1901 Census Report. There is an excellent description and analysis
of the Bengal famines in Hunter, *Annals of Bengal*, 28–55. On the decline of famines in India, see
McAlpin, *Famines*. For a good general account see McAlpin, *Subject to Famine*.
[19] Cassen, *India*, 79; Sen, *Famines*, ch.6; Aykroyd, *Conquest*, ch.7.
[20] Cassen, *Population*, 214.
[21] Seavoy, *Famine*, 263.
[22] Southard, 'Famine' in *Encyclopaedia Social Sciences*, 1st edn.
[23] Aykroyd, *Conquest*, 89–93.

Then came one of the worst famines which resulted from Stalin's policies in 1932–3.[24]

For parts of northern Europe serious famine is recorded from the sixteenth to nineteenth centuries. A contemporary described a terrible famine in Sweden in 1596 as follows: 'People ground and chopped many unsuitable things into bread; such as mash, chaff, bark, buds, nettles, leaves, hay, straw, peatmoss, nutshells, pea-stalks etc. This made people so weak and their bodies so swollen that innumerable people died.'[25] In Finland, the 1696–7 famine was one of the worst in European history; it is estimated that a 'quarter or a third of the Finnish population disappeared at that time.'[26] Famines continued through the eighteenth century in this region. We are told that 'At least nine severe harvest failures were recorded in the Scandinavian countries between 1740 and 1800, each resulting in a substantial rise of the death rate. In Norway, the death rate in 1741 was more than three times as high as in 1736–1740. . . . In Sweden, during the severe famine of 1773, the death rate rose to 52.5 per thousand population.'[27]

Likewise Scotland suffered from famine until the late eighteenth century. 'The years 1635, 1680, 1688 . . . the years 1740, 1756, 1766, 1778, 1782 and 1783 . . . are all mentioned, in different places, as years of very great suffering from want. In the year 1680, so many families perished from this cause that for six miles, in a well-inhabited extent, there was not a smoke remaining.'[28] We are told that in 1623 'many died in the streets and on highway sydes for verie want of food, famished.' Another contemporary described how 'in the end there was a great death of persons of all ranks, but speciallie of the poore, which died through famine in the fields and the hie ways.'[29] Martin Martin described how in the Outer Hebrides 'the late years of scarcity brought them very low, and many of the poor people have died by famine.'[30] The terrible starvation related to the potato blight in Ireland in the mid nineteenth century showed a society still subject to famine until a late date.[31]

Braudel described how 'A privileged country like France is said to have experienced 10 general famines during the tenth century: 26 in the eleventh; 2 in the twelfth; 4 in the fourteenth; 7 in the fifteenth; 13 in the sixteenth; 11 in the seventeenth and 16 in the eighteenth.' Even this summary, Braudel believes, runs a risk of 'over-optimism' because 'it omits the hundreds and hundreds of

---

[24] For a graphic description, see Bennett, 'Famine' in *Encyclopaedia of the Social Sciences*, 2nd edn.
[25] Quoted in Appleby, *Famine*, 133.
[26] Braudel, *Capitalism*, 42; cf also Flinn, *European*, 50.
[27] United Nations, *Determinants*, 51.
[28] Malthus, *Population*, I, 275.
[29] Quoted in Flinn, *European*, 51.
[30] Martin, *Western Islands*, 95.
[31] Smith, *Great Hunger*.

local famines.' The situation was particularly grave in 1662. The Electors of Burgundy, for instance, sent a protest to the King which stated that 'famine this year has put an end to over seventeen thousand families in your province and forced a third of the inhabitants, even in the good towns, to eat wild plants.' A chronicle even alleged that 'Some people ate human flesh.' Ten years earlier 'the people of Lorraine and other surrounding lands are reduced to such extremities that, like animals, they eat the grass in the meadows . . . and are black and thin as skeletons.'[32] E.L.Jones reports a study by Rich and Wilson which suggests that 'death tolls for famine and disease in Louis XIV's France' show a peak of two million in 1692–4, 'or 1.9 per cent of the European population.'[33] We are told that 'the failed harvest of 1693 caused an apocalyptic, medieval-type dearth which killed millions of people in France and the neighbouring countries.'[34]

In Germany, famine continued into the eighteenth century. Taking a lower estimate, East Prussia 'lost 250,000 people or forty-one per cent of its population to starvation and disease in 1708–11.'[35] Famines occurred in Silesia in 1730, in Saxony and southern Germany in 1771–2, in and beyond the boundaries of Bavaria in 1816–17. In northern Italy, a report of 1767 suggested that the '316 preceding years included 111 years of famine compared with only 16 of good harvests.'[36] Cipolla cites a number of descriptions of famines in Italy for the fifteenth and sixteenth century, for instance in the northern Italian town of Bergamo in 1630 a physician described how 'most of these poor wretches are blackened, parched, emaciated, weak and sickly . . . they wander about the city and then fall dead one by one in the streets and piazzas and by the Palazzo.'[37]

Standing back from the details, it would appear that Malthus was correct in believing that famine was still a very serious threat to much of Europe until at least the middle of the eighteenth century. Yet both he and Adam Smith were also right in suggesting that the situation, bad as it was in Europe, was not as serious as that in China and India. Looking back from the vantage point of two centuries later, Jones concludes that 'At the minimum the effective demographic shock in Asia was double that in Europe, and the best of the estimates suggest that it was an order of magnitude greater.'[38] Or as Petersen puts it: 'On the scale of world history Europe's food shortages have been relatively puny. The normal death rate of the great civilizations of Asia,

---

[32] Braudel, *Capitalism*, 39,3,42.
[33] Jones, *Miracle*, 30.
[34] Le Roy Ladurie, *Feast*, 68; for graphic accounts of French famines, see Le Roy Ladurie, *Peasants*, 135,198–9,244.
[35] Jones, *Miracle*, 29.
[36] Braudel, *Capitalism*, 39,39.
[37] Cipolla, *Before*, 159; famines in 1527–9 are alluded to in Flinn, *European*, 53.
[38] Jones, *Miracle*, 30.

on the contrary, "may be said to contain a constant famine factor."[39]

There are, as John Walter and Roger Schofield point out, numerous difficulties in assessing the degree and nature of famine in England. There are difficulties in the sources, in the interpretation, and in evaluation.[40] There were several famines in early medieval England; according to Creighton those of 1143, 1194–6 and 1257–9 being especially severe.[41] After 1258 the pattern becomes a little clearer with Creighton's work supplemented by that of the Victorian economic historian Thorold Rogers, who claimed to have in his possession 'a record of every harvest in England since 1259', covering a period of 628 years. Rogers made the assumption that a famine was 'a scarcity in which the price of wheat rises to more than twice its average price, a dearth when the additional price is from one half the ordinary price to double.' Using this criterion, he concluded that though there were 'particular years with famine prices' they were very exceptional. 'In the fifteenth century there was only one year of famine, 1438, and one year of dearth, 1482. In the sixteenth, there was a year of famine in 1527 and after Henry had committed the enormous crime of issuing base money, famine was endemic.'[42] However, standing back from the evidence he wrote: 'I know of only one distinct period of famine in the whole economical history of England.' That was in the period 1315–21.[43] Creighton wrote that 'There were, of course, years of dearth and scarcities in the centuries following, but there were no great famine-pestilences like those of 1196, 1258 and 1315.'[44] To what extent is their belief that England was relatively free from famine throughout the more than six hundred years after 1320 supported by more recent research?

Though a number of regional famines had been mentioned in chronicles between the Norman Conquest and the end of the thirteenth century, the first national famine in England since the middle of the twelfth century occurred in the period which Rogers notes, namely the years 1315–6.[45] We know that the famine was caused by continuous heavy rains, which followed earlier years of poor harvest. The rain and clouds prevented crops maturing. 'In 1315 and 1316, the average grain yields in England appear to have been about 50 per cent of normal, but in some areas, yields were only 20 per cent of normal.'[46] Animal fodder was also affected, so large numbers of animals died. The wet ground was infected with fungi which killed cattle and 'muddy or flooded pastures caused sheep to suffer epidemics of liver flukes and murrain (rinderpest).' Cattle and

---

[39] Petersen, *Malthus*, 164.

[40] Walter and Schofield (eds), *Famine*, ch.1, esp. 5–9.

[41] Creighton, *Epidemics*, I, ch.1.

[42] Rogers, *Industrial*, I, 59–60.

[43] Rogers, *Six Centuries*, 62.

[44] Creighton, *Epidemics*, I, 49.

[45] For chronicles see Kershaw, *Great Famine*, 26.

[46] Seavoy, *Famine*, 72.

oxen were also decimated by this disease, which lowered their ploughing capacity. The heavy rains affected all of northern Europe and also caused widespread famine on the Continent.[47]

It is impossible to know how many people died. The population of England may have been something like five million at this point, in which case Seavoy's estimate that 'The famine of 1315–6 killed at least 10 per cent of England's population' would represent a loss of at least 500,000 people.[48] Hollingsworth in his summary of some of the figures is not prepared even to make a guess at numbers.[49] Walter and Schofield conclude that its impact 'remains uncertain'. They make the interesting observation, however, that it 'may have been particularly severe in the highland zone.'[50] What is clear, is that many people died. There was a genuine national famine which was also apparently accompanied 'by a virulent and widespread epidemic of an enteric type – perhaps typhoid.'[51] It is the only famine after 1300 in which allegations are made that people were forced to eat taboo food. It was alleged that horse and dog flesh was eaten and even that hungry prisoners in gaols ate new arrivals.[52]

There may have been regional famines in 1321–2 and we are told that 'Prolonged rains in the north of England in 1438–9 produced famine conditions that were aggravated by an epidemic of typhus and other famine related diseases.'[53] The evidence is very sketchy for the rest of the fifteenth century, and hence 'it can only be a supposition that famine is unlikely to have been a serious problem after the mid fourteenth century, even in the highland zone.'[54]

Certainly, historians have not come up with convincing evidence of any serious national famines in the period after 1317, though there were undoubtedly dearths and possibly some regional famines. Among the worst years were 1555 to 1559, but it is not certain that even then there was famine.[55] The period from 1560 to about 1595 was one of good harvests and no notable mortality, and population grew rapidly. At this point there were several very poor harvests caused by bad weather.

The area worst affected was the northern border of England. 'In 1587–8, 1597 and 1623, the northwestern English counties of Cumberland and Westmorland were struck by famine.'[56] The dimensions of the crisis are indicat-

---

[47] Le Roy Ladurie, *Feasts*, 45–7.

[48] Seavoy, *Famine*, 73; for the estimate of five million, see Kershaw, *Great Famine*, 3.

[49] Hollingsworth, *Historical Demography*, 384–5.

[50] Walter and Schofield (eds), *Famine*, 29.

[51] Kershaw, *Great Famine*, 11.

[52] Creighton, *Epidemics*, I, 48.

[53] Seavoy, *Famine*, 74.

[54] Walter and Schofield (eds), *Famine*, 30.

[55] See Walter and Schofield (eds), *Famine*, 59; Appleby, *Diet*, 115.

[56] Appleby, *Famine*, 1.

ed by Andrew Appleby: 'In the parishes of Cumberland and Westmorland burials were three or four times the normal number; famine carried off perhaps one-tenth of the population.'[57] A doubling of the death rate affected other upland areas. Keith Wrightson notes that 'clear evidence of famine deaths has been found in Cumbria, Yorkshire, Northumberland and Durham, Staffordshire and upland Devon.'[58] There was another, much less widespread, rise of death rates, this time concentrated in Cumberland and Westmorland in 1623. These deaths should be put into the context of the nation as a whole. The area affected covered only upland, pastoral, regions, and not even all of these. Appleby concludes: 'I think those parishes that saw their burials double will remain the exception, at least south of the Trent.'[59]

With these exceptions, it is clear that for the rest of the period after about 1560, and perhaps well before, for ninety per cent of the population famine was not an immediate threat. This interesting absence was noted some years ago by Peter Laslett. In *The World we have Lost*, he asked 'Did the peasants really starve?' His answer was basically that there is no evidence that they did. The only exception he could find was in the parish register of Greystoke in Cumberland. He comes to the conclusion that 'Nearly all of the English registers which have been studied so far yield entirely negative conclusions; they contain no examples of harvest years where a conspicuous rise in burials was accompanied by a corresponding fall in conceptions and in marriages.' This is one of the strongest indexes of malnutrition and starvation in the French studies. 'We may here be faced with a sociological discovery of the first historical importance, that our country in the seventeenth century was already immune from these periodical disasters, whereas France and Scotland were not.'[60]

With the exception of Appleby's discoveries for 1596–8, Laslett's tentative guesses have been confirmed by later work on parish registers which in its turn has been given definitive support by the work of Wrigley and Schofield and their collaborators. They remind us that 'The usual assumption is, of course, that periods of economic stress when wages are low will tend to raise mortality levels, that there will be evidence of the operation of the Malthusian positive check.' Yet, 'Of this there is almost no sign.' We are told that 'there is no warrant in the English evidence for the view that *long-term* movements towards lower wages provided higher general mortality, and that a steady rise in real wages brought a saving of life.' There were, of course, mortality crises, but 'short-run fluctuations in the death rate appear to have been very largely determined by

[57] Appleby, *Diet*, 114.
[58] Wrightson, *Society*, 145.
[59] Appleby, *Famine*, 135.
[60] Laslett, *World*, ch.5 *passim*, 120.

variations in factors unrelated to harvest plenty or failure.', in other words by 'the prevalence of lethal micro-organisms.'[61]

Walter and Schofield state that by the middle of the seventeenth century 'England had slipped the shadow of famine, in sharp contrast to the continuing vulnerability of most other west European countries.' They believe that 'Even in the heartland of the previously famine-prone northern highland zone there was little response in mortality levels to the harvest failure of 1630.' They support the work of Appleby who established 'that there was some vulnerability to famine, that it was confined to a particular type of region, and that in contrast to parts of the continent, England both escaped relatively lightly from harvest failure and saw the early disappearance of famine even on a regional level.'[62]

Similarly, Paul Slack writes that 'Major crises of subsistence, harvest failures followed by high mortality over whole regions, have been extraordinarily difficult to find in England, at any rate in the parish-register era. There is no sign of them after 1623 and when there is evidence for them, in 1586–7, 1596–8 and 1622–3, they were confined to particular, largely upland, areas.'[63] Leslie Clarkson concludes that 'famine was rarely a direct cause of death in pre-industrial England.'[64] De Vries looked at the English evidence from a continental perspective and thought that: 'the death rate and the price of grain did not move together sufficiently to generate true crises of subsistence.'[65]

Any remaining threat of famine had retreated by the later seventeenth century. Slack points out an indication of this: English towns 'were sensibly turning their public stocks of corn into stores of fuel' since the major threat was now cold rather than hunger.[66] It was noted some time ago by J.D.Chambers that there was no correlation between food prices and burials in early-eighteenth-century Nottinghamshire and he observed that famine did not seem to be a cause of high mortality in the seventeenth century either.[67] Recently, Roy Porter has found that in the eighteenth century 'one critical watershed *had* been passed. . . . People no longer starved to death "en masse" in Georgian England. Bad harvests gave local short-falls, but not absolute dearth.'[68]

This does not mean that people were not hungry. Dearth, or shortages, especially in the spring, may well have been common until the nineteenth century. Such dearths are widely documented, particularly in the 1590s and 1620s in England. Adam Smith later maintained that such 'Years of dearth, it is

[61] Wrigley and Schofield, *Population*, 415,416,354.
[62] Walter and Schofield (eds), *Famine*, 36,34,3.
[63] Slack, *Dearth*, 8; for similar conclusions see Palliser, *Tawney's Century*, esp. 345.
[64] Clarkson, *Disease*, 36; cf ch.2 of Clarkson for some general description.
[65] De Vries, *Economy*, 8.
[66] Slack, *Dearth*, 17.
[67] Chambers, *Vale of Trent*, 26–7; Chambers, *Population*, 90; Chambers, *Population*, 55,92.
[68] Porter, *Eighteenth*, 12; see also 144,340.

to be observed, are generally among the common people years of sickness and mortality.'[69] That labourers were suffering scarcity at times is well known, for instance in Kent and elsewhere in the seventeenth century.[70] We hear in the 1640s 'That time there was a great dearth and plague in Oswaldstree.'[71] Brian Outhwaite has brought together some of the evidence concerning the effects of such dearths in the sixteenth and seventeenth centuries.[72] This was a condition that continued well into the nineteenth century.[73]

Deaths from malnutrition and starvation were also known. Keith Thomas gives some examples to support the claim that 'In the seventeenth century, however, it was rare, but certainly not unknown, for men to die in the streets from starvation or exposure.'[74] In the eighteenth century, Henry Fielding thought that one to two thousand people died of hunger in the streets of London each year, and Dr Johnson was told that more than twenty people died per week in London from the indirect effects of starvation.[75] People 'are every day dying and rotting by cold and famine.'[76] Writing in the eighteenth century, Short believed that various diseases particularly affected the 'half starved' poor. Here we are dealing with something very different – urban poverty and neglect, which continues up through the nineteenth century, for instance as described in Lancashire in 1827 where the poor died in their hovels.[77]

We have moved from villages and peasants and mass starvation into another phenomenon. A recognition of this change is provided by the earliest English demographer, John Graunt who wrote in 1662 of the burials in London over the previous twenty years: 'Of 229,250 which have died we find not above fifty-one to have been *starved.*' This excluded infants possibly starved by their wet nurses.[78] Some historians have tried to show that famine persisted into the late eighteenth century.[79] Yet they are unable to find evidence of anything beyond extreme hardship, declining nutrition and undoubted misery. In his very detailed study of the effect of food shortages and rising prices in the 1740s, the worst period in the century, J.D.Post concluded that deaths from starvation were uncommon and the temporarily 'rising death rates resulted more from

---

[69] Smith, *Wealth,* I, 92.
[70] Chalkin, *Kent,* 254; for evidece of destitution in 1618–25 in Staffordshire, see Palliser, *Death,* 64.
[71] Gough, *Myddle,* 33.
[72] Outhwaite, *Dearth.*
[73] For example Burnett, *Plenty and Want,* 66; Arch, *From Ploughtail,* 10.
[74] Thomas, *Religion,* 6.
[75] Bayne-Powell, *Travellers,* 113; Wrigley, *Population and History,* 64.
[76] Quoted in George, *London,* 194.
[77] Thompson, *Working Class,* 316.
[78] Quoted in Laslett, *World,* 117.
[79] Wells, *Wretched Faces,* esp. 1, 59–71,318.

abnormally low atmospheric temperatures than from the shortage of food and
elevated cereal prices.'[80]

There are some reasons for expecting that Japan would suffer from
widespread famines and in particular face a similar situation to that in the other
two great agrarian civilizations of Asia. It was heavily dependent on one crop,
rice, the population was extremely dense and the physical environment was very
unpredictable.

Malthus was somewhat puzzled by the evidence for Japan. 'In reading
the preface to Thunberg's account of Japan, it would seem extremely difficult
to trace the checks to the population of a country, the inhabitants of which
are said to live in such happiness and plenty.' He continues, however, that there
is enough evidence in later chapters of Thunberg, and particularly in the
chronicles cited by Kaempfer, to conclude that when compared to China 'With
regard to the positive checks to population from disease and famine, the two
countries seem to be nearly on a level.'[81]

Thunberg was aware that 'it sometimes happens' that even with all their
precautions 'even here famine is felt.'[82] Yet the overwhelming impression he
gives is of a famine-free land. Alcock wrote, with reference to Thunberg, that 'of
the whole catalogue of wonderful conditions' one of the most 'extraordinary and
marvellous to Europeans' must have been that 'hunger and famine (were) almost
unknown in a nation of thirty millions or more, inhabiting a set of islands not
larger than Great Britain and Ireland, and something like the same geographical
position.'[83]

What then was the situation? The matter of famines is a contentious one
among historians of Japan, with sharply varying estimates of the seriousness of
the phenomenon. Little is written about the subject in the period up to 1700. It
is clear that Japan did suffer from periodic regional and some national famines
in the period between the eighth and seventeenth century. Kaempfer cited a
number of great famines mentioned in the Japanese chronicles.[84] There were
other occasions with terrible floods or drought which may have led to famine.
This is clearly an incomplete list. 'In three years 1182, 1230, and 1259 – the
inclement weather induced widespread famine and accompanying sickness. The
Great Famine of 1230 was said to have killed one-third of the population.'[85]
Only the first of these is noted by Kaempfer.

---

[80] Post, *Food Shortage*, 61,62,90,202,218,221,273.
[81] Malthus, *Principle*, I, 138.
[82] Thunberg, *Travels*, IV, 94.
[83] Alcock, *Tycoon*, I, 62.
[84] Kaempfer, *History*, I, 296–332.
[85] Farris in Kiple (ed.), *Disease*, 382.

If we examine general histories of Japan in English, famine appears to play rather a minor role. For instance, Sansom's three volume 'History of Japan', gives little on famine before the eighteenth century. The first volume, covering the period to 1334, has one reference to famine. Sansom's second volume, covering the period 1334–1615, mentions no further famines. It is only in the third volume, covering the period 1615–1837 that we again come across famine.[86] More recently, the *Cambridge History of Japan* has covered the medieval and early modern period in two volumes. No serious famines occurring before 1732 are mentioned in these volumes.[87]

The 1732 famine was known as the Kyoho famine. There are various theories as to what caused it. One author suggests 'swarms of locusts appeared in the Inland Sea area, ruining much of the rice crop of western Japan.' As a result, rice in Edo and Osaka 'cost five to seven times as much as it had during the glut of the previous years.'[88] Kalland and Pedersen state that it was caused by a series of poor harvests, which 'culminated in 1732 when the winter crops of wheat and barley were damaged due to heavy rains from the second month on. . . . This poor harvest was followed by a disastrous rice crop. Rice insects (*unka*) ruined the fields and reports say that only 10 per cent of the fields were unharmed.'[89]

It is estimated that in northern Kyushu, something like 20 per cent of the population in the Fukuoka Domain died during this famine. Given the population of the area at the time, this would mean about fifteen thousand people within the total Japanese population of approximately twenty million. Two things are worth noting. First, that the famine was largely restricted to northern Kyushu. It does not seem to have led to a serious famine for the vast majority of the population who lived on the larger island of Honshu, although some deaths were also reported in the Inland Sea area of western Japan. Even southern Kyushu is not described as being seriously affected. Secondly, this was the last serious famine in this area. Afterwards, 'some people may have starved, but it seems that most managed to survive somehow.' In the data for this area 'there are very few traces of either the Temmei famine (1783–86) or the Tempo famine (1836–38).'[90] Thus, with one exception, the crowded island of Kyushu seems to have been free of famine.

The second of the three major famines, the Temmei famine of 1782–5, occurred in some northern parts of the main island of Honshu. The events are described by Sansom. 'In 1778 there were floods in Kyoto and in parts of Kyushu, and an eruption of the volcano on Shima Island, followed by an eruption of Sakarujima, the volcano near Kagoshima, in 1779. The great famine

[86] Sansom, *History*, I, 393; III, 184–5.
[87] See Saito, *Famine*, for a recent helpful overview of the history of famine in Japan.
[88] Tsuji Tatsuya in *Cambridge History*, 4, 451.
[89] Kalland and Pedersen, *Famine*, 40.
[90] Kalland and Pedersen, *Famine*, 40, 47, 51, 32.

of Temmei began in 1783. In the following year from spring to harvest rain was incessant, and during that period an eruption of the volcano Asama caused great devastation.'[91] It is agreed that the shortages of the 1782–5 period 'were caused by summer cold spells . . . due chiefly to the large amounts of volcanic ash thrown into the atmosphere by an eruption of Mt. Asama.'[92]

'No-one knows how many people died in the great Temmei famine' and there is considerable dispute about the effects. We do know that the shogun's land-tax revenue fell by more than a half.[93] We also know of terrible suffering. Sugae Masumi, an itinerant scholar, travelled through the northern villages in 1785 and came across mounds of bleached bones. A peasant came up to him and explained that 'These are the bones of people who starved to death. During the winter and spring of the year before last, these people collapsed in the snow. . . . Their bodies blocked the road for miles and miles, and passersby had to tread around them carefully. . . . We also used to catch chickens and dogs running around in the open and eat them. When we ran out of animals, we stabbed and killed our children, our brothers, or other people who were on death's door with some disease, and ate their flesh.'[94]

Hanley and Yamamura have argued that the mortality has been exaggerated. They made a study of one of the areas hit by the famine, the Morioka domain in north-east Japan. While the local authorities, arguing for a reduction in rice tax, assessed a domain-wide total of some 64,000 deaths, a study of the local records suggests that the actual totals were less than one tenth of this. The authors believe that the samurai diary of Haruyama Kichisaburo was probably more accurate when it suggested that the crop failures were 'relatively limited' and that the famine was 'not so severe' because of large quantities of goods brought in from outside 'thanks to the developed commerce'[95]

The third serious famine was the Tempo famine of the 1830s. 'It was unusually cold during the spring planting of 1833, exceptionally so during the summer growing season . . . and the autumn saw abnormally early snow falls'. Next year 'the summer was, unfortunately, wet . . . the result was a general crop failure. This affected both rice and the other crops of wheat, barley and even bamboo shoots. The worst areas were again those hit by the Temmei famine, that is north-eastern Japan, the Tohoku. In 1833 only about a third of the normal crop was grown. Nevertheless 'one bad season was an irritation rather than a tragedy.' The next two years were 'only marginally better, and the harvest of 1836 was infinitely worse.' It 'rained almost incessantly throughout the

[91] Sansom, *History*, iii, 184–5.
[92] Furushima Toshio in *Cambridge History*, 4, 496.
[93] Tsuji Tatsuya in *Cambridge History*, 4, 466.
[94] Quoted in Hane, *Rebels*, 8.
[95] Hanley and Yamamura, *Economic*, 150.

summer. It was cold, into the bargain. Once again 'the effects of this extraordinary weather were felt chiefly in the Tohoku.' The harvest 'was estimated to be only 28 percent of normal.'[96]

It is as always difficult to estimate the effects. We know that there was terrible suffering not only on the northern tip, but along the western coast down to Echizen, now part of Fukui prefecture. For instance, W.E.Griffis in 1871 'saw a great heap of skulls, bones, clothes, bowls, utensils, and other relics of the dead. It was the monument of a famine which ravaged Echizen some forty years ago, during which time the poor and the beggars died in such numbers that they could not be consumed or inhumed in the usual manner singly, but were cremated by scores on heaps of brush-wood.'[97] The rice tax received by the Tokugawa government fell from 1.25 million *koku* in 1833 to 1.03 million *koku* in 1836 and rice prices were three times higher in Osaka in 1837 than they had been in 1833.[98]

It is less easy to assess the number of deaths caused by the famine. Harold Bolitho writes that 'In 1836, we are told, over 100,000 starved to death in the Tohuku, and in Echizen the following year the death rate was three times the normal figure. In Tottori, officials were claiming that of a total of 50,000 people in distress, 20,000 died.'[99] As the same author warns us, however, 'these figures were all too often thrown together on the basis of hasty and confused impressions.'[100] It was in the interests of the officials to exaggerate the crisis in order to get aid. On the basis of a detailed study of one area, Bizen, south of Kyoto, Hanley and Yamamura warn of the dangers of accepting the crude estimates: '. . . the figures for the population of Bizen compiled by the Bakufu dropped by just over 8,000 between the years 1834 and 1846.' This decline of about 2.5 per cent, the authors believe, 'reflects the magnitude of the Tempo famine on the domain population' more accurately than later reports.[101] When an author in the recent *Cambridge History* writes of 'tens of thousands of peasants' dying, we must put this in the context of a total Japanese population of over 30 million at this time.[102]

It is worth looking at the area of the famine. Both the Temmei and Tempo famines were worst in the cold northern area but the effects of the Tempo spread further down the north-eastern coast of Honshu to the middle of Japan. This was without doubt the most widespread of the Japanese famines and also the last. The vulnerability of this particular area continued until the 1930s.[103] In

[96] Harold Bolitho in *Cambridge History*, 5, 118.
[97] Griffis, *Mikado*, 513–4.
[98] Harold Bolitho in *Cambridge History*, 5, 119–20.
[99] *Cambridge History*, 5, 119.
[100] *Cambridge History*, 5, 119.
[101] Hanley and Yamamura, *Economic*, 182.
[102] Furushima Toshio in *Cambridge History*, 4, 495.
[103] See Hane, *Rebels*, 114–36.

many ways it was the Japanese equivalent, in terms of climate and agriculture, to the upland area of northern England which, as we have seen, was the one area of that country which suffered from serious famine after the fifteenth century.

The three case studies of Japanese famine, as with England, warn us not to take an easy evolutionary view of the phenomenon. It is not true that there was steady progress from widespread famine, through a gradual elimination, to the eradication of the final pockets. In both England and Japan, famine could occur after a long period of absence. It may well be that the Tempo famine was the only serious famine to hit central Japan during the three hundred years up to its industrial take-off, just as the upland famine in England at the end of the sixteenth century was the only famine in that country in the three hundred years before its industrial revolution.

How we judge the picture of famine in Japan will depend very much on what we compare it with. In comparison to the English case, it is clear that parts of Japan were still relatively vulnerable, suffering some thousands of deaths from starvation long after famine had disappeared in England. It would also be foolish to minimize the horrific suffering, particularly in the north, or to overlook what must have been numerous shortages and acute hunger in other years which did not lead to famine. The ever-present shortages and fear of hunger are well shown in Takashi Nagatsuka's novel about late-nineteenth-century village life.[104] However, compared to its neighbour China, or to India, the scale and devastation caused by famine was only moderate.

The achievement in avoiding famine is magnified when we consider the pressure of population. Japan was more densely populated per acre of cultivated land than anywhere else in Asia. Yet it was able to feed its people and, with the exceptions noted, keep them free from starvation. The developments are particularly impressive when we note the absence of famine in the huge urban centres of central Japan. Although there were high prices, shortages and hunger, there are no accounts of large numbers of starving peasants flooding into the great cities of Osaka, Kyoto or Edo. Nor are there accounts of the urban poor dying in their thousands in these cities, which in total numbered over two million inhabitants by the eighteenth century.

There are a number of possible causes for the early escape from serious famines in Japan and England.[105] When compared to its Asian neighbours, there is certainly nothing special about the soil and terrain of Japan. Over much of England the soil was much better than that in Japan, yet not better than that in

---

[104] Nagatsuka, *Soil*, 67.

[105] For a useful overview of some of the causes of famine and ways in which they were overcome, see McAlpin, *Subject to Famine*, ch.1, 7.

much of the rest of Europe. Both countries did, however, have one great advantage in terms of natural resources. This was the possibility of drawing heavily on the sea which surrounded them. In Japan Kaempfer estimated that 'The Sea and its Productions contribute full as much towards the sustenance of the Natives, as the growth of the Country, Rice only excepted.'[106] In England, likewise, the presence of an alternative and added source of protein and vitamins, which would not be subject to the same rhythms of drought and flood as the land mass, could provide a very useful buffer against starvation.

In terms of climate, it is difficult to see how Japan was more privileged by nature than China or India. It may have suffered less from drought, but the flooding was possibly worse and it suffered numerous typhoons, earthquakes and several massive volcanic eruptions which cut down the sunlight and caused the rice harvests to fail. Certainly, as a region, Europe was more temperate than Asia, and this may help to account for its relatively lower levels of famine. Yet within Europe, it would not be convincing to explain the general absence of famine in England in terms of the weather.

The variability of the climate, however, was important. In both England and Japan the weather varies quite considerably over even short distances, partly as a result of the way the islands lie stretched out north to south, partly because they are islands with diverse ocean currents playing upon their coasts. It would appear that famines tend to be greatest in large continental countries where for hundreds of miles a similar ecology encourages a single agricultural regime. The great plains of China, Russia, India and north Africa are the famous loci of famine. Here, if the staple crop is wiped out, it is extremely difficult to find alternative foodstuffs in the vicinity.

Adam Smith suggested that with its very variable climate and ecology England was a long way from this position. 'The seasons most unfavourable to the crop are those of excessive drought or excessive rain. But, as corn grows equally upon high and low lands, upon grounds that are disposed to be too wet, and upon those that are disposed to be too dry, either the drought or the rain which is hurtful to one part of the country is favourable to another . . . what is lost in one part of the country is in some measure compensated by what is gained in the other.'[107] Furthermore, the mixture of arable and pasture, different cereals and livestock in England over quite short distances was very important as a buffer against famine.

Kaempfer wrote that nature seemed to have designed Japan 'to be a sort of a little world . . . by endowing them plentifully, with whatever is requisite to make the lives of their Inhabitants both delightful and pleasant.' The diversity is well caught in the following passage: 'These many and different islands are,

---

[106] Kaempfer, *History*, I, 213.
[107] Smith, *Wealth*, II, 33.

with regard to the whole Empire, what different Countries and Provinces are with regard to the whole globe: Differing in soil and situation, they were to produce various necessaries of life. And indeed there is scarce any thing that can be wished for, but what is produced in some Province, in some island, or other, and produced in a quantity sufficient to supply the whole Empire.'[108]

Another important factor is the absence of war. Adam Smith believed that the 'waste of war' is one of the two major causes of food shortages. Whether it is civil war or marauding invaders, harvests may be lost, seed destroyed and young men taken away. Any or all of these can lead to a famine. As we have seen, one of the greatest of all blessings which England and Japan have enjoyed over the last thousand years is that they have largely avoided destructive warfare on their own territories.

The ease of communications is another key constituent. In the majority of famines deaths are regional; food exists in other areas, but cannot be obtained quickly or cheaply enough through lack of suitable roads or rivers for the transport of the large supplies needed. If carried by men or animals, the cost of transportation can be prohibitive and too slow. One of the main theories to account for the decline of famine in Asia is the partial eradication of the 'friction of space' by the introduction of railways.[109]

England and Japan had their equivalent of the railways from very early on, namely a bulk-carrying transport system which could convey grain over long distance at a low cost. In Japan there were extensive and very heavily used water communications which made the shipping of grain and other products very widespread from at least the thirteenth century. There were not only the coastal routes, but the large inland sea and navigable lakes. Much of inhabited Japan was within a day of water transport.

Similarly in England there was very extensive coastal shipping in normal times, which could be mobilized if there was a food shortage. By contrast 'in France there was little movement of grain, and it was difficult to compensate for the effects of a poor regional harvest.'[110] For instance, in 1316 merchants from Cornwall were shipping corn to London to help meet shortages.[111] As in Japan, it was not merely a matter of the open sea, but also that England, 'being an island well endowed with navigable rivers, grain could be transported in bulk over long distances relatively easily.'[112]

---

[108] Kaempfer, *History*, I, 102; III, 314.
[109] See for example *Encyclopaedia Britannica*, 'Famine'; Hunter, *Annals of Bengal*, 44,52; Aykroyd, *Conquest*, 56,82.
[110] Dupaquier in Walter and Schofield (eds), *Famine*, 199.
[111] Kershaw, *Great Famine*, 9.
[112] Walter and Schofield (eds), *Famine*, 10.

Yet the experience of other islands in the world which have shared many of these advantages but continued to suffer from famines into the nineteenth century suggests that there is another set of factors, in the political, economic and social realm, which mediate the geographical advantages. Before analyzing the two particular cases, it is worth looking briefly at the two major theories which have been put forward to account for famines and to suggest ways of avoiding them.

The first theory was suggested by Adam Smith in *The Wealth of Nations*. He argued that the cause of famine was political – government interference in the working of the market. Scarcities were caused by war and the weather, but 'a famine has never arisen from any other cause but the violence of government attempting, by improper means, to remedy the inconveniences of a dearth.' He stated that 'In an extensive corn country, between all the different parts of which there is a free commerce and communication, the scarcity occasioned by the most unfavourable seasons can never be so great as to produce a famine.' As long as the market is allowed to operate freely, the laws of supply and demand will prevent a famine. 'When the government, in order to remedy the inconveniences of a dearth, orders all the dealers to sell their corn at what it supposes a reasonable price, it either hinders them from bringing it to market, which may sometimes produce a famine even in the beginning of the season; or if they bring it thither, it enables the people, and thereby encourages them to consume it so fast, as must necessarily produce a famine before the end of the season.'[113]

Smith's views were accepted into the mainstream of political economy, being repeated, for instance, by Dugald Stewart and Malthus.[114] Such views probably condemned millions to death in Ireland, India and elsewhere in the nineteenth century.[115] This was because they were based on the assumption that an integrated market economy, which Smith was describing, where the invisible hand might be active, existed everywhere. That this was not so is explained by Amartya Sen in his book *Poverty and Famines*.

Sen shows that the first half of Smith's argument was correct. Famines are not 'natural', they often occur, as in Bengal in 1943, when there is no absolute shortage of food. But the reasons for some local scarcity turning into famine is not because of government interference. It lies much deeper. Basically, although this is not quite how Sen puts it, we are dealing with pre-market economies. In other words, the laws of supply and demand do not apply. The reason for this, as Sen shows, is that while there is 'demand' in one sense, that is people want the

[113] Smith, *Wealth*, II, 33,33.
[114] Stewart, *Collected Works*, IX, 51ff.
[115] Arnold, *Famine*, 113 outlines some of the disastrous effects of Smith's views in India.

food, there is not 'demand' in another, namely the social and economic and political structure is such that the poor do not have any purchasing power or, as he calls it, 'entitlements'.

He argues, 'A food-centred view tells us rather little about starvation.' We need to look 'at the food going to *particular* groups.' He agrees that the idea that 'starvation may be caused not by food shortage but by the shortage of income and purchasing power', begins to unravel the difficulty, but points out that 'income and purchasing power' assumes a monetized market economy. 'Entitlement' is much wider and catches the idea of what anthropologists call 'embedded' economies. Most peasants do not have 'income' which can be quantified in monetary terms. They have an ability, through labour, land, skills and knowledge to get a living. Thus their 'entitlement' is always weak. In a period of food shortage, it fades away altogether. They are, like the animals which they start to slaughter, expendable.

This is nothing to do with government price-fixing. It is all to do with the development over time of large masses of the population who are politically and socially weak and living on the edge of starvation. 'The entitlement approach places food production within a network of relationships, and shifts in some of these relations can precipitate gigantic famines even without receiving any impulse from food production.'

We are dealing with two very different worlds. In the market-based econo-mies of parts of north-west Europe about which Adam Smith was writing, and in particular the English and Dutch cases, his remarks are probably acceptable. But in the ninety per cent of the world outside this little market-capitalist corner, his assumptions did not hold. 'Adam Smith's proposition is, in fact, concerned with efficiency in meeting a market demand, but it says nothing on meeting a need that has not been translated into effective demand because of lack of market-based entitlement and shortage of purchasing power.'[116] The millions who have sold every scrap they have, including their wives and their children, for a little food to prevent themselves from 'dying by inches' were a long way from the relatively privileged world of eighteenth-century England. Unfortunately Sen's theories are also open to criticism. They do not help us greatly in understanding market-based economies, nor do they give sufficient weight to those non-market cases where there is indeed an absolute and real shortage, as occurred, for example, in the Chinese famine of 1876–9.[117]

It would appear that in both England and Japan there developed an agricul-ture which was able to create sufficient surpluses to sustain a population whose standard of living in normal years was well above subsistence. Its efficiency was

[116] Sen, *Famines*, 154,159,161.
[117] Arnold, *Famine*, 45.

such that it was also able to support a large urban community and a large proto-industrial sector. Both countries had been through an early 'agricultural revolution', which substantially raised agricultural production.[118] The system of rents and taxes was not such as to create a vast poverty-stricken peasantry living just above subsistence who, without any savings or 'entitlements', would perish in their hundreds of thousands when a harvest failed.

There are various aspects to the agricultural development. There is the absolute amount and quality of the grain. Here it would appear that both countries were favoured. For instance, in England, the rapid development of English agriculture is indicated by the growing calls for the de-regulation of the grain trade from the early seventeenth century. In 1621, John Smith of Nibley 'asked for an end to all statutory restraints on the export of grain, since progress in arable agriculture, he asserted, "with God's ordinary blessinge, freeth us from that feare" of dearth.' Fynes Moryson described England at this time as a country with a normal grain surplus and 'scarce once in ten yeeres' needing to import corn.[119] When Blane in the early nineteenth century speculated on the reasons why there had not been 'any recurrence of famine since the year 1448', he thought that 'improvements in agricultural skill, the progress of knowledge, and better policy' had played a part. But much more important

> has been the production of a quantity of corn beyond the bare necessities of the consumer. But as refinement and the arts of life advance, a demand arises for horses, fermented liquors, and the various artificial wants of luxury. This operates virtually as a perpetual granary, so that when a year of scarcity arises the resources of superfluity may be turned into the channels of necessity. To this, and the free commerce of grain, we owe our long exemption from famine in England.[120]

There was a growing diversity of grain crops. This was one of Appleby's main theories to account for the early disappearance of famine in England. 'In the seventeenth century', he argued, 'England benefited from a growing emphasis on spring-sown cereals which meant that all grains did not fail at the same time nor all rise in price to famine levels.' This contrasted with France where 'the continuing stranglehold of winter cereals perpetuated the threat of dearth.'[121] Furthermore there was a considerable 'buffer' against disaster in the wide range of non-grain foodstuffs in both England and Japan.

Famine is ultimately about whether people live at subsistence level in normal years and are pushed under during a short-term crisis. It is related to the normal

---

[118] A good account of the new varieties of rice brought into Japan from the fourteenth century onwards, is given in Saito, *Famine*, 5ff.

[119] Quoted in Palliser, *Tawney's Century*, 346.

[120] Blane, *Dissertations*, 163–4.

[121] Walter and Schofield (eds), *Famine*, 2.

standard of living of a population and the relative affluence of a country was important. 'Where a country is so populous in proportion to the means of subsistence that the average produce of it is but barely sufficient to support the lives of the inhabitants, any deficiency from the badness of seasons must be fatal.'[122] Thus:

> When the common people of a country live principally upon the dearest grain, as they do in England on wheat, they have great resources in a scarcity; and barley, oats, rice, cheap soups, and potatoes, all present themselves . . . but when their habitual food is the lowest in this scale, they appear to be absolutely without resource, except in the bark of trees, like the poor Swedes; and a great portion of them must necessarily be starved.[123]

A number of authors have suggested that the English may have been well above subsistence level by the later sixteenth century.[124] Recent work on expenditure by Carole Shammas suggests that whereas in very poor countries, something like three quarters of the budget will be spent on food, in England even the poor spent only just over half of their income on food.[125] The difference was suggested long ago by Hollingsworth: 'Crises of subsistence . . . come up in almost every French study of parish registers. . . . They are much less common in English registers however, so that it would seem that the English were not living quite so close to the margin of subsistence .'[126] Indeed, it seems likely that the majority of the population were well above subsistence levels by the thirteenth century at least. Creighton approvingly quotes Thorold Rogers to the effect that 'Famine, in the strict sense of the word, has rarely occurred in England, owing to the practice which the inhabitants of this island have persistently maintained of living mainly on the dearest kind of corn. . . . The people living abundantly, and, except when extraordinary scarcity occurred, regularly on the best provision which could be procured.' Creighton had earlier shown that ergotism, a disease caused by eating inferior grains and widespread on the continent in the middle ages, was absent.[127]

The same was also true in much more densely populated Japan. Starting from a base which may already have been higher than in much of Asia, it has been argued that in general the diet of ordinary people improved from the end of the seventeenth century. The introduction of the potato (both sweet and white) at the start of the seventeenth century 'may well have been an important

---

[122] Malthus, *Principle*, 115.
[123] Malthus, *Population*, II, 231.
[124] Walter in Walter and Schofield (eds), *Famine*, 90.
[125] Cited in Walter and Schofield (eds), *Famine*, 86.
[126] Hollingsworth, *Historical Demography*, 165–6.
[127] Creighton, *Epidemics*, I, 222–3,68.

factor in maintaining a dense population in Japan in the eighteenth and nineteenth centuries.'[128] An agricultural revolution whose benefits were not swallowed up by growing population raised living standards.[129]

When historians began to notice the absence of famine in England, they wondered whether this could have been due to governmental action. De Vries suggests that 'In England (where the Poor Law of 1597 imposed on each community the obligation to support its poor) . . .' this may have been one of the reasons why there were not 'true crises of subsistence'.[130] Government activity in this field lasted roughly a century. From the first proclamation in 1527, until the abandonment of the policy in the 1630s, the English government did try, sometimes successfully, to control the flow and price of grain.

Books of Orders were issued which were the basis for searches for hidden stores of grain kept from the market to improve prices. After the 1620s, the stocks of grain were such that the policy was thought unnecessary and people began to anticipate Adam Smith's arguments. As the Somerset justices pointed out, searches for corn caused the prices to rise, causing 'a dearth without scarcity'.[131] The administrative action in connection with these Books of Orders is surveyed by Walter, who shows that 'When prices rose, exports of grain were to be banned, censuses taken of grain stocks, the market regularly supplied and the storage and sale of grain closely regulated.'[132] Yet neither Walter nor Slack suggest that this was a basic reason for the absence of famine deaths in England.

There is some evidence of government intervention to help alleviate food shortages in Japan. It was accepted that there was an obligation to help. In 1798, the philosopher Toshiaki Honda stated that 'Even in bad years, when the crops failed to ripen in one place, there has never been a case when the drought extended to every part of the nation. It is therefore the parental duty of the ruler towards the people to relieve their hunger by shipping grain from provinces with rich harvests to those with poor ones, thus ministering to their wants.'[133] Kaempfer describes how, long ago, 'there being a great famine in Japan . . . the Emperor order'd that from the twentieth day of the first month, for one hundred days successively, boil'd rice should be distributed to the poor, at his own expense, in all parts of the Empire.'[134]

Deliberate measures were taken to provide a buffer against the vagaries of the weather by creating entitlements. From the time of the Kyoho famine, 'Several

[128] Hanley in *Cambridge History*, 4, 682.
[129] Hanley and Yamamura, *Economic*, 168.
[130] De Vries, *Economy*, 7–8.
[131] Slack, *Dearth*, 12.
[132] Walter and Schofield (eds), *Famine*, 117ff.
[133] In Keene, *Discovery*, 201.
[134] Kaempfer, *History*, I, 331.

funds of rice and money were established with the express purpose of providing relief in case of emergencies.' A fund to help poor parents to bring up their children was introduced in parts of Japan from 1736 onwards, helping something like twenty per cent of families.[135]

Alongside the formal mechanisms for creating entitlements in a population, there are a host of informal, customary and institutional mechanisms which are equally important in mitigating the cruelties of nature and man. In relation to England, as Walter has argued, the possible defences against famine in early modern England have been underestimated. One was the possible presence of a form of 'sharecropping', which spread the risk between owner and cultivator. A second was the institution of servanthood, whereby the young were protected for a part of their lives, a 'refuge of the children of the poor'. A third was payments in kind for those with special skills, who escaped the spiral of rising prices. Another was the purchase of grain by labourers from their employers at special prices. Yet another important factor was the widespread availability of credit at reasonable rates of interest. There were also obligations on the rich to help the poor in times of need, part of a general atmosphere of noblesse d'oblige and obligation to charitable giving.[136]

It is not difficult to see similar mechanisms operating in Japan. There were various forms of tenancy similar to sharecropping; Japan was the one country in Asia where the institution of servanthood was important. When this was supplemented by the unique form of adoption it provided exactly that support which Walter suggests for England.[137] Payments in kind, the widespread availability of credit at very low rates of interest, are all to be found in Japan, whereas they are not present in the same way in China or India.

One difficulty with all of this is that many of these institutions are the *products* of a settled and famine-free society. The widespread availability of credit at low interest rates or the large gifts which the middling and rich could make in times of hardship are both only possible in a relatively affluent society. They are important mechanisms for evening out wealth, but they do not explain the relatively high level of wealth in the first place. In order to proceed further, we have to look at the heart of the matter, which concerns the development of the economy.

Peasant societies also have many informal mechanisms for risk sharing and support. Indeed, the constant struggle against political and economic insecurities means that there are usually a battery of institutions, kinship, quasi-kinship, associations, ceremonial funds and so on, which are developed to

---

[135] Kalland and Pedersen, *Famine*, 63,65; for another case of administrative action, see Sansom, *History*, III, 185.

[136] See Walter and Schofield (eds), *Famine*, ch.2.

[137] For the evidence on servanthood and adoption, see the chapter on 'Heirship' below.

try to overcome periodic crises. The problem is that these are usually very short range. When support is needed most, supporters are also drowning. In this respect, the real difference is that in the case which Walter describes, the informal mechanisms spread much more widely in space and in time, through the mediation of that store of wealth and entitlements, namely money. As long as money holds its value, people can draw in assets from elsewhere. We should therefore, make a strong distinction between money-based informal mechanisms, including those which are based on 'contract' (servanthood and adoption, credit, gifts and lowering of prices) on the one hand and face-to-face informal mechanisms, based on 'status', that is neighbourly and kinship support, on the other.

This is related to the general theme of Seavoy's book on famines in peasant societies where he argues that there is an inevitable link between non-market (peasant) economies and famines. He believes that the only way in which famines will be avoided in the future in places such as India or China or Africa is to destroy the 'peasant mode of production' as quickly as possible, and turn people into small rural producers for the market.[138] In essence, the argument is that peasant societies find it very difficult to ensure against periodic fluctuations, to spread risk widely in time and space. Hence they tend to be submerged by temporary fluctuations. Market mechanisms of money, trade, credit and so on are more effective in spreading difficulties and hence lift people above the threshold of famine. Famines and peasants are linked; market capitalism will eliminate famine. It does this by giving everyone minimum entitlements.

Kunstadter argues that 'perhaps as important as the introduction of new food technologies' was the introduction of 'social changes' which 'cushion the temporary fluctuations in availability of foods.' These he lists as 'Money, credit, markets, and wage-labour opportunities' which widen the economic activities 'far beyond the bounds of primitive community ecosystems.'[139] Thus the question we need to ask concerns the timing and depth of the spread of trade, markets and bi-occupations in England and Japan.

The various volumes of the *Cambridge History of Japan* indicate that there was an early development of a sophisticated market economy in Japan from at least the fifteenth century.[140] The same is true of England.[141] This was combined with an unusual social structure whereby there was a large and relatively affluent 'middling group', neither peasants nor lords, but rich farmers, artisans, craftsmen and so on, that gave the two countries a social structure very different from the 'normal' famine-laden societies. If it can be argued that famine and

[138] Seavoy, *Famine*; for serious criticisms of this approach, see Arnold, *Famine*, 57–61.
[139] Quoted in Macfarlane, *Population*, 308.
[140] *Cambridge History*, see especially vol.3, ch.8 and vol.4, chs3,10,11.
[141] Macfarlane, *Origins of Individualism*, esp. ch.6.

traditional 'peasant' social structures are deeply intertwined, it is not surprising that it was the great peasantries of the world, in India, China, central and eastern Europe and Russia, which suffered massive famines. Even in the Americas, where famine, on the whole, has been almost absent, it is in north-east Brazil and Mexico, the two large flat 'peasant' areas that famines occurred.[142] The fact that both Japan and England had moved early into a market dominated and highly commercialized economy, goes a long way towards explaining the relative absence of famine.

This general diversification of the English market is described by Walter and Schofield. 'Increased consumer demand for non-cereal foodstuffs and non-agricultural products promoted mixed farming and a diversification of occupations in the countryside, leading to a better balance between cereal-growing and animal husbandry, and, more generally, to a strengthening of marketing networks.'[143] The diversification and integration into a national market was widely noted in the seventeenth century. 'In the seventeenth century there was no unified national market on the continent, while on the other side of the Channel everything was organised around London.'[144] The latter part of this comment is supported by Walter and Schofield's remark that 'the common movement of regional prices indicates that a national market had indeed been achieved by the late seventeenth century, through which local shortages could be made good from surpluses accruing in other areas.'[145] It could well be argued that the diversification and creation of a national market had progressed a long way well before this date in both England and Japan. The relative absence of famine reflects this fact.

In considering the link between subsistence peasant agriculture and famines, there is a temptation to assume a rather straightforward linear progress, from embedded, peasant, famine-ridden, societies, through various stages, to integrated, food-sufficient, capitalist agriculture.

An implication of such an argument is that on the edges of the central capitalist zones there will be regions which suffer as they are integrated into the market. There is a half truth in this. Yet it may not be that simple. Recent work on the north-west of England in the later sixteenth century, suggests a rather more subtle and interesting idea, which is that it is not necessarily the continuing presence of peasant subsistence agriculture on the edge of capitalist systems that causes the major problems, but rather too precipitous a leap forward.

In the English case, Walter and Schofield argue that 'on closer inspection, the problem afflicting the north-west may not have been so much the region's backwardness as its premature specialisation in pastoral agriculture.' This was

---

[142] Scheper-Hughes, *Death Without Weeping*.
[143] Walter and Schofield (eds), *Famine*, 42.
[144] Dupaquier in Walter and Schofield (eds), *Famine*, 199.
[145] Walter and Schofield (eds), *Famine*, 9.

suggested earlier by Appleby, who is quoted as saying that the rise in grain prices relative to pastoral products during the bad weather at the end of the century 'disrupted the theoretical advantages of specialization.' In other words, 'the famines of the later sixteenth century appear as the penalty to be paid by communities that had engaged in a form of agricultural specialisation in circumstances in which not only had the market failed to reward them adequately' but also there was insufficient grain and no adequate mechanism for obtaining it from elsewhere. This may not be an ancient pattern of continuing subsistence crises, but one shaped more recently by the economic changes of the sixteenth century.[146]

Now the argument that specialization in pastoral agriculture on the edge of a large grain-based market may have considerable costs could be extended further. As these authors suggest, it may help to explain the late vulnerability of Scotland and Ireland. The implications may well extend to famine in Africa, for instance among the pastoralists in East Africa or the Sahel. The way in which certain countries have been pressurized into producing commercial crops such as coffee or cotton or cocoa, whose prices then slump, is a contemporary global example of the same danger.

Specialization may also be a relevant factor in Japan. The first serious famine, in Kyushu, occurred in precisely one of the most advanced areas of Japan, whose population had built up rapidly on the basis of its relative closeness to China. It had become very specialized in craft production. In the crisis of 1732 it may well have suffered not because it was 'backward', but because it was precocious.

A variant of the argument might also help in understanding the one area in Japan where famine continued to be a threat until recently, namely the northern area of Tohoku. This was a region which was unable to produce much grain. It provided fish and forest products for the rest of Japan. Part of its problem may have been that in years of scarcity elsewhere in Japan its specialization made it particularly vulnerable in terms of the 'entitlement' theory.

Through a combination of the factors discussed above, among them the absence of warfare, the good water communications, the varied and advanced agriculture, the developed market economy, Japan, and even more so England, had 'slipped the shadow' of famine unusually early. The second of the great Malthusian sources had largely been circumvented. The solidity and nature of this escape becomes even more apparent in we look at the food supply in Japan and England.

---

[146] Walter and Schofield (eds), *Famine*, 9,32.

6

Food and Nutrition

A search for the reasons for the relatively early disappearance of famine in England and Japan leads us to a wider discussion of the quality and quantity of food. Furthermore, almost every known human disease is influenced in some way by nutrition. Even when it does not directly cause ill health, it will affect mortality and morbidity rates because well fed populations can resist various micro-organisms better than badly fed ones. 'There is no doubt that malnutrition in man produces a severe defect in the function of the immune system.'[1] The reverse is also true. For instance, 'Countries where endemic diseases such as malaria occur, often show a general state of malnutrition, high infant and tuberculosis death rates; lethargy and weakness are often so pronounced as to slow down agricultural activities, and so further lower the nutritional state.'[2]

'The Means of preserving Life, which is Eating and Drinking, has destroy'd more Lives than ever did sword, Famine or Pestilence.'[3] Or as Dr Buchan wrote, 'Unwholesome food, and irregularities in diet, occasion many diseases. There is no doubt but the whole constitution of the body may be changed by diet alone.'[4] William Willis, an English doctor in Japan, noted that 'In very many cases the enlightened doctor knows that it is not medicine so much as good food that is required to bring about the recovery of his patient.'[5] A few years later Griffis

---

[1] Poston, *Immunity*, 190.

[2] Roberts, *Hygiene*, 344; for further discussion of the complex synergy between nutrition, disease and work, see Nevin Scrimshaw in Newman (ed.), *Hunger in History*, 356–8; Neumann in Hunter, *Tropical Medicine*, 870–2; Mascie-Taylor (ed.), *Disease*, 44–56.

[3] An eighteenth century aphorism in *Characters and Observations*, 230.

[4] Buchan, *Domestic*, 62.

[5] Cortazzi, *Willis*, 182.

widened the connection, writing that 'Sydney Smith condensed a volume of dietetic hygiene in his exact statement that "Some men dig their graves with their teeth". The complement of that is found in this: Disease enters by the mouth; or, the mouth is the door of disease.'[6] George Orwell wrote that 'I think it could be plausibly argued that changes of diet are more important than changes of dynasty or even of religion.'[7]

In western Europe over the five hundred years leading up to the industrial revolution, there was a generally favourable position for the majority of the population with regard to food. In 1959 J.T.Krause pointed out that 'Materials for Sweden, Ireland and England show that these pre-industrial western peoples had relatively adequate diets, diets which were far superior to those of the presently less developed countries.'[8] John Hall writes of western Europe, 'the diet of the medieval peasant may seem terrible to our eyes, but it was significantly better than that of the other pre-agrarian civilizations.'[9] Europe's privileged position in comparison to Asia is documented in some detail by Braudel.[10] While the whole of the west European population seems in the main to have had a more varied, protein and vitamin rich diet than Asia, the extreme case was north-west Europe. Thus, 'northern Europe was characterized by a larger consumption of meat, and southern Europe by a larger consumption of carbohydrates.' An interesting, if very preliminary, calorific map of Europe tends to support this view.[11] There were two areas where the quantity and quality of the diet was seen to have been outstanding. One was Holland, the other was England.[12]

Perceptions of the English diet by early English commentators were famously effusive.[13] To take but one example, Fynes Moryson travelled around Europe in 1605–17 and made a dietary survey. He found 'the diet of the Germans is simple, and very modest, if you set aside their intemperate drinking.' The people of the Netherlands had an extremely rich diet of butter, milk, meat and other products. In Denmark the ordinary people 'feed much on divers kinds of dried fishes', which he thought led to their 'leane and withered faces' and they 'likewise feede on bread very black, heavy and windy.' In general in diet 'they are much like the Germans.' Some Italians ate well and others badly. On the whole, however, 'The Italians generally compared with English or

[6] Griffis, *Mikado*, II, 507.
[7] Orwell, *The Road to Wigan Pier*, quoted in Appleby, *Diet*, 3.
[8] Krause, *Neglected Factors*, 535; see also Hajnal, *Marriage Patterns*, 131.
[9] Hall, *Powers and Liberties*, 123.
[10] Braudel, *Capitalism*, ch.2 esp. 133–5; see also Flinn, *European*, 97.
[11] Braudel, *Capitalism*, 89,88.
[12] On Holland see Schama, *Embarrassment*, 169–74.
[13] For example, Anglicus, *Properties*, ii, 734; Fortescue, *Commendation*, 65v,66,81–81v,85–85v; Reynolds, *British Pamphleteers*, 29–33.

French, are most sparing in their diet.' They were 'not so great flesh-eaters as
the Northerne men', but ate a lot of bread and salads. Likewise 'For their dyet,
the Turkes live sparingly.' France abounded with many foodstuffs, yet the
common people had very little good food. 'At this day none eate lesse Bacon or
dried flesh for ordinary diet, than the French.' There were many fish and wild
animals, but the 'countrey people neither do nor may eate them'. 'Their Beef is
neither very good, nor much used. Their Sheep are lesse than ours in England',
though sweet. 'They use not much whitemeats, nor have I tasted there any good
Butter . . .' Even the wealthier lived less well than the English. 'As well the
Gentlemen as Citizens live more sparingly than the English in their ordinary
private diet, and have not their Tables so furnished with variety and number of
dishes.' The Scots 'eate much red Colewort and Cabbage, but little fresh meate
and a lot of porredge.'[14] In Ireland, the 'English-Irish' lived well, but the 'meere
Irish' lived on what he considered a filthy, if nutritious diet including horse
meat, oats and even the blood from living cattle.

As for the English, he believed they had an excellent diet. 'At this day the
English inhabitants eate almost no flesh more than Hennes, and for Geese
they eate them at two seasons. . . . They had also great plenty of Connies
[rabbits] . . .' The English have 'abundance of Whitemeats, of all Kinds of
Flesh, Fowle, and Fish, and of all things good for foods.' They also had many
delicacies which were rare or not known abroad, oysters, many sea birds, fallow
deer, brawn. As for grains, 'The English Husbandmen eate Barley and Rye
browne bread, and preferre it to white bread as abiding longer in the stomack,
and not so soone digested with their labour, but Citizens and Gentlemen eate
most pure white bread, England yeelding (as I have said) all kinds of Corne in
plenty.' As a result of the abundance of food, the English were thought to be the
gluttons of Europe, a charge which Moryson was keen to refute.[15]

The reputation of the English as comparatively well fed continued into the
eighteenth century. Satirical prints, for example showed the fat, roast-beef
stuffed English countrymen and the thin, wasted, herbivorous Frenchmen.[16]
Arthur Young, we are told, 'represents the labouring classes of France, just at
the commencement of the revolution, as "76 per cent worse fed, worse clothed,
and worse supported, both in sickness and health, than the same classes in
England".'[17]

In the early eighteenth century, the Swiss traveller De Saussure noted of
London, 'In these markets an abundance of every kind of salt and fresh water
fish is to be found; also vegetables and poultry of every description.' He wrote

[14] Moryson, *Itinerary*, IV, 24,59,67,93,125,140–1,183; whitemeats are butter, cheese and other milk
     products.
[15] Moryson, *Itinerary*, IV, 171–4.
[16] Duffy, *Englishman and Foreigner*, 39,47,48,74,75,95.
[17] Malthus, *Population*, I, 230–1.

that 'English people are large eaters; they prefer meat to bread, some people scarcely touching the latter. The cooking is simple and uniform, stews are seldom served, and they do not roast or boil their meats as much as we do, which makes it, I think, more succulent and delicate, thereby giving it a better taste.' As for dairy products, 'Outside the town you scarcely see anything but large, fine pastures, where all the year round thousands of cows graze and give an abundance of milk. English people consume of great quantity of dairy produce; they are very fond of cream, milk and butter.' Butter was particularly important, for 'they do not know how to prepare fish and vegetables except with this ingredient melted.' Fruit and vegetables were also in abundance. 'Around London there are numerous fine large gardens, all belonging to gardeners who grow vegetables of every kind and flowers and fruit trees.'[18] La Rochefoucauld a generation later noted that 'The consumption of meat is much greater in England than in any other country whatever; the whole nation eats it and the Englishman, generally speaking, is a flesh-eater.'[19]

Contemporary observations on the variety and quality of foodstuffs in medieval England are supported by historical research.[20] For instance, Christopher Dyer has recently provided a detailed analysis of diet between the thirteenth and fifteenth centuries.[21] He shows that it is a myth that there was no fresh meat available in the winter.[22] There was, in fact, very high meat consumption. For example, looking at the diet of harvest workers, by 1400 the meat allowance was nearly a pound per person per day, not counting extra offal. The Sedgeford records 'give a picture of harvest workers and their dependents of the thirteenth century sitting down to heavy meals of barley bread and cheese, accompanied by a little salt meat or preserved fish, with ale, milk and water to drink. Their successors of the fifteenth century were issued with ample quantities of wheat bread, nearly a gallon of ale per day, and (except on fast days), large portions of fresh meat.'[23] The house of a particular fifteenth century peasant was 'stuffed with bacon, dairy produce, malt, salt-beef onions and garlic.'[24] Kitchen gardens growing an assortment of vegetables were widespread in medieval villages.[25]

From these accounts it would seem that the English diet was varied and substantial. Even in charitable institutions such as St Bartholomew's hospital or in the House of Correction, meat and beer, fish and milk products were served

---

[18] De Saussure, *Foreign*, 171,220–1,133,222,137.
[19] Rochefoucauld, *Frenchman*, 204.
[20] For example, see Drummond, *Food*, ch.3; Rogers, *Six Centuries*, 59.
[21] Dyer, *Everyday Life*, chs5–7.
[22] Dyer, *Diet*, 93.
[23] Dyer, *Everyday Life*, 86,87; see also 91.
[24] Dyer, *Diet*, 210.
[25] Dyer, *Everyday*, ch.7.

daily.[26] However, the evidence from the later eighteenth century and into the nineteenth century is more mixed. Gilbert White writing in 1778, suggested that there had been improvement: 'The plenty of good wheaten bread that is now found among all ranks of people in the south, instead of that miserable sort which used in the old days to be made of barley or beans.' 'Every decent labourer also has his garden, which is half his support, as well as his delight; and common farmers provide plenty of beans, peas, and greens, for their hinds to eat with their bacon.'[27] On the other hand, William Cobbett thought that conditions had deteriorated from a high level in the 1760s, to the present days of 'slavery, of rags, and of hunger' in the 1830s. He wrote that when a boy 'I never knew a labouring man . . . go out to his work in the morning without a bottle of beer and a satchel of victuals, containing cheese, if not bacon, hung upon his crook.'[28]

One revealing source is the enquiry by Sir F.Eden into the state of the poor in the late eighteenth century. Looked at from our present perspective, these suggest, as Dorothy Marshall concludes, that 'the ordinary labourer could depend on his wages to procure no more than the barest living, bread, cheese and weak tea being his staple diet, as the pathetic budgets that Eden and Davies collected testify.'[29] But relative to the condition of most labouring populations, this could be interpreted in a more positive manner:

> the incomplete data for the English poor in a harsh year reveal a per capita consumption of dairy goods which was about twice as great as the estimated India per capita production in 1940. Then, of the 31 families for which Eden has detailed information, 27 families had meat or fish included in their diets, sometimes in sizable quantities. Of the four families without any meat listed in their budgets, three of the men were given some victuals by their employers and thus may have had meat.[30]

Although it is not difficult to show that the English were better fed than many people in contemporary Asia and Africa, it is not easy to judge whether the diet was nutritionally satisfactory. Most believe that the foodstuffs of the wealthier were more than adequate. Appleby concludes that 'By all accounts the food of the well-to-do was both varied and plentiful through the sixteenth century, probably becoming somewhat richer and more elaborate towards the end of the century.' Such people 'enjoyed a varied diet, with adequate amounts of fruit and, at least by the end of the century, vegetables.'[31] The problems were

[26] Drummond, *Food*, 56.

[27] Quoted in Marshall, *English People*, 171; a hind is a farm servant.

[28] Cobbett, *Progress*, 9.

[29] Marshall, *English People*, 173.

[30] Krause, *Neglected Factors*, 535.

[31] Appleby, *Diet*, 98,101.

ones of overeating, and too much meat eating. Anaemia due to a disdain for vegetables, constipation, the stone and were the problems of the rich according to Keith Thomas.[32]

As for the poor, Appleby believes their diet grew worse in the sixteenth century: 'price data gives a general picture of an erosion in the diet throughout the sixteenth century. Apparently there was a switch away from wheat to the lower-priced and less-desired grains.' Yet he admits that 'With our limited knowledge it is very difficult to say whether these people had a qualitatively adequate diet. Did they, for example, eat enough fruits, vegetables or seasoning herbs that contained vitamin C, to ward off scurvy? It is impossible to say.'[33]

Alan Everitt writes of the seventeenth century that although labourers' diet varied regionally, the 'staple articles of his diet were bread, pies and puddings.' The bread was usually made from barley, 'occasionally from oats, wheat and rye.' At times they were forced to mix buck wheat with their barley-flour, though Justices in 1623 said they had not formerly been 'acquainted with (it) and therefore show much loathness to use (it).' Because of their dependence on market purchase, 'When prices rose . . . they were often reduced to extreme misery.' With regard to protein, cheese was widely eaten: 'Even the tin-miners of Devon, the poorest of the poor, reckoned some kind of hard cheese in their diet. With butter and lard, cheese 'probably formed the only fat and protein element in the poorer farmworkers' meals.' But Everitt then proceeds to explain that 'Though few labourers kept pigs of their own, many had fletches of bacon hanging in their roof or chimney. . . . Beef was eaten by labourers who fed at the master's table, but in the inventories of out-labourers it is rarely mentioned.' He admits, however, that they would be unlikely to have meat in such large pieces as to be listed in an inventory. Vegetables and herbs 'were commonly grown in cottage gardens.' There was a lot of wild life and wild fruits and nuts and 'rural labourers profited accordingly. Even the poor had a good deal of milk or ale and beer to drink, all of them nourishing in their way.'[34] The picture is hardly one of total misery. Reasonable bread, widespread use of butter, cheese, milk, some meat and plentiful vegetables, beer and ale.

Another important source of protein was fish. Harrison had mentioned 'all sorts of fish taken upon our coasts and in our fresh rivers'.[35] Fish could also now be brought from further away. Joel Mokyr describes how 'In the late fourteenth century, Dutch fishermen discovered the technique of gutting and salting fresh herring, which allowed preservation for long periods.' Then the 'discovery of huge supplies of codfish off the banks of Newfoundland in 1497 by John Cabot,

[32] Thomas, *Religion*, 6–7.
[33] Appleby, *Diet*, 110,104.
[34] Everitt in Thirsk, *Cambridge Agrarian History*, IV, 450–3.
[35] Harrison, *Description*, 126.

and the use of a new type of line with thousands of hooks, gave the Europeans a new and unexpected supply of dried cod, not appetizing perhaps by modern standards, but rich in protein.'[36]

From this preliminary survey we may draw a few tentative conclusions. As Appleby suggested, 'By continental standards the food eaten by the English was plentiful, with far more meat than was customary across the Channel.'[37] Meat eating was widespread in the sixteenth century and the production and storage of meat increased throughout the period. In the later half of the seventeenth century, Gregory King estimated that half the population only ate meat once a week or less[38] but Kames noted an improvement by the middle of the eighteenth century. 'There is also a remarkable alteration in point of diet. Formerly, people of rank lived on salt meat the greater part of the year: at present, fresh meat is common all the year round. Pot-herbs and roots are now a considerable article of food: about London, in particular, the consumption at the Revolution was not the sixtieth part of what it is now.'[39] The development of new fodder crops had made it possible to keep more animals alive through the winter, hence the fresh meat. Likewise Malthus believed, that 'The price of provisions has risen, but almost invariably the price of labour has risen in a greater proportion; and it is remarked in most parishes that more is consumed among the common people than formerly.'[40] The relative affluence of the English is shown by Shammas in her analysis of household budgets.[41]

Too much meat eating, of course, is dangerous to health. As Buchan commented 'No people in the world eat such quantities of animal food as the English, which is one reason why they are so generally tainted with the scurvy and its numerous train of consequences, indigestion, low spirits, hypochondricism, etc.'[42] Certainly the amounts eaten were huge. In 1778 a Spanish visitor commented that 'More meat is sold in a month [in Leadenhall market, London] than is eaten in the whole of Spain during a year.'[43] It may be, however, that the consumption of meat, which had risen to a very high level between the fifteenth and seventeenth centuries, had begun to decline among the poorer groups from the early eighteenth century, as Shammas argues.

All assessments of whether a diet is 'adequate' are subjective. This is shown, for instance by Shammas' work on English consumers. She found that 'Throughout the early modern period, workhouses seem to have offered a daily

[36] Mokyr, *Lever*, 70.
[37] Appleby, *Diet*, 102.
[38] Cited in Macaulay, *History*, I, 316 n.
[39] Kames, *Sketches*, I, 245.
[40] Malthus, *Population*, I, 268.
[41] Shammas, *Consumer*, 123 and table 5.1, 128 and table 5.2, 124 and table 5.1.
[42] Buchan, *Domestic*, 65.
[43] Quoted in Braudel, *Capitalism*, 131.

diet in the mid to high 2,000 (calories) in adult male equivalent terms'. Or again, she estimated from Eden's late-eighteenth-century survey that the poor had a diet which contained between 2,500 and 3,000 calories a day. She believed that this was a good deal less than what was required.[44] However, when we compare this with figures for South-East Asia in the 1960s, for example, which showed that the calories per day were Pakistan (2,030), India (2,050), Burma (2,150), Thailand (2,185), the English figures do not seem so inadequate.[45] Of course a great deal depends on age, gender, body weights, whether a woman was pregnant or lactating and the nature of work. It is generally thought that the quality of the diet declined through to the middle of the nineteenth century, yet a survey of the consumption of agricultural labourers in 1862 showed that 'the poorest workers in Britain in this period, consumed about 2,700 calories per day per adult male equivalent. But the more highly paid of these workers were consuming over 4,000 calories per day, far above modern consumption levels.'[46]

In terms of traditional agricultural practice one strategy, which the English had adopted, was to have a high protein diet heavily reliant on domesticated animal products. This gives plenty of energy with minimum effort. The explanation for why the Japanese did not take this approach is complex.

In the late nineteenth century Chamberlain observed that until recently the Japanese did not have 'any flocks of sheep and goats, and droves of geese, turkeys or pigs. Even cattle are comparatively scarce, and neither their flesh nor their milk is in general use, beef being still regarded as a luxury, and milk rather as a medicine than a food. The pasture meadow and the farmyard are alike lacking.'[47] Griffis had noted that 'In Japan, sheep and tame geese are unknown, except from reading of them.'[48] Morse commented, 'In riding through the country one soon notices the absence of flocks of hens. A single hen and cock roam together, though they are usually confined under an inverted wicker basket.'[49]

It is not certain when the Japanese gave up eating the products of domesticated animals, meat, milk and eggs. Nor are the reasons clear. One theory is that it was during the reign of the Emperor Temu, whose accession is generally dated 673 AD 'During that reign Buddhism appears to have become a powerful influence at court; for the Emperor practically imposed a vegetarian diet upon the people – proof positive of supreme power in fact as well as in theory.' Lafcadio Hearn explained that 'although fish never ceased to be an article of

[44] Shammas, *Consumer*, 137ff,140,134ff,146.
[45] For the source of these figures and others for Nepal, see Macfarlane, *Resources*, 174.
[46] Gregory Clark in Mokyr (ed.), *Industrial*, 258.
[47] Chamberlain, *Things*, 19.
[48] Griffis, *Mikado*, 449.
[49] Morse, *Day*, I, 53.

food for the laity, we may say that from about this time, the mass of the nation abandoned its habits of diet, and forswore the eating of meat, in accordance with Buddhist teaching.'[50] Kaempfer commented on 'the want there is of Flesh-meat, which Custom and Religion forbid them to eat.' He believed that the result was an efficient agriculture. 'Pythagoras's doctrine of the transmigration of the Soul being receiv'd almost universally, the natives eat no Flesh-meat, and living, as they do, chiefly upon Vegetables, they know how to improve the ground to much better advantage, than by turning it into meadows and pastures for breeding of Cattle.'[51]

The absence of all products of domesticated animals, not only meat but also milk, was evident until the last third of the nineteenth century. Early European travellers had noted that the Japanese would eat wild animals, for example wild boar, hares, wild fowl, but would not 'eate any Milke, because they hold it to bee as bloud, nor tame beasts.'[52] Thunberg observed that the Japanese 'abstain from animals food, are very loath to shed blood, and will not touch any dead body. Wherever any one transgresses in any of these points, he is considered as unclean for a longer or a shorter term, as was the case with the Jews, agreeable to the Levitical law.'[53] J.L.C. Pompe van Meerdevoort, a Dutch doctor, wrote 'Meat is hardly ever used. Before 1859 only slaughtering of pigs for the Dutch at Desima was allowed; later, when more foreigners and especially the English came to Japan, several slaughterhouses appeared, established by Europeans or Americans. The Japanese make little use of them, although it was my experience in the hospital that they liked beef stock and the meat of cows and calves quite well.'[54] Even milk drinking was thought to be both immoral and disgusting. In the 1880s Isabella Bird described how 'I thought that I might get some fresh milk, but the idea of anything but a calf milking a cow was so new to people that there was a universal laugh, and Ito told me that they thought it "most disgusting".'[55]

The change to an animal protein diet started, as Pompe observed, in the middle of the nineteenth century. Dr Willis in the 1860s noted that 'The Japanese display a growing fondness for animal food, especially amongst the soldier class. Butchers shops are springing up in different parts of Edo where none previously existed. I have met Japanese whose taste seemed to have ranged over an extensive number of the animal kingdom.'[56] Ten years later Morse reported that 'A meat shop was a great novelty a few years ago, and even now

[50] Hearn, *Interpretation*, 263,216–17.
[51] Kaempfer, *History*, I, 187,194.
[52] Purchas, *Pilgrims*, 146.
[53] Thunberg, *Travels*, iv, 20.
[54] Wittermans, *Pompe*, 53.
[55] Bird, *Tracks*, 133.
[56] Cortazzi, *Willis*, 160.

only a few are seen in the larger cities.'[57] We are told that 'Meat was hardly ever consumed by the peasants. In fact, even in urban areas, meat was a luxury. In 1889–93, the annual consumption of meat per capita was 0.9 pounds. This rose to 4 pounds by 1922–26, still a minuscule 1.2 ounces per capita per week.'[58] The real shift only occurred after the Second World War.[59] Beardsley and his co-workers' account of the 1950s described how 'Meat was unknown on the table two generations ago. There are old persons still who have never violated the Buddhist taboo against eating "the flesh of four-footed creatures".' Even eggs and chickens were not safe: 'villagers feel themselves extravagant if they eat their own eggs and cruel if they eat their own chickens.'[60]

In the absence of domesticated animals, the Japanese hunted for protein elsewhere. With the long sea coasts and many rivers and lakes, it is easy to understand their omnivorous use of marine products. 'Of all the soft submarine plants there is hardly one, but what the Natives eat. Fishermen's wives wash, sort, and sell them, and they are likewise very dexterous in diving them up from the bottom of the Sea in twenty to forty fathom depth.'[61] 'Almost everything in the sea furnishes food for the masses; not only fish, but sea urchins, sea cucumbers, squids, and even some species of worms are eaten.'[62] 'Every species of fish is eaten, down to the very coarsest.' Fish 'is a standing dish at every Japanese table, answering to the English joint of meat.'[63]

The sea was systematically harvested, not only for every moving form of life, but even for edible seaweeds. 'Dried seaweed is eaten often with rice, the iodine content undoubtedly accounting for the rarity of goitre in Japan.' 'All through the winter and spring on sunny days every little backyard blossomed with rows of wooden frames on which the seaweed carefully picked over and arranged in layers on straw mats was dried.'[64] The nutritional value of seaweeds is considerable. 'The chief carbohydrates in seaweeds are mannitol and the polysaccharides alginic acid and laminarin. They contain less than 1 per cent of fat, but appreciable amounts of protein and a high content of minerals.'[65] Seaweed was, and still is, an important constituent of the Japanese diet.

Whales were particularly important. 'Of all the animal productions of the Japanese Seas, I know none of so extensive an use, for rich and poor, as the Kudsuri or Whale.' Every single part of the whale was used:

---

[57] Morse, *Day*, I, 128.
[58] Hane, *Rebels*, 40.
[59] Hanley in Jansen and Rozman (eds), *Japan*, 455.
[60] Beardsley et al., *Village*, 107.
[61] Kaempfer, *History*, I, 189.
[62] Morse, *Day*, I, 88.
[63] Von Siebold, *Manners*, 132.
[64] Geoffrey, *Immigrant*, 241, 218.
[65] Davidson, *Nutrition*, 185.

Of all these several kinds of Whales nothing is thrown away as useless, excepting only the large Shoulder-bone. The skin which is black in most kinds, the Flesh which is red and looks like Beef, the intestines, which from their remarkable length are call'd Fiaksiro, that is, an hundred fathoms long, and all the inward parts are eat, pickel'd, boil'd, roasted, or fry'd. The fat or blubber is boil'd into Train-oyl and even the sediments of the second boiling are eat.

Kaempfer noted that 'Fisher-men and the common People attribute their good state of health amidst all the injuries of cold and weather, which they are continually expos'd to, chiefly to their eating this flesh.'[66]

Yet it is clear that with a dense population, much of it living away from the sea, marine products were not sufficient. Fish, with the possible exception of whale meat, was half way between a luxury and an ordinary part of the diet. On the one hand, 'Much of the food of the peasantry is raw or half-raw salt fish.'[67] On the other hand, only a small proportion of the food budget could be spent on fish. The annual consumption per person in 1900 was 29 pounds (1bs) of fish – about half a pound a week, or an ounce a day. A survey in the Gunma prefecture in 1910 'showed that 65 per cent of the money spent on food went for rice and other grains . . . less than two percent on fish.'[68]

The Japanese seem to have been equally omnivorous in relation to plants, both cultivated and wild. 'Horse-radishes, Carrots, Gourds, Melons, Cucumbers, Mala insana, Fennel and some sorts of Lettice, which with us are cultivated in Gardens, grow wild in Japan.' Of wild plants generally 'there are very few, but what afford their roots, leaves, flowers and fruits, not only for the sustenance of the common people, but even for the delicious tables of people of quality.'[69] 'Bamboo roots, and various forms of mushrooms (*Agarici*), which with these people are in great request, occur common in the shops, dried for sale, and are besides in almost daily use, both for soups and sauces.'[70] In general, 'it is very common to meet with a great number of culinary vegetables and kitchen-garden plants, growing wild in the open fields, and consequently there are no other gardens, than those which are found near every house, are of a very insignificant size, and are chiefly intended for the sake of ornament.'[71] This last remark, about the absence of kitchen gardens, may have become less true as time went by and particularly in cities. By the middle of the nineteenth century, Laurence Oliphant wrote 'There are kitchen-gardens attached to every establishment, with vegetables, and fruit-trees, and orchards, where the pears are trained on

---

[66] Kaempfer, *History*, I, 213,215,214.
[67] Bird, *Tracks*, 100.
[68] Hane, *Rebels*, 40.
[69] Kaempfer, *History*, I, 189.
[70] Thunberg, *Travels*, iv, 89.
[71] Thunberg, *Travels*, IV, 89,90.

trellises like grapes.'[72] In Gunma prefecture in 1910, some 13.5 per cent of the food budget was spent on vegetables.[73]

As well as vegetables, there were various kinds of nuts. Kaempfer mentioned that 'Chesnut trees grow in great plenty in Japan, particularly in the Province Tsikusen, and they bear chesnuts much larger and better than ours.' 'There are two sorts of Oaks grow in the Country, both different from ours. The acorns of the larger sort are boil'd and eat by the common People.' There was a great variety of fruits. 'Oranges and Lemons grow very plentifully, and of different sorts. That sort of Lemons, which is reckon'd the best, is call'd Mican.' Furthermore, 'With Peaches, Apricocks and Plums they are plentifully supplied.'[74] Because Japan spans several climatic zones, almost any fruit could be grown. 'Hence the southern islands, though generally said not to be hot enough for the sugarcane, teem with most of the fruits of the tropics, while the northern yield those of the temperate zones.'[75]

Kaempfer noticed the importance of root vegetables. 'Turneps grow very plentifully in the Country, and exceeding large ones. Of all the produce of the fields they perhaps contribute most to the sustenance of the Natives.'[76] Thunberg had singled out 'Turnips (*Brassica rapa*)' which were 'sown in abundance, and are much used for food, as are likewise other esculent-rooted and bulbous plants.'[77] There were huge white radishes: 'some weighing fifty to sixty pounds, other types of radishes of fifteen pounds' weight were common.'[78] 'An invariable accompaniment at Japanese meals is the pickled vegetables.'[79] 'The commonest and most useful of them is the garden radish, which is pickled or salted, boiled almost dry with *mirin*, sugar, and bonito shavings, put into soup, or grated to flavour raw or fried fish.'[80] The importance of radish, or *daikon*, was explained by Mrs Geoffrey. She wrote that 'another favorite condiment for the rice is grated or pickled daikon. Daikon might be called the garlic of Japan, so widespread and all-pervading is its aroma, but it is far more disagreeable to the neophyte than garlic. The crop is pretty to look at, for it is marketed in long white roots, as thick as a man's arm, but tapering gracefully, and invariably scrubbed in some dirty pool till it shines as white as sea sand. Its taste brings tears to my eyes, but it is beloved of the Japanese, and science has recently

[72] Oliphant, *Elgin's Mission*, 197–8.
[73] Hane, *Rebels*, 40.
[74] Kaempfer, *History*, I, 180,181,181,181.
[75] Siebold, *Manners*, 229.
[76] Kaempfer, *History*, I, 188.
[77] Thunberg, *Travels*, IV, 88.
[78] Siebold, *Manners*, 234.
[79] Inouye, *Home*, 59.
[80] Inouye, *Home*, 71; for another good account of the ubiquity of radishes, see Morse, *Day*, I, 36–7.

turned up a good reason for their craving for it. Daikon, it seems, is rich in diastase, which assists the process of converting the starch of rice into sugar for energy; so that without daikon, the nation might have acute indigestion over the tons of rice it consumes annually.'[81]

The one vegetable which produces a high level of protein is the bean. 'Of Beans, Peas and Lentils, many sorts are cultivated, both the larger (*Phaseoli*) and the smaller (*Dolichos*).'[82] 'Beans are largely grown, and of numerous varieties – some like the English field bean, and others like the French bean, though both inferior in flavour. They are grown for various purposes, and are eaten as food in a green state, and also when ripe. Some kinds are ground down into powder and made into cakes.'[83]

Two types in particular were noticed by Kaempfer. 'Daidsu, that is, Daidbeans, is a certain sort of Beans, about the Bigness of Turkish Pease, growing after the manner of Lupins. They are next to the rice in use and esteem. Of the Meal of these Beans is made what they call Mudsu, a mealy Pap, which they dress their Victuals withal, as we do with Butter.' The second kind were 'Adsuki, or Sodsu, that is sobeans. They grow likewise after the manner of Lupins, and are black, not unlike Lentils, or the Indian Cajan. The flower is bak'd with sugar into Mansje and other Cakes.'[84] The importance of soya beans in Japanese diet is widely known. 'But in point of utility the soy bean comes next to rice, for our soy sauce which enters into almost all dishes is made from the bean, wheat, and salt. So extensively is this sauce employed that table salt is comparatively little needed. The bean is also the principal ingredient in *miso*, which is a mixture of the soy bean, steamed and pounded, with rice-yeast and salt.'[85] '*Miso* soup, boiled with fish and onions, is eaten by the common people, frequently three times a day, or at each of their customary meals. *Misos* are not unlike lentils, and are small beans, gathered from the *Dolichos soja*.'[86] In the 1950s, the widespread use of soybeans, red beans, broad beans and chick peas continued to be evident.[87] The dietic value of these pulses was increased by fermenting them. All kinds of vegetable sprouts, which contain the maximum nutrition, were to be found for sale. 'Sprouted beans and peas of many kinds and the sprouts of other vegetables, such as onions, are very generally seen in the markets of both China and Japan, at least during the later winter and early spring.'[88] 'The extensive use of sprouts – the germinated beans, peas and lentils

[81] Geoffrey, *Immigrant*, 241.
[82] Thunberg, *Travels*, IV, 88.
[83] Alcock, *Tycoon*, I, 321.
[84] Kaempfer, *History*, I, 188.
[85] Inouye, *Home*, 58.
[86] Thunberg, *Travels*, IV, 38.
[87] Beardsley et al., *Village*, 106.
[88] King, *Farmers*, 134.

of China and India – also has nutritional merit, since essential amino acids, fats, and vitamins become more available in the sprouts as a result of germination. Extensive nutritional experiments have revealed, for example, that the nutritive value of soybeans is significantly greater after germination than before.'[89] In particular, the sprouting may have provided essential vitamin C in the diet.[90]

Another important crop was oil-seed rape. 'Rape is grown for its seed here, as in China, from which large quantities of oil are made, and it forms one of the more important crops.'[91] It was an excellent plant in several ways. For instance, as well as producing valuable oil, 'its young shoots and leaves are succulent, nutritious, readily digested and extensively used as human food, boiled and eaten fresh, or salted for winter use, to be served with rice.' Another great advantage is that it takes very little out of the soil. 'Like the dairy cow, rape produces a fat, in the ratio of about forty pounds of oil to a hundred pounds of seed, which may be eaten, burned or sold without materially robbing the soil of its fertility if the cake and the ashes from the stems are returned to the fields, the carbon, hydrogen and oxygen of which the oil is almost wholly composed coming from the atmosphere rather than from the soil.'[92]

Although it is less efficient for this purpose, 'the protein intake from rice, barley and wheat was of utmost importance during the middle of the nineteenth century.' It is estimated that eighty per cent of the protein in the Japanese diet in the second half of the nineteenth century came from these grains. The amount coming from soybeans was surprisingly small, only about five to six grams out of a total of forty-five to fifty grams per day.[93] The type of grain which was eaten varied by region, period and class. In the Tokugawa and Meiji periods, 'In the westernmost parts of Japan, people ate a higher proportion of *mugi* (wheat and barley) and sweet potatoes, while people in the mountainous areas ate more millet and *hie* (deccan grass).'[94] Rice was the preferred food but many could not afford it. 'Every one lives on it who can afford to do so; but as a rule, the peasantry cannot. Wheat, barley, and especially millet, are the real staples throughout the rural districts, rice being there treated as a luxury to be brought out only on high days and holidays, or to be resorted to in case of sickness.'[95] At the start of the twentieth century, it was estimated that 'In most parts of Japan the grain food of the laboring people is about seventy per cent

[89] Dubos, *Adapting*, 64.
[90] Davidson, *Nutrition*, 179.
[91] Alcock, *Tycoon*, I, 321.
[92] King, *Farmers*, 190–2.
[93] Shunsaku Nishikawa in Jansen and Rozman (eds), *Japan*, 437.
[94] Hanley in Jansen and Rozman (eds), *Japan*, 455.
[95] Chamberlain, *Things*, 21.

naked barley mixed with thirty per cent of rice, both cooked and used in the same manner.'[96]

When it could be obtained, the rice was thought to be extremely good, with a special flavour, extra nutritious and long lasting:

> There are several varieties of Rice grown in the Country. The best sort hath not its equal in the Indies. It is perfectly white, like Snow, and so nourishing and substantial, that Foreigners, who are not used to it, can eat but little of it at a time. The Japanese rice accordingly is esteem'd the best of all Asia, particularly what grows in the Northern Provinces, which will keep many years, and which for this reason they chuse to fill their Store-houses withal, having first wash'd it in muddy water and then dried it.[97]

Thunberg also believed that 'The rice in this country is accounted the best in all the East-Indies and is extremely white, glutinous, and more nutritive than any other.'[98]

What is clear is that whatever the grain, the Japanese had to draw most of their nourishment from it, both carbohydrates and proteins. It is only possible to extract enough protein from grains for the really exhausting physical labour which was common in Japan by a consumption well above average. This led to an attitude towards eating which puzzled and intrigued foreign observers.

As Griffis travelled on the river from Osaka in 1871, he watched the men who, with enormous effort, punted the boat with long poles. 'After a hard night's toil, poling and walking in a nipping frost, I wished to see the breakfast by which they laid the physical basis for another day's work.' He had heard rumours that the Japanese eat some secret form of protein, 'The daily ration of a Japanese labourer was one mouse per diem; so I was once told in America.' But 'I never saw or heard of such animals being eaten during all the time I was in Japan.' Nevertheless he was on the look-out 'for some stimulating food, some piece of flesh diet to be eaten by these men, who had to make muscle and repair the waste of lubricating their joints.' What he observed was as follows: 'The first course was a bowlful of rice and a pair of chopsticks. In the second course history repeated itself. Third course was a dipperful of tea . . . the fourth course was a bowl of rice and two slices of radish; the fifth was the same. A dipperful of tea-liquor finished the meal, and the pole was resumed.'[99]

Eliza Scidmore was aware of the same extraordinary contradiction between simple diet and physical strength. 'The coolies, sitting around this kitchen, fortified their muscle and brawn with thimble cups of green tea, bowls of rice,

---

[96] King, *Farmers*, 379.
[97] Kaempfer, *History*, I, 187,186.
[98] Thunberg, *Travels*, IV, 85.
[99] Griffis, *Mikado*, 409–10.

and a few shreds of pickled fish.' 'The diet of these coolies seems wholly insufficient for the tremendous labor they perform – rice, pickled fish, fermented radish, and green tea affording the thin nutriment of working-days. Yet the most splendid specimens of physical health are reared and kept in prize-fighting condition on what would reduce a foreigner to invalidism in a week.'[100]

Food had to be eaten constantly to replenish energy. 'There is certainly far greater sustaining power in European food, and our medical authorities urge a more extensive use of animal food besides fish. Rice and vegetables, it is true, fill the stomach; indeed, one may even feel surfeited, and yet in a short time the strain disappears and hunger returns. For this reason coolies and others engaged in severe physical labour take four or more meals a day.'[101] 'In general they eat three times a day; about eight o'clock in the morning, two o'clock at noon, and eight in the evening. There are some that observe no regular time for their meals; but eat whenever they are hungry; for which reason the victuals are obliged to be kept in readiness the whole day.'[102] Some people ate even more frequently: 'Japanese farmers even five or six times a day.'[103] 'Rice is the mainstay, and a huge quantity of it is always kept ready boiled, needing only to be warmed up or mixed with hot tea.'[104] 'Rice is boiled in quantities large enough to last for one, or even two days. It is heated over when wanted, or hot tea is poured over the cold rice after it is served.'[105]

'The manner in which it is cooked makes it exceptionally palatable and nutritious, quite different from the Indian process which leaves each grain separate and dry.'[106] Davidson and his colleagues point out how much can be lost in the preparation of rice. 'Rice, as purchased in any bazaar, has to be washed and this washing water must then be discarded. The rice is then cooked in water and this cooking water is usually discarded, though it is sometimes consumed . . . the losses of thiamine particularly may be very high. Similar losses of nicotinic acid also occur. It is probably a safe assumption that for rice half of the water-soluble vitamins which escape the millers are washed away by the housewife and so lost to her family.'[107] The fact that Japanese rice is left in a very wet state, the water not poured away, may indicate that some of this loss was avoided.

How then would we evaluate the nutritional level of the majority of the Japanese population over the centuries? Hanley concludes, 'From the evidence

---

[100] Scidmore, *Jinrikisha*, 142,254.
[101] Inouye, *Home*, 75.
[102] Thunberg, *Travels*, IV, 37.
[103] Morse, *Day*, II, 354.
[104] Arnold, *Seas*, 402.
[105] Scidmore, *Jinrikisha*, 194.
[106] Chamberlain, *Things*, 21.
[107] Davidson, *Nutrition*, 212.

available, it is possible to argue either that the Japanese had a very poor and boring diet in the Tokugawa period or that the diet was rich and varied.'[108] One group of scholars and observers believed the diet to be inadequate. Willis thought 'that butter and milk would be a very useful addition to the sweet potato which formed the ordinary diet of the poor people.' He stressed that 'a mixed diet, one partly vegetable and partly animal, is best suited to the requirements of the human body and the one best suited to the capabilities of this province to produce food for its inhabitants.' A few months later he wrote from Satsuma (now Kagoshima) at the southern tip of Japan: 'It is the duty of the undersigned to speak plainly and to tell the Government that the standard of health and vigour of the inhabitants of this province and indeed throughout Japan falls short of what it should be.' One of the chief causes was, he thought, 'the comparatively poor diet of the population generally.'[109] Certainly visitors from the better fed western middle classes in America or Britain were surprised at how meagre the diet seemed to be. They noted that for many 'even rice was something of a luxury.' 'The shops, such as they are, contain the barest necessaries of life. Millet and buckwheat rather than rice, with the universal *daikon* [radish] are the staples of diet.'[110] This thin diet continued into the 1930s. A newspaper reporter then described the daily meals of a typical family of tenant farmers in western Japan as consisting of 'rice gruel and pickles for breakfast; rice gruel, dregs of soybean cakes, and pickles for lunch; and rice mixed with barley, vegetables and pickles for supper.'[111]

Ironically, it appears that two of the major health problems were caused by the preparation and eating of too much of the food with the highest status, white rice. One was calcium deficiency. The absence of meat and eggs in the diet could be offset by eating cheaper grains. 'It is said that injuries and fractures of the bones heal very slowly and often imperfectly. Rice has but half the ash material of wheat, and the water does not supply sufficient inorganic matter necessary for the bones.'[112]

Equally important was the spread of a curious wasting disease which was finally traced to a particular inadequacy in the diet. This was beri-beri, or *Kakke* as it was known in Japan. 'Kakke is the same disease as that known in India and the Malay peninsula under the name of beri-beri, and may be defined in popular language as a sort of paralysis, as it is characterised by loss of motive power and by numbness, especially in the extremities.' It 'attacks with special frequency and virulence young and otherwise healthy men – women much less often,

---

[108] In *Cambridge History*, 4, 686.
[109] Cortazzi, *Willis*, 181.
[110] Bird, *Tracks*, 128.
[111] Hane, *Rebels*, 41.
[112] Morse, *Day*, I, 40.

scarcely ever indeed except during pregnancy and after childbirth. Children of both sexes enjoy almost absolute immunity.'[113]

Beri-beri is strongly connected with a rice diet.[114] The conventional wisdom among some scholars of Japan is that it is the milling of the rice that caused the problem. 'Obviously, in retrospect, the cause was an increase in the eating of polished rice, resulting in thiamine deficiencies.'[115] 'White, or polished, rice was considered the highest quality, and this tended to be eaten in cities.' This led to the 'Edo affliction' as it was known, which disappeared when people went back into the countryside.[116] That the problem may not only have lain in the milling, but also in the washing, is suggested by others. It is well known that heavy washing of rice was linked to the question of milling. 'In northern China, Korea, and Japan, the rice hulls were traditionally removed before shipment in order to reduce bulk. When the rice reached the cities, it was so crawling with weevils that the subsequently highly-milled rice was covered in weevil juices and thus often treated with talc. Cooking procedures called for the rice to be thoroughly washed several times. The first washing alone removed half of the thiamine.'[117] Certainly a very heavy and exclusive diet of milled white rice, which was particularly common in Tokyo (Edo) where the rice rents were paid to the daimyo, is the root of the problem.

A thoughtful attempt to estimate whether the diet was inadequate in terms of energy during the second half of the nineteenth century has been made by Shunsaku Nishikawa. He gives figures suggesting 'the growth from 1,664 Kcal in the 1840s to 1,902 Kcal in 1887.' Given the size and weight of the Japanese population, he believes that 'A diet providing 1,700–1,900 Kcal and 45–50 g of protein might keep the physique of the Japanese people within certain limits, but was not insufficient for the Japanese of that era.' 'Taking everything into consideration, 2,000 Kcal per day per capita was not a low nutritional standard in 1887. Further, the survey data do not include consumption of unrefined sake, consumed by farmers, which could have provided additional calories needed for hard labor.' In conclusion, he believes that the evidence as a whole shows 'the adequacy of the diet and its long-term stability over a critical half-century of transition.'[118] Hanley likewise believes that there had probably been an increase in the amount of rice consumed per person over the Tokugawa period.[119] At the end of the nineteenth century, Chamberlain wrote that 'Experts say that Japanese food, though poor in nitrogen and especially in fat, is rich in carbon

---

[113] Chamberlain, *Things*, 269.
[114] See Guggenheim, *Nutrition*, ch.9 for a good account.
[115] Hanley in Jansen and Rozman (eds), *Japan*, 455.
[116] Hanley, in *Cambridge History*, 4, 683.
[117] Kiple (ed.), *Disease*, 607.
[118] In Jansen and Rozman (eds), *Japan*, 436,445,492,446.
[119] In *Cambridge History*, 4, 681.

and amply sufficient to support life, provided the muscles be kept in action, but that it is indigestible and even deleterious to those who spend their time squatting on the mats at home.'[120] More recently, Dubos has pointed out that while many American and Europeans 'feel that they need a daily food intake containing more than 2,500 calories and 70 grams of protein. . . . In contrast, whole populations of other ethnic groups seem well adapted to diets providing approximately 1,500 calories and 40 grams of protein, or even less, and often with hardly any meat.'[121]

Nutritional patterns have major consequences for health. In general, the complex mix of vitamins, proteins and carbohydrates influences the effects of disease. Well-fed populations have lower case mortality from many diseases. Furthermore, infection rates are lower. Specifically there are certain nutritional diseases which can be avoided, for example scurvy, beri beri and goitre.

The history of nutrition in England and Japan has been very different. The English relied on animal protein and indeed some may have suffered the health hazards of too rich a diet at times. The Japanese on the other hand had to make up for a shortage of animal protein by way of vegetable and grain protein. On the whole they avoided serious deficiencies of vitamins, proteins and carbohydrates, except in the case of the vitamin B deficiency manifested in beri-beri. We are dealing with two reasonably fed populations. This is an essential background factor in the discussion of disease, the last of the Malthusian scourges.

[120] Chamberlain, *Things*, 180.
[121] Dubos, *Writings*, 183.

Part III

In the Body

7

Dysentery, Typhoid, Cholera and the Water Supply

The third Malthusian scourge was disease. The conquest of war and famine would only exacerbate the threat to mankind from the rapid rise in population. The consequences of increasing density would be the emergence of new diseases and the growing danger from those already present. Formal medical knowledge and technology provided no solution. How was it possible to escape from a threat which is even greater than those of war and famine?

Diseases are transmitted to humans by three main routes, through the mouth by way of contaminated food and drink, by way of insect and other vectors, and through the respiratory route by droplet infection. The first of these, the swallowing of food and water containing dangerous bacteria, is particularly important in relation to the Malthusian argument. Contamination will tend to increase, all else being equal, as human beings live in more crowded conditions, fouling their water supplies and increasing the danger of food pollution. This is a very large topic and in order to simplify it I shall confine myself at this stage to diseases carried through drink and the effects of polluted water.

There is a wide class of water-borne infections, which are often termed 'dysentery' or 'epidemic diarrhoea'. Usually the various diseases are endemic, but there may be epidemic outbreaks. Alfred Crosby describes how enteric infections have killed 'more humans in the last few millenia than any other class of diseases, and are still doing so.'[1] It is estimated that in some tropical areas, more than fifty per cent of the population carry amoebic dysentery.[2] In relation to this disease 'In 1981, it was estimated that there were about 480 million infected people in the world: 290 million in Asia, 80 million in Africa, 90 million

---

[1] Crosby, *Ecological*, 208.
[2] Merck, *Manual*, 826.

in the Americas, and remarkably, 20 million in Europe.'[3] Another guess was that some 750 million people, or a quarter of the world's population, suffered from at least one attack of dysentery in 1963.[4] Diarrhoea is particularly dangerous for young children and many infant deaths are caused by dehydration following diarrhoea. Although many diarrhoeal diseases in children are also caused by viruses as well as bacteria. It is often difficult to distinguish these from other deaths, so that the whole category has been lumped under the term 'pneumonia-diarrhoea complex'. It is estimated that in many developing nations, and probably up to the end of the nineteenth century in a number of western cities, this complex was 'implicated in at least half of all infant deaths and a high proportion of deaths of children aged between 1 and 5 years.'[5] One estimate suggests that, on average, a child in a developing country will suffer two months of diarrhoea per year.[6] 'On average, a rural Gambian child suffered from gastro-enteritis for 13.1 per cent of the time, i.e. on about one day in eight.' The effects of such diarrhoea are considerable. 'Powander has calculated an average loss of 0.6 g of protein/kg/day during most illnesses, but this rises to 0.9 g/kg/day with diarrhoea. At this rate of loss it is easy to understand that when diarrhoea occurs chronically over several weeks or even months, children can become irredeemably wasted.' Peter Lunn concludes, 'data from other parts of the developing world confirm diarrhoeal disease to be the most important cause of child morbidity and mortality.'[7]

Of the English past Wrigley and Schofield write that 'Dysentery has been little noticed in earlier discussions of crisis mortality in England', though 'On the continent dysentery has more readily been acknowledged as a major source of crisis mortality.' They believe that in England 'The seasonal pattern of local crisis mortality that emerges ... suggests that they [intestinal infections] ... may also have been major killers in the pre-industrial period.'[8] This is supported by Leslie Clarkson. 'In London and the provincial towns dysentery was a regular summer visitor, and was an important cause of death among children.'[9] Creighton had noted that dysentery seemed to have increased as a problem in seventeenth-century England.[10] Certainly it was believed at the time that 'Diseases of the Stomach and Intestinal Tube, are very universal and frequent maladies in both sexes, and throughout all orders and ages.'[11] There

---

[3] K.David Patterson in Kiple (ed.), *Disease*, 569.
[4] Cited in Harding et al., *Epidemiology*, 146.
[5] Kunitz, *Speculations*, 352.
[6] Figures quoted in Dasgupta, *Inquiry*, 405.
[7] Peter Lunn in Schofield et al. (eds), *Decline*, 134,136,134.
[8] Wrigley and Schofield, *Population*, 659.
[9] Clarkson, *Disease*, 51.
[10] Creighton, *Epidemics*, I, 412–3: see II, ch.viii for an account of dysentery in England.
[11] Black, *Arithmetical*, 157.

is considerable evidence for its virulence. Basing the estimate on the causes of death given in the Bills of Mortality, 'In London during the years 1667–1720, that is, after the final outbreak of plague, deaths from intestinal infections accounted for between one-fifth and one-third of all deaths. They were highest among infants, infantile diarrhoea being probably the most common single cause of deaths among babies.'[12] 'Gastric disease, apparently linked to deficient water supplies, seems to have been a major killer of older infants and "weanlings" throughout the period and before the latter part of the eighteenth century it may also have claimed many lives among the newborn.'[13]

However there is evidence of a rapid decline of dysentery in eighteenth century London which is puzzling. Instead of the growth of cities leading to rising rates of infection, it would appear that at some point the mortality from dysentery began to drop. In the middle of the eighteenth century, William Black noted that 'dysentery and bloody flux' were beginning to decline in London.[14] Heberden provided a detailed analysis of the bills of mortality to show the decline of dysentery which was particularly marked from the decade 1730–1740.[15] In 1796 he said that several diseases, including 'dysentery', 'have so decreased, that their very name is almost unknown in London.'[16] As we have seen, Malthus thought that, along with the disappearance of bubonic plague, the decline of dysentery was the most important reason for a decline in mortality rates. Place wrote that 'In the latter half of the seventeenth century, the dysentery caused the death of 2,000 persons annually in the metropolis; its prevalence gradually decreased during the last century, and the disease itself is now almost extinguished as a fatal disease. Only fifteen are stated to have died of it in the year 1820.'[17] The decrease may have extended well beyond the city of London. Stephen Kunitz notes that '. . . during the second half of the eighteenth century . . . the pneumonia-diarrhoea complex also appears to have begun to decline in North-west Europe.'[18]

Another bacillary disease, typhoid or enteric fever, is similarly passed through human excreta into the water system, or through food, especially milk.[19] 'Control of typhoid fever depends on maintaining a separation between sewage and drinking water. In certain areas of the world, as many as three percent of adults may be shedding *S.tyhphi*. Thus with poor sanitation, the population is continuously exposed, and the disease is constantly present.' 'Three-quarters of

[12] Clarkson, *Disease*, 51–2.
[13] Landers, *Age Patterns*, 58.
[14] Black, *Arithmetical*, 164.
[15] Heberden, *Observations*, 34–5,40–1.
[16] Quoted in George, *London*, 70,330 n112.
[17] Place, *Illustrations*, 250.
[18] Kunitz, *Speculations*, 353.
[19] Roberts, *Hygiene*, 358.

the world's population live in areas where typhoid is endemic, and 1 out of every 300 of the world's population contracts the disease each year. One million persons die of it annually, mostly children.' The global incidence is reckoned to be some '15 million cases of typhoid fever each year.'[20]

Typhoid was very prevalent in western countries until the middle of the nineteenth century. For a long time it was thought that the disease was spread by 'miasma';[21] it was only in the 1840s that 'the Englishman William Budd virtually inaugurated the science of epidemiology by his demonstration that typhoid was spread from infected individuals to new hosts by means of water and food.' From then on sanitary improvements dramatically lowered the infection rates. 'Where pure water and food can be assured, typhoid transmission is minimal. Solely by improvement of sanitary conditions in the past century in developed countries, the incidence of typhoid fever has declined from 1 in 200 to 1 in 250,000.[22] As a result of improved drainage, there may well have been low exposure to typhoid in late Victorian England.[23]

Cholera is caused by *Vibrio comma* (*V.cholerae*), 'a short, curved, motile, aerobic gram-negative rod.'[24] It is spread through water and food contaminated by the excrement of carriers. Thus 'it will usually be possible to avoid cholera . . . if only cooked food and boiled water are taken.'[25] Cholera is endemic in several parts of Asia, but it became epidemic and spread over much of the world in five great pandemics in the nineteenth century, starting from India. There is currently a seventh world pandemic of cholera, which began in the 1960s, though the old virulent form is being replaced by a milder bacteria.[26]

Cholera first reached England in October 1830, during the second world pandemic. In the years to 1831–2, about 31,000 deaths were ascribed to 'cholera and diarrhoea'. During the third pandemic, some 62,000 died in 1848–9 and about 31,000 in 1853–4. In the fourth and last serious pandemic to strike England, about 15,000 died in 1866. We are told that 'Thereafter the Asian epidemics which spread through the European Continent in 1873, 1884–6 and 1892–3 were repulsed.' The mystery is why, when we compare its incidence in England with Scotland and Ireland, let alone the Continent, it was relatively less severe. England had the fastest growing and largest cities in Europe and yet 'cholera never ravaged Britain as severely as Continental countries, and it de-

---

[20] Charles W.LeBaron and David W.Taylor in Kiple (ed.), *Disease*, 1071,1073.
[21] 'Miasma' is defined by the O.E.D. as 'Infectious or noxious exhalations from putrescent organic matter; poisonous particles floating in and polluting the atmosphere'.
[22] Le Baron and Taylor in Kiple (ed.), *Disease*, 1075, 1074.
[23] Guha, *Decline*, 106.
[24] Merck, *Manual*, 819.
[25] Burnett, *Infectious*, 162.
[26] Patrice Bourdelais in Schofield et al. (eds), *Decline*, 118,124; Ewald, *Infectious*, 72.

parted a generation earlier.[27] There was no effective treatment for cholera and for most of the period the causes were unknown.[28] It was contained and then disappeared before the new town sanitation systems were widespread. As compared to other diseases, such as tuberculosis or scarlet fever, it was a relatively minor killer. Like dysentery in the eighteenth century, its rates are much lower that we might expect.

We would expect enteric disease to be particularly virulent in Japan with its large urban and semi-urban areas and the well-documented use of human manure on the rice fields. There is some evidence of early epidemics. 'The earliest Japanese reference to dysentery is an account that mentions an epidemic in Kyoto in the eighth month of AD 861.'[29] Epidemics of the disease, called *sekiri* or 'red diarrhoea' were noted in 861, 951 and 947, according to Hattori. Further outbreaks occurred in the eleventh to thirteenth centuries, usually coinciding with other epidemics. Yet, after that, as the population grew, the disease became less, rather than more, common. We are told that 'severe, large-scale epidemics seem to have been fairly rare in the early modern period. Fujikawa mentions only seven epidemics of diarrheal diseases for the Tokugawa period in his chronology of epidemics in Japan.'[30] There was an outbreak right at the end of the nineteenth century. Griffis wrote of 1899, 'During this year, also, dysentery raged throughout the empire, there being nearly 9,000 fatalities out of 45,000 cases.' 'Happily in this instance that which caused woe and death became the occasion of a great triumph in science and the healing art, for Dr Kitasato, pupil of the illustrious Dr Koch, of Berlin, discovered the bacillus of dysentery.'[31] The Japanese bacteriologist Kiyoshi Shiga isolated *S.dysenteriae* in 1898.[32]

The relatively low incidence of dysentery in Japan is attested to by Pompe. 'For abdominal disease, the climate is very salubrious; I have never seen endemic diseases of the digestive organs in Japan.' The situation was entirely different from that in China. 'In nearby Shanghai, however, they are found quite frequently and in the most malignant varieties.' Pompe put this down to the swampy, half-saline water of Shanghai, and the temperature. He felt that 'If the patients come to Japan before it is too late, they soon recover without having to use much in the way of medicine; the climate here is the main medicine. If there were direct steamship traffic with Java, Japan would be an excellent sanitarium for dysentery patients.'[33] The most extreme statement comes from Morse,

[27] Smith, *People's Health*, 230,233,237. All figures are very appoximate.
[28] For a good account of nineteenth century cholera, see Creighton, *Epidemics*, II, ch.9.
[29] Jannetta, *Epidemics*, 148.
[30] Jannetta, cited in Kiple (ed.), *Disease*, 379,382,387.
[31] Griffis, *Mikado*, 657.
[32] Kiple (ed.), *Disease*, 606.
[33] Wittermans, *Pompe*, 110.

writing mainly of the vast city of Tokyo in the 1870s: 'those diseases which at home are attributed to bad drainage, imperfect closets, and the like seem to be unknown or rare . . .', and indeed 'dysentery' is 'never known here.' He repeats this extraordinary fact later: the 'severer forms of bowel complaint, such as dysentery and chronic diarrhoea are very rare.'[34] This has been noted again recently: 'Even dysentery . . . was not the killer of children that it was in the West in the nineteenth century.'[35] Jannetta notes that 'Yamazaki's analysis of the Tokugawa and early Meiji literature suggests that severe large-scale dysentery epidemics were uncommon during the Edo period.'[36] A detailed analysis of a particular region supports the view that dysentery in its various forms was insignificant. 'The Hida records provide a clear example of what can only be inferred from descriptive Japanese source materials – that dysentery epidemics were rarely a major cause of high mortality in the late Tokugawa period. Relative to other causes of death, diarrheal diseases were unimportant, and epidemics were rare. Children under age five were those most likely to die of dysentery, but even in this age group other causes of death were much more important.'[37]

We might have expected the large and crowded cities of Japan to be very susceptible to typhoid. Yet we are told, 'typhoid seems not to have been a problem'.[38] Morse believed that 'typhoid' was 'rarely epidemic'.[39] Jannetta surveyed the evidence and found a number of outbreaks of dysentery, but none are definitely typhoid. That of 1829 is the most likely to be a form of typhoid, paratyphoid B, another variety of the deadly salmonella infections. The word for typhoid is of foreign origin, *chifusu*, and the earliest reference to the disease found by Fujikawa in his 'History of Diseases in Japan' was in 1862, and that was in a translation of a Dutch book in that year. Further research is needed, but it does look as if typhoid was far less serious in Japan than in other large and crowded nations and may have been absent until very late. Although a good deal may be concealed, it is difficult not to agree with Jannetta that 'it seems likely that Japan had lower mortality from enteric diseases than other premodern societies.'[40]

We might have expected cholera to be a particular menace in the ancient and great cities of Japan. As Paul Ewald argues:

> Once such a virulent pathogen evolved, the highest density of people infected with the pathogen should occur in the cities with the most extensive contamination of

[34] Morse, *Day*, I, 23,39.
[35] Hanley in *Cambridge History*, 4, 698.
[36] Jannetta, *Epidemics*, 151.
[37] Jannetta, *Epidemics*, 154–5.
[38] Hanley in *Cambridge History*, 4, 698.
[39] Morse, *Day*, I, 40.
[40] Jannetta, *Epidemics*, 149,155.

wells. The older, larger cities should meet this condition more frequently than the younger, smaller settlements; the older drains and wells would have been more prone to cross-connections, and larger cities would have been most able to maintain a steady rate of infections and deaths repelling potential inhabitants.[41]

In fact an analysis of the Japanese pattern shows that 'Japan's geographic position and trading policies provided a highly effective barrier against this destructive disease.'[42] The first great pandemic started in India in 1817 and spread to America and Europe within a year. Yet it only reached Japan in its final year, in 1822, and was confined to western Japan.[43] The second world cholera outbreak did not reach Japan, for Japanese sources 'make no mention of an epidemic resembling cholera in 1831'. Given that this was one of the major epidemic diseases of the nineteenth century, that it was very easily transmitted and travelled all over the rest of the world, that it 'failed to travel the relatively short distance between India and Japan during those years (i.e. 1825–1837) is remarkable.' In the third pandemic in the 1850s, again cholera did not reach Japan until the last years of the outbreak, in 1858. Thus 'until the very end of the Tokugawa period, Japan was spared the serious epidemics of cholera to which other regions of the world were repeatedly exposed.'[44] Certain forms of cholera may never have reached Japan at all; Morse wrote in the 1870s that '*cholera infantum* are never known here.'[45] It was not until 1822 that the disease was first given a name, the foreign onomatopoeic term *korera* or *korori*, according to Fujikawa.[46]

Given a population of upwards of thirty million people in the middle of the nineteenth century, crowded into massive cities and a densely populated countryside, it is very surprising that most of the outbreaks were confined to a matter of thousands of deaths. The control of cholera, like that of dysentery and typhoid, is considerably affected by a set of practices concerning personal cleanliness and sanitation. It seems likely that certain customs and habits of hygiene and waste disposal were of central importance in containing the outbreaks once they had reached Japan.

Another reason lies in the efforts made by the Japanese authorities to contain the outbreaks that did occur. The descriptions of these efforts during the last third of the nineteenth century are particularly vivid and provide a useful insight into the very careful regulation of public health in Japan which was an

---

[41] Ewald, *Infectious*, 78.

[42] Jannetta, *Epidemics*, 157.

[43] Jannetta, *Epidemics*, 159; though Alcock, *Tycoon*, 190, mentions memories of an outbreak in 1818.

[44] Jannetta, *Epidemics*, 161,163,172.

[45] Morse, *Day*, I, 23.

[46] Fujikawa, *History of Diseases*, ch.6.

important background factor in its impressive medical history in relation to other diseases as well as cholera.

After a lull between 1822 and 1858, cholera returned. Pompe was involved in trying to combat it. 'I took all possible precautions to check the disease and assisted the government in taking hygienic measures, which were carried out with a great deal of energy. (In such times an autocratic government has a great deal of value). I explained to the physicians the nature and treatment of cholera and gave, of course as much assistance as I could.' He then disseminated his experience and knowledge widely over Japan. 'I ordered the printing of a short handbook in Japanese in which all characteristics of the disease were described, and this booklet was circulated throughout the country.'[47]

Morse provides detailed accounts of the measures taken. He referred to cholera outbreaks in several Japanese cities, for instance Satsuma and Kyoto. He was particularly impressed by the government measures:

> The dread word has come that Asiatic cholera has broken out in Yokohama and Tokyo. The foresight and thoroughness of the Government is remarkable. The vast city covers an extent of territory three times that of New York City and there are said to be fifty or sixty thousand jinrikishas, every one of which is compelled to carry a box of chloride of lime. Every morning a servant passes through the corridors and entry-ways of the University sprinkling carbolic acid water on the floors and mats; every Government officer, native and foreign, receives a small vial of cholera medicine made by the regular formula of laudanum, rhubarb, camphor etc. with a paper containing printed directions as to when and how to use it. Mine was in terse English.[48]

Sir Edwin Arnold also described the action taken:

> Their central idea is to isolate every case as it occurs, and, the police being pretty well omnipotent, this is not so difficult here as it would prove elsewhere. At the approach of the enemy the executive and civil authorities laid their heads together, got hospitals ready, appointed medical and administrative staffs, decided on the methods to be adopted as to disinfectants, conveyance of patients, isolation of relatives and houses, and disposal of corpses, and then issued clear instructions in every *ken* and *cho*.[49]

Hearn was aware that there were considerable pressures on people to try to conceal the disease. 'The sanitary law forbids the treatment of cholera in private houses; yet people try to hide their sick, in spite of fines and other penalties, because the public cholera-hospitals are overcrowded and roughly managed,

[47] Wittermans, *Pompe*, 91.
[48] Morse, *Day*, I, 336.
[49] Arnold, *Seas*, 539.

and the patients are entirely separated from all who love them.'[50] Similarly, 'Rich and poor people alike naturally hate to be "spotted", cut off, carried to the hospital, and buried with scanty ceremony after demise; so the rich will pay for concealment and the poor will implore it.' 'Now, the hospital is naturally dreaded. Many Japanese women, and even men . . . die actually and positively from the depressing fact of being there – good as the treatment is, kindly and brave the nursing, and fearless and devoted the medical assistance.' Consequently, 'the poor people will not proclaim to the doctors the beginning of their attack. They allow the insidious preliminary symptoms to go on, hoping to pull through.' When the doctors are finally called, they were put under great pressure to conceal the truth. In Tokyo, the authorities 'made an excellent beginning by severely punishing two medical men who concealed cases of cholera . . . after which the danger rather was that zealous doctors would call every casual stomach-ache . . . "cholera" '.[51]

As the cities grew rapidly and Japan opened up to the west and re-organized itself after the Meiji restoration it began to suffer, as did Europe and America, from cholera. Yet the efforts to control it were extremely thorough and a recent appraisal is in essence correct; 'Cholera was absent until the mid-nineteenth century and then was readily contained.'[52]

In relation to enteric disease, though one would expect to find increasing mortality as population grew, especially in cities, yet in England, dysentery started to decline in London and perhaps in other cities in the eighteenth century. In Japan, despite massive cities and dense rural population between the seventeenth and mid nineteenth centuries, dysentery, cholera and typhoid were either absent or largely under control. An explanation could be sought among the factors listed by Macfarlane Burnett: 'Decent sewage disposal, pure water supply, pure food laws, control of milk supply and pasteurization, plus the cult of personal cleanliness . . .'[53]

Because of its climate, England is a country usually bountifully supplied with water through numerous springs, rivers and wells. There are no obvious reasons for thinking, however, that there was anything special about these sources and the way in which drinking water was obtained from them. There were numerous problems of contamination of water supplies, which grew worse as the population doubled from the later sixteenth century and began to grow rapidly again from the middle of the eighteenth century. The horrendous situation in many parts of England described in the sanitary reports of the middle of the nineteenth century cannot be projected back into earlier

[50] Hearn, *Kokoro*, 257.
[51] Arnold, *Seas*, 539–40.
[52] Hanley in *Cambridge History*, 4, 698.
[53] Burnett, *Infectious*, 106.

centuries, but they do indicate how difficult it was to obtain clean water until the latter part of the nineteenth century. For example Edwin Chadwick quotes a number of accounts from health inspectors describing the foul pits, ditches and rivers which the poor were often forced to use for their water supply.[54]

The necessity for large supplies of reasonably clean water for all sorts of purposes was widely recognized. Buchan put succinctly arguments that could be found in writings from the middle ages onwards: 'Water is not only the basis of most liquors, but also composes a great part of our solid food. Good water must therefore be of the greatest importance in diet.' Water was important for personal cleanliness: 'As it is impossible to be thoroughly clean without a sufficient quantity of water, we would earnestly recommend it to the magistrates of great towns to be particularly attentive to this article. Most great towns in Britain are so situated as to be easily supplied with water.' Water was important for urban cleanliness. 'The streets of great towns, where water can be had, ought to be washed every day. This is the only effectual method for keeping them thoroughly clean; and, upon trial, we are persuaded it will be found the cheapest.' It was therefore important to procure as much clean water as possible. 'Before water be brought into great towns, the strictest attention ought to be paid to its qualities, as many diseases may be occasioned or aggravated by bad water; and when once it has been procured at a great expense, people are unwilling to give it up.'[55]

'A piped water supply to towns was in many instances established during the Middle Ages, and certain religious orders, notably the friars, showed a conspicuous initiative in organising and constructing conduits.'[56] We learn that 'pipes or open conduits served Exeter, Bristol and Southampton in the fourteenth century, and Gloucester and Hull in the fifteenth.'[57] We can examine this provision with particular reference to the city where the problems of an adequate water supply were most acute, namely London. It appears that 'The first public cisterns, the Great conduit in West Cheap, was begun in 1285, to store the water thus brought from Paddington. By the end of the sixteenth century, some twenty conduits existed, three of which drew their supply from the Thames, and three of which are still commemorated today in the names of Great Conduit, Lamb's Conduit, and White's Conduit Streets.'[58] A general description of how this conduit system was worked in the sixteenth century is given by F.N.L.Poynter: 'The water supply was conveyed through the city

---

[54] Chadwick, *Report*, 137,141–2.
[55] Buchan, *Domestic*, 68.
[56] Pounds, *Culture*, 161.
[57] Hibbert, *The English*, 103.
[58] Hardy, *Water*, 251.

in wooden pipes from the Thames and stand pipes were placed at street junctions.'[59]

As the city began to grow rapidly in the second half of the sixteenth century, the medieval conduits needed to be supplemented by other supplies. Of course there remained the widespread system of wells and hence it has been argued that 'until the early seventeenth century, London was largely supplied with water from shallow wells, which were sunk both in public places and in the yards and gardens of private establishments.'[60] Yet even this was not enough. In the 1580s a Dutch engineer, Peter Maurice, began to install a new system of water pumps driven by the force of the Thames at London Bridge. 'At the end of this bridge, on the London side, is a curious machine for pumping water and for sending it into different parts of the town. This machine turns in either direction, according to the tide, so that it is always in use.'[61] There were improvements in the sixteenth century, with the water-driven distribution of water along wooden pipes. An interesting insight into the robustness of these wooden water pipes is given by Peter Quennel: 'Going through Red Lion Square, Holborn, about 1930, we saw some of the old wooden water supply pipes being dug up. These were made of elm trunks, bored out to about 6 inches diameter, and according to Mr Austin, the Holborn Surveyor, were laid about 1620.'[62] Another important development in the early seventeenth century was the building of the New River. Blane thought that despite the improvements of the 1580s, 'the supply was scanty till the formation of the New River in the reign of James the First.'[63] Yet, as the city grew even more rapidly, the inadequacy of a system based on wooden pipes and the power of water itself became apparent and a further development was needed.

The new system is best described by De Saussure: 'One of the conveniences of London is that everyone can have an abundance of water.' 'The big reservoir or cistern near Islington, the York Buildings machinery near the Strand, and that of the Bridge supply every quarter abundantly. In every street there is a large principal pipe made of oak wood, and little leaden pipes are adapted to this principal pipe, and carry water into all the houses.' As a result of this, 'Every private individual may have one or two fountains in his house, according to his means, and pays so much a year for each fountain. Water is not obtainable all day, these fountains giving three hours' water in every twenty-four. The large leaden cisterns are replenished during the time the water does not run into the houses.' 'Companies or societies have undertaken this vast enterprise and

---

[59] Wilson, in Nicoll (ed.), *Shakespeare*, 162.
[60] Hardy, *Water*, 251.
[61] De Saussure, *Foreign*, 83.
[62] Quennell, *Things*, III, 93.
[63] Blane, *Dissertations*, 127; see also Heberden, *Observations*, 71.

reap the profits.' Alongside this new system, there was the old. 'Besides the distribution of water by the means of pipes, there are in many streets pumps and wells, where poor people who cannot afford to pay for water can obtain it for nothing.'

How had it suddenly become possible to supply what was becoming the largest city on earth with plentiful water? We note the improved use of metal technology, the lead cisterns, the 'little leaden pipes' attached to the oak main pipes. But the real key lay in a new way of forcing the water to these more distant parts of the expanding city, which could not be reached from the old, water-driven, machine. The provision of water was one of the first fruits of the industrial revolution, the application of machinery based on the use of fossil fuels through steam engines.

Again De Saussure provides a good introductory account:

I have named the York Buildings machinery. This is so curious that I must tell you more about it, for everyone understanding machinery admires it greatly ... smoke issuing with force through a little tube, and corresponding with a large and tightly-covered boiler full of boiling water, sets in motion a large piece of machinery, composed of wheels, counterpoise and pendulum, which in their turn cause two large pumps to work continually. This piece of machinery and the two pumps are placed at the foot of a wooden tower, which is, I think, about one hundred feet in height, its breadth diminishing after the manner of pyramids, gradually. At the summit of this tower, which is octagonal, there is a small leaden cistern or basin, which receives the water the pumps send up, and from thence it flows into the great reservoir or pond of Marylebone.[64]

Thence it could be distributed over a much wider area.

There was a rush of activity to provide piped water throughout London resulting from a combination of steam and the development of joint stock companies. During the 1690s, John Houghton F.R.S. carried a series of advertisements in his news sheets concerning the new conduits that were being laid. In July 1694 he commented in his editorial on the fact that while the making of the New River by Sir Thomas Middleton was a great advance, 'yet seeing we grow so very great' more was needed, which would be provided by the 'City Conduits that's now laying into Houses' which will 'make us abound not only with useful, but more pleasant Waters than ever.' He carried a series of advertisements urging people to join the scheme. The first of these in September 1694 was as follows:

The Conduit water that will wash very well, and is as fine as any other whatever, and much finer than most, is to be Lett, at the Black Horse and Key against the

[64] De Saussure, *Foreign*, 155–6, 156–7.

Poultrey Compter. 'Tis brought through Pipes from Paddington, through St. James' Square, the Strand, Fleet-Street, St. Paul's Churchyard, Cheapside, Lombard-Street, Cornhill, and Threadneedle-Street, to Bishopsgate; with a great many Bye Pipes from them. And wherever Four Persons at least, will agree to take it, within a Hundred Yards of where it now reaches, it shall be laid for them.[65]

The results were impressive. 'The amount of water English people employ is inconceivable, especially for the cleansing of their houses.'[66] In his 1756 *Essay on Waters*, Lucas considered that London was served with water in greater variety and abundance than any city in Europe: 'there is not a considerable street in London which is not furnished with such plenty of water, by way of aqueducts or pipes, from various sources, besides what wells and pumps supply . . . but even the upper story of most houses are, or may be, supplied with water' 'Common cocks in the broadest streets watered them in summer, and cleansed them in winter; the abundance of water removed the need for hawkers of water such as could be seen in Paris and other great cities.'[67] The greater cleanliness the ample supply of water allowed may well be a significant feature in the surprising finding that cities, and particularly London, did not become un-healthier as they rapidly expanded in the eighteenth century. This water supply, Lucas believed 'is one of the causes why our capital is the most healthful great city in the world.'[68] Blane observed in the early nineteenth century: 'A plentiful supply of water promotes health in a great city, not only by its application to various household purposes, but by cleansing the gutters and common sewers.' He further noted that 'the ingenious machinery of the steam-engine has, since the beginning of this century, been applied for conveying and raising it [water] to the tops of the highest houses in all situations . . . affording a degree of abundance and accommodation in this article of life hitherto unknown.'[69] Thus by 1828 'nine London companies served some 164,000 tenants, in a city contain-ing about 200,000 houses, and a population of about 1,500,000.'[70]

The supply of large amounts of fresh water for washing and cleaning was not confined to London. In Nottingham 'The town had formerly been supplied from its numerous wells and by water-carts bringing a supply from the river, but in the last decade of the seventeenth century a company had been formed to supply the town with water from the Leed by means of "an engine", one of

---

[65] Houghton, *Husbandry*, II, 103,112.
[66] De Saussure, *Foreign*, 157.
[67] The first quotation is from Lucas, the second by Hardy, both are in Hardy, *Water*, 255.
[68] Cited in Wright, *Clean*, 93.
[69] Blane, *Dissertations*, 127–8.
[70] Hardy, *Water*, 252. Smith, *People's Health*, 215ff provides a useful account of nineteenth-century water supplies, and Landers, *Death*, 70ff discusses London water supplies in the eighteenth century.

the many joint-stock pumping enterprises undertaken at that time.'[71] In 1693 in Derby 'one Mr George Sorocold has set up a Water-house to convey water-pipes to all the Houses in the Town that desire it, and 'tis likely it will be much used.'[72] It is likely that further research would uncover numerous other examples. From the later seventeenth century, through a combination of technology, government encouragement and the private enterprise water companies, English cities began to gain a special advantage in relation to the supply of reasonably clean water. That this did not solve all the problems is graphically illustrated by Chadwick's survey of the 1840s. Yet even his account serves to underline how much England was already dependent on the application of the new industrial technologies to the solution of the basic need for water. It is not difficult to imagine what would have happened to urban growth from the middle of the eighteenth century if the steam-pumping of waters and the initiatives of the competing water companies had not been available.

Japan has plenty of rivers, rushing down from the mountains to the sea. These were diverted for irrigation and for domestic use, using a variety of techniques. 'In many country villages, where the natural conditions exist, a mountain brook is conducted by a rock-bound canal through the centre of the village street; and thus the water for culinary and other purposes is brought directly to the door of every house on that street.' Supplementary to this, and for taking water into the cities, bamboo was used. 'There are many ways of conveying water to villages by bamboo pipes. In Kioto many places are supplied by water brought in this way from the mountain brooks back of the city.'[73]

These streams were less safe than they looked. Although Kaempfer had been impressed that the rivers which ran through Nagasaki 'provide it with clear and sweet water, very fit for daily drink,'[74] the pollution of the smaller streams was noted by nearly all observers. 'Through these ditches the water is running, and though vitiated by the water from the kitchen and baths is yet sufficiently pure to support quite a number of creatures, such as snails, frogs, and even fishes.'[75] 'In many of the villages there is a running stream down the centre of the street covered in partially in some villages and quite open in others. In a number of places the water appeared to me to be bad and unwholesome and as if containing the drainage from the houses.'[76] Mrs Geoffrey noted the same problem. 'I have walked through picturesque villages where elaborate stone conduits led a stream

[71] Chambers in Glass and Eversley (eds), *Population*, 340.
[72] Houghton, *Husbandry*, I, 38.
[73] Morse, *Homes*, 298,299.
[74] Kaempfer, *History*, II, 90.
[75] Morse, *Homes*, 52.
[76] Cortazzi, *Willis*, 130.

past the door of every house so that each house was entered by a little wooden bridge. Here a woman would be leaning over to wash clothes, while a little lower down another would be dipping up a bucket of water to boil for tea!'[77]

The growth of Tokyo, or Edo as it was once called, more or less directly parallelled that of London and it is worth investigating how a city which soon became the largest in the world was supplied with water. Hanley has given a very good account: 'In 1590, Okubo first went to Edo to assess the situation and make plans. The system he began was so large in scale and so successful that it has been compared to that of the Romans.' The first system to be constructed was the Kanda system which 'drew its water from the Inokashira spring west of the city. Water was carried to the city limits mainly in exposed aqueducts, and then in underground aqueducts or wooden pipes within the city.' Alongside this was another conduit system which took water from the Tama River, bringing much more water over a length of over fifty miles. 'For its underground aqueducts, the Kanda system used square pipes of red pine, but other early systems had pipes made of other kinds of wood, stone, earth, and bamboo.' 'The public was supplied with water from wells built into the aqueduct system; people were required to go to the nearest well and draw water there rather than tap the nearest duct themselves.'[78] The efficient water system may have been based on Chinese models. Needham points out that 'The extent of piped water supplies in ancient China has been very much underestimated by most later writers' and notes the use of bamboo tubing and conduits of earthenware.[79]

Hanley is very impressed with the system in Edo. It delivered water twenty-four hours a day and 'Stoppage of water was so rare that Edo-ites made no backup arrangements for emergencies.' The system was so good that when it was decided to modernize it at the end of the nineteenth century 'the only major change was to replace the wooden pipes with impervious metal ones. Thus the Japanese were able to use the main features of a system constructed in the seventeenth century when converting to a water supply system based on modern technology more than two centuries later.' Other Japanese cities, however, 'relied on rivers and wells for their water supply.'[80] The utilization of river water in Edo was described by Captain Saris in 1613: 'underneath this Cawsey runneth a River, at every fiftie paces there is a Well-head, fitted very substantially of free-stone, with buckets for the neighbours to fetch water, and for danger of fire.'[81]

Hearn described the considerable efforts made to keep the wells clean. His house was visited by 'professional well-cleaners.' He describes how 'once every

---

[77] Geoffrey, *Immigrant*, 46.
[78] Hanley, *Sanitation*, 6,7,8.
[79] Needham, *Clerks*, 361.
[80] Hanley, *Sanitation*, 16–17,8.
[81] In Purchas, *Pilgrims*, 153.

year wells must be emptied and cleansed, lest the God of Wells, Suijin-Sama, be wroth.' This god 'protects all wells, keeping their water sweet and cool, provided that house-owners observe his laws of cleanliness, which are rigid. To those who break them sickness comes, and death.' Once a month 'a Shinto priest visits the homes of pious families having wells, and he repeats certain ancient prayers to the Well-God, and plants *nobori*, little paper flags, which are symbols, at the edge of the well. After the well has been cleaned, also, this is done. Then the first bucket of the new water must be drawn up by a man; for if a woman first draw water, the well will always thereafter remain muddy.' Not only is there a God of the well, but also he has 'little servants to help him in his work. These are the small fishes the Japanese call funa (a sort of small silver carp). One or two funa are kept in every well, to clear the water of larvae. When a well is cleaned, great care is taken of the little fish.' Hearn found the 'water of my well is clear and ice-cold', but could never drink it again without thinking of 'those two small white lives circling always in darkness.'[82]

It may be that the water supply in Japanese cities was as good, if not better, than that in British cities of the same period. On the other hand, it is undoubtedly true that bacteria could accumulate during the process of storing and conveying water. 'As these wells have all wooden sides and a square wooden flooring where washing is done, they present a far from cleanly appearance, and the water is as often as not contaminated, especially in the crowded quarters of the city.'[83] Earlier, Willis had written. 'Another cause of disease is the imperfect state of the water supply, and of the drainage. In a large portion of the town the wells derive their supply of water from the surface drainage. Such water having soaked through a soil saturated with decaying organic matter is in many cases quite unfit for domestic use.'[84] Morse agreed with Willis: 'It is hardly within the province of this work to call attention to the exceeding impurity of much of the well-water in Tokyo and elsewhere in Japan, as shown by many analyses, or to the imperfect way in which water is conveyed from remote places to Tokyo and Yokohama.' As he admitted, 'In their present imperfect method of water-service it is impossible to keep the supply free from local contamination.'[85]

A plentiful supply of relatively fresh water is important in facilitating the cleaning of clothes, houses, streets and human bodies. It would appear that both English and Japanese villages, towns and cities had such a supply by the eighteenth century at the latest. This was an important achievement and would have had considerable consequences on general health. On the other hand, there was no way in which water could be purified sufficiently for it to be safe for drinking. It continued to be one of the major causes of enteric illness until the

---

[82] Hearn, *East*, 97–8.
[83] Inouye, *Home*, 69.
[84] Cortazzi, *Willis*, 260.
[85] Morse, *Homes*, 296,297.

later nineteenth century. Goubert is right in arguing that the 'Conquest of Water', if by that we mean its purification so that it could be drunk safely unboiled, only occurred in the latter half of the nineteenth century.[86] If water was so dangerous and could cause so much illness and death, is there anything about the way in which water was drunk, or the amount that was drunk, that was significant in either England or Japan?

[86] Goubert, *Conquest of Water*.

8

Drink: Milk, Water, Beer and Tea

In the search for the elusive cause of the pattern of decreasing mortality in eighteenth-century England, Thomas McKeown eliminated all except nutrition. That he almost totally ignored drink is explained by his belief that there was no possibility that changes in drinking habits could have had much effect before the later nineteenth century. 'The only successful personal measures – boiling or chemical treatment of water – were unknown at that time.'[1] Yet the relatively light incidence of the water-borne diseases of dysentery, typhoid and, for a long time, cholera, in Japan is likely to be related to drinking habits, and so is the dramatic decline of dysentery in eighteenth-century England.

At first sight, given the rich pastoral agriculture in England, we might have expected milk drinking to have been important. Yet if people had drunk full-fat, unpasteurized and unboiled milk, they would have been in considerable danger. Despite Cobbett's robust belief that 'to suppose the milk contains any thing essentially unwholesome is monstrous',[2] animal milk was a source of human infection. A host of bacteria breed and spread through milk. As the Cleggs describe it: 'milk is a solution of proteins containing a suspension of fat globules, mineral salts, vitamins, and milk sugar. It provides an ideal medium for bacterial growth and multiplication.' The diseases it carries include bovine tuberculosis, Brucella, septic sore throats and scarlet fever, human tuberculosis, bacillary dysentery, infectious hepatitis, typhoid and paratyphoid fevers and diptheria.[3]

The contaminations start in the milk itself. 'Even under the cleanest

---

[1] McKeown, *Food*, 232.
[2] Cobbett, *Cottage*, 112.
[3] Clegg and Clegg, *Man*, 125.

conditions milk which is freshly drawn from a healthy cow is never sterile. A mixed population of bacteria is always present in the milk ducts and teat canals of the udder of a healthy cow, and freshly drawn milk contains about 20,000 bacteria per cubic centimetre of milk.' Dirt accumulates on the udder: 'unless they are kept scrupulously clean, the udder and hind quarters become soiled with excreta, and may even be caked with the dried material.'[4] Further contamination comes from the 'dust and dung in the cow shed, from the vessels used for collection and storage of milk, from the hands and clothes of the milker and the contaminated water used for washing utensils or cooling the milk. Cow dung contains over a million bacteria per gramme, and the litter in a dirty cowshed may contain more than ten times this population per gramme.'[5]

All these dangers assail milk before it even leaves the cow shed. In the conditions of transit before the later nineteenth century, it is not difficult to envisage further pollution. A rather extreme, but graphic, account was given by Tobias Smollett in 1771: 'The milk . . . lowerd with hot water, frothed with bruised snails; carried through the streets in open pails, exposed to foul rinsings, discharged from doors and windows, spittle, snot and tobacco quids, from foot-passengers, overflowings from mud-carts, spatterings from coach wheels, dirt and trash chucked into it by roguish boys for the joke's sake, the spewings of infants . . .'[6]

Although some have argued that the supply of milk improved dramatically in the later eighteenth century,[7] it would appear that nothing very significant could be done about the quality. 'It cannot be said that the bacteriological knowledge which resulted from Pasteur's pioneer studies had much influence on the handling of milk until nearly the end of the century . . . pasteurization was first used in the dairy industry about 1890, more as a means of increasing the "life" of the milk than to kill the germs likely to cause harm to the consumer.' J.C.Drummond adds that only in about 1896 did it begin 'to be appreciated that pasteurization also provided a valuable protection against milk-borne disease.'[8] The only real precaution is to boil milk for a reasonably long time.[9]

In view of all this, how much of this dangerous substance was drunk unboiled by the English population? It is known that there were vast herds of milking animals, which yielded milk for butter and cheese. But was whole milk drunk on its own? Certainly there were large quantities of milk both in cities and the

---

[4] Lane-Claypon, *Hygiene*, 240.
[5] Clegg and Clegg, *Man*, 125–6.
[6] Quoted in Ferguson, *Drink*, 46–7.
[7] Beaver, *Milk*.
[8] Drummond, *Food*, 301.
[9] For further comments on the dangers of milk, see Drummond, *Food*, 72, 193; Smith, *People's Health*, 212ff.

countryside.[10] We also know that it was drunk by labourers in the seventeenth century, but not how it was drunk.[11] There seem to have been strong prejudices against drinking it raw[12] and I have come across little positive evidence that it was drunk in large quantities. It may well be that Ferguson is right in concluding that 'Until the nineteenth century milk was considered more as a source of butter and cheese than as a drink in itself',[13] although 'very considerable quantities of whey were drunk'.[14] Whey is the liquid remaining after taking off the curd to make cheese. It was also drunk after making butter, in the form of skim milk. It is interesting that Cobbett, in arguing vehemently for the wholesomeness of milk, recalled that 'I have drinked little else for the last five years', added, 'Skim-milk I mean'.[15] It may have been important as a supplementary food and in this context it is worth noting Beaver's thesis that the rapid decline in infant mortality from about 1900 was largely due to the pasteurization and bottling of milk and speedier communications.[16]

In the case of Japan, there was no danger of infection by milk until the later nineteenth century. As we have seen, the Japanese did not keep milking animals in any quantity between the tenth and nineteenth centuries. By then even the slightest hint of animal milk made most Japanese metaphorically and literally sick. It would appear that they shared that lactose intolerance which was common to most non-pastoral societies and hence made it impossible for adults to absorb milk products.[17] Thus, for a combination of reasons, the Japanese had reached the position described by von Siebold in the early nineteenth century where 'The use of milk . . . in any form, is unknown, or, at least, strictly prohibited in Japan.'[18] The Japanese may not have had milk protein, but before the discoveries of Pasteur, they probably avoided an immense amount of illness, including tuberculosis and enteric diseases, by never drinking animal milk.

Drinking unboiled water is always dangerous. 'Pure water does not occur in nature except perhaps as rain water as it leaves clouds. All other waters . . . contain some inorganic and organic substances which can support

---

[10] cf. Houghton, *Husbandry*, II, 156 for one estimate of London milk consumption in 1695.

[11] Everitt in Thirsk (ed.), *Agrarian History*, IV, 452–3.

[12] cf. Houghton, *Husbandry*, II, 147.

[13] Ferguson, *Drink*, 46.

[14] Drummond, *Food*, 72.

[15] Cobbett, *Cottage*, 91.

[16] Beaver, *Milk*.

[17] For lactose intolerance, see Pelto and Pelto in Romanucci-Ross et al., *Anthropology of Medicine*, 186; Tannahill, *Food in History*, 124–7; Kiple (ed.), *Diseases*, 813–6. For an overview of lactose intolerance, which was found throughout Japan and China, see Paige and Bayliss, *Lactose Digestion*. For the lactose tolerance of Norse peoples, see Crosby, *Ecological*, 48.

[18] Von Siebold, *Manners*, 121.

some form of microscopic life.' The most directly and obviously transmissible diseases have been outlined – cholera, typhoid and dysentery. Many other micro-bacteria harmful to man can also be carried in unboiled water, although 'All vegetative bacteria and many spores are killed by five minutes boiling'.[19] The danger increases as the population becomes more dense and the amount of refuse and manure, human and animal, accumulates in a crowded environment and leaches into water. If the transmission through drink can be halted, as in modern customs of sterilizing or boiling water, then an immense amount of illness can be avoided.

One of the facts that most struck foreigners about the English between the fourteenth and eighteen centuries was that, partly because of their affluence, partly because of their agricultural surpluses, partly because of their preferences, they were a people who did not drink much water. When Fortescue in the fifteenth century compared England and France, one of the differences he noted was in drink. Many French peasants were miserably poor: 'The people being with these and diverse other calamities plagued and oppressed, do live in great misery, drinking water daily. Neither do the inferior sort taste any other liquor saving only at solemn feasts.' The English, however, were an affluent people: 'the men of that land are rich. . . . They drink no water, unless it be so that some for devotion, and upon a seal of penance do abstain from other drinks.'[20] In the middle of the sixteenth century, John Aylmer contrasted people in continental countries and the English: 'They drink commonly water: and thou good ale and beer.'[21]

The continued avoidance of water in England was evident to De Saussure in 1726:

> Would you believe it, though water is to be had in abundance in London, and of fairly good quality, absolutely none is drunk? The lower classes, even the paupers, do not know what it is to quench their thirst with water. In this country nothing but beer is drunk, and it is made in several qualities. Small beer is what everyone drinks when thirsty; it is used even in the best houses, and costs only a penny the pot. Another kind of beer is called porter, meaning carrier, because the greater quantity of this beer is consumed by the working classes.

He then proceeded to describe ale, a superior clear beer made without hops, and ends: 'It is said that more grain is consumed in England for making beer than for making bread.'[22] This lends support to M.C.Buer's observation that 'it has to be

[19] Clegg and Clegg, *Man*, 131,135.
[20] Fortescue, *Commendation*, 81,85.
[21] Quoted in Macfarlane, *Individualism*, 178.
[22] De Saussure, *Foreign*, 158.

remembered that water was not a usual beverage in the 18th century, even charity children were given small beer.'[23]

There seem to have been several reasons far drinking beer rather than water. One was undoubtedly to avoid illness. Henry VII pronounced that the water of England was undrinkable.[24] Andrew Boorde drew attention to the dangers of water; it was not wholesome if taken neat. The order of goodness of water was rain water, running water, river water, well water, standing water.[25] Even water drunk with wine must be boiled or distilled. Wear quotes advice given by William Vaughan, Robert Burton, Venner and others on what the best water was, but notes that no reference is made as to whether it was drunk or not. He points out that the danger of polluted water was well appreciated.[26]

With the development of spas there were those who advocated the drinking of water as healthful in the eighteenth century,[27] and it was probable that certain water, from deep wells for instance, was not too dangerous.[28] On the whole, however, it has been recognized by most peoples that there was a link between disease and drinking water. The difficulty was what to do about it. One solution was to boil up water with oats and to make a drink called 'water-gruel' which was deemed safe and nutritious. But much better was to make a pleasure of necessity by substituting a drink which the English liked for the dangerous substance.

The history of ale and beer drinking in England is a large and complex one. At first the English drank mainly ale, that is a fermented drink made from barley but without the use of hops. It is possible that ale was sufficiently widespread before the fifteenth century for it to act as a substitute for water. 'That water rather than ale was often drunk is difficult to prove. On the contrary, the constant amercement of brewers in seigneurial courts might suggest an abundance of ale.' Dyer provides other evidence of the very large consumption of ale in medieval households, calculating that about a gallon of ale per person per day was the allowance in lordly households, and that 2.6 pints per person per day may have the norm among 'peasants' in the thirteenth century.[29]

Increasingly ale was supplemented by and then largely replaced by beer. Hops were the special ingredient that made beer different from the earlier ales; 'there is no doubt the hop was known in England before the Conquest, and passages in contemporary writers show that some use was made of the plant by the Saxons in their primitive process.' Yet the 'date of its practical introduction

---

[23] Buer, *Health*, 109.

[24] Shrewsbury, *Philistines*, 69.

[25] Boorde, *Regyment*, 253.

[26] Wear (ed.), *Medicine*, 143.

[27] See Short, *A Rational Discourse*; Curteis, *Essays*, 52.

[28] That deep wells give good water was discussed, for instance, in Murphy, *Our Homes*, 767.

[29] Dyer, *Diet*, 204, 193, 202; see also Dyer, *Everyday Life*, 84–5.

for brewing . . . was most probably the middle of the 15th century.'[30] The rhyme 'Turkies, carps, hoppes, picarell and beere, Came into England all in one yeare' refers to its introduction from Flanders at that time.[31]

Beer grew in popularity and was described by Harrison in the later sixteenth century as the national drink. 'Our drink, whose force and continuance is partly touched already, is made of barley, water, and hops, sodden and mingled together by the industry of our brewers in a certain exact proportion.' It was very cheap, 'so that for my 20s I have ten score gallons of beer or more . . .' which made it available even to the poor.[32] By the early seventeenth century, Fynes Moryson could boast that 'The English Beere is famous in Netherland and lower Germany, which is made of Barley and Hops; for England yeelds plenty of Hops, however they also use Flemish Hops. The Cities of lower Germany upon the sea, forbid the publike selling of English Beere, to satisfie their owne brewers, yet privately swallow it like Nectar. But in Netherland, great and incredible quantity thereof is spent.'[33]

Many people have drawn attention to the nutritional value of beer. Made out of barley and fermented, it added a great deal to the dietary intake. Drummond writes: 'it seems probable that this "small beer" had a calorific value of about 150–200 Cal. per pint. This meant that a young boy drinking about 3 pints a day would get some 500–600 Cal. towards his daily needs of about 2,500.'[34] In other words, the energy value of beer is about 30 to 60 Kcal per 100 ml, about the same as milk.[35] As well as the calories, 'beer would have supplied a modest amount of calcium and appreciable quantities of ribo-flavin, nicotinic acid, pyridoxin, panthonenic acid and perhaps other vitamins.' Drummond concludes by saying that it is certain 'that home-brewed beer was a good, sound, healthful drink and one which could not possibly do any harm to children when drunk in reasonable amounts.'[36]

If beer was to act as a substitute for water, enormous amounts would be needed. A detailed study of liquid consumption suggests that a twelve stone man under 'ordinary circumstances of work and health' requires about four pints of water a day. Half of this is supplied in 'solid' foods, so he will need about two pints more, depending on temperature and activity. If on average people need about two pints of liquid a day, is it possible that as much beer as this was brewed in England? It appears that it was. The excise duty on beer in 1684

[30] *Chambers's Encyclopedia*, 'Beer'.
[31] For the introduction of hops, see Drummond, *Food*, 44.
[32] Harrison, *Description*, 135,138.
[33] Moryson, *Itinerary*, IV, 166.
[34] Drummond, *Food*, 114.
[35] Davidson, *Nutrition*, 206.
[36] Drummond, *Food*, 114.

suggest that 'each member of the population, man, woman and child, consumed . . . nearly a pint a day. But allowance must also be made for the beer brewed privately on which excise was not charged: Gregory King estimated that in 1688 this came to a further seventy per cent of the original total.[37] It would appear that every man, woman and child consumed an average of nearly two pints of beer a day. John Houghton in the 1690s assumed a global figure of two pints per person per day.[38] This would easily be enough, along with lesser drinks such as ale and perry, to supply all the drinking needs of the population.

Other indications of the amount drunk suggest very large quantities. The allowance for Christ's hospital at the end of the eighteenth century was about 2.5 gallons per person per week, or a little under 3 pints per day.[39] In the mid-eighteenth-century Mutiny Act, the allowance of small beer for the soldiers was set at five pints per person per day, and many argued that it should be more, for 'every gentleman's servants each consumed daily six pints.'[40] At the poor house in Heckingham, Norfolk in 1794, Eden noted that 'The men are, each, allowed a pint of beer at every meal, except when they have broth, or gruel. Women, with children at the breast, have the same allowance. Others have two-thirds of a pint.'[41] A little earlier, Rochefoucauld had seen that 'The harvesters have meat three times a day and strong beer to drink in proportion as well as all the small beer they want.'[42] Peter Clark has provided a detailed social history of the English alehouse. He gives figures for the sixteenth century of four pints of beer a day for the English garrison in Boulogne in 1545 and two pints of ale a day for the inhabitants of Coventry (men, women and children) in the 1520s.[43]

The side-effects of this enormous consumption of beer are obvious. The centre of English social life was the ale house.[44] Anyone who has visited an English village or town will know about the pub, which was only one amongst the assembly of inns, ale-houses and other establishments. As Stubbes fulminated, 'every countrey, cittie, towne, village, and other places, hath abundance of ale-houses, tavernes, and innes', which were patronised, being 'so fraught with maultwormes, night and day, that you woulde wonder to see them.'[45]

---

[37] Thomas, *Religion*, 18; cf. Houghton, *Husbandry*, IV, 299, which gives the number of barrels on which customs were paid in 1684–94, which works out at a pint per head, the other pint would come from ale that escaped excise. See Clark, *Alehouse*, 109 also.

[38] Clark, *Alehouse*, 209.

[39] Drummond, *Food*, 114.

[40] Boswell, *Life of Johnson*, II, 10, note.

[41] Drummond, *Food*, 224.

[42] Rochefoucauld, *Frenchman*, 230.

[43] Clark, *Alehouse*, 109.

[44] cf. Clark, *Alehouse*.

[45] Stubbes, *Anatomie*, 113.

Was there something in the beer that gave it any particular medicinal value? Nothing special may have been meant when Henry VI in 1436 commended the new drink of beer made from hops as 'notable, healthy and temperate',[46] yet it may already have been noted that the practice of adding this herb to the drink, made a real difference to health. 'Hops gives beer a bitter flavour and are useful both as an antiseptic and a preservative.'[47] The Italians used hops as a cure for various diseases, a fact noted by an early-eighteenth-century English author who wrote that 'It's most certain that *Hopps* by their grateful Bitterness are excellently suited to the Stomach, and very serviceable to the Digestion.'[48] Recognition of the medical value of beer is shown in an eighteenth-century book by David Davies, quoted by Dugald Stewart: 'Time was when small beer was reckoned one of the necessaries of life, even in poor families . . . it seems to have been designed by Providence for the common drink of the people of this country, being deemed a preservative against some of its worst diseases.'[49]

Once we begin to examine the process of beer-making, and particularly the role of hops, we begin to see that much of the method was concerned, as Pasteur was later to realize, with the problem of avoiding infection by the wrong bacteria. The barley is mixed with water, ferments and turns to malt. It is thoroughly dried and then crushed to make it amenable to further soaking. Boiling water is added and the malt is mashed. The central process, the fermenting of the malt through diastase which converts the modified starch of the malt into sugar and dextrin, takes place. At this point there is a very considerable danger of infection by unwanted bacteria, which would lead the beer to go stale very quickly. So the extract is washed and boiled for two hours with hops, which act as a form of bacteriocide. The liquid is cooled, fermented for at least forty hours, and then stored for some weeks. If it is necessary for the beer to keep for an especially long time, or in a hot climate, as in export ale, further hops are added. Throughout, the water has to be of the purest and everything kept very clean.

What is needed in this process is a selective bacteriocide that will kill off unwanted bacteria. The Germans hit on a specific herb for this purpose, wild hops. 'The hops exert a purifying, a preservative, and an aromatic influence over the wort. The tannin precipitates the excess of albuminous matter, thus ridding it of a certain source of after trouble, while the constituents of the hop in different ways play their preservative part.'[50] There appears to be a natural 'tannin' present which acts as a bacteriocide which has been more recently

---

[46] Drummond, *Food*, 44.
[47] Ferguson, *Drink*, 10.
[48] Curteis, *Essays*, 70.
[49] Stewart, *Collected Works*, IX, 319; my italics.
[50] *Chamber's Encyclopaedia*, 'beer'.

described: 'Hops not only impart a distinctive bitter flavour to the brew but also the perpenes present in them are thought to have antibiotic properties – against chance contaminants.'[51] It may well be that the widespread drinking of beer by the English after about 1530 was of central importance for general health. It may not only have given a nutritious and perfectly safe drink, but have contained considerable amounts of some antibiotic or bacteriostatic substance in the 'tannin', which would go into every beer-drinker's mouth and stomach and act as a general disinfectant or protection against many kinds of bacterial infection.

After hop-based beer was introduced into England there was a period when the health of the nation improved considerably. The second half of the sixteenth century saw one of the healthiest periods in English history when mortality was relatively low and the population grew.

It would appear that up to the eighteenth century 'small beer' was sufficiently cheap for the whole population to drink. Just about the time that De Saussure wrote his description of the beer-drinking nation, the second major change in English drinking habits was beginning, namely the move from beer to tea as the staple drink of the labouring population. David Davies at the end of the eighteenth century, having said what a good drink beer was, and how it had been a 'necessary of life' and 'the common drink of the people', stated that 'on account of the dearness of malt, which, is most unfortunately for them, a principal subject of taxation, small beer has been, these many years, far beyond their ability to use in common.' He explained that 'Under these hard circumstances, the dearness of malt and the difficulty of procuring milk, the only thing remaining for them to moisten their bread with, was *tea*. This was their last resource. Tea (with bread) furnishes one meal for a whole family every day, at no greater expense than about one shilling a week at an average.' To the suggestion that this was a luxury, Davies replied: 'If you mean fine hyson tea, sweetened with refined sugar, and softened with cream, I readily admit it to be so. But *this* is not the tea of the poor. Spring water, just coloured with a few leaves of the lowest-priced tea, and sweetened with the brownest sugar, is the luxury for which you reproach them.' 'To this they have recourse from mere necessity; and were they now to be deprived of this, they would immediately be reduced to bread and water. Tea-drinking is not the cause, but the consequence, of the distresses of the poor.'[52]

In Japan, although some water was drunk, as indicated by the presence of special water carriers and particular wells kept separate from washing wells, on the whole the Japanese tried to avoid drinking ordinary water. Morse was careful

---

[51] Davidson, *Nutrition*, 206.
[52] Quoted in Stewart, Collected *Works*, IX, 320,320.

not 'to drink water, as, in fact, one rarely does in Japan.'[53] The universal drink was tea.

The origins and date of the discovery of tea are uncertain.[54] One theory is that tribal groups living in the mountainous forests on the borders of Assam and Burma used the leaves of a certain species of Camellia bush which when mixed with hot water made a refreshing drink. Tea was perhaps also eaten as a vegetable, chewed, pickled or sniffed like snuff in this area, as it still is today in parts of south east Asia.[55] Several thousands of years before the birth of Christ the knowledge of tea was transferred to China. 'According to certain statements made by ancient Chinese authors, the tea-plant was growing in the Celestial Empire as early as about 2700 BC.' It was domesticated in China and the fact that 'no tea-plants have been found growing wild in China' suggests that it was of Assamese origin, a fact supported by botanical evidence that '*Thea assamica* is now generally considered by botanists to be the parent stock of all cultivated varieties of the tea-plant.' The original stock was considerably modified to bring out its powerful medicinal ingredients. We are told that 'for centuries . . . the Chinese used tea exclusively as a medicine.'[56] According to Okakura it was 'highly prized for possessing the virtues of relieving fatigue, delighting the soul, strengthening the will, and repairing the eye-sight. It was not only administered as an internal dose, but often applied externally in form of paste to alleviate rheumatic pains.'[57] Needham tells us that 'by the 4th century it [tea] had universally conquered Chinese society and was everywhere used as the refreshing drink we know.'[58]

Tea was introduced into Japan as a medicine in the eighth century AD. At first it was cultivated in monastery gardens as a medicinal herb, to heal sickness and to help keep the monks alert during meditation. Its use and influence was restricted to courtly and monastic circles.[59] 'Though encouraged from the first by imperial recommendations, tea culture made little or no progress in Japan till the close of the twelfth century.'[60] Then in 1191 the monk Eisai returned from China, bringing with him Rinzai Zen Buddhism and tea. Eisai gave detailed advice on how it should be picked, prepared and drunk so that its virtues would be maximized. 'Eisai also taught the Japanese the Chinese way of preparing the

[53] Morse, *Day*, I, 25,69–70; II, 245.
[54] I am extremely grateful to DrDerek Bendall and Dr.H.B.F.Dixon of the Department of Biochemistry, University of Cambridge, for reading this chapter and making a number of most helpful suggestions concerning the details of the biochemistry of tea.
[55] Hobhouse, *Seeds*, 124.
[56] Browne, *Tea*, 4,5,87.
[57] Okakura, *Tea*, 44–5.
[58] Needham, *Clerks*, 362.
[59] Tanaka, *Tea Ceremony*, 23.
[60] Chamberlain, *Things*, 453.

leaves: gather them early in the morning before dew-fall, then roast them on a sheet of paper over a very gentle heat so that they do not burn, and keep them in a pot with a stopper made from bamboo leaves.'[61] In this way the green powdered tea was introduced which became central to the tea ceremony and much of Japanese cultural life.[62]

Tea appears to have had many virtues for this great exponent of Zen. He wrote a two-volume work called 'Kissa-yojo-ki' or 'Notes on the curative effects of tea'. 'Tea is the most wonderful medicine for preserving health; it is the secret of long life. It shoots forth its leaves on the hillside like the spirit of the earth. Now, as in the past, it possesses these same extraordinary qualities, and we should make much greater use of it.'[63] Iguchi provides a summary of Eisai's work:

> the health of the five human organs is strengthened through the plentiful intake of the five flavours they each respectively enjoy. Accordingly, the lung enjoys sharp flavours, the liver desires sour flavours, the spleen sweet flavours, the kidney salty flavours and the heart enjoys bitter flavours. But, whilst people absorb the four flavours of sharp, sour, sweet and salty, the bitter flavour necessary for the heart is unpleasant and cannot be taken in. This is the reason, Eisai writes, why Japanese hearts are afflicted and Japanese lives short. We are fortunately able to learn from the people of the continent and we must make our hearts healthy absorbing the bitter flavour of tea.

Hence Eisai 'interprets tea drinking as a secret technique for the prolongation of life.'[64] It gave health to many other parts of the body as well as the heart; 'it was believed to banish sleep and to be effective against liver and skin complaints, rheumatism and beri-beri.'[65] Another summary states that tea drinking was strongly recommended by Eisai 'as a cure for five types of disease: loss of appetite, drinking water disease, paralysis, boils and beri-beri. Tea, he added, is a remedy for all disorders.'[66]

The tea plantations grew and tea drinking became widespread among the Samurai in the thirteenth century and by the Muromachi period (1336 onward), all classes in Japan drank tea.[67] By the later sixteenth century, tea had assumed an immense importance in Japanese life. The tea ceremony, developed by Rikyo and other great masters, became the most important cultural institution in Japan. Vast quantities were grown. In 1678 Willem Ten Rhijne 'was

[61] Frederic, *Daily Life*, 75.
[62] For an excellent account, see Okakura, *Tea*.
[63] Frederic, *Daily Life*, 75.
[64] Karsen, *Tea Ceremony*, 101.
[65] Frederick, *Daily Life*. 75.
[66] Tanaka, *Tea Ceremony*, 25.
[67] Paul Varley in *Cambridge History*, 3, 460.

responsible for the first descriptions and specimens of the tea plant to come to the West. Just a few months after his arrival at Nagasaki (in 1674) he sent an essay on the tea plant, a branch of a camphor tree, and a batch of twigs, leaves, and flowers' back to a friend.[68]

Kaempfer had just the right combination of qualities to appreciate and describe tea. He was by training a doctor but he was also one of the greatest of seventeenth century botanists. Combining these skills with his encyclopaedic knowledge of all aspects of Japanese history and culture, he gives us a portrait of tea in Japan. He was impressed with those medicinal virtues of tea which had been the basis for its acceptance in China and Japan. 'Tsianoki, that is the Tea-shrub, is one of the most useful Plants growing in Japan.' He wrote a special appendix on tea, in which he concluded, 'To sum up the virtues of this liquor in a few words, it opens the obstructions, cleanses the blood, and more particularly washes away that tartarous matter, which is the efficient cause of calculous concretions, nephritick and gouty distempers. This it doth so very effectually, that among the Tea-drinkers of this Country I never met with any, who was troubled either with the gout or stone.' But its virtues were even more general. 'I believe, that there is no Plant as yet known in the world, whose infusion or decoction, taken so very plentifully, as that of Tea is in Japan, sits so easy upon the stomach, passes quicker through the body, or so gently refreshes the drooping animal spirits, and recreates the mind.'[69]

Kaempfer differentiated between the two main types of Japanese tea, the high-quality and costly powdered green tea, and ordinary tea. In the tea houses on the highways, 'The Tea sold at all these places is but a coarse sort, being only the largest leaves, which remain upon the shrub after the youngest and tenderest have been pluck'd off at two different times, for the use of people of fashion, who constantly drink it before or after their meals.' He was aware that the differences in the way it was picked, dried, stored, and boiled, altered its nature. 'The common drink of the Japanese is brew'd of the larger leaves of this Shrub; but the young and tender leaves dried, powder'd and mix'd in a Cup of hot water into a sort of Soup, are drank in the houses of people of quality before and after their meals.'[70] In this they anticipated the findings of modern research: 'The most essential points in making good tea of the finest quality and with the least waste are to have actually boiling water, and tea leaves so crushed and subdivided that the largest possible surface is rapidly exposed to the boiling water in infusing it. This explains why the best tea-infusion in the world is that made by the Japanese from their carefully prepared "tea powder".'[71]

[68] Bowers, *Medical Pioneers*, 36.
[69] Kaempfer, *History*, I, 179; III, 240,241.
[70] Kaempfer, *History*, II, 329; I, 179.
[71] Notter and Firth, *Hygiene*, 166.

Whatever virtues the tea leaf contained would be affected by the way in which it was prepared. 'The leaves must be roasted when fresh, for if they were kept but one night, they would turn black, and lose much of their virtue: For this reason they are brought to these roasting houses the very same day they are gather'd.'[72] 'The process of harvesting the tea, or rather, of storing the harvest, is one of extreme nicety. The leaves are sorted for the finer and coarser teas as they are plucked, and no more of either kind are gathered in a day than can be dried before night.'[73] The tea was 'prepared in the Tsuiusi, as they call them, that is, publick roasting-houses, or laboratories, built for this very purpose, and contrived so, that every body may bring their leaves to be roasted.' The tea could also be roasted at home. 'The Country people go a much shorter way to work, simply and without any great art, roasting their leaves in earthen kettles. Nor is their Tea much the worse for it, which besides, as it costs them no great trouble nor expense, they can afford to sell very cheap.'[74]

An alternative method to preserve as much as possible of the natural juices while cooking the leaves, was described by Chamberlain. 'As soon as possible after being picked, the leaves are placed in a round wooden tray with a brass wire bottom over boiling water. This process of steaming, which is completed in half a minute, brings the natural oil to the surface. The next and principal operation is the firing, which is done in a wooden frame with tough Japanese paper stretched across it, charcoal well-covered with ash being the fuel employed.' The aim was to cure the tea but to do so as lightly as possible and hence not to destroy the natural oils. 'Sometimes – and we believe this to have been the common practice in ancient days – the leaf is not fired at all, but only sun-dried.'[75]

Once the tea had been cured, it was essential to store it carefully. The country people kept it 'in straw baskets made like barrels, which they put under the roofs of their houses, near the hole which lets out the smoak, they being of opinion, that nothing is better than smoak to preserve the virtues of the leaves, and still to fix them more and more.'[76]

'The tea drunk at meals is common tea, which as it consists of old leaves, may be taken in any quantity without affecting the nerves. A handful of the leaves is thrown into an earthen tea-pot and hot water poured into it; and the pot is set over a fire to keep it hot. The infusion is of a reddish-yellow hue and is almost tasteless.'[77] Such tea would be prepared in the morning, and then used throughout the day. 'This kettle is to serve for the whole family all day long, to

---

[72] Kaempfer, *History*, III, 230.
[73] Von Siebold, *Manners*, 232.
[74] Kaempfer, *History*, III, 230,233.
[75] Chamberlain, *Things*, 454.
[76] Kaempfer, *History*, III, 237-8.
[77] Inouye, *Home*, 62.

quench their thirst. Every one, who hath a mind to drink, goes there, when he pleases and with a pail takes out as much of the decoction, as he will.'[78] The tea was kept on the boil and 'from this the brown decoction is poured out for immediate use, and another kettle, filled with cold water, affords them the means of diluting and cooking it.'[79] When visitors came, they were instantly served from this store. 'And it is the custom of the Country to present friends that come to visit them, with one or more dishes of Tea, both when they come and go.'[80] As Morse wrote, 'it is one of the pleasant features of Japan that wherever you go, friend's house or shop, tea is offered you.'[81]

Western travellers found the ordinary Japanese tea somewhat unappetizing at first. 'Tea is the national drink, a weak concoction taken without sugar or milk. One has to get used to this drink slowly, for at first the newcomer might well use it as an emetic; gradually, however, one gets accustomed to it. Wherever a European visits a Japanese home, the first thing offered to him is a cup of tea. The Japanese drink dozens of cups of tea a day.'[82] Morse had found the tea rather uninteresting but later wrote, 'I am getting accustomed to the tea and find it refreshing. It is always very weak, very hot, and is drunk without milk or sugar. It is drunk by everybody, high and low, at intervals through the day.'[83] 'You give a public lecture, and instead of the customary pitcher of cold water and a glass, a tray with a teapot and cup is placed upon your desk.' Institutions had special officers who just made tea: 'At the University one man's whole duty is to prepare tea for the teachers, and at intervals throughout the day he brings to your laboratory a teapot of hot tea.'[84] What was apparent to all was that tea was drunk by all Japanese in huge quantities: 'the grand object of cultivation, next to rice, is the teaplant. . . . Its consumption is now almost unlimited.' It is drunk 'at all their meals, and, indeed, at all times in the day, by every class.' In addition to the large plantations, 'every hedge upon every farm is formed of the teaplant, and furnishes the drink of the farmer's family and labourers.'[85] One estimate is that 'about 3 litres is the daily consumption of the citizens of the empire of the rising sun.'[86] And at the end of their lives the Japanese showed their appreciation for its great virtues and healthy properties: 'Last of all, the vacant spaces in the coffin are filled with bags of tea.'[87]

[78] Kaempfer, *History*, III, 239.
[79] Thunberg, *Travels*, IV, 41; cf. also Oliphant, *Elgin's Mission*, 170.
[80] Kaempfer, *History*, I, 179.
[81] Morse, *Day*, I, 192.
[82] Wittermans, *Pompe*, 53.
[83] Morse, *Day*, I, 51–2.
[84] Morse, *Day*, II, 192.
[85] Von Siebold, *Manners*, 232,133,232.
[86] Brand, *Les Grandes Cultures*, 224.
[87] Bacon, *Japanese Girls*, 278.

The virtues of tea drinking as a preventive to disease lie in two areas. The first is in the obvious fact that it provides a cheap drink which avoids the many dangers of unboiled water. This became particularly apparent in Japan with the dramatic events of the later nineteenth century when cholera was introduced into the country. 'Cholera was very prevalent . . . not a swallow of cold water could be drunk. Tea, tea, tea, morning, noon, and night, and on every possible occasion.'[88] Sir Edwin Arnold wrote during a cholera outbreak in the 1890s, 'I may add that the custom of perpetual tea-drinking greatly helps the Japanese in such a season as this. When they are thirsty they go to the tea-pot, and the boiled water makes them pretty safe against the perils of the neighbouring well.' He had come from India where people were not yet drinking tea except in very restricted circles. He also mentioned interestingly that 'There is beside a general and widespread intelligence as to the advantage of boiling water and milk, and dipping vegetables and fruit in boiling water.'[89]

The link between population density and the boiling of water in China and Japan was pointed out by King. 'The cultivation of tea in China and Japan is another of the great industries of these nations, taking rank with that of sericulture if not above it in the important part it plays in the welfare of the people. There is little reason to doubt that this industry has its foundation in the need of something to render boiled water palatable for drinking purposes.' He added 'The drinking of boiled water is universally adopted in these countries as an individually available and thoroughly efficient safeguard against that class of deadly disease germs which thus far it has been impossible to exclude from the drinking water of any densely peopled country.' He believed that 'This device and the custom are here centuries old and throughout these countries boiled water, as tea, is the universal drink, adopted no doubt as a preventive measure against typhoid fever and allied diseases.'[90]

King was writing explicitly in order to influence policy in the United States, where he was head of the Government Agricultural Bureau. He saw that America and Europe might well have to emulate Japan and China in this respect given the difficulties of supplying safe water. 'So far as may be judged from the success of the most thorough sanitary measures thus far instituted, and taking into consideration the inherent difficulties which must increase enormously with increasing populations, it appears inevitable that modern methods must ultimately fail in sanitary efficiency.' He believed that 'it must not be overlooked that the boiling of drinking water in China and Japan has been demanded quite as much because of congested rural populations as to guard against such dangers in large cities, while as yet our sanitary engineers have dealt only with the urban

[88] Morse, *Day*, II, 192.
[89] Arnold, *Seas*, 543.
[90] King, *Farmers*, 323, 77.

phases of this most vital problem and chiefly, too, thus far, only where it has been possible to procure the water supply in comparatively unpopulated hill lands.'[91]

Morse had earlier stated that 'For centuries the Japanese have realized the danger of drinking water in a country where the sewage is saved and utilized on the farms and rice-fields.'[92] He knew of the danger of contaminating water supplies with night soil, but 'experience has taught the Japanese to drink the water boiled or in the form of tea.'[93] This knowledge may explain the fact that even if the few tea leaves were for some reason not available, then water was still boiled. One of a list of the inversions of Japan as opposed to the west is that 'they drink hot water instead of cold.'[94] Jannetta writes 'It was customary to boil drinking water in Japan . . .'[95] 'The Japanese seldom drink water, although they splash, dabble, or soak in it half the time.'[96]

The drinking of tea has been looked on as a way of making hot water palatable. 'The fact that water must first be boiled before it can be turned into tea is probably one of the most important health measures ever to have been introduced, albeit unconsciously, since unboiled water was, and still is, in some parts of the world, the main channel by which bacterial diseases such as cholera and other enteropathic infections are disseminated.'[97] Yet there are indications that not only were tea leaves attractive as a stimulating infusion, but that they contained some further property of a health-inducing kind.

There are clues throughout the history we have outlined that there is some medically important agent in the specific Camellia leaf which is made into tea. The Dutch physician Cornelis Bontekoe (alias Cornelis Dekker) wrote a *Tractaat* on the excellence of tea, coffee and chocolate.[98] 'He held green tea of Bohea in such high esteem that in one of his works he seriously recommended the sick to take 50, 60, up to 100 cups without stopping, a feat he had accomplished himself in one morning. It was when suffering cruelly from stones, as he had, that he believed had been cured by the copious use that he had made of the Chinese drink. He defended it strongly against those who said it caused convulsions and epilepsy; on the contrary, he attributed to it all sorts of therapeutic virtues.'[99]

A further clue is provided by the Scottish philosopher Kames. In trying to

---

[91] King, *Farmers*, 323–4.
[92] Morse, *Day*, II, 192.
[93] Morse, *Latrines*, 172.
[94] Morse, *Day*, I, 25.
[95] Jannetta, *Epidemics*, 202.
[96] Scidmore, *Jinrikisha*, 62.
[97] Marks, *Clinical Effects*, 709, 711.
[98] Published at The Hague, 1685.
[99] Brand, *Les Grandes Cultures*, 216. The tea cups were presumably miniature.

account for the decline in all types of mortality in the eighteenth century, he wrote that one important factor might be 'the great consumption of tea and sugar, which I am told by physicians to be no inconsiderable antiseptics.'[100] Such an antiseptic would be likely to be bitter and astringent to the taste, and somewhat unpalatable. The description of ordinary Japanese tea by Griffis fits the description very well: 'The drink was the cheapest tea. . . . The third course was a dipperful of tea, apparently one-half a solution of tannic acid, in which a raw hide might have been safely left to tan.' So powerful was this, that Griffis wondered whether 'the disease of ossification of the coats of the stomach, so common in Japan, arises from the constant drinking such astringent liquor.'[101]

What then is tea made of? 'Of the total solids extracted, some 40% are polyphenols, often referred to incorrectly as tannins, 20% are proteins and amino acids, 5% caffeine, 5% inorganic ions and 3% miscellaneous substances including lipids, carbohydrates and vitamins.'[102] Clearly the largest constituent is the polyphenols or 'tannins'. This tannin constituent was emphasized in the Japanese way of drying and making tea. As we have seen, the way of curing the tea seems to have been designed to keep the maximum amount of the natural juices in the leaf. 'The tea for home consumption is only slightly fired and therefore retains most of the aroma. As a consequence lukewarm water is all that is necessary for the first infusion, while with us, 'unless the water boiling be', etc. is a well-known maxim.'[103] There appears to be a contradiction between Morse's statements, which sometimes refers to 'very hot' water being needed for tea, and here talking of 'lukewarm' water. For brownish tea (*bancha* and *hojicha*), the water is very hot. For green teas (*sencha*), the water is boiled, but it should be cooled a little before pouring into a teapot.[104] It is estimated that while the loss of soluble tannins in green tea manufacture is 'slight', in black tea two thirds are lost. It may, however, be the case that the fermentation process of black tea, which increases the micro-organisms in the leaf, may have compensated by creating some useful, bacteriostatic, or possibly antibiotic, substances.[105]

In 1911 tannic acid was 'official in both the British and United States Pharmacopoeias', used in various medical preparations. Its medical value is described thus:

> When applied to broken skin or exposed surfaces it coagulates the albumen in the discharges, forming a protecting layer or coat. It is moreover an astringent to the

---

[100] Kames, *Sketches*, I, 245.
[101] Griffis, *Mikado*, 410.
[102] Marks, *Clinical Effects*, 711.
[103] Morse, *Day*, I, 27.
[104] Saito – personal communication.
[105] For the increase of micro-organisms and the process of fermentation, see Ukers, *Tea*, I, 526–36.

tissues, hindering the further discharge of fluid. It is a powerful local haemostatic, but it only checks haemorrhage when brought directly in contact with the bleeding point. It is used in the treatment of haemoptysis in the form of a fine spray, or taken internally it will check gastric haemorrhage. . . . In the intestine tannic acid controls intestinal bleeding, acting as a powerful astringent and causing constipation; for this reason it has been recommended to check diarrhoea. Tannic acid is largely used in the treatment of various ulcers, sores and moist eruptions. The glycerin is used in tonsillitis and the lozenges in pharyngitis. For bleeding haemorrhoids tannic acid suppositories are useful, or tannic acid can be dusted on directly. The collodium stypticum is a valuable external remedy.[106]

This description of the effects of one of the main ingredients of tea would no doubt have gladdened the heart of Eisai. But we can take the analysis one stage further. We may ask the question, what then is the powerful constituent in tannin which seems to act as such a strong disinfectant? Although this may not be the whole answer, part of it seems to be that tea tannin is another name for one of the most powerful antiseptics known to man, namely phenol.

William Ukers provides a useful overview of the nature of tea tannins.[107] 'Tannins may be subdivided into two groups; one group consists of esters of polhydroxy compounds and phenolic acids . . .'[108] The polyphenol content is of central importance in tea. 'The quality of tea, as drunk, is largely determined by its polyphenol content, which is responsible mainly for the strength and colour of the infusion, its mouth-feel and the ability to form "tea cream" – a precipitate of complexes of polyphenols with caffeine.' These polyphenols 'are formed during conversion of fresh leaf to black tea by oxidation of flavanols, flavandiols and theogallin.'[109] We have seen that 40% of the solid content are polyphenols. What then are the virtues of polyphenols?

'Phenol was the first of the disinfectants and antiseptics and its germicidal activity was dramatically demonstrated by the work of Lister in 1867.'[110] Lister first used 'carbolic acid, the remarkable efficacy of which in deodorizing sewage made Lister regard it as a very powerful germicide.'[111] If we look at carbolic acid, an obsolete name for phenol (hydroxybenzene), 'It has a characteristic smell, and a biting taste . . . and acts as a powerful antiseptic. It dissolves in water . . .' Carbolic acid then 'is an efficient parasiticide, and is largely used in destroying the fungus of ringworm.' Taken in even moderate quantities it is poisonous, but if mixed with soluble sulphate it may be safely consumed. 'Taken

[106] *Encyclopaedia Britannica*, 1911 edn, 'tannin'.
[107] Ukers, *Tea*, I, 516ff.
[108] *Chamber's Encyclopaedia*, 1966 edn, 'tannin'.
[109] Marks, *Clinical Effects*, 729.
[110] Clegg and Clegg, *Man*, 174.
[111] *Encyclopaedia Britannica*, 'Lister'.

internally, in doses of from one to three grams, carbolic acid will often relieve obstinate cases of vomiting and has some value as a gastric antiseptic.'[112]

The polyphenols in tea are 'astringent', 'these compounds are chemically quite distinct from hydrolysable or condensed tannins. Their reactions with protein – unlike those of tannic acid and other commercial tannins – are reversible and there is no evidence that they damage the intestinal mucosa.'[113] Furthermore, it is likely that the tea polyphenols, containing other condensed tannins, act in a different antibacterial way than that of phenol (carbolic acid).

What might be surmised to have happened is as follows. In the Assamese jungles many hundreds of thousands of years ago a plant evolved which in its struggle for survival developed a number of substances in its leaves. One was caffeine, a stimulant which no doubt attracted certain birds and animals. Yet it also had to produce defences against the numerous bacteria in the forest with a very powerful defence mechanism in the form of tannin. This most powerful of germicides or paraciticides was one of the properties which gave it that medicinal virtue which was recognized when it was taken on its long journey to China, Japan and ultimately Europe and the world. When it was cured lightly, the worst of the bitterness removed, it provided a drink attractive for its stimulating effect. 'The ingestion of caffeine in even moderate doses, e.g. 250 mg, significantly increases work production and the ability to withstand prolonged strenuous exercise.'[114] This was obviously welcome to the hard-working Japanese and Chinese populations. The fact that it also stimulates the mind, and encourages wakefulness and concentration, made it attractive for the early religious communities where it was carefully tended. Without this feature, it would never have been spread by humans. Yet it also contained an astringent, bitter, agent which, when boiled in water and even without full boiling, would destroy most harmful bacteria.

Various clues as to the bacteriostatic effects of tea occur throughout the literature. In Assam the seed of tea is 'eaten locally as a cure for dysentery and fever.'[115] It was discovered that tea was a powerful protection against impure water. The Swedish explorer Peter Kalm wrote:

> It is necessary for me to admit that tea has been extremely useful in my travels through savage countries, where one cannot carry wine or other drinks, and where the water is generally undrinkable, being polluted and infected by insects. In such cases the water becomes a very agreeable drink when, having boiled it, one drinks it with an infusion of tea. I cannot sufficiently praise the taste of the water treated

[112] *Encyclopaedia Britannica*, 'carbolic acid'.
[113] Marks, *Clinical Effects*, 730; cf. also Stagg and Millin, *Tea*, 1447.
[114] Marks, *Clinical Effects*, 723.
[115] Kingdon-Ward, *Manipur*, 196.

thus; moreover it restores the strength of the exhausted traveller. In the same way as a number of explorers who have travelled in the virgin forests of America, I have constantly been put to the test. In these tiring excursions tea is as indispensable as food.[116]

A Professor Sheng is quoted as follows: 'Tea is important to prevent the accumulation of the neutral fat in the blood, reduce chloresterol and increase the elasticity of the wall of blood vessels. It plays a certain role in the prevention of atherosclerosis and cerebral apoplexy, and has some effects on chronic nephritis, acute hepatitis, diabetes, and leukemia; it can also help inhibit rheumatic arthritis.'[117]

The most thorough assessment of the possible medical effects of tea has been made by Stagg and Millin. They point out that tea seems to have been found effective against a number of diseases. 'Tea was used extensively in combating plague in Japan during an epidemic in 1951 and this had led to its exploitation as an adjunct in the treatment of several diseases including dysentery (where the diuretic property of caffeine supplements the antibacterial function of polyphenols).' They suggest that it 'probably has therapeutic value in the prevention of dental caries and the prophylaxis and treatment of vascular and coronary disorders including atherosclerosis.' Most importantly they report on tests that have been done with tea, and give a summary of the probable medical benefits. In relation to the tests, 'Infusions of green tea were found to act bacteriostatically *in vitro* on Typhoid bacillus, *Shigella paradysenteriae*, *Shigella dysenteriae*, *Staphylococcus aureas*, *Salmonella typhosa*, *Bivrio cholera* and *Leuconostoc mesenteroides*.'[118] In other words, a number of the worst stomach infections, typhoid, dysentery and cholera among them, are affected by tea.

Stagg and Mikin's findings on typhoid had been anticipated. As early as 1885 it had been noted that 'Infusion with tea and other astringent vegetables is also good in emergencies, and generally renders organic matter harmless. Cases have been observed where typhoid fever has been apparently spread by drinking-water; but the disease was confined to those who drank it in its ordinary condition, whereas those who took it in the form of tea escaped. In such a case protection is doubly afforded by the water having been boiled, and also by the action of the tannin as a coagulating and precipitating agent.'[119] Again, in 1923, an American army doctor, Major J.G. McNaught, is quoted as having shown that 'The typhoid germ, in pure culture, becomes greatly diminished in

---

[116] Brand, *Les Grandes Cultures*, 218.
[117] Goodwin, *Gunpowder Gardens*, 60–1.
[118] Stagg and Millin, *Tea*, 1451, 1453, 1451.
[119] Murphy, *Our Homes*, 797–8.

numbers by an exposure of four hours to tea. After 20 hours it was impossible to recover it at all from the cold tea.'[120]

If this account is basically correct, it helps to explain why a country as thickly populated as Japan suffered so little from enteric disease, in particular bacillary and amoebic dysentery. When the Japanese population were drinking tea they were also daily drinking pints of powerful antiseptic. We may note King's observation that all hygienic measures will fail to provide 'absolute safety' unless they have 'the equivalent effect of boiling water, long ago adopted by the Mongolian races, and which destroys active disease germs at the latest moment before using.'[121] The destruction of the germs at 'the latest moment before using' was doubly efficient because of the antiseptic content of that boiled water. Tea is probably 'after water, the world's most popular beverage,' being cheap, exhilarating and health-inducing.[122] Having conquered the third of the world's population that lived in China and Japan, it then began its next move, to Europe and ironically, by way of the British Empire, to India and beyond.

Tea was first mentioned in European sources in 1559 and Ukers provides a good general survey of the introduction of the beverage into Europe and England.[123] 'The first cargoes of tea are thought to have arrived at Amsterdam in 1610.'[124] In France the new drink is not mentioned until the 1630s. Tea was 'first served to the public in England in 1657', when it was drunk very weak, with sugar but without milk. It was 'brewed, kept in a cask, then drawn and warmed up for customers as they asked for it.'[125]

At first tea was very expensive and hence a great luxury. Famously it was drunk by Mrs Pepys, as Pepys recorded in his Diary on 25 September 1660; it was drunk partly for medicinal reasons as it was thought that it would be good for his wife's cough. When it first reached the London market 'it was sold for the remarkable price of £3-10s a pound.' Then 'the price dropped to about £2 in nine or ten years', when it became available in every coffee house. Yet it remained a luxury drink throughout the seventeenth and early eighteenth century. In noble families, for example the Bedford family of Woburn Abbey, considerable quantities were bought and drunk from 1685 onwards.[126] By

---

[120] Ukers, *Tea*, I, 557.
[121] King, *Farmers*, 323; Needham had noted the remark made in about +1126 in China that 'Even when the common people are travelling they take care only to drink boiled water.' (Needham, *Clerks*, 362).
[122] Marks, *Clinical Effects*, 707.
[123] Ukers, *Tea*, I, chsIII, IV.
[124] Braudel, *Civilization and Capitalism*, 250.
[125] Ferguson, *Drink*, 24.
[126] Scott Thompson, *Noble Household*, 169–70.

1710 in London about half of the tradesmen who left inventories had tea equipment.[127]

In Holland 'even in the 1660s when enough tea was being shipped by the East Indian Company to send the price plummeting from a hundred gilders a pound to ten, it remained too expensive to replace ale as the drink of the people.'[128] By 1700 the importation was about 20,000 lb a year. Ten years later, the 'figure was trebled.' 'In 1715 the market was flooded with Chinese green tea and in 1760 duty was paid on over five million pounds.'[129] We are told that the consumption did not 'become considerable until 1720–30 when direct trade between Europe and China began.' Before then, most tea had come by way of Batavia (Indonesia), carried by the Dutch. By 1787, some 17,800,000 lb was being imported in to England. This massive increase was noted by George Staunton, who estimated that in the century since 1693, there had been a four hundred fold increase in the export of tea from China.[130] Other figures suggest an increase from 4,713 lb imported in 1678 by the East India Company, to 370,323 lb drunk in 1725; to 5,648,000 lb in 1775 to 23,730,150 lb in 1801.[131]

At the end of the eighteenth century in England Staunton estimated that 'more than a pound weight each, in the course of a year, for the individuals of all ranks, ages and sexes' was consumed.[132] Other estimates are higher than this. Some suggest that the average consumption was over 2 lb per person per annum. 'By the end of the century the amount imported was over twenty million pound, that is, about 2 lb per head of the population.' But this was only the official figures. 'It was estimated that in 1766 as much reached England illegally as came through the proper channels.'[133] Hobhouse estimates 2.5 lb per annum, per head.[134] It is suggested that a pound of tea can make almost 300 cups[135] which would suggest that an adult, on average, was drinking at least two cups of tea a day, a lot less than the Japanese but still a large amount. The chronology suggests an amazingly rapid growth from the 1730s onwards, with tea spreading through the whole population. Kames observed how even the poorest recipients of charity would drink tea twice a day.[136]

---

[127] Shammas, *Consumer*, 183.
[128] Schama, *Embarrassment*, 171–2.
[129] Drummond, *Food*, 203.
[130] In Braudel, *Structures*, 251.
[131] *Chamber's Encyclopaedia*, 1895 edn, 'tea'; other figures, different but roughly in line with these, are given in Forrest, *Tea*, 284. See also the same authors *World Tea Trade* for further details. Shammas, *Consumer*, 297, provides figures which show that tea was a mass consumption article by the 1740s.
[132] Quoted in Braudel, *Structures*, 251.
[133] Drummond, *Food*, 203.
[134] Hobhouse, *Seeds*, 114.
[135] Tannahill, *Food in History*, 268.
[136] Kames, *Sketches*, III, 83.

Interestingly, 'only a tiny part of Western Europe – Holland and England – had taken to the new drink on a large scale. France consumed a tenth of its own cargoes at the most, Germany preferred coffee, Spain hardly tried it.' As it spread, the argument about its virtues or possible dangers increased. A medical student defended a thesis on the virtues of tea in France in 1648, but 'Some of our doctors burned a copy of the thesis.' Ten years later, another thesis 'under the patronage of the Chancellor Seguier (who was himself a fervent tea addict) celebrated the virtues of the new drink.'[137] In Holland it was 'first recommended by moral physicians like Johannes van Helmont as a restorative against loss of body fluids from excessive sweating and purges.'[138] In England it was advertized as 'That excellent and by all Physicians approved, China drink, called by the Chineans, Tcha, by other Nations Tay or Tee', and was sold at the Sultans Head near the Royal Exchange.[139] Thomas Trotter in his *View of the Nervous Temperament* argued that tea, as well as other commodities like coffee and tobacco 'had once been used as medicines, but had been reduced to necessities.'[140] Various broadsides and manuscripts extolled its virtues, and doctors and others echoed their praise.[141] Curteis in 1704 thought that it 'comforts the head and Stomach, assisting the Memory and promoting Digestion; dispels Drouziness, Headaches, Vertigo's, &c is friendly to the Nerves; useful to Gouty, Rheumatic, and Hypochondriac Persons; opens Obstructions; cleanses the Blood and Kidneys, and is a good antidote against the Stone or Gravel.' He noted that the '*Chinese* use it as a great remedy in most of these Cases.'[142]

Thomas Short in his *Dissertation upon Tea* of 1730 reported various experiments which showed that when 'salt of tea' was added to blood, it separated the 'blood serum'. It furthermore helped to preserve meat from becoming rotten. He listed the diseases against which it was a good preservative, including 'diseases of the head', 'thickness of the blood', diseases of the eye, ulcers, gout, the stone , obstructions of the bowels and many others.[143] In 1772 the well-known doctor Lettsom wrote a *Natural History of the Tea-Tree, with Observations on the Medical Qualities of Tea* along the same lines. He similarly undertook experiments to show that beef immersed in green tea water took 72 hours to become putrid, while beef immersed in ordinary water was rotten in 48 hours. From this and other experiments he concluded that 'It is evident from these experiments, that both green and bohea Tea posseses an antiseptic (Exper. I) and astringent (Exper. II), applied to the dead animal fibre'. His third

[137] Braudel, *Structures*, 252,250.
[138] Schama, *Embarrassment*, 171.
[139] Ferguson, *Drink*, 241.
[140] Porter and Porter, *In Sickness*, 220.
[141] Ukers, *Tea*, I, 31–2,39–40 quotes a number of the accounts.
[142] Curteis, *Essays*, 100.
[143] Short, *Dissertation*, 40–61.

experiment, injecting tea and ordinary water from the first experiment into the abdomen of a frog showed that while tea had no effect, the ordinary water led to rigidity and loss of motion in the frog's legs.[144]

Others, most famously John Wesley, Jonas Hanway, Arthur Young and William Cobbett, attacked tea-drinking with vehemence.[145] Indeed, the comments of those opposed to tea suggests how widely tea drinking had spread. In 1744 Duncan Forbes wrote: 'But when the opening a Trade with the *East-Indies* . . . brought the Price of Tea . . . so low, that the *meanest* labouring Man could compass the Purchase of it', when connections with Sweden 'introduced the common Use of that Drug amongst the *lowest* of the People' even in Scotland, 'and when Tea and Punch became thus the *Diet* and *Debauch* of all the *Beer* and *Ale* Drinkers, the effects were very *suddenly* and very *severely* felt.'[146]

Tea was very widely drunk from the middle of the eighteenth century. Le Blanc wrote in the 1740s: 'In several parts of England, a farmer's servant drinks his tea, before he goes to plow.'[147] In 1751 Charles Deering published a book about Nottinghamshire. He wrote as follows:

> The People here are not without their Tea, Coffee and Chocolate, especially the first, the Use of which is spread to that Degree, that not only the Gentry and Wealthy Traders drink it constantly, but almost every Seamer, Sizer and Winder, will have her Tea and will enjoy herself over it in a Morning, . . . and even a Common Washerwoman thinks she had not had a proper Breakfast without Tea and hot buttered white Bread . . . being the other Day at a Grocers, I could not forbear looking earnestly and with some Degree of Indignation at a ragged and greasy Creature, who came into the Shop with two Children following her in as dismal a Plight as the Mother, asking for a Pennyworth of Tea and a Half pennyworth of Sugar, which when she was served with, she told the Shop-keeper: Mr N. I do not know how it is with me, but I can assure you I would not desire to live, if I was to be debarred from drinking every Day a little Tea.[148]

In 1784 Rochefoucauld wrote 'Throughout the whole of England the drinking of tea is general. You have it twice a day and, though the expense is considerable, the humblest peasant has his tea twice a day just like the rich man; the total consumption is immense.' Even more specifically he later observed 'that it is reckoned that in the course of the year every single person, man or women, on the average consumes four pounds of tea. That is truly enormous.'[149] In 1809

---

144 Lettsom, *Natural History*, 39ff.
145 Ukers, *Tea*, I, 47–8; Cobbett, *Cottage Economy*, 20–9.
146 Drummond, *Food*, 204.
147 Quoted in George (ed.), *England in Johnson's day*, 15.
148 Quoted in Marshall, *English People*, 172.
149 Rochefoucauld, *Frenchman*, 23,26.

Geijer described how 'Next to water tea is the Englishman's proper element. All classes consume it, and if one is out on the London streets early in the morning, one may see in many places small tables set up under the open sky, round which coal-carters and workmen empty their cups of delicious beverage.'[150]

By the end of the eighteenth century, Eden wrote 'Any person who will give himself the trouble of stepping into the cottages of Middlesex and Surrey at meal-times, will find, that, in poor families, tea is not only the usual beverage in the morning and evening, but is generally drank in large quantities at dinner.' Drummond notes that in Eden's surveys of diet, beer is 'seldom met with in the estimates quoted by Eden. Tea and sugar, on the other hand, are almost universal.' He then quotes Eden to the effect that 'They [farm labourers] seldom, however, can afford to purchase beer, and in its place, have very generally in this part of the country, substituted tea at every meal.' We are told that 'it was not uncommon for two pounds a year to be so spent when the total income was only a matter of forty pounds a year.' Arthur Young was surprised that 'the inmates of the Nacton House of Industry, who were allowed to spend 2d. out of every shilling they earned on food, almost invariably bought tea and sugar with this money.'[131]

Jonas Hanway asked 'When will this evil stop?', after pointing out that no less than four million pounds had been imported a year or so before, he wrote 'Your very *Chambermaids* have lost their bloom, I suppose by *sipping tea*.' Most historians have sided with him when he proclaimed 'What an *army* has *gin* and *tea* destroyed!' and indeed Hanway's harangue against tea may be one of the reasons for its later bad reputation. But his vehemence certainly indicates that its consumption was widespread. 'Nay, your servants servants, down to the very beggars, will not be satisfied unless they consume the produce of so remote a country as China.' Or again, 'There is a certain lane near RICHMOND where BEGGARS are often seen in the summer drinking their tea. You may see it drunk in cinder carts; and what is no less absurd, sold out in cups to hay-makers.' Furthermore, 'Look into all the cellars in LONDON, you will find men and women sipping their tea, in the morning or afternoon, and very often both morning AND afternoon.'[152]

His diatribe was answered by Samuel Johnson[153] who admitted that he was 'a hardened and shameless Tea-drinker, who has for twenty years diluted his meals with only the infusion of this fascinating plant, whose kettle has scarcely time to cool, who with Tea amuses the evening, with Tea solaces the midnight, and with Tea welcomes the morning.'[154] The Rev. Sydney Smith was equally

---

[150] Quoted in Wilson, *Strange Island*, 154.
[151] Quoted in Drummond, *Food*, 104, 210, 204, 204.
[152] Hanway, *Essay on Tea*, 243–5.
[153] Boswell, *Life of Johnson*, I, 313–4; Review of Hanway in Johnson, *Works*, II, 389–404.
[154] Johnson, *Works*, II, 390.

enthusiastic. 'Thank God for tea! What would the world do without tea? I am glad that I was not born before tea.'[155] A more measured approach was shown by Dr Buchan. 'Much has been said on the ill effects of tea in diet. They are, no doubt, numerous; but they proceed rather from the imprudent use of it, than from any bad qualities in the tea itself.' He continued that 'Good tea, taken in moderate quantity, not too strong, nor too hot, nor drank upon an empty stomach, will seldom do harm; but if it be bad, which is often the case, or substituted in the room of solid food, it must have many ill effects.'[156]

The power of tea was thought to lie in an essence or ingredient which people tried to extract. Mr Lawrence at his Toy Shop, in 1709 offered a 'Chimical Quintessence of Bohee-tea, and Cocoa Nuts, wherein the Volatile Salt, oil and spirit of them both, are chymically extracted and united.' Drummond thought he was merely seizing 'the opportunity of making money out of a gullible public by selling them the essential medicinal essence of tea.'[157]

We may conclude that in Japan the drinking of tea played a similar role to that of beer in England. It made it possible for even the poor to avoid unboiled water. Furthermore, tea contained a substance, often earlier called 'tannin', but in fact a mixture of polyphenols, which is a powerful disinfectant. This added to its health-preserving effects and may be one of the major reasons why a dense and urbanized population managed to avoid most of the enteric diseases until the later nineteenth century. Nor was this an entirely unintended consequence, for the earliest writers on tea had been aware of its therapeutic and medicinal value.

These virtues were transferred to England from the early eighteenth century when the craze for tea began. Soon tea was taking over from beer as the national drink. There is not much evidence that it was drunk for its medicinal value, but its stimulating and pleasant effects and relative cheapness made it attractive. The healthful properties were largely an unintended consequence but may have been dramatic. Christopher Hann suggests in relation to the rapid spread of tea in the colder parts of Turkey 'the frequent regular glasses of piping hot tea consumed by those at work, each glass filled with sugar cubes . . . must be satisfying urgent calorific requirements.'[158]

One of the main features of the fall in mortality in the eighteenth century, according to Malthus and others, was the decline in dysentery. A major part of the explanation for this may have been tea-drinking, particularly among the poorer parts of the population and may not only have affected the drinkers themselves. Just as we have become more aware of the indirect effects of 'passive smoking', so the fact that mothers did not have dysentery probably helped to

---

[155] Quoted in Ukers, *Tea*, I, 48.
[156] Buchan, *Domestic*, 66, 67.
[157] Drummond, *Food*, 205.
[158] Hann, *Tea*, 78; Wolf, *People*, 333 makes a similar suggestion.

prevent their infants from suffering those most important of infant killers, infant and weanling diarrhoea.

Another side effect is worth noting. Dorothy George long ago argued that the 'orgy of spirit-drinking' was the main reason for a rise in mortality in London in the period 1720–50. Suddenly after 1751 gin drinking largely disappeared as a problem. She explained this mainly as result of the Act of 1751 and the subsequent increase in excise duty on gin. There was a drop from 6–7 million gallons of gin a year before 1751 to 1–3 million gallons in the period 1760–90, despite a rapid growth in London's population.[159] It seems unlikely that this rapid conversion from gin would have been possible without the sudden influx of a cheap and stimulating substitute which also avoided the necessity of drinking polluted water.

In the first decades of the nineteenth century, as the improvement in health became apparent, several authors suggested that perhaps the reason for this was tea-drinking. Blane wrote that '*Tea* is an article universally grateful to the British population and has to a certain extent supplanted intoxicating liquors in all ranks, to the great advantage of society. . . . The modern use of tea has probably contributed to the longevity of the inhabitants of this country.'[160] Even more interestingly, the founder of the modern census, Rickman, in correspondence with d'Invernois in 1827, modestly wrote, 'It is not for Mr Rickman to assign causes of the decrease of mortality; if he might venture further than in the Preliminary Observations to the Census of 1811 and 1821 . . . he would ascribe it to the general use of tea and sugar.'[161] Neither of them was in a position to see why this association should be there, beyond the replacement of 'intoxicating liquors'. We can now build on their insight. It may help to explain a paradox noted by Shammas, that the eighteenth century witnessed *both* a decline in the nutritional status of the poor *and* an improvement in health. Tea is less nutritionally useful than beer, as we have seen, yet simultaneously led to an improvement in *health*. The same paradox can be found in the case of clothing, where the thin cottons were less satisfactory in many ways in terms of warmth and comfort for ordinary people, but may have been of great importance in improving health.

Most deaths in earlier populations occurred in the first year of life. The effects of changing drinking patterns on infants and their parents is therefore worth particular examination. The puzzle in the English case is two-fold. Firstly, for much of the period up to the later seventeenth century, infant mortality rates, at about 150 per thousand, were relatively low. One important

[159] George, *Some Causes*, 333–5.
[160] Quoted in George, *London*, 329–30, n103.
[161] Minutes of Evidence, Population Bill Committee 1830 quoted in George, *London*, 329–30, n103.

contributory factor here seems to have been infant feeding. As we shall see, it was customary for English infants to be breast-fed by their own mothers for up to about one year. This would give them reasonable protection against enteric disease. It is at this point that another danger emerges, namely the withdrawal of breast-milk and the substitution of other foods and drink. It is here that the widespread availability of a cheap alternative to water, namely small beer, was important in England.

It seems likely that until the 1680s, when the cost of beer went up with increased malt taxes, infants drank beer when they were weaned. Even in the early eighteenth century Thomas Tryon wrote 'Also no Children ought to drink any kind of strong Drink: I could commend Water, as the most wholesome; but it being contrary to our Custom, ordinary Beer may well do, or rather small Ale.'[162] Alice Clark wrote that 'It must be remembered that before the introduction of cheap sugar, beer was considered almost equally essential for human existence as bread. Beer was drunk at every meal, and formed part of the ordinary diet of even small children.'[163] Likewise Keith Thomas writes that 'Beer was a basic ingredient in everyone's diet, children as well as adults.'[164] Pullar concludes that 'water was impure, and children who were weaned had always drunk very small beer.'[165] Drummond noted that 'small beer' was 'the ordinary table drink even of young children.'[166]

Yet as beer became more expensive perhaps poorer families would have had to supplement it with water, or equally damaging, cow's milk. It is therefore unlikely to be a coincidence that the infant mortality rates began suddenly to rise in the decade 1680–90 from the range of 150–60 per thousand to about 175–85 per thousand.[167] They stayed at these higher levels until the decade 1740–50, when they dropped back to the earlier levels. This drop is particularly surprising since it occurred just as London began to expand very fast and other cities became more crowded.

There is no obvious change in breast-feeding in general to account for this since only a tiny part of the population had ever sent their children to wet-nurses. Attention has therefore focused on another theory. This is that the increased use of colostrum, that is the highly beneficial secretion in mother's breasts at birth, caused the reduction in mortality. Ole Benedictow argues that 'It therefore seems that the greater part of the decline in infant mortality . . . must be ascribed to the change back to immediate breast feeding,

---

[162] Tryon, *Cleanliness*, 16.
[163] Clark, *Working Women*, 223.
[164] Thomas, *Religion*, 18.
[165] Pullar, *Consuming Passions*, 155.
[166] Drummond, *Food*, 114.
[167] I am extremely grateful to Dr Roger Schofield for these figures.

a change that was strongly recommended in the proto-scientific works on medicine produced by physicians and midwives during this period.'[168]

Fildes agrees that 'in the absence of any other factor that can be identified as relevant, sufficiently effective, and showing change in the same period, it seems reasonable to attribute the improvement in neonatal survival between the late seventeenth and early nineteenth century to changes in ideas and practice of neonatal feeding, particularly early maternal breastfeeding.' A 'Change towards early maternal breastfeeding during the eighteenth century contributed to a notable decline in mortality (0–28 days) and a decrease in maternal morbidity and mortality from milk fever.'[169]

There are a number of difficulties with this argument. The fall in infant mortality began in the 1740s, while Hunter's experimental feeding scheme, which Fildes argues was the main reason for a change to more immediate breastfeeding and use of colostrum, started in 1750. Furthermore, Fildes' evidence is largely concerned with the upper classes. She can only conjecture that 'It is probable that Hunter's findings would have spread slowly among the poor by word of mouth.'[170] Even this 'slow' spread cannot be assumed. As Landers points out 'Arguments of this kind are often difficult to accept because of the strictly limited influence which "leading edge" medical opinion and practice are likely to have had among the population.'[171] What seems certain is that it would have taken ten or twenty years for the new opinions to spread widely, too late to account for the change.

In fact, it seems likely that the explanation for a dramatic fall in infant and maternal morality in the first three months after birth lies in a combination of other environmental factors. In particular, the rapid growth of tea consumption among the poor and middling groups, starting in London and then spreading over the whole country fits the chronology much better than does the colostrum argument. That the cause of the change lay in wider changes in the environment and not specifically in breast-feeding practices is further supported by the fact that while maternal and infant mortality dropped significantly in the first three months after birth, so, equally, did paternal mortality. Mothers were still six times more likely to die in the sixty days after birth than their co-resident male partners as the changes took place, but the ratio remained roughly the same. Indeed, the ratio moved from 6 : 1 to 7 : 1 in the crucial period between 1750 and 1770.[172] In other words husbands had also dramatically improved their health. In

[168] Benedictow, *Milky*, 28.
[169] Fildes, *Breasts*, 87–9.
[170] Fildes, *Breasts*, 86–7.
[171] Landers, *Death*, 357, n9.
[172] I am most grateful to Dr Jim Oeppen for informing me of this finding, which will appear in the forthcoming work on 'English Population History from Parish Reconstitutions' by Wrigley, E.A, Davies, R.S., Oeppen, J. and Schofield, R.S.

fact the whole family was much healthier. This is more consistent with the effects of general environmental changes, and in particular the effects of tea-drinking which would have cut back the rates of infant diarrhoea (through infections caught from the mother), and adult dysentery and other enteric infections, than it is with the specific mother-infant changes to breast-feeding or greater use of colostrum. The presence of a cheap alternative to water or milk was probably equally important as the child was weaned and helped avoid much of the 'weanling-diarrhoea' complex.

Obviously single-factor explanations are not sufficient. Yet it does seem likely that changes in drinking habits in England were significant. England was noted as the most assiduous beer and then tea-drinking nation in Europe. It was a pattern, in relation to tea, which had been established even earlier in Japan. Drink is likely to have had a very significant effect on the escape from the Malthusian trap on these two islands.

9

Two Methods for the Disposal of Human Excrement

That both England and Japan in their different ways avoided drinking unboiled water is of the first importance in explaining the disease patterns on these two islands. Yet heavily polluted water could still have caused illness in other ways, so we need to look at the treatment of the most serious cause of pollution – animal and human excrement. This topic has wide ramifications for health; for instance, manure is the prime breeding ground for flies, one of the most danger-ous of disease vectors. Is there anything special in the way in which the English and Japanese dealt with the problem of organic waste disposal?

Most societies face major sanitary problems. As the number and density of human beings increase, and likewise the number of the animals upon which they depend, so the excreta of both multiples. This excrement is difficult to dispose of. Normally it is allowed to lie about, or flushed into the water system. Micro-organisms then infect human beings in various ways.

This problem is of marginal importance in lightly settled and mobile hunter-gatherer or pastoral societies, but as population density rises and people live close together in towns and cities, it grows exponentially. While such close and crowded living may well be a successful economic strategy it is likely to lead to high mortality.

It may be that human beings have evolved some primitive instincts which cope with this danger of contamination and which work reasonably well with fairly light populations. People appear to feel a widespread disgust about their excreta. This may be cultural, an aversion to those boundary substances which are neither in the body nor fully outside the body,[1] or it may be some biological

---

[1] Douglas, *Purity and Danger*; Thomas, *Cleanliness*, 81.

drive. Whatever the reason, it has meant that most human beings try to avoid the smell and sight of their own decomposing body matter.

In relation to Japan, we cannot understand how human excrement was dealt with without taking account of geography. In this case, the background was the nature of the soil in Japan and the necessities of feeding the growing population. 'The soil of Japan, in itself, is for the major part, mountainous, rocky and barren' and only through the 'indefatigable care and industry of the Natives' was it made 'fruitful enough to supply them with all manner of necessaries.'[2] Siebold echoed this view. 'The soil is naturally sterile, but the labour bestowed upon it, aided by judicious irrigation, and all the manure that can in any way be collected, conquers its natural defects, and is repaid by abundant harvests.'[3] 'Without manure they do not cultivate; the soil is not rich in productive materials, as it is mostly of volcanic origin. A Japanese saying is, "A new field gives but a small crop." '[4]

The problem was exacerbated by the fact that most of Japan was so mountainous that only a small part could be used for agriculture. 'In this land of mountains, barely twelve per cent of the entire surface can be cultivated, and even the cultivable portion is not highly fertile by nature. It is made so by subsoil working, by minutely careful weeding, by manure judiciously and laboriously applied, by terracing, and by an elaborate method of irrigation.'[5] The application of large amounts of manure was absolutely necessary. The small amount of cultivated land and enormous amount of fertilizer needed was described by King. 'If we state in round numbers the total nitrogen, phosphorus and potassium thus far enumerated which Japanese farmers apply or return annually to their twenty or twenty-one square miles of cultivated fields, the case stands 385,214 tons of nitrogen, 91,656 tons of phosphorus and 255,778 tons of potassium.'[6]

Also related to the ecology of these mountainous islands was the supply of animal manure, the main source of fertilizer in most agrarian civilizations. The number of domestic animals, even chickens, was small and the manure of those animals that did exist was carefully husbanded. Thunberg observed that 'it is a very common spectacle to see old men and children following the horses that are used in travelling, with a shell (*Haliotis tuberculata*) fastened to the end of a stick, in order to collect the ordure from off the highways, which is carried home in a basket.'[7] Morse echoed his observation. 'With the number of pack-horses and

[2] Kaempfer, *History*, I, 161.
[3] Von Siebold, *Manners*, 231.
[4] Morse, *Day*, I, 24.
[5] Chamberlain, *Things*, 19.
[6] King, *Farmers*, 213.
[7] Thunberg, *Travels*, IV, 82.

cattle that one sees on the road one is surprised at the absence of manure. There seems to be a class of men – at least they all are old men – whose duty it is to sweep up this material, not for the road's cleanliness, but for its value as dressing for the land.'[8] The results were impressive. 'There is no part of the world, where manure is gathered with greater care than it is here, insomuch that nothing that can be converted to this use is thrown away or lost.'[9]

'They are very dexterous and skilful in manuring their Ground, which they do in various ways, and with many different substances.'[10] The Japanese used everything they could. 'In some fields they were ploughing in weeds and vege-tables, apparently as manure.' Alcock added that 'horse manure and seaweed are both used, but the latter only suits a certain few crops.'[11] The mountains were scoured for leaves and vegetation which were rotted down or dug into the soil. 'The first cutting of this hill herbage is mainly used on the rice fields as green manure, it being tramped into the mud between the rows.' Then 'The second and third cuttings of herbage from the *genya* lands in Japan are used for the preparation of compost applied on the dry-land fields in the fall or in the spring of the following season.'[12] However, such green vegetation and sea-weed could only supply a small part of the need.

With the long sea–coast, fish manure was another obvious way to try and meet the deficit. Fish were rotted down and spread on the fields. 'Millions of small fish lie drying along shore, to be used as manure.'[13] Morse noted how 'a great many cargoes of fish manure are brought from Hakodate',[14] while Hayami tells us that 'Sardines caught and dried in the fishing villages of eastern Japan could be transported more than 500 kilometres (300 miles) to Osaka to be used as fertilizer for cotton cultivation in the surrounding villages.'[15] The extreme shortage of fertilizer encouraged the development of a sophisticated marketing and transport system:

By the mid-eighteenth century, for example, fish caught off Tohoku were being brought to shore, unloaded, dried, baled, reloaded aboard coasting vessels, shipped south to Choshi, transferred to river boats, hauled up the Tone to its south fork, sent down to Edo, punted over to riverbank warehouses, unloaded and stored, sold, reloaded on boats to go out into the Tama region, punted down the

[8] Morse, *Day*, I, 153, see fig.127.
[9] Thunberg, *Travels*, IV, 82.
[10] Kaempfer, *History*, I, 186.
[11] Alcock, *Tycoon*, II, 143,476.
[12] King, *Farmers*, 209.
[13] Griffis, *Mikado*, 546.
[14] Morse, *Day*, I, 24.
[15] Hayami, *Transformation*, 5.

coast and upstream, unloaded, hauled overland to villages, and finally carried out to the fields and applied.[16]

Yet fish and green manure combined could supply only a small part of what was required. We need therefore to turn to what King described as 'One of the most remarkable agricultural practices adopted by any civilized people' that is the 'centuries-long and well nigh universal conservation and utilization of all human waste in China, Korea and Japan, turning it to marvellous account in the maintenance of soil fertility and in the production of food.'[17]

Speaking of night soil, or human excrement, Morse reported that 'the immense value and importance of this material is so great to the Japanese farmer, who depends entirely upon it for the enrichment of his soil, that in the country personal conveniences for travellers are always arranged by the side of the road, in the shape of buckets or half-barrels sunk in the ground.'[18] This practice had been noticed by Kaempfer: 'care is taken, that the filth of travellers be not lost, and there are in several places, near country people's houses or in their fields, houses of office built for them to do their needs.'[19] Thunberg gave a particularly full account of the collecting of urine from passers by: 'Nay, even urine itself, which the Europeans so seldom turn to the advantage of their fields, is here carefully collected in large earthen pots, which are to be found sunk in the earth here and there in different parts, not only in the villages, but even beside the highways.'[20] Even within built-up areas methods were developed to collect the urine of passers-by. 'A privy, which is necessary for every house, is always built in the Japanese villages towards the street, and at the side of the mansion-house; it is open downwards, so that the passengers may discharge their waters from the outside into a large jar, which is sunk on the inside into the earth.'[21]

In the villages, the precious commodity was carefully collected. In a community near Tokyo in the early twentieth century, 'Once a year, in fact, the terrace people were given what they called "dung cakes". A local farmer used regularly to bring along a cart and buy up all the night soil from the communal toilet; then, at the end of the year, he'd take them some of the special rice used for making rice cakes to thank them for the year's supply of "dung" ... "you can see 'business' has been good this year – there are plenty of dung cakes", we'd joke to each other.' Landlords would build tenements specifically 'to obtain a ready

[16] Totman, *Peasants*, 466.
[17] King, *Farmers*, 193.
[18] Morse, *Homes*, 232.
[19] Kaempfer, *History*, II, 293–4.
[20] Thunberg, *Travels*, IV, 82.
[21] Thunberg, *Travels*, III, 144.

supply of fertilizer for their fields.'[22] Likewise in the towns human excrement had a market value. Morse wrote that 'I was told in Hiroshima in the renting of the poorer tenement houses, if three persons occupied a room together the sewage paid the rent of one, and if five occupied the same room no rent was charged!'[23] The excreta might even be sub-divided. 'The value of human wastes was so high that rights of ownership to its components were assigned to different parties. In Osaka, the rights to fecal matter from the occupants of a dwelling belonged to the owner of the building whereas the urine belonged to the tenants. Feces were considered more valuable and hence commanded a higher price.'[24]

The commodity became more and more valuable, so that 'as the price of fish and other fertilizers rose, the value of night soil rose correspondingly, and vegetables were no longer sufficient to pay for it. By the early eighteenth century, with the increase in new paddies in the Osaka area, the price of fertilizer had jumped to the point that even night soil had to be purchased with silver.' The competition for night soil even led to open conflict. 'In the summer of 1724, two groups of villages from the Yamazaki and Takatsuki areas fought over the rights to collect night soil from various parts of the city.'[25] Even in the 1930s 'every scrap of human manure is used to-day. ... The school and village office rent out the right to collect their night-soil.'[26]

In the early twentieth century a woman recollected how, 'When the mother-in-law stepped out of the house, she did not go beyond the village boundary, because she said, she didn't want to waste any human manure. Whenever the young wife left the house, her mother-in-law would tell her, 'If you feel like relieving yourself while you're out, be sure to run into our field." '[27] Ronald Dore in the 1950s remembered past days 'when people told stories about stingy guests who would hurry home when they felt their sphincters tightening so as not to give away valuable fertilizer.'[28]

The immense amount of human manure applied to the fields was analysed by King. 'Japan produced, in 1908, and applied to her fields, 23,850,295 tons of human manure; 22,812,787 tons of compost; and she imported 753,074 tons of commercial fertilizers, 7,000 of which were phosphates in one form or another.' Human manure alone he estimated as 1.75 tons per acre of cultivated land. Calculating 'the average amount of excreta per day for the adult at 40 ounces, the average annual production per million of adult population is 5,794,300 pounds

[22] Saga, *Silk and Straw*, 23,17; see also 28.

[23] Morse, *Homes*, 232.

[24] Hanley, *Sanitation*, 9.

[25] Hanley, *Sanitation*, 9,10.

[26] Embree, *Suye Mura*, 35.

[27] Hane, *Rebels*, 88.

[28] Dore, *Shinohata*, 74.

of nitrogen; 1,825,000 pounds of potassium, and 775,600 pounds of phosphorus carried in 456,250 tons of excreta.'[29] Particularly important was the urine, which constituted some five-sixths of the weight. The Japanese, King worked out, 'save for plant feeding more than a ton of phosphorus (2712lbs) and more than two tons of potassium (4488lbs) per day for each million of adult population.'[30]

The first stage is the collecting of human excreta. It may be that the perception that excreta was a valuable by-product meant that defecation and urination were not considered indecent or embarrassing in Japan. Margaret Lock explains that a Japanese child 'gradually becomes aware that its body processes and everything that enters and leaves its body are being carefully monitored by its mother, and it is trained to take over these functions from her.' This has several consequences. 'This regular monitoring of the body results in a great sensitivity to bodily functions and an ability on the part of most people to discuss their own bodies in a rather objective way without embarrassment.'[31] Combined with this openness and lack of embarrassment, there is also firm discipline and control. As Gorer described the situation, 'In the life of Japanese children, the most consistent and most severe aspect is ... training in control of the sphincter.'[32]

Furthermore, the Japanese seem to have been brought up in a way which meant that they did not find the smell offensive. That the 'repugnance to faecal odors' was something new in Japan 'being learned more in the schools than at home' is suggested by Beardsley.[33] Cornell and Smith also describe how 'Strong odors invariably announce that nightsoil is being handled. However, no one particularly minds this and, in fact, a farmer of the old school is said to find this odour pleasantly suggestive of the earth's fruitfulness.'[34]

The need for fertilizer and a great concern with cleanliness led to the early development of sanitary toilet facilities. These were aesthetically and functionally designed to capture from each individual the solid and liquid wastes, ensuring that they were preserved in a state that caused minimal risk to health. Kaempfer commented on the great cleanliness of Japanese toilets, specifically the inns which he visited:

> The house of office is built on one side of the back part of the house, and hath two doors to go in. Going in you find at all times, a couple of new small mats, made

---

[29] King, *Farmers*, 194. Recent figures suggest some 4 oz of faeces and 50 oz per day of urine per adult per day (Roberts, *Hygiene*, 459), while others suggest 2.5 oz of solid and 40 oz of liquid excreta per head per day for the whole population (Notter and Firth, *Hygiene*, 227).

[30] King, *Farmers*, 74.

[31] Lock, *Medicine*, 74.

[32] Gorer, *Themes*, 111.

[33] Beardsley et al., *Village*, 88.

[34] Cornell, *Two Villages*, 130; for the strength of the smell to visitors, see Thunberg, *Travels*, III, 144.

either of straw or Spanish broom, lying ready, for the use of those persons, who do not care to touch the ground with their bare feet, although it be kept neat and clean to admiration, being always cover'd with mats. You let drop what you need, sitting after the Asiatic fashion, through a hole cut in the floor. The trough underneath is fill'd with light chaff, wherein the filth loses itself instantly. Upon the arrival of people of quality, the board, which is opposite to your face, sitting in this necessary posture, is cover'd with a clean sheet of paper, as also are the bolts of the two doors or any other part they are likely to lay hold of. Not far from the little house stands a bason fill'd with water, to wash your hands after this business is over. This is commonly an oblong rough stone, the upper part whereof is curiously cut out, into the form of a bason. A new pail of bambous hangs near it, and is cover'd with a neat fir, or cypress board, to which they put a new handle every time it hath been us'd, to wit a fresh stick of the bambou cane, it being a very clean sort of a wood, and in a manner naturally varnish'd.[35]

Many of the distinctive features of the Japanese toilet, the cleanliness, the separation of urine and faeces, the use of paper, the washing of hands, was described at the end of the sixteenth century by the Jesuit visitor Rodrigues: the Japanese

provide their guests with very clean privies set part in an unfrequented place far from the rooms. ... The interior of the privies is kept extremely clean and a perfume-pan and new paper cut for use are placed there. The privy is always clean without any bad smell, for when the guests depart the man in charge cleans it out if necessary and strews clean sand so that the place is left as if it had never been used. A ewer of clean water and other things needed for washing the hands are found nearby, for it is an invariable custom of both nobles and commoners to wash their hands every time after using the privy for their major and minor necessities.[36]

The plentiful supply of cheap paper in Japan from an early period, strong yet bio-degradable, suggests that the Japanese may have emulated the Chinese. According to Needham 'By the time of Sui dynasty the use of paper in lavatories was probably universal, as we can see from a passage written ... about +590.'[37] According to Frederic, in the medieval period 'They wiped themselves clean either with small squares of paper or little wooden sticks (*sutegi*) which they left on the spot.'[38] Thunberg likewise described the three essential features – the urinal, faeces drop and washing place. 'Every house has its *privy*; in the floor of which there is an oblong aperture, and it is over this aperture that the Japanese

---

[35] Kaempfer, *History*, II, 323–4.
[36] Quoted in Hanley, *Sanitation*, 11,19.
[37] Needham, *Clerks*, 373.
[38] Frederick, *Daily Life*, 87.

sit. At the side of the wall is a kind of a box, inclining obliquely outwards, into which they discharge their urine. Near it there is always a China vessel with water in it, with which, on these occasions, they never fail to wash their hands.'[39]

Morse described how 'In the country the privy is usually a little box-like affair removed from the house, the entrance closed half way up by a swinging door. In the city house of the better class it as at one corner of the house, usually at the end of the verandah, and sometimes there are two at diagonal corners.' Once inside, considerable trouble was taken to make the room as pleasant as possible. 'The interior of these apartments is usually simple, though sometimes presenting marvels of cabinet-work. Much skill and taste are often displayed in the approaches and exterior finish of these places.' Morse described how:

> The inner compartment has a rectangular opening cut in the floor, and in the better class of privies this is provided with a cover having a long wooden handle. The woodwork about this opening is sometimes lacquered. Straw sandals or wooden clogs are often provided to be worn in this place. ... The receptacle in the privy consists of a half of an oil barell, or a large earthen vessel, sunk in the ground, with convenient access to it from the outside. ... The urinal is usually of wood, though porcelain ones are often seen. The wooden ones are in the form of a tapering box secured against the wall of the closet. Sometimes sprays of a sweet-scented shrub are placed in these and often replaced. The refinement of the Japanese in these matters is shown by the various names applied by them to the privy, such as *Setsu-in*, snow-hide, *Chodzu-ba*, place to wash hands, *Ben-jo* and *Yo-ba*, place for business, *Koka*, back frame, etc.[40]

The attitude of the Japanese towards the toilet is described by the novelist Tanizaki, writing in 1933. 'It always stands apart from the main building, at the end of a corridor, in a grove fragrant with leaves and moss.' It is here, he believes, that meditation can take place and where, he suspects:

> haiku poets over the ages have come by a great many of their ideas. Indeed one could with some justice claim that of all the elements of Japanese architecture, the toilet is the most aesthetic. Our forebears, making poetry of everything in their lives, transformed what by rights should be the most unsanitary room in the house into a place of unsurpassed elegance. ... Compared to Westerners, who regard the toilet as utterly unclean and avoid even the mention of it in polite conversation, we are far more sensible and certainly in better taste.' The 'absolute cleanliness' which is needed is one of the factors which makes those with a taste for traditional architecture 'agree that the Japanese toilet is perfection.[41]

---

[39] Thunberg, *Travels*, III, 281.

[40] Morse, *Latrines*, 173.

[41] Tanizaki, *Shadows*, 3–5; for more recent accounts of Japanese toilets, see Engel, *The Japanese House*, 239–40; Ohnuki-Tierney, *Illness*, 30–1.

The toilets were emptied 'every few days' though it was unlucky to do so 'on days with the 10, as 10th, 20th, 30th' when 'the latrine must not be cleaned.' They were emptied in Tokyo 'by hundreds of men who have their regular routes. The buckets are suspended on carrying-sticks and the weight of these full buckets would tax a giant.'[42] The excrement of nearly a million inhabitants 'is carried off daily to the farms outside, the vessels in which it is conveyed being long cylindrical buckets borne by men and horses.'[43] 'The occasional passage of a train of porters carrying open pails of liquid manure from the town to the fields, or a string of horses laden with the same precious but "perilous stuff" may, indeed, be objected to. But the conical tubs on the horses are carefully covered over, and form, indeed, a great improvement on the open pails.'[44]

'During our ride to Akashi on the early morning train we passed long processions of carts drawn by cattle, horses or by men, moving along the country road which paralleled the railway, all loaded with the waste of the city of Kobe, going to its destination in the fields, some of it a distance of twelve miles, where it was sold at from 54 cents to $1.63 per ton.' King went on to describe the night soil carts: 'Such carts are even more frequently drawn by men than by cattle or horses, and tightly covered casks supported on saddles are borne on the backs of both cattle and horses, while men carry pails long distances on their shoulders, using the carrying pole.' By this date, certainly, the tubs were closed. 'Here, too, the night soil of the city was being removed in closed receptacles'[45] In other cities, and in earlier centuries, boats were used, as in Osaka.[46]

All this was offensive to foreign residents: ' "violets" was our password when one of these equipages was spied approaching, and was the signal for every one to bury his nose in a handkerchief.'[47] But the smell, as we have earlier seen and according to Chamberlain, 'causes no distress to native noses.'[48] 'This stuff is often transported miles into the countryside where it is allowed to remain in open half oil-barrels for a time and then is distributed to the rice-fields by means of long-handled wooden dippers.'[49] There it joined the waste from the village itself. The widespread presence of tanks where the mixture of urine and faeces were allowed to decompose was noted by Kaempfer:

> Old shoes of horses and men, which are thrown away as useless, are gather'd in the
> same houses, and burnt to ashes, along with the filth, for common dung, which

[42] Morse, *Day*, II, 311; I, 23–4.
[43] Morse, *Homes*, 232.
[44] Alcock, *Tycoon*, I, 120.
[45] King, *Farmers*, 397,197,42.
[46] Hanley, *Sanitation*, 9.
[47] Geoffrey, *Immigrant*, 45.
[48] Chamberlain, *Things*, 20.
[49] Morse, *Day*, I, 23.

they manure all their fields withal. Provisions of this nasty composition are kept in large tubs, or tuns, which are buried even with the ground, in their villages and fields, and being not cover'd, afford full as ungrateful and putrid a smell of radishes (which is the common food of country people) to tender noses, as the neatness and beauty of the road is agreeable to the eyes.[50]

By the twentieth century these 'tubs, or tuns' had become 'cement-lined pits'.[51]

Such storage was essential in two ways. First, it greatly added to the agricultural value of the mixture. 'The wastes of the body, of fuel and of fabric worn beyond other use are taken back to the field; before doing so they are housed against waste from weather, compounded with intelligence and forethought and patiently laboured with through one, three or even six months, to bring them into the most efficient form to serve as manure for the soil or as feed for the crop.'[52] The second, perhaps unintended, consequence, was to kill almost all the harmful micro-organisms. Writing about the dangers of flies in night soil, Roberts described how they could be controlled 'By close-packing the manure and relying on the heat of fermentation to destroy the larvae (220 °F kills in three minutes). The heat of fermentation may usefully conserve by covering the manure with tarpaulins, or by collecting the manure, when fresh and therefore most dangerous, in concrete receptacles.'[53] Furthermore, by keeping the night-soil in containers, the chain of fly reproduction is broken, for it is necessary for the larvae to leave the excrement at a later stage in order to survive. In a tub or barrel, they would not be able to do so and could not turn from maggots into flies.

By the end of some months kept moist in a tub, the mixture would have retained the maximum amount of nitrogen and other useful elements, which are lost in drying, and would have been almost sterile. The Japanese farmer, 'does not carry out his manure either in winter or in summer into his fallow fields, to be dried up there by the scorching heat of the sun, and to have its nutritive qualities weakened by the evaporation of the volatile salts and of its oily particles.'[54] The sterility would have been further ensured when the excreta was spread on the land. 'Throughout most of human history, domestic and industrial sewage was spread over the land. This practice took advantage of the fact that soil possesses certain built-in mechanisms – physical, chemical, and microbial – capable of destroying most substances and micro-organisms, including those

[50] Kaempfer, *History*, II, 294.
[51] King, *Farmers*, 199.
[52] King, *Farmers*, 13,
[53] Roberts, *Hygiene*, 240.
[54] Thunberg, *Travels*, IV, 82–3.

which might be dangerous for man.'[55] Or as King noted in 1911, 'recent bacterial work has shown that faecal matter and house refuse are best destroyed by returning them to clean soil, where natural purification takes place.'[56]

In the Japanese case there were several methods used to prepare the night soil. Sometimes 'the material is worked and reworked, with more water added if necessary, until it becomes a rich complete fertilizer, allowed to become dry and then finely pulverized.'[57] More often it seems to have been spread in liquid form, where it would penetrate with maximum effect to the roots of the plant or into the prepared soil as needed. Isabella Bird noted with disgust how there were 'much-decayed manure heaps, and the women were engaged in breaking them up and treading them into pulp with their bare feet.'[58] Thunberg observed with similar revulsion, 'the disgusting trouble of mixing up manure of various sorts, the excrements both of man and beast, with water and urine, together with every kind of refuse from the kitchen, till it becomes a perfect hodge-podge.'[59] 'In some of the plots men are at work breaking up the soil, in others distributing from buckets the liquid manure.'[60] 'Human manure is given in a liquid state, during the younger stages of the growing crops.'[61] Alcock described 'This collection of manure of every kind of urine and offals, which they had prepared at home, quite thin and fluid, they now carried in two pails on their shoulders to their lands, and there with a scoop poured it out near the roots of the green corn, the blades of which were six inches long. This I was told was done twice each time they sowed.' He saw the great advantage of this, for the young plant 'receives the whole benefit of it, at the same time that the liquor penetrates immediately to the root.' When the corn grew another six inches, 'the farmer has dug up, as it were, these small trenches, and very carefully put earth about the roots, whence the corn has both received manure and been watered.'[62]

There is considerable value in storing night soil in liquid form and then distributing it. 'Liebig, the greatest living authority on agricultural chemistry, states that night-soil loses in drying half its valuable products, that is, half its "nitrogen", for the ammonia escapes into the atmosphere. By irrigation, by the diffusion and conveyance of the manure to the plant in the medium of water the escape of the valuable substance as a noxious and injurious gas is diminished.'

[55] Dubos, *Adapting*, 198.
[56] King, *Farmers*, 199; for early evidence for the purifying influence of earth, see Murphy, *Our Homes*, 755.
[57] King, *Farmers*, 251.
[58] Bird, *Tracks*, 91.
[59] Thunberg, *Travels*, IV, 83.
[60] Morse, *Day*, I, 9–10.
[61] Alcock, *Tycoon*, II, 476.
[62] Thunberg, *Travels*, II, 213; IV, 83,87.

Furthermore, '... it is at the same time stated, the process of applying manure by irrigation, that is, separated and diluted with water, is considered to be productive of less deleterious gas, of less injurious effects, than by spreading it over fields in a solid form, and allowing it to remain until it is decomposed and separated by the atmosphere and conveyed into the soil by rain.'[63]

The immense labour of spreading the liquid manure was reduced considerably by the use of a simple technique. 'When they wish to manure a field, they make a tree do the duty of one man and very much assist and economize the labour of the other by passing a rope through the handle of the pail close to the depot of the manure, one end of which is secured to the tree and the other is held by a labourer to enable him to swing the contents over a wide area. In other cases he is supplied with a large ladle, at the end of a ten feet handle, which gives an equally wide sweep, and with little labour.'[64] A more recent account describes how in some areas the night soil 'is dipped from the buckets by means of a long-handled wooden dipper and dribbled along the rows of plants.'[65] Comparing the methods of American and Asian agriculture, 'The difference is not so much in activity of muscle as it is in alertness and efficiency of the grey matter of the brain. He sees and treats each plant individually, he loosens the ground so that his liquid manure drops immediately beneath the surface within reach of the active roots.'[66] It may also have minimized health risk as the earth and manure were quickly mixed. Care also seems to have been taken to keep the pails in which excrement was carried to the fields as clean as possible. 'The cleanliness of the Japanese is amazing.... The wooden buckets in which the sewage is carried to the fields are white and clean as our milk pails.'[67]

The absence of a piped sewage system in Japan had its advantages. When comparing Japanese and American cities in the 1870s Morse wrote: 'the secret of sewage disposal has been effectually solved by the Japanese for centuries, so that nothing goes to waste.' As a result that 'class of diseases which scourge our communities as a result of our ineffectual efforts in disposing of sewage, the Japanese happily know but little. In that country there are no deep vaults with long accumulations contaminating the ground, or underground pipes conducting sewage to shallow bays and inlets, there to fester and vitiate the air and spread sickness and death.' Thus 'those diseases which at home are attributed to bad drainage, imperfect closets, and the like seem to be unknown or rare, and this freedom from such complaints is probably due to the fact that all excrementious matter is carried out of the city by men who utilize it for their farms or rice-

---

[63] Chadwick, *Report*, 121–2,121.
[64] Alcock, *Tycoon*, I, 297–98.
[65] Cornell, *Two Villages*, 130; this sounds like the method described by Thunberg, *Travels*, IV, 83.
[66] King, *Farmers*, 203.
[67] Morse, *Day*, I, 61.

fields.' 'With us the sewage is allowed to flow into our coves and harbors, polluting the water and killing all aquatic life; and the stenches arising from the decomposition and filth are swept over the community to the misery of all. In Japan this material is scrupulously saved and goes to enrich the soil.'[68] 'The result of the transference of this material into the country leaves the shores of a city absolutely pure. No malarious flats nor noisome odors, arising from littoral areas, curse the inhabitants, as with us.'[69]

Yet, as with almost every positive aspect, there was also a potential serious negative effect. The collecting, moving, disinfecting and distributing of this immense amount of human night soil, some two-fifths of a ton per person per year, was an operation which caused health problems. Rudyard Kipling on his visit to Japan wrote, 'Only one drawback occurred to the Professor and myself at the same time. Crops don't grow to the full limit of the seed on heavily worked ground dotted with villages except at a price. "Cholera?", said I, watching a stretch of well-sweeps. "Cholera", said the Professor. 'Must be, y'know. It's all sewage irrigation." '[70] E.L.Jones notes that when agriculture shifted south, 'Faeces discharged into water made China the world reservoir of lung, liver and intestinal flukes and the Oriental schistosome. . . . Human excreta were used as a fertilizer, and soil-transmitted helminth infestation was an occupational hazard for the farmer.'[71]

Thunberg had noticed a specific form of abdominal disease 'to which the Japanese are most liable' which was called *Senki*.[72] This 'attacks great numbers of people, and likewise strangers, who reside any length of time in the country. The pain is violent and intolerable, and often leaves swellings behind it, in different parts of the body; and it especially productive of the *Hydrocele*.'[73] Kaempfer described a particular form of abdominal complaint called *Senki*, which 'is an endemial distemper of this populous Empire, and withal so common, that there is scarce one in ten grown persons, who hath not some time or other felt its attacks.' 'The name of Senki is not given indifferently to all Belly-achs, but only to that particular sort, which besides a most acute pain in the guts, occasions at the same time convulsions in the groins. For such is the nature and violence of this distemper, that all the membranes and muscles of the abdomen are convulsed by it'. 'Some very particular symptoms of this endemial distemper of Japan are, that mimicking the hysteric affection, it often puts the patient

---

[68] Morse, *Homes*, 233,23.

[69] Morse, *Latrines*, 172.

[70] Quoted in Tames, *Encounters*, 89.

[71] Jones, *Miracle*, 6.

[72] I would like to thank Dr Nicholas Mascie-Taylor for comments on this section.

[73] Thunberg, *Travels*, IV, 76.

under an apprehension of being suffocated, the whole region from the groins up to the false ribs, and higher, being strongly convulsed, that after it hath for a long time miserably tormented the patient, it will end in tumours, and swellings arising in several parts of the body.' The only treatment for the disease, which Kaempfer thought rather effective, was acupuncture. He believed that it was caused by the air, the climate, 'the way of life of the natives, their victuals and drink.'[74]

It seems almost certain that *senki* was in fact schistosomiasis or bilharzia. By the 1950s it had been recognized that schistosomiasis, previously thought to be mainly confined to Egypt, Sudan, South Africa and parts of China, was 'the most important tropical disease in the world, after malaria.'[75] A recent estimate by Nicholas Mascie-Taylor suggests that it 'affects over 200 million people and poses a threat to 400 million more in at least 76 countries.'[76] There have been massive attempts to eradicate it.[77] Yet it 'is continuing to spread despite technical advances and refinements.'[78] As Larry Laughlin points out, the fact that almost everyone in most rural populations in areas of endemic schistosomiasis 'have had an infection sometime during his life', when 'superimposed on the 1.5 billion humans in schistosome endemic areas, easily qualify schistosomiasis as one of the major world public health problems.'[79]

The nature of schistosomiasis was first investigated and explained by Japanese scientists. In 1905 Katsurada 'had described eggs and worms from patients and cats in the Yamanashi district of Japan, and named them *Schistosoma haematobium japonicum.*' Then in 1913, Miyairi and Suzuki 'discovered the snail host into which the miracidia penetrated, and for the first time described the fork-tailed schistosome cercariae emerging from the snails a few weeks later.'[80]

They showed that schistosomiasis is 'a parasitic disease ... due to infection with blood flukes of the genus Schistosoma.' The intermediate hosts are snails. 'Man becomes infected by bathing, wading, or other contact with the free-swimming cercariae forms of the parasite which penetrate the skin.' The Japanese version of the disease, *Schistosoma japonicum* causes 'disturbances in the small intestine, colon and rectum.' It appears that the 'Disease due to *S.japonicum* is more severe than the other two variants and is quite resistant to

---

[74] Kaempfer, *History*, III, 263–4,236,263.
[75] John Farley in Kiple (ed.), *Disease*, 996.
[76] Mascie-Taylor (ed.), *Anthropology of Disease*, 23.
[77] For an excellent account of these, and overview of the disease, see Farley, *Bilharzia*. For another authoritative account see Basch, *Schistosomes*.
[78] Mascie-Taylor (ed.), *Anthropology of Disease*, 23.
[79] In Hunter, *Tropical Medicine*, 715.
[80] John Farley in Kiple (ed.), *Disease*, 996.

treatment.'[81] The best treatment is through the use of tartar emetic, which was only introduced by McDonough in 1918.[82]

S.japonicum is found in Japan, central and southern China, the Philippines, the Celebes. Thus it would appear to fit with irrigated rice cultivation areas in the Far East. The snail requires a good deal of surface water: 'almost without exception, where an irrigation scheme or man-made lake has been constructed in an area where schistomiasis occurs, it has led to an outbreak and increased endemicity.'[83] The water needs to be of a certain temperature and turbulence.[84] The eggs need to be passed through human excreta from the humans to the water. The area of *S.japonicum* lies within the area where human excreta is used in agriculture.

In all these respects most of Japan would appear to provide ideal conditions for very widespread schistosomiasis in the past. Yet there is an oddness. The outbreaks seem to have been localized. Although recent successful control measures complicate the assessment, recent maps of the distribution of schistosomiasis in Japan suggest that it is only found in limited areas: north-west Kyushu, near the southern tip of Honshu, and in the area around Tokyo.[85] Even within an area designated as prone to the disease, its presence and virulence probably varied from valley to valley. In a certain area, schistosomiasis was known as 'Katayama Fever' in the nineteenth century for it was 'seen very often in immigrants to the Katayama River Valley and was said to have led to the prohibition of marriage between people of this area and outsiders because of illness and deaths among new spouses.'[86]

One reason for marked regional differences can only be understood if we look at the link between the human excreta that carry the eggs and the snails in the water. 'Eggs in the excreta perish unless they promptly reach water so that sanitary facilities can prevent this.'[87] If this were generally the case in Japan, the normal methods of storing urine and faeces would be enough to break the chain. Unfortunately, however, while 'Most eggs desiccate and die if they do not come into contact with fresh water soon after leaving the host', it appears that 'mature *S.japonicum* eggs may survive outside the body for up to 80 days under moist conditions, e.g., in China and Japan, where they will hatch and infect snails the following spring.'[88] These particularly hardy eggs might survive the Japanese

[81] Merck, *Manual*, 876.
[82] Hunter, *Tropical Medicine*, 709.
[83] In Feachem et al. (eds), *Water*, 26–7.
[84] Mascie-Taylor (ed.), *Anthropology of Disease*, 25.
[85] Farley, *Bilharzia*, 7; the map in Hunter, *Tropical Medicine*, 714, shows an even more restricted area.
[86] Hunter, *Tropical Medicine*, 723.
[87] In Feachem et al. (eds), *Water*, 26.
[88] Hunter, *Tropical Medicine*, 711.

storage process, unless it was carried out with great thoroughness. The winter months were particularly dangerous. In tests carried out in the 1920s it was found that 'during the summer months the process is so active that all pathogenic bacteria and eggs are dead in a few weeks. In the winter however both may remain alive for months.'[89] Just to take one example of variations which might have large consequences, we are told that of one area 'Unlike the coastal plain to the south there are few cisterns for storing and curing nightsoil'. Instead, it 'is removed from a tank beneath the toilet in each homestead and taken directly to the field ...' where it is spread.[90] This would have allowed the schistosomiasis eggs to flourish and spread the infection to people working in the fields. However the extraordinary pains which most took to carry away all human manure, sterilize it, and then bury it at the roots of the plants, meant that the Japanese achieved a level of sanitation unrivalled by another major nation until the twentieth century.

In western Europe there was the same contradiction between economic efficiency and mounting population on the one hand, and the 'externalities' of excrement on the other. Europe's solution to this problem was different. North-western Europe through the centuries practised mixed arable and pastoral farming and the number of domestic animals per head of population was higher than in any other large settled population. Its agriculture depended on manure, yet without the problem of poor, volcanic soil, with less emphasis on arable farming, and with many more domestic animals the pressure to use night soil was less extreme. Manure for the fields took a number of forms, but its central constituent was animal dung. Grain production produced straw, which could be used to feed large numbers of cows and oxen, whose manure could then be re-cycled. To what extent was there still a need for night soil as a fertilizer?

It would appear from general surveys that in the long period between the twelfth and eighteenth centuries, night soil was not used very much in western Europe, with one notable exception. Braudel wrote of the general position: 'the principal source of manure remained livestock – never human beings, as in the towns and countryside of the Far East ...' The partial exception he noted was that urban refuse was used 'around certain towns, such as Valencia in Spain or some Flemish cities'.[91] The Flemish case is well documented and the arrangements look very similar to those we have described for Japan, with the careful collection of urine and faeces, which were of great commercial value and extensively used on the neighbouring fields.[92]

[89] Wellington, *Report*, 33.
[90] Cornell, *Two Villages*, 130.
[91] Braudel, *Capitalism*, 77.
[92] Chadwick, *Report*, 123; Van Bath, *Agriculture*, 256–7.

It was also a 'most valuable manure, which was quite indispensable to the agriculture around Paris, and consequently to Paris itself.'[93] It was claimed that the French, Prussians and the Germans all used night soil to a certain extent in the nineteenth century.[94] There is some evidence of its use during the nineteenth century in Scotland. For example, in parts of Glasgow, 'There were no privies or drains there, and the dung heaps received all filth which the swarm of wretched inhabitants could give; and we learned that a considerable part of the rent of the house was paid by the produce of the dung heaps.'[95] Yet the use seems to have been relatively small when we compare it to that of China or Japan.

Turning to the English case with its emphasis on pastoralism we would not have expected much use of night soil in smaller towns and villages. But from the middle of the sixteenth century London was emerging as one of the major cities in the world and by 1700 it was the largest city in Europe. It would appear to be in the position of the Flemish and Dutch cities or Paris and hence we might have expected a widespread use of night soil in its environs.

One of the best surveys of the various forms of manuring and fertilizing land in various parts of England from the sixteenth to eighteenth centuries is provided by Mildred Campbell. She describes the use of lime and marl (an enriching earthy substance). Where these were not available all kinds of thing were used:

> Norden says that on the coast of Cornwall a certain kind of seaweed and sea sand were spread over the soil for its enrichment. Pebbles and stones from the shore were burned and spread on the land in Sussex, Kent and Suffolk. Refuse from the streets of London and the city ash heaps was spread over Middlesex farms. Dredges from the river were used in Hampshire. ... Plot tells how chippings of stones were used near Banbury, and 'Taylers shreds' near Watlington.

Animal manure, however, 'was the fertilizer most commonly used by all farmers, and that which received the highest praise from the writers on husbandry.'[96]

What is noticeable in Campbell's review of contemporary accounts is the omission of any mention of 'night soil', though a certain amount might have been included in the 'refuse' that came out of London onto Middlesex farms. Other general surveys of early modern agriculture in England also omit reference to the use of night soil. Lord Ernle's *English Farming, Past and Present*, for instance, mentions a number of manures and fertilizers, almost identical to those

---

[93] Chadwick, *Report*, 133.
[94] *Rural Cyclopedia*, III, 347.
[95] Chadwick, *Report*, 98.
[96] Campbell, *English Yeoman*, 175.

noted by Campbell, but there is no mention of night soil.[97] The most detailed contemporary account we have of farming in the seventeenth century, that of Robert Loder, mentions various experiments with different kinds of manuring. He used cattle and sheep dung, horse and cow dung, mud from the pound, black ashes (probably wood, peat ash or soot), malt waste, and dung from the pigeon-cot but in all of the accounts there is no reference to night soil.[98] Likewise in a detailed diary and letter book of the early eighteenth century: 'The only fertilizers known apart from animal manure, were lime, ashes from the burned moss of undrained land, seaweed and marl . . .'[99] Another account of manuring practices is provided in Ruston and Witney's *Agricultural Evolution of a Yorkshire Village*. They include mud, lime, ashes, pigeon dung and manure, but there is no reference to night soil.[100]

The one explicit reference to the use of night soil to which some writers have drawn attention is that by the early-sixteenth-century writer Thomas Tusser in his *Five Hundred Points of Good Husbandry*. Yet, in the whole of his account, there is but one reference to the matter, under the month of November. The question is explicitly labelled 'Cleansing of privies', in other words, he is giving advice about household cleanliness, not specifically about manuring. The verses explain that 'Foule privies are now to be clensed', and that this 'baggage' if 'buried in garden, in trenches alowe', will 'make very many things better to grow.'[101] Two centuries later in Arthur Young's *Farmer's Calender* there is a good deal about the various stages of manuring, but no mention of night soil.[102] Soil was increasingly given fertility by using the new techniques which are a central feature of the 'agricultural revolution' of the seventeenth and eighteenth century. Clovers, alfalfa, new grasses, turnips were alternated with the cereals in new rotations. Several helped to fix nitrogen in the soil. It appears that with all these alternatives there was no need for night soil as a fertilizer. When Houghton at the end of the seventeenth century examined the potentials of urine and faeces, it was the medicinal value of each that he tried to promote.[103]

However, as London grew, an increasing number of people drew attention to the wasted potential of all the night soil, pointing to what happened in Paris, and working out schemes which would increase both profit and health. A particularly forceful account is provided by articles in the nineteenth-century *Rural*

[97] Ernle, *Farming*, 94,97,109.
[98] Loder, *Farm Accounts*, xviii; the 'pound' was the place where impounded, stray, animals were detained.
[99] Blundell (ed.), *Letter Book*, 135.
[100] Ruston and Witney, *Agricultural*, 106.
[101] Tusser, *Five Hundred Points*, 51.
[102] Young, *Farmer's Kalendar*, 43,224.
[103] Houghton, *Husbandry*, II, nos.158–65.

Cyclopedia. It was pointed out that 'by far the greatest waste of all occurs in the sewerage of our towns and cities. This is of wondrous importance, both for the enormous value which it draws off for agriculture, and for the incalculable evil which it inflicts upon the public health.'[104] While other countries made some use of night soil,

> in our highly refined and civilized country, we send them down our water-closets, to be wasted in the rivers, and finally in the sea; while we send our gold into Russia and Peru, and our ships to Ichaboe and Saldhanna Bay, to bring back to us what we have so wantonly wasted, to be converted into food, and again wasted in its turn. Our hordes of population, instead of being enrichers of the island, in an agricultural point of view, are absolute impoverishers. They draw off the corn, the roots, and the flesh from the land; and they send it away into the sea, by means of the Thames, the Severn, the Humber, the Tees, and Tyne, and scores of other great wasters of the elements of human food. The Medlock, into which not more than the drainage of 100,000 is imperfectly discharged, is said by Mr Grey to contain sufficient phosphoric acid to supply 95,000 acres of wheat, 184,000 acres of potatoes, or 280,000 acres of oats, and to hold in solution a sufficient quantity of silica to supply 50,000 acres of wheat.[105]

The author believed that a solution would soon be found. Various ideas were put forward, for instance that the night soil be dried like the French 'poudrette' and sold under a suitable euphemism. Already foreign companies were marketing it under names such as 'Alkine-vegetative powder' or 'Owen's Animalized Carbon'. Another scheme was to use the power of steam to pump liquid manure out from the cities and to make it available from stand-pipes on every farm. Yet despite the fact that it was calculated that this would reduce the price from ten shillings per ton to seven or eight pence, the schemes were never put into operation. Justus von Liebig thought it was something to do with the 'domestic arrangements peculiar to the English' which 'render it difficult, perhaps even impossible, to collect the immense quantity of phosphates ... which are daily sent into the river in the form of urine and solid excrementa.'[106]

Probably more important were the economics of the situation, caused by the huge abundance of alternative fertilizers and manures. Chadwick noted that 'In the parts of some towns adjacent to the rural districts the cesspools are emptied gratuitously for the sake of the manure; but they only do this when there is a considerable accumulation ...'[107] Although there were numerous experiments to

---

[104] *Rural Cyclopedia*, III, 347.
[105] *Rural Cyclopedia*, III, 347, quoting Liebig.
[106] *Rural Cyclopedia*, 347.
[107] Chadwick, *Report*, 119.

try to make use of the human excrement from nineteenth-century cities,[108] in general, there seemed to be a lack of demand. 'It might have been expected, from the value of the refuse as manure (one of the most powerful known), that the great demand for it would have afforded a price which might have returned, in some degree, the expense and charge of cleansing. But this appears not to be the case in the metropolis.' Chadwick found that 'at present, with the exception of coal-ashes, which are indispensable for making bricks, some description of lees, and a few other inconsiderable exceptions, no refuse in London pays half the expense of removal by cartage.' Indeed, the situation was so bad that night soil could not be given away; 'the evidence of a considerable contractor for scavengering etc. who states, with respect to the most productive manure – "I have given away thousands of loads of night-soil; we knew not what to do with it." '[109] 'The value as manure of the contents of the privies was constantly being stressed by the scientists – it was stated that the amount available in Birmingham in one year was worth $100,000 to the farmers – but the difficulty was to find an economical method of transporting it to the country. It was all very well to say that the "chamber-pot is a penny savings bank" but when it came to collecting the contents by house-to-house visits and transporting them in carboys to distant farms the cost was found to be prohibitive.'[110] Smith describes how after the introduction of guano in the 1840s, whatever market there was for human manure collapsed entirely and though various schemes staggered on, they 'proved neither efficient nor profitable'.[111] Only for specialized purposes, for example when urine was needed for washing cloth in Halifax, does there seem to have been a widespread demand for one form of excrement. Here urine was collected, as in Japan, in large pots.[112]

Whereas in Japan night soil could be used in lieu of rent, in England one had to pay to have it taken away:

> But the expense of this mode operates, as the reports from the large towns show, as a complete barrier to all cleanliness in this respect in the dwellings or streets occupied by the labouring classes. The usual cost of cleansing cesspools of a tenement in London is about 1/- each time. With a population generally in debt at the end of the week, and whose rents are collected weekly, such an outlay may be considered as practically impossible, and the interior landlords delay incurring the expense until the nuisance becomes unbearable.[113]

[108] See for example, Murphy (ed.), *Our Homes*, 758.
[109] Chadwick, *Report*, 118.
[110] Drummond and Wilbraham, *Food*, 310.
[111] Smith, *People's Health*, 220.
[112] Beckman, *Inventions*, II, 97.
[113] Chadwick, *Report*, 117.

With some minor exceptions England was at the opposite extreme to Japan. Whereas in Japan night soil was most highly prized, in England it could not be given away. This created an immense problem. If each person produced some 40 oz of excrementa per day, then the inhabitants of a city like London were producing many thousands of tons each week. It was a growing threat as the cities expanded and was exacerbated by the vast amounts of horse manure. The solution was to be a major contribution by the English to world civilization.

One of the most difficult tasks is to create a system which will capture the excreta efficiently from human beings. In the majority of societies, people tend to go out into the fields and woods. The idea of excreting within an enclosed space is not looked on with favour, as many development experts have found. However, it would appear that the notion of a 'private' room or 'privy' was an early feature in England. Margaret Wood writes that 'Privies or garderobes were more numerous and better planned in the Middle Ages than is generally supposed.'[114] 'Among the lower orders there were some private latrines, as we know from housing ordinances of 1189, requiring that garderobe pits, if not walled, must be at least five and a half feet from the party line; if walled, two and a half feet.' Two centuries later, 'In a contract dated 1370 for the building of 18 shops in London, the mason was to make "ten stone pits for *prevez*, of which pits eight shall be double (i.e. serve two houses) and each in depth ten feet and in length ten feet and in breadth eleven feet." ' A contract for some house repairs in 1450 includes a price for the 'takeying owte of a serteyne of dounge owte of a privey and for to bery ye dounge in ye same pyt (5s 6d).'[115]

There are references to privies in Chaucer's poems and Furnivall gives a good idea of the amount of care and attention devoted to the subject.[116] There is a description of a Lord's toilet, how it is to be kept, the rags, water, seat and so on. This suggests that the English already deviated from the Continental posture in defecation – sitting rather than squatting. It also suggests that rags were used in lieu of toilet paper. On this Pudney writes 'It is a subject I prefer not to explore in detail, except to recall that civilized Romans used perfumed wool and sometimes sponges, that medieval laity were known to use curved sticks and bunches of hay, that ecclesiastics, whose smallest rooms were often well found and often communal, seemed to have favoured the shreds and tatters of their own discarded habits.'[117]

Less obscure is the matter of medieval public latrines, which have been described by Ernest Sabine. He gives considerable evidence of the widespread use of public latrines in London from at least the thirteenth century. He asks, 'If,

---

[114] Wood, *English House*, 377.
[115] Wright, *Clean*, 50,52,52; see also Pounds, *Culture*, 162.
[116] Furnivall (ed.), *Meals*, 64.
[117] Pudney, *Smallest*, 122.

then, citizens so commonly used the public latrines, how many such conveniences were there? Writers upon the subject usually mention only three: one on Temple Bridge (or pier) south of Fleet Street, one at Queenhithe, and one on London Bridge.' A little research revealed many more. 'Certainty has, therefore, been established for the existence of at least thirteen mediaeval London public latrines. The fact . . . that a knowledge of even this number has been successfully gleaned from mere incidental documentary evidence clearly indicates that there must have been many more such public conveniences.' 'London Bridge ... had not merely one common latrine, as has been commonly assumed, but several "necessary houses or wardrobes" for the convenience both of the tenants of the houses built on the bridge and of other people resorting to the place.' They were, 'of no inconsiderable size and importance.' These public latrines 'seem to have been not merely for the relief of the floating business population, but rather primarily for the benefit of those householders and tenants who had access to no private latrines.'[118] Furthermore 'by the late Middle Ages there were public latrines ... at Leicester, Winchester, Southampton, Hull and Exeter and, no doubt, elsewhere.'[119]

The evidence on the 'house of office' becomes more voluminous from the sixteenth century. In the early sixteenth century Andrew Boorde gave a detailed description of the arrangements for the privy – where it was to be built, how used and so on. He also advised that people should get into the regular habit of using it first thing in the morning.[120] Harrison noted that in houses lately built, there were 'houses of office further distant from their lodgings.'[121] Lemnius, visiting England in the mid sixteenth century appreciated the nosegays and fragrant flowers in English 'bedchambers and privy rooms.'[122] In the seventeenth century internal toilets may have been widespread, for instance the popular *Orbis*, included a picture of a house showing an internal toilet.[123] Anecdotal evidence suggests the prevalence of privies. A puritan was described as rushing into the 'house of office', among other places, to pray.[124] It was quite frequent for women to have stillbirths in the 'house of office'.[125] We read of a three year old girl killed when a chair in a privy collapsed in the early seventeenth century.[126]

---

[118]　Sabine, *Latrines*, 307,309,307,306.
[119]　Hibbert, *The English*, 103.
[120]　Boorde, *Regyment*, 236–7,248.
[121]　Harrison, *Description*, 199.
[122]　Rye, *Foreigners*, 78.
[123]　Comenius, *Orbis*, 146–7.
[124]　Watkins, *Puritan Experience*, 94.
[125]　Petty, *Papers*, II, 166.
[126]　Forbes (ed.), *Aldgate*, 140.

There were, of course, those who broke the rules, but even the reactions to this indicate the widespread norms. Country housewives used magic to try to stop boys from defecating outside their front doors.[127] People were often taken to court for urinating or defecating in the wrong place. In London there were supplications for the building of both privies, in specific houses, and 'common' ones, or general lavatories.[128] There were differences between town and country, yet it would appear that in the countryside also, people were getting into the habit of using a receptacle, and not merely going out to the nearest field.

The evidence for the nineteenth century is coloured by the problems caused by the rapid growth of large cities. It is clear that the long-standing institution of the 'privy' was accepted as the ideal, but there were far too few of them. Sanitary inspectors reported that 'There are very few houses in town which can boast of either water-closet or privy, and only two or three public privies in the better part of the place exist for the great bulk of the inhabitants.' Or again, they reported how 'The privies are in a most disgraceful state, inaccessible from filth, and too few for the accommodation of the number of people, the average number being two to 250 people.' In Gateshead, 'The want of convenient offices in the neighbourhood is attended with many very unpleasant circumstances, as it induces the lazy inmates to make use of chamber utensils, which are suffered to remain in the most offensive state for several days, and are then emptied out of the windows.'[129]

Until the municipal sewage systems were laid the normal method was to require householders to get rid of their own accumulated excrement, or to hire people to do this. In the eighteenth-century householders were often provided with barrels 'that had to be emptied at intervals by the householder.' Neither private nor municipal emptying was very satisfactory. Even if the liquid waste could be disposed of separately, the solid waste from a household of six would weigh over 100 stone per year and would be unpleasant to move through the city streets. Marshall describes how in eighteenth-century Manchester, 'Householders preferred the easier way of emptying them over Salford Bridge, or, even worse, of tipping them into the streets or onto the public refuse heaps under cover of darkness.'[130] Chadwick reported that 'It is proved that the present mode of retaining refuse in the house in cesspools and privies is injurious to the health and often extremely dangerous. The process of emptying them by hand labour, and removing the contents by cartage, is very offensive, and often the occasion of serious accidents.'[131]

[127] Thomas, *Religion*, 544.
[128] Forbes (ed.), *Aldgate*, 95.
[129] Chadwick, *Report*, 116,112,95.
[130] Marshall, *English People*, 168.
[131] Chadwick, *Report*, 117.

The real test was London, which had emerged as the largest city in Europe. We would expect health to deteriorate rapidly as the medieval system of privies and chamber-pots could no longer cope with the hundreds of tons of human excrement that were being produced each day. Instead, the pressure caused changes which led to the emergence of a great city which became a model for sanitary reform throughout Europe – not nearly as clean as Tokyo or Osaka, but far more so than Madrid, for instance, where Kames reported that 'Till the year 1760 there was not a privy.'[132]

A full account of what happened would take us into the whole structure of local government in medieval and early modern England and the way in which authorities and people combined to develop a tolerable system of drains and sewers.[133] As Chadwick wrote:

> So much of the structural arrangements as depended on drainage was provided for by the Commissions of Sewers who were invested with valuable powers by the Statute of Henry VIII cap.5.s.1/3; the authority of these Commissions 'to be directed into all parts within this realm where need shall require, according to the form ensuing, to such substantial persons as shall be named by the Lord Chancellor and Lord Treasurer, and the two chief justices, or by three of them, whereof the Lord Chancellor to be one', to cause 'to be made, corrected or repaired, amended, put down or reformed, as the case shall require, walls, ditches, banks, gutters, sewers, gates, cullices, bridges, streams, and other defences by the coasts of the sea and marsh ground.'[134]

There was provision for a sewage and drainage system, but little to say how successfully it was implemented.

The opportunity for a new infrastructure was provided by the Fire of London in 1666. 'Before the city was rebuilt, that ingenious architect Sir Christopher Wren, planned and built the common sewers, as they continue to this day; and they are a lasting monument of his judgment and attention to the health and welfare of its inhabitants' so that 'London and Westminster are now ranked among the most healthy spots in the island.' 'The advantages of drains and sewers are remarkably felt in London, which, before the fire of London, was frequently affected with contagious malignant fevers. Before this period all the waste water and filth remained above ground.'[135] It was these changes which, among others, Thomas Short thought contributed to a lowering of mortality in the eighteenth century: 'some places have been very industrious and successful

---

[132] Kames, *Sketches*, I, 248.
[133] Creighton, *Epidemics*, I, 322ff provides a useful introduction to medieval sanitation.
[134] Chadwick, *Report*, 348.
[135] Franklin, *Works*, VI, 320.

in this Part of the Policy, they have opened and cleaned their Ditches and Sewers, let off their Sludge and nasty standing Water, so that all Filthiness is more easily and better carried off.'[136]

The second great effort, the laying of sewage pipes from individual houses in London and later in other cities, did not come until the middle of the nineteenth century. However, the problem was not removed by merely draining the sewage away. 'The chief objection to the extension of this system is the pollution of the water of the river into which the sewers are discharged.'[137] An anecdote about Cambridge illustrates just one dimension of the problem in relation to the growing use of toilet paper. 'There is a tale of Queen Victoria being shown over Trinity by the Master, Dr Whewell, and saying, as she looked down over the bridge: 'What are all those pieces of paper floating down the river?' To which, with great presence of mind, he replied: "Those, ma'am, are notices that bathing is forbidden." '[138]

With regard to the water closet, it would appear that, like many useful inventions it was discovered and re discovered several times. Medieval latrines and privies used pipes to take away the fluid into the cesspit, thus lessening smell and dirt. But the first noted inventor of the water-closet seems to have been Thomas Brightfield. A description of Brightfield's invention is given by Sabine:

> According to a deed dated February, 1449–50, in the Guildhall Library (London), Thomas Brightfield was to make at his own expense within the house where he lived in the Parish of St. Martin, Vintry Ward, a chimney for a kitchen, a cistern of lead, with a lead pipe in the wall to Narrow Lane, and a privy of stone in the stone wall. Now this cistern was doubtless intended as a receptacle for rainwater collected from the roof, and the pipe as a vent for the excess water accruing during heavy rains, leading it down to the public gutter.[139]

The first written specification of a new system was by Sir John Harrington. His device of the mid-sixteenth century 'embodies all the features of the valve closet.' 'It has a seat with a pan, a cistern above ... an overflow pipe, a flushing pipe, a valve or "stopple" and a waste with a water-seal.'[140] There was 'a bowl which could be filled with water from a cistern to a covering deodorizing depth of two feet, and which could be emptied when necessary through an underlying valve into the cesspit.'[141] This would seal off the stench from the cesspit. Yet, although it was copied and used at the Queen's Palace at Richmond, it was an

---

[136] Short, *Increase*, 35–6.
[137] Chadwick, *Report*, 120.
[138] Pudney, *Smallest*, 115.
[139] Sabine, *Latrines*, 312–8, 313.
[140] Wright, *Clean*, 75.
[141] Grigson and Gibbs-Smith (eds), *Things*, 425–6.

invention which came several centuries too early. It depended on a good supply of water and a sewage pipe flowing out.

The merits of the new system of water closets attracted the attention of Benjamin Franklin:

> It is now well known that the stench arising from stationary privies, may be prevented by a cheap and easy method. The excrements may be received in tubs, so closely connected with the sea, that no air can pass. The lower ends of the tub should be sunk below the surface of water contained in proper cisterns. The excrements are soon dissolved in water, and so carried off, *every time the privy is washed, which should be as often as it is used.*

The first patent for a water closet was taken out by Alexander Cummings, a watchmaker of bond Street, in 1775, incorporating all the elements of the modern valve closet.[142] As for smell, 'The first patent for a stink-trap seems to have been taken out by John Gaillait, a cook, in 1782, for "the invention of an entire new machine a stinck-trap, ... which will entirely prevent the very disagreeable smells from drains and sewers." '[143] 'The efficient water carriage of human wastes on a large scale became possible with Joseph Bramah's introduction of the improved version of the water-closet in the 1770s. Between 1778 and 1797, Bramah supplied over 6,000 water-closets; and by the 1830s they were being widely used in London.'[144] There were still many problems to be overcome, particularly in getting the sewage safely from the water closet to a place of disposal, but an important break-through had been made.[145]

'The modern, individual WC which, in the West, has today superseded all other devices for getting rid of human excrement, is the direct descendant of the British "water closet".'[146] This technological break-through finally allowed urban dwellers to have a clean and sweet-smelling 'house of office' located in a little room in their houses. It is difficult to imagine what New York, Tokyo or Rome would be like today if the water-closet was suddenly abandoned. It was a solution which, in the longer term, was to replace the Japanese system of night soil removal. Yet it was one which could only exist with a huge infrastructure of water pumping and sewage piping. Until the mid nineteenth century the Japanese solution was probably far more efficient for the total population than anything in the West. The effect on health was probably not as dramatic in England as in Japan. Dysentery, typhoid and cholera were more prevalent.

---

[142] Wright, *Clean*, 75,71,107.
[143] Quennell and Quennell, *Things*, III, 97.
[144] Hardy, *Water*, 262–3.
[145] Smith, *People's Health*, 222 and Murphy (ed.), *Our Homes*, 662 describe some of the dangers caused by the early water closets wthen not connected to main drainage.
[146] Goubert, *Conquest*, 97.

Nevertheless, the developing techniques of town planning and the application of capital and ingenuity to the solution of this problem undoubtedly made England as healthy in this respect as any European country, with the exception of Holland which combined the use of night soil with the developing techniques of sanitation.

Thus England had taken a less efficient course in the short term, throwing away enormous quantities of rich fertilizer. In the long term the English solution was adopted by the world and replaced the Japanese one, even in Japan. As Pudney put it with quiet irony, 'In the four corners of the earth, British culture and civilization effortlessly left its mark in those pre-propaganda days, in the polite, untranslated, variously pronounced but highly prized terms *Water-Closet* and *W.C.*'[147]

---

[147] Pudney, *Smallest*, 30.

Part IV

On the Body

10

Vector-borne Diseases: Plague, Typhus and Malaria

As their cities grew, the English and Japanese had both avoided the tendency towards a rapid rise in diseases of the stomach due to infected food and drink. Yet there are other diseases which normally increase in virulence as populations grow more dense. One such set consists of those in which the bacteria are transmitted by way of insect vectors. Three of the most common and deadly of these diseases are plague, typhus and malaria.

Plague, bubonic and pneumonic, was widely regarded as the worst of all epidemics. This was partly due to its suddenness and high case fatality. Its first impact often killed up to half a country's population and then through the centuries it constantly recurred. There had been serious outbreaks previously in history, for instance in the sixth and seventh centuries AD, but it is the consequences of the affliction that covered much of western Europe from the fourteenth to seventeenth centuries that concern us here.[1]

Uncertainty surrounds every aspect of the history of plague. To start with, it is not clear how it is spread. We know that it is caused by a bacillus, which was discovered towards the end of the nineteenth century. 'During the first epidemic at Hong Kong, Kitasata, a Japanese bacteriologist, discovered the plague bacillus.'[2] Almost simultaneously it was discovered by Yersin in the West, hence its name 'Yersinia pestis'. It can, however, be transmitted in various ways. Firstly it can undoubtedly be transmitted by the rat flea but it appears that it can also be transmitted by the human flea, *Pulex irritans*, and hence the presence or

---

[1] For general description see Braudel, *Capitalism*, 46ff; Shrewsbrury, *Bubonic Plague*; Creighton, *Epidemics*; Slack, *Plague*, Hollingsworth, *Historical Demography*, appdx 2.

[2] Burnett, *Infectious*, 228.

absence of rats is not a sufficient factor in itself.[3] Furthermore it can be passed, in the pneumonic form, by way of respiratory secretions and so it cannot be classified as either vector-borne or non-vector-borne.[4]

This diversity of transmission has led to many disputes, one of which questions whether the Black Death was transmitted by the black rat. One survey of the evidence has suggested that it was not and that the epidemic was mainly pneumonic and perhaps partly spread by human fleas,[5] while a recent study of plague in early modern England supports the rat hypothesis.[6]

Having decimated populations in Europe from the time of the Black Death in 1348, in the later seventeenth century plague mysteriously and almost completely disappeared.[7] In England, after a high mortality in 1665 in London, it vanished without trace after three hundred years of depredations. 'After 1657, the plague ceased to visit Italy.'[8] In 1707–14, it 'spread from Russia and Hungary as far as Sweden, Denmark, Prussia and Bavaria', but no further west.[9] In France, the last important epidemic was in Provence in 1720–1.[10] That it disappeared in western Europe, while remaining endemic in its central loci in Asia, is not in doubt.

A number of hypotheses have been put forward to explain this decline. One concerns biological adaptations. It has been argued that there was some accidental mutation in the bacteria, *Yersinia pestis*, or its animal or human host, which caused it suddenly to disappear. Yet there has been no sign of such a mutation. Furthermore, where it continued, as in Turkey, there is 'no sign of any decline in the disease's infectivity or virulence in the later seventeenth century. There are similar objections to the argument that a build-up of human or rodent resistance to the disease explains its withdrawal.'[11] 'The suggestion that bubonic plague disappeared from western Europe as a consequence of acquired natural immunity seems untenable.'[12]

A second hypothesis concerns the favourite vector, the black rat. If plague was carried by *Rattus rattus*, it has been suggested that the surplanting of the black rat by the Asian or brown rat might explain the rapid disappearance of plague. There are two insurmountable problems here. The first is timing. Plague disappeared in western Europe from the 1660s. The brown rat reached

---

[3] Flinn, *European*, 57.

[4] Ewald, *Infectious*, 37.

[5] Davis, *Scarcity*, 459–67.

[6] Slack, *Plague*, 11,314.

[7] Kunitz in Coleman and Schofield (eds), *Population Theory*, 281.

[8] Cipolla in Glass and Eversley (eds), *Population*, 573.

[9] *Chamber's Encyclopedia*, 'plague'.

[10] United Nations, *Determinants*, 144.

[11] Slack, *Plague*, 322.

[12] Post, *Modernization*, 34.

England in about 1728 and most of Europe in the 1750s. This is clearly much too late. The second problem is that it appears that the brown rat was just as lethal as the black. The brown rat 'carries diseases of man and animals – plague, typhus, Trichinella spiralis, rat-bite fever, infectious jaundice, possibly Trench fever, probably foot-and-mouth disease and a form of equine 'influenza'. Its destructiveness is almost unlimited.'[13]

A third hypothesis concerns possible alterations in the material environment. It is suggested that various changes occurred in Europe from the middle of the seventeenth century which made the environment less propitious for rats and fleas. Lord Kames in the middle of the eighteenth century suggested that 'Before the great fire *anno* 1666, the plague was frequent in London; but by widening the streets and enlarging the houses, there has not since been known in that great city, any contagious distemper that deserves the name of a plague.'[14] This was a widespread view among English doctors. Black wrote of 'That fortunate disaster which consumed a magazine of putrefaction; together with widened streets, ventilation, cleanliness, a more plentiful supply of water and many other causes, have all contributed to the extinction of this exotic incendiary.'[15] Malthus thought that the disappearance of plague after 1666 in London was due to 'the removal of nuisances, the construction of drains, the widening of the streets, and the giving more room and air to the houses', which 'had the effect of eradicating completely this dreadful disorder.'[16] Unfortunately for this theory, as Creighton pointed out, the area burnt down in the Fire of London was not that in which plague deaths mainly occurred. However, Creighton did believe that a general rise in the standard of living was probably the main cause for the decline of plague.[17]

This argument does take us some way. It would appear that for a number of years after 1348, plague may have become endemic in western Europe, re-infecting the population. For this to happen, a very dense population of rats and fleas are required to carry the plague on from year to year. It could be argued that in the middle of the fourteenth century and for the next several hundred years the living conditions in terms of housing, sanitation, diet, clothing and cultural patterns were such that plague could remain endemic. For the only time in history western Europe became an epicentre of plague. This form of re-infection from within may have become less possible with the kind of improvements in housing, drainage and other aspects of the material environment which Kames, Black and Malthus described. As Zinsser put it, 'Plague epidemics in

---

[13] Zinsser, *Rats*, 202.
[14] Kames, *Sketches*, II, 89.
[15] Black, *Arithmetical*, 65–6.
[16] Malthus, *Population*, II, 153.
[17] Creighton, *Epidemics*, II, 43,39.

man are usually preceded by widespread epizootics among rats; and under the conditions of housing, food storage, cellar construction, and such, that have gradually developed ... rats do not migrate through cities and villages as they formerly did.'[18] Such conditions may have developed in much of England well before the seventeenth century. Creighton, who provides a detailed account of the plague in England, pointed out that there seems to have been a shift in the location of plague. From about 1465, plague became basically a disease of towns, being largely absent in the countryside. Later it was largely confined to London and one or two big cities.[19]

This fits with the description given by John Saltmarsh: 'At the first onset ... there is very great mortality.... Then follows the aftermath – a prolonged period, perhaps centuries long, of endemic plague on a small scale. ... Towards the end of the plague period, the intervals between outbreaks seem to grow longer, and for the most part they are limited to the towns, especially the larger towns; with a few unimportant exceptions, the countryside is free.'[20]

Changes in the material environment, however, cannot explain the sudden disappearance of plague all over western Europe from the later seventeenth century. There are far fewer signs of the kind of improvements Malthus alluded to in most other European cities. Furthermore, many of the improvements seem to have come after the disappearance, rather than before. While it is reasonable to suggest that 'More frequent changes of linen as standards of living rose in the later seventeenth and early eighteenth centuries no doubt freed many early modern Englishmen from the host of fleas which were a necessary condition for major urban epidemics,' Slack is well aware that this cannot explain the original disappearance. 'By the end of the eighteenth century environmental improvements had no doubt made serious epidemics of plague in the more prosperous parts of Europe unlikely; but they do not explain their complete disappearance as early as the 1660s.'[21]

A further set of hypotheses are based on recent findings concerning the ways in which plague spread geographically. Appleby, Slack and others have argued that plague was 'continually re-imported as a result of overseas trade contacts'.[22] Slack has come to the conclusion in studying English plague epidemics that 'Plague was always imported into Britain. We have seen the role of ports – Hull, Yarmouth and Plymouth as well as London – at the beginning of each epidemic wave. The disease might linger for several years afterwards, as it spread from one town to another; but in the end it disappeared and had to be reintroduced

[18] Zinsser, *Rats*, 93.
[19] Creighton, *Epidemics*, I, 233; II, 42.
[20] Saltmarsh, *Plague and Economic Decline*, 31.
[21] Slack, *Plague*, 322, 322–3.
[22] Walter and Schofield (eds), *Famine*, 62.

from outside.' This was also the case at the European level. 'So far as England is concerned, therefore, plague was an invader. It came in waves at irregular but frequent intervals, causing high mortality to begin with and only slowly dying away. The same might be said about Europe and the Mediterranean lands as a whole.' Thus, 'Studies of plague in Europe show that major epidemics in London and then in other English towns were the consequence of waves of infection sweeping across the whole Continent and coming into England from outside.'[23] For instance, 'The last major plague epidemic in north-western Europe has been traced to Dutch ships returning to Amsterdam from Smyrna in 1663.'[24]

If it was the case that plague was constantly being brought in along trade routes, it focuses attention on macro-changes in such routes. Such explanations are particularly attractive since it is clearly only some very large alteration, affecting all of western Europe, which can account for the simultaneous decline of plague there.

One theory is that there was a switch in the pattern of trade. This theory has several variants. One is that 'the fact that northern Europeans turned to an Atlantic-based trade, shifting markets away from the Mediterranean to colonies in the Western Hemisphere and to the Far East, may be related to the decline of plague first in Great Britain, Scandinavia, and the Low Countries.'[25] This may be a part of the reason, but if the change was spread over a number of decades, it is difficult to see why the 1660s were a turning point. Furthermore, plague vanished equally fast in the western Mediterranean. A supplementary theory was put forward by J.F.D.Shrewsbury. 'Bubonic plague disappeared from London and from England because the maritime importations of Pasteurella [Yersinia] pestis in plague-infected ship rats from European and Levantine ports ceased.' The reason for this is simple; 'the development of the all-sea trade between Europe and India, which abolished the caravan route for merchandise from the East across Asia Minor and with it the 'rodent pipe line' for the transit of P. pestis from its Indian home land to the ports of the Levant.'[26] Again this may be a factor, though the change was too protracted to account for the 1660s decline. What is true, as Slack points out, is that 'If ships from infected ports overseas or passengers and goods leaving infected English towns could be stopped, those epidemic waves which swept across Europe and then across England might be cut short.'[27]

---

[23] Slack, *Plague*, 313,14,13.

[24] Post, *Modernization*, 34.

[25] Ann Carmichael in Kiple (ed.), *Disease*, 282.

[26] Quoted in McKeown, *Modern Rise*, 88.

[27] Slack, *Plague*, 315.

This takes us to the last variant of the theories related to the cutting of the source of infection, namely that conscious national and international measures were taken to set up a *cordon sanitaire* to prevent plague from coming in from the East, and particularly through Turkey from India. 'It is likely that bubonic plague was extinguished in western Europe during the seventeenth century by vigorous local action that prevented the disease from spreading once it appeared and during the eighteenth century by national governmental action that hindered and ultimately prevented the international migration of infection.'[28] This was clearly important in the eighteenth century as contemporary observers noted. Black wrote that plague 'rarely now gains admittance, by stealth, into any of the European ports (Constantinople excepted) or even if imported to our shores, the wise precautions and regulation, enacted by quarantines, soon check its irruption and progress.' He wrote that 'At present, in all the Mediterranean ports they are, from fatal experience, scrupulously vigilant to guard, by a circumvallation of alarm posts, against the pestilential infection, and the clandestine entry of infected goods or merchandise.'[29]

While this may help to explain how plague was kept at bay in the eighteenth century, it is difficult to see how it can explain the sudden disappearance in the 1660s. Attempts had earlier been made to provide a quarantine: 'From the very beginning of the epidemic, however, the populations of a number of European cities – above all, in central and northern Italy, which boasted a highly developed order of municipal and medical institutions – reacted aggressively in a largely futile attempt to protect themselves from the disease.'[30] Why was there suddenly universal success? 'There is no evidence ... that noticeable improvements had occurred in this respect after 1660 until at least the end of the eighteenth century.'[31] We can only conclude with Slack that 'It would therefore be as simplistic to search for a single explanation for changes in the distribution of plague as for a single explanation for a political or an industrial revolution.'[32]

Forty years ago Zinsser wrote that 'When all is said and done, we have no satisfactory explanation for the disappearance of plague epidemics from the Western countries.'[33] Now, after much more research we are still in the same position; we do not know what led to its disappearance. Livi-Bacci concludes that neither 'social adjustment, immunity, selection' nor 'other social or ecological transformations' could explain it. All we know is that 'For reasons not

---

[28] Flinn, *European*, 61.

[29] Black, *Arithmetical*, 66–7,66.

[30] Kiple (ed.), *Disease*, 615; for the history of quarantine, reputedly invented in Italy in the fourteenth century, see Beckman, *Inventions*, I, 375–6.

[31] Cipolla in Glass and Eversley (eds), *Population*. 574.

[32] Slack, *Plague*, 312.

[33] Zinsser, *Rats*, 93.

entirely clear' it happened.[34] The same is true of its disappearance elsewhere. For instance, plague became a very serious epidemic disease in late-nineteenth-century India. From 1896 to 1914 it is estimated that over eight million people died of the disease.[35] Then after 1921 it suddenly disappeared – for reasons as yet unknown.[36]

The experience of Japan tends to support the quarantine argument. Periodic outbreaks of plague were widespread in China from an early date. For this reason McNeill suggested that plague might have reached Japan in 808.[37] Yet there is no description in the very full sources of a disease with plague-like symptoms and consequently 'the existence of plague in Japan during this period remains in doubt.'[38] The word for plague, *pesuto*, is of European derivation.

The fourteenth century world pandemic does not seem to have reached Japan. 'If the Mongols had succeeded in their invasion of the islands, then Japan, too, undoubtedly would have suffered from the plague. But Japan remained plague-free, population continued to grow ...'[39] Nor is there any later evidence of plague. Bubonic plague seems 'not to have affected early modern Japan.'[40] Jannetta writes in her recent survey, 'my search for epidemics of bubonic plague in pre-modern Japan went unrewarded ... the Japanese sources reviewed here reveal no evidence of plague in Japan before the late nineteenth century.'[41] This cannot be explained away by the absence of information, for, as Jannetta shows, the records for the history of disease in Japan are superb. Plague really does seem to have been absent. Japan is the one major country in the world with a dense population which does not seem to have suffered from plague until the very end of the nineteenth century.

The absence of plague in Japan can largely be explained by the fact that the hundred miles of sea between Japan and the mainland created a *cordon sanitaire*. Since Japan was self-sufficient in cereals, ships did not carry grain from China or Korea hence infected rats were less likely to enter the country. This natural barrier was made stronger by the Japanese realization of the connection between plague and rats. Griffis noted that the Japanese 'have guarded their coasts against the advent of diseases from abroad. Especially feared is the pest in the

---

[34] Livi-Bacci, *Population*, 49; cf. also Kunitz in Coleman and Schofield (eds), *Population Theory*, 281; Flinn, *European*, 58.

[35] Roberts, *Hygiene*, 120.

[36] See McAlpin, *Famines*, 362.

[37] According to Farris in Kiple (ed.), *Disease*, 377; McNeill, *Plagues*, 134 states this is 'merely a guess'.

[38] Farris in Kiple (ed.), *Disease* 378.

[39] Farris in Kiple (ed.), *Disease*, 383.

[40] Jannetta in Kiple (ed.), *Disease*, 388.

[41] Jannetta, *Epidemics*, xix.

form of the bubonic plague. It was discovered that rats were the carriers of contagion, and that the rodents were in many lines of analogy as susceptible to disease as man is, the bacillus being common to both.' 'A general slaughter was ordered. The number of rats – numerous in most old Japanese houses – killed in the large cities reached to many hundreds of thousands.'[42] The Tokugawa government's seclusion (*sakoku*) policy provided the general context for the medical precautions.

Such knowledge, however, is not enough as we can see from the European context. We are told that 'Sticker has collected a great many references to this subject from ancient and medieval literature, and has found much evidence in the folklore of medieval Europe which points to the vague recognition of some connection between plague and rats.'[43] As late as 1894, the greatest world authority on the history of bubonic plague, Creighton, frequently noted the association between the death of rats and bubonic plague – yet he thought the dead rats were merely a side-effect of deadly miasma arising from corpses, which was the real cause of plague.[44] The difficulty was proving the link, and doing anything about the rats.

What is clear is that there were rats in Japan. 'The whole Country swarms with Rats and Mice. The rats are tam'd by the Natives and taught to perform several tricks. Rats thus taught are the common diversion of some poor People.'[45] Isabella Bird complained: 'my wretched room was dirty and stifling, and rats gnawed my books and ran away with my cucumbers.' There was a 'rat snake' which lived in the rafters and who 'when he is much gorged, occasionally falls down upon a mosquito net.'[46] Morse described how 'the rats tear around overhead, and the ceiling being made of thin boards papered they make a tremendous noise.'[47] Hearn thought 'it is great fun to feed these birds with dead rats or mice which have been caught in traps over night and subsequently drowned. The instant a dead rat is exposed to view a kite pounces from the sky to bear it away.'[48] It would appear that the black rat, *Rattus rattus* is native to Japan.[49] It was not the absence of rats that seems to have been important, but preventing the influx of infected rats. This strengthens the arguments for the importance of quarantining in the European case.

---

[42] Griffis, *Mikado*, 662.

[43] Zinsser, *Rats*, 191.

[44] Creighton, *Epidemics*, I, 168–9,173; for plague as a virus or miasma emanating from the soil and particularly dead bodies, see Creighton, *Epidemics*, I, 176,337; II, 35.

[45] Kaempfer, *History*, I, 201.

[46] Bird, *Tracks*, 145,144.

[47] Morse, *Day*, I, 257.

[48] Hearn, *Glimpses*, 379; other references to the ubiquity and attitudes to rats see Rein, *Travels*, 414; Scidmore, *Jinrikisha*, 325.

[49] Kodansha, *Encyclopedia*, II, 1248.

Typhus is divided into two variants, epidemic typhus, which is carried by
infected lice, and 'scrub typhus' which is carried from its reservoir of rodents
through mites into the human blood. Here I am concerned only with epidemic
typhus. It is a major killer alongside bubonic plague and the two are often
difficult to differentiate.

The disease is caused by one of the groups of micro-organisms called rickettsia, which are 'small cocci or coccobacilli which occupy a position between the
viruses and the bacteria. . . . Rickettsias differ from bacteria in that they require
the presence of living cells for growth.'[50] 'The body louse is the vector from
patient to patient. It takes up rickettsiae from the blood and is itself fatally
infected in the process. However, it has about a week in which to transfer
the infection to another subject before it dies. In view of this method of
transmission, typhus can flourish only in circumstances of poverty, overcrowd-
ing and filth.'[51]

It is not certain where and how typhus originated. 'In all probability typhus
is an ancient disease of rats and mice, perhaps an even more ancient disease of
the fleas that live on the rodents.' But the 'typical louse-spread typhus is a
modern development'.[52] Furthermore, 'there are no records of typhus fever in
recognizable form in the ancient Oriental, Chinese, and classical literatures, and
none in the chronicles and histories of the early Middle Ages.' 'We can thus
conclude with some confidence that, as an epidemic disease, typhus did not exist
in Europe until the fifteenth century.' It was 'well launched in an epidemic form
in Europe during the last decade of the fifteenth century and throughout the
sixteenth.' It is possible that it originated in America. 'There is much in
the historical evidence which suggests the existence of typhus fever among
the South American nations in pre-Columbian days.' 'In rats, the disease can be
kept going indefinitely, and may easily have survived voyages even longer than
those of the Spaniards.'[53] It also appears that it can be transmitted directly from
rat fleas.[54]

Whatever its origins, it began to spread rapidly through Europe. The ideal
conditions were those of 'famine, abject poverty, homeless wandering and constant warfare'; 'no encampment, no campaigning army, and no besieged city
escaped it.' The wars of the seventeenth and eighteenth centuries encouraged its
spread in Europe. 'The wars of the Spanish, Polish, and Austrian Successions'
in the eighteenth century led to an 'almost uninterrupted succession of typhus
epidemics which spared no byway and corner of Europe throughout the eight-

---

[50] Merck, *Manual*, 866.
[51] Burnett, *Infectious*, 146.
[52] Burnett, *Infectious*, 146,146.
[53] Zinsser, *Rats*, 214,218,246,258,263.
[54] Burnett, *Infectious*, 146.

eenth and a large part of the nineteenth century.'[55] Epidemic typhus 'had an enormous impact on mortality in early modern Europe.'[56] It is another disease which grows directly proportionate to the degree of crowding.

The louse which carried most typhus germs does not actually live on the human skin but clings to clothes. Wool is a particularly attractive home. Andrew Nikiforuk suggests that 'As the continent's supply of sheep grew, plague survivors wore more wool, supported greater lice colonies and became more lousy. Typhus took advantage of the wool craze and spread across Europe in the fifteenth century.'[57] If true, this is an important point to remember in relation to its demise.

Nor is it, unlike other vector-born diseases, a bite that causes the disease but rather, 'the dejecta of arthropods', in other words it is parts of the body and faeces of the louse that are absorbed by the human. This can be done through food or 'In rare instances, infection may be sustained by pulmonary inhalation or conjunctival absorption of air-borne suspensions of the organisms.'[58] 'Faeces dust remains infectious for years, and it is either inhaled or enters through the eyelids. Desiccated infected louse faeces shaken out as dust from winter or cold-weather clothing may explain the seasonal incidence of typhus. The inability to keep warm and clean increases the number of lice, and then families huddling together under heavier textiles, possibly infected with louse faeces, or wandering in crowds, facilitates the spread of the contagion.'[59]

The pattern of epidemic typhus in England can be seen through the overview given by Clarkson. 'By about the middle of the seventeenth century fevers of the typhus type ... had become well established as more or less regular visitors in England causing more deaths, year in and year out, than plague', 'In post-Restoration England typhus fever was practically a part of everyday life.'[60] A number of typhus epidemics affected England in the sixteenth to eighteenth centuries. There is very little doubt that 'the disease which decimated both the parliamentary and the Royal armies at the siege of Reading in 1643 was typhus.'[61] Chambers draws attention to typhus outbreaks in 1679–80 and again in 1741–2.[62]

After 1750, typhus remained one of the few diseases which could reach epidemic proportions. It grew more serious in eighteenth-century London.[63]

[55] Zinsser, *Rats*, 238,283,286,282.

[56] Jannetta, *Epidemics*, 194.

[57] Nikiforuk, *Fourth*, 61.

[58] Merck, *Manual*, 866.

[59] Post, *Modernization*, 30.

[60] Clarkson, *Disease*, 45,46.

[61] Zinsser, *Rats*, 281; for a description, see Creighton, *Epidemics*, I, 549,553.

[62] Chambers, *Population*, 102.

[63] Landers, *Death*, 347.

During the period between 1770 and 1815, according to Creighton, it was generally absent.[64] But then there were particularly severe outbreaks in 1816–8, when more than 100,000 people caught the disease, of whom about 10% probably died.[65] The epidemic was even worse in Ireland, at this time, when some 700,000 of the six million or so inhabitants were affected.[66] Typhus finally declined rapidly from the 1870s, but this decline 'should be seen in the context of long-term decline in the death rate from fevers from the mid eighteenth century.'[67] Creighton believed that typhus and relapsing fevers disappeared in England after the 1870s due to an improved standard of living, in particular as a result of better housing, food and fuel.[68] 'The last great epidemic in Eastern Europe after the First World War, is estimated to have affected 30 million people and killed three million of them.'[69]

The connection with clothing and washing is shown in the seasonal incidence of typhus. 'Epidemic outbreaks of typhus usually begin in winter, when the cold discourages bathing and changing clothes, and disappear with the coming of warm weather.'[70] At the end of the nineteenth century, it was thought to be a 'disease for the most part of temperate climates. At the present day Ireland, Russia, Italy, Persia and North China are its chief seats.'[71] A century later its location had shifted to less temperate climes. It now seems to have been reduced to three main areas, 'the Himalayan region of Asia, the Andean regions of South America, and the horn of Africa, especially famine-ridden Ethiopia.'[72]

Since typhus is associated with crowding and with clothing, bathing and personal hygiene, it is particularly interesting to turn to Japan. We know that it was a crowded country. Does the incidence of typhus reflect this fact? In her monograph on epidemics in Japan, Jannetta records that 'One of the most important findings of this study is that two of the most disastrous epidemic diseases of premodern Europe – bubonic plague and epidemic typhus – do not appear in premodern Japanese accounts.' There are no descriptions of anything like epidemic typhus before it was brought into Japan by westerners in the later nineteenth century. The Japanese approximation of the word 'typhus' is *chifusy*, which was written in *katakana*. This suggests that it was regarded as a new disease. It is not one of the diseases referred to in Fujikawa's *History of Disease*

[64] Creighton, *Epidemics*, II, 133ff,215.
[65] Post, *Modernization*, 31.
[66] Victoria Harden in Kiple (ed.), *Disease*, 1082.
[67] Mercer, *Disease*, 89.
[68] Creighton, *Epidemics*, II, 214.
[69] Busvine, *Insects*, 11.
[70] Appleby, *Famine*, 103; cf. also Kiple (ed.), *Disease*, 1080.
[71] *Chamber's Encyclopedia*, 'typhus'.
[72] Harden in Kiple (ed.), *Disease*, 1081.

in Japan. 'What is clear is that Japanese accounts written before the arrival of Western trade contain no descriptions of epidemics similar to typhus.' It seems to have been a 'new and imported' disease in the late nineteenth century.[73]

Malaria is one of the most complex and deadly of all diseases. Nikiforuk estimates that 'Since the beginning of history malaria has killed half of the men, women and children that have died on the planet. It has outperformed all wars, all famines and all other epidemics.'[74] Burnett gives a brief sketch of its devastating effects in history. 'There is good reason to believe that malaria played a major part in the decline and fall of the Roman Empire, of Greece, and of the ancient civilization and power of Ceylon.'[75] 'It was the great devitalizer of the tropics – much of the backwardness of the Indian peasant has been ascribed to malaria – and it was the main agent of infantile mortality all through history till the end of the Second World War.'[76] This is a view supported by the finding that 'before the post-war era virtually everyone in South Asia was suffering in some manner from malaria.'[77] More precisely, 'In India it was calculated that in 1930 about a hundred million people were infected with the parasite, and that about two million deaths per annum were directly due to malaria.' Burnett believes that 'Of all the infectious diseases there is no doubt that malaria has caused the greatest harm to the greatest number.'[78]

Human malaria is an ancient disease. It seems certain that it is an 'Old World disease in its origins' and it can be traced back to the earliest civilizations.[79] There are many different forms of malaria and it has 'shown no signs of evolving towards benigness.' Furthermore, 'Because the malaria organisms can reproduce sexually during its transmission cycle, it has a great potential for evolving around barriers that we place in its way. This potential is well illustrated by its responses to antimalarial drugs.'[80]

It is because of its immense complexity and continued virulence that malaria poses one of the greatest threats to world health today. It was believed in the 1960s that it would be conquered by the draining of swamps and liberal use of DDT, but now it is regaining ground in many parts of the world.[81] Given its terrible debilitating effects, 'destroying blood, weakening physical resistance

[73] Jannetta, *Epidemics*, 191,195.
[74] Nikiforuk, *Fourth*, 14.
[75] Burnett, *Infectious*, 232; cf. also Boserup, *Scarcity*, 393.
[76] Burnett, *Infectious*, 232.
[77] Myrdal, *Asian Drama*, III, 1569.
[78] Burnett, *Infectious*, 232.
[79] Frederick Dunn in Kiple (ed.), *Disease*, 860.
[80] Ewald, *Infections*, 51.
[81] Dunn in Kiple (ed.), *Disease*, 856.

and ruining mental energy and moral determination',[82] an analysis of the spread of this disease is important.

After the devastations caused by malaria in the early Greek and Roman periods, malaria seemed to have receded in Europe. But as population built up again after the Black Death, it began to spread from those areas in the Mediterranean where it had always been endemic. We are told that 'By the Middle Ages, plasmodia occupied most of temperate Europe.'[83] But 'It is not until the seventeenth and eighteenth centuries that malaria became resurgent in Europe, not only in the south but, in periodic outbreaks, as far north as the Netherlands, Germany, southern Scandinavia, Poland, and Russia.'[84]

Mary Dobson believes that the introduction of malaria into England may have been related to the drainage of south-eastern England. The large amount of water in the Netherlands and Holland had provided a breeding ground for the anopheles mosquito and the malarial parasite *Plasmodium vivax* from at least the fifteenth century. Similar conditions began to be created in the coastal regions of south-east England with the drainage of tidal water, 'creating an ideal breeding place for the local mosquito population.' 'The parasite, itself, may have been introduced from the malarial-infested polderlands of Holland by sixteenth-century Dutch settlers who came to England to help reclaim the fens and marshes.'[85]

The extent of malarial infection in England was largely hidden from both contemporaries and historians. The main strain of malaria was one which did not lead directly to a high case fatality among adults but rather to persistent debilitating illness, the famous 'agues', and to infant and child deaths which were disguised among the numerous other causes of death. 'Case-fatality rates of the most common form in the temperate zone, *Plasmodium vivax*, are low except in infants and children and except among new migrants to an area of endemic malaria.'[86] The problem was recognized by Greenhow in the middle of the nineteenth century: 'When death results from malaria in this country it usually arises from some secondary affection (sic), and is not registered under the name of ague. For this reason the death-rates shown in the tables must by no means be received as correct indications of the amount of mortality caused by malarious poisoning. The total mortality from this cause is probably much larger than is usually believed.' Greenhow believed that even so 'it will in this climate constitute but a very small proportion of the general death rate.'[87] Yet

---

[82] Angelo Celli quoted in Nikiforuk, *Fourth*, 15.
[83] Nikiforuk, *Fourth*, 20.
[84] Kiple (ed.), *Disease*, 861.
[85] Dobson, *Hiccup*, 413; see also Dobson, *Marsh Fever*, 382.
[86] Riley, *Insects*, 846.
[87] Greenhow, *Papers*, 105.

this may well not have been the case from the seventeenth to the mid-eighteenth century.

The detailed work by Dobson has shown the seriousness of the situation. 'Approximate estimates of crude burial rates for 560 south-east England parishes also point repeatedly to the high mortality levels in the marshland parishes during this period.' This was a period when there was a temporary rise in mortality in England and much of it was put down to 'fevers'. They 'assumed particular prominence in the epidemiological sources for this period and, indeed, seem to have contributed to the most extensive and prolonged regional mortality peaks of the late seventeenth century.'[88] Many of these 'fevers' may have been related to the spread of malaria. Nor was the situation limited to East Anglia, but extended to the southern counties of Kent, Surrey and Middlesex.[89]

Indeed it seems likely that even northern England was seriously affected. Chadwick described the prevalence of malaria round the city of Durham[90] and Riley states that 'recent research establishes malaria as a leading cause of death in the eighteenth century in northern England and Sweden.'[91] Malaria was found in southern Scotland up to the nineteenth century.[92] As Riley points out, 'European latitudes and temperatures are not important factors in the existence of this disease, only in its seasonality, which is a function of when vectors carrying the plasmodium are numerous and active.' Most of western Europe was potentially malarial. 'An average isotherm of 60 degrees Fahrenheit, 15.6 degrees centigrade, is sufficient for the activity of most strains of the malarial mosquito, and some strains, *Anopheles claviger*, for example, known to be resistant to cold, tolerate lower temperatures.'[93] Burnett correctly observed that 'Although malaria is preeminently a tropical disease, it was once very prevalent in England and certain coastal districts of the Netherlands.'[94]

Burnett also puts his finger on the ensuing problem. If malaria was widespread in parts of England from the early seventeenth century, why does it seem to have receded rapidly after about the first third of the eighteenth century, not only in England, but, somewhat later, from much of Europe? It is 'difficult to understand why malaria had so largely disappeared from Europe' before any new methods of malaria control were introduced.[95] The rapidity of the change was well set out by Place at the start of the nineteenth century.[96] Yet there were

[88] Dobson, *Hiccup*, 411–12,418.
[89] cf. Howe, *Environment*, 109.
[90] Chadwick, *Report*, 94.
[91] Riley, *Insects*, 846–7.
[92] Bruce-Chwatt, *Malaria*, 136.
[93] Riley, *Insects*, 847.
[94] Burnett, *Infectious*, 236.
[95] Burnett, *Infectious*, 236.
[96] Place, *Illustrations*, 251.

resurgences, for 'ague' was widespread in England and also in Scotland, Holland and parts of Germany in 1826–8.[97] However, by the end of the nineteenth century, indigenous malaria had clinically disappeared from England.[98]

A solution to this puzzle is important for several reasons. Firstly, it looks as if malaria is one of those density-dependent diseases which Malthus predicted would emerge to cut back human populations, hence preventing their further growth. Part of the European 'high-level trap' in the seventeenth century was manifested in the form of increased malaria. Yet somehow England and some other parts of Europe passed out of this malarial phase without introducing any obvious direct measures to combat it. The decline in eighteenth century England may therefore hold one of the clues to the unexpected fall in general mortality during that century. A solution to these puzzles might provide us with insights that would be of value in combating the growing threat of a resurgence of malaria in many parts of the world today.

The case of Japan is even more interesting and important. Most of Japan is well within the temperature zone which would make it liable to various forms of malaria. Maps of malaria distribution show that China and Korea up to a latitude of north central Japan suffered seriously from the disease. It arrived in China before the birth of Christ and 'wise men assumed the new disease was three devils.'[99] Korea had a special strain of malaria.[100]

The system of wet rice agriculture practised in Japan, the many ponds and lakes, the extensive drainage carried on along the coasts from the middle ages, all these would lead one to expect malaria to have been widespread. 'Japan is a land with many swamps; it is interesting to speculate about the effects of malaria on a peasantry trying to convert these low-lying lands into productive rice paddies.'[101] We know that mosquitoes were present in large numbers. 'Evening does not bring coolness, but myriads of flying, creeping, jumping, running creatures, all with power to hurt, which replace the day mosquitoes, villains with spotted legs, which bite and poison one without the warning hum. The night mosquitoes are legion.'[102] 'At night, mosquitoes are numerous, hungry and of good size.'[103] Morse referred to the 'swarms' of mosquitoes he encountered.[104] Chamberlain observed that 'the mosquito is a nightly plague during half the year in all places lying at an altitude of less than 1,500 feet above the sea, and in many even

[97] Creighton, *Epidemics*, II, 378.
[98] Dobson, *Marsh Fever*, 386 and cf. figure on 387.
[99] Nikiforuk, *Fourth*, 17.
[100] Merck, *Manual*, 834.
[101] Kiple (ed.), *Disease*, 380.
[102] Bird, *Tracks*, 119.
[103] Griffis, *Mikado*, 528.
[104] Morse, *Day*, I, 131,160.

exceeding that height.'[105] Another mosquito-borne disease, significantly named 'Japanese B encephalitis' was to be found, carried by the genus *Culex*[106] and the *anopheles* mosquito 'seems to have been present in Japan at all times.'[107]

Unlike the New World, which probably never experienced malaria until it was brought over from Europe,[108] it seems clear that malaria was present in early Japan. In the twelfth century, 'Diaries written by members of the gentry ... refer to the occurrence of malaria.' 'Malaria was called either *okori* or *marawa-yami*, the latter meaning high fever and chills.' Another name, also found in the scrolls of the twelfth century, was *gyaku-shitsu*. 'According to this source, illness was characterized by fever and chills that recurred throughout an individual's life.'[109] Even Prince Genji himself suffered from malaria, as did Muso Kokushi, the Zen priest. Although the association with mosquitoes was not made, 'a court lady seemed to believe that butterflies were common where the disease broke out.'[110] From the twelfth to thirteenth centuries there is evidence of malaria and it would seem likely that it persisted in certain places. In the nineteenth century, 'Bange was malarious; there was so much malarious fever that the Government had sent medical assistance.'[111] Morse noted that 'some fevers due to malaria occur.'[112] Scidmore judged the missionary settlement of Tsukiji to be 'malarial'.[113] A health team noted in 1927 that 'Subtertian malaria is very rare' and 'Quartan malaria' was only found in the Kwawa Prefecture, but 'benign tertian malaria is scattered through the country'. It 'occurs principally in low-lying districts where the conditions favour the propagation of *anopheles sinensis* the carrier in this country. It occurs in the summer.'[114]

Japan was a very densely populated island, with the right temperature, ecology and agriculture for malaria. The mosquitoes were present, the disease was present not only in neighbouring countries but early on in Japan itself. We would therefore expect malaria to have played a significant role in Japanese mortality over the centuries.

However, when we turn to a more detailed analysis of the sources, we find that, to all intents and purposes, malaria has been of minimal importance in Japan for nearly a thousand years. Though there were words for it in the early

---

[105] Chamberlain, *Things*, 528.
[106] Kiple (ed.), *Disease*, 811–812; Busvine, *Insects*, 156.
[107] Shoji Tatsukawa in Kiple (ed.), *Disease*, 374.
[108] Kiple (ed.), *Disease*, 860.
[109] Taksukawa in Kiple (ed.), *Disease*, 374.
[110] Farris in Kiple (ed.), *Disease*, 380,384,380.
[111] Bird, *Tracks*, 106.
[112] Morse, *Day*, I, 23.
[113] Scidmore, *Jinrikisha*, 46.
[114] Wellington, *Hygiene*, 34, Tertian malaria is the mild form, quartan has morbid symptoms and subtertian is the very severe form.

records, these were forgotten and it is now called by the loan word, *mararia*, suggesting its foreign nature. The travellers who visited Japan from the sixteenth to nineteenth centuries attest, either by their remarks or, more often by their silences, to its virtual absence. The doctors Kaempfer and Thunberg in their very detailed descriptions do not refer to malaria. Nineteenth century doctors, von Siebold, Pompe and Willis do not mention malaria as a serious malady.

When they mention it at all, it is clearly an illness which has been caught abroad and brought back to Japan. Willis mentions it twice in 1865: 'Both the Admiral and the Minister are suffering from it to no great extent, however, and I hope a few days will put them both on their legs completely, assisted with liberal doses of quinine.' A few years later Willis 'was very busy attending large numbers of sick men who returned from Formosa suffering from malaria. They required large quantities of quinine, with which fortunately the hospital was well supplied.' Willis observed that 'so far as he had been able to learn, nearly every Satsuma man who had returned was suffering from malarial fever or its effects. Many would never recover.'[115] It is worth noting the susceptibility of the Japanese once they went to a malarial area. Yet the return of large numbers of soldiers infected with malaria, which must have happened before in Japanese history, does not seem to have led to an epidemic of malaria within the country.

Medical historians have confirmed this picture of the low incidence of malaria. Fujikawa's *History of Disease* does not include a chapter on it; it was clearly of less importance than, for example, German measles or chicken pox, both of which he covers. More recently, Jannetta's detailed account of epidemics in Japan has no entry for malaria in the index and does not discuss the disease. Neither Sansom or the four later volumes of the *Cambridge History of Japan* mention malaria. More popular social histories paint the same, or an even more extreme picture. Thus Dunn writes of the Edo period that 'there does not appear to have been any malaria in Japan at the time.'[116] Modern maps of the distribution of malaria show Japan as an area without the disease.[117]

The reasons for the decline in England and Europe, and the virtual absence in Japan, are likely to be complex. We know that human feeding patterns are likely to affect immunity. 'There is some evidence ... that children exposed to malaria remain free of this disease as long as they are breast-fed because human milk is very low in paraaminobenzoic acid.'[118] Other eating habits may also be important. For example, it is likely that a reasonably fed population is less likely to succumb to malaria than a severely malnourished one.

---

[115] Cortazzi, *Willis*, 62,207.
[116] Dunn, *Everyday*, 160–1.
[117] Hunter, *Tropical Medicine*, 517.
[118] Dubos, *Adapting*, 158.

Housing and particularly anything that prevents mosquitoes biting, such as netting, is important. Well before it was realized how malaria was spread, it had been noticed that 'In districts where malaria exists it is found by experience that those who go out of their houses only during the day ... often escape the bad effects of the poison.' It was thought that there was something in the 'morning fogs' and 'evening mists' which was dangerous.[119] It was only in the early part of the twentieth century that Grassi discovered the true cause. 'Since mosquitoes bite mainly at dusk, he persuaded the families to stay inside their screened houses after dusk. Around these protected houses were the unscreened neighbouring station houses.' The occupants of the screened houses did not get malaria, those in the unprotected houses did.[120] Obviously as important as not going out is the nature of the housing. It is well known that 'a large proportion of serious vectors bite humans indoors.'[121] 'Recent studies in Sri Lanka, for example, showed that people living in houses with incomplete mud or palm walls and thatched roofs had both malaria and indoor mosquitoes twice as frequently as people living in houses with complete brick and plaster walls and tile roofs.'[122]

There may be other complex effects as well as merely preventing an infected bite. This has been discussed by Ewald:

> Widespread housing improvement may thus provide a benefit not just for the owners of the improved houses but potentially to all within reach of the malaria transmitted from the region. The most obvious benefit should be a stronger reduction in the frequency of *falciparum* malaria than in the frequencies of the milder ... malarias, but indicators of virulence should show a reduction in the virulent strains within species as well, particularly within *P. falciparum*.

Effective screening by house construction and nets not only reduce illness, but might 'cause an evolutionary suppression of virulence, if they were used comprehensively by all sick individuals.'[123]

Unfortunately, 'We shall not know whether making houses mosquito-proof will cause a strong evolutionary shift toward benignness until we try this intervention on a large scale – one that encompasses an entire interbreeding population of pathogens.' The chances of this happening, Ewald believes, are very small because of the nature of human beings. What is important is that everyone, both the sick and the well, use protection. 'But the motivation to use nets and

---

[119] *Chambers's Encyclopedia*, 'malaria'.
[120] Clegg and Clegg, *Man*, 204.
[121] Busvine, *Insects*, 157.
[122] Ewald, *Infectious*, 52.
[123] Ewald, *Infectious*, 53–4.

repellents is strongest for uninfected individuals who are trying to avoid infection. Infected individuals have relatively less to gain from their use, and, if they are ill, may be less able to use them fastidiously. Ill people do not have to remember to use their own mosquito-proof house, or be motivated to do so.'[124]

Lowering the virulence is one aspect of the problem. Another is breaking the cycle of infection altogether. If buildings can be made free of biting mosquitoes for three years 'the cycle of transmission of man-mosquito-man can be broken. After this period the mosquitoes can be left to breed freely.'[125] The cycle may be even shorter in certain types of environment. Leonard Wilson reminds us that 'in temperate climates, adult *Anopheles* either die or go into hibernation each year with the onset of winter. The following spring, a new generation is hatched from eggs laid in water. *Anopheles* of the new generation will be free of malarial parasites until they bite people with malarial parasites in their peripheral blood.'[126] This would apply to both England and most of Japan. If the cycle could be interrupted by preventing the re-infection for one year, the chain could be broken. Thus the variations between summer and winter climate in England and Japan may be important clues to the relative freedom of malaria in these two cases. On the other hand, 'Man can also act as an infective reservoir of malaria for several years. Thus, a year or period of unfavourable climate for the sexual cycle of the parasite in the mosquito does not interrupt the plasmodium cycle in humans.' Furthermore 'studies of *A.atropparvus* have shown that it can spend the winter in English houses in a state of semi-hibernation.'[127] Cohen points out that malaria has been eliminated by improved drainage, 'but primarily only in temperate parts of the world where the life cycles of the appropriate mosquitoes are relatively fragile.'[128]

The prevalence of malaria and the possibilities of its eradication are very closely linked to the system of land use, agriculture and drainage. There are several different theories here. One concerns the fluctuating relationship between humans and domestic animals. Many species of mosquito will feed on the blood of cattle, even though human malaria itself is not transmitted through animals. Burnett suggests that the absence of malaria in certain parts of the world is sometimes 'because local farming conditions made it much easier for mosquitoes to feed on cattle than on human beings.'[129] If the number of domestic animals suddenly increases, this may draw away mosquitoes. This is one cause

[124] Ewald, *Infectious*, 54.
[125] Clegg, *Man*, 211.
[126] Wilson in Bynum and Porter (eds), *Companion Encyclopedia*, 386.
[127] Dobson, *Marsh Fever*, 380–1.
[128] Cohen, *Health*, 43.
[129] Burnett, *Infectious*, 236.

advanced for the decline of malaria in eighteenth century England.[130] Or again, if cattle barns are remote from houses this may have the same effect.[131] However, it could also be argued that if large domestic animals are almost totally absent mosquitoes will find much less to feed on. The relative scarcity of domesticated animals in Queensland, Australia, has been offered as a reason for the disappearance of malaria in that region despite its prevalence at one time and a climate suitable for its continuation.[132]

Mosquitoes will only breed in certain kinds of water. For example the 'malaria-carrying mosquito of Ceylon breeds in pools of clear water exposed to sunlight, not in overgrown swamps or rice fields nor in flowing streams.' This explains the curious finding that 'Ceylon can be divided into a dry northern area, which is highly malarious and relatively sparsely populated and a large well-watered south-western area, thickly populated and relatively free from malaria in normal years.' If agriculture is disrupted by drought, new areas may emerge, ideal for malarial breedings. This happened in 1934 in Ceylon, when rivers dried up in the south and the stagnant pools that remained were filled with mosquito larvae.[133] The converse of this is that if the agricultural system is very efficient and water control is good, and particularly if all waste land is well drained, malaria is likely to decline.

In nineteenth-century England it was noticed that better drainage seemed to eliminate malaria – people usually ascribing it to some invisible miasma. 'The covering of the surface of towns with roads and buildings, and the drainage of soil, tend to prevent the extrication of malaria, or to remove its cause.'[134] Chadwick cited a number of reports by local health officers which linked malaria to drainage.[135] Several authors have suggested a link,[136] indeed Riley sees drainage as the most important control technique: 'Although it is costly, drainage sharply curtails the breeding sites of insects, reduces the incidence of malaria, and brings into use land that is in most cases exceptionally fertile.'[137]

A few other possible factors may also be mentioned. In 1632 a Spanish priest produced a sample of cinchona bark, taken from a tree in Peru, which was taken to Europe as a medicine for malaria.[138] From then on increasing quantities of 'Peruvian bark' or quinine were used in Europe. This undoubtedly mitigated

---

[130] Riley, *Insects*, 849.
[131] Busvine, *Insects*, 7.
[132] Crosby, *Ecological*, 142.
[133] Burnett, *Infectious*, 235–6,235,236.
[134] Greenhow, *Papers*, 105.
[135] Chadwick, *Report*, 93.
[136] Nikiforuk, *Fourth*, 20; Razzell, *Essays*, 160; Dubos, *Adapting*, 89; Bruce-Chwatt, *Malaria*, 139; Creighton, *Epidemics*, II, 373; Cohen, *Health*, 43.
[137] Riley, *Insects*, 840.
[138] Dunn in Kiple (ed.), *Disease*, 860.

the severity of the disease in England, as elsewhere, even though it did not strike at its root causes.[139] It has also been suggested that people may have developed some antibodies against malaria in areas of endemic malaria.[140] Mild strains of the disease 'may have the potential to act like a vaccine against more virulent strains.'[141] Finally, there are certain ways in which the larvae can be destroyed. 'The larvae can be suffocated by an oil film on the surface of the water, poisoned by Paris green or eaten by small fish.'[142]

Mary Dobson has surveyed a number of the possible reasons for the decline in malaria in eighteenth-century England and particularly in the south-east. There was the drainage of fens and marshes, though this alone 'could not have accounted for the decline of malaria throughout the region'. There were better ventilated and lit houses, Cinchona bark (quinine) and a possibly an increasing tolerance on the part of humans. She concludes that no single explanation is sufficient.[143] Indeed, we might go further and say that even all of the above reasons added together are probably not enough to explain the rapid retreat of malaria in England. There is still a mystery to be solved. It is once again tempting to link this decline in some way to the rapid spread of tea-drinking at this very point in time. Possibly the phenolic acid content of tea had an inhibiting or curative effect in relation to malaria. The seventeenth century Dutch physician Cornelis Bontekoe (also Dekker) observed that 'two glasses of strong tea before an attack and a number of glasses after' was an effective cure for malaria, then a serious disease in parts of Holland.[144] Perhaps he had noted an important link. It would be worth further investigation, particularly since the decline of malaria in Japan in the late medieval period may have coincided with the spread of tea-drinking in that country.

It would appear that in Japan three of the most destructive insect-borne diseases, bubonic plague, epidemic typhus and malaria were largely absent until its isolation from the rest of the world was ended in the later nineteenth century. Given the amount of suffering they have caused in every other large agrarian civilization, the benefits of this for the people of Japan was clearly immense. These diseases have a huge impact on the economy, demography and mentality of a nation. They cause periodic catastrophes, panics and persistent debility and ill health. Japan was the only civilization which largely avoided this set of diseases.

---

[139] For a general account of 'peruvian bark' and the controversies over it, see Creighton, *Epidemics*, II, 320–5.

[140] Burnett, *Infectious*, 51.

[141] Ewald, *Infectious*, 53.

[142] Burnett, *Infectious*, 239.

[143] Dobson, *Marsh Fever*, 384–6.

[144] Quoted in Brand (ed.), *Les Grande Cultures*, 216.

England was far more permeable and suffered recurrent outbreaks of all these diseases. Reasons for their decline or disappearance are likely to be found by looking outside England, but there were also changes within the social and material environment that would have mitigated their effects.

11

Public Environs:
Streets, Fields and Markets

The relationship between humans and the various micro-organisms which cause disease is influenced by patterns of living and almost any aspects of life may have decisive consequences. When Edward Morse travelled through Japan in the 1870s one of the first things to strike him was the absence of rubbish. Here was a very crowded country with huge cities and densely packed towns and villages, presumably generating huge amounts of waste. Yet it was, on the whole, spotless. The civilization he had left in Massachusetts was a very lightly settled and basically agricultural one, with small towns and farms, yet it was far dirtier. He began his speculations by an explicit comparison with the coast of America. There, in the coastal towns 'one sees in hundreds of regions along sea walls in our country, outhouses, refuse, and other abominations.' But as he approached Tokyo by rail in 1877, 'a cove is crossed bordered by a long sea wall lined by simple dwellings, yet everything is neat and refined.' He then widened his reflections to encompass his many journeys through the Japanese countryside and long periods in the massive cities. 'It seems incredible when I recall that in country villages and city alike the houses of rich and poor are never rendered unsightly by garbage, ash piles, and rubbish; one never sees those large communal piles of ashes, clam shells, and the like that are often encountered in the outskirts of our quiet country villages.' The Japanese 'in some mysterious way manage to bury, burn or utilize their waste and rubbish so that it is never in evidence. At all events, the egg-shells, tea-grounds, and all the waste of the house is spirited away so that one never sees it.' The very occasional exceptions only went to prove the rule. In one village 'It was hot and sultry, and in our collecting we came across piles of garbage and refuse of the town, a most unusual sight. ... The stench was dreadful, and I wondered at it, as Japanese towns are generally so clean.'[1]

The cleanliness and absence of public dirt could be found in all aspects of Japanese life. Morse expected to find fishing ports dirty, filled with unwanted bits of fish and innumerable flies. He recalled his American experience 'at Grand Manan where there was an intolerable nuisance of the flies in the village, due to the fish cleanings being scattered about.' Yet 'Enoshima is a fishing village, but the fishermen in cleaning their fish carefully remove all the offal, and do this every day. Then, too, everything they catch they eat, and so little is left to decompose.' Hence, he notes, there are no flies. The boats were equally clean: 'The woodwork is of immaculate cleanliness and one always sees some of the crew scrubbing.' Likewise, industrial plants were spotless. He visited a cotton factory: 'What amazed us beyond expression was the absence of all dirt and grease. Every girl looked clean and neat. ... Ruskin would have thought he was in the seventh heaven.'[2]

The countryside was as carefully tended as the town. Alcock quoted Veitch to the effect that 'There is one particularly striking feature in every Japanese farm; viz, the cleanliness and order everywhere prevalent. Each man seems to take a pride in keeping his land in perfect order and clear of everything in the shape of weeds.' Alcock's own impression was the same: 'Nowhere in the world, perhaps, can the Japanese farmer be matched for the good order in which he keeps his farm. The fields are not only kept scrupulously free from weeds, but in other respects the order and neatness observable are most pleasing.'[3] A similar impression was made on Morse: 'One of the many delights in riding through the country are the beautiful hedges along the road, the clean-swept walks before the doors, and in the houses everything so neat and the various objects in perfect taste.'[4]

Although Isabella Bird found some grubby villages, on the whole even she was impressed by the astounding cleanliness. Of one village she wrote, 'It is a doll's street with small low houses, so finely matted, so exquisitely clean, so finically neat, so light and delicate, that even when I entered them with my boots I felt like a "bull in a china shop", as if my weight must smash through and destroy. The street is so painfully clean that I should no more think of walking over it in muddy boots than over a drawing-room carpet.'[5]

The effects of this general public cleanliness was increased by the purity of the air. As Morse commented, 'With the absence of chimneys and the almost

[1] Morse, *Day*, I, 42,43; II, 153.
[2] Morse, *Day*, I, 206; II, 149,272.
[3] Alcock, *Tycoon*, II, 476; I, 319.
[4] Morse, *Day*, I, 54.
[5] Bird, *Tracks*, 40,53.

universal use of charcoal for heating purposes, the cities have an atmosphere of remarkable clearness and purity.' Hence 'The great sun-obscuring canopy of smoke and fumes that forever shroud some of our great cities is a feature happily unknown in Japan.'[6] The same point was made by Arnold: 'One happy consequence of this omnipresent employment of charcoal for domestic and culinary purposes is that Japanese cities, villages and abodes are perfectly free from smoke. The clear air is always unpolluted by those clouds of defacing and degrading black smuts which blot our rare sunshine in London, and help to create its horrible fogs.'[7]

There were also certain advantages caused by the nature of Japanese agriculture and housing. One huge source of filth, namely animal dung, was absent. 'Horses were not used for transportation, and thus the city streets were not fouled.'[8] With few domestic animals, the villages likewise would be much cleaner. The absence of coal burning took away the pall of soot while the small and low-level housing, combined with numerous wide avenues and parks, helped to keep the cities open and well ventilated.

The cities of Japan struck visitors as very pleasant places in which to live. 'The capital itself, though spreading over a circuit of some twenty miles, with probably a couple of millions of inhabitants, can boast what no capital in Europe can – the most charming rides, beginning even in its centre, and extending in every direction over wooded hills, through smiling valleys and shady lanes, fringed with evergreens and magnificent timber.'[9] 'Tokyo is enchanting – so far! It strikes me as a city of gardens, where streets and houses have grown up by accident – and are of no importance as compared with the flowers still.'[10] Particularly impressive was the absence of noise. 'In Tokyo itself you may enjoy, if you wish, the peace of a country village.'[11] Even the worst parts, the very poorest slums in this huge city, were far pleasanter than their equivalents in the West. Morse accidentally wandered into some densely crowded streets in Tokyo. The area looked 'squalid' to him and he was told that 'it was the lowest and poorest quarter of the city' so he 'went slowly along and examined each alley in turn.' 'I heard no loud cries or shouting, saw no blear-eyed drunkards or particularly dirty children and for a hundred children picked at random from what might be called slums, though slums they were not, I would venture that they were more polite and graceful in manner ... than a hundred children

[6] Morse, *Homes*, 2.
[7] Arnold, *Seas*, 382.
[8] Hanley, *Living*, 189.
[9] Alcock, *Tycoon*, I, 128.
[10] Fraser, *Letters*, I, 6.
[11] Hearn, *Kokoro*, 15.

picked at random from upper Fifth Avenue, New York.'[12] The charm and cleanliness was undoubtedly made easier by the height of the buildings: 'because buildings were usually no more than one and one-half stories high, density per square mile even in the largest cities was far less than in European and American cities, with their multi-storied tenements.'[13]

The problem of how the Japanese kept their environs so clean was one which intrigued Morse. One part of the explanation he thought lay in practical necessity. The rising affluence of America had led to a throw-away culture, while in Japan everything was recycled. 'In our extravagant way of living in contrast to the simple life of the Japanese we have much waste to dispose of and it is truly waste.' The Japanese 'bury, burn or utilize their waste.' And far less waste was produced. There were few egg shells because eggs were hardly eaten, there were no tins, there were few bones, because meat was not much eaten and every scrap of everything was consumed or recycled. 'The ground is kept clean and neat, convenient ditches and outlets are contriv'd to carry the rain water off towards low fields, and strong dikes are cast up to keep off that, which comes down from higher places. This makes the road at all times good and pleasant, unless it be just rainy weather and the ground slimy.' It was particularly easy to keep them clean in the countryside because there was a great demand for any rubbish dropped. 'The Inspectors for repairing the highway, are at no great trouble to get people to clean them; for whatever makes the roads dirty and nasty, is of some use to the neighbouring country people, so that they rather strive, who should first carry it away.'[14]

In the towns there was more of a problem, yet even there the streets were conspicuously clean. 'In other respects, both country roads and streets in the city of Yeddo will bear advantageous comparison with the best kept of either in the West. No squalid misery of accumulations of filth encumber the well-cared-for streets, if a beggar here and there be excepted – a strange but pleasant contrast with every other Asiatic land I have visited, and not a few European cities.' The contrast with China was particularly marked. 'In all these things the Japanese have greatly the advantage over other Eastern races, and notably over the Chinese, whose streets are an abomination to anyone possessing eyes to see, or a nose to smell with.' The cleanliness was helped by the good paving. 'A fair amount of industry and business appeared in the shops, and along the wide streets, down the centre of which there is, in most cases, a fine flag pavement.'[15] Most important was the care and responsibility people felt for road cleaning.

---

[12] Morse, *Day*, II, 370.
[13] Hanley, *Living*, 189.
[14] Kaempfer, *History*, II, 293.
[15] Alcock, *Tycoon*, I, 120,189,82.

Particularly in a hot climate, where the roads were not tarmacadamed, 'Roads should be kept watered in summer to lay the dust, and to prevent it from being blown into the houses.'[16] Morse noted: 'The streets and smaller alleys are generally well watered. The people abutting a street may be seen sprinkling it with large bamboo dippers. In Tokyo men go along the streets having suspended on carrying-poles deep buckets of water. A plug is lifted out of a hole in the bottom of the bucket and a spreading stream of water pours out, the man in the meantime almost running to scatter the water over as wide an area as possible.' Their job was made easier by the fact that they only had to deal with the middle third of the street. 'On inquiring it was learned that the city looks after the middle third of the road, the abutters on either side taking care of the other thirds.' The responsibility of those abutting was taken very seriously. 'It is amazing to see how honestly this work is performed by all.' 'One sees little boys in the street scooping water with their hands from buckets and sprinkling the road, and among all classes one observes the natives either sprinkling the paths about the houses or sweeping them with long-handled brooms.' At the end of each day, the streets were systematically cleaned: 'At about five o'clock in the afternoon everybody seemed to be engaged in sweeping the road in front of his shop and house, in many cases sprinkling before sweeping.'[17] The general effect was to lay the dust and prevent micro-organisms being blown about.

As for any rubbish left lying about by accident, this was effectively disposed of by encouraging natural scavengers. The importance of crows as cleansers is particularly notable. Morse observed that while in America the crows were so persecuted that they kept away from human habitations, in Japan they 'are so gently treated that they flock to the city by thousands.'[18] 'The crows are literally the scavengers of the streets, and are often seen disputing with a dog the possession of a bone or stealing crumbs from the children.'[19]

Behind all this strict cleanliness lay powerful pressures. One was cultural. The outside world was considered to be dirty and polluting, in contrast to the cleanliness of the house. The earth itself was dirty and it was necessary to protect people from its pollution. For walking most people wore high wooden clogs, if possible. 'Children of the poorest classes play in front of the house, but instead of enjoying their fun on the ground a straw matting is spread for them.'[20]

Death was particularly polluting and special attention was paid to keeping the 'dirt' it generated at bay. 'In Japan, if someone dies, the house is locked and a notice is hung on the door that there is a corpse in the house. This is done to

---

[16] Lane-Claypon, *Hygiene*, 77.
[17] Morse, *Day*, I, 24, fig.18; II, 125,125; I, 42,349–50.
[18] Morse, *Day*, I, 264.
[19] Morse, *Day*, II, 80–1.
[20] Morse, *Day*, I, 42.

warn people not to enter, for touching a corpse makes one unclean, and this idea
is often extended to the point that one would prefer to avoid entering the house
in which there is one.' The corpse is soon disposed of. 'Corpses usually remain
three or four days above ground; however, in cases of death through contagious
disease they are buried very quickly in Japan, although never within twenty-four
hours.'[21] Cremation was encouraged during epidemics. This had been an old
practice, for 'Cremation followed Buddhism into Japan about AD700, but never
entirely superseded the older Shinto custom of disposing of the dead by inter-
ment.'[22] Morse visited a crematorium, which he praised: 'The simplicity and
cleanliness of the appliances used in reducing the body to ashes interested us
greatly.'[23] If the body was buried, the graveyard was carefully tended. 'Graves
are cleaned yearly, whitewashed and, if necessary, plastered; the grave markers
are cleaned and the inscriptions painted; constant care is taken that the shrubs
and flowers that usually ornament these places are well cared for. It is really
touching to see with what concern the Japanese care for all this.'[24]

The mechanisms for keeping the environment free from dirt lay partly
within the individual, but also in the strict and highly organized system of local
government which Kaempfer described for Nagasaki, with its spies, committees
and executive officers. This system was parallelled in every Japanese city. 'The
inhabitants of every street are divided into *Goningumi*, that is Companies, or
Corporations of five men, whereof there are ten or fifteen, more or less, in every
street.'[25] Anyone who let their part of the street become dirty would be held
responsible, shamed and punished. Minute regulations led to harsh discipline.
'The strong administrative power of the various levels of government enabled
authorities to maintain well-regulated communities, with well-maintained
streets, bridges and water supply systems.'[26] There was a high degree of regulation in the everyday life of the Japanese. Once we have noted the enormously
high value placed on cleanliness, in keeping matter in its right place, and
combine this with the powerful system of control, it is less surprising that Japan
was so clean in its public sphere.

Given all this care and attention to public tidiness and cleanliness it is
appropriate that the Utopian sanitary city of *Hygeia* should have been modelled
on a Japanese city.[27] Nor is it surprising that visiting doctors should feel that the
West could and should learn from the Japanese. Pompe wrote that:

---

[21] Wittermans, *Pompe*, 106,107.
[22] Chamberlain, *Things*, 108.
[23] Morse, *Day*, I, 20; II, 336.
[24] Wittermans, *Pompe*, 107.
[25] Kaempfer, *History*, II, 111.
[26] Hanley, *Living*, 191.
[27] Dubos, *Adapting*, 354–5.

In many respects the Japanese are more advanced than we are, for in most cities in our country there do indeed exist quite a few hotbeds of filth and contamination, and no one at this time is so ignorant that he does not know that swamps, foul ditches, badly covered sewers, and dunghills are most harmful. Yet little is done to do away with them. And what about the slums in which so many people have to live – if we can call that living when almost all factors required for living are lacking? I hope that we may soon see in our civilized home country that hygienic rules are followed more faithfully than is the case at the present time.[28]

In England a number of features were in complete contrast to the situation in Japan. One was the prevalence of domesticated livestock. The countryside was full of horses, sheep, cows and the animals whose dung when they were alive, and whose flesh, skin and bones when dead, would add enormously to the problem of environmental cleanliness. The cities were likewise full of animals. England, with perhaps the highest ratio of livestock to humans of any large population in Europe, was particularly plagued by this problem. There is a great deal of evidence from local records and literary sources to support the impression of the difficulties caused by the keeping and eating of animals, as well as the prevalence of domestic pets. Marshall writes how 'Into the uncovered and incredibly filthy Fleet Ditch went the offal of the catgut spinners, of the tripe-dressers, of the sausage-makers, a mass of decomposing refuse.' She quotes an early eighteenth century poem:

Fleet-Ditch with disemboguing streams
Rolls the large tribute of dead dogs to Thames
The King of dykes! than whom no sluice of mud
With deeper sable blots the silver flood.[29]

Another growing problem which affected England more than any other country was that of air pollution through the increasing use of coal as fuel. In the *Fumigufium or the Smoake of London*, John Evelyn painted a gloomy picture of the 'hellish and dismal cloud of Sea-coale' over London, which was 'so universally mixed with the otherwise wholesome and excellent Aer, that her Inhabitants breathe nothing but an impure and thick Mist, accompanied with a fuliginous and filthy vapour, which renders them obnoxious to a thousand inconveniences, corrupting the Lungs, and disordering the entire habit of their Bodies; so that Catharrs, Phthisicks, Coughs, and Consumptions, rage more in this one City, than in the whole Earth besides.'[30] A dramatic instance of the

[28] Wittermans, *Pompe*, 94.
[29] Marshall, *English People*, 168.
[30] Quoted in Dubos, *Adapting*, 201.

effects of smoke became famous at about that time; in 'an autopsy on the centenarian "Old Parr", who had died of a "peripneumony" after a visit to London, Harvey stated that "the chief mischief (was) connected with the change of air, which through the whole course of (Parr's) life had been inhaled of perfect clarity", whereas the air to which he was exposed in London was polluted by smoke.'[31] This problem obviously increased rapidly over the next two hundred years. It directly contributed to the high level of pulmonary diseases, particularly tuberculosis. Efforts to keep clothes and houses clean were undermined by the thick layer of grime poured out by house and factory chimneys.

A third pressure was from the very fact of the rapid growth and crowding as the population built up in towns and industrial cities from the 1740s. It was a situation which was likely to lead to a rapidly deteriorating environment. The results were graphically described for the eighteenth century. 'In many great towns the streets are little better than dunghills, being frequently covered with ashes, dung and nastiness of every kind. Even slaughterhouses, or killing shambles are often to be seen in the very centre of great towns. The putrid blood, excrements, etc. with which these places are generally covered, cannot fail to taint the air, and render it unwholesome.'[32] Or again 'In Nottingham, a historian reported "the gathered filth within doors is scattered daily in the dirty passages without ... and many of these streets and lanes, if so they may be so-called, are without any sort of pavement, consequently without regulated water courses." '[33]

The situation seems to have been hanging in the balance. De Saussure noted that 'The streets of London are unpleasantly full either of dust or of mud. This arises from the quantity of houses that are continually being built, and also from the large number of coaches and chariots rolling in the streets day and night.' Yet while 'A number of streets are dirty, narrow and badly built; others again are wide and straight, bordered with fine houses.' Furthermore, 'Carts are used for removing mud, and in the summer time the streets are watered by carts carrying barrels, or casks, pierced with holes, through which the water flows.'[34] He also recorded the effects of the new supplies of water, pumped by steam, which allowed the houses and streets to be washed. 'The quantity of water brought into the city by the New River and other water-works, which runs daily to waste, helps to cleanse and keep the common sewers sweet, and thereby contributes much to the healthiness of the city.'[35]

---

[31] Dubos, *Adapting*, 201.
[32] Buchan, *Domestic*, 101.
[33] Chambers, *Population*, 104.
[34] De Saussure, *Foreign*, 67–8.
[35] Franklin, *Works*, VI, 320.

William Heberden believed that the decline of the plague was largely the result of improvements in municipal sanitation after the Fire of London in 1666. He gives a graphic account of the widening of streets and various measures to keep them clear of all filth. As a result, 'the new town rose up like a phoenix from the fire with increased vigour and beauty.' There was also a demonstration effect, 'for it produced in the country a spirit of improvement which had till then been unknown, but which has never since ceased to exert itself.'[36] Blane likewise draws attention both to the actual rebuilding and to the new vigour of the officials which led to 'the removal of filth, the improvement of the common sewers, the widening and paving of streets.'[37] All judgements, of course, are largely a matter of what we are comparing the situation with. In comparison to the Japanese case, England was pretty filthy throughout the period under consideration. Also, in comparison to the Dutch the English environment was not impressive.[38]

While lagging behind the Dutch and Japanese, what is notable about England is that even with the increasing pressures it managed to provide an environment which seems to have kept mortality constant, or even falling.[39] Considering other European cities, whether Paris, which Arthur Young described as dirtier than London, though a good deal smaller,[40] or Portuguese or Spanish cities, London was relatively clean. Kames described how 'Madrid, their capital, is nauseously nasty: heaps of unmolested dirt in every street, raise in that warm climate a pestiferous steam, which threatens to knock down every stranger. A purgation was lately set on foot by royal authority. But people habituated to dirt are not easily reclaimed: to promote industry is the only effectual remedy.' Or again, 'The nastiness of the streets of Lisbon before the late earthquake, was intolerable; and so is at present the nastiness of the streets of Cadiz.'[41]

The effects were noticed by eighteenth-century demographers, who claimed that London was surprisingly healthy. Short wrote in the mid-eighteenth century that 'It also appears from the Tables and Ages, that virtuous temperate People, of most Constitutions, begotten of the like Parents, often live as long in *London* as their Neighbours in their own native Soil.' He thought that this stemmed from its salubrious surroundings, 'For though *London* lies low, yet it stands and is surrounded with fine dry, sandy, gravelly, pebbly Ground and small rising Hills, from which it is constantly fanned with fine fresh Breezes

---

[36] Heberden, *Observations*, 77.
[37] Blane, *Dissertations*, 129.
[38] Schama, *Embarrassment*, 3.
[39] For an interesting early summary of town improvements in eighteenth-century England, which cites a good deal of Contemporary evidence, see Buer, *Health*, ch.vii.
[40] Quoted in Goubert, *Conquest*, 90.
[41] Kames, *Sketches*, I, 248.

from the neighbourhood of the *Thames*; and is now supplied with good fresh Water, and has no large Forests of Wood, nor putrid stagnant Waters, not extensive Fens; its Filth may be easily washed off twice a Day by the Tide.'[42]

In any discussion of public hygiene and cleanliness the dangers to health caused by the housefly cannot be ignored. In his monumental work on *The Housefly, Its Natural History, Medical Importance and Control*, Luther West quoted an educational pamphlet of 1912 which referred to the housefly as 'the most dangerous insect known.' He commented that 'sanitarians today are still unable to dispute the general truth of this assertion.'[43] Why is it so dangerous? Firstly it is ubiquitous and lives close to humans: 'The housefly is world-wide in its distribution and everywhere lives in close association with human dwellings.'[44] Secondly, it breeds very fast. A figure is quoted that 'A pair of flies beginning operations in April may be progenitive of 191,010,000,000,000,000,000 flies by August. Allowing one-eighth of a cubic inch to a fly, this number would cover the earth 47 feet deep.' We are told that 'From egg to adult fly occupies about three weeks in English summer weather; in the tropics the period may be as short as a week.'[45] It will 'breed in a large number of different substances, (ranging from snuff to spent hops!), of which the only common factor seems to be a moist, fermenting or putrefying condition. Typical examples are (a) the excrement of various animals (pig, horse, calf, man), (b) rotting vegetable matter, especially with a high protein content (seeds, grain), and (c) the heterogeneous mixture which constitutes garbage.' For instance, flies were found to be breeding in about sixty per cent of refuse bins in a London district.[46]

All of this would not be of importance if it were not for the fact that flies carry so many and varied bacteria. Roberts describes how flies may spread 'typhoid and paratyphoid fevers, epidemic diarrhoea, the dysenteries and possibly cholera, anthrax, tuberculosis and other infective disorders.'[47] Riley concludes that 'Flies carry more than a hundred species of pathogenic organisms and are believed to transmit more than sixty-five human and animal diseases.' Their danger to humans is increased by the number, as well as the range, of bacteria they carry. We are told that 'In a study involving 384,193 flies taken in Beijing, China, researchers estimated that, on average, each fly from a slum area carried 3,683,000 bacteria and each fly from the cleanest district carried 1,941,000.'

[42] Short, *Increase*, 20.
[43] West, *Housefly*, 265.
[44] Busvine, *Insects*, 191.
[45] Quoted in May, *Ecology*, 166,166.
[46] Busvine, *Insects*, 192,379.
[47] Roberts, *Hygiene*, 240.

They carry such large numbers that the critical mass to infect foodstuffs is always available.[48] The flies' feeding habits and the way in which it transfers bacteria also contribute to its lethal power. The fly is especially well suited to provide a means of transportation of shigellae and other agents living in excreta. Its proboscis is covered with an abundance of fine hair that collects germs as it picks up food from the surrounding filth. The feet are also covered with hair secreting a glue, which adds to their ability to collect microscopic organisms. Because the fly commonly feeds on excreta, its vomit and droppings contain an abundance of shigellae if any were present in its meal. It thus carries bacteria on its body, vomits frequently, and excretes probably every five minutes or so. Since it is particularly attracted to all sorts of foods used by man, especially milk, butter and cheese, meat and fish as well as human perspiration',[49] its negative health effects can be enormous.

When we turn to the incidence of flies in England, we need to remember that the nineteenth-century equivalent to the problem of car pollution through traffic congestion was the surfeit of horse manure. We are told that 'Thompson estimates that there were almost half a million (487,000) horses in use outside agriculture in 1811.'[50] The number grew rapidly so that 'It has been estimated that there were 1.5 million town horses in the late nineteenth century, each producing 22lbs of manure a day.'[51] The dung heaps in the city streets caused by the large number of animals must have created a considerable health hazard. This was one of the few respects in which the English were potentially worse placed than almost all other nations. The improvement of power available per person through unusually high levels of animal muscle and animal protein was balanced by an increased risk of disease.

On the other hand, it may be that what was by the eighteenth century the most organized and well-run mixed agricultural system in the world helped prevent some of the worst effects of all this dung. The efficient storage and use of animal manure may help to explain the fact that flies do not seem to have been as prevalent in England as in many other countries. Walter and Schofield speculate that the improvements of sewers and drains in the eighteenth century 'Though not intended ... had the consequence of reducing the density of insects, notably flies, thereby diminishing the probability that the latter would spread disease by contaminating food.'[52] De Saussure noticed the absence. Commenting on the practice of cutting off horse's tails in England, he noted

---

[48] Riley, *Insects*, 850,851.
[49] Busvine, *Insects*, 197.
[50] Wrigley, *Urban Growth*, 721, n28.
[51] Wrigley and Schofield, *Population*, 656, n27.
[52] Walter and Schofield (eds), *Famine*, 65–6.

'Luckily for them, they live in this country and not in ours where flies abound.'[53]

Riley has drawn our attention to the growing awareness of the importance of controlling insect pests. 'Until the mid-eighteenth century, insect vectors, especially the fly and mosquito, had made an important contribution to infant and childhood mortality.' He then detects a shift. This was 'not a systematic and persistent campaign resulting in complete insect control but instead a campaign consisting of uncounted local efforts waxing and waning in their effectiveness, which, in many individual places and periods, reduced numbers of arthropods and perhaps also rodents below the threshold necessary to cause epidemics.' He believes that consequently 'a significant part of the first phase of the European mortality decline can be explained by insect control.' He tends to place the emphasis on conscious effort; 'eighteenth-century physicians, public authorities, and others introduced and reintroduced measures likely to have reduced the number of places for insects to breed and feed.'[54]

Turning to the Japanese case, the virtual absence of animal manure in Japan, and the fact that when it did fall it was eagerly scraped up, minimized the threat of fly-borne disease. The effects were particularly significant in the huge cities. The Japanese kept fewer dogs and, more importantly, hardly used horses. As Margaret Lock points out, 'Since horse-drawn carriages were not used, one common source of infection in Europe, that of animal manure, was avoided in Japan.'[55]

The absence of animal and human excreta left lying about in the streets and gardens meant that the Japanese almost managed to eliminate the common house fly, for, as Chamberlain observed, 'the house-fly is a much less common plague than in Europe, except in the silk districts.'[56] It was American visitors who particularly noted the contrast. 'There are very few flies to trouble them. Japan seems to be singularly free from these pests.'[57] 'Common houseflies, strangely enough, were rare ...'[58] As a zoologist on the look out for specimens, Morse wrote that 'The absence of flies of the common kinds in the country is a noteworthy feature and to get one at any moment would be difficult.' This notable absence he ascribed to the absence of refuse and scarcity of horses.[59]

The environs of English homes were certainly not spectacularly clean. First the ubiquity of large domestic animals and the side effects of urbanization and

---

[53] De Saussure, *Foreign*, 293.
[54] Riley, *Insects*, 858,841,854,853.
[55] Lock, *Review of Jannetta*, 525.
[56] Chamberlain, *Things*, 527–8.
[57] Griffis, *Mikado*, 528.
[58] Geoffrey, *Immigrant*, 64.
[59] Morse, *Day*, I, 206,51.

industry, and particularly coal pollution, led to dangers to health. The best that could be said was that the English made strong efforts, some of them successful, to keep waste and rubbish and pollution within bounds. In medieval England, it would appear from legislation that there was a general concern to keep water supplies clean. Pollution of water was dealt with by the common law, by statute law, and by manorial law: 'The corruption of the water is an offence at common law, and was early the subject of a statutory provision. In the earlier periods the power of the legislature was directly exercised for the abatement of nuisances.' For example, 'By stat.12th Rich.II.c.13 – None shall cast any garbage or dung or filth into ditches, waters, or other places within or near any city or town, on pain of punishment by the Lord Chancellor at his discretion.' As for manorial law, 'the protection of the subject against nuisances, for punishing particular violations of it, was vested in the Courts Leet.'[60]

The Japanese case was more impressive. Little waste was generated and filth was carefully cleaned away. An attitude which linked physical and spiritual dirt, the absence of domestic animals, the assiduous and watchful local controls by street or town committees, all combined in Japan to create the cleanest environs of any large civilization. There can be little doubt that this diminished the number of disease vectors, in particular flies.

---

[60] Chadwick, *Report*, 350,351,354.

12

Housing and Health

Moving inwards from the environs, the next layer surrounding humans is provided by their constructed habitations. It is well known that the design and construction of a house has significant effects on human health. By altering the relation between humans and insects, housing directly affects plague, typhus and malaria. Through sanitation it affects water-borne diseases. It also indirectly alters the spread of air-borne diseases. Like water, food and clothing 'the comfort of habitation' is a factor 'of great importance for health that can be controlled, so to speak, outside of man.'[1] Just to take the matter of glass for windows, 'The window allowed sunlight to kill a lot of germs, including tubercles.'[2] Cohen reminds us, 'sunlight is one of the best disinfectants known.'[3] Or again, the amount of dust will alter the disease patterns: 'Schutze took samples of the dust from all manner of places in a house and its furniture, and found that there was a great decrease in bacteria after a floor or a piece of furniture had been polished.'[4]

It was not until the end of the nineteenth century that, thanks to the microscope, people could see the bacteria which explained why it was that altering the arrangements of the house could have such dramatic effects on health. Yet there had long been an awareness of the importance of good housing. Dr Buchan gave much sound advice on the necessity for high standards in the house. He started by pointing out that 'Proper attention to AIR and CLEANLINESS would tend more to preserve the health of mankind, than all the endeavours of the faculty.'

[1] Dubos, *Adapting*, 366.
[2] Nikiforuk, *Fourth*, 141.
[3] Cohen, *Health*, 40.
[4] Lane-Claypon, *Hygiene*, 71.

The 'faculty' were, of course, his fellow doctors and this remark shows an awareness of the importance of environmental health. His major concern was with ventilation: 'In places where great numbers of people are collected, cleanliness becomes of the utmost importance. It is well known that infectious diseases are communicated by tainted air. Everything, therefore, which tends to pollute the air, or spread infection, ought with the utmost care to be guarded against.' 'In all places, where vast numbers of people are crowded together, ventilation becomes absolutely necessary.'[5]

The dangers would be felt by the urban poor in particular. 'Nor are many of the holes, for we cannot call them houses, possessed by the poor in great towns, much better than jails. These low dirty habitations are the very lurking-places of bad air and contagious diseases. Such as live in them seldom enjoy good health; and their children commonly die young.' Yet there were also dangers for the comfortably off. 'The various methods which luxury has invented to make houses close and warm, contribute not a little to render them unwholesome. No house can be wholesome unless the air has a free passage through it. For which reason houses ought daily to be ventilated, by opening opposite windows, and admitting a current of fresh air into every room.' The need for ventilation applied to all aspects of domestic life, for instance to bedding. 'Beds, instead of being made up as soon as people rise out of them, ought to be turned down, and exposed to the fresh air from the open windows through the day.'[6]

Another who saw the virtues of good ventilation was Benjamin Franklin. 'A constant circulation of fresh air is so necessary, so important in fevers and in all feverish disorders, that it ought to be particularly considered in the construction of houses.' It was because of this that the less well constructed houses of the poor were often healthier than those of the rich. 'In these houses the rooms are spacious, cold as ice, where the air plays freely around, with doors and windows that do not half shut. The inhabitants of these shattered houses are pitied; and yet the very circumstance of their being out of repair, is what contributes to the health of those who live in them, and facilitates their cure when diseases reign.'[7]

Every aspect of the house is important; the bedding, the floor coverings, the furniture, whether there are cellars or attics, the gaps under the floorboards, the size of doors and windows. Each will affect the balance between the people who live in the house and the many types of micro-organisms, insects and rodents that co-habit with man. An obvious example are the prevailing customs

[5] Buchan, *Domestic*, 79,101,78.
[6] Buchan, *Domestic*, 77.
[7] Frankin, *Works*, VI, 314,315.

concerning the keeping of pets or domesticated animals within the house or close by.

The ancestors of the English had been settled hut dwellers and not nomadic tent dwellers. The geology provided a stable and earthquake-free environment, with plenty of stone, clay and good timber. The population densities were relatively light. The climate was cool and not humid. The land law saw the house and the ground upon which it was built as a distinct 'property'. The people were in many ways unusually affluent. The substantial houses of those living in late medieval England are still to be seen in many English towns, for instance the Suffolk and Norfolk or Cotswold woollen towns. They have well built timber frames, with good walls and floors, sometimes with cellars. Christopher Dyer has recently provided a survey of ordinary English buildings in the later Middle Ages. He shows a number of important things. After the mid fourteenth century 'People and animals were usually accommodated in separate buildings.' In the West Midlands the peasant's houses were substantial buildings, with stone foundations, walls infilled with wattle and daub, thatched roofs. He notes the large size of the houses, mostly of two or three bays and hence measuring 30 to 45 feet in length, and the high quality of the materials they were made of, including, stone foundations and were 'professionally built using expensive timber.' He concludes that 'peasants lived in houses, not huts.' They had much the same floor area per person as nineteenth-century urban houses, twice as much as an Indian peasant in the 1960s and three times as much as a peasant house in late medieval Provence.[8]

A survey of housing in the 1570s by William Harrison showed the improvements since the medieval period. He noted first the change in the structure and materials of the house. Traditionally, 'The greatest part of our building in the cities and good towns of England consisteth only of timber, for as yet few of the houses of the commonality (except here and there in the West Country towns) are made of stone.' But 'such as be lately builded are commonly either of brick or hard stone or both, their rooms large and comely.' Stone and brick is less likely to harbour rodents. Furthermore, 'The mansion houses (dwellings) of our country towns and villages ... are builded in such sort generally as that they have neither dairy, stable, nor brew house annexed unto them (as in many places beyond the sea and some of the north parts of our country) but all separate from the first and one of them from another.'[9]

A combination of wood and brick or stone rather than wood and plaster meant that walls became load-bearing and hence the houses could be taller and have larger, better ventilated and better lit rooms. But the ventilation and

---

[8] Dyer, *Everyday*, ch.8, 140,153,164.
[9] Harrison, *Description*, 195.

lighting depended very much on other developments. 'There are old men yet dwelling in the village where I remain which have noted three things to be marvelously altered in England within their sound remembrance.'[10] One was 'the multitude of chimneys lately erected, whereas in their young days there were not above two or three, if so many, in most uplandish towns of the realm (the religious houses and manor places of their lords always excepted, and per adventure some great personages), but each one made his fire against a reredos in the hall, where he dined and dressed his meat.' By ridding the rooms of smoke, it was much easier to keep them clean and healthy. Chimneys also suck out stale air from rooms very effectively with the up draught and hence are an excellent form of ventilation.

As important as good ventilation was good lighting, both for the way it would show up dirt and for the beneficial effect of sunlight. Harrison noted that in the past country houses 'instead of glass did use much lattice, and that made either of fine rifts of bark in checkerwise.' But now 'as horn in windows is now quite laid down in every place, so our lattices are also grown into less use, because glass is come to be so plentiful and within a very little so good cheap, if not better than the other.'[11] It is difficult to estimate the effects of the introduction of window glass use on health and hygiene, but they have probably been considerable. Lewis Mumford points out, it is difficult to imagine the spick and span Dutch interiors without the prevalence of glass. He suggests that 'both by what it is and by what it does, glass is favourable to hygiene: the clean window, the scoured floor ...'[12]

Another change was in furnishing. Harrison thought that 'the furniture of our houses also exceedeth and is grown in manner even to passing delicacy; and herein I do not speak of the nobility and gentry only but likewise of the lowest sort in most places of our South Country that have anything at all to take to.' Previously costly furniture was to be found only in the houses of the middling and upper ranks, but 'now it is descended yet lower, even unto the inferior artificers and many farmers, who ... have for the most part learned also to garnish their cupboards with plate, their joint beds with tapestry and silk hangings, and their tables with carpets and fine napery.'[13]

If we discount some of this as exaggerated, there still remains evidence of a real improvement in housing, both in the structure and the contents of the house. All this probably had a very substantial effect on general health. In a famous letter, Erasmus had ascribed the prevalence of the plague in England to

[10] Harrison, *Description*, 195,199,200.
[11] Harrison, *Description*, 200,201,197; for examples of glass in Oxfordshire inventories in the later sixteenth century, see Havinden (ed.), *Household*, 151,304.
[12] Mumford, *Technics*, 128.
[13] Harrison, *Description*, 200.

the dirty rush matting.[14] Only a generation later in 1560, early in the transformation which Harrison was describing, a Dutch physician, Levinus Lemnius visited England. He wrote that 'the neate cleanlines, the exquisite finenesse, the pleasaunte and delightfull furniture in every poynt for household, wonderfully rejoysed mee; their chambers and parlours strawed over with sweete herbes refreshed mee.'[15]

The improvements of the Elizabethan period were consolidated through the seventeenth century. This is part of the change which has been termed the 'great rebuilding' by W.G.Hoskins and which has been documented in detail by M.W.Barley in his account of the two major phases of the 'Housing Revolution' between 1575–1615 and 1615–1642.[16] Although later historians have pointed out that the rebuilding was more regionally diverse and spread out than Hoskins argued, his general characterization of a major improvement has not been overthrown.[17] An account of the house and furniture of the middling yeoman class, for instance, suggests that 'After the Civil War there was a notable increase in the scale of living among the well-to-do yeoman.'[18] The surviving solid stone farm houses of the northern counties mainly date from between 1660 and 1720, suggesting a new wave of prosperity and enlargement of houses in the upland areas. In the cities, the rebuilding of London after the great Fire of 1666, and the building of new elegant terraces in Bath and elsewhere in the early eighteenth century are further evidence of a sustained improvement in a country where per capita wealth was increasing year by year and yesterday's luxuries became today's necessities. Josiah Tucker wrote in the later eighteenth century that 'The English, have better conveniences in their houses, and affect to have more in quantity of clean, neat furniture and a greater variety such as carpets, screens, window curtains, chamber bells, polished brass locks, fenders, etc. – things hardly known abroad among persons of such a rank – than are to be found in any other country in Europe, Holland excepted.'[19]

Razzell has revised his theory that smallpox vaccination caused the mortality fall and now lays primary emphasis on environmental change, and particularly housing, suggesting that 'We can provisionally explore one hypothesis that fits all the known evidence; that the main fall in mortality during the early eighteenth century occurred because of the marked improvement in domestic hygiene associated with the rebuilding of English housing at that time.' He

---

[14] For Erasmus' letter and views on what should be done, see Razzell, *Essays*, 224.
[15] Quoted in Rye, *Foreigners*, 78.
[16] Barley, *English Farmhouse*.
[17] Shammas, *Consumer*, 158–63.
[18] Campbell, *English Yeoman*, 240.
[19] Quoted in Porter, *Eighteenth*, 318.

provides evidence to show that the earthen and rush floors which had predominated until the late seventeenth century began to give way to wooden and stone floors, at least among the middle classes.[20]

De Saussure wrote 'I must own that Englishmen build their houses with taste, it is not possible to make a better use of ground, or to have more comfortable houses.' He praised the cleanliness of the tableware. 'An Englishman's table is remarkably clean, the linen is very white, the plate shines brightly, and knives and forks are changed surprisingly often, that is to say, every time a plate is removed.' This was not confined to town people or the very wealthy. 'I have visited several farmers' homes in the country; their houses are clean and well furnished with all necessaries, and most of them possess silver spoons and mugs.' He contrasted the English and Dutch:

> The amount of water English people employ is inconceivable, especially for the cleansing of their houses. Though they are not slaves to cleanliness, like the Dutch, still they are very remarkable for this virtue. Not a week passes by but well-kept houses are washed twice in the seven days, and that from top to bottom; and even every morning most kitchens, staircase, and entrance are scrubbed. All furniture, and especially all kitchen utensils, are kept with the greatest cleanliness. Even the large hammers and the locks on the door are rubbed and shine brightly.[21]

Rochefoucauld on his travels 'admired the way in which in all these little villages the houses are clean and have an appearance of cosiness in which ours in France are lacking.' He wrote of the wealthy farmers that 'Their houses are always clean and well kept; their barns are in excellent condition and they are always careful to keep one small sitting-room spotlessly clean and sometimes quite elegant.' He concluded that 'In a word there is always a marked superiority in the houses of the common people of England over those of the poor peasants of France, which it often pained me to observe.'[22]

That this concern with cleanliness was not a new feature is shown by Keith Thomas who points out that in the seventeenth century 'Books on household management emphasised that it was the woman's duty to "keep all at home neat and cleane", and that "cleanness in houses, especially in beds", was "a great preserver of health". Cleanlinesse is "such an ornament to a housewife", thought Gervase Markham, "that if hee want any part thereof, shee loseth both that all good names else".' Nor was this just a theory, ' "Most people", observed Thomas Tryon in 1682, "take care that their furnitures are daily brushed and rubbed, and their very floors washed, as though they were to eat their food on

---

[20] Razzell, *Essays*, 203,203–4,225–6.
[21] De Saussure, *Foreign*, 68,222,219–20,157.
[22] Rochefoucauld, *Frenchman*, 213,203,158.

them" ,' 'The amount of energy, particularly female energy, which in the early modern period went into scrubbing floors, boiling clothes, scouring pots and pans and polishing furniture is incalculable.'[23]

It may well be that all these improvements in housing are one of the reasons for the curious fact that as cities expanded, the health of the populace improved. This was the view of certain eighteenth-century writers. Short believed that in London 'many late stately Edifices, large clean Courts, lofty Rooms, large sash Lights etc.' were among the things which 'contribute, not a little to make the city more healthy now' than a hundred years before.[24] At the end of the century Malthus believed that the 'better modes of clearing and building towns' and the fact that people were 'better' and their habits with respect to cleanliness 'decidedly improved', were among the factors leading to the notable decline in mortality.[25]

Despite the pollution, Blane argued for the positive effects of coal burning which were 'almost needless to mention, how much an ample supply of fuel is conducive to health, not merely for warmth and for culinary purposes, but as promoting ventilation, which is does not only by the change of air necessarily induced by the current of air up the chimney, but by enabling the poor to admit fresh air in cold weather. It is the winter season, from want of fuel, that typhous infection is most apt to arise, and also to spread.'[26]

There has been much debate as to the state of the poor during the period of rapid industrial and urban growth. The horrors of the living conditions in many of the cities and rural slums by the middle of the nineteenth century is a powerful reminder that new inventions did not solve all problems and that it would be dangerous to assume an ever-upward movement. It could well be argued that the living conditions of the labouring poor in Victorian Britain were worse than those which had ever existed in England.[27] Indeed, some of the new materials which we tend to think of as improvements may have worsened conditions. Chadwick thought that, 'Wood and wattled houses, such as our forefathers built, are the driest and warmest of all; brick is inferior in both these requisites of a comfortable house; but stone, especially the unhewn stone as it is necessarily employed for cottages, is the very worse material possible for the purpose. I prefer the Irish mud cottages.'[28]

This should make us cautious about the claims made for the effects of the

---

[23] Thomas, *Cleanliness*, 73.

[24] Short, *Increase*, 20.

[25] Malthus, *Population*, I, 315,268.

[26] Blane, *Dissertations*, 127.

[27] For one account of the horrors lurking behind the ivy and rose-covered exteriors of English rural cottages, see Arch, *From Ploughtail*, 44.

[28] Chadwick, *Report*, 329.

growing use of brick instead of wood and plaster from the middle of the seventeenth century.[29] However, Slack points out that 'houses built of brick separated rats from men, and in the end, in the eighteenth century, removed favourable ecological conditions for the black rat and encouraged the growth of the brown rat populations. As early as 1652 the London bricklayers themselves pointed out that the substitution of brick for timber would reduce the risk of plague.'[30]

Whatever the building materials, there are strong grounds for arguing that there were deteriorating standards from the early nineteenth century due to crowding. 'Mr Blick, the medical officer of the Bicester union, states that: "The residences of the poor in that part of the district are most wretched, the majority consisting of only one room below and one above, in which a family of eight or ten (upon an average, I should say five), live and sleep. In one of these rooms I have witnessed a father, mother, three grown-up sons, a daughter, and a child, lying at the same with typhus fever: but few of the adjacent residents escaped the infection.' The extremes were in the lodging houses, dormitories for the factories and mines. 'I went to work in Greenside four years. Our lodging-rooms were such as not to be fit for a swine to live in. In one house there was 16 bedsteads in the room up stairs, and 50 occupied these beds at the same time. We could not always get all in together, but we got in when we could. Often three at a time in the bed, and one at the foot. I have several times had to get out of bed, and sit up all night to make room for my little brothers, who were there as washers.'[31] It would not be difficult to add many literary, accounts in order to show the shocking condition of the poor in the great cities.[32] We are a long way from that merry England which Harrison described.

The houses of the ordinary people in Japan at the end of the seventeenth century struck Kaempfer as very small and simple. 'The house of the common people are very mean sorry buildings, small, low, seldom above one story high. If there be two stories, the uppermost is so low, that it scarce deserves that name.' The houses 'consist of four low walls, cover'd with a thatch'd or shingled roof.'[33] Although there were much more substantial houses, both then and later, the bulk of the population lived in extremely small and simple houses until the end of the nineteenth century. Morse wrote that 'It is true that you pass, now

[29] Razzell, *Essays*, 205–6.

[30] Slack, *Plague*, 322.

[31] Chadwick, *Report*, 191,179.

[32] For example, Taine, *Notes*, 225–6. The appaling conditions of the cellar population are described further in Burnett, *Housing*, 58–60.

[33] Kaempfer, *History*, II, 88,309.

and then, large comfortable houses with their broad thatched roofs, showing evidences of wealth and abundance in the numerous *kura* and outbuildings surrounding them; but where you find one of these you pass hundreds which are barely more than shelters for their inmates.' He described how 'the poor farm-labourer and fisherman, as well as their prototypes in the city, possess houses that are little better than shanties, built, as a friend forcibly expressed it, of "chips, paper and straw".'[34] Within them the rooms were tiny: 'being scarcely higher than steamship cabins, and so narrow that an ordinary mosquito-net could not be suspended in them.'[35]

Yet Morse thought even these tiny and most simple of dwellings 'clustered together as they oftentimes are in the larger cities, are palatial in contrast to the shattered and filthy condition of a like class of tenements in any of the cities of Christian countries.' His realization that size and quality of life were not corre-lated arose from his detailed observation of what went on inside the houses. 'Many of the dwellings are often diminutive in size; and as one looks in at a tiny cottage containing two or three rooms at the most, the entire house hardly bigger than a good-sized room at home, and observes a family of three or four persons living quietly and in a cleanly manner in this limited space, he learns that in Japan, at least, poverty and constricted quarters are not always correlated with coarse manners, filth and crime.'[36]

The size and simplicity was partly a result of limited wealth. Another cause was the compound of cultural and geological features which led the Japanese to regard their houses in a very different way to people in the West. The geological background of constant earthquakes and its effect on housing was described by Alcock: 'They have no architecture. They live on a volcanic soil, the surface of which is affected with a tertian ague, thus denying the first conditions of the builder, a stable foundation, and imposing a law of construction fatal to all architectural pretensions or excellence.'[37] Singer captures the essence of the floating Japanese house on its turbulent foundations: 'Chinese dwellings are cut into the soil, moulded from it, or joined to it in such a way that they appear to be parts of the earth's crust.' On the other hand, 'Japanese houses attach themselves only lightly to the soil; they survive earthquakes and hurri-canes by not relying too much on their slender foundations; their virtue is in their swinging elasticity.' They have to be flexible, for 'Relentlessly this archi-pelago is rocked by seismic shocks, invaded by storms, showered and pelted with rain, encircled by clouds and mists.'[38] They are built almost to float on the

[34] Morse, *Homes*, 49–50,49.
[35] Hearn, *Glimpses*, 343.
[36] Morse, *Homes*, 49,50.
[37] Alcock, *Tycoon*, II, 279.
[38] Singer, *Sword and Jewel*, 145–6,147.

landscape: 'they are built like a ship, or a big piece of furniture, held together internally by interlocking beams, and only the most exceptional shock is capable of wrecking them.'[39]

There also seemed to be something deeply rooted, perhaps in a nomadic past, which made the Japanese shape their houses as a wood, bamboo and thatch materialization of skin tents. Alcock described how 'in architecture, a tent-like house, sometimes one superimposed upon the other in two or three stories, with grotesque curves and twisted borders to the roofs, is the extent of their architectural achievements.'[40] Hearn wrote that 'there is much in Japan besides primitive architectural traditions to indicate a nomadic ancestry for the race. Always and everywhere there is a total absence of what we would call solidity.' He captured the essence of the difference between the Japanese and Western attitudes in the following aphorism: 'Generally speaking, we construct for endurance, the Japanese for impermanency. Few things for common use are made in Japan with a view to durability.' In a more poetic style he described the feel of a Japanese city: 'A Japanese city is still, as it was ten centuries ago, little more than a wilderness of wooden sheds – picturesque, indeed, as paper lanterns are, but scarcely less frail.'[41] The simplicity of the Japanese home would have several effects on health, especially when combined with the widespread Japanese practice of building separate, fire-resistant, 'go-downs' or *kura* for the storage of grain or goods, when the family was prosperous enough.[42]

A peculiarity of Japanese law means that even up to the present there is a firm legal division between the surface of the earth and the ground underneath. Until very recently, it was the case that the land was owned by one person and often the house, owned by another, was 'pitched' like a tent on it – to be moved elsewhere, pulled down and rebuilt or whatever. The householder paid to lease the land, but very often did not own it.[43] One of the many consequences of this was that the idea of burrowing into the earth and creating a much more permanent structure with cellars, foundations etc. was out of the question. This was reinforced by the fact that such foundations would not be strong enough to withstand earthquakes and the cellars would cave in, crushing the inhabitants.

As a result a pattern was developed whereby the house was raised above the ground, on stilts as it were. Hanley believes that 'by the sixteenth century and seventeenth centuries, raised flooring was the standard for the well-to-do and the samurai, whereas the common folk and poor had houses with earthen-floors.'[44] It may, in fact, have been a custom from an even earlier date. Frederic,

[39] Maraini, *Meeting*, 75.
[40] Alcock, *Tycoon*, I, 224.
[41] Hearn, *Kokoro*, 20,18,14.
[42] Thunberg, *Travels*, III, 281; Oliphant, *Elgin's Mission*, 133–4.
[43] I am grateful to Professor Hiroshi Watanabe for pointing this out.
[44] Hanley in *Cambridge History*, 4, 666.

describing life in medieval Japan, writes, 'The floor was raised, sometimes by more than a metre, to provide a hygienic space between it and the ground as a protection against humidity during the rainy seasons. Up to the fifteenth century, the floors of houses were made of polished wooden boards just placed edge to edge so that they could be taken up easily to clean the ground under the house.'[45] Whatever the reasons, the houses increasingly had air blowing beneath the floor of the living area. The contrast with Europe and America was apparent: 'the wind has free play beneath; and while this exposed condition renders the house much colder and more uncomfortable in winter, the inmates are never troubled by the noisome air of the cellar, which ... too often infects our houses at home.'[46]

The way in which the 'paper lantern' was constructed had another effect which would have deeply impressed Buchan, Chadwick and others who saw good ventilation as essential to healthy living. 'Posts hold up a traditional Japanese house, so that walls are not structurally necessary.'[47] The walls were like flaps of a tent that could be lifted up leaving just the posts and roof. The possibilities are well described by Hearn: 'In a Japanese house, during the hot season, everything is thrown open to the breeze. All the *shoji* or sliding paper-screens, which serve for windows; and all the opaque paper-screen (*fusuma*) used in other seasons to separate apartments, are removed. There is nothing left between floor and roof save the frame or skeleton of the building.'[48] Morse noticed as he travelled through the country, 'The farmhouses bordering the road are so open that you notice the polished floors from the light that comes from behind. ... With the open character of the house one cannot help realizing the fresh air available all the time.' 'The whole side of the house is open to the sun and air, and yet snugly closed at night by wooden sliding screens and, in the daytime, if necessary, by light framework screens covered with white paper.'[49] The use of strong white paper made from mulberry bark was a light and efficient alternative to western glass. It made it possible to move the screens with ease, and was probably much safer in the light of constant danger from earthquakes.

There were those who complained that the houses were drafty. 'It is not only the clothing that fails to give sufficient cover; the houses are all, without exception, exceedingly drafty because they are walled on all sides by sliding doors made of paper that is glued on [a frame].'[50] Chamberlain narrated how 'an elderly diplomat, who, during his sojourn in a Japanese hotel, spent well-nigh

[45] Frederic, *Daily Life*, 105.
[46] Morse, *Homes*, 15–16.
[47] Hanley in *Cambridge History*, 4, 666.
[48] Hearn, *Glimpses*, 225.
[49] Morse, *Day*, I, 50,67.
[50] Wittermans, *Pompe*, 41.

his whole time in the vain endeavour to keep doors shut and chinks patched up, used to exclaim to us, "mais les Japonais adorent les courants d'air!".[51]

Yet most agreed that ventilation was of considerable benefit to health. 'I must not forget to mention, that it is very healthful to live in these houses, and that in this particular they are far beyond ours in Europe, because of their being built all of cedar wood, or firs, whereof there is a great plenty in the country, and because of the windows being generally contrived so, that upon opening of them, and upon removing the screens, which separate the rooms, a free passage is left for the air to strike through the whole house.'[52] Morse came to the same conclusion; 'I question whether their cold rooms in winter are not more conducive to health than are our apartments with our blistering stoves, hot furnaces or steam-heaters.'[53] As Chamberlain stated confidently, 'the physicians who have studied Japanese dwelling-houses from the point of view of hygiene, give them a clean bill of health.'[54]

The advantages of the mixture of screens and *shoji* were felt throughout the hot weather, but there were difficulties at night and in the colder weather. One solution to the sleeping problem, of which Isabella Bird disapproved, was to 'seal up their houses as hermetically as they can at night and herd together in numbers in one sleeping-room.'[55] The problem was compounded by the lack of fuel and the dangers of setting fire to the wooden houses. 'Neither *chimnies* nor stoves are known throughout the whole country; although the cold is very intense, and they are obliged to make fires in their apartments from October to March. The fires are made in copper kettles of various sizes, with broad projecting edges.'[56] King felt that 'the solution these people had reached of their fuel problem and of how to keep warm' was 'direct and the simplest possible. Dress to make fuel for warmth of body unnecessary, and burn coarse stems of crops, such as cannot be eaten, fed to animals or otherwise made useful.'[57]

In contrast to the large wood or coal fires of Europe, the Japanese only had a tiny fire box. This was very economical in its use of fuel and led to intense socializing as people crowded round it, whether it was on the floor or in a sunken recess where people could warm the lower half of their bodies in a special seating place. Morse described both the use of the *hibachi* and the general imperviousness to cold: 'The artificial heat of the house is secured from a few bits of charcoal partially buried in ashes and held in a pottery, porcelain, or bronze

---

[51] Chamberlain, *Things*, 37.
[52] Kaempfer, *History*, II, 305–6.
[53] Morse, *Homes*, 12.
[54] Chamberlain, *Things*, 37.
[55] Bird, *Tracks*, 99.
[56] Thunberg, *Travels*, III, 283.
[57] King, *Farmers*, 138.

receptacle. The people do not seem to mind the cold as we do. It is now cold enough to wear a light overcoat, and yet the people are flying about in their thin kimonos and with bare legs, as they were in hot summer.' Or again, 'With a heavy frost on the ground and the ditches along the streets frozen over, the little shops are still wide open, the only source of heat being the little fire box, or *hibachi*, around which they seem to cuddle a little closer to warm their hands over the few coals burning in the ashes.'[58] But it was difficult to use at night in the sleeping quarters because of the risk of fumes and fire. 'The Japanese are too wise to sleep with a large *hibachi* in their apartments. They know well that the deadly gas, being heavy, sinks to the bottom of the room, where their *futons* are spread upon the mats; and they either put the fire-box outside, or are careful to see that it has 'honourable mature charcoal' burning low in it.'[59]

One final aspect of the layout and structure of the house is important. As already mentioned there was a strong symbolic opposition made in Japan between the outside and inside. The way this works was not apparent to Westerners and led to some misunderstanding. As Hanley explains, Japanese houses, particularly the larger ones, were divided into a 'living' area, and a 'service' area.[60] The service area in a large house included a privy, the stables, and the cooking area. Thus the 'service' area is half-way between outside and inside. It is within the 'house' yet it is part of the outside world of dirt. Hence the high standards of cleanliness applied within the living area are not always attempted here. This 'service' area was often built on the earth, the floor being packed mud. The kitchen area was in particular affected by the contact with smoke and the refuse of cooking. Morse described one such kitchen area: 'being on the street too, the kitchen is convenient for the vender of fish and vegetables, and for all the kitchen traffic, which too often with us results in the strewing of our little grass-plots with the wrapping paper of the butcher's bundles and other pleasing reminiscences of the day's dinner.'[61] The pure area, which is raised off the polluting earth, has wooden boards and *tatami* matting and where one has to take off one's outside shoes. This is the living area where cleanliness has to be maintained and where the family sleeps, eats and socializes.

It may be that originally wealthier Japanese houses had boards covered with some kind of straw. The date of the introduction of an original form of floor covering, the *tatami* rush matting which Hanley thinks 'may be one feature of Japanese culture that is truly unique',[62] is not certain. One account suggests that 'Towards the end of the fifteenth century, rectangular mattresses of thick straw

[58] Morse, *Day*, I, 335–6; II, 84.
[59] Arnold, *Seas*, 384.
[60] In *Cambridge History*, 4, 675.
[61] Morse, *Homes*, 185–6.
[62] In *Cambridge History*, 4, 667.

covered with finely woven rush (*tatami*) on which the master of the house used both to sit and to sleep, were made in standard sizes (one *ken* by half a *ken*).[63] The *tatami* area of the house was the area of purity and the real heart of the home. It is eloquently described by Hearn: 'Soft as a hair mattress and always immaculately clean, the floor is at once the couch, the dining table, and most often the writing table.'[64] The cleanliness was affirmed by others. 'The mats are always of an immaculate cleanliness, as is also the white or yellow wood of the floor or of the wainscoting, which are frequently washed, and whose brightness no stain ever tarnishes.'[65] Oliphant wrote that 'All our rooms were matted in the usual way with wadded mats, so scrupulously clean that we began by walking about in our own or Japanese socks, for fear of dirtying them.'[66] 'The Japanese never enter their houses with their shoes on; but leave them in the entry, or place them on a bench near the door, and thus are always barefooted in their houses, so as not to dirty their neat mats.'[67] Isabella Bird, however, was less convinced, feeling that something must lurk beneath: 'The *tatami*, beneath a tolerably fair exterior, swarm with insect life, and are receptacles of dust, organic matters, etc.'[68]

The cleanliness of the home and the relative absence of rodents, insects and places for bacteria and other micro-organisms to lurk was much encouraged by the Japanese attitude to furnishings. Hearn caught the essence: 'There is – no furniture (according to the European sense of the term) in a Japanese home, no beds, tables or chairs.'[69] After a while 'familiarity with Japanese interiors has equally disgusted me with Occidental interiors, no matter how spacious or comfortable or richly furnished.'[70] 'Absolute cleanliness and refinement, with very few objects in sight upon which the eye may rest contentedly, are the main features in household adornment which the Japanese strive after.'[71] 'The furniture in this country is as simple as the stile of building. Here neither cupboards, bureaus, sophas, beds, tables, chairs, watches, looking-glasses, or any thing else of the kind are to be found in the apartments.'[72] Almost everything was done at ground level, and hence, once again like a tent, there was almost

---

[63] Frederic, *Daily Life*, 105; Osamu Saito informs me that 'tatami' was used as a foldimg mat in the age of the Genji.
[64] Hearn, *East*, 150.
[65] Regamey, *Art and Industry*, 238.
[66] Oliphant, *Elgin's Mission*, 54,119.
[67] Thungerg, *Travels*, III, 273–4.
[68] Bird, *Tracks*, 99–100.
[69] Hearn, *East*, 149.
[70] Hearn, *Gleanings*, 174–5.
[71] Morse, *Homes*, 309.
[72] Thunberg, *Travels*, III, 283–4.

nothing above a foot from the ground – no hangings, no large pieces of furniture and few shelves.

What there was was carefully covered with surface materials that were both beautiful and designed for cleanliness such as varnish and lacquer. 'The Urusi or Varnish-Tree, is another of the noblest and most useful Trees of this Country. It affords a milky Juice, which the Japanese made use of to varnish, and as we call it, to japan all their Household goods, dishes, and plates of Wood, and this from the Emperor down to the meanest Peasant.'[73] 'Their habits of life are evidently simple in the highest degree. A bare, matted room – not over large but generally clean; a few shelves or a low *etagers* of lacquer let into some recess; a few lacquer cups and saucers, or porcelain with as many trays on stands, – behold the whole furniture of a well-furnished house, from the Daimio, whose revenue is estimated at a million measures of rice, to the little shopkeeper or peasant who lives from hand to mouth.'[74] Where lacquer and varnish were not used, polishing gave the same effect: 'The floors of these galleries are polished to a wonderful smoothness and surface. They are not varnished, nor oiled, nor waxed, but every morning rubbed with a cloth wrung out of hot bath-water which contains oily matter enough to give, in time, this peculiar lustre.'[75]

This simplicity made it easier to keep the living area of Japanese houses clean, though much effort was also put into keeping houses spotless. 'Feather and bamboo brooms, with plenty of water and air, afford the means of cleanliness,' wrote Alcock.[76] 'The verandah is scrubbed first with a wet cloth and afterwards with an almost dry one to make it shine. In the sitting-room the wiping and polishing of the brazier is a long job, for the housewives of Tokyo pride themselves upon the appearance of their braziers. The wife superintends the cleaning of the rooms and also at times lends a hand.'[77] 'This house-cleaning, even with the small amount of furniture found in a Japanese house, is an elaborate affair. Every box and closet and rubbish-hole in the house is turned out and put in order, the *tatami* are taken up and brushed and beaten, the woodwork from ceiling to floor is carefully washed, the plaster and paper walls flicked with the paper flapper that takes the place in Japan of our feather duster.' Furthermore, from time to time, 'All the quilts and clothing must be sunned and aired, the kakemonos and curios belonging to the family unpacked, carefully dusted, and put back into their wrappings and boxes, and the house and garden put into perfect repair. This work, if thoroughly done, takes about a week.'[78] A visiting

---

[73] Kaempfer, *History*, I, 177.
[74] Alcock, *Tycoon*, I, 301.
[75] Scidmore, *Jinrikisha*, 143.
[76] Alcock, *Tycoon*, I, 301.
[77] Inouye, *Home*, 142.
[78] Bacon, *Japanese Girls*, 282–3.

health team noted in 1926 that 'The interiors are scrupulously clean. ... Every room is swept twice a day. Once or twice a year all articles of furniture and all mats are removed from the rooms and exposed to the sun for three or four hours.'[79]

The negative aspect of the sort of materials used to construct Japanese houses is that they are less durable than a house built of brick. The wood and bamboo expand and contract leaving new cracks for dirt to accumulate in. Also bamboo and wood are prone to insect infestation and are easier for rodents to gnaw. Damp and rot set in. The floor covering, particularly if it is made of natural fibres like rushes or straw, inevitably becomes worn out. Houses in cities, with hundreds of thousands of inhabitants living very close together, were very likely to accumulate dirt as they age. So how could a whole vast city be 'spring-cleaned'? The answer was through that most purging and cleansing, yet destructive, of agents, fire.

It was noted as one of the peculiarities of Japanese cities that they seem to have suffered numerous fires and that their inhabitants almost took the conflagrations as 'natural'. For instance, in Tokyo (Yedo or Edo) 'Fires were known as the "Flowers of Yedo", being as much among the great sights of the city as the cherry blossom on the south-east bank of the River Sumida, the morning-glories of Iriya, or the chrysanthemums of Dangozaka, for which Tokyo is still noted.'[80] Despite the utmost care, 'It is no wonder that acres of the city burn over every year or two, and great destruction of property and even of lives occur from the flimsy and inflammable character of the wooden buildings.', 'they have no such institution as insurance, but the merchants always calculate to be burned out on an average once in seven years and so lay by money every year in view of this calamity,'[81] This figure of seven years is confirmed by Alcock. 'They calculate that the whole of this vast city is consumed in successive portions, to be rebuilt in every seven years! It is certainly very rare that a night passes without the fire-bell of the quarter ringing a fearful alarm, and rousing all the neighbourhood.'[82] Mrs Hugh Fraser was aware that 'there is a whole nomenclature in which every variety of fire is described by a different name – one word expresses a fire kindled by intention, another the accidental outbreak, another the fire caught from the next house, another that kindled by a falling spark and so on.'[83]

Morse was somewhat critical of the methods of fire-fighting at first, but later came to appreciate the skill involved and another visitor a little before him wrote that 'They have numerous fire-brigades, which are well organized, and re-

[79] Wellington, *Report*, 21.
[80] Inouye, *Home*, 29.
[81] Morse, *Day*, I, 135,355.
[82] Alcock, *Tycoon*, I, 124.
[83] Fraser, *Letters*, I, 315.

markably efficient.'[84] What is certain is that the intervals between fires grew longer as fire-fighting methods improved in the later nineteenth century, so that Hearn believed that 'it may be broadly stated that every Japanese city is rebuilt within the time of a generation.'[85] This longer span was not a complete blessing, 'Formerly it was calculated that the average life of a house was about thirty years; but now the lesser frequency of fires would give them a much longer lease. This is comforting to house-owners; but it must be confessed that wooden houses more than thirty years old are not pleasant to live in.'[86]

If we return to the metaphor of a tent, it is as if the whole population periodically stripped the tent down, and then set it up again. After a fire, 'The ground is hardly cold before the carpenters are at work, rebuilding the dwellings which have been destroyed.'[87] The losses were kept to a minimum because the house was so light and cheap, furniture was almost absent and those who had valuable goods in large quantities kept them in fire-proof stores made of brick. It was a terrible purging, yet the loss of life and property that did occur may have not been an entirely wasted sacrifice, for the fires cleaned out the cities.

The effects on public health were dramatic. A massive incineration of vermin, insects and any refuse that had accumulated was achieved, along with mouldering wood, mats and bedding. It has often been pointed out that the Fire of London in 1666 was a turning point in the improvement of health in England. The cities of Japan did not just have one great fire but burnt down again and again. It is, of course, a circular process: the frequent fires and earthquakes encouraged insubstantial housing, and such housing burnt easily. Yet the effects are certainly worth attention in Japan. The symbolic statement of this need to renew wooden buildings every few years is made by the practice whereby the great Shinto shrine at Ise has been rebuilt every twenty years for the last thousand years, moving it a few yards to left or right on each occasion. Renewing and refreshing of one's house has long been a tradition in Japan. Among other things, this helps to explain the extraordinary energy and speed with which Japanese cities were rebuilt after the bombing in 1945.

The combination of these factors probably gave the Japanese the cleanest living spaces that have ever existed in a large agrarian civilization. 'If the houses of the Japanese be not so large, lofty, or so substantially built as ours, they are on the other hand greatly to be admired for their uncommon neatness and cleanliness.'[88]

---

[84] Morse, *Day*, II, 100–1,125–6; Silver, *Sketches*, 7.

[85] Hearn, *Kokoro*, 20–1.

[86] Inouye, *Home*, 30.

[87] Fraser, *Letters*, I, 319.

[88] Kaempfer, *History*, II, 304. For further evidence, see Griffis, *Mikado*, 356; Arnold, *Seas*, 401; Morse *Day*, I, 44,61; Morse, *Homes*, 6.

One final way in which the shape and furnishing of houses in Japan may have had a dramatic effect on health can be shown by considering the most dangerous of tropical disease vectors, the mosquito. As we have seen, there are plenty of mosquitoes in Japan and there was once widespread malaria. Yet by the seventeenth century, at the latest, malaria had become relatively unimportant. How can we explain the most successful case of malarial eradication before the use of DDT?

Part of the explanation may lie in those factors already considered. Furthermore, the Japanese tried to keep the numbers of mosquitoes down using various natural predators. The wells, where mosquitoes would breed, were specifically attended to: 'the small fishes the Japanese call funa. One or two funa are kept in every well, to clear the water of larvae.'[89] A certain frog was 'credited with the power of drawing all the mosquitoes out of a room into its mouth by simply sucking its breath in.'[90] 'The mosquitoes were pursued by a fearsome beetle called 'geji-geji', who is cherished by the Japanese because he eats so many mosquitoes.'[91] Yet the mosquitoes could not be eliminated by any of these alone.

There is one extra factor in the Japanese case which is connected to housing, not so much to the light and ventilation which have previously been mentioned, but to another development – the widespread use of mosquito nets. It seems likely that the idea of using netting against mosquitoes and other biting insects is very widespread. Such nets were known, for instance, among the Romans, for we are told that the mosquito net (*conopeum*) was 'ridiculed by the poets Horace, Juvenal and Propertius.'[92] Again, although the earliest mention of mosquito nets to be found in Needham's work on *Science and Civilization in China* is to a reference by an eighteenth-century botanist, it seems likely that the Chinese must have had the idea earlier.[93] Yet we do not know of any civilization where the ordinary people used mosquito netting on a large scale before the twentieth century, except Japan.

Chamberlain had suggested that the mosquito net was introduced by the Portuguese in the sixteenth century,[94] but, as we shall see, the idea had been present in Japan many centuries before the Portuguese arrived. What he may have been referring to was the period when the use spread from a rather limited group of the wealthy to the general population.

[89] Hearn, *East*, 97.
[90] Hearn, *Glimpses*, 365.
[91] Geoffrey, *Immigrant*, 63.
[92] Winslow, *Conquest*, 84.
[93] Needham et al., *Science and Civilization*, VI, 1,328.
[94] Chamberlain, *Things*, 153.

The history of the mosquito net has been outlined by Koyo Ogawa.[95] Ogawa states that the *kaya* (mosquito net) was called the *kaya-katabira* in the 'ancient period', that is before the twelfth century. Illustrations from this period show the curtained bed belonging to aristocrats.[96] In the twelfth and thirteenth centuries the *kaya* was restricted to the upper class. By the fifteenth century the *kaya* had become a popular gift among the nobility and samurai. At that time they were made in the Nara area and the production took the form of a cottage industry. They were mainly made from raw silk.

By the seventeenth century *kaya* were being mass produced on a large scale, the centre of production having moved from Nara to Oomi (in Shiga prefecture). Wholesale firms (*tonya*) in Oomi imported linen thread from Echizen and managed all the processes of the producing, dyeing, weaving and making of the nets. Travelling merchants sold the *kaya* to many places and later the *tonya* opened branches in Edo (Tokyo) and Osaka. The *kaya* were designed to be fixed to hooks on the walls, such a design was convenient as the netting could be removed in the morning. Before this style was invented, the net was arranged on a frame of bamboo poles. The most popular material was linen, though cotton was sometimes used, as was paper. Finally the green linen *kaya* triumphed, the paper *kaya* only remaining among the poor.

In the eighteenth century *kaya* began to feature in wood block prints as an image of summer. Numerous examples can be found showing scenes with *kaya* draped over, or as a backdrop to, human figures.[97] It would appear that then, at least, the use of mosquito netting was very widespread. Later, even in the poorest houses, it was present. In a late-nineteenth-century peasant's house, 'The loose ends of mosquito nets fluttered in the early autumn breeze.' It appears that people may have walked around at night with their faces covered with small pieces of netting. Nagatsuka described how 'They, too, know that a young man will arrive later that night and stand outside the door, his face wrapped in mosquito netting, waiting to be let inside.'[98] Special nets for infants (*horo-kaya* or *makura-kaya*) were sold, consisting of a bamboo frame and a sheet of cloth.[99] We are even told that cormorant fishermen 'take such care of the birds that they provide them with mosquito-nets during the summer, in order to minister to their comfort.'[100]

The ideal mosquito net is described by Roberts. If mosquitoes cannot be

[95] I am most grateful to Mikiko Ashikari for providing a translated summary of part of Koyo Ogawa's *Mukashi kara atta nihon no beddo* (Tokyo, 1990), 152–7.

[96] Leonard, *Early Japan*, 37.

[97] See for example, Takahashi, *Traditional Woodblock Prints*, 25,67,130; Clark, *Ukiyo-e Paintings*, no.21,30 and various famous works by Utamoro, for instance 'In and out of the mosquito net'.

[98] Nagatsuka, *Soil*, 95,87–8.

[99] Ogawa, as cited four notes above.

[100] Chamberlain, *Things*, 105.

eradicated, 'mosquito bed nets can be used, or bedrooms (or even whole houses) mosquito-proofed. A bed net should have a mesh of at least eighteen to the inch. ... The best type of net is rectangular, the free edge being hemmed with a strip of cotton or other material a foot to eighteen inches wide.'[101] The Japanese seem to have made an ideal mosquito net. Morse described how, when he entered a room, 'A huge green mosquito netting in the form of a square box was hung from the four corners of the room. It was big enough for one to stand upright inside, and nearly filled the room.' On another occasion he went to bed in a room 'literally filled with mosquitoes', but 'I managed to get under the netting without letting one in.' He was driven mad by mosquitoes until 'my Japanese boy brought me a mosquito netting almost filling the entire room, and I slept on the floor.'[102] Hearn appreciated the servant who 'takes down the brown mosquito net, brings a hibachi with freshly kindled charcoal for my morning smoke, and trips away to get our breakfast.'[103] Scidmore observed that 'At night they came to close our amados noisily, and to hang up the mosquito-nets of coarsely-woven green cotton – nets the size of the room itself, fastened by cords at the four corners of the ceiling, and exhaling the musty, mildewed odor that belongs to so many things Japanese, and is so inevitable in the rainy season.'[104]

What is significant about this is the shape and size. The nets were not just over the sleeping area. They protected the whole room. In other words, because of a combination of factors – the small size of rooms, the absence of furniture, the availability of good materials for making netting, fine craft traditions and much labour to manufacture them – it was possible to develop an especially effective type of mosquito netting. The fact that the 'dimensions of every house in the empire conform to certain unvarying rules ... the verandas, or outer galleries of the house, are always exactly three feet wide' and inner rooms always based on a multiple of the basic shape of a tatami mat, made manufacture of mosquito netting to a standard pattern much easier.[105] They could be let down at dusk, as soon as mosquitoes appeared and would protect people during the whole evening, not just when they slept for it is in the evening that the *anopheles* mosquito bites and transmits malaria.

A good description of the nature and effectiveness of the nets is given by Mrs Geoffrey: 'Japanese *kaya* (mosquito nets) designed for Japanese houses are more effective than bed canopies, as they are made exactly the size of the room, fastening in the four corners and giving the effect of a screened porch when in position. We found the *kaya* very satisfactory in our little Japanese summer

---

[101] Roberts, *Hygiene*, 238.
[102] Morse, *Day*, I, 57,131,160.
[103] Hearn, *Glimpses*. 187.
[104] Scidmore, *Jinrikisha*, 323–4.
[105] Scidmore, *Jinrikisha*, 143.

home by the shore.'[106] In other words, the Japanese pitched a mosquito-proof tent within the tent of their house. Thunberg described how

> During our journey down, and in this rainy season, we were molested by gnats (*Culex irritans*) which particularly disturbed us in the night and sometimes prevented us from sleeping. We were therefore under the necessity of purchasing a kind of porous green stuff, for curtains, such as is used every where in this part of the world, for a defence against these blood sucking insects. These curtains are very wide, and are tied over the tester, and spread below over the whole bed, without having any other opening than just the bottom. They are very light and portable, and wove so open, as not to prevent the air from passing through them.[107]

The netting may have been particularly fine and widespread in order to protect people against these and other insects as much as mosquitoes. For instance, Chamberlain mentioned 'the *buyu* – a diminutive kind of gnat' which 'infests many mountainous districts during the summer months.'[108] Yet the result appears to have been that by the eighteenth century, at the latest, malaria was not the killer disease that it was elsewhere in Asia.

We may conclude that the English house was generally solid and durable. It became more comfortable as chimneys, glass windows, better flooring and new furnishings were introduced. Enjoyed by a surprisingly large proportion of the population, English houses were probably reasonably conducive to good health.[109] However, the very solidity made it possible for generations of vermin to live unmolested. Houses built for the rich deteriorated into slums for the poor. The worst period for housing was paradoxically the nineteenth century, when the houses of the poor reached a nadir never before experienced.

The Japanese house was very different. It was light and airy, with little height or depth, and was constantly rebuilt as it decayed or was burnt down. The ventilation was excellent, the furnishings minimal and it was for the most part kept spotlessly clean. In the absence of the cosy but unhealthy fug of the solid English house, though it might be uncomfortably cold in winter, it is difficult to think of more healthful housing.

[106] Geoffrey, *Immigrant*, 63.
[107] Thunberg, *Travels*, III, 214.
[108] Chamberlain, *Things*, 528.
[109] No comparison has been made here with housing on the Continent which, at least at the level of the very rich in certain countries at certain times, was far more luxurious than that in England.

13

Textiles, Clothing and Footwear

Closer than the shell of the house are the various substances which humans use to cover themselves, either in the form of bedding, rugs or clothes, including footwear. A moment's thought will show that what one wears and how one wears it, and how often it is washed will have a significant effect on health. An obvious connection is through the prevalence of fleas, lice, mites and other disease vectors which inhabit cloth. How far then, and in what ways did the English and Japanese solve the contradiction innate in all clothing, which is 'to combine sufficient protection with adequate ventilation?'[1]

Many observers noted over the centuries that the English, along with the Dutch, were the best and most richly clothed people in Europe. Among the reasons for this were a general affluence, the spread of wealth across the population, an obsession with fashion and the availability of a variety of textiles, both imported and home produced. In the fifteenth century, Fortescue wrote of the miserable clothes of the French peasantry among whom he was living: 'Their shamewes [coats] are made of hemp, much like to sack cloth. Woollen clothes they wear none, except it be very coarse, and that only in their coats under their said upper garments. Neither use they any hosen, but from the knee upwards: the residue of their legs go naked. Their women go bare foot saving on holy days.' On the other hand, English country people of a comparable level 'wear fine woollen cloth in all their apparel. They also have abundance of bed coverings in their houses, and of all other woollen stuff.'[2] In the sixteenth century, Aylmer compared the affluent English to the Italian peasants. There 'the best coat he weareth is sacking, his nether stocks of his hose, be his own

[1] Lane-Claypon, *Hygiene*, 90.
[2] Fortescue, *Commendation*, 81–81v, 85–85v.

skin . . .'[3] In the seventeenth century, after travelling over most of Europe, Fynes Moryson thought the 'English on their apparell are become more light than the lightest French, and more sumptuous than the proudest Persians.'[4] In the eighteenth century, Arthur Young estimated that the labouring class of France were '76 percent worse . . . clothed . . . than the same classes in England.'[5] Henry Meister, at the end of the century, also wrote that 'the English labourer is better clothed . . . than the French.'[6] Rochefoucauld in 1784 'observed that all classes of people – peasants from the neighbouring country, servants even – were well clad and remarkably clean.'[7]

De Saussure noted that 'The lower classes are usually well dressed, wearing good cloth and linen. You never see wooden shoes in England, and the poorest individuals never go with naked feet.'[8] The question of bare feet was a particular index of relative wealth. Braudel writes of early modern Europe that 'Usually all went barefoot, or almost so.'[9] The absence of shoes among the poorer Scots was noted by a number of observers.[10] The English had good solid shoes, no doubt partly because of their pastoral agriculture, which made leather widely available.

The love of fine clothes which spread outwards from the rich to the middle sort provoked much criticism. In the sixteenth century the excesses were castigated by Philip Stubbes, among others, who complained that even those who were below the rank of yeomen 'go daiely in silkes, velvettes, satens, damaskes, taffaties, and suche like.' He thought that all other countries in the world were 'faire behind' England in apparel, and 'No people so curious in newe fangles as they of Ailgna.' With somewhat exaggerated rhetoric he complained that in England 'Every pesant hath his stately bandes and monstrous ruffes, how costly soever they bee.' He then proceeded to describe the expensive and luxurious shirts, doublets, hoses, coats and other items worn by the English males. The women's clothing was equally luxurious and sinful.[11] Others joined in complaining about the extravagant clothing in the mid sixteenth century.[12] The complaints continued through the centuries. More recently, social and economic historians have described the ample clothing not only of the wealthy,

[3] Reynolds, *British Pamphleteers*, 29–33.
[4] Moryson, *Itinerary*, IV, 231.
[5] Malthus, *Population*, I, 230.
[6] Quoted in Marshall, *English People*, 160.
[7] Rochefoucauld, *Frenchman*, 4.
[8] De Saussure, *Foreign*, 112–3,204,113.
[9] Braudel, *Capitalism*, 227.
[10] Graham, *Scotland*, 15; Wright, *Autobiography*, 80.
[11] Stubbes, *Anatomie*, 17,41,42ff.
[12] Lamond (ed.), *Discourse*, 82.

but of yeomen, husbandmen and labourers in the sixteenth and seventeenth centuries.[13]

There were those who heeded the warnings of Stubbes and others. From the Protestant sects of the sixteenth century, through the seventeenth-century Puritans, there was always an element of reserve and a pressure towards solid simplicity. This blend of affluence and simplicity was noted, for instance, by De Saussure. 'Quakers' clothes, though of the simplest and plainest cut, are of excellent quality; their hats, clothes and linen are of the finest, and so are the silken tissues the women wear.'[14]

Buchan felt that a variety of clothing was essential for health. 'The continual discharge from our bodies by perspiration, renders frequent change of apparel necessary. Changing apparel greatly promotes the secretion from the skin, so necessary for health. When that matter which ought to be carried off by perspiration, is either retained in the body, or reabsorbed from dirty clothes, it must occasion diseases.' As for the kind of clothing that was most healthful: 'Were we to recommend any particular pattern for dress, it would be that which is worn by the people called Quakers. They are always neat, clean, and often elegant, without any thing superfluous.'[15]

Another important aspect when considering the relation between clothing and health is the type of fabric used. Early on woollen cloth was used extensively. It has the virtue of warmth and durability, but it is not easy to keep clean and it shrinks and mats when washed and certainly cannot be boiled. Furthermore it is an ideal home for lice. In the sixteenth century the introduction of the much lighter 'bays and says' from Flanders and Holland which were less likely to harbour multitudes of insects and dirt led to a significant improvement in clothing.[16]

Also important was the use of linen, both as a cloth worn next to the skin and for table covering. There is plenty of evidence of home production of linen garments during this period, and there is also considerable evidence of its widespread use.[17] For instance, many of the late-sixteenth-century Oxfordshire inventories mention linen.[18] As Tryon wrote in the early eighteenth century, 'Every one that can, will have plentiful Changes both of Linen and Wollen Garments.'[19] Hemp was also used extensively for sheets and other coverings which needed to be strong and durable.[20]

---

[13] cf. Campbell, *English Yeoman*, 251ff; Alan Everitt in Thirsk (ed.), *Agrarian History*, 449–50.

[14] De Saussure, *Foreign*, 324.

[15] Buchan, *Domestic*, 100,93.

[16] For example, see Ramsey, *Woollen Industry*.

[17] Fussell and Fussell, *Countrywoman*, 37–8,41.

[18] Havinden (ed.), *Household*, for example 142,208.

[19] Tryon, *Cleanliness*, 6.

[20] For hemp sheets, see for example Havinden (ed.), *Household*, 174.

Cotton manufacture reached England in the later sixteenth century with
the same Dutch and Walloon immigrants who brought the lighter woollen
cloth techniques. By 1600 fustian (a mixture of wool and cotton) weaving was
established in Lancashire around Bolton and Manchester. Yet it was during
the eighteenth century that the improvements in the mechanization of cotton
manufacturing through the carding machine, spinning jenny, fly-shuttle,
spinning frame and 'mule' revolutionized the cost and quantity of cotton
cloth.[21] From the 1730s 'cotton grew at a rate never before witnessed in textiles,
and is regarded as the quintessential growth industry of the early stages of the
Industrial Revolution.' Some of the reasons for this sudden immense burst of
production are because 'Cotton combined qualities that are attractive to both
consumers and producers; it takes dyes well, launders easily, and ventilates
much better than linen and wool. Compared to its main competitors, wool and
linen, cotton fibres lent themselves easily to mechanization, Moreover, the
supply of the raw material was elastic.'[22]

What were the likely effects of this new cloth on health? Three features
can be noted. Cotton can and should be boiled frequently: 'Cotton absorbs
odours and requires even more frequent washing than wool.'[23] Washing does not
destroy or shrink cotton fibres, in contrast to wool. Most importantly, the lice
and fleas which cause so much human illness, particularly typhus, not only find
it more difficult to maintain their hold on cotton but the regular washing
destroys them. When Chambers was trying to account for the drop in mortality
in Nottingham from the 1770s, no factor could explain it except that 'Nottingham, of course, was a cotton town, the first in fact.' He noted that 'By the end
of the century cotton hosiery, underwear, calicoes, bed-hangings and sheets
would be ousting those of wool; and cotton can be boiled, which is fatal for the
typhus louse. The change to cotton would be especially beneficial to the poor of
the large towns.'[24]

Dorothy Marshall quotes Place to support the view that the use of cotton
cloth was important particularly for women's undergarments. Prior to its
introduction, 'the wives of journeymen, tradesmen and shopkeepers either wore
leather stays, or what were called full-boned stays. . . . These were never washed
although worn day by day for years. The wives and grown daughters of
tradesmen, and gentlemen even, wore petticoats of camblet, lined with dyed
linen, stuffed with wool and horsehair and quilted, these were also worn day by
day till they were rotten.' Place observed that cotton goods 'were found to be less
expensive and as it was necessary to wash them, cleanliness followed almost as

---

[21] cf. Marshall, *English People*, 177–8.
[22] Mokyr, *Lever*, 100.
[23] Lane-Claypon, *Hygiene*, 95.
[24] Chambers, *Population*, 104.

a matter of course. . . . This very material change was not confined to the better sort of the people as they were called . . . it descended, although rather slowly, to the very meanest of people, all of whom so far as respects females, wear washing clothes. Cleanliness in matters of dress was necessarily accompanied by cleanliness in other particulars.'[25] Thus all over the country, in the period between 1700 and 1821, Place thought that the working classes were 'infinitely . . . more cleanly in their persons and their dwellings . . . partly from the success of the cotton manufacture.'[26]

E.L.Jones takes as an illustration of almost invisible, but highly important, changes:

> the introduction of cheap cotton underclothing, replacing the body linen used by the wealthy and giving something new to the working classes. In a world of primitive and collective toilet and washing facilities, the greatest endemic threat to health was gastrointestinal infection, easily passed by unwashed hands that had come into contact with body wastes. The lack of easily cleaned undergarments was an invitation to skin irritation, scratching, and thus transfer of pathogens from body to hands to food to digestive tract.[27]

Likewise, in trying to explain the decline of typhus, Landers comments that Chambers' theory concerning the effects of cotton 'still retains much of its validity.'[28]

There is one other area where there may have been significant improvements, namely in bedding. Harrison provides an account of what his congregation thought was a major revolution in the standards of living during the sixteenth century. This was:

> the great (although not general) amendment of lodging, for (said they) our fathers, yea, and we ourselves also, have lien full oft upon straw pallets, on rough mats covered only with a sheet, under coverlets made of dagswain or hap-harlots (I use their own terms) and a good round log under their heads instead of a bolster or pillow. If it were so that our fathers or the goodman of the house had within seven years after his marriage purchased a mattress or flock-bed and thereto a sack of chaff to rest his head upon, he thought himself to be as well lodged as the lord of the town, that per adventure lay seldom in a bed of down or whole feathers, so well were they contented and with such base kind of furniture. . . . Pillows (said they) were thought meet only for women in childbed. As for servants, if they had any sheet above them it was well, for seldom had they any under their bodies to keep

[25] George, *London*, 72.
[26] Quoted in Marshall, *London*, 72.
[27] In Mokyr (ed.), *Industrial Revolution*, 161 n.25.
[28] Landers, *Death*, 356.

them from the pricking straws that ran oft through the canvas of the pallet and raised their hardened hides.[29]

As Shammas shows, there was a very large expenditure on bedding in the sixteenth century and indeed she terms this 'the Age of the Bed'.[30]

The very wide range of beds and bedding in early modern England is attested to in wills and inventories of possessions made at death. Contemporary evidence of the improvements in bedding in Harrison's county of Essex in the later sixteenth century has been summarized by F.G.Emmison.[31] Among the many lists of substantial bedding in later-sixteenth-century Oxfordshire, one may be cited to show the range of beds and bedding. Anne Dartes of Banbury in about 1573 had the following in her parlour: a feather bed and pair of blankets, six pairs of sheets, six pillows and bolsters, a christening sheet and pair of pillow-cases, two flock beds and two coverings, three bedsteads, two fine pillow-cases and a coarse pillow-case, two pairs of flaxen sheets.[32]

Flock mattresses, sheets and blankets may make sleeping more comfortable, but unless the bedding was washed or aired regularly, beds would be a perfect environment for fleas and other insects. The increasing use of cotton sheets from the middle of the eighteenth century may again have been important here. The dangers were stressed by Tryon: 'Cleanness in Houses, especially in Beds, is a great preserver of Health.' He thought that because beds stood in corners and because they were covered with 'ponderous close Substances', they were particularly likely to be unhealthy. 'From the pernicious Smells and putrified Vapours that do proceed from old Beds, are generated the Vermin called Bugs.' Just as fleas arose from dust, so lice were bred from 'Breathings of the Body' and 'Bed Bugs' from the smells in beds. Hence all sorts of beds and bedding should be washed thoroughly at least three or four times a year.[33]

It is difficult to assess just how clean clothing and bedding was. Certainly, linen undergarments could be washed, but the silks, damasks and velvets would have been ruined if immersed in hot water. Similarly, wool cannot be washed often without matting and shrinkage. Houghton in trying to assess the quantity of soap manufactured in London found 'upon Enquiry that in good Citizens Houses, they wash once a Month, and they use, if they wash all the Cloaths at home, about as many Pounds of *Soap* as there be Heads in the Family, and the higher the People be, the oftner they change, the less pains the Washers are willing to take, and the more *Soap* is used . . . and 'tis probable we may allow a

---

[29] Harrison, *Description*, 201.
[30] Shammas, *Consumer*, 169,171, table 6.3.
[31] Emmison, *Elizabethan Life*, 12–16.
[32] Havinden (ed.), *Household*, 63; another good example is on page 75.
[33] Tryon, *Cleanliness*, 5,7,8,11.

Pound a Head once a Month for every Soul in the Bills of Mortality.'[34] Mrs Pepys seems to have washed at home with the help of servants, but also took her linen to a 'whister' for bleaching, 'this being the first time of her trying this way of washing' in 1667. For this she had to cross the river three days in succession, presumably to oversee the work.[35] A picture of public washing grounds in 1582 shows a cauldron of boiling water, with women beating, scrubbing and drying strips of cloth.[36] Possibly because the washing of clothes was essentially defined as 'women's work' there were few if any improvements in techniques until the invention of the modern washing machine.[37]

Until the end of the sixteenth century the most common form of cloth worn by the ordinary Japanese was linen made from hemp.[38] 'Cotton was grown hardly anywhere in Japan until the early Tokugawa period, when it began to replace hemp in the clothing of the commoners.' Once the change over from hemp to cotton had begun, the transformation was swift; it 'proceeded rapidly owing to cotton's greater warmth, softness, durability, and cheapness, and it was all but complete by the end of the seventeenth century.' Cotton had been introduced from Korea, and after the unification of Japan in the later sixteenth century its growth and manufacture increased dramatically. 'As the volume of exports expanded thereafter, cotton cultivation and commercial ginning, spinning, and weaving spread from Oshima and Kumage (Kaminoseki) counties, where they had first appeared, over the whole domain except for a district along the Japan Sea.'[39] By the 1700s, forty to fifty percent of the land around Osaka was growing cotton.[40] Silk, meanwhile, remained the preferred cloth of the rich. The absence of wool is indicated by Morse's remark that 'The Japanese women are much interested in our woolen fabrics, their cloth being cotton, linen, and silk, and the weave simple.'[41] Cotton was dominant and weaving was widespread: 'the women are busy weaving cotton cloth in narrow breadths on rude looms.'[42]

It is difficult to estimate the frequency of the washing of clothing. Some observers thought that it was not washed enough. The extreme case was put by Isabella Bird who was particularly critical of the dirty and unwashed clothing in

[34] Houghton, *Husbandry*, II, 133.
[35] Pepys, *Diary*, 12 August 1667.
[36] See Fussell and Fussell, *Countrywoman*, plate 11.
[37] For a brief useful account of soap making in England, see Grigson and Gibbs-Smith (eds), *Things*, 'Soap'. See also Fussell and Fussell, *Countrywoman*, 26,19–20,122.
[38] Nagahara Keiji in *Cambridge History*, 3,313.
[39] Smith, *Native Sources*, 74,74,75.
[40] *Cambridge History*, 4, 512.
[41] Morse, *Day*, I, 168.
[42] Griffis, *Mikado*, 546.

some of the villages she visited in the later nineteenth century. Many diseases she thought, 'would never have arisen had cleanliness of clothing . . . been attended to.' 'The absence of soap, the infrequency with which clothing is washed, and the absence of linen next the skin, cause various cutaneous diseases, which are aggravated by the bites and stings of insects'; 'these people wear no linen, and their clothes, which are seldom washed, are constantly worn, night and day, as long as they will hold together;' there were lots of sick people 'and all, sick and well, in truly "vile raiment" lamentably dirty and swarming with vermin.' However, three points should be made. The first is that clothes were washed. Even Isabella herself described how she noticed a stream running down through a village where 'People come back from their work, sit on the planks, take off their muddy clothes and wring them out, and bathe their feet in the current.'[43] The second is that though there was no soap in the western sense, 'For scrubbing the floor or clothes, alkali, obtained by leeching ashes, is put in the water.'[44] This would have been perfectly adequate. The third point is that clothes were looked on rather differently in Japan.

In much of the world, clothing is all in one piece and hence tends to be used and re-used as a whole. In Japan, much clothing was made up of a jig-saw of parts. When it was washed it was taken to pieces and then sewn up again for use. When parts were worn out they were simply replaced. This process is alluded to in a seventeenth-century account: 'Not content with a change of clothes at New Year, Bon, summer, and winter, they buy new dresses for every occasion which offers an excuse, discard them after a brief spell of merciless treatment and use the material as scrap for the sewing box.'[45]

The amount and consequences of embedded dirt in clothing when people are engaged in gruelling manual work is largely affected by two further considerations. The first is the cut and style of the clothing, the second is how much is worn during normal daily activities. In relation to the style, the Japanese seem to have solved the problem of keeping good body ventilation. As the anthropologist Kroeber explained, while much Western dress is fitted, 'Chinese and Japanese dress is also cut and tailored, but it is not fitted. It is cut loose, with ample sleeves, or kimono style, to suggest a broad figure. Trousers are ample, so as to have almost a skirt effect.'[46] The notable looseness of most Japanese dress, suitable for a hot climate, would give plenty of body ventilation and allow much of the sweat of labour to dry on the body, rather than on the cotton, and hence to be more easily cleaned off in the bath. Morse observes, 'simplicity of dress . . . are characteristic, not only of the more favored classes, but the posses-

---

[43] Bird, *Tracks*, 198,99,91.

[44] Griffis, *Mikado*, 356.

[45] Saikuku, *Storehouse*, 98.

[46] Kroeber, *Anthropology*, 332.

sion of the poorest among them.'[47] A doctor described women's clothing as follows 'upper clothing is . . . loose, wide and open, and . . . the chest is for the most part naked, and the thighs and legs are covered only with a thin skirt made of crepe or cotton.'[48] Children's clothing, in particular, was kept very simple and unostentatious, to the point of niggardliness. 'The Japanese children are very meanly clad; and, when accompanying their mothers through the streets; their shabby appearance contrasts most strikingly with the parent's splendid attire.'[49] For much of the time, and particularly when it was warm or there was hard physical work to do, clothing was kept to an absolute minimum. Morse noted: 'As we get into the interior, clothing seems to be used only on state occasions; the children are entirely naked, the men mostly so, the women partially so.' Alcock spoke of 'the summer costume of the lower orders, which with the men is limited to a narrow loin cloth, and the women a petticoat, sadly "scrimped" in the breadths.'[50]

In general, the Japanese had developed a system of clothing which was probably just about as healthy as it could be. Improved dramatically by the cotton revolution of the seventeenth century and given support by the emphasis on simplicity, functionality and minimalism, their working clothing was ideally suited to provide a loose, strong cover for the body when needed, but could be dispensed with almost entirely when superfluous.[51] At the end of the nineteenth century Hearn was impressed by the fact that the Japanese were 'still unimpaired by unhealthy clothing.'[52] Though they had adopted many things from the West. 'Basic clothing did not change significantly for most Japanese during the second half of the nineteenth century, notwithstanding the great popularity of Western goods in the large cities.'[53] For much of the time they wore little, but when 'they take to their clothing' they are 'well and comfortably clad.'[54] 'Take it altogether, the Japanese gentleman's attire and that of the ladies as well, is a highly elegant and sanitary one.'[55]

Three other peripheral elements of 'clothing' in the widest sense are also worth noting. The first are handkerchiefs. Handkerchiefs were seen as one of the 'blessings' which was brought with civilization to benighted third world countries, a mixture of morality, hygiene and good manners; 'printed calicoes and missionary pocket-handkerchiefs' helped to spread a 'layer of western

---

[47] Morse, *Day*, I, 44.
[48] Wittermans, *Pompe*, 41.
[49] Siebold, *Manners*, 126.
[50] Alcock, *Tycoon*, I, 120–1.
[51] For warmer winter clothing, see Morse, *Day*, II, 85.
[52] Hearn, *Kokoro*, 28.
[53] Hanley in Jansen and Rozman (eds), *Japan*, 461.
[54] Alcock, *Tycoon*, I, 300–1.
[55] Chamberlain, *Things*, 123.

civilization' like a 'film of oil' over the planet at large.[56] Whether handkerchiefs improved matters or just harboured germs is difficult say. The Japanese variant is likely to have been more conducive to health as it was disposable. The excellent Japanese paper, both strong and cheap, probably gave the world its first widespread use of paper handkerchiefs. 'Instead of a *handkerchief* I always saw them use thin and soft writing paper, which they constantly carried about them for this purpose, and which they also used for wiping their mouths and fingers, as likewise for wiping off the sweat from their bodies under the arm-pits.'[57] Siebold also noted the 'neat square' of clean white paper, the Japanese substitutes for pocket-handkerchiefs, which, after being used, are dropped into the sleeve until an opportunity offers of throwing them away without soiling the house.'[58]

A second accessory is the shoe. As was pointed out by Lane-Claypon in relation to Britain, 'it is doubtful whether the great mass of the inhabitants in this country, at any rate, realise how much avoidable suffering they undergo on account of the lack of care of their feet.' Hence 'Suitable footgear is of the utmost importance for both sexes. The feet should be warm and dry, not cold and damp.'[59]

The problem for most societies has been cost. Daily work in the fields puts an immense strain on any kind of footgear and the majority of people in most societies have not been able to afford to wear anything on the feet, except on special occasions. This leads to a great amount of ill-health and suffering, not merely from endless cuts, bruises, infections, bites, stings and so on, but through the various diseases which are picked up with bare feet, from various worm infestations through to schistosomiasis (bilharzia).

At first sight it looks as if the Japanese did not wear shoes. Griffis noticed 'that the Japanese wear no boots or shoes.'[60] However, he was referring to American-style shoes, made of leather, which were sold in shops and needed boot-blacking etc. In fact, the Japanese did wear foot-coverings, but without large numbers of domestic animals they were not made of leather. For special occasions and among the reasonably well off, there were the divided socks or *tabi* made of cloth. Wooden clogs (*geta*) 'were useful in the mud and rain' and could be worn with the *tabi*. For ordinary walking or work, 'the poor wore sandals of straw called *waraji* which could be woven very quickly and cheaply and were even worn by horses.'[61] For relaxing and special occasions 'the Japanese wore

[56] Mumford, *Technics*, 289.
[57] Thunberg, *Travels*, III, 277.
[58] Siebold, *Manners*, 24.
[59] Lane-Claypon, *Hygiene*, 117,104.
[60] Griffis, *Mikado*, I, 357.
[61] Hanley in *Cambridge History*, 4, 691; on horses, see Thunberg, *Travels*, III, 152 and Oliphant, *Elgin's Mission*, 110.

zori, a kind of thonged sandal.'[62] Contemporary pictures of workmen in the nineteenth century show them all wearing footgear.[63] *Tabi* and clogs had become the common wear of 'the landless, and even servants' by the early nineteenth century.[64]

The house was maintained as a hygienic and pure area by removing all outdoor footwear. 'One soon gets used to the routine of slipping off one's shoes, and the freedom from dust, mud, and germs as well as the quiet that reigns in the house reconciles one to the slight trouble.'[65] Inside the house, bare feet or *tabi* were perfectly adequate. Hearn compared Japanese footwear favorably to that of the West which 'had distorted the Western foot out of the original shape, and rendered it incapable of the work for which it was evolved.'[66] Unlike China, there is no evidence of foot-binding of women in Japan.

Finally, there is the question of bedding. There is some difference of opinion on this matter. The actual nature of Japanese bedding is described by Morse: 'The bed-clothes consisting of lightly or heavily wadded comforters are spread upon the floor, one or more forming the bed, and another one acting as a covering. The common ones are wadded with cotton; the best ones are made of silk, and are stuffed with floss silk.'[67] Some thought that this bedding was unhygienic. 'People used the innermost room (the *nando*) both for sleeping and for storing household goods, and it must have been the darkest room in the house. It must also have been very unsanitary – according to Yanagita – particularly after the Japanese started using cotton for bedding, which would get damp, musty and sweaty and, being stuffed with cotton batting, would be impossible to clean thoroughly without taking it apart.'[68]

Isabella Bird refers to the problem of the storage of the bedding, describing people 'huddled up in their dirty garments in wadded quilts, which are kept during the day in close cupboards, and are seldom washed from one year's end to another.'[69] Yet it would be hard to argue that it was less clean than bedding left on a bedstead. Furthermore, it seems to have been customary to expose the futons to air and sunlight each day: 'Then the futons were hung over poles or lines to sun.'[70] At inns, 'the bedding is a wadded comforter. . . . The comforters are gathered up in the morning and hung over the balcony rails for an airing, and afterwards piled away in some recess or closet' and there is a 'little cushion

[62] Hanley in *Cambridge History*, 4, 691.
[63] Griffis, *Mikado*, II, 357,416,426.
[64] Quoted by Jansen in *Cambridge History*, 5, 79.
[65] Geoffrey, *Immigrant*, 226.
[66] Hearn, *Kokoro*, 28–9.
[67] Morse, *Homes*, 210; cf. also, Morse, *Day*, I, 87.
[68] Hanley in Jansen and Rozman (eds), *Japan*, 453.
[69] Bird, *Tracks*, 99; see also Scidmore, *Jinrikisha*, 145.
[70] Scidmore, *Jinrikisha*, 161.

stuffed with buckwheat hulls' which served as a pillow and is 'covered with thin Japanese paper' which is disposed of each day and 'a new sheet added'.[71]

The English pattern of clothing was one of affluence which led to an unusually well-dressed population. The materials, particularly animal products such as wool and leather, were in abundance. The quality of the medieval cloths was decisively improved in the sixteenth century with the newly imported technique from Flanders and the Netherlands. That people wore warm, comfortable clothes and good shoes throughout the period is both unusual for a pre-industrial population and of benefit for general health, but it is difficult to judge just how clean they were.

The introduction of cotton cloth which was lighter and gave a less secure home for the louse both required and permitted frequent washing. Yet it would have remained expensive if it had not been for the simultaneous development of the various steam-power driven looms, which suddenly made cotton available at prices that most but the very poorest could afford.

As for Japan, it had benefited from the cotton revolution about two centuries earlier than England, though it was the cheapness and skill of its labour, and the scanty nature of the dress, that allowed the poor to enjoy this form of clothing rather than the invention of new power looms. In design, clothes in Japan were almost perfect in terms of health. Their main defect may have been that they gave inadequate protection from cold.

[71] Morse, *Day*, I, 237; see also 57.

14

Bodily Hygiene:
Bathing and Washing

Changes in bodily hygiene are often thought to be an important factor in explaining improvements in health. In a revision of his ideas, McKeown has widened them from nutrition to include hygiene: 'Second only to nutritional influences over time, and probably in importance, were the improvements in hygiene', which he believes were 'introduced progressively from the second half of the nineteenth century.'[1] Razzell also has switched from theories associated with smallpox vaccination to lay more emphasis on hygiene: 'it was an improvement in personal hygiene rather than a change in public health that was responsible for the reduction in mortality between 1801 and 1841.'[2]

McKeown believed that 'Standards of personal hygiene were low in the eighteenth century, particularly because bathing was uncommon, even among the well-to-do.'[3] The Bushmans write that 'probably not until 1850 did regular personal washing become routine in large numbers of middle-class households.'[4] Plenty of material can be found to support such a view. For instance, a doctor writing in 1801 remarked that 'most men resident in London and many ladies though accustomed to wash their hands and faces daily, neglect washing their bodies from year to year.'[5]

The reports collated by Chadwick paint a picture of considerable personal filthiness: 'When they are washing, the smell of the dirt mixed with the soap is

[1] McKeown, *Food*, 244.
[2] Razzell, *Essays*, 164.
[3] McKeown, *Modern Rise*, 124.
[4] Bushman, *Cleanliness*, 1225.
[5] Quoted in Wright, *Clean*, 138.

the most offensive of all the smells I have to encounter.' Particular cases seemed
to support this vision:

> Mr. John Kennedy, in the course of the examinations of some colliers in
> Lancashire, asked one of them: 'How often do the drawers (those employed
> in drawing coals) wash their bodies?' 'None of the drawers ever wash their bodies.
> I never wash my body; I let my shirt rub the dirt off; my shirt will show
> that. I wash my neck and ears, and face, of course.' 'Do you think it usual
> for the young women (engaged in the colliery) to do the same as you do?'
> 'I do not think it is usual for the lasses to wash their bodies; my sisters
> never wash themselves, and seeing is believing; they wash their faces, necks
> and ears.'[6]

It is often thought that there was a shortage of water which made bodily
washing difficult, and in particular that there was a general absence of hot
water. Washing in cold water is both less effective and less pleasant. Heating
up water for baths is expensive. Yet two developments in eighteenth- and
nineteenth-century England increased the supply of hot water. One was
the increasing use of coal, and the other was the use of hot water which was
a by-product of industrial use. The latter potential is well documented by
Chadwick.[7]

A second necessity is for some receptacle and a private space in which to
wash. Bathrooms in most houses are a fairly recent phenomenon in Europe.
'Although baths had their origins in antiquity, bathrooms, which were first
developed in England, appeared for the first time in France in the 1730s.'[8] Yet
the separate bathroom was pretty much confined to the very richest in the
society until the later nineteenth century. Even in the 1920s it could be stated
that 'In this country the provision of baths in dwelling houses of quite large size
was not usual even some fifty years ago.'[9] It is easy to assume that before the
advent of private bathrooms it was very difficult, if not impossible, for people to
bathe their bodies. There is clearly some truth in this. Affluence may make
privacy easier.

Yet there are also many ways in which, if people wished to do so, they could
bathe their whole body without needing a bathroom. They can do so using a tub
within the house. This is described in Chadwick's report which has to be set
against the image of a filthy working population.[10] There are no reasons why
such an arrangement should not have been used back into the middle ages.

---

[6] Chadwick, *Report*, 135,315.
[7] Chadwick, *Report*, 316–7.
[8] Goubert, *Conquest*, 86.
[9] Lane-Claypon, *Hygiene*, 84.
[10] Chadwick, *Report*, 316.

Indeed, 'some illustrations are to be found of bathrooms as a curtained alcove with a tub in it' for the fourteenth century.[11]

There were also alternatives outside the house. The seventeenth-century Yorkshire diarist, Adam Eyre, recounts on several occasions how he went to the river to bathe.[12] Or again, there were a few public bath houses. It would appear that it was such a bath house to which Pepys' wife went in 1665: 'my wife being busy in going with her woman to a hot-house to bath herself, after her long being within doors in the dirt, so that she now pretends to a resolution of being hereafter very clean.' The editors describe the hot-house as 'A public steam-bath establishment, used for hygienic and medicinal purposes, especially (perhaps exclusively) by women.'[13] The growth of the fashion for 'taking the waters' at health spas in the later seventeenth century was largely limited to the upper middle class and hence was unlikely to affect the general populace in a way comparable to what we shall find in relation to public bathing in Japan.[14]

Comenius's popular *Orbis Sensualium Pictus* described both private and public bathing. 'He that desireth to be washt in cold water, goeth down into a river. In a Bathing-house we wash off the filth either sitting in a Tub or going up into the Hot-house and we are rubbed with a Pumice stone or a Hair cloth.'[15] From the picture accompanying this description, it is clear that the customers were men, though a 'Bath Woman' was there to fetch water in a bucket. The third necessity, to turn the experience into something which will make a real improvement to health, is that the water is hot and that some cleansing agent is used.

It is assumed that soap was very expensive and out of the reach of most people until the later nineteenth century.[16] This may not have been the case. For instance, writing of Elizabethan home life, Byrne states that 'Balls of sweet-scented soap were at most people's disposal for their ablutions, and although it could be bought at about fourpence a pound it was generally made at home, where it was perfumed with such essences as oil of almonds or musk. Sir Hugh Platt has some delightful soap recipes in which rose-leaves and lavender flowers figure prominently.' It could be bought commercially by the barrel, one family bought a barrel for fifty shillings at Stourbridge Fair in 1562.[17]

Most important, however, is the attitude towards bathing. Here, it is often assumed, was the other major obstacle to personal hygiene. Many believe that

[11] Quennell and Quennell, *Things*, I, 168.
[12] Eyre, *Diary*, 48,50,57.
[13] Pepys, *Diary*, VI, 40.
[14] See Turner, *Taking the Cure*, and Mullett, *Public Baths*.
[15] Comenius, *Orbis*, 153.
[16] Nikiforuk, *Fourth*, 34.
[17] Byrne, *Elizabethan Life*, 28–9; for other evidence on soap made in the home, see Fussell, *Countrywoman*, 119–20.

the majority of the population made a virtue of necessity – they were going to be dirty, so they might as well make washing a vice. It is even asserted that there was some kind of folk wisdom which made washing dangerous.[18]

The general nature of the attitudes towards bathing in Europe, and in particular among the French upper classes, has been established by Georges Vigarello's *Concept of Cleanliness*. He shows how up to the fifteenth century, public bathing was widespread and baths were positively regarded but quotes an astounded visitor to Switzerland in the sixteenth century, 'Men and women mix indiscriminately together in baths and steam-baths without any impropriety occurring.' Vigarello continues that 'It was also the practice in thermal baths in the Middle Ages, where naked bodies of both sexes shared the same water.' He gives a number of reasons for the change in attitude from the fifteenth century. He argues that the disappearance of both public and private bathing were the result of a 'progressive intolerance by the human environment of places seen as turbulent, violent and corrupting, and fears of the weakness of the body, based on ideas about dangerous openings and fluxes. The impact of the plague was much greater because it affected a practice already unstable and under threat.'[19]

In England, a similar change in attitude to bathing has been surveyed by Keith Thomas. He reminds us that 'The monastic orders indeed were notable for their rules about daily washing and periodic bathing.' Gradually towards the end of the Middle Ages the enthusiasm for bathing, and particularly public bathing, declined. According to Thomas, by the sixteenth and seventeenth centuries 'In general, bathing was regarded either as a sophisticated form of sensual indulgence or as a medical procedure to be undertaken for some specific therapeutic purpose and only after consultation with a physician.' He believes that it 'might be useful as a means of treating certain complaints, whether at home or in the mineral waters of a spa. But it seems to have been less usual as a method of keeping the body clean than it had been in the later Middle Ages.'[20]

Towards the end of the seventeenth century, medical writers were advocating baths as a means of personal hygiene.[21] One was Sir John Floyer, whose *History of Cold Bathing* was first published in 1697, to see six editions within thirty-five years. According to Mullet, 'Cold bathing had gone out of fashion for some time because chemical doctors had discouraged the practice in order to get patients to take their internal medicines. Disuse had also resulted from the religious changes of the sixteenth century, since the virtues of many wells were imputed to various saints who were no longer worshipped.'[22] But 'Sir John

[18] Goubert, *Conquest*, 84.
[19] Vigarello, *Cleanliness*, 29,34.
[20] Thomas, *Cleanliness*, 61,59,58.
[21] Thomas, *Cleanliness*, 75.
[22] Mullet, *Public Baths*, 19,19–20.

Floyer, declared that if the English could only be brought to understand the value of a bath, they would all want to have one in their houses.' Another advocate was Cheyne, who 'advised all who could "to have a cold bath at their houses to wash their bodies in" and "constantly two or three times a week, summer and winter, to go into it".' Then 'during the eighteenth century it became increasingly common for medical writers to stress the connection between good health and frequent washing, and to lament "the shameless disuse of bathing, hot and cold, that prevales in our days".'[23]

This link was forcefully stressed by Buchan. 'When infectious diseases do break out, cleanliness is the most likely means to prevent their spreading; it is likewise necessary to prevent their returning afterwards, or being conveyed to other places.' He believed that 'Were every person, for example, after visiting the sick, handling a dead body, or touching any thing that might convey infection, to wash before he went into company, or sat down to meat, he would run less hazard either of catching the infection himself, or of communicating it to others.' Washing of all the limbs was beneficial. 'Frequent washing not only removes the filth and sordes which adhere to the skin, but likewise promotes the perspiration, braces the body, and enlivens the spirits.' Anticipating many of Chadwick's reforms he wrote that 'To the same cause must we impute the various kinds of vermin which infect the human body, houses, etc. These may always be banished by cleanliness alone, and wherever they abound, we have reason to believe it is neglected.' In particular, 'Diseases of the skin are chiefly owing to want of cleanliness. They may indeed be caught by infection, or brought on by poor living, unwholesome food, etc but they will seldom continue long where cleanliness prevails.'[24] This is the functionalist, rather than the aesthetic, approach to cleanliness which Vigarello stresses as a major change, partly based on the discoveries of William Harvey.[25]

It is important to note that too much emphasis can be placed on bodily cleanliness. We have been deeply influenced by the nineteenth-century hygienic movement and it is consequently easy to assume that the absence of constant washing in hot water is dangerous. We tend to assume that there is something almost magical in hot water and washing with soap. In fact, the body produces protective oils for the skin which are necessary to health and it is dangerous to scrub them all off. It may well be that even before the nineteenth-century changes, most people in England washed enough for reasonable health. The real dangers come from unwashed hands and faces, or when the body has sores or cuts. The absence of any obvious correlation between washing behaviour and changes in health in eighteenth-century England is therefore not surprising.

---

[23] Quoted in Thomas, *Cleanliness*, 75,76.
[24] Buchan, *Domestic*, 104,103,103–4,100,100. 'Sordes' means filth, uncleanness.
[25] Vigarello, *Cleanliness*, 140–1.

Indeed, the dangers of over-washing are as great as those of washing too little. This becomes evident when we look at Japan:

> Few visitors to Japan fail to remark on the extraordinary Japanese passion for bathing. The early Chinese historians commenting in the third century A.D. on the peculiar habits of their primitive island neighbors to the east, the Christian missionaries and traders of the sixteenth and seventeenth centuries ... all have quickly taken note of the Japanese penchant for frequent bathing, their custom of bathing communally and their delight in soaking in waters so hot as to seem beyond human tolerance.

The peculiarity was shown in the earliest mythical accounts of Japan. 'Izanagi, the principal creator-deity, takes a bath on the very first page of the *Kojiki*, and the divine actors of the subsequent myths about the origins of Japan repeatedly immerse themselves in rivers or the sea and engage in all manner of ritualistic purifications.' Peter Grilli writes, 'repeated references to bathing in the creation myths and subsequent events of Japanese mythology' indicate 'a strong identi- fication of evil and immorality with filth and pollution and – by contrast – of virtue and goodness with cleanliness and purity.'[26] This ancient interest in baths and bathing is unique to Japan. 'Cleanliness is one of the few original items of Japanese civilisation.' 'Almost all other Japanese institutions have their root in China, but not tubs.'[27]

The contrast between the European and Japanese attitudes towards bathing are examined by the anthropologist Fosco Maraini. 'It seems to me that the contempt for the body inherent in Christianity has, over the centuries, resulted in a view of the bath as no more than an unfortunate necessity, as brutish in its way as any other bodily function.' However in Japan, 'the act of bathing is no mere concession to the dreadful tendency of bodies to become soiled. It is, rather, an act of respect – amounting almost to worship – for the corporeal being whose worth, in Japan, is not inferior to that of the spiritual being.' Thus he believes that 'With its roots in ritual ablutions and purifications, bath-time in Tokyo is a pious, auspicious and above all a happy occasion.'[28]

One reason for the difference clearly lies in the cultural and religious atti- tudes alluded to by Maraini and Grilli. Another stems from the geology of Japan which has produced an abundance of hot springs. 'Few places in volcanic Japan do not have a hot spring within easy reach.' Hence 'Few peoples have delighted in bathing as much as the Japanese, blessed since the earliest times with abun- dant hot water from mineral springs located throughout their volcanic land.'

---

[26] Grilli, *Bath*, 15,46,47.
[27] Chamberlain, *Things*, 60.
[28] Maraini, *Tokyo*, 57.

Grilli adds that 'hot springs were the only universal luxury enjoyed by Japanese of all walks of life. The hot water from natural springs cost nothing and could be found almost everywhere.'[29]

The hot water that gushed from the volcanic rocks contained minerals believed to be of medicinal value. This led to the proliferation of the Japanese equivalent of the 'spa', where people 'took the waters'. Kaempfer noted that 'there are besides many and efficacious hot baths in the Country, where they send, as we do, Patients labouring under stubborn and lingring sickness.' In one place 'Not far from the village, on the side of a small river, which falls down from a neighbouring hill, is a hot bath, famous for its vertues in curing the pox, itch, rheumatism, lameness and several other chronical and inveterate distempers.' 'Among others there is a famous hot Bath, which they believe to be an infallible cure for the Venereal Disease, if the Patient for several days together goes in but a few moments a day and washes himself in it.'[30] A century later Thunberg echoed his observations: 'The Japanese use this and other similar baths, with which the country abounds, in venereal complaints, the palsy, itch, rheumatism and many other disorders.'[31]

The variety of minerals in these springs is described in a recent account. 'Beppu, for example, has hot springs of virtually every type found in Japan: sulphurous springs, alkaline springs, simple salt springs, acid springs, ferrous springs, and springs of high radium content.'[32] Morse described how 'One spring was supposed to be good for pain in the chest and leg, another was good for stomach disorders; another for weak eyes; and another for troubles in the head, and so on. Each spring was supposed to have different curative virtues!'[33] Whether they are useful or not is an open question: 'It is unclear whether Dr Balz's assertion that the Kusatsu baths would cure syphilis, rheumatism, and chronic skin diseases was due to the chemical properties of the water or the possibility that the diseases might be boiled out of the sufferers.'[34] The latter theory is implied by Rein. 'There is no doubt that the regular use of warm baths among the Japanese contributes greatly to the maintenance and improvement of their health. Rheumatic complaints . . . are usually checked in the germ, and are therefore much less common than with us.'[35]

Turning to ordinary bathing, the actual process of washing off dirt and bathing was believed to have many benefits. 'In Japan, care of the skin is rightly

---

[29] Grilli, *Bath*, 21,124.
[30] Kaempfer, *History*, III, 319; II, 367; I, 165.
[31] Thunberg, *Travels*, III, 102.
[32] Grilli, *Bath*, 132.
[33] Morse, *Day*, I, 99.
[34] Grilli, *Bath*, 136.
[35] Rein, *Travels*, 413.

considered one of the surest safeguards for a healthy condition. A bath, the Japanese believe, removes harmful gases. These gases have to escape through the pores of the skin, and if these are clogged they are naturally prevented from doing so.'[36] The healthful aspects merged with the therapeutic – the reinvigorating and refreshing effects of hot water. The 'Japanese usually bath, or sweat, after their days journey is over, thinking by this means to refresh themselves and to sweat off their weariness.'[37] 'The peasant, the labour of the day over, can always look forward to the luxury of a hot bath, and a still more luxurious shampooing – if not by his barber or the blind professors of the art, who go about all the evening, with a whistle for their cry, seeking customers – he can always make sure of it by his wife's aid.'[38]

An account of the importance of the bath in a rural village is given in the late-nineteenth-century autobiographical novel, *Soil*. After a hard and cold day's work, Oshina goes off for her bath at a neighbour's house. She is kept waiting, but 'When finally the men were finished Oshina hurriedly took off her clothes, thinking of nothing else but getting into the hot water.... As Oshina felt warmth returning gradually to her body she began to feel revived. She wanted to stay in the soothing water forever.' After her death, her husband 'was too tired at the end of the day of steady labor to do much night work. ... Except for a few occasions when he had made rope he spent the long evening bathing.'[39]

The 'motivations for bathing in Japan go beyond efficiency and transcend physical cleanliness. What the bath offers is a sensual feeling of well-being, of harmony with one's environment and with one's self.'[40] This feeling no doubt reflects some physiological fact. Very hot baths 'tend to pass out of the purview of hygiene and to enter that of therapeutics. They produce definite effects on the circulation which may be beneficial.'[41] The 'total' effect is made clear by Maraini: 'In Japan the bath originated with ritual purification, hence it is a positive, pleasurable act, an essential ingredient in the rest and refreshment which a man takes after the toil of the day, a function as important and vital as sleep or meals.'[42]

Baths were seen as domestic necessities by most according to Morse: 'nearly every house among the higher and middle classes possesses the most ample arrangements for hot baths; and even among the poorer classes, in the country as well as in the city, this convenience is not wanting.'[43] During the 1880s a

---

[36] Wittermans, *Pompe*, 98.
[37] Kaempfer, *History*, II, 324.
[38] Alcock, *Tycoon*, I, 302.
[39] Nagatsuka, *Soil*, 5,123.
[40] Grilli, *Bath*, 22.
[41] Lane-Claypon, *Hygiene*, 84.
[42] Maraini, *Meeting*, 25.
[43] Morse, *Homes*, 203.

report on the conditions in a village in the Kanagawa Prefecture stated that seven or eight houses in ten had a bath tub.[44] 'The old mansion, like all Japanese houses, was provided with a huge cauldron and furnace quite near the house, for heating water for the bath taken daily by every member of every Japanese family.'[45] A group of health officers who visited Japan in 1926 noted that 'even the poor aim at bathing once a day', and that 'Every house except the poorest has its bath tub and those persons who possess none borrow from a neighbour.'[46] 'In my Japanese travels I have seen dwellings of every conceivable type; even the huts of the most poverty-stricken peasants or labourers had their *o-furo* (honourable bath); in the worst cases there would be a big basin in which you washed as best you could. But there was never a complete lack of facilities.'[47]

Alongside the very wide provision of private baths were the 'added convenience' of innumerable public baths. 'Every town and village has its bathhouse, and it is hot-water bathing always.'[48] 'On almost every street public baths are found, where large bathtubs and hot water are available to everyone for a few pennies.'[49]

The bathhouse, preferably naturally heated from a thermal spring, was one of the central institutions of Japan. 'Public bathhouses in Japanese cities have played a role as community gathering places for the last four hundred years, comparable to the central plazas or coffee houses of European towns – centers where neighbors could meet regularly to share news and gossip.' Thus the official function of bathhouses as places to wash 'has been almost secondary to their role as neighborhood centers where friends meet to exchange news and gossip and where the myriad relationships that bind a community are strengthened every day.'[50] 'The public bath-houses, that alternate with the tea-houses in the village streets, have roofs and sides of solid wood, except the street front, which is open and curtainless, and within which men, women and children meet in the hot-water tanks, as at the market-place or street-corners in other countries'[51] It is here that the particularly intense solidarity of the 'small group' society of Japan is both expressed and reaffirmed. The famous Durkheimian 'effervescence' whereby, through rituals, a society expresses and reaffirms itself, occurs in the steam and conviviality of the bath house where friends and neighbours are made equal and close. '*Hadaka no tsukiai* – "companions in

[44] Kunio (ed.), *Manners and Customs*, 287.
[45] Griffis, *Mikado*, 446.
[46] Wellington, *Report*, 8,21.
[47] Maraini, *Meeting*, 25.
[48] Morse, *Day*, I, 42.
[49] Wittermans, *Pompe*, 99.
[50] Grilli, *Bath*, 16,94.
[51] Scidmore, *Jinrikisha*, 169.

nudity" or friends who bathe together, the Japanese say, are the closest friends of all.'[52]

The fact that small villages and towns had bath-houses suggests their importance, as does their prevalence in the great cities. It was calculated in the later nineteenth century that 'There are over eleven hundred public baths in the city of Tokyo in which it is calculated that five hundred thousand persons bathe daily, the usual charge being 2½ *sen* (under three farthings of English money) for adults, two *sen* for children and one and a half *sen* for infants in arms.'[53]

In order for even this large number of bathing establishments to cope with the huge number of clients and to provide them with a cleansing and satisfying experience, several conventions were developed. The first, which applied to private baths as well, was that dirt was washed off outside the bath. The bath was the social and spiritual cleansing. 'It must be understood that each bather first cleans himself outside the bath by ladling water over the body. ... Thus each one enters the bath already clean, to enjoy the luxury of a good boiling.'[54] 'The bather always washes himself on the flooring and gets into the bath only to warm himself.'[55]

Isabella Bird referred to the absence of soap[56] and Griffis notes that 'the Japanese have no word for soap, and have never until these late days used it.' He believed that their outstanding cleanliness is due to the fact that 'Hot water is the detergent and the normal Japanese gets under it at least once a day.'[57] But they also had an alternative to animal-fat based western soap. 'Soap is a foreign innovation; and the same purpose was served by the use of fine bran-powder obtained by sifting rice after its final cleaning in a mortar. A handful of this powder is put into a little cloth bag, which is then wetted and rubbed against the skin; and the turbid water which exudes through the texture of the bag is very efficacious in cleaning the skin. It is now used together with soap.'[58] 'The original national cleanser was the bran bag (*nuka-bukuro*) made by sewing a handful of bran into a small piece of linen, which furnishes a deliciously soft washing material.'[59] In fact, the Japanese had available numerous different 'natural' soaps like their Chinese neighbours who made use of the soap-bean tree, the soap-pod tree and other plants.[60]

---

[52] Grilli, *Bath*, 34.
[53] Chamberlain, *Things*, 60.
[54] Chamberlain, *Things*, 61.
[55] Inouye, *Home*, 54.
[56] Bird, *Tracks*, 198.
[57] Griffis, *Mikado*, 356.
[58] Inouye, *Home*, 120.
[59] Chamberlain, *Things*, 61; Scidmore, *Jinrikisha*, 173, also alludes to these rice-bran bags.
[60] Needham, *Clerks*, 396ff; for various different substances used as soap in the Meiji period, see Keizo (ed.), *Japanese Society*, 45–6.

A major obstacle to the effective use of public baths are usual western social conventions concerning nudity and decency. Japanese baths ran right against Victorian attitudes and we find some interesting descriptions and musing on the subject. The problem is that if people are too aware of their nakedness, they will want to bathe alone, or at least not with the opposite sex, or they may wear clothes – which destroys much of the cleansing effect of the water. The more that privacy and decency has to be protected, the more expensive it becomes to build walls and separate dressing rooms and perhaps individual baths. Public bathing may well soon move out of reach of the mass of the populace as too expensive or too embarrassing.

The social conventions in Japan avoided these problems. 'One can really see some strange things in these public baths. Here, men, women and children bathe in the same tubs, all together and at the same time, and yet this does not give rise to the slightest impropriety; indeed, I would almost say without their even paying attention to the difference in sex.'[61] 'As the editor of the *Japan Mail* has well said, the nude is seen in Japan, but not looked at.'[62] Coming from that most inhibited of civilizations, upper middle class Victorian Britain, Alcock encountered some 'shocking' sights as he walked around the cities. 'Men and women steaming in the bathing houses, raise themselves to the open bars of the lattice fronts to look out.' 'As we approached, an elderly matron stepped out onto the margin, leaving half a dozen of the other sex behind her, to continue their soaking process. The freedom of the lady from all self-consciousness or embarrassment was so perfect of its kind.' He concluded that one really needed to rethink one's idea of decency: 'I cannot help feeling there is some danger of doing great injustice to the womanhood of Japan, if we judge them by our rules of decency and modesty. Where there is no sense of immodesty, no consciousness of wrong doing, there is, or may be, a like absence of any sinful or depraving feeling.'[63]

Morse gives us both the most detailed descriptions of the inside of the public bathing houses and of the entirely different cultural premises upon which they were based. 'The baths are stretched along the side of the streets; rude wooden sheds open in front, within which are the tanks, which are eight feet long and five feet wide, the water pouring out from a wooden pipe at the inner side of the tank, or simply running over the edge of the tank from the spring just behind.' 'In one, six or seven persons were bathing, in a crouching position, with the water up to their shoulders, at times dipping up water and pouring it over their heads.' 'But the most striking sight was to see both sexes in the bath, young and

[61] Wittermans, *Pompe*, 99.
[62] Chamberlain, *Things*, 60.
[63] Alcock, *Tycoon*, I, 253; II, 73; II, 253.

old, and the whole affair open to the street along which many were passing, though a low screen partially intervened.'[64]

Morse tried to inject some cultural relativism into all this. Addressing his American audience he wished to:

> express some plain truths about the subject of nakedness, which in Japan for centuries has not been looked upon as immodest, while we have been brought up to regard it as immodest. The exposure of the body in Japan is only when bathing and everybody minds his own business. On the streets of the city or country I never saw a man looking at the ankles or legs of a girl . . . the Japanese, as well as other Eastern people, have for centuries been accustomed to see nakedness, without its provoking among them the slightest attention, or in any way suggesting immodesty.

He elaborated: 'The missionary should remember that clothes-morality is climatic, and that a certain degree of covering of the body has gradually become in the Northwest associated with morality and piety, the traditions of tropical countries may have equally connected elaborate dress rather with the sensualities of Solomon in his glory than with the purity of the lily as clothed by Nature.' As all observers noted, there was no prurience, no indecency; bodily privacy was just different. 'In Japan, among the lower classes, the sexes bathe together, but with a modesty and propriety that are inconceivable to a foreigner until he has witnessed it. Though naked, there is no indecent exposure of the person. While in the bath they are absorbed in their work, and though chatting and laughing seem utterly unmindful of each other.'[65]

The difference of attitude and the changing practices are well shown in an order issued by the government of Tokyo in 1871:

> The common people of the city, instead of wearing clothes, go out to work or to the bath virtually naked. This is a general custom, and Japanese are not inclined to criticize it, but in foreign countries it is looked down upon. Westerners consider it shameful to reveal their bodies, and they do not do it. Recently we have come into much closer contact with other countries, and many foreigners have come to Japan. If this ugly practice is left as it is, it will bring shame upon our nation.

Henceforward 'no one, not even the poorest people' were to go out almost naked.[66]

How often then did the Japanese bathe? 'Wealthy Japanese bathe everyday.'[67]

[64] Morse, *Day*, I, 97.
[65] Morse, *Homes*, 200,200,201.
[66] Quoted in Keizo, *Japanese Society*, 159.
[67] Wittermans, *Pompe*, 99.

Ordinary people also bathed daily. 'Japan is famed for the cleanliness of her people whose invariable custom is to take a hot bath daily.' To bathe daily in hot water, if spread over the majority of the population, would be surprising enough. Yet it would appear that, if possible, people would bathe several times a day – and for long periods: 'as life is not supportable in Japan unless one has a hot bath once at least, sometimes twice a day, our tub was perpetually being heated, used, and renewed.'[68] Morse observed bathing more often than this among the ordinary population: 'the Japanese working classes – such as the carpenters, masons, and others – often bathe two or three times a day.'[69] Chamberlain recounts how 'In another case, some of the inhabitants of a certain village famed for its hot springs excused themselves to the present writer for their dirtiness during the busy summer months: "For", said they,"we have only time to bathe twice a day". "How often, then, do you bathe in winter?" "Oh about four or five times daily. The children go into the bath whenever they feel cold." '[70] In such a village Isabella Bird noted that the people bathed 'four times a day and remain for an hour at a time.'[71]

The Japanese liked their baths extraordinarily hot: 'the Japanese hot bath is very hot (not less than 110 °F as a general rule) and even the adult foreigner must learn slowly to bear it, and to appreciate its hygienic value.'[72] 'I suppose it is the force of habit, but they certainly bear par-boiling, both men and women, better than any people I ever met with.'[73] Von Siebold in his study of Japanese volcanic spas 'dropped eggs into the waters, and when he retrieved them in a few minutes they were boiled.'[74]

The Japanese became used to such scorching temperatures from infancy. 'Shortly after birth children are bathed – indeed, three times a week in warm water and later, when they are a little older, often even more frequently. The body gets so used to this that every Japanese needs his warm bath as much as his food.'[75] Even 'among the lower classes, where there are few bathing facilities in the houses, babies of a few weeks old are often taken to the public bath house and put into the hot bath.' 'To a baby's delicate skin, the first bath or two is usually a severe trial, but it soon becomes accustomed to a high temperature, and takes its bath, as it does everything else, placidly and in public'[76] Drawings of bath

---

[68] Geoffrey, *Immigrant*, 51,256.
[69] Morse, *Homes*, 202.
[70] Chamberlain, *Things*, 62.
[71] Bird, *Tracks*, 94.
[72] Hearn, *Glimpses*, 339.
[73] Alcock, *Tycoon*, II, 74.
[74] Bowers, *Medical Pioneers*, 118.
[75] Wittermans, *Pompe*, 98.
[76] Bacon, *Japanese Girls*, 8,9.

houses often show mothers sitting accompanied by their tiny infants, who would go with them into the boiling water like everyone else.[77]

The care of the body was not confined to washing. The Japanese paid particular attention to the head and hair. From birth, the head was shaved: 'it is the custom to shave the heads of very small boys and girls.'[78] As children reached three or four, the hair styles of the genders were differentiated. Of a girl, Bacon wrote 'at the age of three, the hair on her small head, which until then has been shaved in fancy patterns is allowed to begin its growth toward the coiffure of womanhood.'[79]

Women's hair-styles were elaborate and appropriate to age and marital status: pre-pubertal, young women, courtship, marriage, young married, old married, widowed and so on; social rank, region and other criteria also varied.[80] An enormous amount of effort was put into perfecting and maintaining the style. 'Both the *shimada* and the *marumage* are heavy as they require false hair. The hair needs also to be well oiled. The hair is done once in three or four days, but is seldom washed, not more than once a month. The head is consequently heated and a headache is often the result.'[81]

The rest of the head was kept absolutely free of hair. 'Not a particle of hair is ever allowed to appear upon their faces.'[82] 'The Japanese woman does not allow any hair or even down to grow on her face, and from time to time shaves the whole face like the other sex. We are not a hairy race, and our women have on the whole very smooth faces.'[83] Married women often even plucked out their eye-brows. Special tweezers were used to pluck out hair from the nostrils, chin and elsewhere. The arrangement of the hair was so elaborate that special sleeping rests had to be used by women, as by men, and hats were again out of the question. 'Women wear nothing on their heads except in mid-winter for fear of deranging their elaborate coiffure.'[84] Thus the one area which was not daily immersed in hot water was as carefully tended as the rest of the body.

Men's hair styles were described by Morse. 'I came across a Japanese book in which were some remarkable studies of queues; also a series of sketches illustrating the various modes of dressing the hair for boys and men – old styles of a hundred years ago and the present styles.' The old styles, however, were disappearing rapidly because of western influence. 'Consider the bother of having the top of one's head shaved every two or three days and the queue waxed and firmly

---

[77] For example see the drawing reproduced in Tames, *Encounters*, facing 66.
[78] Hearn, *Glimpses*, 338.
[79] Bacon, *Japanese Girls*, 19.
[80] See *Kodansha Encyclopedia* (Illustrated), under 'Hair Styles'.
[81] Inouye, *Home*, 113.
[82] Oliphant, *Elgin's Mission*, 157–8.
[83] Inouye, *Home*, 119.
[84] Inouye, *Home*, 130.

arranged on the bald spot. To keep it in place night and day must have been a burden. The fishermen, the farmers, and classes of that kind still adhere to the queue.'[85]

Yet despite all this careful attention to cleanliness the Japanese were not immune to the possibility of infection. While skin diseases were common in Europe and America, those who visited Japan thought that they were even worse in that country. Alcock reported 'there is not the exemption from skin diseases which has been asserted. On the contrary, among the working classes, various forms of cutaneous eruptions are common' which he thought 'perhaps to be accounted for by their habit of washing together in crowds.'[86] Members of the family would bath in the same water, taking it in turns. As the water cooled it would become a good medium for spreading certain germs. Morse recorded that 'skin diseases are common, especially the contagious forms.'[87] Isabella Bird wrote that 'It is painful to see the prevalence of such repulsive maladies as *scabies*, ... and unwholesome-looking eruptions'; 'children covered with skin-diseases. ... men exhibiting painful sores'. Willis noted that 'Skin diseases are also prevalent, in many cases arising from inattention to cleanliness or from the use of overheated baths.' He was amazed at their diversity and gravity. 'I must say the skin diseases are beauties such as one never meets with in England. It is awful beyond description some of the cases.' He then made the significant observation that 'There is still a widespread belief that during disease the skin should not be cleansed at all.'[88]

The worst disease seems to have been scabies, or the 'itch' as it was known in the west. This is 'a transmissible parasitic skin infection', caused by the itch mite, which is seldom found 'in a good hygienic environment'. The female mite burrows into the skin and the larvae hatch and 'then tend to congregate around hair follicles.' The disease is easily transmitted by intimate contact with an infected individual.[89]

Willis speaks of 'a violent sort of itch which by neglect of cleanliness becomes very bad and seems to be the cause of many deaths; in as much as it is considered that all efforts to get rid of the disease are mischievous it is allowed to invade the whole body, and by degrees wears out the strength. It is a common belief that this disease is an effort of nature to throw internal disease to the surface.'[90] 'Itch, too, is a common malady – very common to a distressing degree – and inveterate beyond anything known in Europe! It is almost impossible to get a domestic

---

[85] Morse, *Day*, I, 397–8; a 'queue' is the traditional ornamental male hair-style in Japan.
[86] Alcock, *Tycoon*, I, 190–1.
[87] Morse, *Day*, I, 40.
[88] Cortazzi, *Willis*, 260,213.
[89] Merck, *Manual*, 1412.
[90] Cortazzi, *Willis*, 244.

servant free from this loathsome disease, or keep him so.' This was 'a very inveterate form of itch, which Dr Pompas (sic) in Nagasaki assured me was not to be cured by the ordinary treatment in Europe – yellow soap and sulphur it defies; and it is disgustingly prevalent.'[91]

Another skin disease was a kind of childhood eczema which took a number of forms. The one most vividly described was probably seborrheic infantile eczema or a variant, a form of dermatitis which consists of 'a yellowish scaling and crusted area in the vertex of the scalp.'[92] 'The unpleasant appearance of some Japanese children's heads is simply due to a form of eczema. The ailment is one by no means unknown in Europe, and is easily curable in a week. But as popular superstition invests these scabby heads with a health-giving influence in later life, no attempt is made to cure them.' Chamberlain suggested that it may have been related to the particular way of treating children's hair. 'Probably shaving with dirty razors has something to do with the disease; for it generally ceases when shaving stops, and has noticeably diminished since the foreign custom of allowing children's hair to grow has begun to gain ground.'[93] Bacon thought that 'many babies in Japan are afflicted with disagreeable skin diseases, especially of the scalp and face-troubles which usually disappear as soon as the child becomes accustomed to the regular food of the adult.'[94] She believed the diseases were due to infant diet.

Both scabies and eczema were affected by other Japanese customs. Busvine suggests in relation to scabies that 'Bed sharing, indeed, seems to be the only social factor responsible for increasing infection.' The best chances of scabies spreading are, for example, 'where children sleep together or with their mother.'[95] The custom of infants sleeping with the mother for at least a year after birth, and the constant carrying of infants by parents and older siblings may have been important in spreading the itch mite and eczema to almost all of the Japanese population in their infancy. It is also possible that constant washing in boiling water would remove the protective oil that the skin naturally produces and makes it more vulnerable to infections of this type.

Equally difficult to deal with were eye infections: 'a great many, and particularly old people, were affected with red, sore, and running eyes.' In 1848 Mohnike was struck by the 'prevalence of diseases of the eyes' and Willis developed 'quite a reputation for his treatment of eye disease', including cataracts:

---

[91] Alcock, *Tycoon*, II, 144.
[92] Merck, *Manual*, 1424.
[93] Chamberlain, *Things*, 93.
[94] Bacon, *Japanese Girls*, 10.
[95] Busvine, *Insects*, 281,278.

Eye diseases also occur quite frequently in Japan. Nowhere in the world does one find so many blind people, which to a large extent has to be attributed to a complete ignorance of opthalmology. Many diseases, had they initially been treated correctly, would soon have been cured, but now end up with complete loss of sight. Diseases of the retina are particularly frequent, also cataracts; I saw a few cases of granulation (trachoma), but not an epidemic.[96]

He further described how

there was a lot of material for operations. As I have mentioned, in no other country in the world are there as many eye diseases as in Japan, and if I had to supply statistics, I should say, on the basis of my experience in Nagasaki, that approximately 8 per cent of the population suffer from diseases of the eye. This will surely be different in other places, but eye diseases do occur with great frequency throughout the nation.[97]

'As we moved through town after town, and village after village, in our daily journeys, I observed a good deal of ophthalmia; blind people not infrequently also.'[98] This high level of trachoma in Japan, with rates of nearly ten per cent of the general population suffering from the disease in 1954, and rates of over fifty per cent in particular prefectures, is indeed a puzzle.[99]

Trachoma is a 'chronic contagious viral conjunctivitis' which 'is most contagious in its early stages and may be transmitted by direct contact with trachomatous material or indirectly by handling contaminated articles (e.g. towels, handkerchiefs).'[100] 'Trachoma transmission may also occur by direct touch, by the contamination of clothing or bedding, possibly by bathing in pools in which people swim and wash, and by sexual means.' More generally, eyes may be affected by 'winds and dust, along with smoke in unventilated huts' which 'further irritate the eyes' and exacerbate bacterial infections such as bacterial purulent conjunctivitis.[101] Against these theories we may place those of the various foreigners who tried to explain the very high levels and seriousness of eye infection in Japan.

Morse wrote that 'The prevalence of eye trouble ... becomes very noticeable as one rides through the country; cataract, inflamed eyes, and loss of one eye are seen as well as many blind people.' He gave a suggestion as to the cause of infection. Both men and women's faces were constantly being shaved. 'The entire face is shaved; even women have their noses, cheeks, and all the surface of

[96] Cortazzi, *Willis*, 10,185.
[97] Wittermans, *Pompe*, 109,117.
[98] Alcock, *Tycoon*, II, 144.
[99] See May, *Ecology*, 289.
[100] Merck, *Manual*, 497.
[101] Mary C.Karasch in Kiple (ed.), *Disease*, 898–9.

their face shaved.' He believed that the widespread eye troubles were 'due in part to these travelling barbers.'[102] Another local custom was put forward as an explanation of eye disease by Alcock. This was 'the practice which prevails among the people of having their eyelids daily turned inside out – of which you may see an example as you pass that barber's shop – and then rubbed over, titillated, and polished by a smooth copper spatula' which 'must, I should think, be eminently conductive to disease of one sort or other.'[103]

That the eye complaints were something more than the result of mere infection caused by dirt, and were specific and highly contagious diseases, does not seem to have been widely recognized until quite late. It was not until the 1920s that Geoffrey observed that 'trachoma' was 'widespread among the Japanese' and is 'the bugbear of foreigners, as its germs lurk everywhere.' 'Uneducated Japanese suffer fearfully from this scourge, as they do not seem to grasp the principles of the spread of infection and its prevention.'[104]

The English may not have been assiduous bathers and the typhus epidemics they periodically suffered testify to a certain want of cleanliness. However, the Japanese delight in communal hot baths and constant washing and polishing does not seem to have protected them from serious skin and eye complaints. Personal hygiene is only one factor in the struggle against disease.

---

[102] Morse, *Day*, I, 53.
[103] Alcock, *Tycoon*, I, 463.
[104] Geoffrey, *Immigrant*, 49.

15

Changing Concepts of Dirt and Cleanliness

In considering the various features of the environment which contributed to the unusual pattern of English and Japanese mortality, a central thread running through all of them has been the attitude towards dirt. Analyses of drink, bodily excrement, rubbish in the environment, the house, clothing and bodily hygiene have all demonstrated the way in which perceptions of dirt and efforts to keep certain things clean had dramatic effects on health in England and Japan. Yet how are we to explain what appears to be an unusual attitude towards dirt and the considerable effort that was made to eliminate it, particularly in Japan, but also in England?

To start with, we need to consider what 'dirt' is. One of the definitions of dirt, as analysed by Mary Douglas and others, is that it is 'matter out of place'.[1] It is material which is on a conceptual boundary – as with matter such as excrement, half inside, half outside – or matter which has crossed into the wrong category. Dirt is the product of a classification system which categorizes certain things as 'clean', others as 'dirty'. The first thing is to recognize dirt. Dirt is contextual and can become invisible; so often 'dirt' that would not be tolerated in one setting, for instance in the home, or in the garden, is acceptable if thrown into the street or a convenient ocean. The second thing is the difficulty of doing something about it when one sees it, for eradicating dirt requires effort. There is no such thing as a cost-free clean environment.

The Scottish philosopher Kames believed that the desire for personal cleanliness might well be universal. What suggested this was that 'cleanness is remarkable in several nations which have made little progress in the arts of life.

---

[1] Douglas, *Purity and Danger*. Or as 'A great philosopher' once said 'dirt was only matter in the wrong place.' (Murphy, *Our Homes*, 894.)

The savages of the Caribbee islands, once a numerous tribe, were remarked by writers as neat and cleanly.' Or again, 'The Negroes, particularly those of Ardrah on the slave-coast, have a scrupulous regard to cleanness. They wash morning and evening, and perfume themselves with aromatic herbs. In the city of Benin, women are employed to keep the streets clean; and in that respect they are not outdone by the Dutch.' He concluded that 'cleanness is agreeable to all, and nastiness disagreeable: no person prefers dirt; and even those who are the most accustomed to it are pleased with a cleanly appearance in others.' On the other hand, Kames noted that while all men may be born with a biological instinct towards cleanliness, not all societies are as 'clean', at least by western standards, as others. 'A taste for cleanness is not equally distributed among all men; nor, indeed is any branch of the moral sense equally distributed: and if, by nature, one person be more cleanly than another, a whole nation may be so.'[2]

The curiosity which aroused Kames' interest was that in the eighteenth century, the three 'cleanest' societies, that is the ones which had the highest reputations for bodily and other cleanliness, were also the three most 'advanced' economies, namely Holland, England and Japan. The cleanest of all larger nations, he thought, were the Japanese, 'so finically clean as to find fault even with the Dutch for dirtiness.' This great cleanness 'I judged to be also the case of the English, who, high and low, rich and poor, are remarkable for cleanness all the world over.' At first he toyed with the idea that the similarity between Japan and England might have something to do with being islands. 'I have often amused myself with so singular a resemblance between islanders, removed at the greatest distance from each other.' After further research he was forced to abandon the theory, upon a discovery that 'the English have not always been so clean as at present' which seemed to be shown by certain earlier disparaging comments by Erasmus and others.[3] Of course, if he had proceeded even further, he would have found plenty of islanders who were less spic and span, and many continental dwellers who were scrupulously clean. Yet the puzzle still remains. What correlation, if any, is there between the elimination of dirt and economic development?

Having illuminated the nature of purity and dirt, and its intimate links to religious ideas, Mary Douglas' work unfortunately takes us little of the way towards explaining why different societies are more or less obsessed with dirt, and why their treatment of what is considered dirty changes over time.[4] Let us start with the list of possible factors put forward and discussed by Edward Westermarck. 'The prevalence of cleanly or dirty habits among a certain people may depend on a variety of circumstances: the occupations of life, sufficiency or

---

[2] Kames, *Sketches*, I, 242–6.
[3] Kames, *Sketches*, I, 246.
[4] Douglas, *Purity and Danger*.

want of water, climatic conditions, industry or laziness, wealth or poverty, religious or superstitious beliefs.'[5]

In terms of 'the occupations of life', Westermarck merely suggests that 'Castren observes that filthiness is a characteristic of fishing peoples 'and gives one example.[6] It would be difficult to take this observation much further in relation to England and Japan, except to say that Kames might have argued that town-dwelling, merchant and artisan types of people, which describes the English, Dutch and Japanese world of the eighteenth century, tend to be conspicuously clean. Amsterdam, London, Osaka, were prototypes of a 'clean' sort of civilization and there may be some association between the 'rationality' of business and the 'rationality' of living. Since the reasons for a high state of 'cleanliness' are likely to be multiple, and will re-enforce each other, we may merely note here that the occupational structure of Japan, England and Holland may be one of the factors we need to take into account.

The second factor mentioned by Westermarck is the availability of the main agent that humans use to rid themselves of 'matter out of place', in other words water. Westermarck was able to cite a number of instances where the presence or absence of water made all the difference to standards of cleanliness. Here again, all else being equal, Japan was one of the most water-filled environments in the world, much of it temptingly hot, and the English weather and ubiquity of rivers, put them not far behind, in the same league as the almost amphibious Dutch. Both at the general level, and at the particular, for instance as we have seen in the effect of pumping water through London, these three cultures had, at the least, less excuse than others for being dirty.

Westermarck's next factor was climate, although all he says on the subject is that 'a cold climate, moreover, leads to uncleanliness because it makes garments necessary.'[7] There is little to be said about this beyond what we have noted in relation to Japan, that few clothes were worn for most of the year probably did improve bodily cleanliness. The well-dressed Dutch and English may have been impeded by their clothing, but managed to maintain a reasonable standard of cleanliness despite this.

The next factor is 'industry or laziness'. Here Westermarck explicitly referred to Kames' ideas and gives examples of peoples who 'from their laziness' are 'as dirty as swine'. Since Kames' argument is somewhat deeper than sheer laziness, it is worth summarizing his views.

Having abandoned the theory of the link between islandhood *per se* and cleanliness, Kames still retained the looser link between growing prosperity and cleanliness. He could see how clean the English were, and believed this to be a

---

[5] Westermarck, *Moral*, II, 349.
[6] Westermarck, *Moral*, II, 349.
[7] Westermarck, *Moral*, II, 350.

recent development. 'A change so extraordinary in the taste and manners of the English, rouses our curiosity.' He thought it was caused by some link with industriousness. Indolence breeds dirt, while 'The industrious, on the contrary, are improved in neatness and propriety, by the art or manufacture that constantly employs them: they are never reduced to purge the stable of Augeas; for being prone to action, they suffer not dirt to rest unmolested. Industrious nations accordingly, all the world over are the most cleanly.'[8] His main example was Holland. 'Arts and industry had long flourished in Holland, where Erasmus was born and educated: the people were clean above all their neighbours, because they were industrious above all their neighbours; and, upon that account, the dirtiness of England could not fail to strike a Hollander.[9] Later the English became more industrious and thus cleaner.

The comparison between France and England created something of a problem, for 'the French are less cleanly than the English, though not less industrious.' He thought this could be explained by the distribution of wealth, for 'the lower classes of people being in England more at their ease than in France, have a greater taste for living well, and in particular for keeping themselves clean.' 'Thus cleanness improves gradually with manners, and makes a figure in every industrious nation.'[10]

The idea that if people were busily moving matter from place to place in one aspect of their lives, making and producing, exchanging and behaving in an active way, this would spread into all of their behaviour is an intriguing one. 'The more you do, the more you do', is a generally observed phenomenon. If dirt containment is largely concerned with keeping matter in its right place, it is very similar to commercial activities. It all comes down to the shifting of atoms to places where they can create useful things for humans, away from places where they can do harm. Both are about creating separations, divisions, new order out of disorder. Some sort of 'elective affinity' between industriousness and cleanliness was noted by William Hazlitt: 'a people that are remarkable for cleanliness, will be so for industry, for honesty, for avarice, and *vice versa*.'[11] The same association had a little earlier been noted by Meister. Writing of London, he was impressed by 'the extraordinary neatness of the dwellings, both within and without, by the exertions in point of commerce, and the universal industry which gives animation and spirit to every quarter of the town.'[12]

Holland, England and Japan were notably 'industrious'. Yet, as Kames noticed, sheer hard work is not a sufficient cause of cleanliness. In many societies ordinary people work incredibly hard, are very 'industrious', and yet live, or are

[8] Kames, *Sketches*, I, 247.
[9] Kames, *Sketches*, I, 247.
[10] Kames, *Sketches*, I, 249,247,244.
[11] Quoted in Thomas, *Cleanliness*, 80.
[12] Quoted in Wilson (ed.), *Strange Island*, 139.

forced to live, in a great deal of 'dirt'. Kames added the dimension of wealth to his model. In England, but not France, the poor had some wealth and hence pride. This takes us on to Westermarck's next factor, namely that 'Poverty, also, is for obvious reasons a cause of uncleanliness.'[13] In this respect it is significant that the English and the Dutch were, per capita, the richest nations in seventeenth-century Europe and Japan, though the wealth was at a lower level, was their nearest equivalent in Asia. Getting rid of dirt takes time, effort and often depends on a considerable infrastructure. In particular, in crowded societies it is difficult to keep up high standards if people are living at subsistence levels. The fact that these three nations had risen well above this level was both a cause, and a consequence, of their increasing wealth.

Westermarck also realized that the pressure for cleanliness was largely a social one and hence closely linked to social stratification: 'Very commonly cleanliness is a class distinction.'[14] This is a complicated matter, but it does seem that in societies with a relatively 'open', but quite stratified social system, such as that which characterized England and Japan, degrees of cleanliness, like many other markers, became important in assessing relative position. To have a 'clean' home, became as important as having a 'clean' accent or 'clean' criminal record. This is illustrated by an early-twentieth-century textbook on hygiene: 'Unconsciously, from childhood upwards we have come to make a rapid general estimate of the social status and of the mental state of individuals by noting their appearance in the matter of personal cleanliness, under which heading that of order and disorder may well be included.'[15] The socially aspiring kept themselves and their houses clean. The noted obsession with etiquette and manners among the middling ranks of Japanese and English society for many centuries encompassed 'proper' behaviour in terms of the body, gesture, posture and so on. The controls which Foucault, Elias and others have analysed were largely status-based.[16] It is not inevitable that dirt and cleanliness will become a central marker of status. The point here is that if a scale of physical purity is established, it will lead to ceaseless striving after increased cleanliness. This relation between social status divisions and cleanliness has been stressed by a number of those who have recently written on the reasons for growing interest in cleanliness in England.[17] As Cooley noted in the nineteenth century, 'Dirty and coarse hands are no less marks of slothfulness and low breeding, than clean and delicate hands are of refinement and gentility.'[18]

The final factor put forward by Westermarck is the religious one: 'In many

---

[13] Westermarck, *Moral*, II, 352.

[14] Westermarck, *Moral*, II, 351.

[15] Lane-Claypon, *Hygiene*, 73.

[16] Foucault, *Discipline*; Elias, *Civilizing Process*.

[17] For example, see Thomas, *Cleanliness*, 69–70,80; Bushman, *Cleanliness*, 1220,1222,1231.

[18] Cooley, *Toilet*, 359–60.

cases cleanliness, either temporary or habitual, is also practised from religious or superstitious motives.' He gives as one example, that 'the Shinto priests in Japan bathed and put on clean garments before making the sacred offerings or chanting the liturgies.'[19] He briefly shows that Greek and Roman religion, Zoroastrianism, Hinduism, Buddhism, Judaism and Islam, all link spiritual and physical purity in some way. 'These practices and rules spring from the idea that the contact of a polluting substance with anything holy is followed by injurious consequences.' Furthermore, 'a polluting substance is itself held to contain mysterious energy of a baneful kind' which is dangerous to others. This takes us into the whole area of pollution, taboo, classification which many anthropologists from Robertson-Smith and Steiner through to Douglas, Leach and their successors have seen as central to an understanding of dirt.[20]

Yet Westermarck also felt that 'whilst religious or superstitious beliefs have thus led to ablutions and cleanliness, they have in other instances had the very opposite effect.' He cites a number of cases where religious people have consciously used dirt as a mark of sanctity. This is particularly so in relation to asceticism. Buddhist monks have a rule which 'prescribes that their dress shall be made of rags taken from a dust or refuse heap.' Christians have often welcomed dirt as a sign of grace or 'as penance'. In medieval Christianity 'abstinence from every species of cleanliness was also enjoined as a penance.'[21] 'In the twelfth century one religious writer elaborated upon the "marvellous mystery" of smelly, greasy, matted and verminous beards, with saliva dripping down them, as a revelation of "interior cleanliness, that is divine virtue".'[22] We need, therefore, to examine with some care the nature of the religion to be found in England, Holland and Japan. To what extent is there an emphasis, in their religions, on the necessity for not merely spiritual but also physical purity?

Japan's blend of Shinto, Buddhism and Confucianism seems to have produced a system of belief and classification which gave the Japanese an exceptional attitude towards purity. Buddhism is well known for its insistence on asceticism, simplicity, the orderly elimination of the material world. Although it is quite compatible with personal dirt, it is not difficult to see, as in the Buddhist temples and rituals in Japan, that it can also give support to an ascetic, anti-dirt, system based on the purging of all matter that is not essential. For instance, in the quintessentially Japanese institution derived from Buddhism, the tea ceremony, 'Spotless cleanliness' was required.[23] Confucianism, though not a

---

[19] Westermarck, *Moral*, II, 352.
[20] Much of the literature is discussed in Douglas, *Purity and Danger*.
[21] Westermarck, *Moral*, II, 354,355–6.
[22] Thomas, *Cleanliness*, 60.
[23] Singer, *Sword and Jewel*, 114.

religion, recommended orderliness and self-discipline, which is again a useful ingredient for a society which takes purity to its limits. But it is when these two are blended with a third element, unique to Japan, namely Shintoism, that a strange chemical transformation seems to take place, emphasizing one strand in all of them.

Lafcadio Hearn described how Shinto beliefs emphasized the link between ritual and physical cleanliness and the need for purity in all things. 'From the earliest period Shinto exacted scrupulous cleanliness – indeed, we might say that it regarded physical impurity as identical with moral impurity, and intolerable to the gods.' He notes that 'the most important of all Shinto ceremonies, is the ceremony of purification – *o-harai* as it is called, which term signifies the casting-out or expulsion of evils.'[24] Before praying to the Shinto gods, worshippers need to purify themselves. 'They wash their faces and hands and rinse their mouths, – the customary ablution preliminary to Shinto prayer.'[25] Purification was at the centre of Shinto. 'Purification rituals occurred at all levels of society, from the two great national ceremonies performed on the last day of the sixth and twelfth months, down to household and individual rites.'[26]

What is particularly important is that moral and physical purity, and their reverse, were seen as symbolically and actually intertwined: 'they never venture to approach the homes of their god if they are in any vice impure; for which reason they wash themselves first perfectly clean, dress themselves in their very best apparel, and wash their hands a second time at the entrance of the temple; then advancing with the greatest reverence, they place themselves before the mirror.'[27] 'The most important principle of the cult is ritual purity. Given the divinity of the whole of nature, and hence of the human body, there was no necessity to differentiate between sin and dirt; the essential was to carry out certain rites, for which the requirements were scrupulous personal cleanliness (*misogi*, ablutions), concentration and abstinence (*imi*) and contact with certain purifying things (e.g. branches of *sakaki, Cleyera japonica*).'[28] 'Kato points out . . . that in the ancient documents the ideas of purity and pollution have highly physical connotations and are in no way of an abstract or a moral nature.'[29] This is shown, for example, in the symbolic association between material and spiritual purity in the rites associated with the chief 'priest' of Shinto, the Emperor. Siebold wrote that 'everything about him must be at all times new. No article of dress is ever worn a second time; the places and dishes in which his repasts are served up, the cups or bowls out of which he drinks, and

[24] Hearn, *Interpretation*, 161,160.
[25] Hearn, *Glimpses*, 14.
[26] Lock, *Medicine*, 25–6.
[27] Thunberg, *Travels*, IV, 22.
[28] Maraini, *Meeting*, 148.
[29] Lock, *Medicine*, 25.

even the culinary utensils in which his meals are prepared, must never have been used before.'[30] Newness and purity are clearly associated.

It is of course impossible to know whether the religion reflected a deep concern with purity, or vice versa; probably, as Hearn implies, they were always influencing each other. 'The Japanese love of cleanliness – indicated by the universal practice of daily bathing, and by the irreproachable condition of their homes – has been maintained, and was probably initiated, by their religion.' Certainly it is not difficult to see how the view that ritual and moral purity in the 'Way of the gods' also means physical purity, was extended through all of life. 'Spotless cleanliness being required by the rites of ancestor-worship – in the temple, in the person of the officiant, and in the home – this rule of purity is naturally extended by degrees to all the conditions of existence.'[31] As Morse remarked 'If cleanliness is next to godliness, then verily the Japanese are a godly race.'[32] His remark has a deeper meaning than perhaps he realized. Cleanliness is 'next' to godliness in a literal sense, indeed it is a part of godliness – and cleanliness would indeed be both a sign and expression of godliness. Religion and cleanliness are one: 'It is no exaggeration to say that they have made a religion of cleanliness, for the implications of ritual purification pervade the most ancient Shinto ethos and have remained constant throughout the development of Japanese cultural history.' 'Filth' means both spiritual and material dirt – 'matter out of place' disturbs the Gods. Dirt is evil. 'In the Shinto tradition, evil and immorality have always been associated with filth and impurity, and virtue with cleanliness.' This attitude pervades every aspect of living as we have seen it expressed in previous chapters. 'Described as the "Shinto attitude" for lack of a better term, the notions of natural purity, simplicity, and aesthetic as well as physical cleanliness have influenced all Japanese designs for living: art and architecture, literature and self-expression, the preparation of food, patterns of familial and societal organization, craft and productivity – in short, all activities by which man defines his existence and orders his life.'[33]

Among the special features of the Japanese, noted by the Chinese historians from the third century onwards, were their 'habits of personal cleanliness.'[34] Reciprocally the Japanese thought other nations very dirty, particularly the Chinese, and also the Ainu whom they had systematically pushed out of the Japanese mainland to the northwest island of Hokkaido. As for Europe, 'the travelled Japanese consider our three most prominent characteristics to be dirt, laziness and superstition.'[35] All Europeans were dirty, but some less so than

[30] Von Siebold, *Manners*, 106.
[31] Hearn, *Interpretation*, 162.
[32] Morse, *Homes*, 201.
[33] Grilli, *Bath*, 24,24,24.
[34] Grilli, *Bath*, 24,44.
[35] Chamberlain, *Things*, 263.

others. The Dutch were the least unclean. 'They shave their beards, cut their nails, and are not dirty like the Chinese.'[36] Yet even they were dirty.[37] Later visitors suggested the way in which cleanliness was somehow linked to simplicity and asceticism.[38]

How this great concern with boundaries, with order, with purity, affected health has been explored by Margaret Lock.[39] She shows how the famous opposition between 'outside' and 'inside' in Japanese culture worked in relation to the house and the body. Danger and dirt lay in the 'outside' world and life was a constant battle to keep it at bay. Lock points out that 'In line with the thinking of Douglas (1966), Japanese people symbolically demarcate areas that are considered "outside", dirty and potentially dangerous, from others that are denoted as "inside", sacred and clean. This is true of social relationships, of the use of physical space, and of attitudes toward the body.'[40]

In relation to social relationships, there were certain 'unclean' groups whom one should keep away from, in particular those in contact with 'unclean' things such as blood and death, most particularly the *eta*. 'To write *eta* the Japanese use two ideograms meaning "much impurity", "much dirt".'[41] Outsiders and strangers, whether Chinese or Europeans, were also dirty, hence the very elaborate precautions to keep them out of Japan. Yet it was not just foreigners and polluting quasi-castes; anyone who was sick was also a threat. Lepers were sent to the most distant places for their bodily decomposition was disgusting; those who were ill were ostracized. Long before germs were discovered, there were other reasons for avoiding contact with the sick: 'Illness was also a state that was considered polluting, according to Shinto beliefs, and thus it called for temporary separation and even ostracism from the group.'[42] This could affect a whole family 'Because it was believed that people could transmit their diseases to their family members, sickness could potentially lead to public ostracism of the entire family.'

Another approach is to emphasize the threshold between the 'outside' world of public space, which is dirty and dangerous, and the pure safety of the living space. This is symbolized in many ways such as taking off outside shoes, washing and bathing when one enters the house, and so on. The danger, however, did not merely come from the outside; the body itself was a potential source of contamination to oneself and to others. One obvious form of dirt was blood, particularly menstrual blood. 'Some women today still consider them-

---

[36] Keene, *Discovery*, 170.
[37] Kaempfer, *History*, I, 108.
[38] Rein, *Travels*, 411; Alcock, *Tycoon*, I, 189,301,302.
[39] A similar account is given in Ohnuki-Tierney, *Illness*, 21–37,49,57.
[40] Lock, *Medicine*, 88.
[41] Maraini, *Meeting*, 223.
[42] Lock, *Medicine*, 90.

selves to be "dirty" when menstruating. Underwear worn at these times is usually washed separately from other clothing.' A second is the idea that internal 'corruptions' worked themselves out onto the surface of the body. Some could be washed away, but more serious ones had to be burned away. Hence one of the major techniques in Japanese medicine was the burning of little mounds of mugwort or *moxa* under a cylinder. This was painful: 'until very recently, moxa was often burned to leave extremely obvious scars. The subconscious need to eliminate things that are offensive or "dirty" as radically and as fast as possible could explain this behavior.' 'Such scars are considered highly disfiguring, but they also symbolize that "once I was dirty but now I am clean". Better to be disfigured and remain part of one's group than to be thought of as polluted and thus risk ostracism.'[43]

Thus, from very early on, an association was made between dirt and disease. The environment, the house and the body must all be kept 'clean', matter must be kept in its place and this would help to minimize the dangers of 'corruption', confusion of categories, breakdown of normal 'health'. Constant attention to all forms of cleansing was an obvious corollary of this: 'Avoidance of constipation and the practice of regular bathing and gargling are still central to concepts of health in Japan today – the body must undergo thorough and regular cleansing in order to avoid sickness.' All this is systematically taught to infants and children. 'During early socialization in Japan today young children internalize many Shinto-derived values; they are taught to fear dirt and to make clear distinctions between what is clean and good and what is dirty and bad. I never once heard a mother teach her child about bacterial theories of infection.' To fail in keeping oneself healthy was a threat to oneself and the whole group. An individual who was ill had failed. It was not merely an economic disaster, as it is in many societies, it was also a social disaster. 'From early historical times in Japan, therefore, impurity, uncleanliness, and the occurrence of sickness were inextricably bound up. Shortcomings in the management of one's own body were seen as sources of illness both for the individual and possibly for one's children.'[44]

All this was mixed up with theories of poisonous 'contagion' through dirt. In a curious way, it anticipated the world of bacteria, viruses and other micro-organisms that was only to be discovered at the end of the nineteenth century. Theories of pollution were strong and widespread – but the pollution was associated with symbolic as well as actual dirt, that is with all ambiguous categories:

A second theory of disease causation was also used. By coming into contact with

[43] Lock, *Medicine*, 90,25,88–9,90,91,91,
[44] Lock, *Medicine*, 25,91,26.

polluting agents such as blood, corpses, people with skin disease, and so on, one could get into a state of *ekiakudoku*, which literally means 'having a spirit polluted by bad poison'. Concepts of communicable and inherited diseases were established early in Japan, for it was believed that such a state not only could bring sickness on the individual concerned but could be passed on to the children.[45]

The indirect consequences for health were immense.

Christianity, like most religions, enjoined 'cleanliness'. After all, it was derived from the same set of purity taboos which led to the levitical prohibitions and to the obsession with purity and danger in modern Judaism. As Wear points out, 'Christianity had helped to give a specific moral and even ascetic tone to hygiene. From the days of the early church, the sins of gluttony and drunkenness had been condemned; the health of the body (the house of the soul) had been linked to the health of the soul, and the Christian was enjoined to care for the body as well as for the soul.'[46] The dualism inherent in Christianity whereby man strives to keep pure in an impure world is a significant factor. 'The quest for physical cleanliness sprang from a sense that the body was sacred and should be protected from the pollutions of the world.' This was symbolically shown, for example, in the central rite of baptism: 'the baptismal ceremony preserved the notion of sin as something that could be washed off. "The blood of Christ washeth away sinne, as water doth bodily filthinesse", declared a Jacobean preacher.'[47] This tradition had been mixed with that of the Greeks, which also, according to Dodds, was preoccupied with purity.[48] Yet a religion like Christianity also adapted to its environment and some Catholic countries do not seem to have been obsessed with cleanliness. In the cases of Holland and England, it would seem that a variant of the religion developed which emphasized the association between material and spiritual 'dirt' as had Shinto.

Purification was, of course, central to many of the church's rituals. The infant was 'washed clean' at baptism by the pure element of water. Women were 'washed clean' after the pollution of childbirth in the ceremony of the churching of women.[49] People's sins were 'washed away' by the blood of Christ at the Holy Communion. The dead were washed clean and raised incorruptible. The symbolism of cleansing of the soul and body is of enormous importance. It may well be that as the external rituals were attacked by the Reformers, and the automatic cleansing performed by the Catholic Church was discontinued, the obsession with the need for personal responsibility in cleanliness grew. Each man his own

---

[45] Lock, *Medicine*, 25.
[46] Wear, *Hygiene*, 1292.
[47] Thomas, *Cleanliness*, 78,61.
[48] Dodds, *Greeks*, 154.
[49] See, for example, Thomas, *Religion*, 38.

priest, also meant that each individual was responsible for his or her purity of soul and body. A war against dirt had to be fought by all.

For whatever reasons, the tendency to see a link between spiritual purity, simplicity, the maintaining of boundaries, and physical behaviour and dirt, grew more pronounced after the Reformation. It is not for nothing that the new sects were called 'Puritans'. There was a constant equation between physical and spiritual 'dirt'; speech, gestures, sexual relations could all be described as 'filthy' or 'foul'. God's grace would 'purge', 'cleanse', turn those born in corruption into the incorruptible. The most extreme expression of cleanliness was to be found among the Quakers, famous for their spotless dress, manners and speech.

Purity, self-discipline, orderliness, all were closely linked to godliness long before John Wesley. Yet it was Wesley who made the connection most famously: 'Let it be observed, that slovenliness is no part of religion: that neither this, nor any text of Scripture, condemns neatness of apparel. Certainly this is a duty, not a sin. 'Cleanliness is, indeed, next to godliness.'[50] In this instance he referred specifically to dress, but in a letter of 1769 he urged his followers to 'take pattern by the Quakers'; 'avoid all nastiness, dirt, slovenliness, both in your person, clothes, house and all about you, Do not stink above ground. . . . Clean yourselves of lice. . . . Do not cut off your hair, but clean it, and keep it clean.'[51] Wesley's comments are interesting because he explicitly linked morality, disease and hard work. 'In his *Primitive Physick*, as well as providing medical prescriptions and hygienic advice (the latter drawn from Cheyne), Wesley put health and illness into a religious context.'[52] It is not surprising that Dean Swift should have seen the dislike of dirt as the main characteristic of Yahoos and humans.

The religious and ritual associations between dirt and spiritual danger are therefore very deep-rooted in English culture, as they are in Japanese. Both are unusually 'puritan' and ascetic cultures, with that curious mix of self-control, asceticism, piety, guilt, which so many analysts have tried to pin down. Most famously, as Fukuyama summarizes the Weber thesis, in the case of Protestants, 'Their frugality, self-discipline, honesty, cleanliness, and aversion to simple pleasures constituted a "this-worldly asceticism" which he understood as a transmutation of the Calvinist doctrine of predestination.'[53]

The subtle blend of religious and medical ideas which developed into the cult of hygiene in the nineteenth century is well analysed in a number of articles by Ginnie Smith. She shows how Greek science had incorporated a strong concept linking hygiene and health. 'In the classical period, Galen (AD 129 – c.200/210)

---

[50] John Wesley, 'On Dress', (various editions).
[51] Quoted in Thomas, *Cleanliness*, 65.
[52] Wear, *Hygiene*, 1296.
[53] Fukuyama, *End of History*, 227.

wrote that medicine was divided into hygiene and therapeutics, into the art of staying healthy and preventing disease, and into the art of treating disease.'[54] This continued through the medieval period, but something new was added by Puritanism: 'Rapid reading suggests that an actual cult of the body was associated with Puritanism, whereas the earlier medieval practices were more functional.'[55] The most notable expression of the new cult of hygiene was in the work of Thomas Tryon in the later seventeenth century: 'In many respects, Tryon's conception of the cleansing of the body of gross humours emerges as a seventeenth-century version, in full religious mystical language, of what has been described as "cult hygiene".' He mixed physical and moral cleanliness in all his writings, 'His Rules of Cleanliness frequently included the sexual reference. The mind could either have "clean inclinations" or become "a cage of unclean thoughts"; the body should be "clean, chaste and healthy", a "well-prepared Temple to receive the sweet influence of god's spirit and company of good angels".'[56]

As Clerget put it, 'Cleanliness calls to cleanliness, clean houses demand clean clothes, clean bodies, and, in consequence, clean morals.'[57] What seems to have happened is that a number of separate streams joined together in eighteenth- and nineteenth-century England to create an obsession with hygiene. There were the early pressures of Christianity and Greek medical science. There was the particular interest of Puritanism. At first this concern was somewhat limited to externals, particularly dress. Keith Thomas points out that most of these moralising injunctions related primarily to visible cleanliness, particularly clean clothes and clean houses. The Puritans and Quakers 'said very little about the desirability of washing all over.' This was because the concern was mainly with symbolic dirt. 'Clean clothes symbolised moral purity: "In fairest weeds are cleanest thoughts and purest minds." '[58] Foreigners suspected that the English were mainly concerned with external cleanliness. Rochefoucauld wrote:

> At first I was quite astonished at all this and did all that I could to make sure whether this cleanliness was natural to the English and so pervaded all their activities, or whether it was a superficial refinement. I was led to see quite clearly that it was only external: everything that you are supposed to see partakes of this most desirable quality, but the English contrive to neglect it in what you are not supposed to see.[59]

Yet the symbolic and ritual merged with the medical and with social

[54] Wear, *Hygiene*, 1283.
[55] Smith, *Prescribing*, 281.
[56] Smith, *Tryon*, 58,59.
[57] Clerget (1843), quoted in Vigarello, *Cleanliness*, 193.
[58] Thomas, *Cleanliness*, 66,62.
[59] Rochefoucauld, *Frenchman*, 43.

snobbery from early on. They created that world of hygiene obsession which is so remarkable a feature of nineteenth-century Britain and America:

> Religion, gentility, and health merged and intermingled in the writings on clean-
> liness. Alcott, who emphasized health, had in addition no doubt 'that he who
> neglects his person and dress will be found lower in the scale of morals, other
> things being equal, than he who pays a due regard to cleanliness.' In Alcott's mind,
> health and morals were opposite sides of the same coin.[60]

It prepared the ground for the medical revolution of the later nineteenth century, which demonstrated how it was that health, morals and cleanliness were indeed linked through the germ theory of disease. Bodily dirt, it was shown, 'forms a favourable medium for the absorption, and the transmission to the internal portions of the body, of noxious effluvia, vapours and gases, mias-mata, and the aerial germs of infectious and contagious diseases.'[61] The Japanese and West Europeans were the first to benefit from this finding. A different constellation was to be found in other civilizations.[62]

---

[60] Bushman, *Cleanliness*, 1224.

[61] Cooley, *Toilet*, 186.

[62] For the interesting contrasted case of India where ritual and physical dirt are dealt with differently, see Khare, *Ritual*, 244–8.

Part V

In the Air

16

Air-borne Diseases:
Smallpox, Measles and
Tuberculosis

War and famine are both, to some degree, within mankind's control. The incidence of enteric and vector-borne diseases can be lessened by attention to diet and hygiene. However, that group of diseases which is spread through the air, consisting of air-borne bacteria and the most minute of the micro-organisms, viruses, are much more difficult to influence. Environmental improvements would have less effect on these diseases and all of them are thought to reach epidemic proportions only in very large and dense populations.

Historians have stressed that sickness spread by droplet infection has long been one of the most deadly branches of disease. 'It has been calculated that about half of all episodes of human illness are caused by respiratory viruses. Most of these are of course quite trivial infections like the most frequent of them all, the common cold.'[1] In England and Wales in 1850, infectious diseases 'were responsible for some 60 per cent of all deaths, air-borne diseases being about twice as significant as water and food-borne.'[2] 'Droplet infection' continues to be 'by far the commonest and most important in civilized countries'. Add to colds and 'flu 'the fact that most of the generalized infections of childhood such as measles, chickenpox, mumps and rubella are also spread by the respiratory route and it becomes clear that, in advanced countries, droplet infection is much the most important route by which infectious diseases spread.'[3] The minute viruses which cause most of these diseases could only be observed with powerful electron microscopes developed in the twentieth century. Only in the case of smallpox was some early action possible. Yet, as we shall see, while human

[1] Burnett, *Infectious*, 107,109.
[2] Schofield et al. (eds), *Decline*, 171.
[3] Burnett, *Infectious*, 109.

beings were largely unable to deal with these threats directly, the cumulative effect of the reduction of malnutrition and increasing general health may well help to explain what has hitherto been the inexplicable decline of some of these diseases. Here I will consider just three of the most serious of these droplet borne diseases, smallpox, measles and tuberculosis.[4]

Smallpox (variola) was a major scourge of human populations until the nineteenth century. It was a particularly painful and deadly disease. Apart from its gruesome symptoms, smallpox is significant both for its high case mortality and because of its ability to survive outside the human host. 'Leading the pack is the smallpox virus which kills one in ten and can survive for more than a decade outside of the host.'[5] It has been suggested that 'The virus first appeared in Europe before the tenth century where it probably established itself as a minor flu-like nuisance.'[6] Something happened to change this in the sixteenth and seventeenth centuries and it grew increasingly virulent, decimating parts of the New World as well as the Old.[7] The fluctuations could be quite abrupt. We are told that 'Smallpox mortality itself evidently rose sharply in the early decades of the eighteenth century and fell again after 1750.'[8] As Malthus observed, 'The small-pox is certainly one of the channels, and a very broad one, which nature has opened for the last thousand years to keep down the population to the level of the means of subsistence.'[9]

Creighton provided a useful general account of smallpox. He believed that the earliest reliable references to it in England occurred in a letter of 1514.[10] At first it was a fairly mild childhood disease, but became more serious in the early seventeenth century. The first literary reference was in 1602, and the first epidemic occurred in 1628. There were increasing references to the disease after 1660. Thus, it is principally a disease which rose to prominence from the middle of the seventeenth century.[11]

Some estimates of mortality from smallpox and other diseases can be derived from bills of mortality. Some figures for eighteenth-century England suggest that about 15 per cent of deaths were due to smallpox,[12] yet Landers thought that the proportion of deaths caused by smallpox in London in the eighteenth

---

[4] There are, of course, many other important air-borne diseases which could be included in a longer treatment, in particular pneumonic plague and influenza.

[5] Ewald, *Infectious*, 63.

[6] Nikiforuk, *Fourth*, 66.

[7] For some of the terrible effects on third world peoples, see Crosby, *Ecological*, 200ff.

[8] Landers, *Age Patterns*, 55.

[9] Malthus, *Population*, II, 183.

[10] Creighton, *Epidemics*, I, 456.

[11] Creighton, *Epidemics*, II, ch.iv.

[12] Razzell, in Drake (ed.), *Industrialization*, 146.

century was only 7.6 per cent.[13] This is the opposite of what one might have expected, considering the high population density of the city. Yet it may well have been that very high density which lowered the case mortality of the disease. Another explanation which needs to be considered is the development of inoculation and vaccination.

Although inoculation against smallpox had been practiced in India from 'remotest antiquity',[14] the technique only came into western Europe through Turkey and China in the early eighteenth century. Lady Wortley Montagu described the Turkish custom of ingrafting and inoculation, which she helped to introduce into England.[15] At first there was considerable opposition to the method. Thomas Wright in his Autobiography described how 'my children were attacked by that dreadful distemper the small-pox.' 'They had often begged to be inoculated, but as their grandparents were bitterly prejudiced against the practice, to oblige them I had forbore to do it.' He himself was inoculated very early, in 1736, and gives a graphic account of the operation.[16]

The dangers caused by inoculation were considerable. 'Administered without asepsis, the inoculation could infect the patient with other germs, and unless he was segregated during its course he could spread smallpox to others. In one instance, a single inoculated child infected seventeen persons, of whom eight died of the disease.'[17] A similar point was made in 1896: 'Smallpox inoculation protected the individual, but, by spreading the disease, increased rather than diminished the total number of deaths.'[18] As Heberden commented in the later eighteenth century, 'however beneficial inoculation prove to individuals, or indeed to the nation at large, the bills of mortality incontestably show, that in London more persons have died of the small pox since the introduction of that practice.' One reason for this, he thought, was that 'while the inoculation of the wealthy keeps up a perpetual source of infection, many others who either cannot afford, or do not chuse, to adopt the same method, are continually exposed to the distemper.'[19] It may not have been until Jenner's introduction of 'vaccination' in 1796–8 that this type of preventive method spread widely and made a significant impact.[20]

There is disagreement as to the effects of smallpox inoculation. There are grounds for believing that, at least until the end of the eighteenth century, the

---

[13] Landers, *Metropolis*, 72.

[14] Shrewsbury, *Philistines*, 124.

[15] Montagu, *Letters*, I, 303.

[16] Wright, *Autobiography*, 152,21.

[17] Petersen, *Malthus*, 160.

[18] *Chambers's Encyclopaedia*, 'smallpox'.

[19] Heberden, *Observations*, 35–6.

[20] Instead of introducing the virus from those who had smallpox, as in inoculation, vaccination used a milder form of the diseae from infected cows and was both more effective and less dangerous.

numbers inoculated were not very large and the methods used were not very effective. While being strong advocates of inoculation, neither Malthus nor Black believed that inoculation was yet of great significance. The latter wrote that 'Even in the London smallpox hospital, since its first institution, forty years ago there have not been inoculated altogether 25,000.' Furthermore, Black pointed out that a situation where 'none under seven years of age are inoculated' was hardly likely to make much impact on a disease where five out of every six of those affected were under the age of seven.[21] Creighton lucidly demonstrated how the effects of smallpox inoculation were too little and too late to have had more than a marginal effect, hardly touching ordinary people.[22] Razzell original-ly argued that 'Inoculation against smallpox could theoretically explain the whole of the increase in population.'[23] He has now modified his views arguing that smallpox inoculation probably played only a minor part in the mortality changes of the eighteenth century.[24] This fits with Blane's contemporary view of the effects of vaccination, that 'the decrease of burials took place some years before that notable discovery.'[25]

What seems to have happened is that the incidence of smallpox changed; increasingly it became a disease of towns and childhood. This point was made by Creighton a century ago and Burnett believed, according to Chambers, that 'by 1750 almost every child born in London or larger provincial towns must have been exposed to smallpox.' 'It then became almost entirely a disease of child-hood where the level of immunity was at its lowest.'[26]

According to Jannetta, smallpox was the most deadly of Japanese epidemic diseases.[27] Japan was relatively heavily populated well before Europe and this may help to explain why smallpox became prevalent there a good deal earlier. The first recorded smallpox epidemic in China occurred around AD 495, carried to Japan by Buddhist missionaries in about AD 552. There were a series of epidemics from that year to 582.[28] The native Japanese terms of *toso* or *hoso* were first used of the disease in 735,[29] when an unusually severe epidemic of smallpox spread through Japan.[30] 'In the year 737 alone, the province of Izumi near the capital lost 44 percent of its adult populace, while Bungo in northern Kyushu

[21] Black, *Arithmetical*, 61,265.

[22] Creighton, *Epidemics*, II, 504ff, esp. 511.

[23] Drake (ed.), *Industrialization*, 154.

[24] Razzell, *Essays*, 3,150,220.

[25] Blane, *Dissertations*, 172.

[26] Creighton, *Epidemics*, II, 556; Chambers, *Population*, 102.

[27] Jannetta, *Epidemics*, 70.

[28] Tatsukawa in Kiple (ed.), *Disease*, 375.

[29] Fujikawa, *History of Diseases*; I am grateful to Osamu Saito for translating the Fujikawa references.

[30] For further accounts of the eighth-century epidemic, see Farris, *Population*, 53ff.

and Suruga in eastern Japan sustained death rates of about 30 percent.' In the epidemic of 812–14 'almost half' of the population died.[31] Over the next eleven centuries it occurred with increasing frequency. 'In the early centuries the intervals between epidemics were relatively long, and the smallpox virus probably died out between epidemics.' But in later centuries, epidemics became more frequent and 'at some point fairly early in Japanese history, smallpox became an endemic disease.' This probably occurred before the twelfth century, according to Jannetta.[32]

The incidence of smallpox was very patchy. It would appear in a group of villages or one part of the country and not in others; in Sendai for instance, 'smallpox was epidemic in different villages and towns at different times.' The length of an outbreak varied; sometimes it lasted for two months, sometimes for more than two years. It tended to be concentrated in major cities and it became 'primarily a disease of children'.[33] With urban growth and larger cities, this happened in Japan much earlier than in England, probably by the twelfth century.[34]

The impact of the disease on children was considerable. It was the 'most important epidemic disease in the Hida villages and a major cause of premature deaths.' There, in the period between 1771 and 1852, smallpox deaths constituted some 10 to 12 per cent of all deaths. Furthermore, 'Smallpox accounted for 26 per cent of the deaths of all children who died before the age of 10. It was the most important identifiable cause of death in early childhood.' Jannetta estimates that perhaps '10 percent of all children born died of smallpox.' Almost all children had had smallpox.[35]

In the sixteenth century the Portuguese missionary Luis Frois 'wrote that nearly all Japanese bore pockmarks from smallpox, and he believed that the ailment was more severe among the Japanese than the Europeans.'[36] Thunberg thought 'The *Small-pox* and the *Measles* have been long prevalent in this country, and are not more dreaded here than in other places. I did not see a great many people that were much defaced by them: they are unacquainted with Inoculation.'[37] However Oliphant noted in the late 1850s, 'From the numbers of people marked with small-pox, that disease must rage with virulence in Japan, but the appalling sights so familiar in China are unknown there.'[38] Griffis in

[31] Farris in Kiple (ed.), *Disease*, 378.
[32] Jannetta, *Epidemics*, 67,67,104.
[33] Jannetta, *Epidemics*, 73,86,104,106.
[34] Farris in Kiple (ed.), *Disease*, 381.
[35] Jannetta, *Epidemics*, 76,77,91,92.
[36] Farris in Kiple (ed.), *Disease*, 383.
[37] Thunberg, *Travels*, IV, 77.
[38] Oliphant, *Elgin's Mission*, 206.

the 1870s wrote that 'in older days ... fully one-third of the living had pitted faces ...'[39] and Isabella Bird found that 'fully 30 percent of the village people are badly seamed with smallpox.'[40]

The Japanese did what they could. As early as the AD 737 outbreak they made forceful attempts to try to contain the disease by quarantine and other measures.[41] We are told that in 1795 'When his town was ravaged by smallpox, Ogata, following the technique that he had learned in a Chinese medical text, powdered the scabs from patients and used the product for successful vaccinations.'[42] Yet this cannot have been widely done before this period, for it was von Siebold and other foreign doctors who started to propagate the new method of vaccinations. When von Seibold arrived in 1823, 'smallpox was widespread and he brought a small batch of immunizing lymph from Batavia to demonstrate the value of vaccination.' Unfortunately, the lymph had lost its potency in the journey, and no vaccinia resulted.[43] Vaccination seems to have been successfully introduced from Russia in about 1824.[44]

Once the idea of vaccination was introduced, the Japanese took to it with enthusiasm. Pompe wrote in the middle of the nineteenth century that 'The Japanese have been amenable to vaccination. In this respect they again show that they willingly adopt from the European what is to their advantage.' 'In some provinces the Daimios have made vaccination compulsory, and in Satsuma every child two years of age has to be inoculated. If this has not been done, it will be done forcefully. In Jedo there is an establishment where poor people can have their children inoculated.'[45]

Some were dismissive of the efforts,[46] and others noted that some of the early measures were ineffective. 'The smallpox epidemics became more severe, and the mortality must have been very high in 1854 and 1855. Part of this was the result of the inefficient way of taking care of smallpox patients; patients were allowed to leave the bed, the room, indeed the house, too soon, long before the illness was entirely gone.'[47] It is clear that it did indeed take time for the new treatments to take effect. In 1863, Willis noted, 'the fleet has smallpox; at present it is spreading; if it increases, it may go far to cripple the efficiency of the force.' Two weeks later, however, the smallpox in the fleet had 'disappeared'. A

[39] Griffis, *Mikado*, 662.

[40] Bird, *Tracks*, 81.

[41] Farris, *Population*, 60–1.

[42] Bowers, *Medical Pioneers*, 110; the Chinese had been using a method of inoculation, using the contents of smallpox pustules from the nose, from about AD 1000 (Needham, *Clerks*, 375).

[43] Bowers, *Medical Pioneers*, 110.

[44] Veith, *Mutual Indebtedness*, 397.

[45] Wittermans, *Pompe*, 110,111.

[46] See von Baelz quoted in Hane, *Rebels*, 45.

[47] Pompe, *Wittermans*, 111.

year later 'Smallpox is very common amongst the Japanese just now and some foreigners have it.'[48]

By the 1870s a remarkable change was occurring. Griffis, who spent several years in Japan at that time wrote that 'so great has been the triumph of the hygienic art in Japan that . . . whereas . . . one-third of the living had pitted faces, the average crowd in Japan of today shows no more visible traces of this horrible disease than the same number of human beings in other civilized countries.'[49] Morse saw some beggars who had 'been rendered blind by smallpox', but commented that 'since the common sense of the nation saw the merits of vaccination and promptly adopted it this loathsome disease has been banished forever from the country.' He commented on a blind masseur: 'The amma was made blind by smallpox, at one time a dreadful scourge in the country, but now happily unknown.'[50]

Measles is another epidemic disease which has often decimated populations and over which humans had very little control before the discovery of the virus and preventive treatment in the twentieth century. We are reminded that in eighteenth and nineteenth century western Europe, 'measles resembled the severe disease that is found today in underdeveloped and isolated countries.'[51] It was far more virulent than it is today and could cause heavy mortality.[52] 'Measles is a disease that is highly dependent on a large, densely settled population' for the virus can only survive for a few hours outside its human host.[53] The virus has to be passed quickly from person to person, within a few days, or else it dies out: the infectious period is short. 'In measles the virus appears to be liberated into the secretions of mouth and nose for only a few days during the stage just before and just after the appearance of the rash, so that infection can be spread only during that period.'[54] A pool of at least three to five hundred thousand individuals living in close proximity is needed in order for measles to become an endemic disease.[55] Measles is one of the very best illustrations of the type of negative feedback Malthus wrote about. Countries with light population densities would avoid measles, unless it was introduced as in the conquest of America or in other remote tribal areas. Yet as the populations built up in Europe, countries would reach levels which would begin to give shelter to endemic measles.

[48] Cortazzi, *Willis*, 59.
[49] Griffis, *Mikado*, 662.
[50] Morse, *Day*, I, 21,219–20.
[51] Jannetta, *Epidemics*, 112.
[52] For example, Shrewsbury, *Philistines*, 93.
[53] Jannetta, *Epidemics*, 109.
[54] Burnett, *Infectious*, 124.
[55] Cohen, *Health*, 49.

However, its severity and fluctuations are still a mystery.[56] There is evidence that it became more virulent in England in certain periods. 'William Heberden asserted in 1785 that measles "are usually attended with very little danger; it is not often that a physician is employed in this distemper."'[57] Black in 1789 thought that 'Few escape this exotick contagion, especially in childhood and in cities.' But he estimated that the mortality rate of measles was only between one tenth and one twelfth that of smallpox. He thought that the case fatality was 'at 1 of 77 whom it attacks.'[58] Creighton recorded that measles was epidemic in seventeenth- and eighteenth-century England, but that it was less virulent than in the nineteenth century.[59] Yet 'In 1804 measles caused as many deaths, chiefly among adults, as did smallpox, and actually surpassed the latter in 1808.'[60] Having apparently become more dangerous, it then changed again, also for unknown reasons, so that along with other diseases, measles became less serious after about 1880, both in incidence and mortality. However, 'The change began well before modern preventive methods had exerted any noticeable influence.'[61] Its curious behaviour is well illustrated by the Japanese case.

With its enormous cities surrounded by crowded villages, Japan was probably the most densely populated area in the world in the eighteenth and nineteenth centuries and 'one would expect to find epidemics occurring frequently.' It is one of the major surprises of Jannetta's book, and the principal finding of theoretical importance in the field of epidemiology, that this was not so. The Japanese sources 'indicate that during the Tokugawa period measles epidemics were infrequent, occurring at intervals of about twenty or thirty years.'[62] It is clear that measles is a very old disease in Japan; we are told that there were two epidemics of the 'red pox' (*akamaogasa*) in 998 and 1015 AD.[63] Fujikawa however gives the first certain reference to measles (*hashika*) as occurring in the Kamakura (1185–1333) era; before then it tended to be conflated with smallpox.[64] There were some thirty-six epidemics between 998 and 1862, and 'there is no evidence of a trend toward more frequent epidemics as the Japanese population grew larger.' One can trace the route of some of the later epidemics; they 'did not start in the largest cities and radiate outward to other parts of the country, but invariably moved from Nagasaki.'[65] This suggests that the infection

[56] For a still useful general account, see Creighton, *Epidemics*, II, ch.v.
[57] Dubos, *Adapting*, 168.
[58] Black, *Arithmetical*, 64.
[59] Creighton, *Epidemics*, II, 647.
[60] Dubos, *Adapting*, 168.
[61] Zinsser, *Rats*, 67.
[62] Jannetta, *Epidemics*, 109.
[63] Farris in Kiple (ed.), *Disease*, 379.
[64] Fujikawa, *History of Diseases*.
[65] Jannetta, *Epidemics*, 115–7,133.

was introduced through Japan's only open port. Despite its dense population, Japan did not develop endemic measles.

It would also appear that while a serious illness, the disease was not a major killer. Yamazaki wrote that '. . . the average fatality was only three to five persons per hundred cases.' Measles 'had little impact on mortality in the Hida villages. . . . Measles deaths accounted for only .004 percent of all deaths.' Consequently, Jannetta suggests that 'measles mortality in early modern Japan may have been considerably lower than in either early modern Europe or present-day West Africa.'[66]

Any explanation for the muted nature of the disease has to take into account several factors. Obviously Japan's sea-barrier and conscious policy of isolation was important and 'reduced her exposure to one of the major epidemic diseases of the early modern period.' Yet this does not explain why, once it reached Japan, measles did not become endemic. This is a puzzle which still needs a solution. Given its adaptation to north European climates it cannot be that southern Japan was too cold for the virus. It has been suggested that there may be some correlation with living standards; 'People who are malnourished are believed to be more susceptible to the secondary infections and complications that are the major causes of measles mortality.'[67] Yet, as Jannetta points out, the patterns in late-nineteenth-century Europe, which were particularly severe, do not suggest a straight association with wealth or nutrition. We do not know why measles did not become endemic and why the periodic invasions of the virus did not kill more people.

Tuberculosis is one of the most important causes of mortality in early modern societies. There are three types, the human, the bovine and the avian. The bacillus is 'a rod-shaped acid-fast organism', which may enter the body by 'inhalation, ingestion, or direct inoculation. Inhalation of bacilli spread in droplet form by coughing, sneezing, or expectorations from tuberculous patients with open cavities is by far the most common method of spread. . . . Intestinal infection also may result from ingestion of milk-borne bovine bacilli.'[68]

Tuberculosis is an ancient disease, 'one of the oldest diseases known to humanity.'[69] It was known in Britain by Anglo-Saxon times,[70] but it was from the seventeenth century that it became a major killer. We are told that 'In the seventeenth and eighteenth centuries it was responsible for about one-fifth of all deaths in London, except during years when epidemics of plague raged.'[71]

[66] Jannetta, *Epidemics*, 139,144.
[67] Jannetta, *Epidemics*, 144,112.
[68] Merck, *Manual*, 1335.
[69] Farris in Kiple (ed.), *Disease*, 379.
[70] Howe, *Environment*, 103.
[71] Clarkson, *Disease*, 39.

There was widespread awareness of both its serious nature and of the difficulty of disentangling its different forms. The latter difficulty is shown in the terminology: 'For example the pulmonary forms were commonly called phthisis or pulmonary consumption; infections of the lymph glands surrounding the neck were termed scrofula; and those of the skin referred to as lupus vulgaris.'[72] Black in the eighteenth century was aware of both the serious nature of the disease and the vagueness of terminology used to describe its various manifestations:

> From one *fifth* to one *sixth* of all the mortality in London is from consumption; which is nearly double to that even of smallpox. But consumption is a term too lax and indefinite. Into this gulph, no doubt, are thrown many febrile and slow hectick emaciations, from infancy to old age, in both sexes; and there are few diseases from acute and chronic sources, especially in their fatal termination, without termination, without emaciation and cachexy.[73]

Yet there can be little doubt as to its seriousness. 'Behold here one of the great caravans of dead to the stygian ferry; and tottering myriads crowding to the same shambles. Every introspection of morbid registers, and the unanimous observations of the medical profession, concord in proclaiming the notoriety of the consumptive throng, and their ruinous domination.'[74] In the middle of the nineteenth century, various authorities estimated that between one quarter and one third of all deaths were caused by consumption.[75] 'As killers, both cholera and typhus were dwarfed by tuberculosis.' It was reckoned by contemporaries to be 'the most lethal disease of the nineteenth century, and probably of several centuries before.'[76] Flinn states that 'There is evidence that this disease accounted for a higher proportion of all deaths in some European countries than any other cause of death by the early nineteenth century, so that it is clear that already by the eighteenth century it was a major killer, if not *the* major killer.'[77]

Although tuberculosis pre-dated industrialization, it does seem to be closely associated with both that process and urbanization.[78] This explains why 'Physicians on the continent allege, that phthisis is more prevalent in Britain than in any other kingdom of Europe.'[79] At the end of the eighteenth century, Place noted that 'The only fatal disease which seems to have much increased in

---

[72] William D. Johnston in Kiple (ed.), *Disease*, 1061.
[73] Black, *Arithmetical*, 93.
[74] Black, *Arithmetical*, 92.
[75] Greenhow, *Papers*, 47.
[76] Chadwick, *Report*, 11.
[77] Flinn, *European*, 62.
[78] Johnston in Kiple (ed.), *Disease*, 1059.
[79] Black, *Arithmetical*, 93.

London, is consumption.'[80] The reasons were known to contemporaries: 'Tuberculosis thrives in deprived bodies: its allies are undernourishment, debilitation, unventilated living and working accommodation, and squalor. Until the end of the nineteenth century it was almost exclusively an urban disease.'[81] As a contemporary put it:

> amongst the lower orders universally, and more especially those penned up in the foul atmosphere of cities ... phthisis is more fatal than amongst those who browse in the pure air of the country. In accommodation, clothing, noxious trades, etc. the indigent have also the disadvantage; and during sickness, from the same causes, their recovery is more desperate. With respect to seasons, winter and autumn in our climate is the most pernicious to pulmonick maladies.[82]

It was noticed that 'The pulmonary death-rate is usually excessive in towns where both males and females are largely employed in the manufacture of textile fabrics.'[83] But other occupations were also dangerous. 'Textile mill laborers, masons, pottery factory operatives, metal grinders, and other workers in the "dusty trades" inhale particulate matter that inflames the lungs and increases their risk of developing the disease. The physical exertion and stress of exhausting work also magnify an individual's risk of developing tuberculosis, as does smoking.'[84] 'Poor diet, crowded conditions in housing and at work and poor ventilation contribute to high tuberculosis mortality.'[85] In relation to diet, for example, there is evidence of 'the importance of protein in resistance to tuberculosis.'[86]

The decline of tuberculosis in parts of the world is consistent with the view that it is the environment which is the important factor. It is agreed that 'In most European countries ... tuberculosis mortality has been declining at an almost constant rate for more than a century without the benefit of vaccination or antimycobacterial drugs.'[87] 'In the light of present-day knowledge it is most unlikely that medical treatment as such had anything to do with the slow but persistent fall in mortality up to 1939. It is doubtful whether treatment ever did more than delay the fatal event in those who would have died without treatment.' What changed were living conditions. 'In all probability the diminution resulted mainly from the steady advance in the standard of living over the

---

[80] Place, *Illustrations*, 251.
[81] M.W. Flinn, introduction to Chadwick, *Report*, 11.
[82] Black, *Arithmetical*, 94.
[83] Greenhow, *Papers*, 74.
[84] Johnston in Kiple (ed.), *Disease*, 1061.
[85] Mercer, *Disease*, 104.
[86] Johnston in Kiple (ed.), *Disease*, 1061.
[87] Dubos, *Adapting*, 236.

period. By 1939 the average person in a civilized community was eating more and better food, was housed in greater comfort, had more opportunity for fresh air and sunlight, and was more cleanly in his habits than in the nineteenth century.' The result is that while most of us still carry the infection 'Today most of the cases and the deaths in Western countries, occur in old men, often derelicts and drunkards from the city slums.'[88] As Greenwood noted, tuberculosis was not conquered, just held in abeyance, in certain parts of the world.[89] It is now again on the increase and a recent survey shows that in 1990 it caused almost two million deaths of those aged over five, far outstripping diseases such as malaria, AIDS or even diarrhoea.[90]

Since tuberculosis was so obviously associated with urbanism and industrialism in the West, it is of considerable interest to see the long-term pattern in Japan. It looks as if pulmonary tuberculosis may have been present in tenth and eleventh century Japan, as there are possible references in the *Genji* and other literature and in excerpts from Chinese medical books.[91] The word for respiratory TB, *Kekkaku (hai-kekkaku)* is a native Japanese term and not a European loan word. Yet in the ensuing centuries, despite the fact that large cities grew on these highly crowded islands, and despite the presence of many 'dusty trades', particularly textiles and pottery, what seems remarkable is the relative absence of widespread tuberculosis mortality in Japan until very late. Jannetta does not include tuberculosis in the index of her book on epidemics in Japan, let alone discuss it. Equally significant is the fact that tuberculosis is not one of the nine diseases to which a chapter is devoted in Fujikawa's classic *History of Diseases in Japan*. Chicken pox, German measles, Influenza and other ailments are there, but not TB.

It would appear that from about the middle of the nineteenth century, as western contact increased and Japan began to move into its industrial phase, tuberculosis began to increase. Willis did not single out tuberculosis or associated diseases as especially prevalent. In his account; 'the principal diseases appear to have been those of a venereal character, eye disease, and leprosy.'[92] Later Morse wrote that 'phthisis (tuberculosis of the lung) is not more common than in the Middle States of our country.'[93] However, Pompe wrote that 'By far the most prevalent diseases found in Japan are those of the chest including the lungs, the bronchial tubes, and the heart. Lung tuberculosis occurs quite

[88] Burnett, *Infectious*, 218,218,216; see also Dubos, *Writings*, 109–10.

[89] Greenwood, *Epidemics*, 360.

[90] WHO 1994, cited in *New Internationalist* 272 (Oct. 1995) 15; there is now serious concern of a massive world epidemic of tuberculosis and over three million people are reported to have died of it in 1995.

[91] Tatsukawa in Kiple (ed.), *Disease*, 374.

[92] Cortazzi, *Willis*, 259.

[93] Morse, *Day*, I, 39.

frequently in all its varieties and also bronchial diseases.' Some statistical impression of what 'quite frequently' means is given when we are told that 'Of 700 patients seen by Pompe, 42 were diagnosed as tuberculosis, and of this number, 36 died.'[94]

The situation appears to have become much worse towards the end of the nineteenth century and some Japanese thought that the disease was a new one. In Natsume Soseki's novel *I am a Cat*, written in 1904–5, one character says 'Indeed these days one cannot be too careful. What with the increases in all these new diseases like tuberculosis and the black plague.' These were 'Things that did not exist in the days of the Shogunate.'[95] We are told that 'tuberculosis epidemics were just starting at the end of the nineteenth century.'[96] This may have been related to the entry of large numbers of young women into the labour force, where they worked and lived in crowded workshops and dormitories.[97] Certainly by the 1905 edition of *Japanese Things*, Chamberlain thought that consumption was one of the three most serious diseases in Japan.[98] Hane provides some figures for this period: 'In 1889, 0.15 percent of the population died of the disease; in 1900, 0.17 percent; in 1904, 0.185 percent; and in 1935, 0.19 percent.'[99] According to a Health Officer's Report of 1927, 'Tuberculosis ranks first as the cause of death in Japan. In all its forms it caused during the year 1915 to 1920 an average death rate of 2.3 per 1,000 for the whole country and 3.6 per 100 for the cities exceeding 50,000 in population.'[100] Although the absolute numbers and the percentages are still small, it was clearly an important source of illness and death. After 1945 the rates began to drop, again probably more the result of improved living conditions than medical treatment.[101]

A particular difference between England and Japan is worth noting. We have been considering pulmonary tuberculosis. The other main form, bovine tuberculosis is, of course, associated with cattle. The widespread keeping of cows and use of dairy products in England clearly raised the bovine tuberculosis level. Even as late as the early twentieth century, Lane-Claypon thought that 'Tuberculosis is certainly the most serious infection owing to the wide prevalence of the disease among cows.' She thought that at least a quarter of the cows were infected.[102] On the other hand, the virtual absence of cows from Japan until the later nineteenth century, and the correlated absence of dairy products, must

---

[94] Wittermans, *Pompe*, 109.
[95] Natsume, *I am a Cat*, 102–3.
[96] Johnston in Kiple (ed.), *Disease*, 1063.
[97] Jannetta, *Two Centuries*, 432–3.
[98] Chamberlain, *Things*, 251.
[99] Hane, *Rebels*, 46.
[100] Wellington, *Report*, 27.
[101] For other figures see Johnston in Kiple (ed.), *Disease*, 1066.
[102] Lane-Claypon, *Hygiene*, 235.

have minimized this potent cause of one type of tuberculosis and may be a reason for the dramatic increase after that when meat eating became more widespread.

In considering the general patterns of air-borne diseases, it is important to remember that 'infectious diseases are not static conditions, but depend upon a constantly changing relationship between parasite and invaded species, which is bound to result in modifications both of clinical and of epidemiological manifestations.'[103] One particular manifestation of this seems to be the way in which certain diseases which begin as epidemics, killing large numbers of people, later become less virulent. Kunitz speculates that 'in large populations these crowd diseases [measles and smallpox] will turn into childhood diseases.'[104] Commenting on their decline in North America, he explains that 'Smallpox and measles began to recede in the late eighteenth century for the same reasons as in Europe: with the growth of population and development of communications, they increasingly afflicted children rather than adults.'[105] Thus, growing contact between parts of England and the rise in population size 'meant that measles and smallpox became endemic and affected primarily younger age groups.' These 'density-dependent crowd diseases' became 'childhood diseases'.[106] The same point has been elaborated by Cohen, who shows the advantages of a large population and the consequent change of certain epidemic diseases into childhood complaints in Europe.[107] Likewise Kiple has argued that the 'taming of diseases by rendering them endemic' is 'the next great change in the ecology of human disease' after the transition to sedentary populations. He suggests that 'Such a phenomenon occurred gradually for ... between 5,000 and 40,000 new hosts are required annually for it to become endemic. But, sooner or later, cities that had previously suffered from epidemics ... became populous enough to produce through births enough non-immune individuals to retain the diseases permanently.'[108]

If there is a threshold of population above which certain diseases, particularly viral ones including smallpox and measles, become endemic and less disastrous, it may be that Japan passed over this threshold very early, perhaps in the eighth to eleventh centuries, and thereafter a number of common diseases were less virulent. In England the change may have occurred in the eighteenth century.

---

[103] Zinsser, *Rats*, 88.
[104] Kunitz, *Speculations*, 352.
[105] Kunitz in Coleman and Schofield (eds), *Population*, 285.
[106] Kunitz, *Speculations*, 354; for an interesting earlier suggestion of this approach see Schofield, *Review of McKeown*, 180.
[107] Cohen, *Health*, 54.
[108] Kiple, in Bynum and Porter (eds), *Companion Encyclopedia*, 364–5.

This is a possible background factor, yet it can only explain a little of the puzzle of the fluctuations in these diseases.

Viruses are notoriously volatile and some of the puzzles may in this case be explained by changes in the strain. The sudden influenza epidemics, increasingly virulent attacks of smallpox and measles, and the equally sudden decline of measles, all these might be thought to be partly explained by viral transformations.

It is also not clear to what extent the prevalence and case mortality rates are influenced by changes in the environment. On the one hand, it could be argued that air-borne diseases are the least susceptible to external environmental changes. On the other hand it is likely that the case mortality, particularly of measles and tuberculosis, are considerably affected by the standard of living of the population. A well-fed and generally healthy population may be much less prone to high mortality.

Another type of argument might be termed the 'disease load' theory. Respiratory diseases interact with other diseases. The viruses do not act alone. They also 'enter into relationships' with the relatively large micro-organisms, for instance bacteria. This added complexity is well described by Burnett. In the case of the influenza epidemic of 1918, 'It seems as if a very active virus swept over the whole world, finding almost all individuals susceptible to it, and in its passage made all sorts of temporary alliances with pathogenic bacteria spread by the same respiratory route. The virus initiated the illness in every case, but when a fatal outcome resulted it was almost always the bacteria which were finally responsible.' There is in any relatively dense human population 'a constant interchange of the viruses and bacteria which can occupy the upper respiratory tract.'[109] It is often impossible to specify what is the cause of death; a pack of causes is at work.

If a country becomes heavily populated it is likely to suffer from numerous diseases of density – including a wide range of bacterial and viral infections. Each exacerbates the other. It is likely that the cumulative effect will be to bring population growth to a halt with a series of inter-related epidemics, each feeding off the other. Yet this need not happen. The diseases spread through water or by insect and other vectors are directly affected by changes in the physical environment in a way which is not the case with droplet spread infections. If it is indeed the case that the English and Japanese were able to alleviate the effects of some of the vector-borne and water-borne diseases unusually early, the indirect effect would be to make it possible for them to recover more easily from respiratory epidemics.

The old picture of the body fighting off the assault of deadly germs is now obsolete. All of life is filled with potentially lethal pathogens. 'Would time

[109] Burnett, *Infectious*, 122,133.

permit, one could list many examples of infections caused by either protozoa, fungi, bacteria, rickettsia, or viruses that are ubiquitous in their distribution among human, animal, or plant communities but remain in a latent, essentially inactive state under ordinary "normal" circumstances. These latent infections express themselves in the form of disease only after some physiological or environmental factor has caused a primary disturbance that allows the microbial agent to manifest its potential pathogenicity.'[110] We have witnessed this delicate balance in the history of England and Japan. 'Environmental factors' including changes in drink, clothing and housing, shifted the balance and diseases waxed and waned without any change in their innate power of multiplication, pathogenic seriousness or infectivity or any help from the medical profession. If 'Disease is life under altered conditions' as Virchow claimed, then, in reverse, health is equally 'life under altered conditions', and the conditions did alter, dramatically, over the centuries.

By a set of curious chances, none of them predictable or determined at the time, the effects of the three main branches of human disease were mitigated. In both England and Japan this resulted in a decline in mortality. In both cases this contradicted Malthus' early predictions. People on these islands had successfully escaped, for a time, from the third part of the Malthusian trap.

[110] Dubos, *Writings*, 123.

Part VI

In the Womb

17

Fertility, Marriage and Sexual Relations

We have seen that England and Japan had escaped early from the constant crises that the great thinkers of the eighteenth century had assumed were inevitable. In both these countries, war, famine and epidemic disease, which periodically decimated the populations of other agrarian civilizations, were muted in their effects. We have begun to explore a number of the factors which lay behind this unusual passage from a world of recurring disaster.

At this point, with mortality well below the normal, the second stage of the Malthusian trap will usually be sprung. The natural fertility of human beings and their usual patterns of marital and sexual relations will lead people to produce numerous offspring. A cohabiting couple is likely to produce an average of at least ten children over a life time. If the mortality caused by either periodic crises or endemic mortality was as low as they appear to have been in England and Japan, and if there was not massive out-migration, the population will double every generation, at least. At this rate, for instance, an English population of three million in 1500 would have been about three billion in 1800. Yet we know that it was in fact less then ten million. The growth from a higher base in Japan would have been even greater. In reality one of the most striking facts about the populations of both countries is that in the very period when mortality was relatively low, their populations were static for a period of about five generations. This suggests that both mortality and fertility rates were low.

How was it that these two countries could escape from the second of Malthus' laws, that if mortality is checked the population will grow very rapidly? This was a world where there was no effective artificial contraception. How then could these two islands escape from the tendency towards rapidly rising population which soon wipes out all the gains made by reducing high mortality?

Malthus likened food production to a tortoise and the rapid growth of population caused by the high human fertility potential to a hare. Having discovered that it is impossible to produce enough food for a naturally growing population, 'our next attempt should naturally be to proportion the population to the food. If we can persuade the hare to go to sleep, the tortoise may have some chance of overtaking her.'[1] It should be possible to control fertility more easily than to control mortality, for it is much more within the realm of conscious human effort and institutions.

Before looking in more detail at possible causes, it is necessary to establish a little more firmly that we are right in assuming that the fertility rate was indeed well below the theoretical maximum. Most would assume that in the pre-contraceptive age, fertility would be at the upper level which is normal in a 'natural' situation.

If we look at the birth rates, in the majority of agrarian societies outside Europe before the 1950s, these were usually in the range between 45 and 55 per thousand.[2] A rate of 45 per thousand was not unusual.[3] The rates in historical Europe were probably not as high as this. By the middle of the nineteenth century, west European populations had birth rates of about 35 per thousand per year.[4] Up to the middle of the eighteenth century, the rates were probably normally higher, of the order of 40 per thousand, as in eighteenth century France.[5] In England the rates were lower. It has now been established that during the second half of the seventeenth century and early eighteenth century, birth rates were well below the expected 45 per thousand of a 'normal' pre-industrial population. They fluctuated around 30 per thousand or so, in other words about 15 points below the expected level. These low birth rates then rose during the industrial revolution to figures closer to those we would associate with an agrarian population.[6]

If we look at Japanese fertility, we find that when the results of detailed studies began to emerge in the 1950s the birth rates were 'so low as to be inconceivable.'[7] Smith's study of Nakahara suggested that 'Compared to rates in underdeveloped countries today, which run consistently in the 40s and 50s, the Nakahara average is distinctly low', though it was 'about the average for the

---

[1] Malthus, *Population*, II, 172.

[2] These are 'crude birth rates', because they do not take account of the sex, age or marital status composition of the population. They are reckoned by calculating the number of livebirths per thousand persons per year in the population under scrutiny.

[3] Nag, *Human Fertility*, 174; Clark, *Population Growth*, ch.1.

[4] Coale, *Malthus*, 8.

[5] Wrigley and Schofield, *Population*, 479.

[6] For some figures and discussion, see Hollingsworth, *Historical Demography*, 148–52; Jones and Mingay (eds), *Land, Labour and Population*, 195–200; Deane and Cole, *British Economic Growth*, 127; Chambers, *Population*, ch.3.

[7] Taeuber, *Population of Japan*, 33.

Japanese communities.' The adjusted figures between 1721 and 1820 fluctuated between 25 and 43 per thousand per year.[8] Hanley and Yamamura made detailed studies of four villages over periods from 1693 to 1871. In Fujito, the birth rate fluctuated between 15.4 and 33.1, with a mean of 24.2; in Fukiage, between 19.4 and 31.9, with a mean of 26; in Numa, between 15.7 and 24.9, with a mean of 19.6; in Nishikata, between 16.7 and 19.9, with a mean of 18.5. As the authors conclude, this shows birth rates which 'seem extraordinarily low for a premodern society', for 'If we envision preindustrial societies as resembling many of the underdeveloped countries of the mid-twentieth century, then we would expect birth rates nearly double those calculated for these Tokugawa villages.'[9]

Let us examine some other features of the fertility situation. Firstly there is the question of age-specific fertility, that is rates which take into account the age and sex structure of the population in question. Thomas Smith found that the results of his study of this index for Nakahara showed that age-specific fertility was 'low compared with all of the European parishes' with two interesting exceptions, Colyton in England between 1647 and 1719, and a parish 'in the region of puzzlingly low fertility in southwestern France.'[10]

A second feature is the gap between childbirths. If we take France in the seventeenth and eighteenth century as a fairly typical pre-contracepting population, then we find birth intervals between first and second births which varied between 19 and 28 months in three different parishes.[11] In the parish of Crulai, there was normally a birth interval of 29.6 months, but only 20.7 months when the preceding child died before reaching its first birthday.[12] It would therefore seem reasonable to see an interval of between 20 and 30 months as 'normal', depending on the birth order and whether the previous child had died. Flinn gives a table showing birth intervals of 14, 28 and 31 months for first, second and third births in England, and 16, 23 and 26 months for France. For Germany the intervals were 20 and 24 months for second and third births, and for Switzerland, 20 and 23 months.[13]

It may well be that the intervals were at least a year longer than this in Japan. Feeney and Kiyoshi state that in Japan they were about three and a half years.[14] Kalland and Pedersen claim that 'there typically were about three years between each child.'[15] If it is indeed the case that there was between six months and a year

[8] Smith, *Nakahara*, 39,40; the un-adjusted figures taken from the *shumon aratame-cho* seriously under-record births.

[9] Hanley and Yamamura, *Economic*, 211, table 8.4; 212.

[10] Smith, *Native Sources*, table 4.1 and fig.4.1, 106–7,105; for European figures, see Flinn, *European*, table 3.3, 31.

[11] Glass and Eversley (eds), *Population*, 617.

[12] Wrigley, *Population and History*, 124.

[13] Flinn, *European*, 33, table 3.5.

[14] Feeney and Kiyoshi, *Rice*, 24.

[15] Kalland and Pedersen, *Famine*, 54.

longer gap in Japan than in most other societies, this may provide a clue to the mechanisms of the preventive check.

The result of the low birth rates was a smaller completed family size. In four out of the five French parishes which Smith tabulated, the completed family size lay between 8.2 and 10.4 live births.[16] In England, the figures for Colyton 1647–1719 were much lower. For instance, for those who married at under 24, the mean completed family size was about 5.[17] But Japan was lower still. For instance, in Yokouchi 1701–50 it was 5, in 1751–1800 it was 4, and after 1800 it was 4.2. Other villages were higher, but none exceeded 7. Nakahara, for instance, was 6.5 in 1717–1830.[18] The study of four villages by Hanley and Yamamura has found figures in line with those for Yokouchi. 'The number of children ever born averaged from just under three to between three and four for all of the villages. While the average was around three, the modal number of children born was sometimes only two, as was the case of Fukiage between 1773 and 1801.'[19] Elsewhere Hayami reports completed family size of under 4, except in the highest class.[20] To achieve an average of between three and six live births per marriage, with long periods at around three or four, is very unusual.

What then are the factors which affect fertility? In this analysis of the constraints on fertility rates in England and Japan I will use a framework proposed by Kingsley Davis and Judith Blake. They used a threefold classification of the ways in which human fertility can be affected; in allowing intercourse in the first place (intercourse variables), in allowing or preventing conception to occur after such intercourse (conception variables), and in allowing or preventing the result of any conception to be born and live (gestation variables).[21] In this chapter I shall look at the first of these, intercourse variables, that is the pattern of marriage and sexual relations.

In the years that followed the first publication of the *Essay on Population* in 1798, Malthus read much more widely and made several trips round Europe. What he found led him to revise his theory. In the almost totally new second edition of the *Essay* published in 1803 Malthus no longer saw the argument he had earlier elaborated as based on 'iron laws', but rather as a description of 'tendencies'. The normal demographic situation was one of crisis and negative feedback, yet this was only a 'normal' pressure which could, and occasionally had been, overcome. The way to avoid it was to introduce a new element, what Malthus called the 'preventive checks'.

---

[16] Smith, *Native Sources*, 106, table 4.1.
[17] Wrigley, *Family Limitation*, 97.
[18] Smith, *Native Sources*, table 4.1, 106.
[19] Hanley and Yamamura, *Economic*, 228.
[20] Hayami, *Class Differences*, 13; these figures, however, do not include unrecorded births.
[21] Davis and Blake, *Analytic Framework*.

Malthus had noticed that while many great civilizations encouraged marriage at as early an age as possible, this was not the case in western Europe. During travels in Norway between the two editions of the *Essay* he had noticed the various pressures which led to the postponement of marriages. He began to realize that this was a feature of much of western Europe. 'It can scarcely be doubted that in modern Europe a much larger proportion of women pass a considerable part of their lives in the exercise of this virtue (i.e. late age at marriage) than in past times and among uncivilised nations.' Thus a delay in marriage, he believed, was 'the most powerful of the checks which in modern Europe keep down the population to the level of the means of subsistence.' He found that the most extreme case of the preventive checks of late marriage and non-marriage was England itself: 'The most cursory view of society in this country must convince us, that throughout all ranks the preventive check to population prevails in a considerable degree.'[22] He then attempted to explain why and how it had begun to operate.

What Malthus was suggesting was that there were signs that a new pattern different from the 'crisis' one was emerging. Population was held in check through the operation of lower fertility rates rather than through rising mortality. 'I think it appears that in modern Europe the positive checks to population prevail less and the preventive checks more than in past times, and in the more uncivilised parts of the world.'[23] Considering these views some years later, he concluded that 'probably it may be said with truth, that, in almost all the more improved countries of modern Europe, the principal check which at present keeps the population down to the level of the actual means of subsistence is the prudential restraint on marriage.'[24]

It is now well known that the age at marriage (and hence entry into sexual union) and the proportion not marrying was the central mechanism which affected fertility rates in north-western Europe, and particularly England, in the centuries leading up to the industrial revolution. In the majority of human societies, women marry and enter sexual union at or soon after puberty, that is in their middle or late teens. As a result of work by John Hajnal, we know that western Europe had an exceptional marriage pattern whereby women often entered their first sexual union after a delay of up to ten years beyond puberty, in other words in their middle twenties. This seems to have been the case since at least the sixteenth century.[25] Indeed, there is now evidence that the 'Hajnal' pattern was present in England from at least the thirteenth century.[26]

England was the most extreme case. As Wrigley shows, during several peri-

[22] Malthus, *Population*, I, 116,119,129,315,236.
[23] Malthus, *Population*, I, 315.
[24] Malthus, *Summary*, 254.
[25] Hajnal, *Marriage Patterns*. For Europe in general, see Flinn, *European*, 28, table 3.1.
[26] See e.g. Richard Smith in Landers and Reynolds (eds), *Fertility*, 173.

ods in the seventeenth and eighteenth centuries, women were marrying for the first time at an average age of 26 or older. This greatly shortened their period of being 'at risk' of having children. This helps to account for much of the restrained fertility in England. Then the population started to grow rapidly in the middle of the eighteenth century. Wrigley argues that this was caused by a drop of three years in the mean age at first marriage, from about 25 to about 22. This drop would lead to a cumulative rise in marital fertility of about 25 per cent (from 4.42 to 5.5 children). This means that 'Earlier marriage alone would therefore account for more than half of the rise' in the Gross Reproduction Rate.[27] Part of Wrigley's views have been challenged by Goldstone who argues 'Changes in the proportions ever married, rather than in age at marriage, must thus bear the brunt of explaining fertility shifts before 1700.' He agrees that the rising fertility of the later eighteenth century was caused by a fall in the age at marriage, but suggests that this was not caused by a general fall in age at marriage but a specific change. 'A close look at the age distribution at marriage shows that after 1750 age at marriage did not shift generally towards younger ages. Instead, what occurred was a dramatic rise in first marriages by men aged 19–23, and by women aged 22 and under.' 'The great population boom of the late eighteenth century appears to be the result of a relatively confined effect, a major shift to much younger first marriage by some 20 per cent of the marrying population.'[28] Whichever view prevails, it is clear that age at marriage and proportion marrying are crucial variables.

When we turn to Japan, if we take the two extremes of age at first marriage for women, namely the 'normal' pattern of human societies, at between 15 and 18, and the seventeenth century English pattern of between 25 and 27, Japan lies about half way between. Hayami's early work on Suwa county shows age at marriage in various regions and periods between 1671 and 1871. The lowest figure for any period and place is 18.3 years, the highest is 22.0. The average of the averages is 20.4 years. In Yokouchi village, of which he made a special study, the figures were identical, lying between 18.5 and 21.[29] In his study of Nakahara, Thomas Smith found similar ranges. The overall mean was 19.9 years, with the smaller landholders marrying at an average age of 22.6 and the larger landholders at an average age of 17.6 years.[30] On the basis of this work, Smith concludes that the figures for Nakahara 'clearly belong to the non-European marriage pattern', though he also admits that they were 'considerably above that in many underdeveloped countries today.' 'Nuptiality made only a marginal contribution to low fertility, marriage for females was young.'[31]

[27] Wrigley, *Population and History*, 256.
[28] Goldstone, *Demographic*, 10,19,29.
[29] In Laslett and Wall (eds), *Household*, 502,508; Hayami's figures are in Japanese age (*sai*) and hence at least a year needs to be subtracted from them (see the note two paragraphs below).
[30] Smith, *Nakahara*, 93 and 94 (table), *Native Sources*, 121.
[31] Smith, *Nakahara*, 93,11,100.

Hanley and Yamamura, however, put a different emphasis on the findings. Firstly, they found slightly higher ages, though a similar difference between the rich and the poor. Women from richer families 'married at just over 21 while families with extremely little or no land married at over 25.' They argue that the 'custom for women to first marry at from 22 to 25 was prevalent at least throughout central and western Japan.'[32] Hanley and Yamamura cite the following figures for mean age at first marriages for various communities: '23.3 in Fujito, 23.4 in Fukiage, 23.4 in Nishikata, 23.5 in Numa.'[33] The result was that in the most fertile period, 20–4, many Japanese women were still unmarried. 'The 20s are considered the most fertile years for women but, in a sample of twenty-one years from the four villages, the percentage of women in the 20–24 age group who were married was under 40 percent in thirteen of these years.' This was not a new pattern in the later Tokugawa period; in the village of Fukiage in 1683 'only 37.5 per cent of women aged 20–24 were married.' Hanley and Yamamura therefore conclude that 'the average age at first marriage for women was relatively high for women in a preindustrial society.'[34]

More recent work by Hayami has emphasized the class and regional differences in Japan. In terms of class, in one study class I women married at an average age of 19 *sai* and had 6.2 live births, class III women at 22 *sai* and had 4.6 live births.[35] In another case 'Nishijo village in Mino Province – age at first marriage for the wives of the 1773–1835 cohort differed conspicuously according to landholding. In the upper class of peasants, age at first marriage was 21.5 *sai* while in the lower class of peasants, it was 24.5 *sai*.' The regional variations are very important. Hayami concluded that 'it is possible to suggest that there were two patterns of marriage in Japan in the late nineteenth century – a pattern of early marriage in eastern Japan and one of late marriage in the western Japan.' He related this to the relative prosperity and inheritance customs of the two regions.[36]

What is clear is that there was a firm idea that a girl would be both marriageable and likely to marry in an age band that began at about 18 or a little older. This can be seen most delightfully in the indicative hair styles of women. We are told that 'after twenty-one' a girl would wear certain hair styles, for 'she was now at an age when she might get married very soon, so she'd want a graceful style that wasn't too conspicuous.'[37] These styles divided the hair – showing the incipient break from her parents. The 'various styles of dressing the hair of girls'

---

[32] Hanley and Yamamura, *Economic*, 286,246.

[33] Hanley in Hanley and Wolf (eds), *Family*, 216.

[34] Hanley and Yamamura, *Economic*, 248,250,246.

[35] Hayami, *Class Differences*, 15. 'Sai' means years of age, Japanese style, that is to say one year old when born, becoming two on New Year's Day. Class I are the richest, Class III the poorest.

[36] Hayami, *Fossa*, 59,70,70–1.

[37] Saga, *Silk and Straw*, 152.

allowed one to 'form a pretty accurate estimate of any girl's age up to her marriage, when the *coiffure* undergoes a definite change.'[38]

The very late age at marriage of men in Japan, which meant that husbands were on average about eight years older than their wives, may also be important. 'In Kyushu men were enjoined not to marry until age 30 or later',[39] though the ages were usually a little under 30. The late age at marriage for men is shown in Smith's study of Nakahara where 'the proportion of all males who were likely to be still single did not drop below half until almost age 30.'[40]

The age at which sexual relations began, which was largely synonymous with marriage in Japan, needs to be considered alongside the period at which co-habitation ceased. Here we come across a curious but significant feature of the Japanese fertility pattern which differentiated it from every other agrarian population of which we have records, namely the very young age at which women stopped bearing children. A man marrying at 30 to a girl of 22 would already be in his mid-forties by the time she approached her usual period of ending childbirth.

In the majority of societies, the mean age at last childbirth, assuming both partners are still alive, is roughly 40. With reference to twentieth century populations, 'the meagre evidence available suggests that the mean age at last birth seems to vary little among populations which do not practice birth control; it was 40.9 among the well-nourished Hutterites and 41.7 in a poorly nourished English population cited by Frisch.'[41] Flinn reviewed some historical European figures for before 1750 derived from reconstitution studies and found mean ages at birth of last child of 40.9 for Belgium, 40.4 for France, 40.0 for Germany and 38.5 for England.[42] In the classic French study of Crulai 'the age of women at the time of their last confinement lies between 38 and 41 years. In Geneva the average of mothers of whose families we have complete records is, at their last confinement, round about 38 or 39 between 1600 and 1649.' In three other French parishes, it varied between 39 and 41.8, the mode being over 41.[43]

In contrast, Hanley and Yamamura noted in their study of four Japanese villages that 'The highest average age at last birth' was 37 in Fukiage, 'while the lowest averages, around 33, were for Numa and Nishikata.' In Fujito village there was an average age of 34 at last birth. Women in the sample villages were bearing their last child in the middle or early thirties, 'while living with their husbands at least through age 43.'[44] The importance of this curious pattern is

[38] Bird, *Tracks*, 80.
[39] Taeuber, *Population of Japan*, 29.
[40] Smith, *Nakahara*, 91.
[41] Menken et al., *Nutrition*, 433.
[42] Flinn, *European*, 29.
[43] Deprez in Glass and Eversley (eds), *Population*, 616.
[44] Hanley and Yamamura, *Economic*, 236,241,324.

emphasized by Thomas Smith who notes that 'farm size affected family size by the age of marriage and the age of stopping, not by the spacing of children.'[45] In other words, somewhat like England, the number of women at risk was being constrained, but much of the constraint in Japan seems to have come from the five or so years cut off the end of childbearing. Although these were less fertile years, this would nevertheless have reduced the average number of births by at least one or two children. It is both significant and puzzling that 'Nineteenth-century Japanese women, on the average, stopped bearing children five or six years earlier than did their contemporary European counterparts.'[46] The pattern was one where in the case of 'women in the first half of the childbearing years we observe high marital fertility but a low proportion married, whereas for women in the second half of the childbearing years we see low marital fertility but a relatively high proportion married.'[47]

In England from the mid sixteenth to early eighteenth century, the effective period of childbirth was 25–40, in Japan it was 22–35. As Hanley and Yamamura point out, 'An average age of 23.6 at first birth and of 34 at last birth, as in Fujito, leaves only a decade for childbearing.'[48] The fact that there were longer spaces between births in Japan, and the shorter duration of years of childbearing, meant that its total fertility was even lower than that in England.

This only suggests other questions. For instance, in what way and for what reasons did the Japanese manage to end their childbearing so early? Although it is as yet only a surmise, it might well be that they influenced their fertility through an unusual form of marital abstinence. This was not the classic case of *coitus interruptus*, but rather interrupted marriage.

Dr Emiko Namihira informs me that there is a Japanese phrase which can be translated as 'divorce within marriage'. There are grounds for believing that there were strong pressures within the traditional Japanese family which controlled the occurrence of sex within marriage. One of these concerned an apparently strong taboo against older women having children or perhaps even sex. In a novel we are told that 'We Japanese have always considered it disgraceful for a couple in their forties to have a child.'[49] This attitude is suggested by the memories of a woman who recalled the tragic death of her mistress after a failed abortion. 'She must have been about forty-one at the time. In those days it was considered a great disgrace to have a baby after the age of forty – they were usually either aborted or killed at birth. A middle-aged woman only had to look tired or slack off from work and tongues would start wagging.' When a middle-aged woman became pregnant, her mother-in-law, 'used to come along almost

[45] Smith *Native*, 121.
[46] Hanley and Yamamura, *Economic*, 246.
[47] Sasaki in Hanley and Wolf (eds), *Family*, 140.
[48] Hanley and Yamamura, *Economic*, 241.
[49] Ariyoshi, *The Twilight Years*, 135.

every day and bait her about it: "It's disgusting a woman your age having a baby – you want to get rid of it just as soon as you can," she'd say.[50] Other writers suggest that part of the problem lay in the structural relations between the mother and daughter-in-law. Hanley and Yamamura cite evidence from Tosa that 'it was not considered proper for a woman to have a child if she had a daughter-in-law bearing children.'[51] Taeuber reports that '"Elderly" couples in their late thirties or early forties felt it somewhat improper to have a child, especially if there was a daughter-in-law in the house.'[52]

Further clues concerning sexual patterns emerge from a recent work on Japanese family planning by Samuel Coleman. He shows a set of characteristics which may be significant. 'Japanese sexuality is still largely confined to this dichotomy of "sex for pleasure" and "sex for reproduction" . . . the idea of sex as "communication" is all the more alien. Japanese sex specialists have recognized this tendency to place sex in a separate dimension from interpersonal relationships.'[53]

This has several effects. The sexual relationship between men and women is conceived of as a duty – for the production of children. Since this duty was fulfilled when a certain number of children were safely born or a woman reached a certain age, at that point men may have stopped having sexual intercourse with their wives. 'For husbands, sexual intercourse was a duty to produce offspring, summarized in the expression "obligatory fuck" (*giri man*).'[54] The end of this obligation was possibly a relief for the women as well. It might well be that, partly as a result of the grinding hard work, the considerable burden of breast-feeding, carrying children and the threat of unwanted extra children, husbands and wives stopped sleeping together when the men were in their mid-forties and women their mid-thirties. If this were so, it would explain the particularly early age at which the last childbirth occurred.

The stopping of sexual relations within marriage, and more widely the whole of marital life, was clearly deeply influenced by the attitude towards sexuality in Japan. This is a very large subject and one which it is difficult to deal with briefly. It is obvious that prostitution, brothels, extra-marital sex, bastardy and much else was widespread in the countries from which early travellers to Japan came. In England, for instance, there is now an extensive historical literature on many of these topics.[55] The following account is therefore not meant to imply superiority or inferiority in Japanese moral values. What I hope to show is that visitors to Japan, and particularly observant doctors, sensed that the attitude

[50] Saga, *Silk and Straw*, 210.
[51] Hanley and Yamamura, *Economic*, 265.
[52] Taeuber, *Population of Japan*, 30.
[53] Coleman, *Family Planning*, 173.
[54] Coleman, *Family Planning*, 175.
[55] For example, see Laslett et al. (eds), *Bastardy*.

towards the body, sexuality and marriage was very different from that in the often hypocritical puritan countries from which they had come. The impressionistic account they give would need to be deepened by evidence based on Japanese sources for a proper analysis, but until that is done the following will provide some idea of a few of the differences.

Kaempfer encountered the very widespread existence of brothels in Japan, particularly in the towns and villages along the main highways: 'It is unquestionably true, that there is hardly a publick Inn upon the great Island Nipon, but what may be call'd a bawdy-house; and if there by too many customers resort to one place, the neighbouring Inn-keepers will friendly and willingly lend their own wenches, on condition, that what money they get shall be faithfully paid them.' He gave a description of two particularly well known villages: 'The two villages Akasaki and Goy, lying near one another, are particularly famous on this account, all the houses therein being so many Inns, or rather bawdy-houses, each furnish'd with no less than three, six or seven of these wenches, for which reason also they are call'd the great store-house of Japanese whores, and by way of banter, the common grind-mill.' Travellers who passed along the highways took sex in the same way as they took food. 'Very seldom any Japanese pass thro' these villages, but they pick up some of these whores and have to do with them.'[56]

Thunberg added further touches. 'In all the sea ports great care has been taken to establish a brothel (and for the most part several) even in the smallest villages. They were commonly the handsomest houses in the place.' He also noted a contradiction in the sexual morality. On the one hand, Japan was a monogamous society. 'In this country the men are not allowed a plurality of wives, as in China, but each man is confined to one, who has liberty to go out and show herself in company, and is not shut up in a recluse and separate apartment, as is the custom with their neighbours.' On the other, there was widespread concubinage. 'In this country likewise the dishonourable practice of keeping mistresses obtains with some; but the children they bring into the world cannot inherit, and the mistresses are considered as servants of the house.' The contradiction between strictness and laxness struck him forcefully. 'Fornication is very prevalent in this country; notwithstanding which, chastity is frequently held in such high veneration both with married and single, that when they have been injured in this point, they sometimes lay violent hands upon themselves.'[57]

Pompe, gave a detailed and sensitive account of sexual morality. In the capital alone, he thought, there were some sixty thousand prostitutes. Prostitution in Japan, he argued, was 'such a remarkable phenomenon, so deeply rooted in the social structure and at the same time so pitiful that every right-minded person

---

[56] Kaempfer, *History*, II, 346.
[57] Thunberg, *Travels*, III, 125; IV, 52.

can only wish that it could be prohibited at the government level.' The attitude towards the inmates of the brothels was strangely tolerant: 'The Japanese society does not look with contempt on these public brothels, precisely because they are *public*. For them this excludes every connection with crime.' This was part of a wider attitude. 'The Japanese does not regard a free sex life as bad, much less as sin; the word "vice" is therefore not the right term for it. Neither the religion nor the society prohibits intercourse with women outside of marriage, and this is the cause for all the remarkable acts which arouse our amazement.'[58]

The sense of shame and sin was very different from that in the west. 'Many people have observed, as I have, that the Japanese talk about natural situations with a great deal of frankness, which surprises newcomers. They tell stories in the presence of their wives which exceed every sense of shame, without apparently offending the ladies.' This meant, for example, that girls who had worked in the brothels could make good marriages afterwards, despite the fact being known. 'After reaching their twenty-fifth year, these girls are set free. Their bondage is over, and I am sure people would be surprised to hear that they return to society as decent women, and yet this is absolutely true.' On the other hand, because of poverty and disease, their life was often miserable. 'The humiliations they have to undergo weigh heavily on many of them, and I bear testimony to the fact that I have often treated such girls in my clinic, who were dying of lung tuberculosis as a result of distress about the role they had to fulfil.'[59]

Many of the earlier observations were confirmed, and sometimes given statistical depth, by Willis. He found brothels particularly prevalent in the sea ports as outside influence built up. In one port he found 'The number of prostitutes is out of all proportion to the population, a circumstance due it is said to the crowds of native sailors who visit the place in summer in junks.' In particular, 'It is computed that there are about one thousand prostitutes at Yokohama, of which number between two and three hundred are employed as mistresses of foreigners, with an average wage, at the present time, of fifteen to twenty dollars a month each.' But such institutions were widely spread through Japan. 'I found that brothels were common in the larger villages and towns, and where brothels did not exist the tea house women acted as prostitutes.' 'In several places in the province of Shinano [Nagano prefecture] the waiting women at Inns act as prostitutes, in which capacity their services when rendered form an item of charge included in the bill furnished by the landlord.' More generally, 'Many tea-houses have degenerated into brotheles; and houses of ill-fame, of one kind or another, are very generally distributed over Japan.'[60]

[58] Wittermans, *Pompe*, 47,112,113.
[59] Wittermans, *Pompe*, 40,115,114.
[60] Cortazzi, *Willis*, 140,243,245,129,161,245.

He suggested that there was probably an increase in the incidence of brothels, as wealth increased. 'Married men to a considerable extent frequent them, and they have been largely on the increase during the last thirty years, arising it is believed from the increase of wealth and desire of enjoying it amongst all classes.' Like Pompe, he noted the tolerance towards such activity: 'when a woman returns to her relations after serving a term at a brothel, she is not looked upon as having forfeited all claim to respectability, and she occasionally marries.' Likewise, the keeping of mistresses was not considered a vice: 'keeping concubines is very common and implies no depravity. Anyone married or single, who can afford the expense, is at liberty to keep a mistress without loss of respectability.' He, too, found awful conditions and estimated that 'One third of all prostitutes die before the term of their office expires of syphilitic and other diseases.' One new fact added by Willis concerns the recruitment of the prostitutes. 'Prostitutes are procured from the poor and necessitous classes of towns, being generally the daughters of small shop-keepers, artisans or coolies. The farming class contributes but few owing to the shame it would bring upon the relations of the prostitute.' Often it was want that drove people to sell their relatives, or themselves, into the sex trade. 'In Japan it not unfrequently happens that when a man is reduced to poverty his daughter or wife volunteers to sell herself for a term to a brothel, and such an act is looked upon as the highest evidence of filial or conjugal affection.'[61]

The acceptance of a high level of extra-marital sexuality by husbands, or of sexual encounters by those men who were unable to marry, is clearly related to the absence, in Japan, of the Christian belief that marriage and sex are inexorably linked. The idea that sex outside marriage was 'sinful', an old tradition in the west, is hardly developed in Japan, as one can see whether one looks at the great novels such as the *Genji* or the long history of open 'pornography' in art.

A further study of this topic might suggest that extra-marital sex, or just flirtation with women other than one's wife, may have been a very important part of a pattern which kept down marital fertility, particularly once a certain desired number of children had been reached, or a man had lost his wife. Other aspects of the pattern, including the long gaps between childbirths and absence of widow remarriage, could all have been importantly affected by the ease of extra-marital liaisons for men, whether with prostitute, concubine or geisha. It has been observed that the separation of sex for pleasure and for reproduction means that 'Pleasureful sex is extramarital' for many men in modern Japan.[62] Once the need for heirs was satisfied, the man might often have ended sexual relations with his wife. 'Concubinage, the privilege of the rich, had its evil side; but it had also the effect of relieving the wife from the physical strain of rearing

[61] Cortazzi, *Willis*, 245,243,241,242.
[62] Coleman, *Family Planning*, 175.

many children in rapid succession.'[63] As for the fertility of the prostitutes and concubines, it would require further research to see what happened in such cases. The bizarre theory of the eighteenth-century demographer, Short, for instance, shows a realization of the problem involved and suggested a mechanism for lowered fertility among such a group: 'From a Mixture of several genital Liquors of the same Species, or by excessive Venery, both Male and Female become barren: Hence common Prostitutes (whilst such) rarely conceive; who yet, when married, and faithful to their Husbands, breed and bear as well as other Women.'[64]

The ages at starting and 'ending' marriage were combined with the second feature of the 'west European marriage pattern', namely the proportion ever married. In the majority of human societies, almost all able-bodied women marry and have children. Only in western Europe, did relatively large numbers of women never marry. England was again an extreme case. In the period 1600–49, some 20.5 per cent of women never married, and in 1650–99 the proportion was even higher at 22.9 per cent.[65] For a pre-industrial agrarian population to have nearly one quarter of its women never marrying is very unusual. There were even periods when the rates were up to nearly 300 per thousand, or nearly a third of all women did not marry.[66] This rate fluctuated so that in 1700–49 the never marrying proportion dropped to 11.6 per cent and in 1750–99 to 5.9 per cent.[67] By then the levels were beginning to approach those normal in other, non-European, societies.

The general position in Japan does not fit readily into a 'non-western' pattern of universal marriage. We are told that 'Birthrates dropped along with nuptiality in the eighteenth century as increasing numbers of individuals failed to marry and as women married late and shortened their span of childbearing.'[68] Not only were marriages postponed even later in 'years of economic hardship', but 'It was also the custom for only one son in each household to marry'[69] for 'marriage was largely restricted to the head of the household or his successor.' Even in the early seventeenth century there is evidence that 'a sizable number of agricultural labourers dependent on and perhaps residing with patrimonial landlords did not marry.' This trend continued. 'Various village studies have demonstrated a gradual and long-term decrease in the percentage of married women that accompanied the decline in household size.'[70]

---

[63] Hearn, *Kokoro*, 149.
[64] Short, *Increase*, 28.
[65] Wrigley and Schofield, *Reconstitution*, 176.
[66] Wrigley and Schofield, *Population*, see graph, 262.
[67] Wrigley and Schofield, *Reconstruction*, 176.
[68] Rozman in *Cambridge History*, 5, 554
[69] Hanley in *Cambridge History*, 4, 700.
[70] Rozman in *Cambridge History*, 5, 553.

The specific figures, however, are not entirely satisfactory. Hayami showed in his study of Suwa county that the proportion of women aged 21–40 who were married tended to vary from 70–80 per cent, with an average of 77 per cent.[71] This includes those aged 21–3 who would shortly marry. But even allowing for that, it would seem that we might be getting rates of 15 per cent of non-married women, which is not far from the European pattern. Hanley and Yamamura also found that 'the percentage of women never married was higher than it is today' and that in most periods '80 percent of the women aged 35–39 were married.' Though they warn us that 'these percentages should not be misconstrued as representing women ever married; they are for women living with their husbands at the time', they are not inconsistent with a figure of 15 per cent of women never married.[72] This also fits with their statement that 'On the average, most households contained one woman in the childbearing ages, but nearly a third of these were unmarried.'[73] More recent work by Yoichiro Sasaki and Susan Hanley again suggests that perhaps 20 per cent of those aged 30–9 were not currently married, though in some cases this was caused by death of a spouse or divorce.[74] Kalland and Pedersen believe that 'Many people remained unmarried and households with bachelors and spinsters were common',[75] though Feeney and Kiyoshi cite some evidence which tends to suggest a modification of the high figures of non-marriage[76] and Cornell has argued forcefully that spinsters were rare in pre-modern Japan. As she points out, it is significant that there is no word equivalent to 'spinster', meaning an unmarried woman.[77]

In terms of proportion ever-marrying, the Japanese pattern was again probably less extreme than the English, but there was much more non-marriage than in most Asian societies. 'In Japan, although the proportion marrying was higher than in the West, it did not reach 100 percent at any age.'[78] The Japanese figures, however, may be brought more or less into line with the English by a second feature which is less often noticed, that is the question of what happens when a husband dies.

In England, there was a custom which demographers have sometimes described as 'serial monogamy', namely that after a marriage was broken by the death of a spouse the widow or widower usually, and fairly swiftly, remarried. For instance, on the basis of a listing of a seventeenth century English parish, Laslett found that of the 72 husbands in a village, no less than 21 were recorded as having been married more than once: 'once a man reached the marriage age

---

[71] Hayami in Laslett and Wall, *Household*, 501.
[72] Hanley and Yamamura, *Economic*, 250; Hayami's figures are likewise for those currently married.
[73] Hanley and Yamamura, *Economic*, 250.
[74] Hanley and Wolf (eds), *Family*, 140–1,213–6.
[75] Kalland and Pedersen, *Famine*, 54.
[76] Feeney and Kiyoshi, *Rice*, 29.
[77] Cornell, *Spinsters*, *passim* esp. 338,335.
[78] Hayami, *Fossa*, 61.

he would tend to go on getting married whenever he found himself without a wife. . . . The law holds for women too, but is weaker in their case.'[79] With fairly high adult mortality, this would keep women, in particular, in the 'at risk of conception' category. In England, according to Burn, both common law and church law in the seventeenth century allowed a widow to remarry at any time.[80]

However, in a couple of asides, Smith suggests that this may not have been so in Japan. He noted that 'remarriage was less frequent than we had imagined', elaborating on this as follows: 'We had expected a higher rate of remarriage in incomplete marriages than we found. Only one in three widowers and one in five widows remarried.'[81] It may well be that once again the demographic statistics have uncovered a cultural attitude which was both powerful and deserves more attention. A hint of this is given in the classic film about post-war Japan, *Tokyo Story*, where towards the end of the film the widowed daughter-in-law is urged by her parents in law to marry again. They are aware of how difficult this is for her to contemplate, but stress that 'The old days are gone when a widow couldn't re-marry.' It is quite consistent with the structure of a Japanese family that once a daughter-in-law had some children and settled in, it would be very disruptive if she re-married. A hint at the difficulties of the situation was given by Inouye: 'A widow is, as long as she remains in the family, maintained by her son or daughter's husband. Until recently she had, if she wishes to remarry, first to return to her own family and become a spinster again, so to speak, by re-assuming her maiden name.'[82] The low level of remarriage would reinforce the short duration of the period of childbearing in Japan by terminating it unusually early in cases where a husband died.

Thus in terms of the use of the 'intercourse variables', England was at the extreme end of the continuum. It was through delayed and selective marriage that fertility was mainly held in check. This is a very unusual situation and one which Malthus came to emphasize as the major way to escape his iron laws. Although the case was not so extreme, in Japan the number of women 'at risk' of intercourse was lowered by a combination of middling marriage age, some non-marriage, and apparently an early age at which many people stopped inter-course within their marriages. Yet in neither case would the natural fertility of women have been brought into line with unusually low mortality by the use of marriage strategies alone. We therefore need to look at the next way in which fertility is influenced, through the biological and contraceptive inhibitions which determine whether intercourse leads to conception.

---

[79] Laslett, *World*, 104.
[80] Burn, *Ecclesiastical Law*, II, 416.
[81] Smith, *Nakahara*, 14,100.
[82] Inouye, *Home*, 218.

18

Biology and Contraception

The second set of determinants of fertility lie in the area of 'conception varia-bles', that is to say those factors which determine whether a woman becomes pregnant after sexual intercourse. It is important to point out that I am not here talking about the genetic make-up of a population, in other words some intrinsic fecundity level. Thomas Smith rightly points out that 'It seems unlikely that Japanese women were relatively less fertile in any biological sense'[1] and the same is true of English women. What I am concerned with is the way in which cultural factors, for example breast-feeding habits, nutrition or the work patterns of women, affect women's bodies so that the fertility rates are altered.

One of the main factors that is most likely to affect female fecundity is the working condition of women. Women characteristically have three major roles in agrarian societies, as child bearers and nurturers, as house maintainers, and as workers in agriculture and other productive enterprises. The amount and nature of what they have to do will naturally affect their bodies and hence both their fertility and mortality. There is little evidence of an unusual strain in the case of English women. Their conditions of giving birth, the breast-feeding practices, and the way in which they reared their children do not seem unusual.

In contrast, Japanese women were unusual in two respects. Firstly, as we shall see, breast-feeding was prolonged, perhaps being twice as long as that in European populations. Apart from any contraceptive effect, this would also have a more generalized effect on their health and strength. A second factor was the pressures exerted by the economy and in particular the growing strain on women's bodies produced by the peculiar nature of Japanese agriculture and economic organization.

[1] Smith, *Nakahara*, 11.

The involvement of women in every aspect of the agricultural economy in Japan meant that their bodies were under very great strain. Parts of the argument have been advanced in several recent publications by Osamu Saito. He suggests that 'farming became extremely intensive' and that 'it is likely that this tendency had adverse effects on women's fecundity, and hence, fertility levels.'[2] In particular he argues that women's work-load increased in the later Tokugawa period and this may have led to a decrease in marital fertility.[3] The difficulty, however, is to show how, exactly, the causal connection worked. The only direct link he suggests relates to the fact that pregnant women worked until delivery, and soon after. 'Case studies, moreover, have shown that even when women were pregnant, they usually continued to work right up to the week the baby was due, and then started working soon after the birth.'[4] Somehow this was connected to 'high death rate of newborn babies.' Evidence concerning the rush to get back to work is given by Pompe: 'When the child is born, there comes for the mother a period of real suffering; Japanese midwives have the idea that "rest" after the delivery is particularly harmful, and they do not even allow the woman in childbed the sleep which contributes so much to restore the forces spent during delivery.'[5] There may, however, have been some limitations on women's work after childbirth at certain times and places.[6]

The sort of situation Saito alludes to is described in *Silk and Straw*.[7] The interviewee remembered how she 'saw Mother coming back down the road from the mountains, where she'd been chopping wood. She was carrying an enormous bundle of branches on her back.' She was also 'carrying a large round object wrapped up in her apron.' This turned out to be a baby. 'Afterward I realized she must have given birth to the baby alone up in the mountains, cut its umbilical cord with her billhook, and then carried it the five or six miles back home. She didn't want to leave all the firewood she'd collected . . . so she'd lugged it all the way back as well.' Another account based on a woman's memories of conditions before the Second World war gives the same impression. 'I had seven children. I didn't stay in bed for three days. No one said to me, "you did a fine job". Soon after childbirth I would carry a three *to* (1 *to* equal 4.76 US gallons) sack to the watermill and didn't ask anybody to help me. When I was in

---

[2] Saito, *Infanticide*, 378–9.
[3] Saito, *Gender*, 23–4.
[4] Saito, *Gender* 24.
[5] Wittermans, *Pompe*, 42.
[6] Folklore studies for nineteenth-century Japan suggest that there was a taboo on working for three days after childbirth; this was because the woman was polluted. If she worked, she would harm the rice field. There was furthermore a thirty-day taboo on working. If a woman had to go out before this, she would take a small umbrella or wear a cloth on her head, so that her pollution would not affect the sacred sun. I am grateful to Dr Namihira for this information.
[7] Saga, *Silk and Straw*, 206.

bed I was given just a slice of pickle. That was enough'.[8] It does seem likely that the rate of fetal loss, which is usually very high in agrarian societies, often leading to termination of up to a third of all conceptions,[9] would be raised by such work practices. It also seems probable that it may have raised maternal mortality at childbirth and to have led, as Saito suggests, to a 'high death rate of newborn babies.'[10]

Another factor is nutrition. Recent work on the relation between food and fertility has tended to minimize the influence of nutrition. There is obviously an effect in extreme cases. 'When food supplies are so short as to cause starvation, there is little doubt that fertility is lowered.' On the other hand, once above the level of starvation, at a level of severe malnourishment or above, the influence is much less. 'When malnourishment is chronic and nutritional intake is above starvation levels, it is not clear that fertility is affected by any physiological mechanism determined by nutritional status.' Menken, Trussell and Watkins conclude that 'the differences that appear to be due to nutritional level are slight, and would explain very little of the evident variation in fertility among populations.'[11] It would appear that both English and Japanese diets were well above the level where they would drastically effect fertility.

The health status of both men and women also contributes to fertility levels. The four diseases which immediately spring to mind as likely to affect fertility are smallpox, typhus, malaria and venereal diseases. Jannetta writes that 'Smallpox also checked population growth by lowering fertility. Recent research indicates that smallpox caused significantly reduced fertility in males who survived the disease.'[12] Since the medieval period, a high proportion of the Japanese population probably had smallpox in their youth, and this may have lowered fertility. Smallpox was also to be found in England and the West. It is reported that typhus has a 'known sterilizing effect on the male'.[13] Typhus was absent in Japan until the late nineteenth century but its rise in England may have had some influence. Malaria was not common in Japan by the seventeenth century and this may be an important absence since it again is thought to affect fertility. Venereal disease on the other hand, was quite widespread, at least in some cities, and this again probably affected fertility, though by how much we do not know.[14]

---

[8] Quoted in Hane, *Rebels*, 89.
[9] Wrigley, *Population and History*, 93.
[10] Saito, *Gender*, 24; see also Laslett, *Illicit Love*, 229.
[11] Menken et al., *Nutrition*, 439,437; see also 425 and Diggory et al. (eds), *Natural Human Fertility*, 137.
[12] Jannetta, *Epidemics*, 189; cf. also Mercer, *Disease*, 154.
[13] McLaren, *Breast Feeding*, 383.
[14] For the prevalence of venereal diseases in Japan from the sixteenth to nineteenth centuries, see Jannetta in Kiple (ed.), *Disease*, 388; Thunberg, *Travels*, III, 143,199; Wittermans, *Pompe*, 116; Cortazzi, *Willis*, 60,141,144,185,244–5,257,259.

The mean age at sexual maturity for women usually varies within the range of thirteen to sixteen, for men between fourteen and seventeen. Thus Pearl found that the mean of the means for women in 169 groups was 15.7 years.[15] It can be lower, as in North America in the 1970s with a mean age for women of twelve,[16] but it is seldom much higher. Contemporaries in seventeenth-century England noted considerable variations: there were some women 'who being Married very young, Conceive not till they are Nineteen, Twenty or Twenty two or three years of Age, or more, and . . . others that Marrying betimes have Children at Fourteen or Fifteen.'[17] Mrs Sharp noted an instance of a five-year old girl who was menstruating.[18] But there was a consensus that the normal age was about fourteen. Culpeper stated that first menstruation occurred 'usually in the fourteenth year of their Age, seldom before the thirteenth, never before the twelfth.'[19] Jorden thought menstruation usually began at 'about 14 years old, and in some sooner.'[20] Mrs Sharp stated that while 'fulnes of blood and plenty of nutriment brings them down sometimes at twelve years . . . it was commonly in Climacterical or twice seven years they break forth.'[21] By law it was assumed impossible for a male to procreate under the age of eight,[22] and it was a presumption by church law that consummation of marriage could not occur under the age of fourteen for boys, twelve for girls.[23] While stressing, therefore, that there were likely to be differences not only between different regions and socio-economic levels, but also over time, it can be assumed that fourteen and sixteen are reasonable ages. This is six to ten years before women actually tended to marry. Age at sexual maturity is therefore unlikely to have had any significant effect in England. We await information on this matter for Japan, but in its absence it seems reasonable to assume that a Japanese woman marrying at between eighteen and twenty-two was fecund.

Another factor affecting fertility is breast-feeding. 'The mechanism linking the two is believed to be a neurally mediated hormonal reflex initiated by the suckling stimulus, whereby increases in the pituitary hormone prolactin act either upon the hypothalamus or directly on the ovaries to prevent ovulation.'[24] Interestingly, the levels of prolactin increases as the level of nutrition of the

[15] Nag, *Human Fertility*, 105.
[16] Laslett, *World*, 91–2.
[17] Jorden, *Weaknesses*, 57.
[18] Sharp, *Midwives Book*, 289.
[19] Culpeper, *Midwives*, 71.
[20] Jorden, *Weaknesses*, 1.
[21] Sharp, *Midwives*, 84.
[22] Burn, *Ecclesiastical Law*, I, 110.
[23] Howard, *Matrimontal*, I, 357.
[24] Wilson, *Proximate*, 219.

mother falls, hence perhaps acting as an automatic contraceptive device during periods of hardship.[25] There is evidence that the hormonal effects only last a few hours. If infants are only breast-fed infrequently, the contraceptive effect will be a good deal less than if they are fed on demand, or at least every four or five hours. 'The duration of postpartum amenorrhoea is related to the nursing pattern; the suckling duration (more minutes per episode), the suckling frequency (more frequent day and night-time feeds) and number of episodes per night are the most important factors for the delay in onset of post-partum menstruation.'[26]

It is not known exactly how much protection is given by breast-feeding and indeed it probably varies considerably. One study suggests that fertility is reduced by about twenty percent, a second that the reduction is about twenty-five per cent.[27] Historical studies suggest even higher protection. Knodel, for instance, has shown that the interval between births may vary from about twenty-four months with no breast-feeding, to about thirty-nine months with prolonged breast-feeding.[28] In relation to wet-nursing Wilson notes that 'In non-breast-feeding areas such as Flanders and Bavaria, the non-susceptible period was as short as three or four months and mothers had very high fertility.'[29] Whereas in areas where it was customary for mothers to breast-feed their own babies rather than hand them over to wet-nurses there was a non-susceptible period of ten to twelve months.[30] 'Extensive international research has shown that the *lower and upper limits of amenorrhea related to childbirth as 2 and 18 months respectively*. The average in poor, developing countries is about *10 months*. Two of these 10 months follow automatically after childbirth irrespective of breast feeding.'[31] The range is usually narrower than above. 'The net contraceptive effect of prolonged breast feeding in an underdeveloped country where people enjoy a poor (suboptimal) level of nutrition is usually 6 to 10 months, which produces a birth interval of about 30 months.'[32]

It is known that long breast-feeding is characteristic of hunter-gatherer groups which have been most successful in keeping their populations in balance with their environments. A 'distinctive feature of hunting-gathering life around the world has been the extremely heavy reliance upon lactation to feed infants. Typically hunter-gatherer babies are carried by their mothers next to a naked

[25] Benedictow, *Milky*, 36,n57.
[26] Jones in Landers and Reynolds (eds), *Fertility*, 25.
[27] Myrdal, *Asia*, II, 1429, n1; Nag, *Factors Affecting*, 78–9.
[28] Wrigley, *Population*, 347, n112.
[29] Quoted by Richard Smith in Bynum and Porter, *Companion Encyclopedia*, 1684.
[30] Wilson. *Proximate*, 220.
[31] Benedictow, *Milky*, 32.
[32] Benedictow, *Milky*, 37. Some useful figures are contained in Diggory et al. (eds), *Natural Human Fertility*, 105.

breast all day and night, and babies take milk very frequently throughout the day.' The breast-feeding goes on until after the next child is born. We are told that 'Few babies in hunter-gatherer societies are weaned before their mother becomes pregnant again: instead the typical pattern is that the mother feeds her baby until she becomes pregnant again, and then weans the child early in the next pregnancy.' This is not done consciously as a contraceptive device.[33] Yet the unintended consequence is to reduce fecundity.

In Japan numerous observers attested to the fact that almost all infants were breast-fed. 'Japanese mothers have as a rule abundant nourishment for their children, and suckle them until they are from two to five years old, and wean themselves of their own accord. . . . This long-continued suckling may be partly accounted for by the absence of any other suitable food for children in the shape of the milk of animals.'[34]

There is also evidence that the Japanese practiced unusually long breast-feeding. A survey of duration around the world suggested that twelve months of maternal breast-feeding is normal, with occasional instances of societies with up to twenty-five months (Nepal) or even twenty-eight months (Bangladesh).[35] Japan perhaps even exceeded Bangladesh. 'Up to the mid-twentieth century, it was common for rural women in particular to nurse children up to the age of three or over.'[36] One author suggests that in the middle of the nineteenth century 'Mothers suckled their children till they were six or seven years old.'[37] The comments of several visitors support this view. 'Her boy was five years old, and was still unweaned,'[38] Morse recounted how a woman was sitting in a jinrikisha 'with a large-sized child in her lap, the child holding in her hand a half-consumed sweet potato and tugging away at the maternal font for the milk to go with it.' 'Some [Japanese] show a remarkable protrusion of the incisors, and this deformation has been ascribed to the custom of children nursing so late; children nurse until they are six or seven years old and this is supposed to pull their teeth forward.'[39] 'Japanese infants are not weaned till they are two or three, sometimes not till they are five years old.'[40] Pompe gave a slightly lower age: 'The children there get the mother's, or at least human, milk for a much longer period than anywhere in Europe. Two years is the average period for breastfeeding. . . . As long as the mother has milk she will suckle her child, and I rarely heard complaints that milk was lacking.'[41]

[33] Nancy Howell in Coleman and Schofield (eds), *Population*, 178,179.
[34] Rein, *Travels*, 426; see similarly Bacon, *Japanese Girls*, 9.
[35] Dyson and Murphy, *Fertility Transition*, 426, table 5.
[36] Hanley and Yamamura, *Economic*, 244.
[37] Keizo, *Japanese Society*, 57.
[38] Bird, *Tracks*, 100.
[39] Morse, *Day*, I, 263,40.
[40] Chamberlain, *Things*, 93.
[41] Wittermans, *Pompe*, 43.

If there are long intervals between each feeding, the inhibiting effects of breast-feeding are much reduced. At first sight, we might expect Japan to be a strong example of the abandoning of infants at home while the mother went off to work. Not only was Japanese agriculture one of the most labour-intensive in the world, but women were heavily engaged in almost all stages of agricultural production. When not doing heavy farm work, they were very busy in bi-occupations, such as spinning and weaving.

One of the customs which struck visitors to Japan was the way in which infants were carried everywhere. Furthermore, breast-feeding was undertaken wherever the mothers went. Morse saw 'women nursing their children in the streets, in the shops, and even while riding in the jinrikishas.' 'Here comes a woman nursing her child in her arms as she travels along, and soon we pass another, naked to the waist, browned by the sun, leading a pack-horse, and actually holding a baby under her arm like a bundle and the baby nursing in this uncomfortable position.'[42] At noon 'everybody taking a siesta lying on the floor; children nursing from sleeping mothers.'[43] 'I was met by groups of fishermen, with their wives and children – the wife suckling her baby, and carrying the fish.' Elsewhere, 'almost every woman has at least one at the breast, and often another at the back.[44]

The Japanese custom of carrying infants was both important and universal. They seem to have been carried to the fields where their mothers worked, either by the mother or an older sibling. 'Little children are never left alone in the house, but are tied to the back of the mother or one of the older children.' 'I have never yet seen a cradle, nor have I seen a baby left alone to squall its eyes out; indeed, it is the rarest sound in Japan – a baby's cry.' Infants were 'forever riding on their mother's back or somebody's else back.'[45] There are numerous other descriptions of an institution which had a very substantial influence on Japanese mortality and fertility.[46]

The effects of all these practices has been commented on by demographers. Hanley and Yamamura note a three year period of suckling and write that 'Women who nursed that long would experience the maximum postpartum amenorrhoea, which would explain why there were so few children born within one year of each other.'[47] More recently Saito has written that 'Tokugawa Japan's . . . was a breast-fed population and this must have kept the natural fertility level lower than the theoretically expected level.'[48]

---

[42] Morse, *Day*, I, 262,95.
[43] Morse, *Day*, I, 60; for a picture of this, see Morse, *Day*, I, 176.
[44] Alcock, *Tycoon*, I, 452,82.
[45] Morse, *Day*, I, 351,115,41.
[46] For other descriptions of this customs of carrying infants, see Morse, *Day*, I, 10,176; Bacon, *Japanese Girls*, 6; Alcock, *Tycoon*, I, 122; Griffis, *Mikado*, 356.
[47] Hanley and Yamamura, *Economic*, 244.
[48] Saito, *Infanticide*, 380, n3.

When we turn to the west, it would appear that much of continental Europe, at least in the cities and among the middle classes and above, was characterized by widespread wet-nursing, from at least the sixteenth century. Evidence in relation to France, Italy, Germany and Flanders is now abundant.[49] The major exception on mainland Europe was Holland where, as Schama has documented, maternal breast-feeding was the norm in the sixteenth to eighteenth centuries.[50]

England was also somewhat exceptional. Bartholomaeus Anglicus in about 1230 wrote that children were breast-fed by their mothers.[51] There are also hints of maternal breast-feeding in literary sources of the fourteenth century.[52] The evidence becomes more abundant from the sixteenth century and has been analysed in great detail by Valerie Fildes who has shown that wet nursing was to be found among some wealthy families, particularly in London, during the sixteenth to eighteenth centuries. On the other hand, she concludes in general that 'The impression gained over years of study is that the great majority of British infants were breastfed at home by their mothers.'[53] Even in relation to the most wet-nurse prone of groups, wealthy London citizens in the seventeenth century, the work of Roger Finlay suggests 'that the practice was limited to a handful of particularly wealthy parishes'.[54] Demographic studies based on reconstituting populations suggest a pattern which is consistent with breast feeding by the mother.[55] For the early modern period, wet-nursing 'seems unlikely to have involved more than a tiny minority of urban infants . . . an untypical minority of families.' 'Most infants were nursed at home, and by their mothers.'[56]

As to the duration of breast-feeding, Fildes using literary sources such as medical texts and diaries shows that the age recommended by writers was 21–4 months in the sixteenth to seventeenth century, but dropped to ten months in the later eighteenth century. The mean average actual age was 14.5 months in the sixteenth century, 13.75 months in the seventeenth, and 8 months in the eighteenth.[57] There is much literary advice and diary evidence for the length of breast-feeding in England to support her views.[58] These figures also fit well with

---

[49] See for example Ariès, *Centuries*, 374; Hunt, *Parents*, 100–1; Flandrin, Families, 203ff; Fildes, *Wet Nursing*, 122; Flinn, *European*, 40; Stone, *Sex and Marriage*, 426ff; De Mause (ed.), *Childhood*, 185; Goody, *Family*; Richard Smith in Bynum and Porter (eds), *Companion Encyclopedia*, 1684.

[50] Schama, *Embarrassment*, 538–40.

[51] Anglicus, *Properties*, I, 303 (spelling partly modernized).

[52] For example, Chaucer, 'Reeves Tale', *Works*, 57.

[53] Fildes, *Wet Nursing*, 98.

[54] Wilson, *Proximate*, 205.

[55] Wilson, *Proximate*, 223; McLaren, *Breast Feeding*, 381,387.

[56] Wrightson, *Society*, 108.

[57] Fildes, *Breasts*, 325ff; for other evidence, see Flinn, *European*, 32.

[58] For example, Culpeper, *Midwives*, 214–5; Sharp, *The Midwives Book*, 367,174–5.

recent analyses of the phenomenon as suggested by studies which link baptisms and marriages. On the basis of sixteen individual parishes in the sixteenth to eighteenth centuries, Wilson found intervals between live births which, depending on factors such as 'the frequency of suckling and the amount of supplementary food given to infants', would be associated with fourteen to eighteen months of breastfeeding. Wilson concludes that breastfeeding 'is unlikely to have been less than a year, and was probably somewhat longer.'[59]

As regards the frequency of breast-feeding it would seem that the majority opinion among professionals was that babies should be fed on demand:

> As for the feeding schedule, few writers advised a strict routine. The child should be fed when he was hungry. Most advisers showed a compassionate attitude to the baby, urging adults to heed the child's cry. Some sterner voices pointed out that babies who were given the breast whenever they cried were 'almost continually sucking, and never satisfied', but the mainstream of advice to mothers was to satisfy their babies.[60]

Fildes surveys the evidence and concludes that 'the normal procedure in Britain, France and some other parts of Europe before the mid-eighteenth century was to feed infants on demand.'[61]

The comparatively low level of fertility in England led demographers to believe that some form of family limitation must have been practised.[62] There is evidence that the idea of contraception was not unknown. Place referred to the importance of 'Aristotle's Complete Master-Piece' a well-known book of advice containing information on intimate female matters including contraception.[63] In the middle of the eighteenth century the popular *Whole Duty of Man* asked its readers whether they had 'taken anything to prevent conception or cause miscarriages.'[64] In the later sixteenth century a curate was accused, among other things, of teaching birth control to unmarried persons.[65] One can go back to Lollard tracts in the fifteenth century and even earlier references to similar practices.[66] It is less easy to know what, exactly, was available and how often contraceptive methods were used.

There are various mentions of herbs and potions in Himes' classic work though we do not have many explicit references to their use for early modern

[59] Wilson, *Proximate*, 224.
[60] Crawford, *Suckling*, 31.
[61] Fildes in Diggory et al. (eds), *Natural Human Fertility*, 123, and Fildes, *Wet Nursing*, 118–20.
[62] For example, Wrigley, '*Family Limitation*'.
[63] Place, *Autobiography*, 45.
[64] *Whole Duty of Man*, 495.
[65] Marchant, *Church Under Law*, 222, n4.
[66] Du Boulay, *Ambition*, 106; Himes, *Contraception*, 161,163,172.

England.[67] 'One emetic designed to purge the desire for intercourse consisted of radish root, agarick, and saram boiled in barley water, to be taken when cool.' Other ingredients included 'rue calamine, castor oil, endive, sallow flowers, woodbine, cucumbers.'[68] However, most of the remedies associated with child-bearing were designed to increase, rather than lower fertility, though Lilly's adopted son was said to have sold astrological sigils at four shillings each, for use as contraceptives to servant girls.[69]

There is some evidence of mechanical contraceptives. There may have been some knowledge of a female tampon or pessary supposedly first described by Fallopius in 1564 as a protection against syphilis. We are told that 'A typical pessary to be inserted into the vagina was composed of bitter almonds blanched and ground. Another pessary used castoreum mixed in rue and the ground roots of lilies and nenufar.'[70] But such pessaries may also have been intended for medical use, or even to increase fertility. Thus, in the middle of the seventeenth century Culpeper explained that 'The Runnet of an Hare mixed in a little Cotten, and put up the womb as a Pessary, and remaining there a day, is an excellent remedy. But let it be done presently upon the stopping of the Men-struis, and tied up in a linnen cloth, and a string tied to it, that so you may draw it out again.'[71] There were also various ointments to put on the penis. Even though they may have had little direct contraceptive effect, as Schnucker points out, 'The use of such juices, oils, and ointments probably were effective to some extent, for it would be difficult to maintain an erection while the penis was bathed in a cool liquid, particularly, a slightly anaesthetic one.'[72]

Even the purpose of the male condom, or contraceptive sheath, is not abso-lutely clear. The condom was supposedly first described by Fallopius as a linen shield to give protection against venereal disease, and there are examples of its use in the seventeenth century.[73] Condoms were improved by substituting animal skin (probably dried gut of a sheep) for linen and were described by Casanova as 'the little shields which the English have invented to keep the fair sex from worrying.'[74] James Boswell used them as much to try to protect himself against venereal disease as to protect his partner.[75] They were advertized for sale in London in the later eighteenth century.[76] McLaren gives some further de-

[67] Himes, *Contraception.*
[68] Schnucker, *Elizabethan*, 657.
[69] Thomas, *Religion*, 188–9,635; a 'sigil' is a seal or signet.
[70] Schnucker, *Elizabethan*, 657.
[71] Culpeper, *Midwives*, 97.
[72] Schnucker, *Elizabethan*, 657.
[73] Himes, *Contraception*, 188ff; Bloch, *Sexual Life*, 312.
[74] Quoted in Bloch, *Sexual Life*, 313.
[75] Boswell, *London Journal*, 49; *In Search of a Wife*, 150,152,153.
[76] Hibbert, *The English*, 398.

scription of their use in the eighteenth century.[77] It seems likely that it was not until the 1850s that 'the basic processes of rubber manufacturing had been worked out and the manufacture of "questionable rubber goods" was booming at least in the United States.'[78] If we take all these herbal and mechanical methods together, it would seem that they were little used and of limited effectiveness before the late nineteenth century.

When we turn to Japan, the evidence suggests a similar absence of any effective contraceptives. The major works on the subject by Taeuber, Hanley and Yamamura, Saito, Smith and others do not mention any widespread use. Hanley and Yamamura remark that 'After a child was born or aborted, women often tried to prevent becoming pregnant again. It was thought effective to drink a bowlful of salt water every night before going to bed. Urinating immediately after intercourse was supposed to prevent conception.'[79] The latter method was also believed to be effective in England.[80] Another hint, true or untrue, comes from a remark that 'The Chinese and Japanese girls, in the houses of prostitution, simply use rounds of oiled silk paper, which they insert in the womb, to cover the head of the duct.'[81] There also seems to have been some reliance on a variant of the rhythm method. 'There was a folklore belief that if a couple avoided intercourse in certain periods, they would not have children. A man called Ogino, basing himself on this idea, did surveys which showed the idea was correct and hence the Ogino method was originated. The idea was to avoid the 15 days from the commencement of menstruation. After that one could have intercourse. My mother's generation used this method.'[82] Another curious allusion was made in 1926 to the fact that 'Marriage between lepers is allowed – sterilization by vasectomy is practised by request'. The operation was 'a bloodless one and finished in twenty minutes.'[83] One wonders how recent and widespread such an operation was in Japan. It would seem that few effective contraceptives were used in either Japan or England. What then could couples do to avoid conception?

The most extreme action was to avoid or limit sexual intercourse within marriage. There is some evidence of an anecdotal kind that a few people did this, a method which had been ascribed to the medieval Italian peasantry.[84] Stories were told of people who came to a bad end as a consequence. 'Mr Bonham's wife

---

[77] McLaren, *Birth Control*, 21ff.

[78] Petersen, *Malthus*, 204; cf. also Mumford, *Technics*, 260.

[79] Hanley and Yamamura, *Economic*, 234.

[80] Garfield, *Wandering Whore*, 12ff.

[81] *Untrodden Fields of Anthropology*, 101.

[82] Emiko Namihira, personal communication; Osamu Saito informs me that 'Ogino's method was first advocated in a woman's magazine in the late 1920s.'

[83] Wellington, *Report*, 29.

[84] Coulton, *Medieval Village*, 244.

had two children at one birth, the first time; and he being troubled at it travelled and was absent seven years.' After his return 'she was delivered of seven children at one birth'[85] To avoid offspring the alternatives were to live apart, or take protective action. There were herbal remedies such as the drink which a doctor recommended to quench sexual desire.[86] Or one could try sewing up one's blankets to prevent temptation as in the ballad in the Pepysian collection titled 'The discontented bride; or a brief account of Will the baker who sew'd himself up in a blanket every night going to bed, for fear of enlarging his family.'[87]

Such total abstention, however, is unlikely to have been widespread partly because it went completely against Christian teaching concerning 'conjugal duties'. For instance the German theologian Bullinger warned that some people, fearing surplus children, 'wil not geve himselfe to labour.'[88] It was also contrary to desire and the 'passion between the sexes.' It might, however, be a method used later in marriage. As a Danish vicar noted in 1772 'moreover some married couples are living in abstinence because they wish not to have more children.'[89] If one's wife died, another option was to marry an older woman. Thomas Wright in the eighteenth century described how after his first wife, the mother of seven children, died, 'some people advised me to marry an old woman that would have no more children.'[90]

A method to detect the widespread and effective use of contraception in historical populations was developed in the 1950s by French demographers. It involved looking at the gaps between successive children, particularly the last few, and to see how far this deviated from 'natural' fertility. Using this method, it has now been established that certain groups in Europe began to use some form of contraception from the later seventeenth century. The citizens of Geneva were among the first, and aristocratic families in France at about the same time.[91] Other areas such as parts of Denmark, Norway, Spain and much of France followed in the eighteenth century.[92] The method that was used seems to have been *coitus interruptus*. This is a method which is known in many societies, even the simplest.[93] We are told that 'a small number of texts . . . suggest the possibility that by the early fourteenth century the practice of *coitus interruptus* had spread quite widely among married couples in parts of western Europe.'[94] It was used to a limited extent in sixteenth century

---

[85] Aubrey, *Natural History*, 71.
[86] Cogan, *Haven*, 246.
[87] Pepys Ballad Collection, vol.iv, 119 (Magdalene College, Cambridge).
[88] Translated in Coverdale, *Matrimony*, 26.
[89] Steensberg, *Fertility and Esteem*, 43.
[90] Wright, *Autobiography*, 144.
[91] Laslett, *World*, 237; Hawthorn, *Fertility*, 36,38.
[92] Lofgren, *Family*, 36; Daedalus, *Historical*, 531; Drake, *Norway*, 70.
[93] See Nag, *Human Fertility*, 216, table 70.
[94] Biller, *Birth-Control*, 20.

Germany,[95] and was clearly known in England.[96] Indeed, there were those who thought that it was quite common. Culpeper in the middle of the seventeenth century suggested that *coitus interruptus* ('Onan's sin') was widespread; 'for this god slew him. I believe God hath been more merciful to many in *England* in the same case.'[97] There is some evidence of *coitus interruptus* in eighteenth-century sources.[98] It is also clear that *coitus interruptus* was known and used effectively over much of Europe in the nineteenth century to bring down fertility. 'In the West almost the entire fertility transition took place by means of traditional methods like coitus interruptus. In fact, in most of the West the distribution and advertisement of birth control methods was illegal until after World War II.'[99]

However, when we look at the many studies of English population, it now appears that *coitus interruptus* was not used widely enough before 1850 to have any discernible effects on fertility. One of the earliest family reconstitutions, that of Colyton in Devon, seemed to show the distinctive pattern of birth control.[100] A few other local studies also seemed to reveal some birth control.[101] Yet subsequent research on English parishes has not detected this pattern.[102] In the *Population History of England* Wrigley and Schofield only mention *coitus interruptus* once, in passing, and hardly consider birth control before the late nineteenth century. It seems likely that while there was some use of contraception among the aristocracy from the later seventeenth century,[103] in general its use was very limited before the nineteenth century. Most were probably in the position of Thomas Wright who admitted that having many children added to his difficulties, 'but as this is the common lot of humanity, and we cannot help it, we must endeavour to be as content as we possibly can.'[104]

When we turn to Japan the evidence from the growing number of family reconstitutions points in the same direction as that for England. Smith found that the study of age-specific marital fertility showed that 'the tests devised by Louis Henry for family limitation did not yield a positive result', for the shape of its fertility curve is of the kind usually associated with the absence of such limitation.[105] Hanley and Yamamura likewise note that 'We have found no mention of *coitus interruptus* in Japan.' and concludes that 'There is no evidence

---

[95] Wrigley, '*Family Limitation*', 105, n1, citing Helleiner.
[96] For a good description of 'withdrawal' in the early sixteenth century, see T.Wright in the *Camden Society* (1843), 97.
[97] Culpeper, *Midwives*, 70.
[98] McLaren, *Birth Control*, 25ff.
[99] Livi-Bacci, *Population*, 169, n32.
[100] Wrigley, '*Family Limitation*'.
[101] For example, Jones, *Population*, 20,23.
[102] Flinn, *European*, 45–6; see also Wilson, *Proximate*, 206.
[103] Stone, *Sex and Marriage*, 415ff; Flinn, *European*, 45.
[104] Wright, *Autobiography*, 146.
[105] Smith, *Nakahara*, 14.

that there was widespread knowledge of any effective birth control measures other than infanticide and abortion.'[106] It is worth noting that this tendency to ignore or avoid contraception is still a powerful force in Japan. As Coleman has pointed out, Japan is the only advanced industrial country which hardly makes use of modern contraceptive technology.[107]

A consideration of the pressures determining whether a woman conceived after intercourse suggests that in England and even more so Japan, long and frequent breast-feeding by the mother was an important factor. By lengthening birth intervals it reduced fertility quite considerably. On the other hand, in neither case does contraception appear to have been important before the later nineteenth century. This leaves us with one final area where fertility could be influenced, namely the circumstances of a woman if she became pregnant.

---

[106] Hanley and Yamamura, *Economic*, 315,215.
[107] Coleman, *Family Planning*, 3.

19

Abortion and Infanticide

A combination of lowered natural fertility, late age at marriage and the possibility for women to remain unmarried is enough to explain the unusual English fertility pattern. Yet a puzzle still remains in the case of Japan. On the one hand, marriage was more or less universal for women and the age at marriage somewhat lower, and on the other hand, the achieved fertility in Japan was, in certain periods, even lower than that in England. Having considered 'exposure to intercourse' and 'exposure to conception' variables, the only remaining area where control could be exercised was in relation to 'gestation' variables, that is to say in practices which would affect the period between conception and a safe and protected birth. This takes us to the controversial topics of abortion and infanticide.

Abortion is a contentious and difficult topic to study. One problem is caused by the various legal and moral attitudes towards it. A number of studies have shown that many societies see little wrong with abortion and practice it extensively.[1] Both Plato and Aristotle approved of abortion in certain circumstances. In the ancient Germanic laws, abortion practised on another was a crime, but not when practised on oneself.[2]

The legal and moral situation in England is the product of a long and complex history. The Jewish tradition sees abortion and infanticide as 'heathen abominations'.[3] This may have been absorbed into Christianity and then become mixed with the more tolerant attitude stemming from the Germanic and Greek traditions. The result was a set of contradictions.

---

[1] Westermarck, *Moral*, I, 414; Davis and Blake, *Analytic Framework*, 229; Nag, *Human Fertility*, 219ff (table 73); Hawthorn, *Fertility*, 47.

[2] Sumner, *Folk Ways*, 315.

[3] Sumner, *Folk Ways*, 315.

Part of the complex history is summarized by Westermarck:

> 'Prevention of birth', says Tertullian, 'is a precipitation of murder; nor does it
> matter whether one take away a life when formed, or drive it away while forming.
> He also is a man who is about to be one. Even every fruit already exists in its seed.'
> St. Augustine . . . makes a distinction between an embryo which has already been
> formed, and an embryo as yet unformed. From the creation of Adam, he says, it
> appears that the body is made before the soul. Before the embryo has been
> endowed with a soul it is an *embryo informatus*, and its artificial abortion is to be
> punished with a fine only; but the *embryo formatus* is an animate being, and to
> destroy it is nothing less than murder, a crime punishable with death. This
> distinction between an animate and inanimate fetus was embodied both in Canon
> and Justinian law, and passed subsequently into various lawbooks. And a woman
> who destroyed her animate embryo was punished with death.

The situation was further complicated by the idea that the *embryo formatus*,
being a person with an immortal soul, needed baptism. St. Fulgentius said that
these aborted fetuses would be treated 'with everlasting punishment in eternal
fire', not through any sin of their own, but because of original sin. Later,
however, St Thomas Aquinas suggested the possibility of salvation for an infant
who died before birth.[4]

The situation under English law was both complicated and subject to change.
It appears that for most of the period under consideration, abortion was not a
felony unless by attempting to procure it the mother died of the injuries. If the
fetus in the womb died, it could not be certain that its death had been caused by
the attempted abortion and in any case it was not *in rerum natura*, the natural
world. Hence abortion was not a crime. It was only brought to the ecclesiastical
courts in relation to cases of bastardy.[5]

This may help to explain the virtual absence of cases of abortion in English
secular courts. Another reason why it may have been very uncommon to pros-
ecute is the difficulty of proving that an abortion has been artificially procured.
One reason for this is the very high rate of 'natural' abortion in all societies.
Before considering the evidence for artificial abortion in England, we need to
have some sense of the 'natural' abortion rates.

It has been reckoned that in modern populations with satisfactory conditions
of health and living, roughly ten to fifteen per cent of all pregnancies will
terminate in spontaneous abortion.[6] Although some 'developing' societies have
similar rates[7] it is likely that many also have higher ones. It is impossible to know

---

[4] Westermarck, *Moral*, I, 416,417.
[5] Hale, *Pleas*, I, 429–30,433; see also Burn, *Justice*, II, 592; Burn, *Ecclesiastical Law*, I, 122; Blackstone, *Commentaries*, IV, pt.1, 198, n42.
[6] Studies quoted in Myrdal, *Asian*, II, 1437; Roberts, *Hygiene*, 272.
[7] cf. Ardener, *Divorce*, 51.

what rates were customary in early modern England. One historian has guessed that they were 'well over ten per cent in past centuries' on the grounds that they must have been a good deal higher than the seven to eleven per cent of all pregnancies terminating in spontaneous abortion in England in 1950, and 2.3 percent in stillbirths.[8] Two, admittedly fallible, pieces of evidence bear on this problem. One comes from the bills of mortality, which give the cause of death. Graunt estimated from these bills that 'the abortives and stillborn are about the twentieth part [fifty per thousand] of those that are christened.'[9] These would only later be well formed fetuses and this is also a problem likely to affect the other source, namely the handful of parish registers which noted stillbirths and abortions.

One register which records 'abortions' is Hawkshead in Lancashire between 1581 and 1710. It is estimated that roughly one in twenty births were stillborn, with rates varying from sixteen to ninety-six per thousand, as compared to fifteen per thousand in England and Wales in 1967.[10] In Ashton-under-Lyne, the parish register gives burials of abortions, and in 1623 these reached their highest figure of seven per cent.[11] Stillbirth rates in certain hamlets of the Cumberland parish of Greystoke in the late sixteenth and early seventeenth centuries were around nine per cent of all births.[12] Again these figures would only apply to mature stillbirths. Mrs Cellier, in her plan to set up a hospital at the end of the seventeenth century, recorded that because of unskilled midwifery many fetuses were lost: 'That within the Space of twenty years last past, above six thousand women have died in child-bed, more than thirteen thousand children have been born abortive, and about five thousand chrysome infants have been buried within the weekly bills of mortality.'[13]

The real problem is that spontaneous abortions in the first few months would not be registered and yet this is often a period of particular vulnerability. Landers quotes figures from Leridon which suggest that 'Perhaps 8 percent are lost in the first four to seven weeks, and less than 1 percent after the 20th week.'[14] A popular book of anonymous advice under the pseudonym 'Aristotle' speculated on the problem: 'Q. Why do women easily miscarry when they are first with child, viz, the first, second, or third month? A. as apples and pears easily fall at first, because the knots and ligaments are weak, so it is with a child in the womb. Q. Why is it hard to miscarry in the 3rd, 4th, 5th or 6th months? A. Because then

---

[8] Hair, *Bridal Pregnancy*, 235, n10.

[9] Quoted in Forbes (ed.), *Aldgate*, 64.

[10] Schofield, *Perinatal Mortality*, 13.

[11] Laslett, *World*, 130.

[12] Armstrong, *Birth*, 36.

[13] Quoted in Clark, *Working Women*, 274.

[14] A.G.Hill in Landers and Reynolds (eds), *Fertility*, 154.

the ligaments are stronger and well fortified.'[15] This was recognized by midwives and doctors. For instance Culpeper wrote that 'women are most subject to suffer abortion or miscarriage in the two first months of their conception.' Women who normally menstruated heavily 'suffer abortion [i.e. miscarriage] upon every slight occasion.'[16]

> Every pregnant woman is more or less in danger of abortion. This should be guarded against with the greatest care, as it not only weakens the constitution, but renders the woman liable to the same misfortune afterwards. Abortion may happen at any period of pregnancy, but it is most common the second or third month. Sometimes, however, it happens in the fourth or fifth. If it happens within the first month, it is usually called a false conception; if after the seventh month, the child may often be kept alive by proper care.[17]

Another difficulty for the historian, and an indicative one, is that the terminology made no distinction between 'natural' and 'artificial' abortion. This is probably one of the reasons why Westermarck uses the term 'feticide' to describe deliberate abortion.[18] As one seventeenth-century author described it, 'They call abortion the sudden exclusion of the child, already formed, and alive, before the perfect maturity thereof.'[19] It was synonymous with miscarriage, meaning 'when a woman is delivered of hir childe before hir time.'[20] Combined with the high natural wastage rates, this semantic confusion makes it impossible to estimate any sort of rate of artificially induced abortions in early modern England. We just have tantalizing hints. 'One in five of the men who tried to conceal the pregnancy of their sexual partners' suggested using some kind of abortion in certain seventeenth-century church court proceedings.[21] This is obviously a very biased sample. John Graunt assumed that it was usual for women in cases of fornication to use abortion.[22] In the eighteenth century, Swift wrote a satire in which he suggested that surplus children should be eaten. One of the advantages would be that 'it will prevent those voluntary abortions, and that horrid practice of women murdering their Bastard Children, alas! too frequent among us.'[23] Buchan thought that though dangerous, it was relatively common. 'Every mother who procures an abortion does it at the hazard of her

[15] Aristotle, *Works*, 264–5.
[16] Culpeper, *Midwives*, 111,79.
[17] Buchan, *Domestic*, 531.
[18] Westermarck, *Moral*, I, 413.
[19] Willoughby, *Midwifery*, 263.
[20] Boorde, *Breviarie*, fols.7v–8; cf. also Culpeper, *Midwives*, 79.
[21] Quaife, *Wanton*, 118.
[22] Graunt, *Natural Observations*, 103.
[23] Reynolds, *British Pamphleteers*, 228.

life; yet there are not a few who run this risk merely to prevent the trouble of bearing and bringing up children.'[24]

All we can do is gain a feeling for the kind of situation in which abortion would be used and for what purposes.[25] The first thing to note here is that by the eighteenth century, at least, there do seem to have been professional abortionists available, or those who gave advice: 'criminal advertisements' for the 'relieving' of women appeared in the papers, and a 'certain White living in St. Paul's Churchyard practised abortion as his calling.'[26] Buchan referred to 'Those wretches who daily advertise their assistance to women in this business' who deserved 'the most severe of all human punishments.'[27]

It had long been envisaged in English law, that 'potions' might be given to women 'to destroy the child within her'. Culpeper gave various herbal remedies to bring on menstruation, but he warned midwives, 'Give not any of these to any that is with Child, least you turn Murderers.'[28] Boorde also stated that there were certain laxatives which caused 'abortion' and that 'light women', that is immoral women, might use them.[29] The danger was formally recognized in midwives' certificates; one for 1722 included the clause 'Item, you shall not give Counsel, nor Minister any herb, Medicine, potion, or any other thing to any woman being with Child, thereby to destroy or cast out what she goeth withall before her time.'[30]

It is likely that there were a number of known abortifacients. A recent article suggested that hemp was 'grown quite extensively in the eastern counties and was called "The Devil's Flower" and was used to procure miscarriages.'[31] However, the most important seems to have been savin, or juniper. According to an authority on abortion referred to by Bloch, 'English women use mainly Juniperus Sabina, the needles of the yew';[32] 'Savin is strongly poisonous; it possesses emmenogogic properties, and hence was a common means of procuring abortion.'[33] The same drug was good for helping with menstrual disorders, but in a large dose when a woman was with child would cause a miscarriage. Dryden in 1693 wrote 'Help her to make Manslaughter; let her bleed. And never want for

---

[24] Buchan, *Domestic*, 531.

[25] For some general remarks and literary evidence for the eighteenth century, see McLaren, *Birth Control*, 31–6.

[26] Cited in Bloch, *Sexual Life*, 313.

[27] Buchan, *Domestic*, 531.

[28] Culpeper, *Midwives*, 78.

[29] Boorde, *Breviarie*, 8.

[30] In *Local Population Studies*, 4, (Spring 1970).

[31] *Country Fair*, March 1970, 29; Hilda Martin tells me that another favourite was 'penny royal'.

[32] Bloch, *Sexual Life*, 313.

[33] *Oxford English Dictionary*, 'savin'. 'Emmenagogic' means to have the power to cause menstrual discharge.

Savin at her need.'[34] 'Savin' continued to be used into the nineteenth century.[35] Blackstone refers to the allegations of the use of a '*decoction* of savin' and of 'oil of savin' in two of the most important early-nineteenth-century trials concerning abortion.[36]

Another method seems to have been to batter the body physically, as described in two bastardy cases in the ecclesiastical courts. In one case a girl was entreated 'to bruise her body thereby to destroy the child.'[37] In a sixteenth-century case, a priest's pregnant mistress 'tightened her girdle and performed exercises with a rolling pin in order to destroy the fetus.'[38] Finally, there were a number of pessaries or suppositories which were 'apparently to induce enough vaginal bleeding so that the fetus would be flushed out of the womb.'[39]

In the absence of effective contraception, abortion was quite widely used to try to avert the consequences of illicit sexual relations. However, there is no evidence that abortion within marriage was widespread. Most of the writers on women's matters stressed the demand for measures to overcome barrenness, rather than any pressure to limit families.

Attention was drawn to the phenomenon of abortion in Japan by Taeuber. She cites Professor Honjo who believed that 'abortion served to limit family size in Edo, Osaka and Kyoto', while infanticide was the preferred method among peasants. She quotes a late Tokugawa account as follows:

> Many women become pregnant, but they can not nurse their children. They murder their babies or procure abortion. By travelling around our country, I know this custom prevails. It is a very terrible fact that in a village consisting of ten houses, every year over two babies are killed. . . . In Chugoku, Shikoku, and Kyushu abortion is universal. Even in the provinces of Dewa and Oshu alone, every year about sixteen or seventeen thousand babies are killed.

She cites a proclamation of 1667 by the fourth shogun who 'forbade the use of signs to indicate the availability of abortion facilities. Punishment for violation was banishment from the city. This regulation pertained only to the city of Edo; elsewhere proscriptions were local or non-existent.' From the evidence, Taeuber thought that abortions were 'countless'. 'Many medicines were sold quite openly until 1667' which were 'predominantly abortifaciants, either *oroshi-kusuri*, "putting-down medicine", or *jiyu-gan*. "freeing capsule". . . .

---

[34] Quoted in *OED*, 'savin'.

[35] Smith, *People's Health*, 75. According to Hibbert, savin was popularly known as 'Cover Shame' (Hibbert, *The English*, 398).

[36] Blackstone, *Commentaries*, IV, pt.1,198, n42.

[37] Quaife, *Wanton*, 118.

[38] Houlbrooke, *Church*, 160.

[39] Schnucker, *Elizabethan*, 658,659.

Mechanical methods of abortion were more common than medicinal in both ancient and Tokugawa times.'[40] More recently Hanley and Yamamura have added to the references on the subject. 'Many books were published during the Tokugawa period on methods of abortion, the earliest dated 1692. A common method seems to have been to apply continuous pressure to the belly or to vibrate it until abortion was induced. The practice of inserting a stick-like object into the head of the uterus had been perfected by the mid-seventeenth century and was used by professionals – usually midwives – from this time on.' Furthermore, medicines were available. 'Many names exist for the medicines used to induce miscarriages, which were sold as *gekkei yaku* (menstrual medicine) A common medicine was a mercurial compound. . . . The most frequently mentioned plant with the reputation of inducing menstruation was the *goshitsu*, also known as *inokozuchi*, a member of the burdock family.'[41] Thunberg noted that 'The root of the *Dracontium Polyphyllum* is used by dissolute women, for the purpose of procuring abortion.'[42] Elsewhere Hanley and Yamamura tell us that to try to induce abortion 'Okayama women used to cauterize the navel with moxa, or brew the seeds of the white morning glory and drink the resulting tea. They tried eating carp before they were two months pregnant, and they vigorously massaged the belly.' During the early nineteenth century 'Kagawa Mitsusada published extremely detailed instructions on how to perform an abortion . . . specifying among other things that the procedure was not to be used on women more than three months pregnant.'[43] More recently Hanley has written that 'descriptions of abortion, abortionists, and the effects of this practice are abundant, this form of birth control is known to have been widely practiced throughout Japan. Abortion was an undesirable practice but was not a "sin".'[44]

Alcock wrote that 'Abortion in the unmarried is said, upon good authority, to be not infrequent, and there are female professors of the art'[45] and a little earlier Willis noted that 'If a prostitute becomes with child abortion is procured about the fifth month, by means of drugs or instruments introduced into the uterus by experts.'[46] A detailed account of abortion methods was given by Pompe:

> In Nagasaki, there were two old women who were notorious because of their way of practising abortus by means of a lance which they were able to handle quite well.

[40] Taeuber, *Population*, 29,30,31,29.

[41] Hanley and Yamamura, *Economic*, 233–4.

[42] Thunberg, *Travels*, III, 163.

[43] Hanley and Yamamura, *Economic*, 234.

[44] Hanley in *Cambridge History*, 4, 700; for a further summary of evidence of widespread abortion in Tokugawa village studies, see Hanely and Wolf (eds), *Family*, 5–6.

[45] Alcock, *Tycoon*, I, 122.

[46] Cortazzi, *Willis*, 245.

To these and similar individuals, people in Japan sometimes go for help, and I must say that it is specifically the wealthier ones, those who would be quite able to support their children, who most frequently do this. Another woman achieved the same effect with live mercury; she did not have such a large practice because the results were not always successful.[47]

Another method was described by Nagatsuka, when Oshina dies as a result of a botched self-abortion; 'perhaps the bacillus had been on the winter cherry root she had used to break through into her uterus.'[48]

The difference of attitude as between Japanese and Europeans was shown by Pompe:

As soon as I had sufficient proof of the actual existence of these crimes, I discussed this with the authorities in charge, but they found my complaints exaggerated. It is true that murder was outlawed in the country, but then the victim would be alive first, and an unborn fruit was not considered to be a living individual as yet. It belonged to the mother, they said, as part of her body, and she was free to do what she wanted with that body. I did not succeed in bringing about any improvement in this state of affairs, and both ill-famed women still carry on a thriving practice as 'famous abortionists'.[49]

Further evidence of the importance of abortion is provided by the recent history of family planning in Japan. Kingsley Davis noted that while Europeans achieved their demographic transition by contraception and notably *coitus interruptus*, 'The resort to abortion has been the leading cause of probably the fastest drop in the birth rate ever exhibited by an entire nation.'[50] A village study showed that in the year 1952, for instance, of the registered hospital cases, at least 'forty-three per cent of local pregnancies ended in abortion.'[51] Currently, abortion is one of the major forms of 'family planning' in Japan, despite the fact that 'fewer Japanese approve of the use of abortion than do Americans.' There was in the 1970s a rate of about 84 abortions for every thousand women of childbearing age, one of the highest rates in the world. In some years, pregnancies 'were more likely to end in abortions than in live births.'[52] The ability of the Japanese to control their fertility through abortion is shown by what happened in 1966. In that year, when it was unlucky to have children (the year of fire-horse), the births declined by 25 per cent. This was accomplished 'largely

[47] Wittermans, *Pompe*, 39 n4.
[48] Nagatsuka, *Soil*, 28.
[49] Wittermans, *Pompe*, 39 n4.
[50] Davis, *Change*, 345.
[51] Beardsley et al., *Village*, 335.
[52] Coleman, *Family Planning*, 68,4.

through induced abortion.'[53] A recent comparison of abortion rates in Japan and America shows that over half of pregnancies are terminated by abortion in Japan, while in America roughly a quarter are so terminated.[54]

Although it seems likely that the literature has over-stressed abortion, it might be safe to assume that combined with infanticide it lowered the birth rate by between two and five births per thousand. The importance of abortion fluctuated over time and region, rising in certain cities and among the middling groups of artisans and merchants, perhaps being far less important in villages and among the hard-pressed farming wives who may have let the child come to term and then used the last method available, infanticide. The difference between the cities, where abortion was the principal method, and rural areas, where infanticide was favoured, was observed in a study by Bonsen Takahashi.[55]

There was probably considerable regional variation over Japan. Even neighbouring villages might have very different rates, as is suggested by the figures for the four adjacent communities studied by Beardsley and his collaborators.[56] There were also temporal fluctuations. It seems likely that during the rapid population boom of the seventeenth and late nineteenth and early twentieth centuries, abortions were much less frequent. During the latter period, they were strongly forbidden by the Meiji and subsequent governments along with infanticide, and this probably led to a sharp drop in abortions among a population as law-abiding as the Japanese. The use of abortion rose again rapidly from the 1940s when Japan's fertility was dramatically reduced. In general then, abortion has been one of the major tools to adjust fertility rates in Japan.

Like abortion, infanticide is and was very widespread in many parts of the world. In a survey of the subject, Westermarck gave instances from all types of civilization. He outlined some of the motives at the start of the twentieth century: 'Among a great number of uncivilised peoples it is usual to kill an infant if it is a bastard, or if its mother dies, or if it is deformed or diseased, or if it for some reason or other is regarded as an unlucky child.' In some societies 'it is the custom that, if a woman gives birth to twins, one or both of them are destroyed.' Or again, 'Among some peoples mothers are said to kill their new-born infants on account of the trouble of rearing them, or the consequent loss of beauty.' Westermarck continues that 'In another respect, also, the long suckling-time is an inducement to infanticide; among certain Australian tribes an infant is killed immediately on birth "when the mother is, or thinks she is, unable to rear it owing to there being a young child whom she is still feeding".'[57]

[53] D.Eleanor Westney and Samuel Coleman in Kodansha, *Encyclopaedia*, 'Population', 225.
[54] Roger V. Short in Diggory et al. (eds), *Natural Human Fertility*, 21.
[55] Cited in Nakamura and Miyamato, *Population*, 250.
[56] Beardsley et al. *Village*, 335.
[57] Westermarck, *Moral*, I, 394,395,398–9,399.

Birdsell suggests that 'systematic infanticide has been a necessary procedure for spacing human children, presumably beginning after man's entry into the niche of bi-pedalism, and lasting until the development of advanced agriculture. It involved between fifteen and fifty percent of the total number of births.'[58] Others put the figures even higher. Howell writes that 'all observers agree that infanticide is a universal or near-universal trait in hunter-gatherer societies.'[59] For instance, among a group called the Eipo, 'an unusually careful study shows that between a quarter and a third of all live births are killed, especially births of girls.'[60]

Among many peoples 'infanticide is not restricted to more or less exceptional cases, but is practised on a much larger scale. Custom often decides how many children are to be reared in each family, and not infrequently the majority of infants are destroyed.' In particular it is thought to be related to scarce resources. 'Urgent want is frequently represented by our authorities as the main cause of infanticide; and their statements are corroborated by the conspicuous prevalence of this custom among poor tribes and in islands whose inhabitants are confined to a narrow territory with limited resources.'[61]

The anthropological literature warns us against making any deductions from the level of infanticide to the presence or absence of love of children. 'In ancient Greece exposure often proceeded from affection for the previous children, from a desire to procure for them a standard of living which numbers would have made impossible.'[62] Nadel observed that Eskimos and Chinese practised infanticide extensively, 'in spite of their love of children and their desire for progeny.'[63] 'That the custom of infanticide is generally restricted to the destruction of new-born babies also appears from various statements as to the parental love of those peoples who are addicted to this practice. In Fiji "such children as are allowed to live are treated with a foolish fondness." Among the Narrinyeri, "only let it be determined that an infant's life shall be saved, and there are no bounds to the fondness and indulgence with which it is treated".'[64] We need to bear this in mind when studying an institution which, as David Hume wrote, is 'shocking to nature',[65] and of which most of us have no experience.

If we turn first to the case of Europe and specifically of England, it is clear that the authorities firmly condemned infanticide. Although Greek thinkers,

---

[58] Birdsell, *Some Predictions*, 236.
[59] Howell in Coleman and Schofield (eds), *Population Theory*, 182.
[60] Coleman in Coleman and Schofield (eds), *Population Theory*, 30.
[61] Westermarck, *Moral*, I, 396,400–1.
[62] Hocart in *Encyclopaedia of Social Sciences*, 'infanticide'.
[63] Nadel, *Foundation*, 271.
[64] Westermarck, *Moral*, I, 404–5.
[65] Hume, *Essays*, 235.

such as Plato and Aristotle, had seen infanticide as justified and indeed mandatory in certain situations, the Christian authorities condemned it vehemently.[66]
How far this ran against popular pressures we cannot say, for the actual incidence of infanticide is impossible to determine. The widespread abandonment
of infants in many European cities during the early modern period suggests that
infanticide, whether direct, or through the appalling death rates of 'foundling'
children, may have been common. It is estimated that 'By the end of the third
quarter of the eighteenth century about a third of all the babies born in Paris'
ended up in a foundling institution. Up to a third of these died within a year.[67]
Others give an even lower survival rate, of between one in ten and one in fifty of
them surviving to the age of twenty.[68] On the other hand, there were clearly
some countries, particularly Holland, where abandonment was infrequent.[69]

An influential article by William Langer some years ago argued that 'infanticide flourished in England'. His account is based on mid-nineteenth-century
evidence. A century earlier, according to Chambers, 'Exposure in the streets,
desertion by parents, and a deliberate destruction of infant life by parish authorities were everyday occurrences in London, perhaps especially in the first half of
the eighteenth century.'[70]

However, concern about infanticide seems to have been almost totally restricted to the consequences of illegitimacy. Wrightson's conclusion is that,
'Contemporary statements on the actual practice of infanticide significantly
narrowed the field of its discussion. Infanticide was referred to not as a widely
practiced custom, but as a crime associated primarily with attempts on the part
of bearers of illegitimate children to either conceal their offence or to rid
themselves of the unwanted child.' He notes that in the Essex Assizes between
1601 and 1665 in cases of infanticide 'fifty-three of the sixty-two children
are unambiguously described as bastards.'[71] There was an economic motive
in that an unwed mother would have been unable to provide for a child
without enormous difficulty. Mrs Cellier thought that 'many infanticides
were for want of fit ways to conceal their shame and provide for their children.'[72]
But it was all to do with illegitimacy. 'Illegitimate birth, which has been a
common cause of infanticide, has remained practically the only cause in modern
Europe . . .'[73]

[66] Westermarck, *Moral*, I, 408–9,411–12.
[67] Wrigley, *Population and History*, 125.
[68] Sauvy, *Population*, 342; cf. Langer in Heer (ed.), *Readings*, 7ff for further French figures cf. also Tilly et al., *Abandonment*.
[69] Schama, *Embarrassment*, 522.
[70] Chambers, *Population*, 78.
[71] Wrightson, *Infanticide*, 11–12.
[72] Cellier, *Royal Hospital*, 191.
[73] Hocart in *Encyclopedia of Social Sciences*, 'infanticide'.

This is indicated in another way. In the majority of societies where infanticide is practised on a large scale within marriage as a form of birth control, the gender of the infants is an important matter:

> In Rome, Greece, Arabia, India and China women of the upper classes, relieved by the males of the harder tasks both as an effort to keep them young and as a sign of rank, became an economic burden; and consequently infanticide fell mainly on the females. The necessity of finding a dowry for daughters contributed to a selection of female children for infanticide in China and India. Ancestor cults of Greece, Rome, India and China, which could be transmitted only through the males, also resulted in the destruction of girl infants.[74]

None of those who have studied the English material have found any gender bias. Hoffer found 'Between 1560 and 1603, the comparable statistics for victims were twelve females and twelve males; from 1636 to 1650, nine females and eight males.'[75] On the basis of the Essex Assize records, Wrightson found 'No marked sex differential in the children allegedly murdered, there being twenty-nine male and thirty-three female victims.'[76] Malcolmson concluded that 'the sex of the baby was an irrelevant consideration in English infanticides, unlike those in some other societies. Boy babies had no better chance of survival than girl babies; the circumstances of the mother provided the rationale for infanticide, not the sex of her infant.'[77]

Hoffer asks whether 'infanticide may have been a form of birth control' and answers, 'In fact, it was not.' Her evidence is mainly from the sex ratio.[78] Wrightson agrees with this view, concluding that 'It seems most unlikely . . . that infanticide has a distinct role in the earlier period as a means of population control. . . . The evidence of the practice of infanticide would suggest that it was an offence committed under exceptional circumstances, related largely to the concealment or disposal of illegitimate children.'[79]

Even though we cannot ever know for certain about infanticide within marriage, Malcolmson feels that 'any significant correlation between infanticide and population control would appear to be unlikely.' He quotes J.D. Chambers to the effect that 'compared to the natural causes which hovered over them from the moment of birth, death by direct or indirect human agency was of minor significance, a mere eddy on the tide of mortality that swept away the generations.'[80] Even if we include the 'foundling' phenomenon, and even if we accept

---

[74] Hocart in *Encyclopaedia of Social Sciences*, 'infanticide'.
[75] Hoffer, *Mothers*, 114.
[76] Wrightson, *Infanticide*, 12.
[77] In Cockburn (ed.), *Crime*, 192.
[78] Hoffer, *Mothers*, 114.
[79] Wrightson, *Infanticide*, 19.
[80] In Cockburn, *Crime*, 207.

that the high mortality among those upper-class infants sent out to wet nurses was some kind of indirect, subconscious, form of infanticide, the numbers affected would have been insignificant when compared to the total numbers of births and of infant deaths in England by 'natural' causes. When we turn to the case of Japan, we find a very different situation and one which brings the English absence of widespread infanticide into sharper relief.

It was the literary and legal evidence for infanticide which first attracted attention and much of it is gathered together in Taeuber's work. She cites a report of the late Tokugawa period: 'Many of the poor peasants in the remote regions do not raise their children. Their humanity is below that of the animals. The practice [of infanticide] is beyond description, but it has become a custom and people do not think it strange. It is reported frequently that the custom [of infanticide] has penetrated even to persons of high character.' 'This practice is most common in the Hyuga region [of Kyushu]. Here it is said that if a birth occurs to a person of high character and the decision is made to raise the child, [people] offer them congratulations. If [people] learn that the child is not to be raised they pretend ignorance; [under these circumstances] they do not offer congratulations. Generally only the first son is raised, and the others are not. If two or three sons are raised the family is ridiculed for undue attachment. This is a shocking situation.'[81]

Taeuber continues, 'The literature would indicate that in many areas of Kyushu two of each five children were killed, while in Tosa-Kuni of Shikoku one boy and two girls were the maximum number allowed to survive.' 'In Hyuga, all except the first-born were killed. In some districts nine of each ten births reported were those of boys; presumably, therefore, seven or eight of each nine girl babies were destroyed. There are reports that the *samurai* saved only the first-born.' 'The locale of the various reports on family limitation suggests that practices of destruction were diffused throughout the islands. Abortion and infanticide were believed to be so rife on *bakufu* lands and imperial estates that the cultivation of the lands, the production of rice, and hence the rice levies were jeopardized.' 'In the Nankai region limitation was widespread, even among the *samurai*. Families were reported as raising two sons and one daughter; if another baby was expected, the midwife was instructed as to disposal if the sex should prove otherwise than that needed to complete the desired family.'[82]

Now it may well be the case, as some Japanese scholars who have checked her quotations suggest, that some of these remarks are misunderstood or mistranslated.[83] Yet even if we discount a good deal, there does still seem to be a fair

---

[81] Taeuber, *Population* 29–30; the square brackets are Taeuber's.

[82] Taeuber, *Population*, 30.

[83] Dr Namihira informs me that Tokuji Chiba checked Taeuber's quotations and cast doubt on their accuracy.

amount of evidence of infanticide at certain times and in certain places. Honda, writing in the eighteenth century described how 'If they do have a child, they secretly destroy it, calling the process by the euphemism of "thinning out". This practice is most prevalent in the thirteen provinces from the Kanto to Ou [these include most of the east and north of Japan]. It is an evil custom that inevitably arises when there has been a protracted peace, and it is due also to the lack of any governmental system of guidance.'[84] Kyurinsai is quoted to the effect that 'If humble persons living in huts have large numbers of children, they will let the first one or two live, but after that, they often kill the children born. They call this *mabiku* [to thin out]. Female infants by custom are mostly killed.' *Mabiki*, Hanley and Yamamura explain 'usually refers to the thinning of seedlings'.[85]

The literary evidence is supported by detailed village studies based on family reconstitution. One of the most thorough analyses is of the village of Nakahara by Thomas Smith. The main method was through an analysis of sex ratios at birth. This led Smith to believe that 'infanticide was widely practiced in the village.' The sort of evidence is as follows:

> We must suppose . . . that the sex of the next child was to some extent a matter of choice, carried out by infanticide, and that families tended to eliminate infants of the sex that they had more of, and to eliminate girls somewhat more often than boys. Otherwise, it is quite inexplicable that families with predominantly male children tended to have females in the next child by a ratio significantly different from normal; that those where females predominated tended to have males by a ratio significantly different from normal; and that those with an equal number of both sexes, although tending to have more males than females, did *not* do so by a significant margin.[86]

Given the fact that we are only trying to explain a small part of the fertility reduction in Japan, we should be careful not to exaggerate the extent or uniformity of infanticide. A recent survey has pointed out that 'sex-selectiveness of the sort Smith detected in Nakahara has not been found elsewhere. Hayami has applied Smith's method to Nishijo, a village only 5 km north-east of Nakahara . . . and has found no consistent variation in the sex ratio.' We are told that 'there did exist some villages which did not show *any* sign of family limitation.'[87] As further research is undertaken, we are likely to find very considerable variation between region and region, and even between nearby villages. What does not seem disputable from the evidence, however, is that infanticide was unusually prevalent in early modern Japan. Even in the early twentieth century

---

[84] Keene, *Discovery*, 114.
[85] Hanley and Yamamura, *Economic*, 238.
[86] Smith, *Native Sources*, 110,112–13.
[87] Saito, *Infanticide*, 374.

it was probably widespread. In *Silk and Straw* the village blacksmith described how

> Because everyone was so hard up around here 'thinning out' the newborn was quite widely practiced. The number of children killed just depended, I'm told, on how strict the local policeman was . . . if a slack new policeman was appointed to the area, the 'thinning out' rate would rapidly increase. The situation was so bad that the number of kids in each grade of the primary school varied a good deal, depending on who'd been the local constable at the time they were born.[88]

Two keys to the prevalence of infanticide lie in the methods used and the attitude towards it: 'According to the ancient tales, when the woman in a poor family was delivered, the midwife asked the family whether to let the infant remain, *okimasu-ka*, or whether to return it, *modashi maskuka*. The midwife either cared for the infant who must be assisted to survive or managed the death of the infant for whom there was no room.'[89] But how the 'managing' was done is not explained. The only description I have come across is by Hanley and Yamamura who write in passing that the 'Japanese usually let the child die at birth, preventing its first cries or smothering it as soon after as possible.' 'Thus, it would be difficult if not impossible in many cases for anyone but the mother and the midwife to know if the birth had been a stillbirth or not.'[90]

Some descriptions of the methods are given in *Silk and Straw*. 'Killing off a newborn baby was a simple enough business. You just moistened a piece of paper with spittle and put it over the baby's nose and mouth; in no time at all it would stop breathing.'[91] The idea of using paper for this purpose may strike a western reader as implausible. Yet one has to take into account that Japanese paper (*washi*) was immensely strong. Japanese paper was employed not only for the usual purposes, but also for bags, umbrellas, lanterns, and sliding screens. Oiled, it was used for raincoats, it was also made into other forms of clothing, for fireworks, for rope, and even during the second world war for huge balloons to carry bombs. In particular, it was used for homicide:

> *washi* has also been used successfully for generations to suffocate those one wishes to be rid of but leave no marks upon . . . the killer lays a wet piece of *washi* over the victim's mouth and nose just after a breath is exhaled . . . and does whatever necessary to keep the victim from removing the paper . . . in the end all he has to do is peel away the damp paper. The victim shows no signs of foul play, and, once

[88] Saga, *Silk and Straw*, 28.
[89] Taeuber, *Population*, 29.
[90] Hanley and Yamamura, *Economic*, 315.
[91] Saga, *Silk and Straw*, 203.

dried, the highly durable *washi* proves perfectly serviceable for sending letters or writing poems.[92]

If the paper method failed, then occasionally they resorted to '*usugoro*' ('mortar killing'). The 'woman went alone into one of the buildings outside and had the baby lying on a straw mat. She wrapped the thing in two straw sack lids, tied it up with rope, and laid it on the mat. She then rolled a heavy wooden mortar over it. When the baby was dead, she took it outside and buried it herself.'[93]

A passive form of infanticide was exposure of the infant. A woman described how her mother had delivered her own baby in the fields, and lugged it home with the firewood. 'When we got into the house, Mother left the baby on a straw mat in front of the kitchen stove. You know, she didn't even wrap it up to keep it warm. . . . The baby was bawling its head off and I went to see if it was all right, but Mother said, "Leave it alone. If it's a weak thing it's going to die anyway, so let it get on with it".' The author remembered another baby. 'When I went to look, there was a newborn baby lying on a mat in front of the stove, completely naked though it was the middle of December. I seem to remember a couple of babies died soon after they were born but I'm not absolutely certain.'[94] In such cases it would be extremely difficult for the authorities to prove infanticide.

After the effort and suffering of carrying the child in the womb, and the pain of childbirth, the decision as to whether it would then be necessary to get rid of it would have been influenced quite considerably by beliefs about what one was getting rid of. Is it already human, with a separate existence, and what will happen to it after it dies? One aspect of the problem is alluded to by Dore: 'the doctrines of the transmigration of souls and of the ultimate destiny of the soul to lose its identity by merging with the absolute would make infanticide seem less of a crime than in Christian countries where each soul is given only one chance of redemption of which it would be sinful to deprive it.'[95] Hanley notes that 'Infanticide was even condoned by the euphemism that it was a means of "returning" an infant at birth before it had become an individual and a part of society. Thus it was thought of as a form of postpartum birth control.'[96]

It has been suggested that Buddhism does not put pressure on people to avoid abortion. We are told that aborted fetuses are referred to in Buddhist

---

[92] Barrett, *Japanese Papermaking*, 8.

[93] Saga, *Silk and Straw*, 210.

[94] Saga, *Silk and Straw*, 207.

[95] Dore, *Fertility*, 82.

[96] In *Cambridge History*, 4, 700. Scheper-Hughes writes of the Catholic Brazilian 'At least some of these little "angels" have been freely "offered up" to Jesus and His Mother, although "returned" to whence they came is closer to the popular idiom.' (Scheper-Hughes, *Death Without Weeping*, 343).

terminology as 'water child' or *mizuko* and that 'The belief regarding the spirits of the unborn in the Edo Era held that they were "sent back" but not permanently; mothers prayed to them to be born into their families again in the future, a sentiment attested to by the practice of burying the remains under the house veranda or floors. In the meantime these spirits were in the Children's Limbo.'[97] As for infanticide, 'if you wanted a boy but the newborn was a girl, you'd make it a "day visitor", as they used to say.'[98] There seems to have been an idea of a kind of watery reservoir or purgatory, where infant souls would normally reside. One description of this area, to which all infants and children whether killed or dying naturally would go, is given by Kaempfer:

> These blind superstitious people believe, that the bottom of this lake is the purgatory for children, which die before seven years of age, and are there tormented, till their redemption is brought about by some way or other. They are told so by their priests, who for their comfort assure them, that as soon as the water washes off the names and characters of the Gods and Saints, which are writ upon the papers they give them, the children at the bottom feel great relief, if they do not obtain a full and effectual redemption.[99]

This 'return' to the 'Children's Limbo' and the idea of rebirth need not just apply to the fetus in the womb. For a period after birth the infant is still in a state where it can safely be 'returned', to be kept in store as a 'spare' if needed at a later point. Whereas in the west the moment a child is born and shows signs of life, to deprive it of life is murder, Hanley and Yamamura suggests that this may not be the case in Japan: 'the Japanese child has traditionally not been a true member of society at birth, and hence letting it die – or killing it – before it became a member of village society was not the offence that murder was.'[100] In the 1930s John Embree wrote: 'During the first thirty days or so of a child's life his soul is not very well fixed in his body – it is a period of danger and uncertainty.' The naming ceremony, *Hiaki*, 'therefore, represents the end of the birth period. . . . The child has now passed another stage. From now on he may be carried on the back and may cross water safely, for he is now recognized by the gods as well as by the people of his world.'[101]

We should treat the 'thinning' process as occurring from pregnancy to this naming ceremony, in other words not make the absolute distinction between abortion and infanticide that western ethical systems suggest, just as we need to reconsider the distinction between active killing, and passive allowing a child to

[97] Coleman, *Family Planning*, 60.
[98] Saga, *Silk and Straw*, 203.
[99] Kaempfer, *History*, III, 61.
[100] Hanley and Yamamura, *Economic*, 316.
[101] Embree, *Suye Mura*, 136–7, quoted in Hanley and Yamamura, *Economic*, 316.

die. Such blurring is now of increasing comprehensibility in a world where our technology has again confused the boundaries between the child in the womb and outside it. The ambivalence, guilt, pressures, idea of 'sending back', all are movingly described in the words of an old woman who had killed several of her infants:

> In order to survive I had no choice. To keep the children we already had, the others had to be sent back. Even now, rocks mark the spots where the babies were buried under the floor of the house. Every night I sleep right above where they're buried. Of course, I feel love and compassion for the babies I sent back. I know I will go to hell when I die. I have a feeling the babies are there, too. When I die I want to go to hell so that I can protect them as best I can.[102]

The relatively low mortality rates in Japan combined with the bounded and difficult geographical location created an enormous problem. The Malthusian prediction of mass starvation always faced the Japanese. In the absence of any effective contraception and with a marriage system that allowed most women to marry in their early twenties only a combination of long lactation and periodically high rates of abortion and infanticide within marriage kept the dangers at bay. In England the unusual pattern of late and selective marriage, combined with maternal breast-feeding, meant that the pressure to control fertility through selective abortion and infanticide was absent. These expedients were almost entirely restricted to cases where an unmarried woman became pregnant and could not face the shame and expense of having a baby. Yet even when we have said this we are faced with a puzzle, for neither in England or Japan did people wait until they were at the very edge of disaster. They took pre-emptive action and at certain times kept their fertility low even when material wealth was growing. In the next chapter I will try to explain why this happened.

---

[102] Quoted in Hane, *Rebels*, 82.

20

Strategies of Heirship

In terms of the proximate ways in which the final Malthusian trap was avoided we appear to be moving towards a solution. In England, the age at marriage and proportion marrying 'were on a large enough scale in themselves to move population growth rates between the minimum and maximum to be found in pre-industrial societies.'[1] 'Natural' fertility of roughly 50 per thousand was lowered by a combination of biological factors (nutrition, disease, lactation) and the marriage pattern of late and selective marriage, to between 30 and 35 per thousand.

In the Japanese case, it would appear that a combination of middling marriage age, early termination of child-bearing, some non-marriage and pressures against remarriage had a significant impact. Combined with customs of infant feeding, abortion and infanticide, this reduced fertility to an even lower level than in England, reaching some 25 per thousand in certain periods, about half the 'natural' level.

Yet, having solved the problem of how fertility was regulated, we are still faced with complex questions of why it was often held below the normal level. The control of fertility in these two agrarian societies which were growing in wealth is sufficiently unusual to make us wonder what conditions could have encouraged people to use marital and other techniques to circumvent biology and control fertility. How was it that there could emerge in both countries a pattern in which overall wealth could increase, but the expected Malthusian upsurge in fertility did not, for a time, occur?

Normally, pre-industrial populations aim at the maximum number of children, as many as God or the gods will give, offspring who are both useful

[1] Wrigley, *Population History*, 216.

economically, and desirable in many other ways.[2] Even in the very restrained atmosphere of early modern England, where children were often considered a 'burden' and a cost, and where marriage had to be postponed until one could 'afford' it, once a person was married there seems to have been little, if any, discussion of what should be the maximum number of children one should aim at. There was no widely accepted 'normal' family size above which one should not go.[3]

When we turn to Japan, we find a different situation. We have seen that the achieved family size in Japan in the eighteenth and early nineteenth centuries was usually in the range of 3–6 children, often with a low average of 3.5 children. Connected to this is the strong impression that the Japanese consciously aimed at about this figure. Evidence of a widespread norm stipulating an upper number of children in Japan would go far towards suggesting an attempt to balance fertility and resources. A low upper ceiling is, of course, one of the major features of post-demographic transition populations which have strong beliefs that two or three children are 'enough'.

In an early article on Japanese fertility, Dore reported 'A survey of a sample of nearly 500 farmers from four villages in different parts of Japan' which 'gave the average number of children considered desirable as 3.8.' There were considerable variations, between 3.2 and somewhat higher, but the figures were all low. This idea in a survey undertaken in the 1950s might be thought to be recent and a sign of the demographic transition. Yet Dore cites an article of 1934 where in a northern village the writer was told 'In our family it is a tradition that we never rear more than five children in each generation.'[4] Taeuber reports that 'In Kyushu . . . it was regarded as somehow disgraceful to have more than three children.'[5]

While there was an upper limit both in numbers and age, there was also a lower threshold. It was important for a marriage to be fertile. Whereas it was not permissible in England for a marriage to be terminated on account of barrenness, in Japan we are told 'one practice, especially prevalent in rural areas, was to delay registration of the marriage until the wife had a live birth. An old saying – still widely quoted – held that "the bride who bears no children leaves after three years." '[6] It is interesting that such a long period was given; in many societies it would have been one or two years. The statistics bear out the saying. Thomas Smith reports that 'ten of thirteen divorces in the village ended childless marriages after an average of 3.0 years of conjugal living. In other words, childless marriages never became complete marriages.'[7]

---

[2] For the high desire for children, and some reasons for it, see Macfarlane, *Population*.
[3] See Macfarlane, *Marriage*, part II and ch.8.
[4] Dore, *Fertility*, 80,81.
[5] Taeuber, *Population of Japan*, 29.
[6] Coleman, *Family Planning*, 175.
[7] Smith, *Native Sources*, 117.

This upper and lower limit suggests that parents were consciously planning their family size and composition, a fact also born out by Thomas Smith's work. It suggests, as Hanley and Yamamura note, that 'Parents sought to rear a family of about three to four children.'[8]

It would seem that the main reasons for conscious family limitation in Europe were mainly of two kinds. To avoid shame and punishment in having unwanted and often illegitimate children, or, occasionally, to prevent the over-burdening of a house with children. In the Japanese case a distinction needs to be made between two types of cause. One explains why certain children were kept and others encouraged to die, the other explains why families set an upper threshold of live births. Amongst the former, Mrs Suzuki described conditions in the early twentieth century:

> It was thought bad luck to have twins, for example, so you got rid of one before the neighbours found out. Deformed babies were also bumped off. . . . In my case, I wasn't deformed, I was downright ugly. My parents and grandparents were very shocked apparently. 'We'll never be able to find her a husband – not with those looks', they said. My mother told me that when she first saw my face, she thought, 'What a waste of time, giving birth to a thing like that.'

So attempts were made to stifle the infant.[9]

The destruction of malformed babies who could not work or marry is attested to by several visitors. Morse had observed the 'marked absence of deformations or malformations among the people'. He ascribed this 'first, to the personal attention given to children, and, secondly, to the almost universal one-storied house with absence of flight of stairs down which children might fall.'[10] He does not seem to have made the connection suggested by Griffis: 'In their method of rearing infants, only the hardy ones can survive the exposure to which they are subject. Deformity is strikingly rare.' 'It is probable that the people do not always take extraordinary pains to rear deformed infants.'[11]

What we need to concentrate on are the systematic reasons for the very low and controlled fertility rate, the mix of all the different techniques we have discussed, which for a century and a half balanced the Japanese population so that it did not grow despite relatively low mortality rates.

Kingsley Davis used the Japanese case to argue that the main pressure which keeps down fertility in most societies is not poverty but a desire to increase wealth. He concentrated his attention on the later nineteenth century onwards and suggested that 'Under a prolonged drop in mortality with industrialization, people in northwest Europe and Japan found that their accustomed demograph-

---

[8] Hanley and Yamamura, *Economic*, 227.
[9] Saga, *Silk and Straw*, 203.
[10] Morse, *Day*, I, 116,34,116.
[11] Griffis, *Mikado*, I, 570.

ic behaviour was handicapping them in their effort to take advantage of the opportunities being provided by the emerging economy.' He argued that 'faced with a persistent high rate of natural increase resulting from past success in controlling mortality, families tended to use every demographic means possible to maximize their new opportunities and to avoid relative loss of status.' The central thesis is that it was not absolute poverty but, as Malthus had suggested, the desire for wealth, which drove west European and Japanese populations to break out of the vicious cycle. 'Fear of hunger as a principal motive may fit some groups in an extreme stage of social disorganisation . . . but it fits none with which I am familiar and certainly none of the advanced peoples of western Europe and Japan. The fear of invidious deprivation apparently has greater force.' It was not poverty which caused the demographic transition but, miraculously, wealth. It was 'in a sense the rising prosperity itself, viewed from the standpoint of the individual's desire to get ahead and appear respectable, that forced a modification of his reproductive behaviour.'[12] He was here echoing the views of others that 'human beings do not regulate their populations in relation to the food supply, but in relation to the prestige supply.'[13]

Now that the pattern of pre-industrial Japan and England is at last visible to us in detail we can test the thesis which Davis suggested. We know that mortality was partially brought under control several hundred years before either nation industrialized. We know that both countries were faced with the possibilities of rocketing population within a pre-industrial economy, and indeed that in the sixteenth century in England and the seventeenth century in Japan, rapid growth did occur for a while. Rather than succumbing to the usual Malthusian 'positive' checks there is evidence of 'preventive' action.

The idea that it was the desire for wealth, as much as present poverty, which motivated people in Japan was early noticed by contemporaries. With reference to the small size of families, one author started by arguing that 'All this is ascribable to their poverty. They prefer leading as best a life as they can without encumbrances to bringing up many children to hunger and penury, and restrict the number of their children to two or three.' But he went on to admit that 'Even rich families are contaminated by this evil custom, and deliberately restrict the number of their children.' The same memorial of 1754 stated that while fifty years before, farmers had brought up 'five or six or even seven or eight children', 'in recent years it has become fashion among the farmers not to rear more than one or two children between a couple.' He was not absolutely certain 'whether this is due to the luxurious habits that prevail among them or some other causes' but was sure that 'As soon as a baby is born, its parents put it to death.'[14]

---

[12] Davis, *Change*, 352,362,352.

[13] Burton Benedict in Allison (ed.), *Population Control*, 178.

[14] Ro-Tozan in Taeuber, *Population of Japan*, 30.

The evidence for the way in which infanticide was a form of birth control within respectable families, a way of adjusting reproduction and production, was provided by Thomas Smith. His detailed reconstruction of a village population on the basis of excellent demographic records produced several unexpected findings. Firstly, it began to appear that infanticide was not mainly a response to poverty and was not just practiced by the poorest households. 'Infanticide seems to have been widely practiced there by the most respectable and stable part of the population.'[15] He found that 'What is surprising is that the practice does not appear to have been primarily a response to poverty: large landholders practiced it as well as small, and registered births were as numerous in bad as in good growing years.'[16] Or again, 'Although large holders had somewhat larger families than small, this balancing tendency was present in both groups, so infanticide seemed not to be wholly a function of poverty.'[17]

Parents were very consciously exercising planning; using selective infanticide to adjust family size and composition. 'Among the apparent objectives of infanticide in Nakahara were overall family limitation; an equilibrium of some sort between family size and farm size; an advantageous distribution of the sexes in children and possibly, also, the spacing of children in a way convenient to the mother; and the avoidance of an unlucky sex in the next child.' Thus infanticide was 'practiced less as part of a struggle for survival than as a way of planning the sex composition, sex sequence, spacing, and ultimate number of children.'[18] Thomas Smith's suggestion as to the reason for this practice is that it 'may lie in the fiercely competitive nature of farming as reflected in the land registers, and in the relation of family size and composition to farm size and farming efficiency.'[19]

He develops this speculation. 'Our guess is that all families wanted at minimum one or two male children on account of their value as labour and as male and replacement heirs. Small families were predominantly male, therefore, because they accepted male children, tended to eliminate females, and stopped procreation early.' Yet having achieved a certain minimum number of males, families then did not want any more 'for fear of causing future competition for the family headship and creating problems about the division of property and the care of non inheriting sons.' Thus, after a couple of males, 'female children were as desirable as males or more so . . . they could inherit in the event of the failure of the male line or be used to recruit an adoptive heir by marriage.

[15] Smith, *Native Sources*, 131.
[16] Smith, *Nakahara*, 147.
[17] Smith, *Native Sources*, 9.
[18] Smith, *Native Sources*, 9,131,110.
[19] Smith, *Nakahara*, 14.

Consequently, the greater the number of children a family had, the higher the proportion of girls was likely to be.'[20]

The desire to increase economic efficiency to a maximum is commented on by Hanley and Yamamura: 'These consistently high proportions in the working ages, even in periods of economic prosperity, combined with efforts to decrease even further the number of dependents during the economic troughs . . . lead us to conclude that people actively sought to achieve an age composition favourable to economic production.' For instance, 'In a period of an expanding economy, younger brothers who would normally leave home or remain unmarried were permitted to marry and remain in the village.' As a region's economy developed, birth rates rose, and then declined as the growth levelled off.[21]

Although Smith does not explicitly make the connection, we could take the word 'thinning', used as a synonym for infanticide, to its logical conclusion and suggest that births of children became part of the general strategy of farming. Just as one had very carefully to manipulate rice seedlings, water and the occasional animal, likewise one had to balance very delicately the family labour force through the 'cultivation' of the right number of children. In an economy which, as we have seen, was almost totally dependent on human labour, too much labour was as bad as too little. Like water or night soil on the rice fields, just the right amount had to be applied. Miscalculation would mean disaster for the whole family enterprise. Too many children would imperil older siblings and other members of the family in that highly precarious and competitive world of Japanese agriculture which Thomas Smith has so excellently described.

The situation of Japanese parents was well stated in the early eighteenth century by the Japanese philosopher Honda: 'Whenever there has been a period of continued peace, husbands and wives are fearful lest it become increasingly difficult for them to earn a living. Aware that if they have many children they will not have any property to leave them, they confer and decide that rather than rear children who in later years will have great difficulty in making a decent living, it is better to take precautions before they are born and not add another mouth to feed.'[22] Two features made the parents particularly conscious of the dangers. The first was the exceedingly high population density in Japan. Because only a very small part of Japan could be cultivated, densities were far greater even than in China: 'Japan at the end of the Tokugawa period had a population of about 35 million and a density of 100 persons per square kilometre. China at the end of the Ch'ing dynasty probably had a population of more than 400 million, more than 11 times greater than that of Japan – but with a density of only 40 per square kilometre.' There was also no 'open frontier' for

[20] Smith, *Native Sources*, 127.
[21] Hanley and Yamamura, *Economic*, 262,227,212.
[22] Quoted in Keene, *Discovery*, 114.

the Japanese. 'The possibility of leaving congested villages for sparsely settled regions or foreign countries probably made population control a less urgent matter for the Chinese than for the Japanese.'[23]

Secondly, the organizational units of Japan were small and strong, the famous 'small group' society had a deep influence. As Dr Namihira explains, 'All of Japan was divided into very small units of responsibility and mutual control; all were limited. The borders were very strong; for instance, the borders of the village were very strong. Every small child knew exactly where the invisible line was between his village and any other. Thus there was self-limitation both at the family and the village level.' These two factors united to put an enormous pressure on individuals, especially when combined with the ecological constraints imposed by wet rice cultivation:

> Rice has both a symbolic meaning and an ecological constraint. Rice is grown in the dry season, hence there is always a shortage of water. One family is supposed to be able to be supported by one hectare of rice land. The number of families and the size of the families is restricted by the amount of water available. The size of the rice fields decides the family ranking in a community. Furthermore, each village had its own rank. This village ranking was decided in the fourteenth to fifteenth centuries and changed little. The rank of the village decided how much water it would get.[24]

This fits with Daniel Scott Smith's argument that infanticide may often have been the result of village pressure, rather than individual family wishes: 'By limiting family size, villages avoided the potentially disrupting force of a large landless population, even though excess children would not reduce family assets.'[25] Furthermore the 'Japanese like to keep a certain standard of life. Too many children means that the standard of living dropped. The ranking of the family within the village was crucial. The need to divide land among many children, for instance, would lower this.'[26] Or as Nakamura and Miyamato put it, 'In Japan, the tendency was for all families to have a small number of offspring so that each would be able to maintain its position in the village hierarchy.'[27]

It is very rare to obtain an account of how the pressures worked on an individual but one fictional account in the late nineteenth century is revealing. It shows that fear of poverty is inseparable from desire for wealth. Oshina had her first child, a daughter, at nineteen. When she became pregnant again the

[23] Nakamura, *Population*, 235,248.
[24] Namihira, personal communication.
[25] Smith, *Nakahara*, 194.
[26] Namihira, personal communication.
[27] Nakamura, *Population*, 265.

next year, 'They were barely surviving as it was, so another child was out of the question.' So her mother performed an abortion on her. She did not have another child for thirteen years and they looked forward to the birth, which turned out to be a boy. She became pregnant again. They had planned to send the daughter off to service which would have earnt money. If they did so and the mother had two infants to look after, she 'would be unable to do as much work as before.' The loss of her income would be 'a major blow'. She discussed the problem with her husband. 'It's your belly,' he would say, 'so you just do what you want.' He was concerned but could not order her to do anything. She could not decide what to do, so time passed. Finally at four months, she performed an abortion on herself – and died in terrible pain from the ensuing infection.[28]

Expected high mortality rates and the necessity for family labour leads, in most societies, to the need for as many children as possible. In Japan the situation was already present where planned parenthood was necessary. Biological, marital and sexual patterns could be relied on to produce nearly the right number, but in the absence of any form of effective contraception the final adjustments had to be made by the most direct forms of birth control, namely abortion and infanticide. Of these, infanticide was in many ways preferable.

The reasons for this have been explained with reference to those other groups which have used infanticide as a form of birth control over long periods, namely hunter-gatherers. 'The advantage of infanticide as a method of population control as opposed to methods that prevent pregnancy is that the infant can be examined before the decision is made, so that the sex and physical condition and appearance of the baby can enter into the decision.' Thus, as a form of *post-facto* contraception, it has some advantages over abortion. 'From this point of view, infanticide is rational and eugenic; the investment of parents and especially mothers in the infant is stopped just at the point when the most "expensive" portion of the investment, lactation, is about to start. The sunk cost of the pregnancy and the childbirth has been paid, and the mother has the advantage of being able to see and judge the viability of the infant before making a decision.'[29] As we have seen in the Japanese case, she can also use the Darwinian technique of a form of speeded-up natural selection, by making obstacles to survival. If the infant survives, he or she is likely to be strong enough to face the incredibly gruelling work load that most Japanese faced through the centuries.

I will now consider some of the more general causes of a peculiarly calculative attitude towards fertility. In this analysis will be found several of those factors which, for the first time in history, created two large agrarian populations which withstood the natural tendency towards maximum reproduction steadfastly

[28] Nagatsuka, *Soil*, 28.
[29] Howell in Coleman and Schofield (eds), *Population Theory*, 182.

enough to break out of the Malthusian fertility trap. The achievement was surprising, and our modern world rests upon it. But it was at a considerable cost. In essence, forces strong enough to stand up to the biological urge to procreate had to be developed. A wedge had to be driven between the biological and the social. In relation to fertility we know the broad dimensions of the methods that were used. In England until the later nineteenth century, the check lay almost entirely in limiting the population 'at risk' by various marriage strategies. The solutions will thus lie in an analysis of the place of marriage in society. In Japan part of the force was biological. Another part was to do with marriage and particularly sexual relationships within marriage. Other parts lie in the practice of deliberate abortion and infanticide. We thus need now to turn briefly to the environment which produced such unusual fertility regimes, whose only long-term antecedents are to be found in some hunter-gatherer societies.

One way of expressing what happened is as follows. A true market economy had developed in which children were weighed against other benefits, as they are today. In Japan, for example, 'As the economy grew, farming became increasingly commercially oriented, and the rural villages were gradually woven into a highly monetized and consumption-oriented society, people began to choose to "trade off" additional children for goods and services or the accumulation of wealth needed to improve or maintain their standard of living and their status within village society.'[30] The umbilical link between production and reproduction had been cut. This was the central peculiarity and the central similarity between Japan and England, which distinguished them, as far as we know, from all other large agrarian civilizations. The causes for this need further exploration, for they cannot be found purely within a demographic discussion.

In my work on English marriage and childbearing, I advanced the argument that the main reason for the control on childbearing in England was that the capitalist and money-conscious society had converted children into commodities; they were to be considered as 'goods' which one might 'afford' or not, as the case might be. They had 'costs' as well as 'benefits'.[31] If we look at the Japanese case, we are struck by an almost identical attitude. Thus Hanley writes that the 'measures taken to lower to the minimum the number of nonproductive members in the household lead us to conclude that the Japanese were seeking to create a population favourable to economic production.'[32] Rozman tells us that 'the viewpoint appears to have prevailed that additional children represented a burden to be avoided if possible. Wealth must not be dispersed; status must be maintained.' The Japanese, like the English, were carefully calculating their labour force requirements in a very unusual manner. 'Analysis of household

---

[30] Hanley and Yamamura, *Economic*, 36.
[31] Macfarlane, *Marriage*, ch.4.
[32] Hanley in *Cambridge History*, 4, 700.

registration data, albeit for a small number of villages, strongly indicates that Japanese households deliberately limited the number of children they had and controlled the timing and sexual distribution of those that survived.[33]

This is precisely the attitude which Malthus had advocated for Europe. It is the motivation which seems to lie at the heart of the rapid fertility decline we are now seeing in parts of south-East Asia and elsewhere. People sought to maintain a balance between resources and population, rather than an unquestioning drive to seek maximum fertility. Yet such an attitude is so unusual that we are still left puzzled as to what caused or allowed such a view. One way of starting to look for a solution is by looking at the danger of having too few heirs.

How could one be sure of an heir and a right mix of surviving children? This is the problem which, along with high mortality rates, leads people in many societies to have higher fertility than they may actually need or even desire. They aim above the target because the dangers inherent in its falling too low – a ghastly old age with no heirs to support one or attend to one's funeral pyre – are greater than the increased hardship of a large family. Faced with the choice of too few or too many, most people, bearing in mind their past experiences, opt for 'too many'. In fact, given the political, economic and religious advantages of children, the very concept of 'too many' is not one that seems to apply. The more children the more wealth.[34]

How was the problem of heirship solved in these two cases? In England the solution was the idiosyncratic one of not worrying too much. It is one of the central peculiarities of England that from very early on there is little preoccupation, at least below the level of the nobility, with the need for heirs. An advanced market economy, with the possibility of hiring in labour and protection against sickness and old age through non-familial mechanisms, meant that to be childless did not mean either spiritual or economic disaster. We see this in the fact that many people never married, that there was no evidence of sex-selective preference for male children, and that there was no 'ancestor cult'.[35] Heirship was relatively unimportant for most people in England.

One index of this lack of concern was the situation in relation to adoption. Anthropologists have drawn attention to the fact that in the majority of agrarian societies the pressure to maintain the family landholding and other assets in situations where demography may cheat one of an heir has led to a vast array of 'adoption' devices.[36] Jack Goody has provided an overview of the various 'strategies of heirship', of which adoption is a central technique in India, China,

---

[33] Rozman in *Cambridge History*, 5, 554–5 citing the work of Hanley and Yamamura.

[34] cf. Mamdani, *Myth, passim*, esp. 77,130–1.

[35] See Macfarlane, *Marriage*, ch.4.

[36] For example Maine, *Dissertations*, 96ff; Lowie, 'Adoption and Fostering' (in *Encyclopedia of Social Sciences*, 1st edn.).

Rome and elsewhere.[37] He has suggested that adoption is important in all areas where there is a great desire to have children because the mode of production is based on family labour and on the transmission of landed property. He notes, however, that there is much less emphasis on adoption in early modern western Europe and curiously that the extreme case is England.[38]

In English common law, as Goody notes, there is a total absence of legal adoption until the twentieth century.[39] The point was made long ago by lawyers, for instance Sir Thomas Smith in the sixteenth century wrote 'nor we have no manner to make lawefull children but by mariage, and therefore we knowe not what is *adoptio* nor *arragatio*.'[40] The legal position from the Anglo-Saxon period through to the nineteenth century was clearly stated by Maitland: 'we have no adoption in England.'[41] Of course one could make a person one's heir by various devises, for instance by will, but one could not legally adopt them.

If we place India and England at the two extremes, Japanese history presents a case which fits at neither end, but combines elements of both in a novel and unusual manner. In Japan, from at least the fourteenth century, there was a developed money economy and a widespread use of non-familial labour in the form of servants. Yet the Japanese were more dependent on family labour than the English and we might have expected the normal strong need to have plenty of children. The need for at least one child to support the parents in old age, and the strong stress on the continuity of the 'house' or '*ie*', made it essential to have an heir. Japan would thus appear to have been in a position very different from England and much closer to that of India or China. Instead there was a device in Japan, special to that society, which had been elaborated over the centuries and which provided just the right mechanism for obtaining both goals – a good family labour force, and one which was not determined by the accidental and uncontrollable forces of mortality and natural fertility. This was that most powerful form of *post-facto* birth control, Japanese adoption. This is the final and necessary part of the jigsaw in trying to understand the Japanese fertility pattern.

Von Siebold noticed that adoption was 'the uniform practice in Japan with the childless, whether sovereign or subject.'[42] Pompe wrote that 'The adoption of children is an easy matter in Japan. If someone who has many sons wants to secure their future careers, he will look around among his kinsmen to see

---

[37] See Goody '*Adoption*', *passim*; Goody, *Production and Reproduction*, 49,55,66ff; Goody, *Family*, 72–3.

[38] Goody, *Production and Reproduction*, 75.

[39] Goody, *Family*, 73.

[40] Smith, *De Republica*, 134.

[41] Pollock and Maitland, *History of English Law*, II, 399.

[42] Von Siebold, *Manners*, 177.

whether there are people willing to adopt one of his sons, for which a certain sum of money may be paid. The child is then completely taken care of by the adoptive parents; he receives their name and will later succeed the adoptive father in his profession.'[43] Adoption, in fact, was mandatory: 'an aged and childless widow, last representative of her family is not permitted to remain without an heir. She must adopt a son if she can: if she cannot, because of poverty, or for other reasons, the local authorities will provide a son for her, – that is to say, a male heir to maintain the family worship.' If one failed to do so, the estate would be forfeit. 'The childless man was obliged to adopt a son; and the 47th article of the Legacy ordained that the family estate of a person dying without male issue, and without having adopted a son, should be "forfeited without any regard to his relatives or connexions".'[44]

Once a person was adopted, he could not be replaced by a subsequent blood relative, however close. 'The Commissioners brought us the intelligence that, the Tycoon being childless, he had within the last few days adopted a son. This lad was to be his successor, and in the event of his subsequently having a son of his own, he would be compelled to give him away rather than dispossess the adopted one.'[45] This shows the closeness of the link formed by adoption, which is confirmed by other accounts. Longford described how there were '*Relations in the First degree* – Parents, adopted parents, husband, child, adopted child. *Relations in the Second Degree* – Grandparents, stepmother, uncles and aunts, brothers and sisters, husband's parents, wife, concubine, nephew, grandchild, daughter-in-law etc.'[46] An adopted child was closer than a grandparent or sibling – adoption created as strong a bond as the closest blood relative. This was shown by the length of mourning for relatives. As Chamberlain explained, 'Real parents . . . 13 months (garments) . . . 50 days (food). Adopted parents . . . 13 months . . . 50 days.'[47]

The closeness, in itself, would not be enormously significant if it were not for two other associated features. The first is the vast number and kinds of adoption. Chamberlain in the later nineteenth century draws attention to the frequency and complexity: 'So completely has adoption become part and parcel of the national life that Mr. Shigeno An-eki, the best Japanese authority on the subject, enumerates no less than ten different categories of adopted persons.' He concluded that 'Galton's books could never have been written in Japan; for though genealogies are carefully kept, they mean nothing, at least from a scientific point of view – so universal is the practice of adoption, from the top of society to the bottom.' And he suggests a couple of reasons for its universality: 'a man with too

[43] Wittermans, *Pompe*, 49.
[44] Hearn, *Interpretation*, 422–3, 381.
[45] Oliphant, *Elgin's Mission*, 158–9.
[46] Longford, *Japan*, 202–3.
[47] Chamberlain, *Things*, 337.

many children hands over one or more of them to some friend who has none. To adopt a person is also the simplest way to leave him money, it not being usual in Japan to nominate strangers as one's heirs.'[48]

The second feature is that those who were adopted were not necessarily or even primarily blood relatives. Chamberlain described the effects of this: 'It is strange, but true, that you may often go into a Japanese family and find half-a-dozen persons calling each other parent and child, brother and sister, uncle and nephew and yet being really either no blood-relations at all, or else relations in quite different degrees from those conventionally assumed.'[49] The subversion of the blood family which this caused, and the turning of the family into an artificial corporation is dealt with by Ratzell. 'The high importance assigned to family cohesion led to the wide spread of adoption, especially in Japan . . . this custom, which in course of time became extraordinarily widespread, had a destructive effect on the family. This, on adoption becoming customary, sank to a corporation; and, with the admission of fresh strangers, the reputation of natural kindred grew to be an abuse.'[50] Rein noted 'the further right of expelling members of the family and introducing strangers into it.' He continued that 'In this way the Japanese family lost much of its natural character, and assumed the aspect of a corporation.'[51] The same point was made more recently by Robert Smith: 'The frequent adoption of successors shows clearly that the Japanese household is essentially an enterprise group, not a descent organization, and that passing over a son in favor of an adopted successor for the headship among merchants, craftsmen, and artists is a manifestation of a universalistic element in the definition of the role of the household head.'[52]

The unusual nature of non-blood adoption is apparent when we compare Japan with China: 'Such non-agnatic adoptions, however, were considered by many Confucians an unfilial breach of the natural father-son relationship.'[53] Practice and theory diverged greatly. 'Despite lip-service to the Chinese notions of the importance of blood-relationships, and the consequent insistence that the adopted son should be a patrilineal kinsman, in actual fact blood ties have not been considered an essential for formal perpetuation of the family.'[54] Attempts were also made to keep adoption within social strata, but these were equally ineffective. 'The clans refused to submit to the edict of 1615, which limited adoption of male heirs to the same class, on pain of state confiscation of the property, and this edict was repealed in 1651. When an heir could be set aside

[48] Chamberlain, *Things*, 17.
[49] Chamberlain, *Things*, 17.
[50] Ratzell, *History*, III, 497.
[51] Rein, *Travels*, 422.
[52] Smith, *Japanese*, 89–90.
[53] McMullen, *Rulers*, 89.
[54] Dore, *City*, 145.

on grounds of incompetence, it became in fact possible to exclude the natural heir and adopt any other male.'[55] As Chie Nakane points out 'Not only may outsiders with not the remotest kinship tie be invited to be heirs and successors, but servants and clerks are usually incorporated as members of the household and treated as family members by the head of the household.'[56] The observation about servants is illustrated in the case of one mountain village by Thomas Smith's study of Tokugawa agriculture where he concludes that 'Many of these servants were literally adopted, from impoverished parents, usually at the age of about ten.'[57]

Another custom was to adopt an in-marrying son-in-law. Thus 'a house-master without male issue might adopt a man betrothed to his daughter ('*muko-yoshi*'). Such an adopted son was invested with all the rights and responsibility of a natural heir. In case of divorce, however, these rights immediately reverted to the original household.'[58] People tended not to adopt infants or little children, for 'More common than the adoption of children was the adoption of young adults, either a husband for a daughter in a family with no sons, or a young man who would himself become their heir.'[59] Adoption became a mechanism for social mobility. 'Adoption into a *samurai* family was also a commodity on the open market and the price fluctuated at different periods.'[60] 'The increasingly impoverished warriors sought solvency by setting aside their own heirs and adopting the sons of rich merchants in their stead.'[61]

Adoption overlapped with marriage strategies, giving families the flexibility to deal with problems of both absence of heirs and shortage of cash. The general feature was that an apparent 'descent groups', the lineage or '*ie*' was not based on birth (blood) but on choice (contract). 'The widespread practice of a bewildering variety of forms of adoption involves yet another principle. People do not generally unite to form groups, not even households, but are instead recruited into them.' The main considerations, Robert Smith writes, are 'the highly pragmatic ones of competence and availability.'[62]

This pragmatic drive towards flexibility and efficiency, keeping the emotional form and force of the family, combined with the choice and pragmatism of a meritocracy, is of course one of the central reasons for the modern success of Japan, with its family-like firms, based on talent and not blood. W.J.Goode spoke of the distinctive nature of this blending of two principles, again in contrast to China:

---

[55] Jacobs, *Capitalism*, 159.

[56] Nakane, *Japanese Society*, 5.

[57] Smith, *Agrarian Origins*, 21.

[58] Jacobs, *Capitalism*, 154.

[59] Hanley in Hanley and Wolf (eds), *Family*, 219.

[60] Bellah, *Tokugawa*, 32.

[61] Jacobs, *Capitalism*, 159.

[62] Smith, *Japanese*, 90.

Perhaps the single most striking contrast illustrating the difference between the
family structures of China and Japan is that the Japanese father, at any class level,
could supplant his heir by adopting a son of superior ability – thus further
guaranteeing the success of his *ie* [the 'house'] and obtaining a protege who
discarded his allegiance to his former family – whereas adoption in China was
extremely difficult and rare, and viewed as impractical because the young man
would always feel loyal towards the family from which he came.[63]

The force of these effects will, of course, depend on how widespread and
frequent adoptions actually were. Hanley and Yamamura have given one of the
most detailed accounts of what happened. In the four villages they studied,
'persons of all ages were adopted, even some elderly women after the Tempo
famine of the 1830s.' The statistics are impressive. 'Of 105 families for whom
records exist for at least two or more generations, 56 families, or 53 percent,
adopted sons or other relatives.' Families even allowed their younger sons to
leave home and be adopted elsewhere, and then when their older son died,
rather than bringing back the younger, they adopted another person. Indeed
'Adoptions were so widely practiced that in Numa in the period 1860–1871
there were more adoptions recorded than marriages.'[64]

As regards fertility rates the important thing is that this type of frequent and
open adoption provided the solution to the problem of how to have very low
fertility and yet ensure the continuity of the house. The way in which this
worked and relieved the pressure to have large families is well described by
Thomas Smith. The culture offers 'a happy evasion' from the problem of having
no heirs. 'It has always been possible in Japan to adopt a male heir, even of adult
age, as a husband for a daughter or outright, so long as there is property to
inherit. . . . Moreover, he is in every sense but sentimentally, and perhaps not
always with that exception – legally, socially, religiously, even genealogically –
the exact equal of a natural heir; and he has the bonus advantage that if he works
out badly, he can be disinherited and replaced.'[65] Adoption in and out, and the
relative ease of getting rid of 'spares' through out-migration, were essential
features of the Japanese pattern, just as the possibility of hiring in servants to
replace children was an essential part of the English. Both broke the nexus
between production and reproduction, blood and labour, which is to be found in
all other large agrarian civilizations.

Thus the whole question of old age and support in sickness was solved in a
novel way. Usually these dire problems are solved by blood kin, who combine to
help. Two alternative strategies devised to find non-blood support were developed in our two cases. In England, this was through the use of paid support,
through servanthood. In Japan, it was through creating 'as if' blood kin when

---

[63] Goode, *World*, 325.
[64] Hanley and Yamamura, *Economic*, 229,232,230.
[65] Smith, *Native Sources*, 36.

needed, as well as through the same mechanisms of money and servanthood as in England.

This takes us out more generally into the relationship between kinship and economy, and particularly the central matter of the nature of property. Ultimately, what happened was that production became more important than reproduction – that the individual members of a family, real kin, were sacrificed for an ideal. As with so many things, the way this worked itself out in the two cases was different. In England, it took the form of the idolization of private, individual, property rights – to which everything else was sacrificed, including the link between parents and children. Property came before blood. In Japan, the ideal was the '*ie*' or family – but ironically, it was not a blood family, but an artificially constructed continuity. If necessary, the actual children had to be sacrificed for the ideal. Thus, in different ways, a form of non-domestic mode of production grew up. The great split between the social and the economic of which Weber wrote, had occurred.[66]

Another way of looking at this is to examine the connection between inheritance systems and the growth of population. Kingsley Davis long ago suggested that a particular inheritance pattern can raise or lower the age at marriage.[67] The point has been made specifically in relation to Japan. Jacobs noted that the system of partible inheritance in China helped encourage fertility: 'Overpopulation is an old and familiar story in China . . . the rural areas are permanently condemned to overpopulation.'[68] This is contrasted to the situation in Japan, with single-heir inheritance. At about the same time, Dore showed how inheritance systems influenced Japanese fertility, for example by affecting the age at marriage.[69] Likewise, Thomas Smith, discussed the effects of inheritance customs in Japan on population growth.[70] Robert Smith and Chie Nakane had suggested some intrinsic link between 'one-son' succession and industrialization, though they did not explicitly link this to fertility.[71]

We need to go beyond the distinction between partible and impartible inheritance. As a result of multiple causes, it would appear that the size of family and number of children was sensitive to economic pressures on these two islands. But it is important to note that while this differentiated both Japan and England from most 'peasant' civilizations, the mechanisms were different. In the Japanese case, a notion of very fixed 'slots' or ecological spaces, seems appropriate. These were not easily expandable, partly because of shortage of land, particular-

---

[66] For further discussion see Macfarlane, *Individualism*.
[67] Davis and Blake, *Analytic Framework*, 217–8.
[68] Jacobs, *Capitalism*, 156–7.
[69] Dore, *Fertility*, 66.
[70] Smith, *Pre-Modern Growth*, 150.
[71] In Laslett and Wall (eds), *Family*, 441,517; for a fuller discussion, see Macfarlane, *Individualism*.

ly of rice land, partly because of organization and taxation constraints. Even when wealth increased considerably through the growth of bi-employments from the seventeenth century, this did not lead to larger families. The reason for this is given by Smith, namely that 'non-agricultural occupations continue to be carried on mainly in conjunction with family farming.'[72]

The families may get richer, but not larger. The system of single-heir inheritance, which is so unusual, yet widespread in Japan, reflects this ecological constraint. In each generation there is one heir; additional children are a problem: 'primogeniture and associated institutions were probably important factors limiting the size of families in Tokugawa Japan because the presence and favoured treatment of the heir led to inevitable dissension and conflict within the family, an intolerable condition within the *ie* structure.'[73] Of course, as Hayami points out, single-heir inheritance was not universal, yet it was the dominant form and primogeniture does not authorize 'the formation of families by sons other than the eldest.' Sometimes there was ultimogeniture, sometimes it was the oldest child of whichever sex, as in parts of north-east Japan.[74] The important point is that there were slots, or breeding spaces, and that they were constrained: 'A large number of children on a small farm was almost as disastrous as no children at all.'[75] The Japanese case has one element of the 'peasant' model, namely the idea of fixed spaces, determined largely by agricultural resources. On the other hand it is very different from other cases in only allowing one heir to succeed to such a space – and often choosing a non-blood heir to fill the niche.

At one time it was thought that a similar model would be appropriate for England, namely that there were 'niches' which had to be filled and that such things as age at marriage, proportions marrying, numbers of children, could be explained best by analogies with animal populations and breeding territories. It has become increasingly apparent that this is not a useful approach. It is not the problem of filling of 'niches' through strategies of heirship which is important, but a much wider problem of earning a living in a market economy. Landers writes that 'Recent research on early modern England, however, has led to a greatly reduced emphasis on the demographic significance of inheritance, whilst enhancing that of a normative living standard or, "culturally determined moral economy".' In relation to the costs of children, 'The criterion on which the model is based is a predominant concern to minimize the current cost of children over a finite period of dependency, rather than a preoccupation with the problems of inheritance or "heirship".'[76] Richard Smith writes: 'Attempts to

[72] Smith, *Native Sources*, 35 cf. also 97.
[73] Nakamura, *Population*, 256.
[74] Hayami, *Myth*, 3–4,4,28.
[75] Hanley and Wolf (eds), *Family*, 197.
[76] Landers and Reynolds (eds), *Fertility*, 112.

understand European marriage characteristics and their associated fertility consequences through models that rely heavily on property, its mode of transmission, and its social distribution have had limited explanatory success.' And hence, 'In the individualistic society, fertility is likely to be determined by influences that are mediated through markets, both domestic and international, and geographical movements that can be both internal and external; it is also susceptible to influences of welfare policy and policy shifts on the part of those who fund and manage welfare systems.'[77]

This shift of emphasis has been exemplified by Goldstone. He stresses that the fluctuations in fertility are determined by changes in employment opportunities and real wages, rather than the number of 'ecological niches' available. For instance, 'Empirical evidence of the nuptiality response to short-term harvest and mortality fluctuations shows that in early modern England people tended to follow *welfare-dependent* nuptiality control. That is, fluctuations in harvest quality and wheat prices did evoke corresponding fluctuations in nuptiality, while fluctuations in mortality appear not to have evoked increases in the formation of new households.' One could, to a certain extent, adapt this to the 'ecological niche' argument in the sense that Goldstone suggests that from the middle of the eighteenth century, growing industrialization provided new opportunities for people to marry and set up homes.[78] Yet it is a very different situation from the normal agrarian environment, for people are now dependent on fluctuations in wages and job opportunities rather than inheriting land or traditional craft occupations.

As with so many comparisons between England and Japan we find that while the outcome was the same, the causes were different. In this case an unusually early separation of production from reproduction occurred on both islands. At the important decision-making level of the reproductive couple, people did not feel those pressures to have as many children as possible in order to be successful. Indeed they felt the opposite. They found that children had many costs as well as many benefits. In England this arose from a highly mobile, individualistic, system where the major unit of ownership and production was no longer the larger family. In Japan it was paradoxically the very strength of the ideal of keeping the 'family' going on a very restricted area that meant that people needed to keep exactly the right balance of land and labour and hence limit their fertility. In both cases the last part of the Malthusian trap had been avoided, though the cost of these solutions in terms of frustration, loneliness and, in Japan, the strain on women's bodies, was immense.

---

[77] In Landers and Reynolds (eds), *Fertility*, 107,112,178,181.
[78] cf. Goldstone, *Demographic*, 16,25–9.

Part VII

Outcome

21

Design and Chance

We can now see more clearly how the normal 'Malthusian' population tendencies failed to work in England and Japan. What happened does not fit with the picture of a single demographic transition from high mortality and fertility up to the nineteenth century and then low mortality and fertility after that. It would appear instead that by the fifteenth century, at least, the birth and death rates had stabilized at a lower level than is normally found in agrarian societies. There followed a second phase in England in the eighteenth century when mortality dropped further and fertility rose. What we normally think of as the 'demographic transition', the very rapid reduction in mortality and fertility in the late nineteenth and early twentieth century, is but the last of several waves.

While it is now easier to see what happened, it is still difficult to understand at a deeper level why it happened. We know the effects, the pattern of the past, but to study the causes which led to those effects, to reason backwards analytically from effect to cause, is much harder. Some of the difficulties can be illustrated by considering speculations concerning the fall in mortality.

Thomas McKeown has addressed the question of why mortality fell in England in the eighteenth century.[1] He suggested that there were four areas where the solution might lie: changes in the nature of infective organisms and/or their hosts, changes in medical knowledge and provision, wider changes in the environment (hygiene, sanitation, housing, clothing), and nutritional improvements caused by changes in food supply. McKeown then proceeded to show that the first three of these could not account for the change. By the method of exclusion he was left with only one possible cause, nutritional levels, which, 'however improbable', must be the truth. The difficulty is that there is

---

[1] His major survey is McKeown, *Modern Rise.*

no evidence of a sustained improvement in nutrition for the majority of the population in eighteenth-century England, but rather the reverse. Although McKeown's own theory has been undermined, no historian has been able to provide a credible alternative.

We may look again at McKeown's four suspects but lengthen the time frame. The argument that changes in the infective organism and its host may help explain the sudden and inexplicable disappearances of a number of diseases, for instance leprosy and plague was once widely canvassed. The unexplained decline of a number of diseases was alluded to by Creighton and more recently by Greenwood who wrote of the mysterious decline of tuberculosis and scarlet fever in the later nineteenth century.[2] In relation to bubonic plague it has been suggested that its sudden disappearance may have been due to changes in the behaviour of the rat or flea, which had nothing to do with human intervention. 'If this is true, it is perhaps the most gigantic example of good luck in the recorded history of mankind: the dietetic peculiarities of the free-ranging flea, apparently enabled the industrial Revolution to proceed on its way.'[3]

It now appears that 'although there have undoubtedly been changes in the character of individual infections, it is unreasonable to attribute to this alone the progressive decline in mortality from infection as a whole, after many centuries in which mortality remained high.'[4] Kunitz argues 'Certainly there were adjustments between parasites and hosts, but it is unlikely that either the waning of virulence of the former, or the rapid selection for resistance of the latter, are adequate explanations of the decline in European mortality.' In relation to inherited resistance, there is 'very little evidence from recent epidemiological studies that inherited resistance is significant in any infectious disease, with the exception of the association between the haemoglobinophies and malaria.'[5] Kunitz is likely to be right about the short term (a hundred years or so). There is no good evidence (yet) that changes in immune systems of humans are sufficiently rapid to account for the decline of diseases such as plague. However, it must be the case that long-term changes have occurred in the human immune system.

Conversely, it would be wrong to go to the other extreme and leave out entirely changes in the degree to which the micro-organisms responsible for diseases have altered. The consideration of various diseases in this book suggests that there may have been very substantial changes in bacterial and viral virulence over time. Not only do diseases influence each other but if we take the interplay between diseases and other environmental conditions, such as population density and nutrition, we may well be witnessing interactions involving

[2] Creighton, *Epidemics*, I, 280; Greenwood, Crowd Diseases, 65.
[3] Chambers, *Population*, 151.
[4] McKeown and Brown, *Medical Evidence*, 306.
[5] Kunitz, *Speculations*, 364,350.

bacterial and viral virulence levels which partly account for the rise and fall of many epidemic diseases. Creighton pointed out on several occasions that there are interactions between different diseases so that it is possible that as one increases it may lead to a decrease or increase in others. He showed that as typhus declined, typhoid rose, or as measles increased, smallpox declined.[6] This synergy of diseases has recently been noted by Cohen, who shows how the spread of malaria and hookworm is associated with the incidence of measles.[7]

The implication is that we have to study all the major diseases alongside each other. Furthermore, a long time perspective is needed in order to notice the patterns. Creighton wrote in conclusion to his work, 'In the long period covered by this history we have seen much coming and going among the epidemic infections, in some cases a dramatic and abrupt entrance, or exit, in other cases a gradual and unperceived substitution.' This leads him to his principal theory when trying to explain the mysterious disappearance of diseases like sweating sickness or plague, namely 'the only law of extinct disease-species which our scanty knowledge points to – the law of succession, or superseding, or supplanting of one epidemic type by another.'[8]

The changing virulence of diseases can be reinstated as one part of a set of interacting causes and effects, rather than being largely discounted as having little to do with the explanation of the mortality decline. It is not the sole explanation, but it is a significant link in the chain that leads us to the explanation. For instance a decline in virulence might lead to denser populations, which would in turn affect the disease organisms.

Turning to the second area considered by McKeown, we may agree with his conclusion that formal medical knowledge and practice is not an important part of the explanation for declining mortality in the period before the later nineteenth century. Almost all historians are agreed that medical advances played little part.[9] Only changes in the treatment of smallpox could have been significant and even Razzell, who most strongly argued for the importance of inoculation, has changed his mind.[10] Neither in England nor in Japan is it possible to explain the fluctuations in general mortality rates before the later nineteenth century in terms of medical practices. 'It is hard for modern man to assimilate the fact that until the twentieth century the contribution of medicine and medical institutions to the reduction of mortality was so slight as to be almost insignificant.'[11] Yet it happens to be the case. Here the causation flows the other

---

[6] Creighton, *Epidemics*, II, 202,629,659.
[7] Cohen, *Health*, 54.
[8] Creighton, *Epidemics*, II, 631; I, 280.
[9] See for example, Nikiforuk, *Fourth*, 138; Dubos, *Adapting*, 236; Szreter, *Mortality*, 3; Flinn, *European*, 99–100,336,368–9; Porter, *Disease*, 62–3.
[10] Razzell, *Essays*, 3,222 and ch.6.
[11] Petersen, *Malthus*, 160.

way. Improvements in life expectancy led to a demographic situation which in turn stimulated an industrial revolution which provided the wealth and technology (particularly the microscope) which made medical science at last of some value in the fight against infective disease.

That the growth in understanding happened very recently is shown if we look at the situation in England as late as the middle of the 1890s, long after the dramatic changes in mortality with which we have been concerned had already occurred. Creighton's *History of Epidemic Diseases* showed that a leading medical historian had little idea of what caused most major epidemics. Influenza, he believed, was caused by earthquakes; plague, cholera and typhoid by the miasma from decomposing bodies; typhus by cold and poverty, dysentery by miasma of faecal origin and leprosy by eating too much salty meat and by rough clothing.[12]

The authors writing on various diseases in *Chamber's Encyclopedia* of 1895 were likewise unsure of the causes of most of them. Smallpox 'is universally acknowledged to be a specific contagion of whose nature we are in the most profound ignorance.' Measles was one of 'the group of blood diseases', but no cause was given. Influenza 'is connected with some particular condition of the atmosphere, but what that condition is is not known.' The cause of plague was unknown, though it seemed to be carried in clothes, bedding and through direct contact. For typhus 'no characteristic organism has been discovered.' Malaria was the result of miasma, 'an earth-born poison which is generated in soils . . . it is impossible to state definitely what the morbific agent really is.' The causes of cholera were still disputed, but it was probably, like typhoid, the result of a germ found in water and milk, as Koch had argued. Dysentery was a disease of the blood found in low and swampy regions. 'Some authorities . . . regard dysentery as itself a malarial disease; but this is not certain.'[13] Given this state of almost total ignorance of causes, it is not surprising that the medical profession was largely unable to provide a cure.

On the other hand it is important to realize that in dealing with formal treatment we may overlook another kind of change in medical thought which is of fundamental significance. While it may be true that without any knowledge of the cause of specific diseases and without particular remedies, doctors and hospitals played little or no direct and short-term part, one needs to distinguish this from a much more generalized change that began to take place at least two and a half thousand years ago and which was made explicit in Greek medicine. This was the growing separation of the spiritual and material causes of suffering.

It would appear that over time in certain civilizations a decreasing emphasis was placed on supernatural causes, leaving material causes more exposed and important. Though people continued to be ignorant of the exact cause, they

---

[12] Creighton, *Epidemics*, II, 415; I, 176,337; I, 162; II, 214; II, 217–8; I, 111.
[13] See *Chamber's Encyclopaedia* under these disease names.

increasingly came to believe that the origins of disease might lie in the material environment. Thus they began to take preventive action such as keeping their houses clean, preferring pure water or avoiding drinking water altogether, encouraging bodily hygiene and sanitation, and instituting quarantine measures when diseases broke out. We have seen many of these preventive actions throughout this book, both in England and Japan.

In trying to explain this change one is aware that it is not exactly formal medical knowledge, but more a generalized growth of an interest in this-worldly and non-spiritual causes of suffering so that 'taking arms against a sea of troubles' people began to vanquish them. It was really a change in perception or cosmology. People began to be aware that different life styles gave you a less pain-filled life. Magical explanations were not disproved, but were 'outflanked', in other words became increasingly irrelevant. There was a growth of useful knowledge and observation of patterns of sickness, so people increasingly avoided, if possible, dangerous situations. There was a growing feeling that dirt was dangerous as well as unpleasant – that somewhere in it lay disease.

A way of looking at this is to reiterate the famous distinction proposed by Edward Evans-Pritchard between 'why' and 'how' causation.[14] In the period from about 1200–1880 in western Europe there was not much progress in understanding the precise nature of how infectious diseases occurred, primarily because the minute size of the micro-organisms made them invisible to the naked eye. Yet there was a shift in the answer to the 'why' questions, from remote 'first causes' (God/chance) which leave one with no room for action (except ritual and magic) and little hope of success, towards explanations of the 'why' which were located in secondary causes firmly situated in the material environment. Even if these were still very generalized, that is to say such things as 'other people', 'dirt', 'miasma' and so on, the shift was important. No-one knew precisely how most diseases were spread, but by locating the 'why' at this level several things followed.

People started to try to control their environment in order to improve their protection against what they guessed was the area from which trouble was likely to come. They instituted quarantine for plague, tried to improve the quality of water and food, tried to reduce 'miasma' and smells by drainage and sanitation, tried to keep houses and air 'clean'. In other words they actively encouraged many of the changes I record in my book. Thus many of the actions are the results not merely of 'blind chance' or the by-products of improved living standards, but also reflect a cosmological change which encouraged people to distance themselves from what they dimly perceived were the causes of disease – other people or the environment. They tried to control their social and natural world because they came to believe that it was in this material and physical

---

[14] Evans-Pritchard, *Witchcraft and Magic.*

world, rather than in the spiritual one, that the origins of diseases lay. This was in many ways a relearning of the Greek medical views that most illness lay in earth, air and water. It is a change which is partly incorporated into scientific texts, but is best seen in those everyday practices with which we have been concerned.

Through a process of 'selective retention' of successful, accidental, discoveries, people came to appreciate what the ancient Greeks had known and the Chinese independently discovered, namely the largely material basis of infective disease. We have seen that the rise of Western medicine was almost entirely based on an increasing perception of the importance of the material, non-supernatural, causes of disease. This has culminated today in a world where infective disease is studied as the interaction, at the atomic and electronic level, of particular patterns of atoms on the pathogen and particular patterns of atoms on the host. This is the ultimate in materialistic explanations.

The long route to this current form of explanation is paved with instances of the gradual assimilation and recognition of behaviour which distances the individual from the presumed, material, cause of disease or, as in the case of boiled water and tea, renders the presumed but unidentified cause of disease ineffective. It is not unreasonable to look upon this as an example of 'Selective Retention' at work, steadily operating over a very long period and through millions of individual decisions and cultural changes.[15]

This explanation connects with the third area examined by McKeown, namely general environmental changes. He looked at the way diseases were transmitted through water, food and insect vectors and was unable to find any significant improvements which would have led to a lowered mortality rate before the later nineteenth century. The only exception he found was a possible improvement in standards of hygiene which might have affected typhus, but this came late in the eighteenth century amongst the well-to-do and its effects only reached the majority of the population in the nineteenth century, after the events he was trying to understand occurred.

Subsequent studies tended to support McKeown's negative assessment. Although sanitary reforms and public health have been suggested as the explanation of the health changes of the later nineteenth century by Simon Szreter,[16] it was widely believed that this was a less convincing explanation in relation to the earlier health transitions for the period up to 1840. Demographic historians, taking account of the awful conditions created by the urban growth in England,

---

[15] For a further discussion of the Darwinian concept of blind variation and selective retention, see Campbell, *Selective Retention*. I am very grateful to Gerry Martin for his suggestions on this matter.

[16] Szreter, *Importance*, 17,26; for an attack on this view and a refutation, see Guha, *Decline* and Szreter, *Mortality*.

ruled this out. Petersen writes, 'during Malthus's lifetime hygienic conditions probably worsened or, at best, improved far too slowly to account for the decline in mortality from roughly 1760 to 1840.'[17] Schofield and Reher concluded, 'there is little evidence that in most areas sanitation and public-health measures improved during the period', thus 'it is very difficult to argue in favour of the importance of public-health measures in Europe before the second half of the nineteenth century.'[18]

One of the many paradoxes was noted by Helleiner. Speaking of the growth of cities from the sixteenth century, he wrote that 'It needs little imagination to realize that the emergence of these large human anthills created a host of problems – food, water, and fuel supply, sewage and garbage disposal, housing, paving etc.' Despite this, the 'same period which witnessed an unprecedented concentration of human beings in large cities, creating conditions favourable to epidemic outbreaks, paradoxically enough saw the beginnings of a development that was to end with the extinction of plague.'[19]

Much of this book has been concerned with showing the ways in which this picture is altered if we examine the complex links between health and environment in more detail. It has become obvious that a combination of the numerous features of the environment, including the absence of war, the nature of the material environment, and changes in patterns of behaviour, did affect health. As the decline in mortality occurred in eighteenth-century England, a number of contemporaries agreed that they were caused by changes in the environment.[20] They drew particular attention to clothing, ventilation and cleanliness of people, houses and streets. It turns out that they were right, though they could only show the associations, not the exact ways in which the disease chains worked.

The final area, which McKeown thought provided the most likely solution, was nutrition. At a simple level of cause and effect it is not difficult for McKeown's critics to show that changing food resources, by themselves, cannot be the main reason for the decline in mortality in eighteenth-century England. Historians have not found evidence of nutritional improvements and the results from studies of height and weight suggests, if anything, a deterioration in levels of nutrition.[21] There is no evidence of improvement in the first half of the eighteenth century when mortality began to fall. There was probably a decline in height between about 1750 and 1790, in the very period of most rapid

[17] Petersen, *Malthus*, 159.
[18] Schofield et al. (eds), *Decline*, 5,9.
[19] Helleiner, *Vital Revolution*, 83,84.
[20] Black, *Arithmetical*, 234; Place, *Illustrations*, 253,257–8; Malthus, *Population*, II, 182; Heberden, *Observations*, 95–6; Blane, *Dissertations*, 122,173,181.
[21] See Mercer, *Disease*, 35,152,169; Razzell, *Essays*, 152,157; Schofield and Rehr in Schofield et al. (eds), *Decline*, 9,21.

mortality decline, and certainly there was no marked improvement until the second half of the nineteenth century.[22] If we take the more cautious view stated by Fogel and others, that 'England appears to have been at least half a century into its Industrial Revolution before witnessing a marked improvement in the heights or nutrition of its labouring classes' we are left with the puzzle indicated by Kunitz, that 'mortality began to decline at least half a century before the height data indicate a significant improvement in nutrition.'[23] Or as Drummond pointed out some time ago, 'It is a remarkable fact that the second half of the eighteenth century saw a striking improvement in the general health of the people in spite of the declining standard of living among a large section.'[24]

This paradox can partly be solved by way of the set of interacting features I have elaborated. For instance, we need to consider drink as much as food. If we do so we can see how people could be much healthier as a result of drinking tea, although their height and weight might not be improved. More widely, we should not go too far in discounting food. While changes in nutrition may not have caused corresponding changes in mortality, the background level and nature of food is vital to understanding everything else. We know that almost all diseases both influence and are influenced by nutrition. The fact that both the Japanese and the English were relatively well fed and, on the whole, managed to avoid periodic famine from early on is a central part of the explanation. Food is important as one part of the causation, though on its own it explains little. The mistake is to concentrate on each causal element in isolation. It is only when we consider all the aspects in the complex interactions that we can begin to understand any single part. That the English ate a lot of meat or the Japanese a large amount of sea produce is, in itself, a neutral and meaningless fact. It is only when it is seen in context with all the other elements that we can begin to judge its significance. The situation which we face, as Mathias put it some years ago, is that the 'influences which combine to affect health, morbidity and mortality . . . are manifold and their interactions are still largely unravelled.'[25]

In order to proceed towards this 'unravelling' it is helpful to think of the causal problems in terms of chains, as a series of linked causes and effects. The causal flows are not continuous like string, but made up of discrete elements, each joined to the next. If we conceive of the problem in this way, we will at least be able to understand why it has been so difficult to solve the mystery of the escape from the Malthusian trap.

Before discussing these chains it is sensible to remind ourselves of the dis-

[22] See Steckel, *Heights*, 185–6; Fogel et al., *Stature*, 466; Razzell, *Essays*, 220; Shammas, *Consumer*, 122.

[23] Fogel et al., *Stature*, 480; Kunitz, *Height*, 278.

[24] Drummond, *Food*, 250.

[25] Mathias, *Transformation*, 283.

tinction between two types of cause. *Necessary* causes are those without which something could not have happened. For example, it might be argued that the absence of internal warfare for at least a century was a necessary cause for the first industrial revolution. But peace will not, in itself, cause industrial development. It will merely provide one element of the 'fertile ground' without which industrialism could not have occurred. *Necessary and sufficient* causes, on the other hand, are those without which something could not have happened and which, in themselves, were sufficient to explain why the consequence was bound to follow. An example would be the fact that after the pasteurization of milk, bovine TB was bound to decrease.

In pursuing such 'causal chain' analysis we should note that chains may be short or long, with few or many links in them. Often a single-link chain appears at first sight to provide an adequate 'explanation'. Thus, in 'explaining' moderate fertility in seventeenth-century England we might posit late age at first marriage as causing restrained fertility. In relation to mortality we might suggest links between cotton clothing and the absence of typhus; island status and the absence of war; volcanic hot springs and hygienic hot baths. Yet usually, on closer inspection, these causal links turn out to be only parts of lengthier and more complex chains, which are better understood as a set of necessary but never sufficient causes.

Many of the arguments put forward in this book have been based on two link chains: tea caused boiled water to be used, which caused dysentery to be minimized; an absence of large domestic animals caused there to be few flies which caused an absence of certain diseases; strong paper permitted handkerchiefs which caused less disease spread by nasal infection. Often in such two link chains the first link is explicit and intentional. People have to boil water to make tea, they like to use paper handkerchiefs to conceal unseemly body matter. The second link can be often incidental and unnoticed. Even the first link is often unintended. People in Japan did not keep domestic animals for a number of reasons, none of which is principally related to the fly problem. People in England did not turn to the use of china utensils because they were more hygienic, but principally because they were seized by a zeal for hot drinks and particularly tea.[26] The fact that people do not themselves see the links makes it more difficult for the analyst who has to undertake a thought experiment to discover them.

Even more difficult to perceive are three, four, five or longer chains.[27] An

[26] See Buer, *Health*, 60 on the effects of the use of china utensils.
[27] Chains can, of course, be much longer. A delightful example of a nine link chain is given in a tale told to a traveller in eighteenth-century Japan. A man claimed he had decided to invest in the making of boxes, using the following links: a high wind in Tokyo > dust clouds > sore eyes > blindness > need to learn musical instrument (samisen) to make money > samisen makers need gut for strings > kill cats > increase in rats > rats gnaw goods > high demand for boxes.

example of a four-link chain in the field of mortality might be: an earthquake prone geology caused the building of flexible, light houses which caused the absence of load-bearing walls which permitted movable sides for houses and allowed maximum ventilation which diminished certain diseases. An example of a five-link chain would be: a Buddhist belief about the sin of eating animals caused the absence of large domestic animals which caused the absence of animal manure which forced the use of night soil which permitted clean cities which caused less enteric disease.

In these cases, the chain is so long that it is unlikely that there is any intentional link between the start and end of the causal sequence. People observe the earthquakes, they have to build light houses and so on. But at each stage there are usually choices as well as constraints. Although the walls were not load-bearing, a whole set of other factors then enter. The presence of very good paper and bamboo in Japan permitted the building of houses with movable walls. The hot climate made it desirable to do so.

This added complication arises from the fact that at each link of the chain there are usually multiple causes and multiple effects. It is thus not a simple matter of tracing a series whereby A permits or causes B, which permits or causes C. We can consider this in its two aspects.

Each link may have a variable number of effects. Starting with at least two effects of one link in the chain, we could note that the drinking of tea had the double effect of making people boil water and of filling their stomach with a powerful disinfectant. Cotton clothes both allowed and necessitated frequent washing with boiling water and also, in contrast to wool, consisted of a vegetable fibre which gave lice a less attractive home. Glass both lets sunlight in, which kills certain bacteria and makes it easier for people to see and remove the 'dirt' in their houses.

The multiple effects of what might be considered merely a single link in certain chains, is well shown by the question of the presence or absence of large numbers of domesticated animals. In England, the very widespread use of cows, sheep, horses and pigs had numerous effects, both positive and negative. It permitted the wearing of good shoes, good clothing, an ample supply of animal protein, manure, and non-human labour. It also caused the public health problems of rotting carcasses and a huge amount of animal excrement. In reverse, the relative absence of domesticated animals in Japan caused protein shortages, long hours of work and a shortage of manure. But it also reduced such problems as tapeworm infestation, animal waste and fly infestation, and other diseases such

---

(Hizakurige, *Shank's Mare*, 73). Marc Bloch's famous, half-facetious, set of links from heavy ploughs > long fields > housing patterns > social structure used to explain the difference between southern and northern France is a classic example of this kind of analysis (See Bloch, *French Rural History*, 52–6).

as influenza which are associated with animals. A single link in a chain can thus have numerous consequences which usually have both positive and negative results.

Furthermore, a link in a chain is usually the result of multiple causation. It is seldom that we find a single cause, single effect, chain. Even two-cause explanations often seem unduly over-simple. Thus, while we can see that personal cleanliness in Japan might be the result of only two causes, plenty of hot water and Shinto beliefs about purity and dirt, we sense that these are only permissive and not fully causal. Or again, when we wonder whether the introduction of hops into England caused an improvement in health, we need to add in other 'causes'. We are forced to ask why beer drinking was so widespread in England and not, say, in Scotland or France. Part of the explanation is ecological: beer requires barley, which grows best in an English type of moist climate, the grape belt had its own drinks. Yet more than this is required. For beer drinking to have a dramatic effect the country had to be wealthy enough to be able to devote almost half of its grain crop to the making of drink. Few pre-industrial countries are that rich. We need at least three permitting causes to produce this effect.

Very often the causes are partly material, partly cultural. The chain which leads from the geological phenomenon of plentiful hot springs, through communal baths, to body hygiene is strongly affected by concepts of decency and modesty and by Shinto beliefs about the need for physical purity and the washing away of bodily dirt. At a deeper level, the very material 'facts' themselves are shaped by concepts. Many societies have straw but seldom do people use it to make shoes. This is not just a matter of comfort but is linked to the ideas of the danger and dirt inherent in the soil and the 'outside' world which then contributes to constituting the house as a pure and clean haven where 'outside' shoes are not used.

Examples of at least three causes acting together in the English case would be needed for the explanation of the English house: geography and geology (stone, wood, no earthquakes), widespread affluence and security, a legal system allowing private property in building and land, were all necessary for the final solution to be reached. Or again, English clothing was the result of abundant wool and leather, widespread wealth and craft skills. The absence of bubonic plague through Japanese history up to the late nineteenth century required a wide sea, quarantine at the ports and the absence of the necessity for grain imports.

Examples of four causes being necessary are equally numerous. In relation to abortion in Japan we have to consider simultaneously the absence of widespread mechanical contraception, a perceived shortage of resources, the attitude to the fetus in the womb, the attitude to women's bodies. These four-cause links can frequently be found in relation to mortality as well. To explain the development of the mosquito net in Japan we need to take into account the shape of rooms, the furnishing of the rooms, the availability of suitable materials out of which to make the netting, the necessary craft skills.

Often one finds there are many causes working together. Two examples of at least six causes may be given. Thus, in order to understand breast-feeding rates and practices one needs to consider the attitude to women's bodies, the status of women, the nature of women's work, the attitude towards the relations of men and animals, the views on what is proper food, the availability of alternative foodstuffs (such as animal milk). An example of a multi-causal link can be found in the study of famine. The degree to which famine will be a serious problem in a country depends on at least the following: the availability of food from the sea, the variability of climate over small areas, the absence or presence of epidemic diseases and particularly malaria, the availability of cheap bulk transport, the productivity of the agriculture, the degree to which wealth is left with the populace or siphoned off by the powerful, the degree of market integration and monetary economy, the level of warfare.

If we consider the complexity of possible causal chain analysis, we are faced with a daunting prospect. Suppose we had a seven link chain, each link producing four consequences. It has been calculated that this would create 21,844 possible 'paths' from the first to last link.[28] Even this does not capture the complexity because there are two further features to consider.

The first is that there are various kinds of loops and symbioses between cause and effect. Thus, war causes famine and disease, disease leads to more famine and so on. The complex relations between nutrition, disease, work and animals has been central to this book. Even within each of these features there are multiple interactions. Diseases mutually influence each other, for example malaria weakens people so that they become susceptible to other infections. Effects feed back and then become causes in a longer chain, for example the relative absence of widespread malaria in Japan added to the strength and efficiency and possibly the optimism of the population, leading to improvements in agriculture, which meant better-fed populations and improved health and more efficient agricultural techniques, all of which would make malaria less of a threat. The processes are often cumulative which helps to explain the increasing divergence of Japan and, to a lesser extent, England from their continental neighbours.

The loops can often lead to a vicious circle: high fertility frequently leads to high infant and maternal mortality, which leads to a desire for more children, which leads to a shortening of breast-feeding and younger age at marriage, which leads to even higher fertility and so on. It was these vicious loops, in particular the sequence of increased wealth leading to increased population

---

[28] Campbell, *Selective Retention*, 394, n4.

leading to increased mortality which in turn caused a decrease in wealth, with which we started in relation to the Malthusian formulation. But there are virtuous loops as well. We have seen a number of these in action, for instance increased wealth, leading to improved living conditions and more cleanliness, leading to less of a disease load on humans making them more hopeful, energetic and capable of increasing wealth further – that virtuous loop which somehow began to emerge in England and Japan.[29]

It is this kind of symbiosis between economic growth and population patterns which has attracted much of the attention of theorists. A brief summary of some of the arguments will illustrate the complexity of the feedback loops. As early as 1959 Krause had suggested that the European demographic pattern was an important cause of the industrial revolution, the slow growth of population at certain periods allowing capital accumulation.[30] Similar suggestions were put forward by John Hajnal in 1965, and more recently by Wrigley and Schofield.[31] Three causal links have been suggested in relation to the English case. The relatively slow population growth in the three generations before industrialization allowed capital saving and infra-structural improvement.[32] The economy grew faster than the population, and wealth accumulated. Then, when the economy began to accelerate rapidly from the middle of the mid eighteenth century, the delicate feedback mechanisms worked in another way and the expanding economy encouraged a rapid growth of population. At this point the rapid population growth, bringing economies of scale, a larger market and the required labour force, was as important as the restrained growth of the earlier period.

Other ways in which the population pattern interacted with economic growth have also been suggested. The middling mortality and fertility meant that the age structure was not dominated by very young and non-productive dependents.[33] Relatively low mortality, including the absence of war and famine, may have raised confidence and the ability to plan and invest which in turn encouraged economic activity.[34]

The theory that unusual economic development in England was somehow linked to its peculiar demographic pattern has been given support by similar arguments for Japan. It would appear that a particular and unusual relation between demography and economy was important, a similar mixture of slow

[29] For a good early description of the wealth-health-wealth loop, see Buer, *Health*, in particular 59–62.

[30] Krause, *Neglected Factors*, especially 536–7.

[31] Hajnal in Glass and Eversley, *Population*, 132; Wrigley and Schofield, *Population*, 439.

[32] See Spengler, *Demographic*, 92.

[33] Wrigley and Schofield, *Population*, 444–9.

[34] Livi-Bacci, *Population*, 107, quoting Helleiner; Mokyr, *Lever*, 155 quoting Boulding; Slack, *Plague*, 19.

growth of population when capital was being built up, with spurts of population in periods and areas where labour was needed.[35] A particularly detailed analysis of the symbiotic relationship has been made by Hanley and Yamamura who suggest similar causal links to those in the English case. Improvements in technology and a stationary population for over a hundred years before Japanese industrialization led to capital accumulation and an improved infrastructure. Likewise a propitious age structure and a low dependency ratio was a considerable advantage.[36]

Considering the two cases together makes it possible to see how complex the causal chains were. For industrialization it was not enough to have a suitable population pattern; there is little sign that Japan was developing towards an indigenous industrial revolution. Many other ingredients were needed. It was not sufficient just to have a stationary population – at times it needed to grow very fast. It is not enough to see population patterns as cause and economic growth as effect. As we have noted above, the causal chains were often circular. A propitious demography encouraged economic growth, which improved living conditions, which lowered mortality. It was at this point that Malthus feared the virtuous circle would break down. What was essential was that there be mechanisms to delay the rapid increase in fertility. These, as we have seen, were present in both countries. To understand such loops of causation we obviously have to consider all parts of the chain simultaneously. In doing so we have to add a further complexity.

The final complication arises from the importance of the order, timing and 'weight' of each link. To take a very simple example of timing, if tea had been introduced to England in the thirteenth rather than the seventeenth century its effects would have been different. Or again, in respect to 'weight' or volume, if the transportation system from Asia in the eighteenth century had only been able to deliver small quantities of tea, then its effect would have been minimal. Or, to take an example from the interactions of population and economic growth, it is not just the nature of each that is important, but the timing and order of events. Wrigley shows that it was not the homeostatic relations between population and resources that was important in England, but 'the remarkable slowness of response between economic (real wage) and demographic (fertility) changes.'[37] It was the fifty year gap in the feedback mechanism, that was essential.

If we multiply these relatively simple examples a hundred times to take into account the introduction of the many technologies and philosophies into England and Japan over the thousand years preceding the nineteenth century, it is

---

[35] See Hayami, *Population Growth*; Smith, *Native Sources*, 16,96.
[36] Hanley and Yamamura, *Economic*, especially, 310ff.
[37] Wrigley and Schofield, *Population*, 451.

possible to glimpse how the causal chains became even more random and complex. There is no necessary and inevitable progress from A to B to C. Instead the process is much closer to the 'Blind Variation and Selective Retention' model beloved of evolutionary biology.[38] Many of the chains were 'successful' for a time, having considerable effects, and then died out. The Japanese use of night soil, or of paper for windows were extremely 'successful' for a time. In the end, however, they were replaced respectively by the English water closet and by plate glass. A diagram of what happened, with causes bouncing off other causes, and effects leading to other effects or back in loops, would look like the tracks of vast flocks of wading birds across the sands of time.

There are some methodological implications of this kind of causal chain analysis. The first is the need for a holistic or total approach to apparently narrow problems. In order to understand the absence of malaria or widespread enteric illness in Japan, or the general prevalence of breast-feeding in England, we have to examine the whole of the culture. The causal chains will zig-zag back and forth between different domains. They will certainly not remain within medicine or biology. They often lead in unexpected ways into religion, law, economics and elsewhere.

A second point is that since the chains are often long and extremely complex, the effects are unintended and usually unknown to the people who are affected by them. To discover what they are likely to be requires a combination of systematic intuition and techniques of testing links which bears a close resemblance to the 'backward' analytic method used by detective story writers. One cannot proceed by the method of conscious, logical, steps. 'Logic is an unreliable instrument for the discovery of the truth, for its use implies knowledge of all the components of an argument – in most cases an unjustified assumption.'[39] One part of this backward analytic technique lies in the use of the comparative method. If one only considers one case, England for example, or Japan, many of the links lie invisible both to the actors themselves and to later analysts. Only when we look at two or, preferably, three cases, do the links and chains become visible.

If we now return explicitly to the central puzzle behind this book, namely how England and Japan managed, at least partially, to escape from the Malthusian trap, we will find that the idea of unintended and apparently random chains of cause and effect helps to make us aware of the ways in which something so unpredictable might have occurred.

The problem of explanation is particularly difficult in the case of mortality where there appeared to be an impasse. One cannot have a society sophisticated

[38] For a good overview, see Campbell, *Selective Retention*.
[39] Dubos quoted in Bynum and Porter (eds), *Companion Encyclopaedia*, 473.

enough to make the powerful microscopes which made it possible to see bacteria until many developments have occurred, in mathematics, in glass manufacture, in precision engineering and so on. It requires a large set of interrelated developments which only flourished after the first industrial revolution. Medicine could only be really effective after an industrial revolution, yet such an industrial revolution depended on mortality being controlled. If the machine for giving the knowledge to conquer many diseases could only come after a reasonable plateau of disease had been reached, how could that be reached without the appropriate knowledge?

The answer seems to lie in the theory of unintended consequences or accidents. People often do the right thing for the wrong reason, or rather, do a thing for one reason and then find that it has other effects. The case of tea-drinking is an excellent example. In China and Japan tea drinking was introduced to improve health. In the west, apart from a few enthusiasts, it was mainly drunk for its reviving effects, though the health benefits were enormous. The same was true of cotton. Or again, maternal breast-feeding was encouraged in England and Japan for numerous reasons but few of them had anything to do with the conscious effort to lower mortality and fertility.

Often the changes only had to be slight. This was noticed by Creighton in relation to leprosy, which he thought was largely caused by poverty, so that 'it was easily shaken off by the national life when the conditions changed ever so little.'[40] The same slight tipping of the balance may apply to many diseases. 'An adequate level of nutrition, a tolerably pure water supply, a fairly low level of contact with serious infectious disease and an absence of opportunities for the rapid multiplication of disease vectors . . . may permit an average life span of half a century even though medical knowledge is slight and medical practitioners may be few and ignorant.'[41] Szreter also emphasizes that one of the main lessons of the British case is that life saving through improved public health can occur without advanced medical technology.[42] This is even more forcefully shown by the Japanese example. Their social and bodily habits eliminated most of the major epidemic diseases well before the advent of modern medicine.

The reasons for the changes were thus only incidentally to do with medicine. 'Europe made the transition to a demographic regime in which people lived longer and died from chronic rather than acute disease', partly 'because people washed their hands, their bodies, and their houses; learned not to spit in public, killed flies, kept food from going bad.'[43] They did many of these things largely

[40] Creighton, *Epidemics*, II, 112.
[41] Wrigley, *Death*, 144.
[42] Szreter, *Importance*, 37.
[43] Wear, in Bynum and Porter (eds), *Companion Encyclopaedia*, 1305.

for reasons which had little do with health in itself, a number were socially conditioned. There are numerous ways in which human pride, conceit, love of status has unintended consequences, leading to changes in clothing, body decoration, food and housing which cumulatively had considerable effects. Whatever the reasons, Riley and others are surely right in arguing that 'if there was a revolution in medicine at the end of the eighteenth century . . . it involved the medicine of the individual; the revolution in the medicine of groups came earlier.'[44]

That revolution in the medicine of groups is most clearly seen in the case of Japan and it is the Japanese example which has made it possible to disentangle some of the ways it worked in England. In the English case the causal chains are particularly complicated because the patterns of mortality and fertility are so intertwined with the first industrial revolution as both cause and effect. In Japan we can hold technology fairly constant and watch the way in which the organization of the society and cultural values led to an impressive control of mortality and fertility.

Observing the two cases also emphasizes the different paths which may lead to roughly the same end. In almost every respect the Japanese and English differed in their strategies, starting from entirely different cultural and geological foundations in many ways the end results were not that dissimilar. Chains which start in different places and move through contrasted links may end with the same results.

Another implication of this book is that almost every change has negative as well as positive effects. There is almost always a contradiction or tension in 'progress'. The control of fertility helped the English and Japanese to avoid the worst excesses of famine, but it was at the cost of much frustration and unhappiness at delayed or absent marriages in England and an heavy cost to women's bodies and minds through abortion and infanticide in Japan. The presence or absence of large numbers of domestic animals, as we have seen, both had their costs. Zealous washing and bodily care in Japan helped avoid certain diseases but encouraged others, notably of the skin and eye, in their stead. Drinking tea led to better health, but, when compared to beer, worse nutrition. The use of night soil in agriculture in Japan helped lower enteric disease, but increased schistosomiasis. The wearing of cotton in England lowered the incidence of typhus, but was less warm and pleasant than woollen clothing. The rapidly increasing use of coal in England 'made possible better warmed houses, better cooked food and greater cleanliness' through the supply of pumped water,[45] but it also aggravated air-pollution and hence pulmonary diseases. The contradictory consequences are numerous and remind us that for almost every two steps forward on one

[44] Ramsey, *Environment*, 613, summarizing Riley.
[45] Buer, *Health*, 60.

front, there is a step back on another, a lesson we are constantly reminded of as
we watch the 'progress' of industrial capitalism today.

A further methodological implication was discussed by Sorokin. He pointed
out that multiple causation theory and the analysis of long chains can easily
degenerate into vagueness. It soon becomes impossible to separate the important
from the trivial. Almost everything is relevant, to a limited degree, as Chaos
Theory has recently re-emphasized.[46] In order to overcome some of these difficulties, Sorokin suggests that 'more fruitful seems to be the way of discovery of
the main, the necessary cause of these phenomena with an indication of the
supplementary factors that facilitate and inhibit the effects of the main cause'.[47]

In the case of this book, the single central necessary cause was islandhood. I
have considered some of the numerous supplementary causes which were also
needed to lead to the exceptional development of these islands, even when
compared to others. Yet it does seem to be the case that islandhood was the
necessary if not sufficient condition for what happened. If England and Japan
had not been large islands, it seems inconceivable that they would have developed in such an unusual way. This can be shown briefly in relation to the link
between islandhood and war.

In terms of international warfare, England for many centuries was in an ideal
position. It could benefit from any technological advances made during the
conflict of European powers, particularly in metalworking. It could raid its
neighbours' wealth. Yet it was not pillaged or even very seriously threatened for
many hundreds of years. It was as if a windbreak had been accidentally formed
around this small plot of fertile ground. This shelter was undoubtedly a key
factor in the later economic miracle. As Nef puts it, the advantages of its position
'allowed Great Britain a long respite from exhausting military effort', an advantage 'not shared by most European states'.[48] Holland had some of the advantages
through its man-made water defences in the century after 1580. But these
became stretched as the power of France increased and the thinness of the flood
dike defences became apparent.

The English in contrast developed a virtuous spiral. The protected position
enabled taxes to be relatively low, encouraged its merchants and trade, which
built up the fleet and hence increased security. They never suffered from the
total shattering which occurred when, in every other large country in Europe or
Asia with the exception of Japan, a foreign nation conquered its soil and took
control. Marc Bloch, E.L.Jones and Joel Mokyr have all pointed to the seeming-
ly curious fact that 'Only those parts of Eurasia that were spared the conquests
of Mongols – Japan and western Europe – were able to generate sustained

---

[46] Sorokin, *Sociological Theories*, 103; Sorokin, *Society*, 505.
[47] Sorokin, *Society*, 507.
[48] Nef, *War*, 116.

technological progress.'[49] We can take the argument one step further and note that even within the favoured area of western Europe, England was enormously lucky to be spared invasions and land wars on its territory.

Yet of course, even if it avoids invasion by others an island can easily be wracked by civil war, as we see so clearly in the contemporary case of Sri Lanka. Thus the relative absence of civil war in England cannot be explained by geography alone, though not having powerful states on one's land borders was an enormous advantage. The avoidance of prolonged and civil strife was the result of constant political effort and of a judicial system that was developed from the twelfth century to iron out disputes without recourse to physical violence. The system was extremely effective in preventing damaging civil wars. Even when disputes did break out, as in the Wars of the Roses, the Pilgrimage of Grace or Monmouth's Rebellion, there was usually little destruction.

This double absence of war explains why to travel round England now is to see an ancient, prosperous, landscape, where many medieval churches and buildings remain. Unlike almost every other country in the world, it has not been periodically destroyed by foreign armies or civil wars. The ancient buildings are the outward manifestation of a gradual and peaceful accumulation of wealth, a slow build-up which provided the necessary fertile ground for the unprecedented increase in productivity of the eighteenth century.

While the connections between islandhood and absence of war might look accidental if we considered England alone, we have also seen that Japan reaped the same advantages from its island position. Peace, prosperity, a balance of political power and islandhood seem to be linked in these two cases.

There is always a strong tendency to impose a pattern on the past and to assume an inevitability in events. There appears to be design, necessity, even calculation. Yet, as Chambers noted long ago, 'changes in the long-term trend of population appear to have sprung from forces that were, from an economic point of view fortuitous'.[50] It was not only from an economic point of view, however. What happened was not only a gigantic accident, but also an enormous exception. It was a strange occurrence that ought not to have happened, nearly did not happen, yet by a set of coincidences and chances, did happen – twice. The point is well made by Mokyr: 'The study of technological progress is therefore a study of exceptionalism, of cases in which as a result of rare circumstances, the normal tendency of societies to slide towards stasis and equilibrium was broken. The unprecedented prosperity enjoyed today by a substantial proportion of humanity stems from accidental factors to a degree greater than is commonly supposed.'[51]

[49] Mokyr, *Lever*, 186.
[50] Chambers, *Population*, 59; see also 151.
[51] Mokyr, *Lever*, 16.

Given this set of curious chances, it is not surprising that many of the most intelligent observers living some two hundred years ago on a small island had little inkling of the vast transformation that was already underway. Adam Smith, Edward Gibbon, Thomas Malthus could not share our hindsight. Only now can we understand some of the incredibly complex, usually chance, links and chains which would make it possible for the first time to reverse the conditions of production and reproduction so that hundreds of millions could be reasonably fed, clothed, housed and at least temporarily freed from the daily fear of war, famine and epidemic disease.

Bibliography

The bibliography includes all works referred to in the text. All books are published in London, unless otherwise indicated.

The following abbreviations have been used.

Am.	American
Econ.	Economic
ed.	edited or editor
edn	edition
eds	editors
Hist.	Historical
Jnl.	Journal
n.d.	no date
n.s.	new series
no.	number
pt.	part
Proc.	Proceedings
Pub.	Publications
Rev.	Review
Soc.	Society
tr.	translated by
Trans.	Transactions
Univ.	University
vol.	volume

Aberle, S.B.D., 'Child Mortality among Pueblo Indians', *American Jnl. of Physical Anthropology*, vol.xvi, no.3, 1932.

Alcock, Sir Rutherford, *The Capital of the Tycoon: A Narrative of a Three Years' Residence in Japan*, 1863.

Allison, A., (ed.), *Population Control*, 1970.

Anglicus, Bartholomaeus, *On the Properties of Things [De Proprietatibus Rerum, c.1230]*. tr. John Trevisa, 1975 reprint.

Appleby, Andrew, 'Diet in Sixteenth-century England: Sources, Problems, Possibilities' in Charles Webster (ed.), *Health, Medicine and Mortality in the Sixteenth Century*, 1979.

Appleby, Andrew, *Famine in Tudor and Stuart England*, 1978.

Arch, Joseph, *From Ploughtail to Parliament, An Autobiography*, (originally written 1892–3), reprinted, 1986.

Ardener, Edwin, *Divorce and Fertility, an African Study*, 1962.

Armstrong, David, 'Birth, Marriage and Death in Elizabethan Cumbria', *Local Population Studies*, no.53, Autumn 1994.

Ariès, Philippe, *Centuries of Childhood*, tr. Robert Baldick, 1962.

Aristotle, *The Works of Aristotle*. New improved edn no date (early nineteenth century; published by Miller, Law and Cater).

Ariyoshi, Sawako, *The Twilight Years*, tr. Mildred Tahara, 1984.

Arnold, David, *Famine, Social Crisis and Historical Change*, 1988.

Arnold, Sir Edwin, *Seas and Lands*, 1895.

Aubrey, John, *The Natural History of Wiltshire*, John Britton (ed.), Wilts. Topographical Society Pub., 1847.

Aykroyd, W.R., *The Conquest of Famine*, 1974.

Bacon, Alice M., *Japanese Girls and Women*, 1902.

Bairoch, Paul, *Cities and Economic Development from the Dawn of History to the Present*, 1988.

Barley, M.W., *The English Farmhouse and Cottage*, 1961.

Barrett, Timothy, *Japanese Papermaking, Traditions, Tools, and Techniques*, New York, 1983.

Basch, Paul F., *Schistosomes: Development, Reproduction and Host Relations*, Oxford, 1991.

Bayne-Powell, Rosamond, *Travellers in Eighteenth-Century England*, 1951.

Beardsley, Richard, K., Hall, John W., and Ward, Robert E., *Village Japan*, Chicago, 1959.

Beaver, M.W., 'Population, Infant Mortality and Milk', *Population Studies*, vol.xxvii, no.2, 1973.

Beckmann, John A., *A History of Inventions, Discoveries and Origins*. tr. William Johnston, revised and enlarged by William Francis and J.W.Griffith, 1846.

Behn, Aphra, (attr.), *The Ten Pleasures of Marriage, and the second part, The Confessions of the New Married Couple* (1682–3), reprint, 1922.

Bellah, Robert N., *Tokugawa Religion, the Values of Pre-Industrial Japan*, Illinois, 1957.

Benedictow, Ole J., 'The Milky Way in History: Breast Feeding, Antagonism Between the Sexes and Infant Mortality in Medieval Norway', *Scandinavian Jnl. of History*, vol.10, no.1, 1985.

Bennett, H.S., *The Pastons and their England*, 1968.

Biller, P.P.A., 'Birth-Control in the Medieval West', *Past and Present*, no.94, Feb. 1982.

Bird, Isabella, *Unbeaten Tracks in Japan* (1880), reprint 1984.

Birdsell, Joseph, 'Some Predictions for the Pleistocene Based on Equilibrium Systems Among Recent Hunter-Gatherers' in Richard Lee and Irven DeVore (eds), *Man the Hunter*, Chicago, 1968.

Black, William, *An Arithmetical and Medical Analysis of the Diseases and Mortality of the Human Species*, 1789.

Blackstone, William, *Commentaries on the Laws of England with an Analysis of the Work*, 1829.

Blane, Sir Gilbert, *Select Dissertations on Several Subjects of Medical Science*, 1822.

Bloch, Ivan, *Sexual Life in England Past and Present*. tr. William H. Forstern, 1938.

Bloch, Marc, *French Rural History, An Essay on its Basic Characteristics*. tr. Janet Sondheimer, 1966.

Blundell, Margaret, (ed.), *Blundell's Diary and Letter Book, 1702–1728*, 1952.

Boorde, Andrew, *A Compendyous Regyment or a Dyetary of Health* (1542), F.J.Furnivall (ed.), 1870.

Boorde, Andrew, *The Breviarie of Health*, 1575.

Boserup, Ester, *Population and Technology*, 1981.

Boserup, Ester, 'The Impact of Scarcity and Plenty on Development', *Jnl. of Interdisciplinary History*, vol.xiv no.2, Autumn 1983.

Boswell, James, *Boswell in Search of a Wife 1766–1769*. James Brady, Frank Pottle and Frederick Pottle, (eds), 1957.

Boswell, James, *Life of Johnson*, George B.Hill (ed.), Oxford, 1887.

Boswell, James, *London Journal 1762–3*, Frederick Pottle (ed.), 1951.

Bowers, John Z., *Western Medical Pioneers in Feudal Japan*, Baltimore, 1970.

Brand, van Someran, (ed.), *Les Grandes Cultures du Monde*, Paris, n.d. c.1900.

Braudel, Fernand, *Afterthoughts on Material Civilization and Capitalism*, tr. Patricia M.Ranum, 1977.

Braudel, Fernand, *Capitalism and Material Life 1400–1800*, 1967.

Braudel, Fernand, *Civilization and Capitalism 15th–18th Century*, 1981–4.

Browne, Edith A., *Tea*, 1917.

Bruce-Chwatt, Leonard J., and De Zulueta, Julian, *The Rise and Fall of Malaria in Europe*, Oxford, 1980.

Buchan, William, *Domestic Medicine: or, A Treatise on the Prevention and Cure of Diseases*, 11th edn, 1790.

Buer, M.C., *Health, Wealth, and Population in the Early Days of the Industrial Revolution*, 1926.

Burn, Richard, *Ecclesiastical Law*, 5th edn, 1788.

Burn, Richard, *The Justice of the Peace and Parish Officer*, 16th edn, 1788.

Burnett, John, *Plenty and Want*, 1979.

Burnett, John, *Social History of Housing 1815–1970*, Newton Abbott, 1978.

Burnett, Macfarlane, and White, David, *Natural History of Infectious Disease*, 1972.

Bushman, Richard L., and Bushman, Claudio L., 'The Early History of Cleanliness in America', *The Jnl. of Am. History*, vol.74, no.4, March 1988.

Busvine, James R, *Insects and Hygiene*, 1980.

Bynum, W.F., and Porter, R., (eds), *Companion Encyclopaedia of the History of Medicine*, 1993.

Byrne, M., St.Clare, *Elizabethan Life In Town and Country*, 1934.

Cambridge History of Japan, vol.1. Ancient Japan, Delmer M.Brown (ed.), 1993.

Cambridge History of Japan, vol.3. Medieval Japan, Kozo Yamamura (ed.), 1990.

Cambridge History of Japan, vol.4. Early Modern Japan, John Whitney Hall (ed.), 1991.

Cambridge History of Japan, vol.5. The Nineteenth Century, Marius B.Jansen (ed.), 1989.

Cambridge History of Japan, vol.6. The Twentieth Century, Peter Duus, (ed.), 1988.

Campbell, Donald T., 'Blind Variation and Selective Retention in Creative thought as in Other Knowledge Processes', *Psychological Review*, no.67, 1960.

Campbell, Mildred, *The English Yeoman under Elizabeth and the Early Stuarts*, New Haven, 1942.

Cassen, R.H., *India: Population, Economy, Society*, 1978.

Cellier, Mrs Elizabeth, 'A Scheme for the Foundation of a Royal Hospital', *Harleian Miscellany*, vol.ix, 1810.

Chadwick, Edwin, *Report on the Sanitary Condition of the Labouring Population of Gt. Britain* (1842), ed. with intro. by M.W. Flinn, 1965.

Chalkin, C.W., *Seventeenth Century Kent. A Social and Economic History*, 1965.

Chamberlain, Basil Hall, *Japanese Things, Being Notes on Various Subjects Connected with Japan*, (originally published as 'Things Japanese, in 1904), Tokyo, 1990.

Chamber's Encyclopaedia, New Edition, 1895.

Chambers, J.D., *Population, Economy, and Society in Pre-Industrial England*, 1972.

Chambers, J.D., 'The Vale of Trent, 1670–1800', *Economic Hist. Rev. Supplement*, 3, 1957.

Characters and Observations, an 18th Century Manuscript, 1930.

Chaucer, Geoffrey, *The Works*, Alfred W. Pollard (ed.), 1965.

Cipolla, Carlo, *Before the Industrial Revolution, European Society and Economy 1000–1700*, 1981.

Cipolla, Carlo, *The Economic History of World Population*, 1962.

Clark, Alice, *Working Life of Women in the Seventeenth Century*, New York, 1919.

Clark, Colin, *Population Growth and Land Use*, 1968.

Clark, Timothy, *Ukiyo-e Paintings in the British Museum*, 1992.

Clark, Peter, *The English Alehouse, a Social History 1200–1830*, 1983.

Clarkson, Leslie, *Death, Disease and Famine in Pre-Industrial England*, Dublin, 1975.

Clearly, Thomas, *The Japanese Art of War, Understanding the Culture of Strategy*, 1991.

Clegg, A.G., and Clegg, P.C., *Man Against Disease*, 1980.

Coale, Ansley J., 'T.R.Malthus and the Population Trends of His Day and Ours', *Encyclopaedia Britannica Lecture*, Edinburgh, 1978.

Cobbett, William, *Cottage Economy*, 1823.

Cobbett, William, *The Progress of a Plough-boy to a Seat in Parliament*, William Reitzel (ed.), 1933.

Cockburn, J.S., (ed.), *Crime in England 1550–1800*, 1977.

Cogan, Thomas, *The Haven of Health*, 1589.

Cohen, Mark Nathan, *Health and the Rise of Civilization*, New Haven, 1989.

Coleman, David, and Schofield, Roger, (eds), *The State of Population Theory, forward from Malthus*, 1986.

Coleman, Samuel, *Family Planning in Japanese Society. Traditional Birth Control in a Modern Urban Culture*, Princeton, 1983.

Comenius, Johannes Amos, *Orbis Sensualium Pictus*, 1672.

Conder, Joseph, *Landscape Gardening in Japan* (1912), New York, 1964.

Cooley, Arnold J., *The Toilet in Ancient and Modern Times with a Review of the Different Theories of Beauty and Copious Allied Information Social, Hygienic, and Medical* (1866), New York, 1970.

Cornell, J.B., and Smith, R.J., *Two Japanese Villages. Matsunagi, a Japanese Mountain Community and Kurusu, a Japanese Agricultural Community*, New York, 1969.

Cornell, Laurel L., 'Why Are There No Spinsters in Japan?,' *Jnl. of Family History*, Winter, 1984.

Cortazzi, Hugh, *Dr Willis in Japan, British Medical Pioneer 1862–1877*, 1985.

Coulton, G.G., *Medieval Village, Manor, and Monastery*, New York, 1960.

Coverdale, Myles, *The Christian State of Matrimony*, (translation of Bullinger), 1575.

Crawford, Patricia, ' "The Suckling Child": Adult Attitudes to Child Care in the First Year of Life in Seventeenth-century England', *Continuity and Change*, vol.1, 23–51, 1986.

Creighton, Charles, *A History of Epidemics in Britain*, 2 vols, 1891 and 1894.

Crosby, Alfred W., *Ecological Imperialism, the biological expansion of Europe, 900–1900*, 1994.

Culpeper, Nicholas, *A Directory of Midwives*, 1656.

Curteis, Thomas, *Essays on the Preservation and Recovery of Health*, 1704.

Curtis, Donald, Hubbard, Michael, and Shepherd, Andrew, *Preventing Famine, Policies and Prospects for Africa*, 1988.

Daedalus, Historical Population Studies, *Jnl. of the American Academy of Arts and Sciences*, Spring 1968.

Dasgupta, Partha, *An Inquiry into Well-Being and Destitution*, Oxford, 1993.

Davidson, Stanley, Passmore, R., and Brock, J.F., *Human Nutrition and Dietetics*, 1973.

Davies, Maude F., *Life in an English Village*, 1909.

Davis, David E., 'The Scarcity of Rats and the Black Death: An Ecological History', *Jnl. of Interdisciplinary History*, vol.xvi, no.3, Winter 1986.

Davis, K., and Blake, J., 'Social Structure and Fertility: An Analytic Framework', *Economic Development and Social Change*, vol.4, no.3, 1956.

Davis, Kingsley, 'The Theory of Change and Response in Modern Demographic History', *Population Index*, vol.xxix, 1963.

De Mause, Lloyd, (ed.), *The History of Childhood, the Evolution of Parent-Child Relationships as a Factor in History*, 1976.

De Saussure, Cesar, *A Foreign View of England in the Reigns of George I and George II, the Letters of Monsieur Cesar de Saussure to his Family*, Madame van Muyden (ed.), 1902.

De Tocqueville, Alexis, *Memoir, Letters, and Remains of Alexis de Tocqueville*, 1861.

De Vries, Jan, *The Economy of Europe in an Age of Crisis, 1600–1750*, 1976.

Deane, Phyllis, and Cole, W.A., *British Economic Growth 1688–1959. Trends and Structure*, 1962.

Diggory, Peter, Potts, Malcolm, and Teper, Sue, (eds), *Natural Human Fertility, Social* and Biological Determinants. *Proceedings of the Twenty-third Annual Symposium of the Eugenic Society*, London, 1986, 1988.

Dobson, Mary J., '"Marsh Fever" – the geography of malaria in England', *Jnl. of Historical Geography*, vol.6, no.4, 1980.

Dobson, Mary J., 'The Last Hiccup of the Old Demographic Regime: Population Stagnation and Decline in Late Seventeenth and Early Eighteenth-century South-east England', *Continuity and Change* 4, vol.3, 1989.

Dodds, E.R., *The Greeks and the Irrational*, California, 1966.

Dore, R.P., *City Life in Japan, a Study of a Tokyo Ward*, California, 1971.

Dore, R.P., 'Japanese Rural Fertility; some Social and Economic Factors', *Population Studies*, vol.vii, no.1, July 1953.

Dore, Ronald, *Shinohata, a Portrait of a Japanese Village*, 1978.

Douglas, Mary, *Purity and Danger, an Analysis of Concepts of Pollution and Taboo*, 1966.

Drake, Michael, *Population and Society in Norway 1735–1865*, 1969.

Drake, Michael, (ed.), *Population in Industrialization*, 1969.

Drummond, J.C., and Wilbraham, Anne, *The Englishman's Food, a History of Five Centuries of English Diet*, revised with a new chapter by Dorothy Hollingsworth, 1969.

Du Boulay, F.R.H., *An Age of Ambition. English Society in the Late Middle Ages*, 1970.

Dubos, Rene, *Man Adapting*, New Haven, 1968.

Dubos, Rene, *The World of Rene Dubos: A Collection from his Writings*, Gerard Piel and Osborn Segerberg (eds), New York, 1990.

Duffy, Michael, *The Englishman and the Foreigner, The English Satirical Print 1600–1832*, 1986.

Dumond, D.F., 'Population Growth and Cultural Change', *Southwestern Jnl. of Anthropology*, vol.21, 1965.

Dunn, C.J., *Everyday Life in Traditional Japan*, 1969.

Dyer, Christopher, 'English Diet in the Later Middle Ages', in *Social Relations and Ideas: Essays in Honour of R.H. Hilton*, T.H. Aston et al. (eds), 1983.

Dyer, Christopher, *Everyday Life in Medieval England*, 1994.

Dyson, Tim, 'On the Demography of South Asian Famines Part 1', *Population Studies*, no.45, 1991.

Dyson, Tim, and Murray, Mike, 'The Onset of Fertility Transition', *Population and Development Review*, vol.11, no.3, 1985.

Earle, Peter, *The Making of the English Middle Class*, 1989.

Ehrlich, Paul, and Ehrlich, Anne, *Population, Resources, Environment: Issues in Human Ecology*, San Francisco, 1970.

Elias, Norbert, *The Civilizing Process, The History of Manners*, 1978.

Embree, John F., *A Japanese Village, Suye Mura*, 1946.

Emerson, Ralph Waldo, *English Traits*, Boston, 1884.

Emmison, F.G. *Elizabethan Life; Home, Work and Land*, Chelmsford, 1976.

Encyclopaedia Britannica, 11th edn., 1910–1.

Encyclopaedia of the Social Sciences, Edwin R.Seligman (ed.), 1st edn, New York, 1935; David L. Sills (ed.) 2nd edn, 1968.

Engel, Heinrich, *The Japanese House, a Tradition for Contemporary Architecture*, Vermont, 1974.

Ernle, Lord, *English Farming Past and Present*, new edition, Sir A.D.Hall (ed.), 1936.

Evans-Pritchard, E.E., *Witchcraft, Oracles and Magic among the Azande*, Oxford, 1937.

Ewald, Paul W., *Evolution of Infectious Disease*, Oxford, 1994.

Eyre, Adam, 'Diary', in *Yorkshire Diaries and Autobiographies in the 17th and 18th Centuries*, H.J.Morehouse (ed.), Surtees Society, vol.xv, 1875.

Fairbank, John King, 'The Paradox of Growth without Development' in *China A New History*, Harvard, 1992.

Farley, John, *Bilharzia, a History of Imperial Tropical Medicine*, 1991.

Farris, William Wayne, *Population, Disease and Land in Early Japan*, Harvard 1985.

Feachem, Richard, et al., (eds), *Water, Wastes and Health in Hot Climates*, New York, 1977.

Feeney, Griffith, and Kiyoshi, Hamano, 'Rice Price Fluctuations and Fertility in Late Tokugawa Japan', *Jnl. of Japanese Studies*, vol.16, no.1, 1990.

Ferguson, Adam, *An Essay on the History of Civil Society*, 1767, Duncan Forbes (ed.), 1966.

Ferguson, Sheila, *Drink*, 1975.

Fildes, Valerie, *Breasts, Bottles and Babies. A History of Infant Feeding*, Edinburgh, 1986.

Fildes, Valerie, *Wet Nursing, A History from Antiquity to the Present*, 1988.

Fisher, F.J., 'Development of the London Food Market, 1540–1640', *Economic Hist. Rev.*, vol.v, 1935.

Flandrin, Jean-Louis, *Families in Former Times, Kinship, Household and Sexuality*, 1979.

Flinn, Michael W., *The European Demographic System 1500–1820*, Baltimore, 1981.

Fogel, Robert W., et al, 'Secular Changes in American and British Stature and Nutrition', *Jnl. of Interdisciplinary History*, vol.xiv, no.2, Autumn 1983.

Forbes, Thomas Roger, (ed.), *Chronicle from Aldgate, Life and Death in Shakespeare's London*, New Haven, 1971.

Forrest, Denys, *Tea for the British: The Social and Economic History of a Famous Trade*, 1973.

Forrest, Denys, *The World Tea Trade: A Survey of the Production, Distribution and Consumption of Tea*, Cambridge, 1985.

Fortescue, John, *Learned Commendation of the Politique Laws of England*, 1567. (originally written in 1461–1471).

Foucault, Michel, *Discipline and Punish, the Birth of the Prison*, 1977.

Franklin, Benjamin, *The Works of Benjamin Franklin*, Jared Sparks (ed.), Boston, 1840.

Fraser, Hugh (Mrs), *Letters from Japan, a Record of Modern Life in the Island Empire*, 1899.

Frederic, Louis, *Daily Life in Japan, at the time of the Samurai, 1185–1603*, 1972.

Fujikawa, Y., *History of Diseases in Japan*, Tokyo, 1912 (in Japanese).

Fukuyama, Francis, *The End of History and the Last Man*, 1992.

Fukuzawa, Jukichi, *An Outline of a Thory of Civilization*, tr. D.Dilworth and G.Cameron, Tokyo, 1973.

Furnivall, F.J., (ed.), *Early English Meals and Manners*, Early English Text Society, 1931.

Fussell, G.E., *The Classical Tradition in West European Farming*, 1972.

Fussell, G.E., and Fussell K.R., *The English Countrywoman, Her life in Farmhouse and Field*, 1953.

Fussell, G.E., and Fussell, K.R., *The English Countryman, His Life and Work from Tudor Times to the Victorian Age*, 1985.

Galloway, P.R., 'Annual Variations in Deaths by Age, Deaths by Cause, Prices, and Weather in London 1670 to 1830', *Population Studies*, vol.39, 1985.

Gardiner, Robert S., *Japan as We Saw It*, Boston, 1892.

Garfield, John, *The Wandering Whore: A Dialogue*. Numbers 1–5, 1660–1, reprinted, The Rota, Exeter Univ., 1977.

Geoffrey, Theodate, *An Immigrant in Japan*, 1926.

George, M. Dorothy, (ed.), *England in Johnson's Day*, 1942.

George, M. Dorothy, *London Life in the Eighteenth Century*, 1965.

George, M. Dorothy, 'Some Causes of the Increase of Population in the Eighteenth Century as Illustrated by London', *Economic Jnl.*, vol.xxxii, 1922.

Geyl, Pieter, *Encounters in History*, 1967.

Gibbon, Edward, *Autobiography*, Lord Sheffield (ed.), World Classics edn, 1959, (originally published in 1796).

Glass, D.V., and Eversley, D.E.C., (eds), *Population in History*, 1965.

Goldstone, J.A., 'The Demographic Revolution in England: a Re-examination', *Population Studies*, vol.49, 1986.

Goode, William J., *World Revolution and Family Patterns*, New York, 1968.

Goodwin, Jason, *The Gunpowder Gardens. Travels through India and China in search of Tea*, Vintage edn, 1993.

Goody, Jack, 'Adoption in Cross-Cultural Perspective', *Comparative Studies in Society and History*, vol.11, no.1, Jan. 1969.

Goody, Jack, *Production and Reproduction. A Comparative Study of the Domestic Domain*, 1976.

Goody, Jack, *The Development of the Family and Marriage in Europe*, 1983.

Goody, Jack, Thirsk, Joan, and Thompson, E.P., (eds), *Family and Inheritance, Rural Society in Western Europe 1200–1800*, 1976.

Gorer, Geoffrey, 'Themes in Japanese Culture', *Trans. New York Academy of Sciences*, series ii, vol.5, 1943.

Goubert, Jean-Pierre, *The Conquest of Water, the Advent of Health in the Industrial Age*, Cambridge, 1989.

Gouge, William, *Of Domesticall Duties*, 1622.

Gough, Richard, *Antiquities and Memoirs of the Parish of Myddle*, (n.d., seventeenth century), 1875.

Graham, H.G., *The Social Life of Scotland in the Eighteenth Century*, 1909.

Graunt, John, *Natural and Political Observations mentioned in a following index and made upon the Bills of Mortality*, 1665.

Greenhow, E.H., *Papers Relating to the Sanitary State of the People of England*, 1858.

Greenwood, Major, *Epidemics and Crowd-diseases, an Introduction to the Study of Epidemiology*, 1935.

Griffis, W.E., *The Mikado's Empire*, 10th edn, New York, 1903.

Grigson, Geoffrey, and Gibbs-Smith, C.H., (eds), *Things, A Volume about the Origin and Early History of Many Things*, n.d., c.1950.

Grilli, Peter, *Pleasures of the Japanese Bath*, 1992.

Guggenheim, Karl Y., *Nutrition and Nutritional Diseases, the Evolution of Concepts*, Lexington, 1981.

Guha, Sumit, 'The Importance of Social Intervention in England's Mortality Decline: The Evidence Reviewed', *Social History of Medicine*, vol.7, no.1, 1994.

Hair, P.E.H., 'Bridal Pregnancy in Rural England in Earlier Centuries', *Population Studies*, vol.xx, no.2, Nov. 1966.

Hajnal, John, 'European Marriage Patterns in Perspective', in D.V.Glass and D.E.C.Eversley (eds), *Population in History, Essays in Historical Demography*, 1965.

Hale, Matthew, *The History of the Pleas of the Crown*, 1736, (Professional Books reprint, 1971).

Hale, Matthew, *Pleas of the Crown: or, a Methodical Summary of the principal matters relating to that Subject*, 1678.

Hall, John A., *Powers and Liberties. The Causes and Consequences of the Rise of the West*, 1985.

Hane, Mikiso, *Peasants, Rebels and Outcastes, the Underside of Modern Japan*, New York, 1982.

Hanley, Susan B., 'Fertility, Mortality and Life Expectancy in Pre-Modern Japan', *Population Studies*, vol.28, no.1, March 1974.

Hanley, Susan B., 'A High Standard of Living in Nineteenth-Century Japan: Fact or Fantasy?' *Jnl. Economic History*, vol.43, no.1, March 1983.

Hanley, Susan B., 'Urban Sanitation in Pre-Industrial Japan', *Jnl. of Interdisciplinary History*, vol.xviii, no.1, Summer 1987.

Hanley, Susan B., and Wolf, Arthur P., (eds), *Family and Population in East Asian History*, Stanford, 1985.

Hanley, Susan B., and Yamamura, Kozo, *Economic and Demographic Change in Pre-Industrial Japan 1600–1868*, Princeton, 1977.

Hann, C.M., *Tea and the Domestication of the Turkish State*, Modern Turkish Studies Programme, Occasional Papers 1, 1990.

Hanway, Joseph, *A Journal of Eight Day Journey. . . . To which is added an Essay on Tea*, 1756.

Hardy, Anne, 'Water and the Search for Public Health in London in the Eighteenth and Nineteenth Centuries', *Medical History*, no.28, 1984.

Harrison, G.A., and Boyce, A.J., (eds), *The Structure of Human Populations*, 1972.

Harrison, William, *The Description of England (1587)*, Georges Edelen (ed.), Cornell, 1968.

Havinden, M.A., (ed.), *Household and Farm Inventories in Oxfordshire, 1550–1590*, 1965.

Hawthorn, Geoffrey, *The Sociology of Fertility*, 1970.

Hayami, Akira, 'A Great Transformation: Social and Economic Change in Sixteenth and Seventeenth Century Japan', *Bonner Zeitschrift fur Japanologie*, vol.8, Bonn, 1986.

Hayami, Akira, 'Another Fossa Magna: Proportion Marrying in Late Nineteenth-Century Japan', *Jnl. of Family History*, vol.12, nos 1–3, 1987.

Hayami, Akira, 'Class Differences in Marriage and Fertility among Tokugawa Villages in Mino Province', *Keio Economic Studies*, vol.17, no.1, 1980.

Hayami, Akira, 'Labor Migration in a Pre-Industrial Society: a Study Tracing the Life Histories of the Inhabitants of a Village', *Keio Economic Studies*, vol.10, no.2, 1973.

Hayami, Akira, 'The Myth of Primogeniture and Impartible Inheritance in Tokugawa Japan' *Jnl. of Family History*, Spring 1983.

Hayami, Akira, 'Population Growth in Pre-Industrial Japan', in *Evolution Agraire et Croissance Demographique*, Antoinette Fauve-Chamoux (ed.), Liege, 1987.

Hearn, Lafcadio, *Glimpses of Unfamiliar Japan (1894)*, Tokyo, 1991.

Hearn, Lafcadio, *Japan, an Attempt at Interpretation*, New York, 1910.

Hearn, Lafcadio, *Kokoro, Hints and Echoes of Japanese Inner Life (1896)*, Tokyo, 1991.

Hearn, Lafcadio, *Out of the East. Reveries and Studies in New Japan*, 1927.

Heberden, William, *Observations on the Increase and Decrease of Different Diseases, and Particularly the Plague*, 1801.

Heer, M. David, (ed.), *Readings on Population*, New Jersey, 1968.

Helleiner, K.F., 'The Population of Europe from the Black Death to the Eve of the Vital Revolution', in *The Cambridge Economic History of Europe*, vol.IV, E.E.Rich and C.H.Wilson (eds), 1967.

Hibbert, Christopher, *The English, a Social History 1066–1945*, 1989.

Himes, Norman, *Medical History of Contraception*, 1936.

Hirschman, Albert O., *The Passions and the Interests, Political Arguments for Capitalism Before its Triumph*, Princeton, 1968.

Hobhouse, Henry, *Seeds of Change*, 1985.

Hoffer, Peter C., and Hull, N.E.H., *Murdering Mothers: Infanticide in England and New England 1558–1803*, 1981.

Hollingsworth, T.H. *Historical Demography. The Sources of History: Studies in the Uses of Historical Evidence*, 1969.

Hopkins, Keith, 'Contraception in the Roman Empire', *Comparative Studies in Society and History*, vol.viii, no.1, Oct. 1965.

Hoskins, W.G., *Essays in Leicestershire History*, Liverpool, 1950.

Hoskins, W.G., 'The Rebuilding of Rural England, 1570–1640', in W.G.Hoskins, *Provincial England*, 1964.

Houghton, John, *A Collection for Improvement of Husbandry and Trade (1692)*, 1969.

Houlbrook, Ralph, *Church Courts and People in the Diocese of Norwich, 1519–1570*, Oxford University, D.Phil. thesis, 1970.

Howard, George Elliott, *A History of Matrimonial Institutions*, Chicago, 1904.

Howe, G. Melvyn, *Man, Environment and Disease in Britain, a Medical Geography of Britain through the Ages*, 1972.

Hume, David, *Essays, Literary, Moral and Political*, 1873 reprint.

Hunt, Daivd, *Parents and Children in History, The Psychology of Family Life in Early Modern France*, 1970.

Hunter, W.W., *Statistical Account of Assam*, (1879), Delhi, 1982.

Hunter, W.W., *The Annals of Rural Bengal*, 1871.

Hunter, W.W., *The Indian Empire: its people, history, and products*, 1886.

Hunter, *Hunter's Tropical Medicine*, revised by Thomas G.Strickland, 6th edn, Washington, 1984.

Inouye, Jukichi, *Home Life in Japan*, Tokyo, 1910.

Jacobs, Norman, *The Origin of Modern Capitalism and Eastern Asia*, Hong Kong, 1958, reprinted, Conneticut, 1990.

Jannetta, Ann Bowman, *Epidemics and Mortality in Early Modern Japan*, Princeton, 1986.

Jannetta, Ann Bowman, and Preston, Samuel H., 'Two Centuries of Mortality Change in Central Japan: The Evidence from a Temple Death Register', *Population Studies*, vol.45, 1991.

Jansen, Marius B, and Rozman, Gilbert, (eds), *Japan in Transition from Tokugawa to Meiji*, Princeton, 1988.

Jippensha, Ikku, *Shank's Mare. Being a translation of the Tokaido volumes of Hizakurige*, Tokyo, 1988.

Johnson, Samuel, *Works*, new edn by Arthur Murphy, 1810.

Jones, E.L., and Mingay, G.E., (eds), *Land, Labour and Population in the Industrial Revolution*, 1967.

Jones, E.L., *The European Miracle, Environments, Economies, and Geopolitics in the History of Europe and Asia*, 1983.

Jones, R.E., 'Population and Agrarian Change in an Eighteenth century Shropshire Parish', *Local Population Studies*, no.1, Autumn 1968.

Jorden, E, *A Rational Account of the Naturall Weaknesses of Women*, 2nd edn, 1716.

Kaempfer, Engelbert, *The History of Japan, together with a Description of the Kingdom of Siam, 1690–1692*, (1727), tr. J.G. Scheuchzer, 1906.

Kaisen, Iguchi, *Tea Ceremony*, Osaka, 1990.

Kalland, Arne, and Pedersen, Jon, 'Famine and Population in Fukuoka Domain During the Tokugawa Period', *Jnl. of Japanese Studies*, vol.10, no.1, 1984.

Kamen, Henry, *The Iron Century, Social Change in Europe 1550–1660*, 1971.

Kames, (Lord), *Sketches of the History of Man*, Basil (Basle), 1796.

Keene, Donald, *The Japanese Discovery of Europe, 1720–1830*, Stanford, 1989.

Keizo, Shibusawa, (ed.), *Japanese Society in the Meiji Era*, Tokyo, 1958.

Kershaw, Ian, 'The Great Famine and Agrarian Crisis in England 1315–1322', *Past and Present*, no.59, 1973.

Khare, R.S., 'Ritual Purity and Pollution in Relation to Domestic Sanitation', in *Culture, Disease and Healing*, David Landy (ed.), New York, 1977.

King, F.H., *Farmers of Forty Centuries, or Permanent Agriculture in China, Korea and Japan*, 1911.

King-Hall, Magdalen, *The Story of the Nursery*, 1958.

Kingdon-Ward, F., *Plant Hunter in Manipur*, 1952.

Kiple, Kenneth F., (ed.), *The Cambridge World History of Human Disease*, 1994.

Kodansha, *Japan. An Illustrated Encyclopaedia*, Kodansha, Tokyo, 1993.

Kodansha, *Kodansha Encyclopaedia of Japan*, Tokyo, 1983.

Krause, J.T., 'Some Neglected Factors in the English Industrial Revolution' *Jnl. Ec. History*, vol.xix, Dec. 1959.

Kroeber, A.L., *Anthropology*, New York, 1948.

Kunio, Yanagida, (ed.), *Japanese Manners and Customs in the Meiji Era*, Tokyo, 1957.

Kunitz, Stephen, 'Speculations on the European Mortality Decline', *Ec. History Rev*, 2nd series, vol.36, no.3, 1983.

Kunitz, Stephen, 'Making a Long Story Short: A Note on Men's Height and Mortality in England from the First through the Nineteenth Centuries', *Medical History*, vol. 31, 1987.

Lamond, Elizabeth, (ed.), *A Discourse of the Common Weal of this Realm of England*, (first printed in 1581 and commonly attributed to W.S.), 1954.

Landers, John, 'Age Patterns of Mortality in London During the "Long Eighteenth Century": a Test of the "High Potential" Model of Metropolitan Mortality', *Soc. Hist. Medicine*, vol.3, no.1, April 1990.

Landers, John, *Death and the Metropolis. Studies in the Demographic History of London 1670–1830*, 1993.

Landers, John, and Reynolds, Vernon, (eds), *Fertility and Resources*, Cambridge, 1990.

Landers, John, 'Mortality and Metropolis: the Case of London 1675–1825', *Population Studies*, no.41, 1987.

Landes, David S., *The Unbound Prometheus, Technological Change and Industrial Development in Western Europe from 1750 to the Present*, 1975.

Lane-Claypon, Janet E., *Hygiene of Women and Children*, 1921.

Laslett, Peter, *Family Life and Illicit Love in Earlier Generations. Essays in Historical Sociology*, 1977.

Laslett, Peter, *The World we have Lost*, 2nd edn, 1971.

Laslett, Peter, Oosterveen, Karla, and Smith, Richard M., (eds), *Bastardy and its Comparative History*, 1980.

Laslett, Peter, with Wall, Richard, (eds), *Household and Family in Past Time*, 1972.

Le Riche, W. Harding, and Milner, Jean, *A Short History of Epidemiology*, 1971.

Le Riche, W. Harding, and Milner, Jean, *Epidemiology as Medical Ecology*, 1971.

Le Roy Ladurie, Emmanuel, *The Peasants of Languedoc*, tr. with an introduction by John Day, 1974.

Le Roy Ladurie, Emmanuel, *Times of Feast, Times of Famine, a History of Climate Since the Year 1000*, 1972.

Leach, Edmund, *Culture and Communication, the Logic by which Symbols are Connected*, 1976.

Lee, Richard B., and Devore, Irven, (eds), *Man the Hunter*, New York, 1968.

Leonard, Jonathon N., *Early Japan*, Netherlands, 1974.

Lettsom, John Coakley, *The Natural History of the Tea-Trea, with Observations on the Medical Qualities of Tea . . .* , 1772.

Lisle, Edward, *Observations in Husbandry*, 1757.

Livi-Bacci, Massimo, *A Concise History of World Population*, 1992.

Lock, Margaret, *East Asian Medicine in Urban Japan, Varieties of Medical Experience*, California, 1980.

Lock, Margaret, 'Epidemics and Mortality in Early Japan', Review of Jannetta in *Jnl. of Japanese Studies*, vol.14, no.2, 1988.

Loder, Robert, *Farm Accounts 1610–1620*, G.E.Fussell (ed.), Camden Society, vol.53, 1936.

Lofgren, Orvar, 'Family and Household among Scandinvaian Peasantry', *Ethnologia Scandinavica*, 1974.

Lofgren, Orvar, 'Historical Perspectives on Scandinavian Peasantries', *Annual Review of Anthropology*, vol.9, 187–216, 1980.

Longford, Joseph M., *Japan of the Japanese*, 1915.

Loschky, David, and Childers, Ben D., 'Early English Mortality', *Jnl. of Interdisciplinary History*, vol.xxiv, no.1, 85–97, Summer 1993.

Macaulay, Thomas Babington, *A History of England*, Everyman edn, 1957.

Macfarlane, Alan, 'Death, Disease and Curing in a Himalayan Village', in C.von Fürer-Haimendorf (ed.), *Asian Highland Society in Anthropological Perspective*, New Delhi, 1984.

Macfarlane, Alan, *Marriage and Love in England, Modes of Reproduction 1300–1840*, Oxford, 1986.

Macfarlane, Alan, 'Modes of Reproduction' in *Population and Development*, Geoffrey Hawthorn (ed.), 1978.

Macfarlane, Alan, 'On Individualism', *Proceedings of the British Academy*, vol.82, 1993.

Macfarlane, Alan, in collaboration with Sarah Harrison and Charles Jardine, *Reconstructing Historical Communities*, Cambridge, 1977.

Macfarlane, Alan, *Resources and Population, a Study of the Gurungs of Nepal*, Cambridge, 1976.

Macfarlane, Alan, *The Culture of Capitalism*, Oxford, 1987.

Macfarlane, Alan, *The Origins of English Individualism*, Oxford, 1978.

Mackenzie, W.C., *History of the Outer Hebrides*, 1903.

Maher, Vanessa, (ed.), *Breast-Feeding in Cross-Cultural Perspective: Paradoxes and Proposals*, 1992.

Maine, Henry Sumner, *Dissertations on Early Law and Custom*, 1901.

Malthus, T.R., *An Essay on Population*, 2nd edn, 1803. Everyman edition, two volumes, no date.

Malthus, Thomas Robert, *An Essay on the Principle of Population and A Summary View of the Principle of Population*, Anthony Flew (ed.), 1982. (An essay originally published in 1798).

Mamdani, Mahmood, *The Myth of Population Control, Family, Caste and Class in an Indian village*, New York, 1972.

Maraini, Fosco, *Meeting with Japan*, 1959.

Maraini, Fosco, *Tokyo*, Amsterdam, 1978.

Marchant, Ronald A., *The Church Under the Law, Justice, Administration and Discipline in the Diocese of York 1560–1640*, 1969.

Marks, V., 'Physiological and Clinical Effects of Tea', in K.C. Willson and M.N. Clifford (eds), *Tea: Cultivation and Consumption*, 1992.

Marshall, Dorothy, *English People in the Eighteenth Century*, 1956.

Martin, M., *Description of the Western Islands of Scotland circa 1695*, Donald J. Macleod (ed.), 1934.

Mascie-Taylor, C.G.N., (ed.), *The Anthropology of Disease*, 1993.

Mathias, Peter, *The Brewing Industry in England*, 1700–1830, Cambridge, 1959.

Mathias, Peter, *The Transformation of England*, 1979.

May, Jacques M., *The Ecology of Human Disease*, New York, 1958.

McAlpin, Michelle B., 'Famines, Epidemics, and Population Growth: The Case of India', *Jnl. of Interdisciplinary History*, vol.xiv, no.2, Autumn 1983.

McAlpin, Michelle B., *Subject to Famine: Food Crises and Economic Change in Western India, 1860–1920*, Princeton, 1983.

McKeown, Thomas, 'Food, Infection and Population', *Jnl. of Interdisciplinary History*, vol.xiv, no.2, Autumn 1983.

McKeown, Thomas, *Medicine in Modern Society*, 1965.

McKeown, Thomas, *The Modern Rise of Population*, 1976.

McKeown, Thomas, and Brown, R.G., 'Medical Evidence Relation to English Population Change in the Eighteenth Century' in David Glass and D.E.C.Eversley (eds), *Population in History*, 1965.

McLaren, Angus, *Birth Control in Nineteenth-Century England*, New York, 1978.

McLaren, Dorothy, 'Fertility, Infant Mortality, and Breast Feeding in the Seventeenth Century', *Medical History*, no.22, 1978.

McMullen, I.F., 'Rulers or Fathers? A Casuistical Problem in Early Modern Japanese Thought', *Past and Present*, no.116, Aug. 1987.

McNeill, William H., *Plagues and Peoples*, 1961.

McNeill, William, H., *The Pursuit of Power, Technology, Armed Force and Society Since AD 1000*, 1983.

Menken, Jane, Trussell, James, and Watkins, Susan, 'The Nutrition Fertility Link: An Evaluation of the Evidence', *Jnl. of Interdisciplinary History*, vol.XI, no.3, Winter 1981.

Mercer, Alex, *Disease, Mortality and Population in Transition, Epidemiological-Demographic Change in England Since the Eighteenth Century as Part of a Global Phenomenon*, 1990.

Merck, *The Merck Manual of Diagnosis and Therapy*, 11th edn, 1966.

Mokyr, Joel, (ed.), *The British Industrial Revolution, an Economic Perspective*, Oxford, 1993.

Mokyr, Joel, *The Lever of Riches, Technological Creativity and Economic Progress*, 1992.

Montagu, Mary Wortley, *The Letters and Works*, Lord Wharncliffe (ed.), 1837.

Morioka, Heinz, and Sasaki, Miyoki, *Rakugo: the Popular Narrative Art of Japan*, 1990.

Morris, Ivan, *The World of the Shining Prince, Court life in Ancient Japan*, 1969.

Morse, Edward S., *Japan Day by Day. 1877, 1878–79, 1882–83*, 2 vols, Tokyo, 1936.

Morse, Edward S., *Japanese Homes and Their Surroundings*, 1886, New York, 1961.

Morse, Edward S., 'Latrines of the East', *American Architect and Building News*, vol.xxxix, no.899, 170–4, 1893.

Moryson, Fynes, *An Itinerary, containing his Ten Yeeres Travell through the Twelve Dominions . . . (1617)*, 1907–8.

Mosk, Carl, *Patriarchy and Fertility: Japan and Sweden, 1880–1960*, 1983.

Mousnier, Roland, *Peasant Uprisings in Seventeenth Century France, Russia and China*, 1971.

Mullett, Charles F., 'Public Baths and Health in England, 16th–18th Century', Supplement to the *Bulletin of the History of Medicine*, no.5, Baltimore, 1946.

Mumford, Lewis, *Technics and Civilization*, 1947.

Murphy, Shirley Foster, (ed.), *Our Homes, and How to make them Healthy*, 1885.

Myrdal, Gunnar, *Asian Drama, an Enquiry into the Poverty of Nations*, 1968.

Nadel, S.F., *The Foundations of Social Anthropology*, 1963.

Nag, Moni, *Factors Affecting Human Fertility in Non-Industrial Societies*, New Haven, 1962.

Nagatsuka, Takashi, *The Soil, a Portrait of Rural Life in Meiji Japan*, tr. Ann Waswo, California, 1993.

Nakamura, James I., and Miyamoto, Matoa, 'Social Structure and Population Change: A Comparative Study of Tokugawa Japan and Chi'ing China.' *Econ. Development and Cultural Change*, vol.30, no.2, 1982.

Nakane, Chie, *Japanese Society*, 1970.

Natsume, Soseki, *I am a Cat*, Tokyo, 1992.

Needham, Joseph, *Clerks and Craftsmen in China and the West*, Cambridge, 1970.

Needham, Joseph, *The Shorter Science and Civilisation in China*, 2 vols, 1980.

Needham, Joseph, et al., *Science and Civilization in China*, various volumes, Cambridge, 1962 on.

Nef, John U., *Industry and Government in France and England 1540–1640*, 1957.

Nef, John U., *Western Civilization Since the Renaissance. Peace, War, Industry and the Arts*, New York 1963.

Newman, Lucille F., (ed.), *Hunger in History*, 1990.

Nicoll, Allardyce, (ed.), *Shakespeare in his Own Age*, 1964.

Nikiforuk, Andrew, *The Fourth Horseman, a Short History of Epidemics, Plagues and other Scourges*, 1991.

Notter, J. Lane, and Firth, R.H., *Hygiene*, 1895.

Ohnuki-Tierney, Emiko, *Illness and Culture in Contemporary Japan, an Anthropological View*, 1984.

Okakura, Kakuzo, *The Book of Tea*, Tokyo, 1991.

Oliphant, Laurence, *Narrative of The Earl of Elgin's Mission to China and Japan in the years 1857, '58, '59*, 1859.

Origo, Iris, *The Merchant of Prato, Francesco di Marco Datini*, 1963.

Outhwaite, R.B., *Dearth, Public Policy and Social Disturbance in England, 1550–1800*, 1981.

Paige, David, and Bayliss, T.M., (eds), *Lactose Digestion. Clinical and Nutritional Implications*, Baltimore, 1981.

Palliser, David, 'Death and Disease in Staffordshire, 1540–1670' in C.W.Chalkin, and M.A.Havinden (eds), *Rural Change and Urban Growth 1500–1800*, 1974.

Palliser, D.M.,'Tawney's Century: Brave New World or Malthusian Trap?' *Economic History Review*, 2nd Series, vol.xxxv, no.3, Aug. 1982.

Pepys, Samuel, *Diary*, (ed.), by Robert Latham and William Matthews, 1971–83.

Perrin, Noel,*Giving up the Gun; Japan's Reversion to the Sword 1543–1879*, New York, 1979.

Petersen, William, *Malthus*, Harvard, 1979.

Petty, William, *The Petty Papers, Some Unpublished Writings*, edited from the Bowood Papers by the Marquis of Lansdowne, 1927.

Place, Francis, *Illustrations and Proofs of the Principle of Population*, 1967.

Place, Francis, *The Autobiography of Francis Place (1771–1854)*, Mary Thrale (ed.), Cambridge, 1972.

Polgar, Steven, 'Evolution and the Ills of Mankind' in Sol Tax (ed.), *Horizons of Anthropology*, 1965.

Pollock, Frederick, and Maitland, Frederick William, *The History of English Law, before the Time of Edward I*, 2nd edn, Cambridge, 1968.

Porter, Roy, *Disease, Medicine and Society in England, 1550–1860*, 2nd edn, 1993.

Porter, Roy, *English Society in the Eighteenth Century*, 1990.

Porter, Roy, and Porter, Dorothy, *In Sickness and in Health. The British Experience 1650–1850*, 1988.

Post, John D., 'Famine, Mortality, and Epidemic Disease in the Process of Modernization', *Economic History Review*, 2nd Series, vol.xxix, no.1, Feb. 1976.

Post, John D., *Food Shortage, Climatic Variability, and Epidemic Disease in Preindustrial Europe. The Mortality Peak in the Early 1740s*, Cornell, 1985.

Poston, R.N., 'Nutrition and Immunity', in R.J.Jarrett (ed.), *Nutrition and Disease*, 1979.

Pounds, N.J.G., *The Culture of the English People, Iron Age to the Industrial Revolution*, 1994.

Pudney, John, *The Smallest Room, a Discreet Survey through the Ages*, 1954.

Pullar, Philippa, *Consuming Passions, A History of English Food and Appetite*, 1972.

Purchas, Samuel, *Purchas His Pilgrims in Japan, extracted from Hakluyts Posthumus . . .*, ed. by Cyril Wild, Kobe, Japan, c.1938.

Quaife, G.R., *Wanton Wenches and Wayward Wives*, New York, 1979.

Quennell, Marjorie, and Quennell, C.H.B., *A History of Everyday Things in England 1066–1942*, 1937–42.

R.C. *The Compleat Midwife's Practice Enlarged*, 1659.

Ramsay, G.D., *The English Woollen Industry 1500–1750*, 1982.

Ramsey, Matthew, 'Environment, Health, and Medicine in the Old Regime', *Jnl. Interdisciplinary History*, vol.xix, no.4, Spring 1989.

Ratzel, Friedrich, *The History of Mankind*, 3 vols, trans. A.J. Butler, 1896.

Razzell, Peter, *Essays in English Population History*, 1994.

Razzell, Peter, *The Conquest of Smallpox*, 1977.

Regamey, Felix, *Japan in Art and Industry, with a Glance at Japanese Manners and Customs*, 1892.

Rein, J.J., *Travels and Researches*, 1884.

Review Symposium, 'The Population History of England 1541–1871: A review symposium', *Social History*, vol.8. no.1, May 1983.

Reynolds, Reginald, and Orwell, George, (eds), *British Pamphleteers. Vol.1. From the Sixteenth Century to the French Revolution*, 1948.

Richards, Audrey I., *Land, Labour and Diet in Northern Rhodesia, an Economic Study of the Bemba tribe*, 1969.

Riley, James C., 'Insects and the European Mortality Decline', *American Historical Review*, vol.91, no.4, Oct. 1986.

Riley, James C., *Sickness, Recovery and Death*, 1989.

Roberts, Llywelyn A. assisted by Kathleen Shaw, *Synopsis of Hygiene*, 1958.

Rochefoucauld, François de la, *A Frenchman in England 1784, Being the Melanges sur L'Angleterre of Francois de la Rochefoucauld*, Jean Marchand (ed.), 1933.

Rogers, James E. Thorold, *Industrial and Commercial History of England*, 1902.

Rogers, James E. Thorold, *Six Centuries of Work and Wages, a History of English labour*, 1917.

Rollins, H.E., (ed.), *A Pepysian Garland, Black-letter Broadside Ballads of the Years 1595–1639, chiefly from the collection of Samuel Pepys*, 1922.

Romanucci-Ross, Lola, Moerman, Daniel E., and Tancredi, Laurence R., *The Anthropology of Medicine, from Culture to Method*, Massachusetts, 1983.

Rural Cyclopedia or a General Dictionary of Agriculture, John M. Wilson (ed.), 1848.

Russell, Claire, and Russell, W.M.S., *Violence, Monkeys and Man*, 1968.

Ruston, Arthur G., and Witney, Denis, *Hooton Pagnell, The Agricultural Evolution of a Yorkshire Village*, 1934.

Rye, William, *England as seen by Foreigners in the Days of Elizabeth and James the First*, 1865.

Sabine, Ernest L., 'Latrines and Cesspools of Mediaeval London', *Speculum*, vol.IX, 1934.

Saga, Junichi, *Memories of Silk and Straw, a Self-Portrait of Small-Town Japan*, Tokyo, 1990.

Sahlins, Marshall D., *Tribesmen*, New Jersey, 1968.

Saikaku, Ihara, *The Japanese Family Storehouse, or the Millionaires Gospel Modernised*, tr. G.W. Sargent. from 'Nippon Eitai-gura 1688', 1969.

Saito, Osamu, 'Famine and Mortality in the Japanese Past: with Special Reference to the Eighteenth and Nineteenth Centuries, Paper prepared for the IUSSP Conference on Asian Population History, Taipei, January, 1996.

Saito, Osamu, *Gender, Workload and Agricultural Progress: Japan's Historical Progress in Perspective*, Discussion Paper A., no.268, Institute of Economic Research, Hitotsubashi Univ. Tokyo, 1993.

Saito, Osamu, 'Infanticide, Fertility and "Population Stagnation": The State of Tokugawa Historical Demography', *Japan Forum*, vol.4, no.2, October 1992.

Saito, Osamu, 'Population and the Peasant Family Economy in Proto-Industrial Japan', *Keio Economic Society Discussion Paper Series*, no.3, June 1981.

Saltmarsh, John, 'Plague and Economic Decline in England', *Cambridge Hist. Jnl.*, vol.vii, no.1, 1941.

Sansom, George, *A History of Japan, 1334–1615*, 3 vols, 1961.

Sauvy, Alfred, *General Theory of Population*, 1974.

Schama, Simon, *The Embarrassment of Riches, an Interpretation of Dutch Culture in the Golden Age*, 1988.

Scheper-Hughes, Nancy, *Death Without Weeping, the Violence of Everyday Life in Brazil*, California, 1992.

Schnucker, Robert V., 'Elizabethan Birth Control and Puritan Attitudes', *Jnl. of Interdisciplinary History*, vol.v, no.4, Spring 1975.

Schofield, R.S., 'Perinatal Mortality in Hawkshead, Lancashire 1581–1710', *Local Population Studies*, no.4, Spring 1970.

Schofield, Roger, 'Review of Thomas McKeown's "The Modern Rise of Population"', *Population Studies*, no.37, 1977.

Schofield, R., Reher, D., and Bideau, A., (eds), *The Decline of Mortality in Europe*, Oxford, 1991.

Scidmore, Eliza R., *Jinrikisha Days in Japan*, New York, 1891.

Seavoy, Ronald E., *Famine in Peasant Societies*, New York, 1986.

Semple, Ellen Churchill, *Influences of Geographic Environment on the Basis of Ratzel's System of Anthropo-Geography*, New York, 1911.

Sen, Amartya, *Poverty and Famines, an Essay on Entitlement and Deprivation*, 1982.

Shammas, Carole, *The Pre-Industrial Consumer in England and America*, Oxford, 1990.

Sharp, Mrs Jane, *The Midwives Book*, 1671.

Short, Thomas,*Comparative History of the Increase and Decrease of Mankind*, 1767.

Short, Thomas, *A Rational Discourse of the Inward Use of Water*, 1725.

Shrewsbury, J.F.D., *A History of Bubonic Plague in the British Isles*, 1970.

Shrewsbury, J.F.D.,*The Plague of the Philistines*, 1964.

Silver, J.M.W., *Sketches of Japanese Manners and Customs*, 1867.

Singer, Kurt, *Mirror, Sword and Jewel, the Geometry of Japanese life*, 1973, Tokyo, 1990 edn.

Slack, Paul, 'Dearth and Social Policy in Early Modern England', *Social History of Medicine*, vol.5, no.1, April 1992.

Slack, Paul,*The Impact of Plague in Tudor and Stuart England*, 1990.

Smith, Adam, *An Inquiry into the Nature and Causes of the Wealth of Nations (1776)*, edited Edwin Cannon, with new preface by George J. Stigler, Chicago, 1976.

Smith, C., Woodham, *The Great Hunger: Ireland 1845–9*, 1962.

Smith, Daniel Scott, 'Review of "Nakahara" ', *Jnl. of Japanese Studies*, vol.5, no.1, 1979.

Smith, F.B., *The People's Health, 1830–1910*, Canberra, 1979.

Smith, Ginnie, 'Prescribing the Rules of Health: Self-help and advice in the Late Eighteenth Century', in Roy Porter (ed.), *Patients and Practitioners*, Cambridge, 1985.

Smith, Ginnie, 'Thomas Tryon's Regiment for Women: Sectarian Health in the Seventeenth Century', in *The Sexual Dynamics of History*, London Feminist History Group, 1983.

Smith, Richard, 'Demographic Developments in Rural England, 1300–48: a Survey', in Bruce Campbell (ed.), *Before the Black Death*, Manchester, 1991.

Smith, Robert J.,*Japanese Society, Tradition, Self and the Social Order*, New York, 1985.

Smith, Thomas Sir, *De Republica Anglorum (1583)*, ed. by Mary Dewar, 1982.

Smith, Thomas C., *Nakahara, Family farming and Population in a Japanese village, 1717–1830*, Stanford, 1977.

Smith, Thomas C., *Native Sources of Japanese Industrialization 1750–1920*, California, 1988.

Smith, Thomas C., 'Pre-Modern Economic Growth: Japan and the West', *Past and Present*, no.60, August 1973.

Smith, Thomas C., *The Agrarian Origins of Modern Japan*, Stanford, 1965.

Sneyd, C.A., (tr.) *A Relation, or Rather a True Account of the Islands of England. . . . About the Year 1500*, Camden Society, 1848.

Sorokin, Pitirim, *Contemporary Sociological Theories*, New York, 1928.

Sorokin, Pitirim, *Society, Culture and Personality: their Structure and Dynamics, a System of General Sociology*, New York, 1947.

Spence, Jonathan D., *The Search for Modern China*, 1990.

Spencer, Joseph E., *Asia – East by South, a Cultural Geography*, New York, 1954.

Spengler, Joseph J., 'Demographic factors and early modern economic development', in D.V.Glass, and Roger Revelle (eds), *Population and Social Change*, 1972.

Stagg, Geoffrey V., and Millin, David J., 'The Nutritional and Therapeutic Value of Tea – a Review', *Jnl. Sci. Food and Agriculture*, no.26, 1975.

Steckel, Richard H., 'Heights, Living Standards, and History. A Review Essay', *Historical Methods*, vol.24, no.4, Fall 1991.

Steensberg, Axel, 'Economy, Fertility and Esteem in a Zealand Village 1675–1754', in J.Szabadfalvi and J.Ujvary (eds), *Studia Ethnographica et Folkloristica in Honorem Bela Gunda*, 1971.

Steiner, Franz, *Taboo*, 1967.

Stewart, Dugald, *Collected Works*, Sir William Hamilton (ed.), 1856.

Stone, Lawrence, *The Family, Sex and Marriage in England 1500–1800*, 1977.

Stubbes, Philip, *The Anatomie of Abuses* (1585), reprinted 1836.

Summer, William, Graham, *Folkways, a Study of the Sociological Importance of Usages, Manners, Customs, Mores and Morals*, 1934.

Szreter, Simon, 'Mortality in England in the Eighteenth and Nineteenth Centuries: A Reply to Sumit Guha', *Social History of Medicine*, vol.7, no.2, 1994.

Szreter, Simon, 'The Importance of Social Intervention in Britain's Mortality Decline c.1850–1914: a Re-Interpretation of the Role of Public Health', *Social History of Medicine*, vol.1, no.1, April 1988.

Taeuber, Irene B., *The Population of Japan*, Princeton, 1958.

Takahashi, Seiichiro, *Traditional Woodblock Prints of Japan*, New York, 1972.

Taine, Hippolyte,*Notes on England*, 1957.

Tames, Richard, *Encounters with Japan*, 1991.

Tanaka, Sem'o,*The Tea Ceremony*, Tokyo, 1982.

Tanizaki, Junichiro, *In Praise of Shadows*, Tokyo, 1992.

Tannahill, Reay, *Food in History*, 1988.

Taylor, G. Rattray, *Sex in History*, 1953.

Thirsk, Joan, (ed.), *The Agrarian History of England and Wales*, vol.iv, 1500–1640, 1967.

Thomas, Keith, 'Cleanliness and godliness in early modern England', in Anthony Fletcher and Peter Roberts (eds), *Religion, Culture and Society in Early Modern Britain*, Cambridge, 1995.

Thomas, Keith,*Religion and the Decline of Magic, Studies in Popular Beliefs in Sixteenth and Seventeenth Century England*, 1970, 2nd impression, 1971.

Thompson, E.P., *The Making of the English Working Class*, 1968.

Thompson, Gladys Scott, *Life in a Noble Household 1641–1700*, 1940.

Thunberg, Charles Peter,*Travels in Europe, Africa and Asia*, 3rd edn, 1796, (originally published in 1793).

Tilly, Louise, A. et al., 'Child Abandonment in European History: A Symposium', *Jnl. of Family History*, vol.17, no.1, 1992.

Totman, Conrad, 'Tokugawa Peasants: Win, Lose or Draw?', *Monumenta Nipponica*, vol.41, no.4, 1986.

Tryon, Thomas, *A Treatise of Cleanliness*, 1682.

Turner, E.S., *Taking the Cure*, 1967.

Tusser, Thomas, *Five Hundred Points of Good Husbandry*, 1984.

Ukers, William H., *All About Tea*, New York, 1935.

Untrodden Fields of Anthropology, Observations on the Esoteric Manners and Customs of Semi-Civilized Peoples . . . , by a French Army Surgeon, New York, 1931.

United Nations, *Determinants and Consequences of Population Trends*, 1973.

United Nations, 'The Determinants and Consequences of Population Trends', *Population Studies*, no.17, 1953.

Van Bath, B.H. Slicker, *The Agrarian History of Western Europe, AD 500–1850*, 1966.

Veith, Ilza, 'On the Mutual Indebtedness of Japanese and Western Medicine', *Bulletin of History of Medicine*, vol.52, no.3, Fall 1978.

Vigarello, Georges, *Concept of Cleanliness, Changing Attitudes in France since the Middle Ages*, 1988.

Von Siebold, Philipp Franz, *Manners and Customs of the Japanese in the 19th Century, from the Accounts of Dutch Residents in Japan*, Tokyo, 1985.

Walter, John, and Schofield, Roger, (eds), *Famine, Disease and Crisis Mortality in Early Modern Society*, 1989.

Watkins, Owen C., *The Puritan Experience*, 1972.

Watkins, Susan, and Menken, Jane, 'Famines in Historical Perspective', *Population and Development Review*, vol.11, no.4, December 1985.

Wear, Andrew, (ed.), *Medicine in Society. Historical Essays*, Cambridge, 1992.

Weir, David R., 'Life Under Pressure: France and England, 1670–1870', *Jnl. Economic History*, vol.xliv, no.1, March 1984.

Wellington, A.R., *Hygiene and Public Health in Japan, Chosen and Manchuria: Report on Conditions Met with During the Tour of the League of Nations Interchange of Health Officers*, Kuala Lumpur, 1927.

Wells, Roger, *Wretched Faces. Famine in Wartime England: 1793–1801*, 1988.

West, Luther S., *The Housefly: Its Natural History, Medical Importance and Control*, New York, 1951.

Westermarck, Edward, *The Origin and Development of the Moral Ideas*, 1906.

Whole Duty of Man, *The New Whole Duty of Man*, 22nd edn, 1750.

Willoughby, Percivall, *Observations of Midwifery*, ed. by Henry Blenkinsop, 1863.

Wilson, Charles, *England's Apprenticeship 1603–1763*, 1971.

Wilson, Chris, 'The Proximate Determinants of Marital Fertility in England 1600–1799', in Lloyd Bonfield, Richard M. Smith, and Keith Wrightson (eds), *The World we Have Gained. Histories of Population and Social Structure*, 1986.

Wilson, Francesca M., (ed.), *Strange Island. Britain through Foreign Eyes 1395–1940*, 1955.

Winslow, Charles-Edward Amory, *The Conquest of Epidemic Disease, a Chapter in the History of Ideas*, Wisconsin, 1980.

Winter, J.M., (ed.),*War and Economic Development. Essays in Memory of David Joslin*, 1975.

Wittermans, Elizabeth P., (tr.), *Doctor on Desima, Selected Chapters from JHR J.L.C. Pompe van Meerdervoort's Vijf Jaren in Japan [Five Years in Japan] (1857–1863)*, Tokyo, 1970.

Wolf, Eric R., *Europe and the People without History*, 1990.

Wood, Margaret, *The English Medieval House*, 1965.

Wright, Lawrence, *Clean and Decent, the Fascinating History of the Bathroom and the WC*, 1960.

Wright, Thomas, *Autobiography of Thomas Wright of Birkenshaw in the County of York, 1736–1797*, ed. by his grandson, 1864.

Wrightson, Keith, *English Society 1580–1680*, 1982.

Wrightson, Keith, 'Infanticide in Earlier Seventeenth-Century England', *Local Population Studies*, no.15, Autumn 1975.

Wrigley, E.A., 'Family Limitation in Pre-Industrial England', *Economic History Review*, 2nd series, vol.xix, no.1, Apr. 1966.

Wrigley, E.A., 'No Death Without Birth: The Implications of English Mortality in the Early Modern Period', in Roy Porter and Andrew Wear (eds), *Problems and Methods in the History of Medicine*, 1987.

Wrigley, E.A., *Population and History*, 1969.

Wrigley, E.A., 'Two Kinds of Capitalism, Two Kinds of Growth', *LSE Quarterly*, vol.2, no.2, Summer 1988.

Wrigley, E.A., 'Urban Growth and Agricultural Change: England and the Continent in the Early Modern Period.' *Jnl. of Interdisciplinary History*, vol.xv, no.4, Spring, 1985.

Wrigley, E.A., and Schofield, R.S., 'English Population History from Family Reconstitution: Summary Results 1600–1799', *Population Studies*, no.37, 1983.

Wrigley, E.A., and Schofield, R.S., *The Population History of England 1541–1871, a Reconstruction*, 1981. The 1989 paper edn with a new introduction is used.

Yamamoto, Hirofumi, (ed.), *Technological Innovation and the Development of Transportation in Japan*, Tokyo, 1993.

Young, Arthur, *The Farmer's Kalendar (1771)*, reprinted, 1973.

Young, Arthur, *Travels in France during the Years 1787, 1788, 1789*, reprinted, 1889.

Zinsser, Hans, *Rats, Lice and History, The Life History of Typhus Fever*, Boston, 1935.

Index

Printed in the United States
150260LV00004B/8/P